Catalyst 2.0

The Online Learning Center for *A Writer's Resource,* Third Edition (http://www.mhhe.com/awr3) provides full coverage of writing, researching, and editing, featuring diagnostic quizzes that help students assess their knowledge of usage, grammar, punctuation, mechanics, and spelling. A list of print and online resources in 30 disciplines provides a starting point for student research projects. "How to Use This Book" tutorials teach students to locate information in the textbook with ease.

The site features all the resources of Catalyst 2.0, the premiere online tool for writing, research, and editing.

To access premium Catalyst content, please go to the Online Learning Center for *A Writer's Resource* Third Edition at http://www.mhhe.com/awr3 and click on the "Enter Catalyst 2.0" graphic shown below in the middle of the home page.

Catalyst 2.0 features interactive tutorials on document design and visual rhetoric, guides for avoiding plagiarism and evaluating sources, electronic writing tutors for composing a range of essays, and more than 4,500 exercises with feedback in grammar, usage, and punctuation.

A Writer's Resource

A Handbook for Writing and Research

Third Edition

Elaine P. Maimon
Governors State University

Janice H. Peritz
Queens College,
City University of New York

Kathleen Blake Yancey
Florida State University

Mc
Graw
Hill

Boston   Burr Ridge, IL   Dubuque, IA   Madison, WI   New York
San Francisco   St. Louis   Bangkok   Bogotá   Caracas   Kuala Lumpur
Lisbon   London   Madrid   Mexico City   Milan   Montreal   New Delhi
Santiago   Seoul   Singapore   Sydney   Taipei   Toronto

Published by McGraw-Hill, an imprint of The McGraw-Hill Companies, Inc.,
1221 Avenue of the Americas, New York, NY 10020. Copyright © 2010, 2007,
2003. All rights reserved. No part of this publication may be reproduced or
distributed in any form or by any means, or stored in a database or retrieval
system, without the prior written consent of The McGraw-Hill Companies, Inc.,
including but not limited to, in any network or other electronic storage or
transmission, or broadcast for distance learning.

1 2 3 4 5 6 7 8 9 0 DOW DOC 0 9

Comb: ISBN: 978-0-07-338377-4   Spiral: ISBN: 978-0-07-730075-3
        MHID: 0-07-338377-5   MHID: 0-07-730075-0

Vice President and Editor in Chief: Manuscript Editor: *Margaret Moore*
   Michael Ryan   Lead Designer: *Cassandra Chu*
Publisher: *David S. Patterson*   Interior and Cover Designer:
Senior Sponsoring Editor: *Maureen McCutcheon*
   Christopher Bennem   Art and Photo Editor: *Sonia Brown*
Director of Development: Production Supervisors:
   Dawn Groundwater   *Randy Hurst, Richard DeVitto*
Development Editor: *Anne Kemper*   Lead Media Project Manager:
Executive Marketing Manager: *Ron Nelms*
   Allison Jones   Composition: *9 / 11 New Century*
Market Development Manager: *Schoolbook by Thompson Type*
   Molly Meneely   Printing: *45# Pub Matte Thinbulk by*
Lead Production Editor: *Brett Coker*   *R.R. Donnelley & Sons*

Cover images: (*from left to right*) © *Philadelphia Museum of Art / CORBIS;*
© *NASA / Roger Ressmeyer/CORBIS; Nevros / Folio, Inc.;* © *Jon Hicks / CORBIS*

Credits: *The credits section for this book begins on page C-1 and is considered
an extension of the copyright page.*

Library of Congress Cataloging-in-Publication Data
Maimon, Elaine P.
   A writer's resource: a handbook for writing and research / Elaine P.
Maimon, Janice H. Peritz, Kathleen Blake Yancey.—3rd ed.
      p. cm.
   Includes bibliographical references and indexes.
   ISBN-13: 978-0-07-338377-4 (alk. paper)
   ISBN-10: 0-07-338377-5 (alk. paper)
   1. English language—Rhetoric—Handbooks, manuals, etc. 2. English
language—Grammar—Handbooks, manuals, etc. 3. Report writing—
Handbooks, manuals, etc. I. Peritz, Janice. II. Yancey, Kathleen Blake, 1950–
III. Title.

PE1408.M3366 2009
808'.042—dc22   2008047101

The Internet addresses listed in the text were accurate at the time of publication. The inclusion of a Web site does not indicate an endorsement by the
authors or McGraw-Hill, and McGraw-Hill does not guarantee the accuracy
of the information presented at these sites.

www.mhhe.com

Preface

As we wrote the first edition of *A Writer's Resource,* our students were always on our minds. We knew that today's students' perspectives on college life were different from those of previous generations of students, and so were their expectations. Most college students today have never known a world without the Internet. Advances in technologies ensure that they are constantly connected to a wealth of information on almost any topic, as well as to one another. Raised on the Web, television, and advertising, they are highly attuned to visual images. At the same time, students with careers and families are entering, and reentering, academia with their own rich set of experiences and expectations. More than ever before, today's students represent an abundance of linguistic and cultural backgrounds, needing a variety of approaches to writing and editing at the college level. Multitasking at unprecedented levels, they need a handbook they can rely on in all their courses: whether that means learning about revision in their English composition class, preparing PowerPoints for a speech course, or looking for help with integrating sources into a history assignment.

Students are different,

the tools are different,

but the goals are the same:

writing well and succeeding in college and beyond.

As students change, so, too, do the tools that students use for writing and research. Research occurs online via databases and the Web, and the greatest challenges students face are not in finding sources, but in choosing and evaluating the most appropriate sources and using them effectively in their projects. Word processing and presentation software and writing for the Web have increased the importance of visuals and design in writing. Many composition courses make use of digital technologies such as electronic portfolios or blogs and use Blackboard or other course-management systems to foster student collaboration and online peer review.

Even though the occasions, tools, and audiences for writing seem more varied than ever, the fundamental goals of composition courses persist. Instructors strive to produce students who can think critically, recognize rhetorical situations, communicate clearly and effectively, write in a variety of genres, and edit their own work. Students must be discerning and ethical researchers, acknowledging the contributions of others and documenting sources appropriately. And composition courses still aim to build writing skills that students will carry with them into their other courses, their work in the community, and their professional lives. In response to these goals—suggested by the Writing Program Administrators Outcomes Statement for First-Year Composition (reproduced on p. xiv) and those of many colleges and universities—*A Writer's Resource* pays new attention to commonly identified outcomes for composition to help students track their progress and understand how they may be assessed.

Today's students need a handbook with state-of-the-art, accessible resources on writing, researching, editing, and design—a handbook they can rely on for all their academic writing.

In revising this text, we have dedicated ourselves to making *A Writer's Resource* an even stronger, more current, and more versatile resource for achieving excellence in the ever-changing environments that students encounter in college.

Features of *A Writer's Resource*

Specific, student- and instructor-tested features of *A Writer's Resource* equip today's students with tools for learning, writing, researching, and editing. The book also provides students and teachers with access to powerful online resources.

A Ready Resource

The third edition of *A Writer's Resource* meets the needs of busy students with new, quickly accessible features that make it an even more convenient reference tool.

New Resources for Writers: Identifying and Editing Common Problems foldout

This handy reference presents easy access to fixes for the most common errors students make when editing for clarity, grammatical conventions, and correctness (punctuation, mechanics, and spelling). On the back of this foldout, students will find **Quick Reference for Multilingual Writers,** a chart offering help with the most common problems that affect Generation 1.5 students and English language learners alike.

Revised and Expanded Resources for Writers foldouts for documenting in MLA and APA style

These foldouts reflect the most recent changes to these two styles of citation. On the front of each foldout, **Identifying and Documenting Sources,** flowcharts help guide students to the correct model citations in the text. On the reverse side, each panel includes visual guidelines for citing sources, showing where students can find the bibliographic information for a book, periodical, Web site, selection from an online database (MLA), or online article with Digital Object Identifier (APA). On the back of each foldout, flowcharts help guide students to the correct model citations in the text.

New Resources for Writers: Discipline-Specific Resources and World Map foldout

Since research forms a vital part of college writing, this pullout section includes up-to-date information on reference works and resources from a variety of disciplines. More reliable than a Google search, this listing of academically vetted sources provides students with a quick-reference guide to the places online and in the library where the research might reasonably start. A revised, full-color map of the world is found on the back of the foldout.

New attention to key writing outcomes

Writing Outcomes boxes at the beginning of each section indicate where students can find key material that will help them master aspects of writing such as rhetorical knowledge, the writing process, and critical thinking. Based on the WPA Outcomes Statement for First-Year Composition (reproduced on p. xiv), this feature helps students find the support they need to address the key issues in their writing on which they are likely to be assessed.

New checklists for self-assessment
These checklists on topics such as editing for style and avoiding plagiarism help students evaluate their work and reflect on processes for improving their writing.

New online interactive tutorials
The handbook offers important guidance for students throughout their college career and beyond, and these online guides help students get the most out of this valuable resource. Brief visual overviews to using the text accompany interactive quizzes that help students become more familiar with the text.

A Resource for Writing
A Writer's Resource recognizes the importance of critical thinking and academic writing in first-year composition.

Guidelines for the most common college writing assignments
Tab 3: Common Assignments across the Curriculum gives students step-by-step advice on writing the three most commonly assigned types of papers (informative, interpretive, and argumentative essays), as well as guidance on other common assignments including personal essays, case studies, lab reports, in-class essay exams, oral presentations with PowerPoint, and multimedia assignments. Three full student papers appear in this section as models.

A focus on critical thinking and effective writing across the curriculum
Although instructors in various disciplines may approach subject matter differently, thinking critically and writing logically are underlying expectations across the curriculum. For this reason, Tab 2: Writing and Designing Texts begins with a chapter on the connections among critical reading, thinking, and writing.

Real student writing
Because students learn best from models that relate to their actual experience, *A Writer's Resource* provides plentiful samples of student and professional writing for a variety of purposes—to inform, interpret, and argue. The chapter on revising presents a full-length edited student essay; the document design chapter contains a student's reflective essay from an electronic portfolio; the common assignments

chapters include three student papers; and the MLA and APA documentation chapters each feature a complete student research report.

This edition includes three *new* student sample papers:

- Reflective essay from an electronic portfolio
- Informative report in the social sciences
- Argument paper

New expanded coverage of argument and visual argument

The third edition further equips students for success in this important genre, with fuller treatment of the classical appeals, fallacies, counterarguments, and the classical, Toulmin, and Rogerian structures of argument. New material in Chapter 4: Reading, Thinking, Writing: The Critical Connection and Chapter 11: Arguments invites students to recognize the persuasive messages that surround them and help them to use those techniques in their own arguments.

New visual rhetoric icon complements integrated coverage of visual rhetoric

This image appears throughout the text and in the table of contents on the tabs. It guides students and instructors to sections dealing with the use of visuals—a complete listing also appears in the Quick Guide to Key Resources at the back of the book. *A Writer's Resource* includes a chapter on Learning in a Multimedia World in Tab 1: Learning across the Curriculum and a chapter on Finding and Creating Effective Visuals in Tab 5: Researching. Coverage is also integrated throughout the text, particularly in Tab 2: Writing and Designing Texts. In addition, the book itself includes visuals drawn from various disciplines, time periods, and cultures.

New updated coverage of today's technologies

Today's student has more opportunities to write than ever before, including Facebook and MySpace pages, e-mail and texting, chat rooms, and blogs. The text gives advice on using online tools for learning; practical suggestions for using online resources to collaborate and revise; a chapter on designing papers and preparing print and online portfolios; advice for writing scannable résumés; and TextConnex boxes with advice on technology and useful links throughout the text.

Preparation for writing at work and in the community

Tab 4: Writing beyond College demonstrates how writing in college prepares students for success in the professional world. Special topics include applying for internships, producing résumés, service learning, and creating brochures and newsletters. In addition, Writing beyond College boxes throughout the book illustrate the variety of writing situations students are likely to encounter outside of college.

A Resource for Researching
A Writer's Resource helps students navigate the complexities of research today.

New updated and expanded coverage of MLA, APA, and CSE documentation
Tabs 6–8 now conform to the seventh edition of the *MLA Handbook for Writers of Research Papers* (2009), the *APA Style Guide to Electronic References* (2007), and the seventh edition of the *CSE Manual for Authors, Editors, and Publishers* (2006). The text also includes up-to-date coverage of *Chicago Manual of Style* documentation. This expanded section contains 120 MLA citation models and 68 APA citation models.

New chapter on plagiarism, copyright, and intellectual property
Chapter 23: Plagiarism, Copyright, and Intellectual Property provides an overview of the issues of copyright, plagiarism, and fair use.

New expanded sections on integrating sources
In Chapter 24, more examples and guidelines give students additional advice on using sources effectively in their papers. More thorough explanation of acceptable and unacceptable paraphrases, summaries, and quotations enables students to avoid accidental plagiarism. An expanded overview of copyright, plagiarism, and fair use appears in Chapter 20: Plagiarism, Copyright, and Intellectual Property.

New Source Smart boxes
Appearing throughout Tab 5: Researching, these boxes offer students tips on researching wisely. Topics include creating a research strategy, conducting interviews, avoiding plagiarism, and integrating sources via summary, paraphrase, and quotation.

New expanded sections on how to evaluate and use online sources appropriately
Chapter 21 now includes an examination of the reliability of three Web sites. These guidelines help students conduct Web research wisely and choose sources appropriately. Chapter 24 helps students draw on a full range of media in their writing, with examples that include blog entries and audio podcasts.

New discussion of annotated bibliography
Chapter 24 includes a sample annotated bibliography. It shows students how to complete this common research assignment, enabling them to assess and track their sources.

A unique chapter on finding and creating effective visuals
Chapter 20: Finding and Creating Effective Visuals includes discussions of why and when students should—or should not—use images to reinforce a point and gives them practical advice on displaying information visually.

A Resource for Editing
A Writer's Resource helps today's students see how grammar fits into the writing process, so they can learn to become effective editors of their work.

Grammar in the context of editing
Most of the chapters in Tabs 9–11, which cover the conventions of English grammar, usage, punctuation, and mechanics, are structured first to teach students to identify a particular problem and then to edit to eliminate the problem in a way that strengthens their writing.

Identify and Edit boxes
These boxes appear in key style, grammar, and punctuation chapters. They give students (especially visual learners) strategies for identifying their most serious sentence problems and are especially useful for quick reference.

New common issues icon ✓
This new icon appears throughout the text and in the table of contents, highlighting sections that discuss students' most common difficulties with grammar, style, word choice, punctuation, and mechanics. These sections are listed in the Quick Guide to Key Resources at the back of the book and referenced, for quick consultation, on the Resources for Writers: Identifying and Editing Common Problems foldout.

New interactive online Test Yourself diagnostic quizzes
These interactive online diagnostics provide immediate feedback to students to let them know where they need improvement and where to find help in those areas. They help students gauge their strengths and weaknesses on the conventions of MLA and APA documentation, grammar, style, punctuation, and mechanics.

Advice on using grammar and style checkers
Boxes appearing near the beginning of most chapters in Tabs 9–11 warn students of the pitfalls of relying too much on computer grammar and style checkers when editing their work, empowering students to become their own grammar checkers.

A Resource for Learning
A Writer's Resource is unique in the amount of support it provides students to help them meet the challenges of learning in college.

A guide for success in college through writing

Tab 1: Learning across the Curriculum introduces students to the new territory of college and to college writing. In this unique section, we define concepts such as *discipline* and explain how to use writing as a tool for learning. New tips in Chapter 1 help students set priorities, take notes, and succeed in all their courses.

Abundant resources for multilingual writers

Starting in the very first tab, *A Writer's Resource* offers non-native speakers of English support for learning and writing in college. Chapter 3 advises multilingual students on how to use writing to deal with their unique challenges. Numerous For Multilingual Students boxes throughout the book and Tips for Multilingual Writers in Tab 12 (prepared by Maria Zlateva, director of ESL at Boston University) provide targeted advice on every stage of the writing process. A separate index for multilingual writers follows the main index. A complete list of all the For Multilingual Students boxes also appears in the back of the book. The Quick Reference for Multilingual Writers foldout offers handy grammar tips in a convenient format.

New attention to Generation 1.5 of English language learners

Chapter 3: Learning in a Multilingual World now addresses both traditional ESL students and members of Generation 1.5, who have marginal proficiency in English as well as one or more other languages.

Further resources for learning

The innovative final section of the book (Tab 13: Further Resources for Learning) provides students with a variety of resources—a timeline of world history, a glossary of selected terms from across the curriculum, a pullout map of the world, and a directory of print and online discipline-specific resources—that will come in handy for students in a wide variety of courses.

Charting the Territory boxes

These boxes provide students with examples of how requirements and conventions vary across the curriculum. They present relevant information on such topics as interpretive assignments in different disciplines and the function of the passive voice in scientific writing.

A Resource for Technology

Online Learning Center (www.mhhe.com/awr3)

Throughout *A Writer's Resource,* Web references in the margin let students know where they can find additional resources on the text's comprehensive Web site. Access to the site—which is powered by *Catalyst 2.0,* the premier online resource for writing, research, and editing—is free with every copy of *A Writer's Resource.* The site includes the following resources for students:

- Interactive tutorials on document design and visual rhetoric
- Guides for avoiding plagiarism and evaluating sources
- Electronic writing tutors for composing informative, interpretive, and argumentative papers
- Over 4,500 exercises with feedback in grammar, usage, and punctuation

Additional options online:

Connect Composition for *A Writer's Resource*
This online premium companion to the text provides students and instructors with:

- **Interactive exercises and assignments keyed to the chapters of the text** allow students to practice the material in the text and submit assignments online.

- **Digital diagnostics and study plan** allow students to test themselves and find where they might need help; Connect Composition will then suggest a course of study including video instruction, practice exercises, and a post-test.

- **Online peer review tools** allow instructors to administer peer review in a flexible, easy-to-use electronic format that helps students throughout the process of inventing, drafting, and revising their work.

- **Live, online tutors** via Net Tutor offer students help with their writing when instructors or writing centers might not be available.

- **Numerous additional interactive resources for writing and research,** including interactive writing tutors and tutorials for visual rhetoric and avoiding plagiarism, provide students with help throughout the writing process.

Connect Composition Plus: *The McGraw-Hill Handbook Online*
This interactive, economic alternative to the print text includes all of the features contained in Connect Composition *plus:*

- **All the content of the full handbook online,** optimized for online reading—with material broken out in easy-to-read chunks of information, with interactive elements integrated contextually throughout.

- **A state-of-the-art search portal** which allows students to explore the whole text using numerous digital navigational tools including text and advanced text search options, hyperlinked indexes and table of contents, interactive resources for writers pages for help with the most common problems, and multimedia quick links that offer instant access to all of the text's multimedia instruction in one place.

- **Over 100 Ask the Author video segments** integrated throughout the digital text, providing students with instant access multimedia guidance on the most commonly asked questions about writing, researching, editing, and designing their work.

- **An economical price** providing students access to the interactive text for approximately half the price of the print text.

CourseSmart is a new way for faculty to find and review eTextbooks. It is also a great option for students who are interested in accessing their course materials digitally and saving money. CourseSmart offers thousands of the most commonly adopted textbooks across hundreds of courses from a wide variety of higher education publishers. It is the only place for faculty to review and compare the full text of a textbook online, providing immediate access without the environmental impact of requesting a print exam copy. At CourseSmart, students can save up to 50% off the cost of a print book, reduce their impact on the environment, and gain access to powerful web tools for learning including full text search, notes and highlighting, and e-mail tools for sharing notes between classmates.

McGraw Hill ⓣegrity campus

Tegrity Campus is a service that makes class time available all the time by automatically capturing every lecture in a searchable format for students to review when they study and complete assignments. With a simple one-click start and stop process, you capture all computer screens and corresponding audio. Students replay any part of any class with easy-to-use browser-based viewing on a PC or Mac.

Educators know that the more students can see, hear, and experience class resources, the better they learn. With Tegrity Campus, students quickly recall key moments by using Tegrity Campus's unique search feature. This search helps students efficiently find what they need, when they need it across an entire semester of class recordings. Help turn all your students' study time into learning moments immediately supported by your lecture.

To learn more about Tegrity, watch a two-minute Flash demo at http://tegritycampus.mhhe.com.

WPA Outcomes Statement for First-Year Composition

Adopted by the Council of Writing Program Administrators (WPA), April 2000. For further information about the development of the Outcomes Statement, please see http://comppile .tamucc.edu/ WPAoutcomes/continue.html

For further information about the Council of Writing Program Administrators, please see http://www.wpacouncil.org

A version of this statement was published in WPA: Writing Program Administration 23.1/2 (fall/winter 1999): 59–66

Introduction

This statement describes the common knowledge, skills, and attitudes sought by first-year composition programs in American postsecondary education. To some extent, we seek to regularize what can be expected to be taught in first-year composition; to this end the document is not merely a compilation or summary of what currently takes place. Rather, the following statement articulates what composition teachers nationwide have learned from practice, research, and theory. This document intentionally defines only "outcomes," or types of results, and not "standards," or precise levels of achievement. The setting of standards should be left to specific institutions or specific groups of institutions.

Learning to write is a complex process, both individual and social, that takes place over time with continued practice and informed guidance. Therefore, it is important that teachers, administrators, and a concerned public do not imagine that these outcomes can be taught in reduced or simple ways. Helping students demonstrate these outcomes requires expert understanding of how students actually learn to write. For this reason we expect the primary audience for this document to be well-prepared college writing teachers and college writing program administrators. In some places, we have chosen to write in their professional language. Among such readers, terms such as "rhetorical" and "genre" convey a rich meaning that is not easily simplified. While we have also aimed at writing a document that the general public can understand, in limited cases we have aimed first at communicating effectively with expert writing teachers and writing program administrators.

These statements describe only what we expect to find at the end of first-year composition, at most schools a required general education course or sequence of courses. As writers move beyond first-year composition, their writing abilities do not merely improve. Rather, students' abilities not only diversify along disciplinary and professional lines but also move into whole new levels where expected outcomes expand, multiply, and diverge. For this reason, each statement of outcomes for first-year composition is followed by suggestions for further work that builds on these outcomes.

Rhetorical Knowledge

By the end of first-year composition, students should
- Focus on a purpose
- Respond to the needs of different audiences

- Respond appropriately to different kinds of rhetorical situations
- Use conventions of format and structure appropriate to the rhetorical situation
- Adopt appropriate voice, tone, and level of formality
- Understand how genres shape reading and writing
- Write in several genres

Faculty in all programs and departments can build on this preparation
by helping students learn
- The main features of writing in their fields
- The main uses of writing in their fields
- The expectations of readers in their fields

Critical Thinking, Reading, and Writing
By the end of first-year composition, students should
- Use writing and reading for inquiry, learning, thinking, and communicating
- Understand a writing assignment as a series of tasks, including finding, evaluating, analyzing, and synthesizing appropriate primary and secondary sources
- Integrate their own ideas with those of others
- Understand the relationships among language, knowledge, and power

Faculty in all programs and departments can build on this preparation
by helping students learn
- The uses of writing as a critical thinking method
- The interactions among critical thinking, critical reading, and writing
- The relationships among language, knowledge, and power in their fields

Processes
By the end of first-year composition, students should
- Be aware that it usually takes multiple drafts to create and complete a successful text
- Develop flexible strategies for generating, revising, editing, and proof-reading
- Understand writing as an open process that permits writers to use later invention and re-thinking to revise their work
- Understand the collaborative and social aspects of writing processes
- Learn to critique their own and others' works
- Learn to balance the advantages of relying on others with the responsibility of doing their part
- Use a variety of technologies to address a range of audiences

Faculty in all programs and departments can build on this preparation
by helping students learn
- To build final results in stages
- To review work-in-progress in collaborative peer groups for purposes other than editing
- To save extensive editing for later parts of the writing process
- To apply the technologies commonly used to research and communicate within their fields

Knowledge of Conventions

By the end of first-year composition, students should
- Learn common formats for different kinds of texts
- Develop knowledge of genre conventions ranging from structure and paragraphing to tone and mechanics
- Practice appropriate means of documenting their work
- Control such surface features as syntax, grammar, punctuation, and spelling

Faculty in all programs and departments can build on this preparation by helping students learn
- The conventions of usage, specialized vocabulary, format, and documentation in their fields
- Strategies through which better control of conventions can be achieved [http://www.wpacouncil.org/positions/outcomes.html, accessed 10/17/2008]

Supplements to *A Writer's Resource*

Instructor's Manual **(available online in printable format)** **(www.mhhe.com/awr3)**
Deborah Coxwell Teague, Florida State University; Dan Melzer, California State University, Sacramento; Thomas Dinsmore, University of Cincinnati

MLA Quick Reference Guide **(ISBN 0-07-730080-7)**
Carol Schuck, Ivy Tech Community College
This handy card features the basic guidelines for MLA citation in a convenient, portable format.

APA Quick Reference Guide **(ISBN 0-07-730076-9)**
This handy card features the basic guidelines for APA citation in a convenient, portable format.

Partners in Teaching: Instructor Resource Portal for Composition **(www.mhhe.com/englishcommunity)**
McGraw-Hill is proud to partner with many of the top names in the field to build a *community of teachers helping teachers. Partners in Teaching* features up-to-date scholarly discourse, practical teaching advice, and community support for new and experienced instructors.

The McGraw-Hill Exercise Book **(ISBN 0-07-326032-0)**
Santi Buscemi, Middlesex College and Susan Popham, University of Memphis
This workbook features numerous sentence-level and paragraph-level editing exercises, as well as exercises in research, documentation, and the writing process.

The McGraw-Hill Exercise Book for Multilingual Writers
(ISBN 0-07-326030-4)
Maggie Sokolik, University of California, Berkeley
This workbook features numerous sentence-level and paragraph-level editing exercises tailored specifically for multilingual students.

The McGraw-Hill Writer's Journal **(ISBN 0-07-326031-2)**
Lynée Gaillet, Georgia State University
This elegant journal for students includes quotes on writing from famous authors as well as advice and tips on writing and the writing process.

Dictionary and Vocabulary Resources

McGraw-Hill, in partnership with Merriam Webster, offers a wide variety of language references for students. From the *Collegiate Dictionary* to the *Notebook Thesaurus,* these resources can be packaged with *A Writer's Resource* at an affordable price. Please contact your McGraw-Hill representative directly, email english@mcgraw-hill.com, or call 800-338-3987 for details.

Acknowledgments

When we wrote *A Writer's Resource,* we started with the premise that it takes a campus to teach a writer. It is also the case that it takes a community to write a handbook. This text has been a major collaborative effort for all three of us. And over the years, that ever-widening circle of collaboration has included reviewers, editors, librarians, faculty colleagues, and family members.

Let us start close to home. Mort Maimon brought to this project his years of insight and experience as a writer and as a secondary and post-secondary English teacher. Gillian Maimon, a first-grade teacher, a PhD candidate, and a writing workshop leader, and Alan Maimon, a journalist who is expert in using every resource available to writers, inspired and encouraged their mother in this project. Elaine also drew inspiration from her young granddaughters, Dasia and Madison Stewart and Annabelle Elaine Maimon, who already show promise of becoming writers. Rudy Peritz and Lynne Haney reviewed drafts of a number of chapters, bringing to our cross-curricular mix the pedagogical and writerly perspectives of, respectively, a law professor and a sociologist. Jess Peritz, a recent college graduate, was consulted on numerous occasions for her expert advice on making examples both up-to-date and understandable. David, Genevieve, and Matthew Yancey—whose combined writing experience includes the fields of biology, psychology, medicine, computer engineering, mathematics, industrial engineering, and information technology—helped with examples as well as with their understandings of writing both inside and outside of the academy.

At Governors State University, Diane Dates Casey, dean of Library Science and Academic Computing, provided research support, while Executive Assistant Penny Purdue was always ready with overall encouragement. At Arizona State University West, Beverly Buddee, executive assistant to the provost, worried with us over this project for many years. Our deepest gratitude goes to Lisa Kammerlocher and Dennis Isbell for the guidelines on critically evaluating Web resources in Chapter 18, as well as to Sharon Wilson. Thanks, too, go to C. J. Jeney and Cheryl Warren for providing assistance. ASU West professors Thomas McGovern and Martin Meznar shared assignments and student papers with us. In the chancellor's office at the University of Alaska Anchorage, Denise Burger, and Christine Tullius showed admirable support and patience.

Several colleagues at Queens College and elsewhere not only shared their insights on teaching and writing, but also gave us valuable classroom materials to use as we saw fit. Our thanks go to Fred Buell, Stuart Cochran, Nancy Comley, Ann Davison, Joan Dupre, Hugh English, Sue Goldhaber, Marci Goodman, Steve Kruger, Eric Lehman, Norman Lewis, Charles Molesworth, Beth Stickney, Amy Tucker, and Stan Walker. We are also grateful to Jane Collins, Jane Hathaway, Jan Tecklin, Christine Timm, Scott Zaluda, Diane Zannoni, and Richard Zeikowitz. The Queens College librarians also gave us help with the researching and documentation chapters, and we thank them, especially Sharon Bonk, Alexandra DeLuise, Isabella Taler, and Manny Sanudo.

We want to give special thanks to the students whose papers we include in full: Ken Tinnes, John Terrell, Rajeev Bector, Matt Shadwell, Esther Hoffman, and Audrey Galeano. We also want to acknowledge the following students who allowed us to use substantial excerpts from their work: Diano Chen, Jennifer Koehler, Ilona Bouzoukashvili, Wilma Ferrarella, Jacob Grossman, and Umawattie Roopnarian.

Our thanks also go to Judy Williamson and Trent Batson for contributing their expertise on writing and computers as well as for sharing what they learned from the Epiphany Project. We are grateful to Harvey Wiener and the late Richard Marius for their permission to draw on their explanations of grammatical points in *The McGraw-Hill Handbook*. We also appreciate the work of Andras Tapolcai and of Charlotte Smith of Adirondack Community College, who collected many of the examples used in the documentation chapters. Maria Zlateva of Boston University, Karen Batchelor of City College of San Francisco, and Daria Ruzicka prepared the ESL materials. Thanks also go to librarians Debora Person, University of Wyoming, and Ronelle K. H. Thompson, Augustana College, who provided us with helpful comments on Tab 5: Researching. Our colleague Don McQuade has inspired us, advised us, and encouraged us throughout the years of this project.

Within the McGraw-Hill organization, many wonderful people have been our true teammates. Tim Julet believed in this project initially and signed us on to what has become a major life commitment. From 1999, Lisa Moore, first as executive editor for the composition list, then as publisher for English, and now as publisher for special projects in Art, Humanities, and Literature, has creatively, expertly, and tirelessly led the group of development editors and in-house experts who have helped us find the appropriate form to bring our insights as composition teachers to the widest possible group of students. We have learned a great deal from Lisa. Thanks also to Christopher Bennem, who had the unenviable job of filling Lisa's shoes as sponsoring editor. Crucial support also came from Beth Mejia, editorial director; David Patterson, publisher for English; and Molly Meneely, market development manager. This book has benefited enormously from three extraordinary development editors: Anne Kemper, development editor; Carla Samodulski, senior development editor; and David Chodoff, senior development editor. All were true collaborators; as the chapters on editing show, the book has benefited enormously from their care and intelligence. Other editorial kudos go out to Meredith Grant, Drew Henry, Karen Herter, Bruce Thaler, Joanna Imm, Judy Voss, Sarah Caldwell, Laura Olson, Elsa Peterson, Aaron Zook, Karen Mauk, Steven Kemper, and Margaret Farley for their tireless work on this project. Thanks as well to Paul Banks, Andrea Pasquarelli, Todd Vaccaro, Alex Rohrs, and Manoj Mehta, without whom there would be no *Catalyst 2.0.* Chanda Feldman and Brett Coker, lead project managers, monitored every detail of production; Cassandra Chu, lead designer, supervised every aspect of the striking text design and cover; and Robin Mouat and Sonia Brown, art editors, were responsible for the stunning visuals that appear throughout the book. Allison Jones, marketing manager and Ray Kelley, Paula Radosevich, Byron Hopkins, Barbara Siry, and Brian Gore, field publishers, have worked tirelessly and enthusiastically to market *A Writer's Resource.* Jeff Brick provided valuable promotional support for the project. We also appreciate the hands-on attention of McGraw-Hill senior executives Mike Ryan, editor-in-chief of the Humanities, Social Sciences, and World Languages group; and Steve Debow, president of the Humanities, Social Sciences, and World Languages group.

Finally, many, many thanks go to the reviewers who read this text, generously shared their perceptions, and had confidence in us as we shaped this book to address the needs of their students. We wish to thank the following instructors:

Content Consultants and Reviewers

Kristina Ambrosia-Conn, Cleveland State University
Frank Ancona, Sussex County Community College

Suzanne Ashby, Pima Community College
James Baskin, Joliet Junior College
Julie Basler, Platt College

Paula Battistelli, Austin Community College
Gary Bays, Wayne College
Nicholas Bekas, Valencia Community College

Michael Benton, Bluegrass Community and Technical College

Paula Berggren, Bernard M. Baruch College

Angela Bilia, University of Akron

Jacqueline Blackwell, Thomas Nelson Community College

Laurel Bollinger, University of Alabama, Huntsville

Eric Branscomb, Salem State College

Tamara Brattoli, Joliet Junior College

Beth Buyserie, Washington State University

Jeffrey Cain, Sacred Heart University

Steve Calatrello, Calhoun Community College

Richard Carr, University of Alaska, Fairbanks

Kathleen J. Cassity, Hawaii Pacific University

Andrew Cavanaugh, University of Maryland

John Chapin, University of Baltimore

Stephanie Clark-Graham, University of Maryland

Joseph Colicchio, Hudson County Community College

Tami Comstock, Arapahoe Community College

Preston Cooper, Austin Community College

Linda Damas, University of Hawaii, Hilo

Mary Ellen Daniloff-Merrill, Southwest Minnesota State University

Michael Day, Northern Illinois University

Rose Day, Central New Mexico Community College

Robert Detmering, Northern Kentucky University

Tom Dow, Moraine Valley Community College

Taylor Emery, Austin Peay State University

Nancy Enright, Seton Hall University

Priscilla Faucette, University of Hawaii, Manoa

Paul J. Ferlazzo, Northern Arizona University

Jason Fichtel, Joliet Junior College

David Fleming, University of Massachusetts–Amherst

Thom Foy, University of Michigan, Dearborn

Lynée Gaillet, Georgia State University

Fernando Ganivett, Florida International University, Miami

Ruth Gerik, University of Texas at Arlington

Mary Val Gerstle, University of Cincinnati

Sam Goldstein, Daytona Beach Community College

Dwonna Goldstone, Austin Peay State University

John Gooch, University of Texas at Dallas

Gary Goodman, University of California, Davis

Nate Gordon, Kishwaukee College

Creed Greer, University of Florida, Gainesville

John Griffith, Butler County Community College

Lynn Grow, Broward Community College

Elizabeth Grundhoffer, New Mexico State University, Alamogordo

Billie Hara, Texas Christian University

Carolyn Harrison, Oakland Community College, Royal Oak

Kimberly Harrison, Florida International University, Biscayne

Cynthia Haynes, Clemson University

Harold Hellwig, Idaho State University

Bruce Henderson, Fullerton College

Matt Hollrah, University of Central Oklahoma

Dedria A. Humphries, Lansing Community College

Jeffrey Ihlenfeldt, Harrisburg Area Community College, Lancaster

Rebecca Ingalls, Drexell University

Tammy Jabin, Chemeketa Community College

Kim Jacobs-Beck, University of Cincinnati, Clermont College

Doris Jellig, Tidewater Community College

Melanie Jenkins, Snow College

Debra Johanyak, Wayne College

Allen Johnson, Christian Brothers University

Matthew Johnson, Southern Illinois University, Edwardsville

Tracy Johnson, Butte College

Meryl Junious, Kennedy-King College

Judith La Fourest, Ivy Tech Community College, Central Indiana

Jessica Lang, Bernard M. Baruch College

Patricia Lonchar, University of the Incarnate Word

Michael Lynch, Kent State University, Trumbull

Joyce Malek, University of Cincinnati

Tammy Mata, Tarrant County College

Donna Matsumoto, Leeward Community College

Gretchen McCroskey, Northeast State Technical Community College

Jeanne McDonald, Waubonsee Community College

John McDonald, University of Portland

Hildy Miller, Portland State University

Thomas Moretti, University of Maryland

Robin Murray, Eastern Illinois University

Mary Anne Nagler, Oakland Community College

Bev Neiderman, Kent State University

Paul Nolan, Cayuga Community College

Torria Norman, Black Hawk College

Kelly O'Connor-Salomon, Russell Sage College
Marilyn Palkovacs, University of Cincinnati
Melinda D. Papaccio, Seton Hall University
Martha Payne, Ball State University
Sarah Quirk, Waubonsee Community College
Christa Raney, University of North Alabama
Peggy Richards, University of Akron
Barbara Rico, Loyola Marymount University

Rebecca Rios-Harris, Cedar Valley College
Kathy Roark-Diehl, New Mexico State University, Alamogordo
Robert Royer, Morehead State University
David Salomon, Russell Sage College
Mary Seel, Broome Community College
Marti Singer, Georgia State University
Wayne Stein, University of Central Oklahoma
Sheilah Stokes, Fullerton College

Margaret Strain, University of Dayton
Linda Tetzlaff, Normandale Community College
Beth Thames, Calhoun Community College
Jo Ann Thompson, University of Cincinnati
Elizabeth Wardle, University of Central Florida
Kathie White, Pima Community College
Anita Wyman, Hillsboro Community College

Editorial Board of Advisors

Steve Adkison, Idaho State University
Robert Eddy, Washington State University
Paula Eschliman, Richland College
Randall McClure, Florida Gulf Coast University
K. J. Peters, Loyola Marymount University
William Thelin, University of Akron

Freshman Composition Symposia

Every year McGraw-Hill conducts Freshman Composition Symposia, which are attended by instructors from across the country. These events are an opportunity for editors from McGraw-Hill to gather information about the needs and challenges of instructors teaching the Freshman Composition course. They also offer a forum for the attendees to exchange ideas and experiences with colleagues they might not have otherwise met. The feedback we have received has been invaluable and has contributed—directly or indirectly—to the development of *A Writer's Resource* and its supplements.

Ellen Arnold, Coastal Carolina University
Tony Atkins, University of North Carolina, Wilmington
Edith Baker, Bradley University
Evan Balkan, Community College of Baltimore
Carolyn Barr, Broward Community College
Laura Basso, Joliet Junior College
Linda Bergmann, Purdue University
Karen Bilda, Cardinal Stritch University
Carol Bledsoe, Florida Gulf Coast University
Kimberly Bovee, Tidewater Community College

Charley Boyd, Genesee Community College
Charlotte Brammer, Samford University
Amy Braziller, Red Rocks Community College
Bob Broad, Illinois State University
Cheryl Brown, Towson University
Liz Bryant, Purdue University, Calumet, Hammond
JoAnn Buck, Guilford Technical Community College
Monica Busby, University of Louisiana, Lafayette
Jonathan Bush, Western Michigan University

Steve Calatrello, Calhoun Community College
Susan Callendar, Sinclair Community College
Diane Canow, Johnson County Community College
Richard Carpenter, Valdosta State University
Sandy Clark, Anderson University
Keith Comer, University of Canterbury
Jennifer Cooper, University of Texas, Arlington
Deborah Coxwell-Teague, Florida State University
Mary Ann Crawford, Central Michigan University

The compass has long been a tool for explorers and mapmakers. This book was designed to be a compass for writing in any discipline.

1

The adequate study of culture, our own and those on the opposite side of the globe, can press on to fulfillment only as we learn today from the humanities as well as from the scientists.

—RUTH BENEDICT

Learning across the Curriculum

1

Learning across the Curriculum

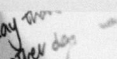 Section dealing with visual rhetoric. For a complete listing, see the Quick Guide to Key Resources at the back of this book.

WRITING OUTCOMES

Tab 1: Learning across the Curriculum
This section will help you answer questions such as:

Rhetorical Knowledge
Why is it fine for me to use emoticons and abbreviations in text messages but not in a college paper? **(2b)**
How can belonging to more than one culture help my writing? **(3)**

Critical Thinking, Reading, and Writing
How can writing help me learn in all my college courses? **(1b)**
How can I plan my time in college? **(1c)**
How can writing help me develop fluency in English? **(3)**

Processes
How can technology help me work with other students on writing projects? **(2b)**
What does social networking have to do with college writing? **(2b)**

Knowledge of Conventions
What is a discipline? **(1a)**
How can I tell what my instructors expect of me in college? **(1c)**

1 Writing to Learn

College is a place for exploration, where you will travel through many courses, participating in numerous conversations—oral and written—about nature, society, and culture. As you navigate your college experience, use this book as your map and guide:

- **As a map:** this text will help you understand the different approaches to knowledge and see how your studies relate to the larger world of learning.
- **As a guide:** this text will help you write everything from notes to exams to research papers.

1a Study the world through a range of academic disciplines.

www.mhhe.com/awr3
For discipline-related resources, go to
Learning > Links across the Curriculum

Each department in your college represents a specialized field of academic study, or area of inquiry, called a **discipline.** Each discipline has its own history, terminology, issues, and subgroups. Sociology, for example, is concerned with the conditions, patterns, and problems of people in groups and societies. Sociologists collect, analyze, and interpret data about groups and societies; they also debate the data's reliability and various ways to interpret the data. These debates occur in journals, books, conferences, and classrooms.

Your college curriculum is likely to include distribution requirements that will expose you to a range of disciplines. You may be asked to take one or two courses in the humanities (the disciplines of literature, music, and philosophy, for example), the social sciences (sociology, economics, and psychology, for example), and the natural sciences (physics, biology, and chemistry, for example). When you write in each discipline—taking notes, writing papers, answering essay-exam questions—you will join the academic conversation, deepen your understanding of how knowledge is constructed, and learn to see and think about the world from different vantage points.

1b Use writing as a tool for learning.

www.mhhe.com/awr3
For activities to help strengthen your active reading skills, go to
Learning > Writing to Learn Exercises

One goal of this handbook is to help you research and write assignments well. As you go from course to course, however, remember that writing itself is a great aid to learning. Think of the way a simple shopping list aids your memory once you get to the store. Writing helps you remember, understand, and create.

CHARTING the TERRITORY

Getting the Most from a Course

When you take a course, your purpose is not just to amass information. Your purpose is also to understand the kinds of questions people who work in the discipline ask.

- In an art history class, you might ask how a work relates to an artist's life and times.
- In a math class, you might ask what the practical applications of a particular concept are.

- **Writing aids memory.** From taking class notes to jotting down ideas for later development, writing ensures that you will be able to retrieve important information. Many students find it useful to use an informal outline for lecture notes (*see Figure 1.1*) and then fill in details after class. Also write down ideas inspired by your course work—in any form or order. These ideas can be seeds for research projects or some other critical inquiry.

- **Writing sharpens observations.** When you record what you see, hear, taste, smell, and feel, you increase the powers of your senses. Note the smells during a chemistry experiment, and you will detect changes caused by reactions more readily.

- **Writing clarifies thought.** Carefully reading your own early drafts helps you pinpoint what you really want to say. Often, the last paragraph of a first draft becomes the first paragraph of the next one.

- **Writing uncovers connections.** Maybe a character in a short story reminds you of your next-door neighbor, or an image in a poem makes you feel sad. Writing down the reasons you make connections like these can help you learn more about the work, and possibly more about yourself.

- **Writing improves reading.** When you read, taking notes on the main ideas and drafting a brief summary of the writer's points sharpens your reading skills and helps you retain what you have read. Writing a personal reaction to the reading enhances your understanding. (*For a detailed discussion of critical reading and writing, see Chapter 4.*)

- **Writing strengthens argument.** In the academic disciplines, an **argument** is not a fiery disagreement but rather a path of reasoning to a position. When you write an argument,

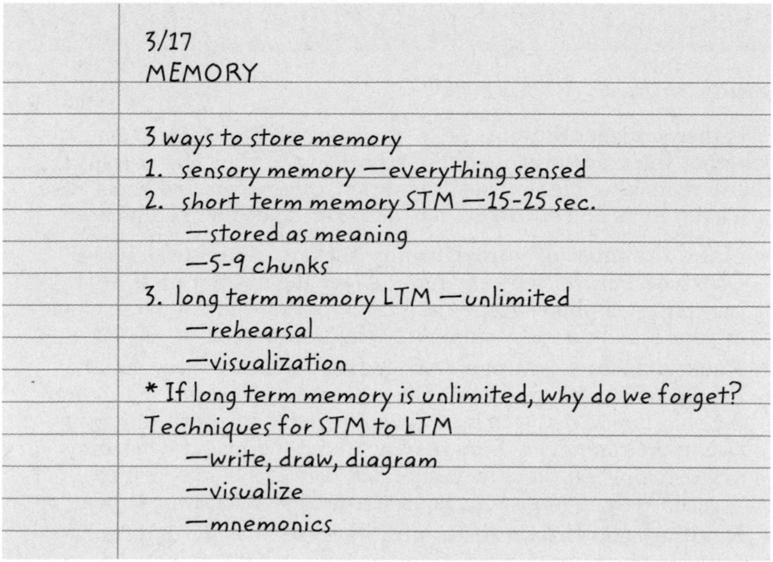

> 3/17
> MEMORY
>
> 3 ways to store memory
> 1. sensory memory — everything sensed
> 2. short term memory STM — 15-25 sec.
>   — stored as meaning
>   — 5-9 chunks
> 3. long term memory LTM — unlimited
>   — rehearsal
>   — visualization
>   * If long term memory is unlimited, why do we forget?
> Techniques for STM to LTM
>   — write, draw, diagram
>   — visualize
>   — mnemonics

FIGURE 1.1 An outline for lecture notes. Jotting down the main ideas of a lecture and the questions they raise helps you become a more active listener.

you work out the connections between your ideas—uncovering both flaws that force you to rethink your position and new connections that make your position even stronger. Writing also requires you to consider your audience and the objections they might raise. (*For a detailed discussion of argument, see Chapter 11.*)

1c Take responsibility for reading, writing, and research.

www.mhhe.com/awr3

For help with college survival techniques, go to

Learning > Study Skills Tutor

The academic community assumes that you are an independent learner, capable of managing your workload without supervision. For most courses, the syllabus will be your primary guide to what is expected of you. Use the syllabus to map out your weekly schedule for reading, research, and writing. (*For tips on how to schedule a research paper, see Chapter 18, pp. 197–203.*)

If you are collaborating with a group on a project, plan a series of meetings well in advance to avoid schedule conflicts. Also, make time for your solo projects away from all distractions. You will be much more efficient if you work in shorter blocks of concentrated time than if you let your reading and writing drag on for interruption-filled hours.

Tips

LEARNING in COLLEGE

Study Skills

Whether academic pursuits are a struggle or come easily to you, whether you are fresh out of high school or are returning to school many years after high school graduation, college is a challenge. Here are a few hints and strategies for taking on these new challenges.

- **Make the most of your time by setting clear priorities.** Deal with surprises by saying "no," getting away from it all, taking control of phone and e-mail interruptions, and leaving slack in your schedule to accommodate the unexpected.
- **Recognize how you prefer to learn.** *Tactile learners* prefer hands-on learning that comes about through touching, manipulating objects, and doing things. *Visual learners* like to see information in their mind, favoring reading and watching over touching and listening. *Auditory learners* favor listening as the best approach. Work on improving your less-preferred learning styles.
- **Evaluate the information you gather.** Consider how authoritative the source is, whether the author has any potential biases, how recent the information is, and whether anything important is missing from the research. In college, critical thinking is essential.
- **Take good notes.** The central feature of good note taking is listening and distilling important information—not writing down everything that is said.
- **Build reading and listening skills.** When you read, identify the main ideas, prioritize them, think critically about the arguments, and explain the writer's ideas to someone else. Listen actively: focus on what is being said, pay attention to nonverbal messages, listen for what is not being said, and take notes.
- **Improve your memory.** Rehearsal is the key strategy in remembering information. Repeat the information, summarize it, associate it with other memories, and above all, think about it when you first come across it.

Source: Based on Robert S. Feldman, *P.O.W.E.R. Learning: Strategies for Success in College and Life,* 2nd ed., New York: McGraw-Hill, 2003.

1d Recognize that writing improves with practice.

Composition courses will help you learn to write at the college level, but your development as a writer does not end there. Writing in all your courses will enable you to mature as a writer while preparing you for more writing after college.

2 Learning in a Multimedia World

More people than ever are using electronic media to write in school, in social situations, and in the workplace. Writing today includes sending a text message to a friend or an instant message to a relative in another city. You might have posted photos on a social networking Web site like MySpace or Facebook, or on your own blog (Web log). Perhaps you added an original video to a content-sharing site like YouTube. These sites are part of Web 2.0, a second generation of Internet sites and tools that foster user creativity and community. Their growth has led many people to write for different purposes and audiences: to stay in touch with friends or to develop a research project with an international colleague. Today's college writers read and compose verbal, audio, and visual texts.

2a Become aware of the persuasive power of images.

As a student, you will not only analyze images but also create them. Images, like words, require careful, critical analysis. A misleading chart, such as the one shown in Figure 2.1 on page 8, or an altered photograph can easily distort your perception of a subject. The ability not only to understand visual information but also to evaluate its credibility is an essential tool for learning and writing. (*For details on evaluating visuals, see Chapter 4: Reading, Thinking, Writing, pp. 21–37, and Chapter 11: Arguments, pp. 126–39.*)

2b Make effective use of multimedia elements.

Technology allows you to include images and other nonverbal elements in your writing to convey ideas more efficienty or powerfully. You can create these elements yourself or import them from other sources and place them where you want them. This passage from Beethoven's Fifth Symphony is one example:

A photograph or diagram or chart can contain information that adds details and makes relationships clearer. In a project for a geography course, for example, photographs can illustrate at a glance the effects

FIGURE 2.1 Misleading (top) and reliable charts. The graph on top, from a 1979 article in the *Wall Street Journal,* shows a dramatic and accelerating increase in currency in circulation in the United States between 1953 and 1979. As a measure of the purchasing power of the people who held the currency, however, the graph is misleading because it fails to take inflation into account. The second graph, corrected for inflation, reveals a steady but far less dramatic rate of increase.

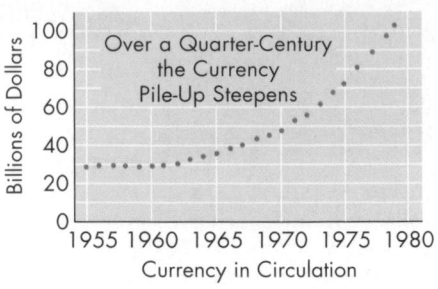

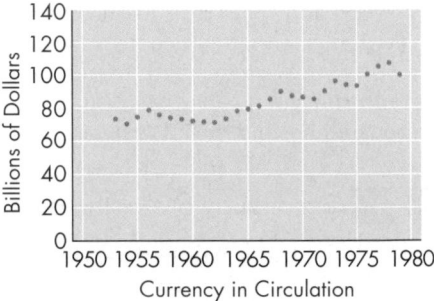

of a hurricane and the scale of recovery, as the images in Figure 2.2 on page 9 demonstrate.

A graph can effectively illustrate important trends for a history paper, as Figure 2.3 on page 10 shows. Similarly, a timeline, like the one in the "Further Resources for Learning" section at the end of this book, can help readers grasp the relationships among important events.

If you can post your composition online or deliver it as an electronic file to be read on a computer, you can include an even greater variety of media. You can supplement a musical passage, for example, with a link to an audio file of the passage.

Presentation software such as PowerPoint allows you to integrate audio and visual features into oral or stand-alone presentations. While effects such as animation can enliven your presentation, do not use multimedia elements solely for decoration.

(*For details on creating effective visuals, see Chapter 5: Planning and Shaping, pp. 54–56; Chapter 6: Drafting Text and Visuals, p. 72; Chapter 7: Revising and Editing, pp. 85–86; and Chapter 8: Designing Academic Papers and Portfolios. For information on creating oral and multimedia presentations, see Chapter 13: Oral Presentations and Chapter 14: Multimedia Writing. For help with finding appropriate visuals, see Chapter 20: Finding and Creating Effective Visuals.*)

FIGURE 2.2 Recovery from Hurricane Katrina. These photos show the same bridge over the Industrial Canal to the Lower Ninth Ward of New Orleans. The top photo dates from a few days after the storm hit in August 2005, while the bottom photo, taken nearly a year later, shows the city's recovery.

2c Take advantage of online and other electronic tools for learning.

www.mhhe.com/ awr3
For more about online resources, go to
Learning > Additional Links on Learning

Technology now makes it possible to transcend the constraints of the clock, the calendar, and the car and engage in educational activities 24/7, or twenty-four hours a day, seven days a week.

Different electronic tools work best for different purposes (*see the TextConnex box on p. 11*).

1. Communicating with e-mail

E-mail is one of the most frequently used forms of written communication in the world today. In some classes, you can use e-mail to communicate with your professor and other students. You can also e-mail a consultant in your school's writing center.

2. Using instant messaging

Instant messaging (IM) can be used to further your learning in much the same way as e-mail. Some instructors may encourage you

Total U.S. Resident Population 1800–1900, by decade (in thousands)

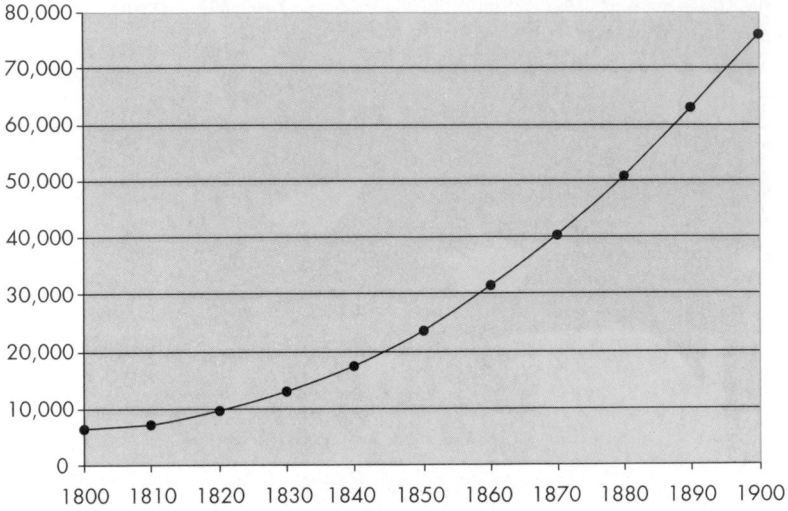

FIGURE 2.3 A line graph showing trends over time.

to contact them in this way. Like all other technologies, IM can distract you from your course work and should be used with care.

3. Consulting course Web sites

Your instructor may have a Web site for your course. If so, check it for late-breaking announcements, the course syllabus, assignments (and their due dates), and course-related links as well as other Web resources. (*For sites that are part of Web-based software offered by companies such as Blackboard, see Using course management software, p. 13.*)

4. Learning in networked classrooms and virtual classrooms

Some colleges and instructors are experimenting with **networked classrooms**—classrooms in which each student works at one of a network of linked computers. For example, your instructor might post daily assignments and discussion topics, and you might be assigned to work collaboratively on a writing project. Computers and the Internet also make it possible for students to engage in distance learning—from almost anywhere in the world—in courses conducted entirely online in **virtual classrooms.** Because you are interacting in writing rather than in spoken discussion, you can save ideas and comments for use in the first draft of a composition.

TEXTCONNEX

Digital Communication Tools: Best Uses

This table shows the most appropriate academic uses of six electronic communication tools.

	PEER REVIEW	GROUP PROJECT	FORMAL CONVER-SATION	INFORMAL CONVER-SATION	QUICK QUESTION	EXTENDED DISCUSSION
E-mail	X	X	X	X	X	X
Instant Message/ Chat	X	X		X	X	
Text Message				X	X	
Listserv		X	X	X	X	X
Blog	X	X		X		X
Wiki	X	X				X

5. Exchanging ideas through blogs

A **blog** is a continually updated Web site that features dated entries with commentary on a variety of topics, links to Web sites the authors find interesting, and (sometimes) a forum for readers' comments. In college classes students sometimes use blogs to summarize and reflect on readings. A class blog may allow students to comment on one another's drafts. Faculty may also use blogs as sites for sharing assignments. (*See Tab 3: Common Assignments across the Curriculum, pp. 170–72.*)

6. Using podcasts

Instructors often record their lectures as downloadable audio or video **podcasts,** making them available to the class for repeated listening and/or viewing on a computer or an MP3 player. Scholarly conference presentations often are podcast. Popular radio shows, television shows, and newspapers frequently include podcasts: the *New York Times,* for example, has a podcast of book reviews. Reputable podcasts are often important sources for research projects.

7. Sending text messages

Much like the shorthand once used by stenographers, text messages rely on abbreviations, but they also include emoticons, combinations of

TextConnex

Netiquette

The term **netiquette** combines the words *Internet* and *etiquette* to form a new word that stands for good manners online. Here are some netiquette guidelines:

- **Remember that most forms of electronic communication can be reproduced.** Avoid saying anything you would not want attributed to you or forwarded to others. Do not forward another person's words without consent.
- **Remember that you are interacting with real humans,** not machines, and practice kindness, patience, and good humor.
- **Use words economically,** and edit carefully. Readers become impatient and their eyes tire when they encounter all lowercase letters or text that lacks appropriate punctuation.
- **Bear in mind that without cues such as facial expressions, body language, and vocal intonation, your message can easily be misunderstood.** Be extra careful about humor that could be misread as sarcasm. Misunderstandings can escalate quickly into *flaming*—the sending of angry, inflammatory posts that use heated langauge.
- **Avoid ALL CAPS.** Typing in all caps is considered shouting.
- **Always seek permission to use other people's ideas** and acknowledge them properly.
- **Never copy other people's words and present them as your own.** This practice, known as *plagiarism,* is always wrong. (*See Tabs 6–8 for help with citing Internet sources.*)
- **Limit e-mails to a single topic and use accurate subject headers. Include a sufficient portion of the previous text** when responding to an e-mail, or use a dash to keep the conversation flowing and to provide context. **Include your name and contact information at the end of every e-mail you send.**
- **When sending text messages, use abbreviations in moderation.** Keep messages brief, but do not use so many abbreviations and emoticons that your meaning is obscured.

characters that look like images, such as :-). Emoticons and abbreviations should not be used in formal college or professional writing situations. Texting is especially useful for very short messages, and its abbreviations can be used in class notes to make note taking faster.

8. Creating and sharing videos

Outside school and in some college classes, many students and instructors create short videos, which they may post on video sharing sites such

TEXTCONNEX

Web 2.0

The Machine Is Us/ing Us, a video by Michael Wesch of Kansas State University, shows some defining features of Web 2.0. <http://mediatedcultures.net/mediatedcultures.htm>

as YouTube. While such compositions usually have a specific intended audience, many Web sites allow them to be viewed by anyone with Internet access. In academic contexts, creating videos helps students analyze the persuasive videos (e.g., advertisements) that surround us.

9. Social networking

Social networking sites (like MySpace and Facebook) allow users to create personal profiles and connect to their friends' profiles. Sometimes, people use these sites to discuss writing projects, conduct surveys, and locate experts. Such sites include two kinds of postings: private, from person to person; and public, from one person to many. Remember that the information you post on these sites is potentially public and visible to possible employers.

10. Collaborating through wikis

A **wiki** comprises interlinking Web pages created collaboratively, which form databases of information. Multiple people create and edit pages on the site. College students and instructors often use wikis to create collaborative projects. The popular online encyclopedia Wikipedia is not always accurate because almost anyone can create or edit its content. The content of some other wikis is created and monitored by experts. Always learn enough about a wiki to assess its reliability (*see Tab 5: Researching, p. 207 and pp. 227–32*).

11. Exploring virtual environments

Some college students and instructors use virtual spaces for group projects. These include graphic **virtual worlds** such as SecondLife.com as well as older text-based technologies such as **MUDs** (multiuser dimensions) and **MOOs** (multiuser object-oriented dimensions). (*See Tab 5: Researching, p. 219.*)

12. Using course management software

Many colleges offer some kind of course management software (CMS) like Blackboard. Although these programs vary, they typically include common features that students can access at any time via a password-protected course Web page.

"Distribution" features allow instructors to present the course syllabus, assignments, and readings. "Contribution" features promote class participation and communication. These features may include e-mail systems; bulletin boards and chat rooms for class discussions; and folders where students can post their work to be read and commented on by classmates and the instructor. **Chat rooms** are online spaces that permit real-time communication. All participants in a chat see the text of the others as they type. Often the CMS will save a transcript of the chat for future reference.

www.mhhe.com/
awr3
To explore *Catalyst*,
go to
Home

Some CMS software includes tools for **peer review,** in which students comment on one another's writing at specific stages in the writing process. Specialized software, like the writing environment in the *Catalyst* Web site that accompanies this book, makes peer review an efficient and accessible learning tool.

If your course has a home page, take time to become familiar with its features—as well as any related course requirements—at the beginning of the semester. (*For more on chat rooms, see Tab 2: Writing and Designing Texts, p. 47.*)

3 Learning in a Multilingual World

To some extent, all college students navigate multiple cultures and languages. The language of anthropology, for example, probably sounds strange and new to most students. In college, students who know two or more languages have an advantage over those who know only English. As a multilingual student, you will be able to contribute insights about other cultures. Your knowledge may ultimately provide more career opportunities in a rapidly globalizing world.

This book uses the term "multilingual" to address students from varied cultural, national, and linguistic backgrounds. You may be an international student learning to speak and write English. You may have grown up speaking standard American English at school and another language or dialect at home. Perhaps your family has close ties to another part of the world. You may have moved between the United States and another country more than once. If you came to the United States at a young age, you may read and write English better than you do your parents' native language. You may speak a blended language such as Spanglish, a mixture of English and Spanish. Because the way we talk influences the way we write, blended and other nonstandard forms of English often appear in college students' writing. There is no single "correct" English, but there is a type typically used in academic contexts. The sections and boxes for multilingual students in this book can help you write in academic English.

Learning to read and write academic English can pose special challenges to multilingual students. Academic language is formal, with an expanded vocabulary as well as complex grammar patterns and culturally specific usage patterns. However, the learning strategies discussed in this section will help you succeed in college.

3a Become aware of cultural differences in communication.

If you are familiar with at least two languages and cultures, you already know that there is more than one way to interact politely and effectively with other people. Your classmates may pride themselves on being direct, but you may think that they sound almost impolite in their enthusiasm to make a point. They may consider themselves to be explicit and precise; you may wonder why they are explaining things attentive people should be able to figure out on their own.

Colleges in the United States emphasize openly exchanging views, clearly stating opinions, and explicitly supporting judgments with examples, observations, and reasons. You may be concerned about an "accent" or about the fine points of grammar or pronunciation. Don't worry. Gather up your confidence and join the conversation. In some cultures, asking a question indicates that the student has not done the homework or has not been paying attention. In contrast, instructors in the United States generally encourage their students to ask questions and participate in class discussion. Students who need advice can approach the instructor or fellow students outside class.

During the first few sessions of a class, observe how students show their interest through body language. Usually, American students are expected to sit up straight, look at the instructor, and take notes. Notice your classmates' posture, their facial expressions, and the gestures they make. Do they raise their hands to ask a question? Do they wait until the end of class and speak with the instructor privately? Just as students are not all the same, neither are instructors. Does the instructor tell students to ask their questions after class? Another good way to learn an instructor's preferences is to visit him or her during office hours and ask questions.

Instructors in the United States also often ask students to form small groups to discuss an issue or solve a problem. All the members of such a group are expected to contribute to the conversation and offer ideas. Students usually speak and interact much more informally in these groups than they do with the instructor in class. (For example, you would not raise your hand before speaking in a small group.)

In every class, students must read and think critically. You will be asked to question the statements in the text or the author's reasons for writing. You will also be expected to write about what you have read and share your opinions.

3b Use reading, writing, and speaking to learn more about English.

To develop your fluency in English, get into the habit of reading, writing, and speaking in English every day.

- **Keep a reading and writing notebook.** Write down thoughts, comments, and questions about the reading assignments in your courses. Try to put ideas from the readings into your own words (and note the source). Make a list of new words and phrases that you find in your reading or that you overhear. Many of them may be **idioms,** words and phrases that have a special meaning not always included in a simple dictionary definition. Go over these lists with a tutor, a friend, or your writing group.

- **Write a personal journal or blog.** Using English to explore your thoughts, feelings, and questions about your studies and your life in college will help make you feel more at home in the language.

- **Join a study group.** Most college students can benefit from belonging to a study group. When you get together and discuss an assignment, you often understand it better. Study groups also provide opportunities to practice some of those new words on your list.

- **Write letters in English.** Letters are a good way to practice the informal style used in conversation. Write to out-of-town acquaintances who don't speak your first language. Write a letter to the college newspaper. You can also write brief notes, either on paper or through e-mail, to instructors, tutors, librarians, secretaries, and other native speakers of English.

3c Use learning tools that are available for multilingual students.

The following kinds of reference books can help you as you write papers for your college courses. You can purchase them at your college bookstore or find copies in the reference section of your college library.

1. Consulting an ESL dictionary

A good dictionary designed especially for second-language students can be a useful source of information about word meanings. Ordinary dictionaries frequently define difficult words with other difficult words. In the *American Heritage Dictionary,* for example, the word *haze* is defined as "Atmospheric moisture, dust, smoke, and vapor suspended to form a partially opaque condition." An ESL dictionary defines it more simply as "A light mist or smoke."

Do not confuse ESL dictionaries with bilingual or "translation" dictionaries. Translation dictionaries frequently oversimplify word meanings. So, too, do abridged dictionaries because they do not indicate shades of meaning.

Like all standard English dictionaries, an ESL dictionary includes instructions that explain the abbreviations used in the entries. They also list the special notations used for words classified as *slang, vulgar, informal, nonstandard,* or another category worthy of special attention. In the ESL/Learner's Edition of the *Random House Webster's Dictionary of American English* (1997), you will find "pig out" as the sixth entry under the word *pig:*

> **Pig out** (no obj) Slang. to eat too much food: *We pigged out on pizza last night.*

The entry tells you that "pig out" does not take a direct object ("no obj") and that its use is very informal ("Slang"), appropriate in talking with classmates but not in writing projects. You will hear a great deal of slang on your college campus, on the radio, and on television. Make a list of slang phrases, and look them up later. If you do not find them listed in your standard or ESL dictionary, check for them in a dictionary of American slang.

The dictionary will help you with spelling, syllabication, pronunciation, definitions, word origins, and usage. The several meanings of a word are arranged first according to part of speech and then from most common to least common meaning. Examine the entry for the word *academic* in the ESL/Learner's Edition:

> **ac.a.dem.ic** /'ækə'dɛmɪk/ *adj.* **1.** (before a noun) Of or relating to a school, esp. one for higher education: *an academic institution.* **2.** Of or relating to school subjects that teach general intellectual skills rather than specific job skills: *academic subjects like English and mathematics.* **3.** Not practical or directly useful: *Whether she wanted to come or not is an academic question because she's here now.—n.* (count) **4.** A student or teacher at a college or university—**ac'a.dem'i.cal.ly,** *adv.*

Note that nouns are identified as count or noncount, indicating whether you can place a number in front of the noun and make it plural. You can

www.mhf awr3

For access to on dictionaries, go

Dictionaries and Thesauri

say, "Four academics joined the group," so when *academic* is used as a noun, it is a count noun. *Honesty* is a noncount noun.

When you look up words or phrases in the dictionary, add them to your personal list. Talk about your list with classmates. They will be happy to explain up-to-date uses of the words and phrases you are learning.

2. Consulting a dictionary of American idioms

As we explained earlier, an idiom is an expression that is peculiar to a particular language and cannot be understood by looking at the individual words. "To catch a bus" is an idiom.

3. Using a desk encyclopedia

In the reference section of your college library, you will find one-volume encyclopedias on every subject from U.S. history to classical or biblical allusions. You may find it helpful to look up people, places, and events that are new to you for a quick identification, especially if the person, place, or event is referred to often in U.S. culture.

4. Referring to a thesaurus

Look up a word in a thesaurus to find other words with related meanings. The thesaurus can help you expand your vocabulary. However, always look up synonyms in a dictionary before using them, since the meaning may not be identical to that of the original word.

*The way the
butterfly in this
image emerges on
a computer
screen, as if from
a cocoon of
written text,
suggests the way
writers transform
words and visuals
into finished works
through careful
planning, drafting,
revision, and
design.*

I like to do first drafts at night, when
I'm tired, and then do the surgical work
in the morning when I'm sharp.

—ALEX HALEY

Writing and Designing Texts

2 Writing and Designing Texts

👁 Section dealing with visual rhetoric. For a complete listing, see the Quick Guide to Key Resources at the back of this book.

Tab 2: Writing and Designing Texts
This section will help you answer questions such as:

Rhetorical Knowledge
What is a writing situation? **(5a)**
When should I use visuals in my writing? What type of visuals fit my writing situation? **(5e)**

Critical Thinking, Reading, and Writing
How can annotation and summary help me with reading assignments? **(4a)**
How can I analyze photographs and other images? **(4a, b)**

Processes
What are the components of the writing process? **(5, 7)**
What is a thesis statement? **(5c)**
How should I give feedback on my classmates' work? **(7a)**
How do I create an electronic portfolio? **(8d)**

Knowledge of Conventions
How can I make my paragraphs clear and effective? **(6c)**
What aspects of document design can help convey my meaning? **(8c)**

4 Reading, Thinking, Writing: The Critical Connection

Critical readers, thinkers, and writers get intellectually involved. They recognize that meanings and values are made, not found, so they pose pertinent questions, note significant features, and examine the credibility of various kinds of texts.

In this context, the word *critical* means "thoughtful." When you read critically, for example, you recognize the literal meaning of the text, make inferences about unstated meanings, and then make your own judgments in response.

Advances in technology have made it easier than ever to obtain information in a variety of ways. It is essential to be able to "read" critically not just written texts but visuals, sounds, video, and spoken texts as well. We use the word *text,* then, to refer to works that readers, viewers, or listeners invest with meaning and that can be critically analyzed.

21

CHECKLIST

Reading Critically

☐ **Preview** the piece before you read it.

☐ **Read** the selection for its topic and point.

☐ **Analyze** the who, what, and why of the piece by **annotating** it as you reread it and **summarizing** what you have read.

☐ **Synthesize** through making connections.

☐ **Evaluate** what you've read.

👁 **4a** Read critically.

1. Previewing

Critical reading begins with **previewing**—a quick review of the author, publication information, title, headings, visuals, and key sentences or paragraphs.

www.mhhe.com/
awr3
For help with
evaluating sources,
go to

**Research > CARS
Source Evaluation
Tutor**

Previewing written texts   As you preview, be skeptical: just because something is in print does not mean that it is true. Whenever possible, ask questions about the following:

- **Author:** Who wrote this piece? What are the writer's credentials? Who is the writer's employer? What is the writer's occupation? Age? What are his or her interests and values?

- **Purpose:** What do the title and first and last paragraphs tell you about the purpose of this piece? Do the headings and visuals provide clues to its purpose? What might have motivated the author to write it? Is the main purpose to inform, to interpret, to argue, to entertain, or is it to accomplish something else?

- **Audience:** Who is the target of the author's information or persuasion? Is the author addressing you or readers like you?

- **Content:** What does the title tell you about the piece? Does the first paragraph include the main point? What do the headings tell you about the gist of the piece? Does the conclusion say what the author has focused on?

- **Context:** Is the publication date current? Does the date matter? What kind of publication is it? Where and by whom was it published? If it has been published electronically, was it posted by the author? By an organization with a special interest?

Previewing visuals   You can use most of the previewing questions for written texts to preview visuals. You should also ask some additional questions, however. For example, suppose you were asked to preview the public service advertisement shown in Figure 4.1.

Here are some preview questions you might ask and the answers you could give to them:

- **In what context does the visual appear?** This public service advertisement appeared in several publications targeted to college students. As the logo in the lower right-hand corner indicates, the ad was produced by the Peace Corps to recruit volunteers.

- **What does the visual depict? What is the first thing you notice in the visual?** The scene is a bare schoolroom in Botswana. (*Look at the world map in Tab 13: Further Resources, to find Botswana in Africa.*) As sun streams from a window, one young man in the foreground looks on as a younger boy erases a blackboard. On the blackboard, a handwritten poster appears with points of advice, for example, "Accept responsibility for your decision." The sunlight shining directly on the boy at the blackboard draws the viewer's attention to him.

FIGURE 4.1 Peace Corps advertisement. The text superimposed on this photograph reads: **What happens in Botswana doesn't stay in Botswana.** When you help make a better life for others abroad, you also develop skills and experience that will serve your community back home. Life is calling. How far will you go?

Tips

Evaluating Context in Different Kinds of Publications

■ **For a book:** Are you looking at the original publication or a reprint? What is the publisher's reputation? University presses, for example, are very selective and usually publish scholarly works. A vanity press—one that requires authors to pay to publish their work—is not selective at all.

■ **For an article in a periodical:** Look at the list of editors and their affiliations. What do you know about the journal, magazine, or newspaper in which this piece appears? Are the articles reviewed by experts in a particular field before they are published?

■ **For a Web page:** Who created the page? A Web page named for a political candidate, for example, may actually have been put on the Web by opponents. (*See the box on p. 233.*)

■ **Is the visual accompanied by audio or printed text?** Bold text appears in the center of the image, followed by smaller print directly addressed to the viewer. The phone number and Web address for the Peace Corps are printed in the lower left, and another appeal to the viewer, followed by the Peace Corps logo, is printed in the lower right.

2. Reading and recording initial impressions

Read the selection for its literal meaning. Identify the main topic and the main point the writer makes about the topic. If possible, read the work in one sitting. Note difficult passages to come back to as well as interesting ideas. Record your initial impressions:

■ If the text or image is an argument, what opinion is being expressed? Were you persuaded by the argument?

■ Did you have an emotional response to the text or image? Were you surprised, amused, or angered by anything in it?

■ What was your initial sense of the writer or speaker?

■ What key ideas did you take away from the work?

3. Using annotation and summary to analyze a text

Once you understand the literal or surface meaning of a text, dig deeper by analyzing and interpreting it. To **analyze** a text is to break it down into significant parts and examine how those parts relate to each other. We analyze a text in order to **interpret** it and come to a fuller understanding of its meanings.

Using annotation and summary **Annotation** combines reading with analysis. To annotate a text, read through it slowly and carefully while asking yourself the *who, what, how,* and *why* questions. As you read, underline or make separate notes about words, phrases, and sentences that strike you as significant or puzzling, and write down questions and observations.

SAMPLE ANNOTATED PASSAGE

Opens with a story about his childhood

Both my parents were immigrants from Russia. In my neighborhood, Yiddish was a first and second language. I grew up in the depths of the Great Depression. There were weeks when my father came home with $5 or less. My mother walked blocks to save a few cents on food.

Establishes his authority—he's experienced multiculturalism

I went to public school. Some of my friends were sent to the yeshiva—an Orthodox Jewish religious school—but my parents, having experienced the vicious, pervasive anti-Semitism in the Old Country, wanted me to learn what America was all about.

At Boston Latin School and Northeastern University—a working-class college—I took classes that taught a great deal about the fundamental rights and liberties that had to be fought for during this still "unfinished American revolution," as Thurgood Marshall called it. These were required courses, and inspired my lifelong involvement in civil rights and civil liberties.

Essential? Supreme Court. Does he assume they would inspire everyone

—NAT HENTOFF, "Misguided Multiculturalism"

A **summary** conveys the basic content of a text. When you summarize, your goal is to communicate the text's main points in your own words, not to say what you think of it. A summary of an essay or article is typically about one paragraph in length. Even when you are writing a fuller summary of a longer work, use the fewest words possible. Although writing a summary requires simplification, be careful to avoid misrepresenting a writer's points by *oversimplifying* them. (*For specific instructions on how to write a summary, see Chapter 24: Working with Sources and Avoiding Plagiarism, pp. 258–60.*)

Questioning the text Analysis and interpretation require a critical understanding of the *who, what, how,* and *why* of a text:

- **What is the writer's *stance*, or attitude toward the subject?** Does the writer appear to be objective, or does she or he seem to have personal feelings about the subject?

- **What is the writer's *voice*?** Is it like that of a reasonable judge, an enthusiastic preacher, or a reassuring friend?

- **What assumptions does the writer seem to be making about the audience?** Does the writer assume that the reader agrees with him or her, or does the writer try to build agreement? Does the writer seem to choose examples and evidence with a certain audience in mind?

- **What is the writer's primary purpose?** Is it to present findings, offer an objective analysis, or argue for a particular action or opinion?

- **How does the writer develop ideas?** Does the writer define key terms? Include supporting facts? Tell relevant stories? Provide logical reasons?

- **Does the text appeal to emotions?** Does the writer use words, phrases, clichés, images, or examples that are emotionally charged?

- **Is the text fair?** Does the writer consider opposing ideas, arguments, or evidence? Does he or she deal with them fairly?

- **Is the evidence strong?** Does the writer provide sufficient evidence for his or her position? Where is the argument strongest and weakest?

- **Is the text effective?** Have your beliefs on this subject been changed by the text?

Visuals, too, can be subjected to critical analysis, as the comments a reader made on the Peace Corps ad indicate (*see Figure 4.2*).

CHARTING the TERRITORY

Mapping Your Topic

When you are analyzing a text within the framework of a particular discipline, you might begin your analysis by comparing the text you are studying with other texts written on the same topic but from different perspectives—from different places on the disciplinary map.

- **What issues might the topic raise for members of different disciplines?** For historians, the reunification of Germany might raise issues about top-down versus bottom-up modes of change. For economists, the interesting issue might be the unemployment caused by privatizing the former East Germany's industry.

- **How would members of different disciplines investigate the issues that interest them?** What data would historians or economists want? Where and how would they get the data?

- **What kinds of conclusions do members of different disciplines tend to expect and accept?** Historians expect and accept arguments about how people have or have not changed their lives, conditions, or ideas over time. Economists tend to expect and accept conclusions based on some more or less unchanging law or principle, such as the law of supply and demand.

Composition of the photograph like Vermeer's paintings of sunlight illuminating an indoor scene. Subtle appeal to students of art history?

Reference to Las Vegas slogan, "What happens here stays here." Secrets of Las Vegas (superficial fun) stay there because of shame. Working with the Peace Corps (worthwhile life direction) in Botswana illuminates your life—and the world (Reference to sunlight?).

The boy is reaching up to erase or wash something from the blackboard. An older boy watches—also "reaching"? A poster covering part of the board lists principles valuable in Botswana and in the U.S.A.

Smaller print elaborates on win/win opportunity of the Peace Corps vs. odds of losing games in Las Vegas.

The Peace Corps logo combines the globe with the American flag—a global view of patriotism. How far will you go geographically and personally?

FIGURE 4.2 Sample annotations on the Peace Corps ad.

4. Synthesizing your observations in a critical-response paper

To **synthesize** means to bring together, to make something out of different parts. In the last stage of critical reading, you pull your summary, analysis, and interpretation together into a coherent whole. Whether you realize it or not, you synthesize material every day. When you hear contrasting accounts of a party from two different people, you assess the reliability of each source; you select the information that is most pertinent to you; you evaluate the story that each one tells; and finally, you create a composite, or synthesis, of what you think really went on. When you synthesize information from two or more texts, you follow the same process.

👁 4b Think critically.

Critical thinkers never simply gather information and present it without question. They inquire about what they see, hear, and read. They evaluate a text's argument to figure out its strengths and weaknesses.

1. Recognizing an argument

Rather than a shouting match, an **argument** means a path of reasoning aimed at persuading people to accept or reject an assertion. The assertion must be on an issue about which reasonable people can disagree and for which evidence can be gathered. For example, the assertion that women should be allowed to try out for all college sports teams is arguable.

2. Analyzing and evaluating an argument

Three common methods of analyzing verbal and visual arguments are (1) to concentrate on the type of reasoning the writer is using; (2) to question the logical relation of a writer's claims, grounds, and warrants, using the Toulmin method; and (3) to examine the ways an argument appeals to its audience.

Types of reasoning   When writers use **inductive reasoning,** they do not prove that the statements that make up the argument are true; instead, they convince reasonable people that if the statements are true (on the basis of facts, statistics, anecdotes, and expert opinion), the argument is probable. When writers use **deductive reasoning,** they are making the claim that a conclusion follows necessarily from a set of assertions, or **premises**—in other words, that if the premises are true and if the relationship between the premises is valid, the conclusion must be true.

For example, a journalism student writing for the school paper might make the following assertion:

> As Saturday's game shows, the Buckeyes are on their way to winning the Big Ten title.

If the student is reasoning inductively, she will present a number of facts—her evidence—that support her claim but do not prove it conclusively:

FACT **1**	With three games remaining, the Buckeyes have a two-game lead over the second-place Badgers.
FACT **2**	The Buckeyes' final three opponents have a combined record of 10 wins and 17 losses.
FACT **3**	The Badgers lost their two star players to season-ending injuries last week.
FACT **4**	The Buckeyes' last three games will be played at home, where they are undefeated this season.

A reader would evaluate this student's argument by judging the quality of her evidence, using the criteria listed in the Tips box.

Tips LEARNING in COLLEGE

Assessing Evidence in an Inductive Argument

- **Is it accurate?** Make sure that any facts presented as evidence are correct and not taken out of context.
- **Is it relevant?** Check to see if the evidence is clearly connected to the point being made.
- **Is it representative?** Make sure that the writer's conclusion is supported by evidence gathered from a sample that accurately reflects the larger population (for example, it has the same proportion of men and women, older and younger people, and so on). If the writer is using an example, make sure that the example is typical and not a unique situation.
- **Is it sufficient?** Evaluate whether there is enough evidence to satisfy questioning readers.

Inductive reasoning is a feature of the **scientific method.** Scientists gather data from experiments, surveys, and careful observations to formulate hypotheses—arguments—that explain the data. Then they test their hypotheses by collecting additional information.

The basic structure of a deductive argument is the **syllogism.** It contains a **major premise,** or general statement; **minor premise,** or specific case; and conclusion, which follows when the general statement is applied to the specific case. Suppose the journalism student is using deductive reasoning in an article about great baseball teams; in that case, the truth of her conclusion will depend on the truth of her premises:

MAJOR PREMISE	Any baseball team that wins the World Series more than twenty-five times in a hundred years is one of the greatest teams in history.
MINOR PREMISE	The New York Yankees have won the World Series more than twenty-five times in the past hundred years.
CONCLUSION	The New York Yankees are one of the greatest baseball teams in history.

This is a deductive argument. For it to be true, the relationship between the premises must be valid, and both premises must be true. True premises do not prove a conclusion that does not follow. For example, it is not accurate to say: "The train is late. Jane is late. Therefore, Jane must be on the train." However, if the train is late and Jane is on the train, Jane must be late. If the logical relationship between the premises is valid, a reader must then evaluate their truth. Do you think, for example, that the number of World Series wins is a proper measure of a team's greatness? If not, you could claim that the major premise is false and does not support the conclusion.

In college, deductive reasoning predominates in mathematics and philosophy and some other humanities disciplines. However, you should be alert to both types of reasoning in all your college courses and in your life.

The Toulmin method Philosopher Stephen Toulmin's analysis of arguments is based on claims (assertions about a topic), grounds (reasons and evidence), and warrants (assumptions or principles that link the grounds to the claims). Consider the following sentence from an argument by a student:

> The death penalty should be abolished because innocent people could be executed.

This example, like all logical arguments, has three facets:

CLAIM The death penalty should be abolished.

GROUNDS Innocent people could be executed (related stories and statistics).

WARRANT It is not possible to be completely sure of a person's guilt.

- **The argument makes a claim.** A **claim** is the same thing as a point or a thesis: it is an assertion about a topic. A strong claim responds to an issue of real interest to an audience in clear, precise terms. It also allows for some uncertainty by including qualifying words such as *might* or *possibly*. A weak claim is merely a statement of fact or a statement that few would argue with. Personal feelings are not debatable and thus are not an appropriate claim for an argument.

  WEAK CLAIMS The death penalty is highly controversial.

  The death penalty makes me sick.

- **The argument presents grounds for the claim.** Here, **grounds** consist of the reasons and evidence (facts and statistics, anecdotes, and expert opinion) that support the claim. A strong argument relies on evidence that is varied, relevant to the claim, and sufficient to support the claim. As grounds for the claim in the example, the student would present anecdotes and statistics related to innocent people being executed. The box on the facing page should help you assess the evidence supporting a claim.

- **The argument depends on assumptions that link the grounds to the claim.** When you analyze an argument, be aware of the **warrants,** or unstated assumptions, that underlie both the claim and the grounds that support it. The warrants underlying the example argument against the death penalty include the idea that it is not possible to be sure of a person's guilt.

  Warrants differ from discipline to discipline and from one school of thought to another. If you were studying the topic of bullfighting and its place in Spanish society in a sociology course, for example, you would probably make different arguments with different warrants than would the writer of a literary analysis of Ernest Hemingway's book about bullfighting, *Death in the Afternoon.* You might argue that bullfighting serves as a safe outlet for its fans' aggressive feelings. Your warrant would be that sports can have socially useful purposes. A more controversial warrant would be that it is acceptable to kill animals for entertainment.

  As you read the writings of others and as you write yourself, look for unstated assumptions. What does the reader have to assume—take for granted—to accept the evidence in support of the claim? In particular, hidden assumptions sometimes show **bias**—positive or negative inclinations that can manipulate unwary readers.

3. Analyzing appeals

Arguments support claims by way of three types of appeals to readers, categorized by the Greek words **logos** (logic), **pathos** (emotions), and **ethos** (character).

TYPES of EVIDENCE for CLAIMS

- **Facts and statistics:** Facts and statistics can be convincing support for a claim. You should be aware, however, that people on different sides of an issue can interpret the same facts and statistics differently or can cite different facts and statistics to support their point.
- **Anecdotes:** An anecdote is a brief story used as an illustration to support a claim. Stories appeal to the emotions as well as to the intellect and can be very effective in making an argument. Be especially careful to check anecdotes for logical fallacies (*see pp. 32–35*).
- **Expert opinion:** The views of authorities in a given field can also be powerful support for a claim. Check that the expert cited has proper credentials to comment on the issue.

- **Logical appeals** offer facts, such as statistics, and reasoning, such as the previous examples of inductive and deductive reasoning.
- **Emotional appeals** engage an audience's feelings and invoke beliefs that the author and audience share.
- **Ethical appeals** present the author as fair and trustworthy, and provide the testimony of experts.

Most arguments draw on all three appeals. A proposal for more nutritious school lunches might cite statistics about childhood obesity, a logical appeal. The argument might appeal to the audience's sense of fairness by stating that all children deserve nutritious meals. It might quote a doctor explaining that healthful food aids concentration. Tailor the type and content of appeals to the appropriate audience.

4. Recognizing common logical fallacies

In their enthusiasm to make a point, writers sometimes commit errors called **fallacies,** or mistakes in reasoning. They can be understood as misuses of the three appeals. Learn to identify fallacies when you read and avoid them when you write.

Logical fallacies involve errors in the inductive and deductive reasoning processes previously discussed:

- **Non sequitur:** A conclusion that does not logically follow from the evidence presented or one that is based on irrelevant evidence.

  EXAMPLE   Students who default on their student loans have no sense of responsibility. [*Students might default on loans due to medical bills or unemployment.*]

Generalizing based on evidence is an important tactic of argument. However, the evidence must be relevant. Non sequiturs also stem from dubious assumptions.

- **False cause:** An argument that falsely assumes that because one thing happens after another, the first event was a cause of the second event. Also known as post hoc.

  EXAMPLE   I drank green tea and my headache went away; therefore, green tea makes headaches go away. [*Perhaps the headache went away for another reason.*]

While writers frequently describe causes and effects in argument, fallacies result when they oversimplify complex relationships.

- **Self-contradiction:** An argument that contradicts itself.

EXAMPLE No absolute statement can be true. [*The statement itself is an absolute.*]

- **Circular reasoning:** An argument that restates the point rather than supporting it with reasonable evidence.

  EXAMPLE The wealthy should pay more taxes because taxes should be higher for people with higher incomes. [*Why should wealthy people pay more taxes? The rest of the statement does not answer this question; it just restates the position.*]

Claims must be backed with evidence, which is missing here.

- **Begging the question:** A form of circular reasoning that assumes the truth of a questionable opinion.

  EXAMPLE The president's poor relationship with the military has weakened the armed forces. [*Does the president really have a poor relationship with the military?*]

Some claims contain assumptions that must be proven first. The author of the above claim must first support the assertion that the president has a poor relationship with the military.

- **Hasty generalization:** A conclusion based on inadequate evidence.

  EXAMPLE It took me over an hour to find a parking spot downtown. Therefore, the city should build a new parking garage. [*Is this evidence enough to prove this very broad conclusion?*]

- **Sweeping generalization:** An overly broad statement made in absolute terms. When about a group of people, a sweeping generalization is a **stereotype.**

  EXAMPLE College students are carefree. [*What about students who work to put themselves through school?*]

Legitimate generalizations must be based on evidence that is accurate, relevant, representative, and sufficient (*see the box on p. 29*).

- **Either/or fallacy:** The idea that a complicated issue can be resolved by resorting to one of only two options when in reality there are additional options.

  EXAMPLE Either the state legislature will raise taxes or our state's economy will falter. [*Are these really the only two possibilities?*]

Frequently, arguments consider different courses of action. Authors demonstrate their fairness by addressing a range of options.

Ethical fallacies undermine a writer's credibility by showing lack of fairness to opposing views and lack of expertise on the subject of the argument.

■ **Ad hominem:** A personal attack on someone who disagrees with you rather than on the person's argument.

> EXAMPLE The district attorney is a lazy political hack, so naturally she opposes streamlining the court system. [*Even if the district attorney usually supports her party's position, does that make her wrong about this issue?*]

This fallacy closes off debate by leaving the subject of the argument altogether.

■ **Guilt by association:** Discrediting a person because of problems with that person's associates, friends, or family.

> EXAMPLE Smith's friend has been convicted of fraud, so Smith cannot be trusted. [*Is Smith responsible for his friend's actions?*]

This tactic undermines an opponent's credibility and is based on a dubious assumption: if a person's associates are untrustworthy, that person is also untrustworthy.

■ **False authority:** Presenting the testimony of an unqualified person to support a claim.

> EXAMPLE As the actor who plays Dr. Fine on *The Emergency Room,* I recommend this weight-loss drug because . . ." [*Is an actor qualified to judge the benefits and dangers of a diet drug?*]

While expert testimony can strengthen an argument, the person must be an authority on the subject in question. This fallacy frequently underlies celebrity endorsements of products.

Emotional fallacies stir audiences' sympathies at the expense of their reasoning.

■ **False analogy:** A comparison in which a surface similarity masks a significant difference.

> EXAMPLE Governments and businesses both work within a budget to accomplish their goals. Just as business must focus on the bottom line, so should government. [*Is the goal of government to make a profit? Does government instead have other, more important, goals?*]

Analogies can enliven an argument and deepen an audience's understanding of a subject, provided the things being compared actually are similar.

- **Bandwagon:** An argument that depends on going along with the crowd, on the false assumption that truth can be determined by a popularity contest.

  EXAMPLE Everybody knows that Toni Morrison is preoccupied with the theme of death in her novels. [*How do we know that "everybody" agrees with this statement?*]

- **Red herring:** An argument that diverts attention from the true issue by concentrating on something irrelevant.

  EXAMPLE Hemingway's book *Death in the Afternoon* is unsuccessful because it glorifies the brutal sport of bullfighting. [*Why can't a book about a brutal sport be successful? The statement is irrelevant.*]

5. Reading visual argument

Like written arguments, visual arguments support claims with reasons and evidence, rely on assumptions, and may contain fallacies. They make logical appeals, such as a graph of experimental data; emotional appeals, such as a photograph of a hungry child; and ethical appeals, such as a corporate logo. Like all written works, visual arguments are created by an author for an audience and to achieve a purpose, within a context. (*For more, see Chapter 5, pp. 37–39*).

X CHECKLIST

Reading Visual Arguments Critically

Review the questions for previewing a visual on pages 23–24 and add the following:

- ☐ What can you tell about the visual's creator or sponsor?

- ☐ What seems to be the visual's purpose? Is a product or message promoted?

- ☐ Who do you think is the intended audience? What aspects of the visual suggest this audience? How?

- ☐ How do aspects of design such as size, position, color, and shape affect its message?

- ☐ What is the effect of any text, audio, or video that accompanies the visual?

Consider an example of Toulmin analysis (*see pp. 30–31*) on an image. A photograph of a politician with her family members makes a claim (X is a good public servant) and offers grounds (because she cares for her family). The warrant is that a person's family life indicates how she will perform in office. Unstated assumptions play a large role in visual arguments because claims and grounds often are not stated explicitly.

Advertisements combine text and images to promote a product or message to an audience. They use the resources of visual design: type of image, position, color, light and shadows, fonts, and white space. (*See the questions on previewing a visual on pp. 23–24 and the discussion of design in Chapter 8, pp. 95–101.*). Most advertisements function in a very specific social context. Consider the public-service ad in Figure 4.3, developed by the nonprofit advocacy group Adbusters.

The ad's text and design evoke a popular series of ads for a brand of vodka. Its uncluttered design focuses the viewer's attention on the shape of a bottle, the outline of which consists of chairs. The text at the bottom refers to AA: Alcoholics Anonymous. By association, the text and images in this public-service ad remind readers that liquor can lead to alcoholism (and then to AA). In contrast with those it spoofs, this ad evokes an unexpected threat, creating a powerful emotional appeal.

What claims do you think this ad makes? One might be that "alcohol is dangerous." The evidence is supplied by the reader's prior

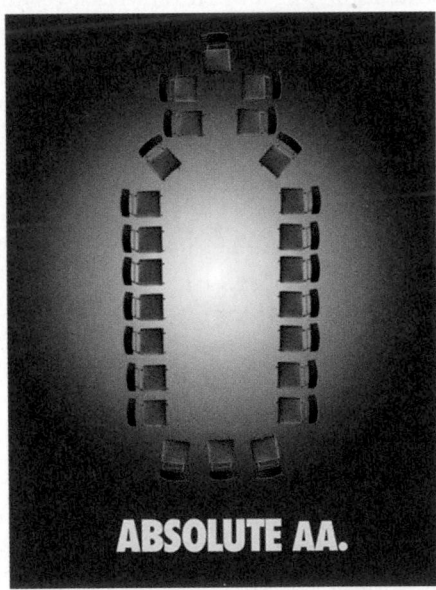

FIGURE 4.3 A visual argument: Adbusters public-service advertisement

knowledge about alcoholism. The argument's assumptions include that viewers will be familiar with both the original liquor campaign and the initials "AA" for Alcoholics Anonymous.

Fallacies frequently occur in visual arguments. For example, celebrity endorsements of products rely on our respect for the celebrity's character. However, an athlete's endorsement of a type of car is an example of false authority, unless she also happens to be an expert on cars. (*See p. 34.*)

4c Write critically.

Sharpening your ability to think critically and to express your views effectively is one of the main purposes of undergraduate study. When you write critically, you gain a voice in the important discussions and decisions of our society. Writing can make a difference.

In college and beyond, you will apply critical-thinking skills to different writing purposes. Tab 3 of this book (*Common Assignments across the Curriculum*) focuses on writing to **inform** (*Chapter 9, pp. 109–18*), to **analyze** (*Chapter 10, pp. 118–26*), and to **argue** (*Chapter 11, pp. 126–39*). In each case, you will present evidence that supports a central point, or **thesis.** For your writing to be convincing and effective, you will need to consider your audience and the context of your assignment.

5 Planning and Shaping

The advice in this chapter will help you determine the kind of writing a particular assignment requires and get you started on a first draft.

5a Learn how to approach assignments.

1. Understanding the writing situation

Writers respond to **writing (or rhetorical) situations.** Figure 5.1 on page 38 shows some components of a writing situation. When you write a lab report for a science class, create a flyer for a candidate for student government, or send an e-mail inviting a friend for coffee, you shape the communication (**message**) to suit the purpose, audience, and context. The results will look much different. All communication occurs

FIGURE 5.1 Elements of a writing situation.

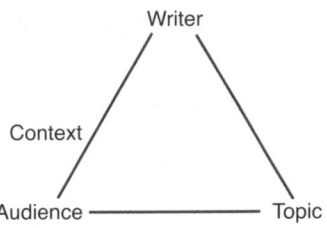

when something is at stake (**exigence**), which could be an assignment, an issue in the community, or your need for coffee and companionship. The **audience** receives the message. Audience members may be friendly or hostile to the writer's message, and their cultures and backgrounds will influence their reactions. Your **purpose** may be to inform them or to move them to action. **Context** includes the means of communication, current events, and the environment in which the communication takes place.

CHECKLIST

Understanding the Writing Situation

Ask yourself these questions as you approach a writing assignment.

Topic (*see 5a.2*)

- ☐ What are you being asked to write about?
- ☐ Have you narrowed your topic to a question that interests you?
- ☐ What genre or format would suit your assignment?
- ☐ What kind of visuals would be appropriate for this topic, if any?
- ☐ What types of sources will help you explore this topic? Where will you look for them?

Purpose (*see 5a.3*)

- ☐ What do you want your writing to accomplish? Are you trying to inform, analyze, or argue?
- ☐ Do you want to intensify, clarify, complicate, or change your audience's assumptions or opinions?

CHECKLIST *(continued)*

Audience (*see 5a.4*)

- [ ] What group do you imagine as your primary readers? How much do they know about the topic at hand?

- [ ] What are your audience's demographics (education level, social status, gender, cultural background, and language)? How diverse is your audience?

- [ ] What common assumptions and different opinions do they bring to the issue? What values do they hold?

- [ ] Are they likely to agree with you, or will you have to persuade them?

- [ ] What is your relationship to them?

- [ ] What sort of voice would appeal to this audience: informal, entertaining, reasonable, or forceful?

Context (*see 5a.5*)

- [ ] Does your topic deal with issues of interest to the public or to members of an academic discipline?

- [ ] What have other writers said recently about this topic?

- [ ] How much time do you have to complete the assignment?

- [ ] What is the specified number of pages?

- [ ] What medium are you using (print essay, video podcast, Web site, presentation software)?

2. Writing about a question

Most of your academic writing will be in response to assignments that pose a question or ask you to formulate one. The particular course you are taking defines a range of questions that are appropriate within a given discipline. Here are examples of the way your course would help define the questions you might ask if, for example, you were writing about Thomas Jefferson:

U.S. history: How did Jefferson's ownership of slaves affect his public stance on slavery?

Political science: To what extent did Jefferson's conflict with the courts redefine the balance of power among the three branches of government?

Education: Given his beliefs about the relationship between democracy and public education, what would Jefferson think about contemporary proposals for a school voucher system?

3. Being clear about your purpose

What kind of assignment are you doing? Think beyond the simple statement "I have to write an essay." Are you expected to inform, interpret, or argue?

- **Informing:** writing to transmit knowledge. Terms like *classify, illustrate, report,* and *survey* are often associated with the task of informing.

- **Interpreting:** writing to produce understanding. Terms like *analyze, compare, explain,* and *reflect* are more likely to appear when the purpose is interpreting.

- **Arguing:** writing to assert and negotiate matters of public debate. Terms like *agree, assess, defend,* and *refute* go with the task of arguing.

Some terms, such as *comment, consider,* and *discuss,* do not point to a particular purpose, but many others do. If you are not clear about the kind of work you are expected to do, ask your professor.

4. Asking questions about your audience

Who makes up your audience? In college, instructors are usually your primary readers, of course, but they represent a larger group of readers who have an interest or a stake in your topic. An education professor reads and evaluates a paper as a representative of other students in the course, experts in educational policy, school board members, public school principals, and parents of school-age children, among others. See the box on page 39 for questions to answer about your audience.

5. Considering context

Writing does not take place in isolation. Your assignment provides some guidance on particular circumstances: due date, length, type of writing (genre). You must also consider the medium: print or digital. The academic discipline you are studying has a history of debate on certain topics, and your paper may have an appropriate role in those debates. Finally, the college or community setting and your place within it will influence your writing, particularly on public issues.

6. Selecting the genre and using appropriate language

Genre simply means kind of writing. Poems, stories, and plays are genres of literature.

Sometimes an assignment will specify the kind of work, or genre, you are being asked to produce. For example, you may be asked to write a report (an informative genre), a comparative analysis (an interpretive genre), or a critique (an argumentative genre).

Some genres, like the case study, are common in a particular field such as sociology but not in other disciplines. Understanding the genre that is called for is very important in successfully fulfilling an assignment. If you are supposed to write a description of a snake for a field guide, you will not be successful if you write a poem—even a very good poem—about a snake. (*See Tab 3: Common Assignments across the Curriculum, pp. 107–72.*) Understanding genre helps you make decisions about language. For a description of a snake in a field guide, you would use highly specific terms to differentiate one type of snake from another. A poem would incorporate striking images, vivid words and phrases that evoke the senses, and other forms of literary language.

 **Tips** LEARNING in COLLEGE

Understanding Assignments

It often is helpful to talk with the instructor after receiving and reviewing an assignment. It is far better to ask for clarification before you start an assignment than to have to start over or to turn in something that does not fulfill the assignment.

7. Choosing an appropriate voice

We hear **voices** when we read, and we create voices when we write. The following two passages both deal with the death of a sportswriter named Steve Schoenfeld. Read both passages aloud, and listen to the different voices:

> Tobin originally planned his news conference for Wednesday but postponed it out of respect for Valley sports journalist Steve Schoenfeld, who was killed Tuesday night in a hit-and-run accident in downtown Tempe.
>
> —LEE SHAPPELL, *Arizona Republic*

> Steve Schoenfeld probably would find it amusing that the NFL plans to honor him with a moment of silence in press boxes before games on Sunday and Monday. He was hardly ever quiet in the press box or anywhere else.
>
> —MARK ARMIJO AND KENT SOMERS, *Arizona Republic*

The first passage is written in an even tone that emphasizes factual reporting. The second passage is written in a poignant style that quietly and movingly celebrates the sportswriter's life.

Different writing situations and assignments allow you to try out different voices. As a college student, you will usually want to inspire trust by sounding informed, reasonable, and fair. Your **stance**—where you stand in relation to your audience and your subject—is seldom that of an expert. Instead, you are writing as an educated person who is sharing what you have learned and what you think about it.

Readers tend to appreciate an even tone of voice, a style that values the middle ground and avoids the extremes of the impersonal or the intimate, the stuffy or the casual. Read your work aloud to yourself or to classmates so that you can literally hear your voice. Does it suit the assignment's topic, purpose, and audience? (*For more about style, see Tab 9: Editing for Clarity, pp. 389–442.*)

www.mhhe.com/
awr3

For more on strategies for exploring your ideas, go to

Writing >
Paragraph/Essay
Development >
Prewriting

5b   Explore your ideas.

You usually explore ideas when you are getting started on a project, but exploration also helps when you are feeling stuck. The following strategies will help you brainstorm and come up with ideas at any stage. You can do much of your exploratory writing in a **journal** (print or electronic), which is simply a place to record your thoughts on a regular basis. (*For more on journals, see p. 46.*) Your class notes constitute a type of academic journal, as do the notes you take on your reading and research.

CHECKLIST

Activities for Exploring Your Ideas

Try one or several of the following when you begin an assignment.

☐ Freewrite. (See 5b.1.)

☐ List. (See 5b.2.)

☐ Cluster. (See 5b.3.)

☐ Question. (See 5b.4.)

☐ Review your notes and annotations. (See 5b.5.)

☐ Keep a journal. (See 5b.6.)

☐ Browse in the library. (See 5b.7.)

☐ Search the Internet. (See 5b.7.)

☐ Exchange ideas. (See 5b.8.)

As you explore, turn off your internal critic and generate as much material as possible.

1. Freewriting

When you feel blocked or unsure about what you think, try **freewriting.** Just write whatever occurs to you about a topic. If nothing comes to mind, then write "nothing comes to mind" until something else occurs to you. The trick is to keep pushing forward without stopping or worrying about spelling, punctuation, or grammar rules. Usually, you will discover some implicit point in your seemingly random writing. You might then try doing some **focused freewriting,** where you begin with a point or a specific question. The following is a student's freewriting on the topic of work:

> I want to talk about the difference between a job and work—between a job and a career. If you don't get paid, is it work? If it is, what's the difference between work and play? There are some things I would only do for money—like work as a waiter. But there are other things I would do even if I weren't paid—garden or ride my bike or play with kids. The trick is to find a career that would allow me to get paid for doing those things.

TextConnex

Digital Tools for Exploring Ideas

Some students use a separate file on a word processor to record and work with ideas. This material can then be copied and pasted into a draft. Web sites such as bubbl.us <http://www.bubbl.us> allow individuals and groups to generate ideas and link them in a visual cluster, which can be e-mailed to one or more recipients.

2. Listing

The key to brainstorming is to turn off your internal editor and just jot things down. Start with a topic and list the words, phrases, images, and ideas that come to mind. Later, you can review this list, underline one or more key terms, add or delete items, and look for patterns and connections. You can then zero in on the areas of most interest, add new ideas, and arrange the items into main points and subpoints. Here is a list a student produced on the topic of work:

> Work—what is it?
> Skilled/unskilled
> Most jobs today in service industries
> Work and retirement
> My dad's retired, but has he stopped working?

If you never want to retire, is your job still considered work?
Jobs I have had: babysitter, camp counselor, salesclerk, office worker—I'd be
happy to retire from those, especially the salesclerk job
Standing all day
Do this, do that
Punch the clock
Do it over again and again
Difference between work and career
I want a career, not a job

3. Clustering

Clustering, sometimes called **mapping,** is a brainstorming technique that generates categories and connections from the beginning. To make an idea cluster, do the following:

- Write your topic in the center of a piece of paper, and circle it.
- Surround the topic with subtopics that interest you. Circle each, and draw a line from it to the center circle.
- Brainstorm more ideas, connecting each one to a subtopic already on the sheet or making it into a new subtopic.

Web sites such as bubbl.us allow you to use this technique on the computer, alone or in groups. (*See the TextConnex box on p. 43.*)

Working as a group, the students in a composition course produced the cluster in Figure 5.2 on the topic of "Work in the U.S. today."

4. Questioning

The journalist's five *w*'s and an *h* (*who? what? where? when? why?* and *how?*) can help you find specific ideas and details. For example, a student group assigned to research and write a paper about some aspect of work came up with the following questions:

- In terms of age, gender, and ethnicity, who is working in Web design?
- What are the working conditions, benefits, and job security of those employed in the current U.S. service economy?
- Where are all the manufacturing jobs these days?

For MULTILINGUAL STUDENTS

Using Another Language to Explore Ideas

Consider exploring your topic using your native language. You won't have to worry about grammar, spelling, or vocabulary, so these issues won't interfere with your creative thought. Once you have some ideas, it is best to work with them in English.

FIGURE 5.2 A cluster on the topic of work.

- When is it best for people to retire from jobs?
- Why are so many U.S. businesses downsizing?
- How do people prepare themselves for career changes?

For other examples of what to question and how, you should take note of the problems or questions your professor poses in class discussions. If you are using a textbook in your course, check out the study questions.

5. Reviewing your notes and annotations

Review your notes and annotations on your reading or research. (*For details on annotating, see Chapter 4. For details on keeping a research journal, see Chapter 24.*) If you are writing about something you have

Different Questions Lead to Different Answers

Always consider what questions make the most sense in the context of the course you are taking. Scholars in different disciplines pose questions related to their fields.

- **Sociology:** A sociologist might ask questions about the ways management and workers interact in the high-tech workplace.
- **History:** A historian might ask how women's roles in the workplace have—or have not—changed since 1960.
- **Economics:** An economist might wonder what effect, if any, the North American Free Trade Agreement (NAFTA) has had on factory layoffs and closings in the United States.

observed, review any notes or sketches you made. These immediate comments and reactions are one of your best sources for ideas.

6. Keeping a journal or notebook

You may find it helpful to go beyond note taking and start recording ideas and questions connected to your classes or your exploratory writing. For example, you might write about connections between your personal life and your academic subjects, connections among your subjects, or ideas touched on in class that you would like to know more about. Jotting down one or two thoughts at the end of class and exploring those ideas at greater length later in the day will help you build a store of essay ideas.

> My economics textbook says that moving jobs to companies overseas ultimately does more good than harm to the economy, but how can that be? When the electronics factory closed, it devastated my town.

TextConnex

Blogging as a Writing Process Tool

As a site for invention, a blog provides space for your notes. It also can function as a research notebook in which you link to online sources and record your own ideas, and it allows you to ask readers questions about issues you encounter in an assignment. (*For more on blogs, see Tab 3: Common Assignments across the Curriculum, pp. 170–72.*)

7. Browsing in the library or searching the Internet

Your college library is filled with ideas—and it can be a great inspiration when you need to come up with your own. Browse the bookshelves containing texts that relate to a topic of interest. Exploring a subject on the Web is the electronic equivalent of browsing in the library. Type keywords related to your topic into a search engine such as Google, and visit several sites on the list that results. (*See Tab 5: Researching, pp. 209–13.*)

8. Exchanging ideas

Writing is a social activity. Most authors thank family members, editors, librarians, and colleagues for help on work in progress. Talking about your writing with your classmates, friends, and family can be a source of ideas.

Online tools that are available to writers offer additional ways to collaborate with others on your papers. Discuss your assignments by exchanging e-mail, instant messages, and text messages. You also might use a blog to exchange ideas and drafts with your classmates (*see the TextConnex box*). If your class has a course Web site, you might exchange ideas in chat rooms. Other options include virtual environments such as SecondLife.com.

Writing e-mail   When you work on papers with classmates, you can use e-mail in the following ways:

- To check out your understanding of the assignment
- To try out various topics
- To ask each other questions
- To share freewriting, listing, and other exploratory writing
- To respond to each other's ideas

Chatting about ideas   You can also use online chat rooms as well as other virtual spaces to share ideas. Your instructor may include **chat** or **MOO** activities, in which you go into virtual rooms to work on assignments in small groups or visit and interact with classes at other colleges. You also can exchange ideas in virtual worlds such as SecondLife.com. **Instant messaging (IM)** also permits real-time online communication. Exchanging ideas with other writers via IM can help you clarify your thinking on a topic. In the exchange shown in Figure 5.3 on page 48, two students use instant messaging to share ideas about volunteerism.

Exchanging text messages   **Text messaging**—the exchange of brief messages between cell phones—can be useful to writers in two ways. First, you can text your ideas for an assignment to a classmate

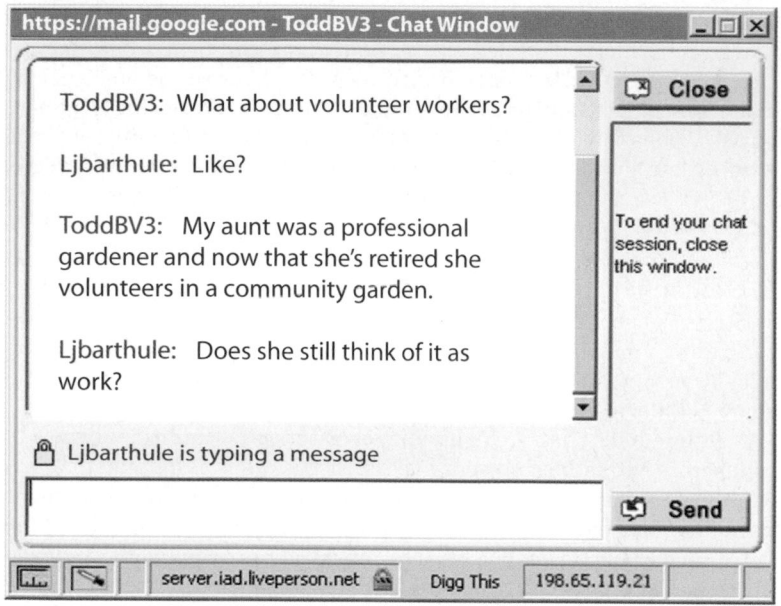

FIGURE 5.3 An online discussion. Chatting online with classmates allows you to test ideas, as in this exchange.

(or—with permission—your instructor) for response. Second, you can use abbreviations commonly used in texting for speedier note taking both in class and for research projects. Such shorthand should *never* be used in assignments.

www.mhhe.com/ awr3

For more help with developing a thesis, go to

Writing > Paragraph/Essay Development > Thesis/Cenetral Idea

5c Develop a working thesis.

The **thesis** is the central idea of your paper. It should communicate a specific point about your topic and suit the purpose of the assignment. As you explore your topic, ideas for your thesis will begin to emerge. You can focus these ideas by drafting a preliminary or working **thesis statement,** which can be one or more sentences long. As you draft and revise your paper, you may change your thesis several times to make it stronger.

To develop a thesis, answer a question posed by your assignment. (*For more about questions, see pp. 44–45.*) For example, an assignment in a political science class might ask you to defend or critique "Healthy Inequality," an article by George Will on the increasing gap between rich and poor in the United States. The question your thesis must answer is, "Is George Will's position that inequality is healthy correct?"

To create a strong thesis, you will need to think critically, developing a point of view based on reading course materials and doing research. Not all theses can be stated in one sentence, but all strong theses are suitable, specific, and significant.

1. Making sure your thesis is suitable

A suitable thesis fits the paper's main purpose. All theses make an assertion, but while a thesis for an argument will take a clear position on an issue or recommend an action, a thesis for an informative or interpretive paper will often preview the paper's content or express the writer's insight into the topic. All of the following theses are on the same topic, but each is for a paper with a different purpose:

THESIS TO INFORM

In terms of income and wealth, the gap between rich and poor has increased substantially during the past decade.

THESIS TO INTERPRET

The economic ideas George Will expresses in "Healthy Inequality" are politically conservative.

THESIS TO ARGUE

George Will is wrong about economic inequality being good for the United States.

2. Making sure your thesis is specific

Vague theses usually lead to weak, unfocused papers. Watch out in particular for thesis statements that simply announce your topic, state an obvious fact about it, or offer a general observation:

ANNOUNCEMENT

I will discuss the article "Healthy Inequality" by George Will. [*What is the writer's point about the article?*]

STATEMENT OF FACT

The article "Healthy Inequality" by George Will is about the gap between rich and poor. [*This thesis gives us information about the article, but it does not make a specific point about it.*]

GENERAL OBSERVATION

George Will's article "Healthy Inequality" is interesting. [*While this thesis makes a point about the article, the point could apply to many articles. What makes this article worth reading?*]

In contrast, a specific thesis signals a focused, well-developed paper.

SPECIFIC

George Will's argument that economic inequality is healthy for the United States should not be accepted. His interpretation of the recent increase in income inequality is questionable. His reasoning about history is flawed. Above all, his idea of what is healthy is too narrow.

In this example, the thesis expresses the writer's particular point—there are three reasons to reject Will's argument. It also forecasts the structure of the whole paper.

> ***Note:*** A thesis statement can be longer than one sentence (if necessary) to provide a framework for your main idea. All of the sentences taken together, though, should build to one specific, significant point that fits the purpose of your assignment. (Some instructors may prefer that you limit your thesis statements to one sentence.)

3. Making sure your thesis is significant

A topic that makes a difference to you is much more likely to make a difference to your readers. When you are looking for possible theses, be sure to challenge yourself to develop one that you care about.

TextConnex

Using Presentation Software as a Writing Process Tool

Many students have discovered that presentation software slides provide a useful tool for exploring and organizing their ideas prior to drafting. The slides also give you another way to get feedback from peer reviewers and others, using the following process:

- Well before a paper is due, create a very brief, three- to five-slide presentation—with visuals if appropriate—that previews the key points you intend to make in the paper.
- Present the preview to an audience—friends, classmates, or perhaps even your instructor. Ask for reactions, suggestions for improvement, and advice for developing the presentation into a written text.

5d Plan a structure that suits your assignment.

Every paper needs the following components:

- A beginning, or **introduction,** that hooks readers and usually states the thesis
- A middle, or **body,** that develops the main idea of the paper in a series of paragraphs—each making a point supported by specific details

■ An ending, or **conclusion,** that gives readers a sense of completion, often by offering a final comment on the thesis

Typically, state your thesis in the introduction. However, in personal, narrative, or descriptive writing, the thesis may be implied by details and evidence. In other cases, the thesis may be most effective at the end of the essay. This tactic works well when you are arguing for a position that your audience is likely to oppose.

It is not essential to have an outline before you start drafting; indeed, some writers prefer to discover how to connect and develop their ideas as they compose. However, an outline of your first draft will help you spot organizational problems or places where the support for your thesis is weak.

For MULTILINGUAL STUDENTS

State Your Thesis Directly

In U.S. academic and business settings, readers expect writers to state the main idea right away. Some other cultures may use an indirect style, telling stories and giving facts but not stating the central idea in an obvious way. When assessing a writing situation, consider your readers' expectations and values.

1. Preparing an informal plan

A **scratch outline** is a simple list of points, without the levels of subordination found in more complex outlines. Scratch outlines are useful for briefer papers. Here is a scratch outline for a paper on an exhibit of photographs by Sebastião Salgado:

www.mhhe.com/awr3

For more on outlines, go to

Writing > Paragraph/Essay Development > Outlines

■ Photojournalism should be informative, but it can be beautiful and artful too, as Salgado's *Migrations* exhibit illustrates.

■ The exhibit overall—powerful pictures of people uprooted, taken in 39 countries over 7 years. Salgado documents a global crisis; over 100 million displaced due to war, resource depletion, overpopulation, natural disasters, poverty.

■ Specific picture—"Orphanage"—describe subjects, framing, lighting, emotions it evokes.

■ Salgado on the purpose of his photographs. Quote.

A **do/say plan** is a more detailed type of informal outline. To come up with such a plan, review your notes and other relevant material. Then write down your working thesis, and list what you will say for each of the following "do" categories: introduce, support and develop, and conclude. Here is an example:

Thesis: George Will is wrong about economic inequality being good for the United States.

1. **Introduce** the issue and my focus.

   - Use two examples to contrast rich and poor: "approximately 17,000 Americans declared more than $1 million of annual income on their 1985 tax returns" (Mantsios 196). Between 1979 and 1992, there was a 15% decrease in the manufacturing workforce, and in 1993, Sears eliminated 50,000 merchandising jobs (Rifkin 2).

   - Say that the issue is how to evaluate increasing economic inequality, and introduce Will's article "Healthy Inequality." Summarize Will's argument.

   - Give Will credit for raising issue, but then state thesis: he's wrong about more inequality being good for the United States.

2. **Support and develop** thesis that Will's argument is wrong.

   - Point out that Will relies on economic interpretations of Greenwood and Yorukoglu. They see decline ("modest") in labor productivity beginning in 1974. But Rifkin says "manufacturing productivity is soaring"—up 35%.

   - Point out one thing Will and Rifkin agree on: computer revolution is affecting economy/jobs. But Will thinks effects are like "economic turbulence" caused in 1770 by steam engine and in 1840 by electricity.

   - Show that these analogies aren't convincing. Too many differences. Use Aronowitz on "jobless future" and Rifkin for support.

   - Say that Will makes fun of those who "decr[y] . . . injustice," people like Rifkin and Aronowitz. Will thinks inequality motivates people to learn new skills so they can compete. A skilled workforce makes society better/healthy.

   - Will's idea of healthy society is narrow. An economic idea only. And who will pay to train unemployed workers?

3. **Conclude** that Will doesn't ask or answer such key questions because he denies that there is any problem. Earlier he says "suffering is good." Where would he draw the line? Maybe quote from Max Weber?

In outlining his plan, this student has already begun drafting because as he works on the outline, he gets a clearer sense of what he thinks is wrong with Will's argument. He starts writing sentences that he is likely to include in the first complete draft.

2. Preparing a formal outline

A **formal outline** classifies and divides the information you have gathered, showing main points, supporting ideas, and specific details by organizing them into levels of subordination.

A **topic outline** uses single words or phrases; a **sentence outline** states every idea in a sentence. Because the process of division always results in at least two parts, in a formal outline every I must have a II; every A, a B; and so on. Also, items placed at the same level must be of the same kind; for example, if I is London, then II can be New York City but not the Bronx or Wall Street. Items at the same level should also be grammatically parallel; if A is "Choosing screen icons," then B can be "Creating away messages" but not "Away messages."

Here is a formal sentence outline for a paper on Salgado's *Migrations* exhibit:

Thesis: Like a photojournalist, Salgado brings us images of newsworthy events, but he goes beyond objective reporting, imparting his compassion for refugees and migrants to the viewer.

I. The images in *Migrations,* an exhibit of his work, suggest that Salgado does more then simply point and shoot.

II. Salgado's photograph "Orphanage attached to the hospital at Kibumba, Number One Camp, Goma Zaire" illustrates the power of his work.

   A. The photograph depicts three infants who are victims of the war in Rwanda.

      1. The label indicates that there are 4,000 orphans in the camp and 100,000 orphans overall.

      2. The numbers are abstractions that the photo makes real.

   B. Salgado's use of black and white gives the photo a documentary feel, but he also uses contrasts of light and dark to create a dramatic image of the babies.

      1. The vertical black-and-white stripes of the blanket direct viewers' eyes to the infants' faces and hands.

      2. The whites of their eyes stand out against the darkness of the blankets.

      3. The camera's lens focuses sharply on the babies' faces, highlighting their expressions.

         a. The baby on the left has a heart-wrenching look.

         b. The baby in the center has a startled look.

         c. The baby on the right has a glazed and sunken look and is near death.

   C. The vantage point of this photograph is one of a parent standing directly over his or her child.

      1. The infants seem to belong to the viewer.

www.mhhe.com/awr3
For help with outlining, go to
Writing > Outlining Tutor

2. The photo is framed so that the babies take up the entire space, consuming the viewer with their innocence and vulnerability.

III. Salgado uses his artistic skill to get viewers to look closely at painful subjects, illustrating a big, complex topic with a collection of intimate, intensely moving images.

👁 5e Use visuals effectively.

Visuals such as tables, charts, and graphs make complex data or ideas clear. Effective visuals are used for a specific purpose, and each type of visual illustrates some kinds of material better than others. For example, compare the table and the line graph on the facing page. Both present similar types of data, but do both have the same effect? Does one strike you as clearer or more powerful than the other?

When you use data or visuals created by someone else, always credit your source. Most images are protected by copyright. If the visual will be republished (including on the Web), you will usually need to obtain permission from the copyright holder. (*For information about finding visuals, see Tab 5: Researching, pp. 219–26.*)

> **Caution:** Because the use of visual elements is more accepted in some fields than in others, you may want to ask your instructor for advice before planning to include visuals in your composition.

TextConnex

Preparing Tables

You can usually create and edit tables using your word-processing software. You can also create tables using database, spreadsheet, presentation, and Web site construction software.

Types of Visuals and Their Uses

TABLES

Tables organize precise data for readers. Because the measurements in the example include decimals, it would be difficult to plot them on a graph.

Emissions from Waste (Tg CO_2 Eq.)

Gas/Source	1990	1995	2000	2001	2002	2003	2004	2005
CH_4	185.8	182.2	158.3	153.5	156.2	160.5	157.8	157.4
Landfills	161.0	157.1	131.9	127.6	130.4	134.9	132.1	132.0
Wastewater treatment	24.8	25.1	26.4	25.9	25.8	25.6	25.7	25.4
N_2O	6.4	6.9	7.6	7.6	7.7	7.8	7.9	8.0
Domestic wastewater treatment	6.4	6.9	7.6	7.6	7.7	7.8	7.9	8.0
Total	**192.2**	**189.1**	**165.9**	**161.1**	**163.9**	**168.4**	**165.7**	**165.4**

Note: Totals may not sum due to independent rounding.
SOURCE: U.S. Environmental Protection Agency. *Inventory of U.S. Greenhouse Gas Emissions and Sinks: 1996–2006.* U.S. Environmental Protection Agency, Apr. 2008. Web. 9 June 2008. p. 8-1.

BAR GRAPHS

Bar graphs highlight comparisons between two or more variables, such as the cost of tuition and fees at different public universities. They allow readers to see relative sizes quickly.

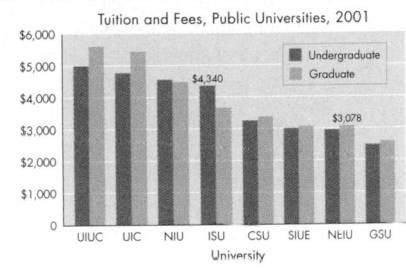

PIE CHARTS

Pie charts show the size of parts in relation to the whole. The segments must add up to 100% of something, differences in segment size must be sizeable, and there should not be too many segments.

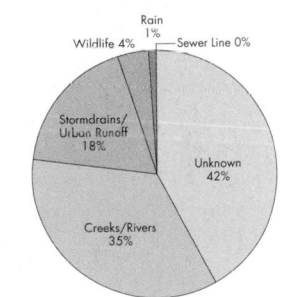

LINE GRAPHS

Line graphs show changes in one or more variables over time. The example shows three sources of nitrous oxide emissions over a 16-year period.

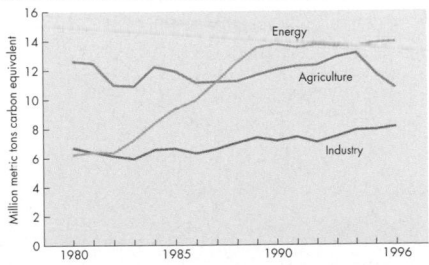

(continued on next page)

Types of Visuals and Their Uses (*continued*)

DIAGRAMS

Diagrams show processes or structures visually. Common in technical writing, they include timelines, organization charts, and decision trees. The example shows the factors involved in the decision to commit a burglary.

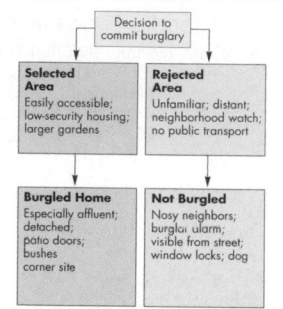

PHOTOS

Photos can reinforce your point by showing readers what your subject actually looks like or how it has been affected. This image of Kurt Cobain could support a portrayal of him as a talented but conflicted artist.

MAPS

Maps highlight locations and spatial relationships. This one shows population densities in China.

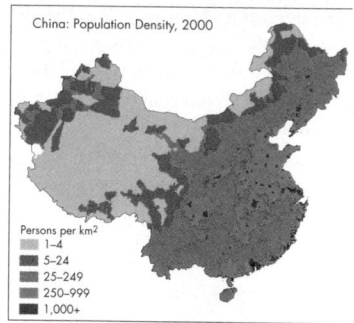

ILLUSTRATIONS

Like photographs, illustrations make a point dramatically. (*A larger version of this image appears on p. 36.*)

6 Drafting Text and Visuals

Think of drafting as an attempt to discover a beginning, a middle, and an end for what you have to say, but remember that a draft is preliminary. Avoid putting pressure on yourself to make it perfect, and leave ample time to revise and edit.

6a Use electronic tools for drafting.

The following tips will make this process go smoothly:

- **Save your work.** Always protect your hard-won drafts from power surges and other mishaps. Save often, and make backups.
- **Label revised drafts with different file names.** Use a different file name for each successive version of your paper. For

www.mhhe.com/awr3

For more on drafting, go to

Writing > Paragraph/Essay Development > Drafting and Revising

Tips LEARNING in COLLEGE

Avoiding Writer's Block

While it is important to allot time for generating and organizing your ideas, do not put off writing the first draft. If you find it difficult to get started, consider these tips:

- **Resist the temptation to be a perfectionist.** For your first draft, do not worry about getting the right word, the stylish phrase, or even the correct spelling.
- **Take it "bird by bird."** Writer Anne Lamott counsels students to break down writing assignments into manageable units and then make a commitment to finishing each unit in one session. She passes along her father's advice to her brother, who had procrastinated on a report about birds and was paralyzed by the enormity of the project: "Bird by bird, buddy. Just take it bird by bird."
- **Start anywhere.** If you are stuck on the beginning, pick a section where you have a clearer sense of what you want to say. You can go back later and work out the transitions. Writers often compose the introduction after drafting a complete text.
- **Generate more ideas.** If you hit a section where you are drawing a blank, you may need to do more reading, research, or brainstorming. Be careful, though, not to use reading and research as a stalling tactic.
- **Set aside time and find a suitable place.** Make sure you have somewhere you can work undisturbed for at least half an hour at a stretch.

example, you might save drafts of a paper on work as Work1, Work2, Work3, and so on.

■ **Print hard copies early and often.** If you save and print the original, you can feel free to experiment.

TEXTCONNEX

Using Hypertext as a Writing Process Tool

Some students insert links in their essays during the writing process. For example, they might include a link to additional research, or to a source that refutes an argument, or to interesting information that is not directly relevant. These links can help writers refer to supplemental material without undermining the coherence of the text. If a reader of an early draft—an instructor or a classmate—thinks the linked material should be in the essay itself, the writer can include it in the next draft.

◉ 6b Develop ideas and use visuals strategically.

www.mhhe.com/
awr3

For more on
developing
paragraphs, go to

Writing >
Paragraph
Patterns

The following strategies can help you develop the ideas that support your thesis into a complete draft. Depending on the purpose of your composition, you may use a few of these strategies throughout or a mix of all of them.

Visuals can also serve as rhetorical strategies. As with paragraphs, you can use a mix of visuals in a paper. Keep in mind, though, that any visuals you use should always serve the overall purpose of your work. (*See pp. 54–56, for more on types of visuals and their purposes.*)

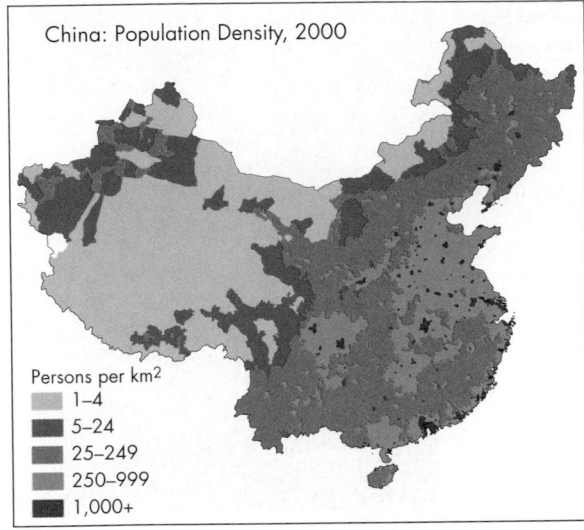

FIGURE 6.1
Visuals that illustrate. This map illustrates the population densities in various regions of China in the year 2000.

1. Illustration

No matter what your purpose and point may be, to appeal to readers you will have to show as well as tell. Detailed examples and well-chosen visuals (*see Figure 6.1*) can make abstractions more concrete and generalizations more specific, as the following paragraph shows:

> As Rubin explains, "for much of the Accord era, the ideal-typical family . . . was composed of a 'stay-at-home-mom,' a working father, and dependent children. He earned wages; she cooked, cleaned, cared for the home, managed the family's social life, and nurtured the family members" (97). Just such an arrangement characterized my grandmother's married life. My grandmother, who had four children, stayed at home with them, while her husband went off to work as a safety engineer. Sadly, when he died, she was left with nothing. She needed to support herself, yet had no work experience, no credit, and little education. But even though society frowned on her for seeking employment, my grandmother eventually found a clerical position—a low-level job with few perks.
>
> —JENNIFER KOEHLER, "Women's Work in the United States: The 1950s and 1990s," student paper

> ***Caution:*** Although any image you choose to include in your paper will be illustrative, images should not function merely as decoration. Ask yourself if each image you are considering truly adds information to your paper.

FIGURE 6.2 Visuals that narrate. Images that narrate can reinforce a message or portray events you discuss in your paper. Images like this one help tell one of many stories about the war in Iraq.

www.mhhe.com/ awr3

For help with the use of narration, go to

**Writing >
Writing Tutors >
Narration**

2. Narration

When you narrate, you tell a story. (*See Figure 6.2 for an example of a narrative visual.*) The following paragraph comes from a personal essay on the goods that result from "a lifetime of production":

> My dad changed too. He had come to that job feeling—as I do now—that everything was still possible. He'd served his time in the Air Force during the Korean War. Then, while my mother worked as a secretary to support them, he earned a college degree courtesy of the GI Bill. After graduation, my father painted houses for a season until he was offered a position scheduling the production of corrugated board. He took it, though he has told me that he never planned to stay. It was not something he envisioned as his life's work. I try to imagine what it is like suddenly to look up from a stack of orders and discover that the job you started one December day has watched you age.
>
> —MICHELLE M. DUCHARME, "A Lifetime of Production"

Notice that Ducharme begins with two sentences that state the topic and point of her narration. Then, using the past tense, she recounts in chronological sequence some key events that led to her father's taking a job in the box manufacturing business.

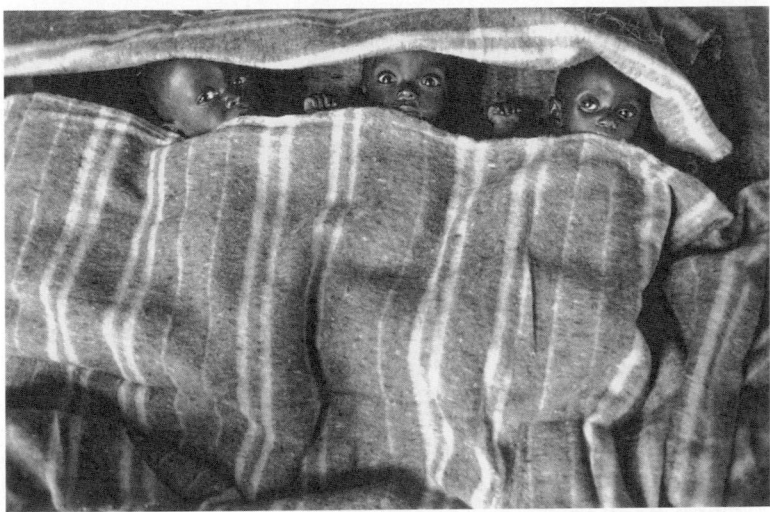

FIGURE 6.3 Visuals that describe. Pay careful attention to the effect a particular image will have on your paper. This photograph by Sebastião Salgado, for example, appeals to the viewer's emotions, evoking sympathy for the refugee children's plight.

3. Description

To make an object, person, or activity vivid for your readers, describe it in concrete, specific words that appeal to the senses of sight, sound, taste, smell, and touch. (*See Figure 6.3 for an example of a descriptive visual.*) In the following paragraph, Diane Chen describes her impression of the photograph in Figure 6.3:

> The vertical black-and-white stripes of the blanket direct our eyes to the infants' faces and hands, which are framed by a horizontal white stripe. The whites of their eyes in particular stand out against the darkness created by the shell of the blankets. The camera's lens also seems to be in sharper focus on the faces than on the blankets, again focusing our attention on the babies' expressions.
>
> —DIANE CHEN, "The Caring Eye of Sebastião Salgado,"
> student paper

www.mhhe.com/
awr3
For help with the use
of description, go to

Writing >
Writing Tutors >
Description

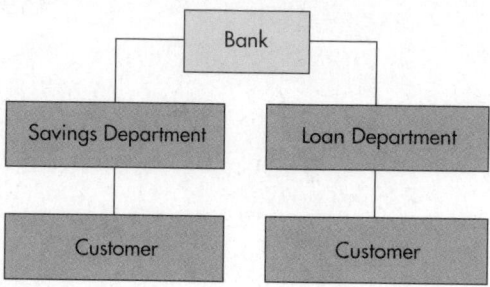

FIGURE 6.4 **Visuals that classify or divide.** An image can help you make the categories in or parts of complex systems or organizations easier to understand. The image shown here, for example, helps readers comprehend the structure of a business.

www.mhhe.com/
awr3

For help with the use of classification, go to

Writing >
Writing Tutors >
Classification

4. Classification

Classification is a useful way of grouping individual entities into identifiable categories. (*See Figure 6.4.*) Classifying occurs in all academic disciplines and often appears with its complement—**division,** or breaking a whole entity into its parts.

In the following passage, Robert Reich first classifies future work into two broad categories: complex services and person-to-person services. Then in the next paragraph, he develops the idea of complex services in more detail, in part by dividing that category into more specific—and familiar—categories like engineering and advertising.

> [M]ost of America's traditional, routinized manufacturing jobs will disappear. So will routinized service jobs that can be done from remote locations, like keypunching of data transmitted by satellite. Instead, you will be engaged in one of two broad categories of work: either complex services, some of which will be sold to the rest of the world to pay for whatever Americans want to buy from the rest of the world, or person-to-person services, which foreigners can't provide for us because (apart from new immigrants and illegal aliens) they aren't here to provide them.
>
> Complex services involve the manipulation of data and abstract symbols. Included in this category are insurance, engineering, law, finance, computer programming, and advertising. Such activities now account for almost 25 percent of our GNP, up from 13 percent in 1950. They have already surpassed manufacturing (down to about 20 percent of GNP).
>
> —ROBERT REICH, "The Future of Work"

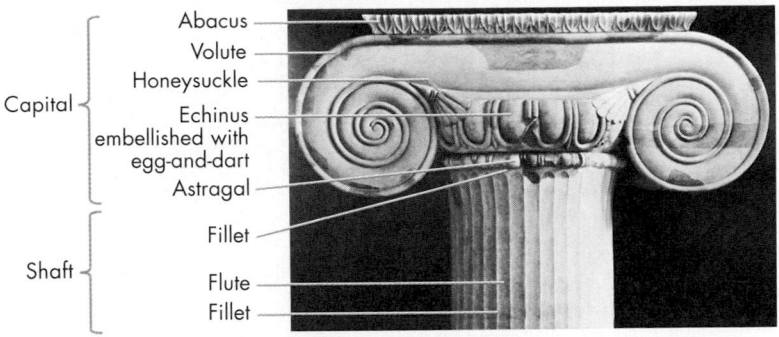

FIGURE 6.5 Visuals that define. Visuals can be extremely effective when used to support a written definition or to identify parts of a whole. This image uses labels and leader lines to identify the characteristics of an Ionic column.

5. Definition

You should define any concepts that readers might need to understand to follow your ideas. (*See Figure 6.5 for an example of a visual that defines.*) Interpretations and arguments often depend on one or two key ideas that cannot be quickly and easily defined. In the following example, John Berger defines "image," a key idea in his televised lectures on the way we see things:

www.mhhe.com/
awr3
For help with the use
of definition, go to
**Writing > Writing
Tutors > Definition**

> An image is a sight which has been recreated or reproduced. It is an appearance, or a set of appearances, which has been detached from the place and time in which it first made its appearance and preserved—for a few moments or centuries. Every image embodies a way of seeing. Even a photograph. For photographs are not, as is often assumed, a mechanical record. Every time we look at a photograph, we are aware, however slightly, of the photographer selecting that sight from an infinity of other possible sights. This is true even in the most casual family snapshot. The photographer's way of seeing is reflected in his choice of subject.
>
> —JOHN BERGER, *Ways of Seeing*

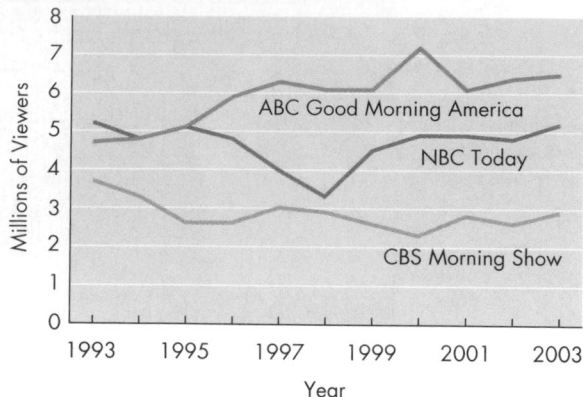

FIGURE 6.6 Visuals that compare and contrast.
Graphs and charts are effective for comparing parallel
sets of data. This line graph tracks the population of
viewers for the three most popular morning shows
over ten years.

www.mhhe.com/
awr3

For help with the use
of comparison and
contrast, go to

Writing >
Writing Tutors >
Comparison/
Contrast

6. Comparison and contrast

When you *compare,* you explore the similarities and differences among
various items. When the term *compare* is used along with the term
contrast, compare has a narrower meaning: "to spell out key similarities." *Contrast* always means "to itemize important differences." (*See
Figure 6.6.*)

In the following example, the student writer uses a **subject-by-
subject** pattern to contrast the ideas of two social commentators,
Jeremy Rifkin and George Will:

> Rifkin and Will have different opinions about unemployment
> due to downsizing and the widening income gap between rich
> and poor. Rifkin sees both the decrease in employment and the
> increase in income disparity as evils that must be immediately
> dealt with lest society fall apart: "If no measures are taken to pro-
> vide financial opportunities for millions of Americans in an era of
> diminishing jobs, then . . . violent crime is going to increase" (3).
> Will, on the other hand, seems to believe that both unemployment
> and income differences are necessary to the health of American
> society. Will writes, "A society that chafes against stratification
> derived from disparities of talents will be a society that discour-
> ages individual talents" (92). Apparently, the society that Rifkin
> wants is just the kind of society that Will rejects.
>
> —JACOB GROSSMAN, "Dark Comes before Dawn,"
> student paper

Notice that Grossman comments on Rifkin first and then turns to his second subject, Will. To ensure paragraph unity, he begins with a topic sentence that mentions both subjects.

In the following paragraph, the student writer organizes her comparison **point by point** rather than subject by subject. Instead of saying everything about Smith's picture before commenting on the AP photo, she moves back and forth between the two images as she makes and supports two points: (1) that the images differ in figure and scene and (2) that they are similar in theme.

> Divided by an ocean, two photographers took pictures that at first glance seem absolutely different. W. Eugene Smith's well-known *Tomoko in the Bath* and the less well-known AP photo *A Paratrooper Works to Save the Life of a Buddy* portray distinctively different settings and people. Smith brings us into a darkened room where a Japanese woman is lovingly bathing her malformed child, while the AP staff photographer captures two soldiers on the battlefield, one intently performing CPR on his wounded friend. But even though the two images seem as different as women and men, peace and war, or life and death, both pictures figure something similar: a time of suffering. It is the early 1970s—a time when the hopes and dreams that modernity promoted are being exposed as deadly to human beings. Perhaps that is why the bodies in both pictures seem humbled. Grief pulls you down onto your knees. Terror impels you to crawl along the ground.
>
> —ILONA BOUZOUKASHVILI, "On Reading Photographs,"
> student paper

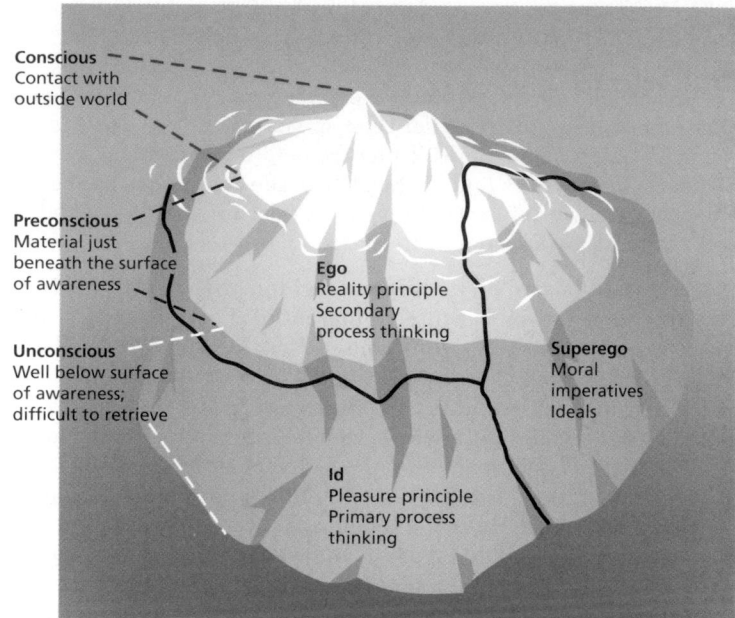

FIGURE 6.7 Visuals as analogies. Visual analogies operate in the same way as written analogies. This figure uses the image of an iceberg to illustrate Freud's theory of the unconscious. The portion of the iceberg below the surface of the water represents the preconscious and unconscious mind.

7. Analogy

An **analogy** compares topics that at first glance seem quite different (*see Figure 6.7*). A well-chosen analogy can make new or technical information appear more commonplace and understandable:

> The human eye provides a good starting point for learning how a camera works. The lens of the eye is like the *lens* of the camera. In both instruments the lens focuses an image of the surroundings on a *light-sensitive surface*—the *retina* of the eye and the *film* in the camera. In both, the light-sensitive material is protected within a light-tight container—the *eyeball* of the eye and the *body* of the camera. Both eye and camera have a mechanism for shutting off light passing through the lens to the interior of the container—the *lid* of the eye and the *shutter* of the camera. In both, the size of the lens opening, or *aperture,* is regulated by an *iris diaphragm.*
>
> —MARVIN ROSEN, *Introduction to Photography*

FIGURE 6.8
Visuals that show a process. Flow charts and diagrams are especially useful when illustrating a process. This one shows the scientific method used in disciplines throughout the sciences and social sciences.

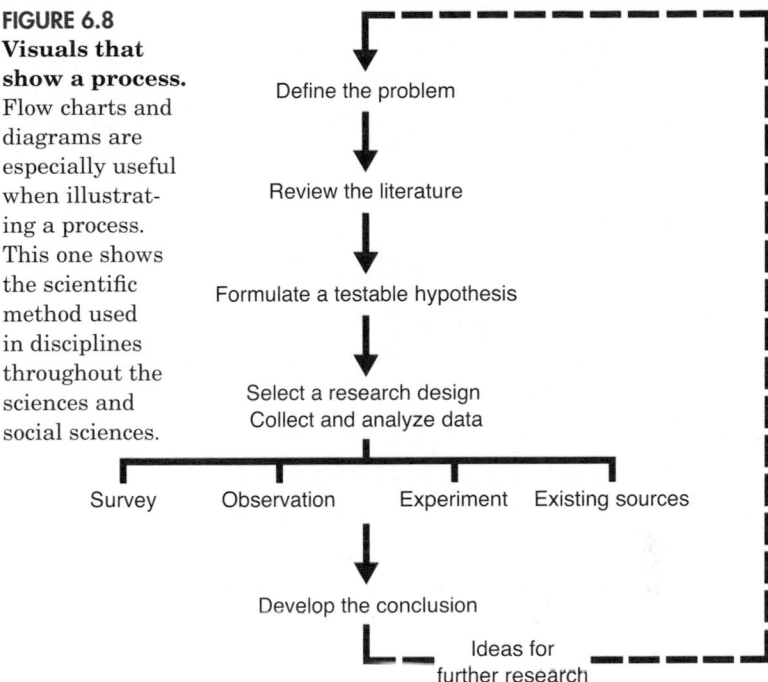

8. Process

When you need to explain how to do something or show readers how something is done, you use process analysis (*see Figure 6.8*), explaining each step in the process in chronological order, as in the following example:

www.mhhe.com/ awr3
For help with describing a process, go to

Writing >
Writing Tutors >
Process Analysis

> To end our Hawan ritual of thanks, *aarti* is performed. First, my mother lights a piece of camphor in a metal plate called a *taree.* Holding the taree with her right hand, she moves the fire in a circular, clockwise movement in front of the altar. Next, she stands in front of my father and again moves the fiery *taree* in a circular, clockwise direction. After touching his feet and receiving his blessing, she attends to each of us children in turn, moving the fire in a clockwise direction before kissing us, one by one. When she is done, my father performs his *aarti* in a similar way and then my sister and I do ours. When everyone is done, we say some prayers and sit down.
>
> —U. ROOPNARIAN, "A Family Ritual," student paper

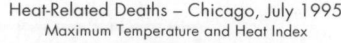

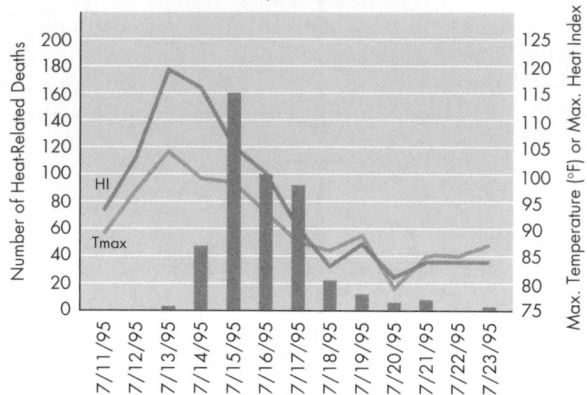

This graph tracks maximum temperature (Tmax), heat index (HI), and heat-related deaths in Chicago each day from July 11 to 23, 1995. The orange line shows maximum daily temperature, the green line shows the heat index, and the bars indicate number of deaths for the day.

FIGURE 6.9 Visuals that show cause and effect. Visuals can provide powerful evidence when you are writing about causes and effects. Although graphs like this one may seem self-explanatory, you will still need to analyze and interpret them for your readers.

9. Cause and effect

This strategy can help you trace the causes of some event or situation, to describe its effects, or both (*see Figure 6.9*). In the following example, Rajeev Bector explains the reasons for a character's feelings and actions in a short story:

> Given the differences between Mrs. Chestny's and her son's values, as well as the oppressiveness of Mrs. Chestny's racist views, we can understand why Julian struggles to "teach" his mother "a lesson" (185) throughout the entire bus ride. Goffman would point out that "each individual is engaged in providing evidence to establish a definition of himself at the expense of what can remain for the other" (29). But in the end, neither character wins the contest. Julian's mother loses her sense of self when she is pushed down to the ground by a "colored woman" wearing a hat identical to hers (187). Faced with his mother's breakdown, Julian feels his own identity being overwhelmed by "the world of guilt and sorrow."
>
> —RAJEEV BECTOR, "The Character Contest in Flannery O'Connor's 'Everything That Rises Must Converge,'" student paper

6c Write focused, clearly organized paragraphs.

Paragraphs break the text into blocks for your readers, allowing them to see how your essay builds step by step and providing a rhythm for their reading. Introductory and concluding paragraphs have special functions, but all paragraphs should have a single, clear focus and a clear organization. (Paragraphs on the Web tend to be short, with links at the ends so readers do not navigate away.)

1. Focusing on one main point or example

In a strong paragraph, the sentences form a unit that explores one main point or elaborates on one main example. When you are drafting, start a new paragraph when you introduce a new reason in support of your thesis, a new step in a process, or a new element in an analysis. New paragraphs also signal shifts in time and place, changing speakers in dialogue, contrasts with earlier material, and changes in level of emphasis. As you draft, bear in mind that each paragraph develops a main point or example.

In the following example, the paragraph focuses on a theory that the writer will refer to later in his essay. The main idea is highlighted:

> Current thinking on the topic of loss and mourning rests on foundations constructed by the British psychiatrist, John Bowlby. Using examples from animal and human behavior, Bowlby (1977) posited "attachment theory" as a means of understanding the powerful bonds between humans and the disruption that comes when the bonds are jeopardized or destroyed. The bonds are formed because of a need for security and safety, are developed early in life, are long enduring, and are directed toward a few special individuals. In normal maturation, the child becomes ever more independent, moving away from the figure of attachment, and returning periodically for safety and security. If the bonds are threatened, the individual will try to restore them through crying, clinging, or other types of coercion; if they are destroyed, withdrawal, apathy, and despair will follow.

Details of attachment theory are developed in the rest of the paragraph.

> —JONATHAN FAST, "After Columbine: How People Mourn Sudden Death"

2. Signaling the main idea of your paragraph with a topic sentence

A topic sentence can be a helpful starting point as you draft a paragraph. In the following paragraph, the topic sentence (highlighted) provides the writer with a launching point for a series of details:

> The excavation also revealed dramatic evidence for the commemorative rituals that took place after the burial. Four cattle

The topic sentence announces that the paragraph will focus on a certain kind of evidence.

had been decapitated and their skulls symbolically placed in a ditch enclosing the burial pit. In the soil above the skulls archaeologists found the butchered bones of at least 250 slaughtered cattle, evidence for a huge ceremonial feast. Clearly this was an expensive way to commemorate a leader. Indeed, the huge quantity of meat suggests that the entire tribe may have gathered at the grave to take part in a ritual feast. Perhaps this was one way the bonds between scattered communities were strengthened.

—Damian Robinson, "Riding into the Afterlife"

Sometimes the sentences in a paragraph will lead to a unifying conclusion (highlighted), as in this example:

Table 1 presents the 15 mechanisms for gaining prestige that were reported for girls and for boys. There were few differences in the avenues to prestige between those in public and private high schools, particularly for girls. Avenues to prestige for girls that focus on their physical attributes, such as attractiveness, popularity with boys, clothes, sexual activity, and participation in sports, were more prominent in public schools than in private schools. In private schools the avenues more indicative of personality attributes, such as general sociability, having a good reputation/virginity, and participating in school clubs/government and cheerleading, were more prominent. Contrary to what parents may expect, avenues considered to be more negative, such as partying and being class clown, appeared more prevalent in private schools than in public schools. However, only clothes remained a significantly more important route to prestige for girls in public schools compared to girls in private schools once controls were introduced for region, size of community, year of graduation, and gender of respondent. Thus, taken together, type of high school had little effect on the ways in which girls accrued prestige in high school.

—J. Jill Suitor, Rebecca Powers, and Rachel Brown, "Avenues to Prestige among Adolescents"

If a topic sentence would simply state the obvious, it can be omitted. In the following example, it is not necessary to state that the paragraph is about Igor Stravinsky's preprofessional life:

Stravinsky was born in Russia, near St. Petersburg, grew up in a musical atmosphere, and studied with Nikolai Rimsky-Korsakov. He had his first important opportunity in 1909, when the great impresario Sergei Diaghilev heard his music.

—Roger Kamien, *Music: An Appreciation*

3. Writing paragraphs that have a clear organization

The sentences in your final draft need to be clearly related to one another. As you are drafting, make connections among your ideas and information as a way of moving your writing forward. The strategies covered in 6b are ways of developing your ideas. Another way to make your ideas work together is to use one of the common organizational schemes for paragraphs, which can also be used for essays as a whole. (*For advice on using repetition, pronouns, and transitions to relate sentences to one another, see Chapter 7, pp. 81–86.*)

www.mhhe.com/
awr3
For more on
paragraphs, go to

**Writing >
Paragraph Patterns**

- **Chronological organization:** The sentences in a paragraph with a chronological organization describe a series of events, steps, or observations as they occur in time: this happened, then that, and so on.
- **Spatial organization:** The sentences in a paragraph with a spatial organization present details as they appear to a viewer: from top to bottom, outside to inside, east to west, and so on.
- **General-to-specific organization:** As we have seen, paragraphs often start with a general topic sentence that states the main idea and then proceed with specifics that elaborate on that idea. The general topic sentence can include a question that the paragraph then answers or a problem that the paragraph goes on to solve.
- **Specific-to-general organization:** The general topic sentence can come at the end of the paragraph, with the specific details leading up to that general conclusion (*see the paragraph from "Avenues to Prestige among Adolescents," p. 70*). This organization is especially effective when you are preparing readers for a revelation.

4. Drafting introductions and conclusions

As you begin your first draft, you may want to skip the introduction and focus on the body of your paper. After your paper has taken shape, you can go back and sketch out the main ideas for your introduction.

www.mhhe.com/
awr3
For more on
introductions and
conclusions, go to

**Writing >
Paragraph/Essay
Development**

To get readers' attention, show why the topic matters. The opening of your paper should encourage readers to share your view of its importance. Outside of essay exams, it's best not to refer directly to the assignment or to your intentions ("In this paper I will . . ."). Avoid vague general statements ("Jane Austen is a famous author"), and try instead to find a way to arouse readers' interest. Here are some opening strategies:

- Tell a brief story related to the issue your thesis raises.
- Begin with a relevant, attention-getting quotation.
- Begin with a paraphrase of a commonly held view that you immediately question.

- State a working hypothesis.
- Define a key term, but avoid the tired opener that begins, "According to the dictionary . . ." .
- Pose an important question.

For informative reports, arguments, and other types of essays, your opening paragraph or paragraphs will include a thesis statement, usually at the beginning or near the end of the introduction. If your purpose is interpretive, however, you may instead choose to build up to your thesis. For some types of writing, such as narratives, an explicitly stated thesis may not be needed if the main idea is clear without it.

Just as the opening makes a first impression and motivates readers to continue reading, the closing makes a final impression and motivates readers to think further. While you should not merely repeat the main idea that you introduced at the beginning of the paper, you should also avoid overgeneralizing or introducing a completely new topic. Your conclusion should remind readers of your paper's significance and satisfy those who might be asking, "So what?" Here are some good strategies for concluding a paper:

- Refer to the story or quotation you used in your introduction.
- Answer the question you posed in your introduction.
- Summarize your main point.
- Call for some action on your readers' part.
- Present a powerful image or forceful example.
- Suggest some implications for the future.

👁 6d Integrate visuals effectively.

If you decide to use a table, chart, diagram, or photograph in your composition, keep this general advice in mind:

- **Number tables and other figures** consecutively throughout your paper, and label them appropriately: Table 1, Table 2, and so on. Do not abbreviate *Table. Figure* may be abbreviated as *Fig*.

- **Refer to the visual element in your text** before it appears, placing the visual as close as possible to the paragraph in which you state why you are including it. If your project contains complex tables or many other visuals, however, you may want to group them in an appendix. Always refer to a visual by its label—for example, "See Figure 1."

- **Give each visual a title and caption** that clearly explains what the visual shows. A visual with its caption should be clear without the discussion in the text, and the discussion of the visual in the text should be clear without the visual itself.

- **Include explanatory notes below the visuals.** If you want to explain a specific element within the visual, use a super-script letter (not a number) both after the specific element and before the note. The explanation should appear directly beneath the graphic, not at the foot of the page or at the end of your paper.

- **Credit sources for visuals.** If you use a visual element from a source, you need to credit the source. Unless you have specific guidelines to follow, you can use the word *Source,* followed by a colon and complete documentation of the source, including the author, title, publication information, and page number if applicable.

Note: The Modern Language Association (MLA) and the American Psychological Association (APA) provide guidelines for figure captions and crediting sources of visuals that differ from the preceding guidelines. (*See Chapter 29: MLA Style: Paper Format, pp. 310–11, and Chapter 33: APA Style: Paper Format, pp. 347–48.*)

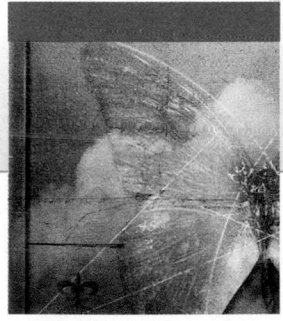

7 Revising and Editing

In the **revising** stage of the writing process, you review the whole composition, adding, deleting, and moving text as necessary. After you are satisfied with the substance of your paper, **editing** begins. When you edit, you polish sentences so that you say what you want to say as effectively as possible.

This chapter focuses on revising. It also introduces the concepts and principles of editing, which are covered in greater detail in Tabs 9–12.

7a Get comments from readers.

Asking actual readers to comment on your draft is the best way to get fresh perspectives on your writing. (Be sure that your professor allows this kind of collaboration.)

1. Using peer review

Peer review involves reading and critiquing your classmates' work while they review yours. You can send your draft to your peer reviewers by e-mail (also print out a hard copy for yourself), or you can exchange drafts in person.

Most readers want to be helpful. Help your readers help you by giving them information and asking them specific questions. When you share a draft with readers, give them answers to the following questions:

- **What is the assignment?** Readers need to understand the context for your project—especially your intended purpose and audience.

- **How close is the project to being finished?** Your answer lets readers know where you are in the writing process and how best to assist you in taking the next step.

- **What steps do you plan to take to complete the project?** If readers know your plans, they can either question the direction you are taking or give you more specific advice, such as the titles of additional sources you might consult.

- **What kind of feedback do you need?** Do you want readers to summarize your main points so you can determine if you have communicated them clearly? Do you want a response to the logic of your argument or the development of your thesis?

Tips   LEARNING in COLLEGE

Re-Visioning Your Paper

Revising is a process of "re-visioning"—of looking at your work through the eyes of your audience. Here are some tips for getting a fresh perspective on your paper:

- **Get feedback from other readers.** Candid, respectful feedback can help you discover the strong and weak areas of your paper.
- **Let your draft cool.** Try to schedule a break between drafting and revising. A good night's sleep, a movie break, or some physical exercise will help you view your paper more objectively.
- **Read your paper aloud.** Some people find that reading aloud helps them "hear" their paper the way their audience will.
- **Use revising and editing checklists.** The checklists on pages 79, 85, 88, and 91 will assist you in evaluating your paper systematically.

CHECKLIST

Guidelines for Giving Feedback

☐ **Focus on strengths as well as weaknesses.** Writers need to know what parts of their paper are strongest so that they can retain those sections when they revise and use them as models as they work to improve weaker sections. Do not withhold constructive criticism, or you will deprive the writer of an opportunity to improve the paper.

☐ **Be specific.** Give examples to back up your general reactions.

☐ **Be constructive.** Instead of saying that an example is a bad choice, explain that you did not understand how the example was connected to the main point, and suggest a way to make the connection clearer.

☐ **Ask questions.** Jot down any questions that occur to you while reading. Ask for clarification or note an objection that readers of the final version might make.

(For help giving feedback, see the Checklist for Revising Content and Organization on p. 79.)

Guidelines for Receiving Feedback

☐ **Resist any tendency to be defensive.** Keep in mind that readers are discussing your paper, not you, and their feedback offers a way for you to see your paper differently. Be respectful of their time and effort. Remember that you, not your readers, are in charge of decisions about your paper.

☐ **Ask for more feedback if you need it.** Some readers may be hesitant to share all of their reactions, and you may need to do some coaxing.

Reading other writers' drafts will help you view your own work more objectively, and comments from readers will help you see your own writing as others see it. As you gain more objectivity, you will become more adept at revising your work. In addition, the approaches that you see your classmates taking to the assignment will give you ideas for new directions in your own writing.

The *Catalyst* Web site that accompanies this book can make it easier for you to obtain and review comments from your readers.

2. Responding to readers

Consider and evaluate your readers' suggestions, but remember that you are under no obligation to do what they say. Sometimes you will receive contradictory advice: one reader may like a particular sentence that a second reader suggests you eliminate. Is there common ground? Yes. Both readers stopped at that sentence. Ask yourself why—and whether you want readers to pause there.

For MULTILINGUAL STUDENTS

Peer Review

Respectful peer review will challenge you to view your writing critically and present ideas to a diverse audience. It also will show you that many errors you make are quite common; it will improve your ability to detect mistakes and decide what to correct first. Your unique perspective can help native speakers improve their writing, as much as they can help you with the subtleties of English idioms.

7b Use campus, Internet, and community resources.

You can call on a number of resources outside of the classroom for feedback on your paper.

1. Using the campus writing center

Tutors in the writing center can read and comment on drafts of your work. They can also help you find and correct problems with grammar and punctuation.

2. Using online writing labs (OWLs)

www.mhhe.com/
awr3
For links to OWLs, go to
Writing > Writing Web Links

Most OWLs offer information about writing, including lists of useful online resources that you can access anytime. Some OWLs are staffed by tutors who support students working on specific writing assignments. OWLs with tutors can be useful in the following ways:

- You can submit a draft via e-mail for feedback. OWL tutors will return your work, often within forty-eight hours.

- You can post your text in a public access space where you will receive feedback from more than just one or two readers.

- You can read compositions online and learn how others are handling writing issues.

You can learn more about what OWLs have to offer by checking out the following Web sites:

- Purdue University's Online Writing Lab: <http://owl.english.purdue.edu>
- Writing Labs and Writing Centers on the Web (visit almost fifty OWLs): <http://owl.english.purdue.edu/internet/owls/writing-labs.html>

3. Working with experts and instructors

In addition to sharing your work with peers in class, through e-mail, or in online environments, you can use e-mail to consult your instructor or other experts.

Your instructor's comments on an early draft are especially valuable. He or she will raise questions and make suggestions, but remember that it is your responsibility to address the issues your instructor raises and to revise your work accordingly.

7c Use electronic tools for revising.

www.mhhe.com/awr3
For help with revising, go to
Writing >
Paragraph/Essay
Development >
Drafting and
Revising

It is always a good idea to print a copy of your draft because the print copy, unlike the computer screen, allows you to see your paper as a whole. Be sure to check for problems in content, structure, and style. Move paragraphs around, add details, and delete irrelevant sentences.

To work efficiently, you should become familiar with the revising and editing tools in your word-processing program.

- **Comments:** Many word-processing programs have a "Comments" feature that allows you to add marginal notes or notes that pop up when readers run the cursor over highlighted text, as shown in Figure 7.1. This feature is useful for giving

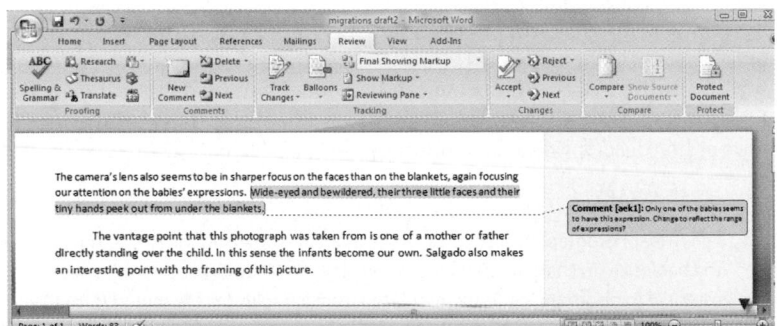

FIGURE 7.1 Using Microsoft Word 2007's Comments feature.

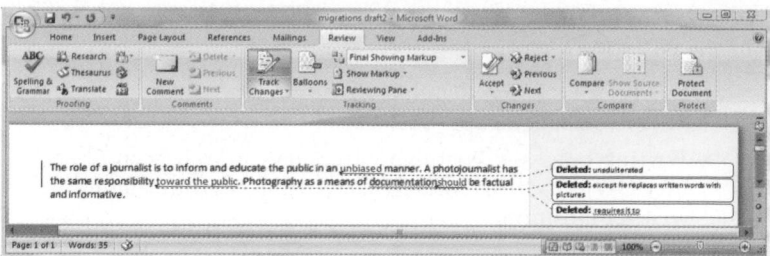

FIGURE 7.2 Showing revisions with Track Changes.

feedback on someone else's draft. Some writers also use it to make notes to themselves.

■ **Track changes:** The "Track Changes" feature allows you to edit a piece of writing while also maintaining the original text. Usually, marginal notes or strike-through marks show what you have deleted or replaced, as shown in Figure 7.2. Because you can still see the original text, you can judge whether a change has improved the paper. If you change your mind, you can restore the deleted text. When collaborating with another writer, do not print the changes, or save the Track Changes version as a separate file.

In addition, many Web-based tools such as Google Docs enable work to be shared, edited, and revised online.

7d   Focus on the purpose of your writing.

As you reread your paper and decide how to revise it, base your decisions on the purpose of your paper. Is your primary purpose to inform, to interpret, or to argue? (*For more on purpose, see Tab 2: Writing and Designing Texts, p. 38.*)

Clarity about your purpose is especially important when an assignment calls for interpretation. A description is not the same as an interpretation. With this principle in mind, Diane Chen read over the first draft of her paper on the *Migrations* photography exhibit. Here is part of her description of the photograph she chose to discuss in detail:

FIRST DRAFT

The photograph is black and white, as are the others in the show. The faces of the babies are in sharp focus while the blanket is a bit defocused. Light, which is essential to photography, is disseminated from a single source coming from the upper left-hand corner of the picture. The light source is not too bright as to bathe the babies in light, but just bright enough to illuminate their faces, which have

---

<table><tr><td>X✓✗✗</td><td>CHECKLIST</td></tr></table>

Revising Content and Organization

☐ 1. **Purpose:** What is the purpose of the text? If it is not clear, what changes would make it apparent?

☐ 2. **Thesis:** What is the thesis? Is it clear and specific? What revisions would make it clearer?

☐ 3. **Audience:** How does the approach—including evidence and tone—appeal to the intended readers?

☐ 4. **Structure:** How does the order of the key points support the thesis? Would another order be more effective? How might overly long or short sections be revised?

☐ 5. **Paragraphs:** How might the development, unity, and coherence of each paragraph be improved?

☐ 6. **Visuals:** Do visuals communicate the intended meaning clearly, without unnecessary clutter? How might they be improved?

---

expressions of interest and puzzlement. Perhaps they are wondering who Salgado is or what is that strange contraption he is holding.

Keeping her purpose in mind, Chen realized that she needed to discuss the significance of her observations—to interpret and analyze the details. She wanted to show her readers how the formal elements of the photograph functioned. Her revision makes this interpretation clearer.

REVISION

The orphanage photograph is shot in black and white, as are the other images in the show, giving it a documentary feel that emphasizes the truth of the situation. But Salgado's choice of black-and-white photography is also an artistic decision. He uses the contrasts of light and dark to create a dramatic image of the three babies.

The vertical black-and-white stripes of the blanket direct our eyes to the infants' faces and hands, which are framed by a horizontal white stripe . . .

7e Test your thesis.

Remember that a thesis makes an assertion about a topic. It links the *what* and the *why*. Is your thesis evident on the first page of your

**www.mhhe.com/
awr3**

For help with
developing a strong
thesis, go to

Writing >
Paragraph/Essay
Development >
Thesis/Central Idea

draft? Before readers get very far along, they expect an answer to the question "What is the point of all this?" If you do not find the point on the first page, its absence is a signal to revise, unless you are deliberately waiting until the end to share your thesis. (*For more on strong theses, see Chapter 5, pp. 48–50.*)

Many writers start with a working thesis, which often evolves into a more specific, complex assertion as they develop their ideas. One of the key challenges of revising is to compose a clear statement of this revised thesis. When she drafted a paper on Germany's economic prospects, Jennifer Koehler stated her working thesis as follows:

WORKING THESIS

Germany is experiencing a great deal of change.

During the revision process, Koehler realized that her working thesis was weak. A weak thesis is predictable: readers read it, agree, and that's that. A strong thesis, on the other hand, stimulates thoughtful inquiry. Koehler's revised thesis provokes questions:

REVISED THESIS

With proper follow-through, Germany can become one of the world's primary sources of direct investment and maintain its status as one of the world's preeminent exporters.

Sometimes writers find that their ideas change altogether, and the working thesis needs to be completely revised.

Your thesis should evolve throughout the paper. Readers need to see a statement of the main idea on the first page, but they also expect a more complex or general statement near the end. After presenting evidence to support her revised thesis, Koehler concludes her paper by stating her thesis in a more general way:

If the government efforts continue, the economy will strengthen over the next decade, and Germany will reinforce its position as an integral nation in the global economy.

7f　Review the structure of your paper.

Does the paper have a beginning, a middle, and an end, with bridges between those parts? When you revise you can refine and even change this structure so that it supports what you want to say more effectively.

One way to review your structure is by outlining the first draft. (*For help with outlining, see Chapter 5, pp. 50–54.*) Try listing the key points of your draft in sentence form; whenever possible, use sentences that actually appear in the draft. This kind of point-by-point outlining will allow you to see the draft's logic (or lack thereof). Ask yourself if the key points are arranged effectively or if another arrangement would work better. The following structures are typical ways of organizing compositions:

- **Informative:** sets out the key parts of a topic.
- **Exploratory:** begins with a question or problem and works step-by-step to discover an answer or a solution.
- **Argumentative:** presents a set of linked reasons plus supporting evidence.

7g Revise for paragraph development, paragraph unity, and coherence.

As you revise, examine each paragraph, asking yourself what role it plays—or should play—in the work as a whole. Keeping this role in mind, check the paragraph for development and unity. You should also check each paragraph for coherence—and consider whether all of the paragraphs together contribute to the work as a whole. Does the length of sections reflect their relative importance? (*For more on paragraphs, see Chapter 6: Drafting Text and Visuals, pp. 69–72.*)

1. Paragraph development

Does each paragraph provide enough detail? Paragraphs in academic papers are usually about a hundred words long. Consider dividing any that exceed two hundred words or that are especially dense. Although sometimes you will deliberately use a one- or two-sentence paragraph for emphasis, short paragraphs generally should be developed more fully or combined with other paragraphs. Would more information make the point clearer? Should a term be defined? Do generalizations need to be supported with examples?

Note how this writer developed one of her paragraphs, adding details and examples to make her argument more effective:

FIRST DRAFT

A 1913 advertisement for Shredded Wheat illustrates Kellner's claim that advertisements sell self-images. The ad suggests that serving Shredded Wheat will give women the same sense of accomplishment as gaining the right to vote.

REVISION

According to Kellner, "advertising is as concerned with selling lifestyles and socially desirable identities . . . as with selling the products themselves" (193). A 1913 ad for Shredded Wheat shows how the selling of self-images works. At first glance, this ad seems to be promoting the women's suffrage movement. In big, bold letters, "Votes for Women" is emblazoned across the top of the ad. But a closer look reveals that the ad is for Shredded Wheat cereal. Holding a piece of the cereal in her hand, a woman stands behind a large bowlful of Shredded Wheat biscuits that is made to look like a voting box. The text claims that "every biscuit is a vote for health, happiness, and domestic freedom." Like the rest of the advertisement, this claim suggests that serving Shredded Wheat will give women the same sense of accomplishment as gaining the right to vote.

—HOLLY MUSETTI, "Targeting Women,"
student paper

www.mhhe.com/
awr3
For more help with
paragraph unity, go to

Writing >
Paragraph/Essay
Development >
Unity

2. Paragraph unity

A unified paragraph has a single, clear focus. To check for **unity,** identify the paragraph's topic sentence (*see pp. 69–70*). Everything in the paragraph should be clearly connected to the topic sentence. Ideas unrelated to the topic sentence should be deleted or developed into separate paragraphs. Another option is to revise the topic sentence.

Compare the first draft of the following paragraph with its revision, and note how the addition of a topic sentence (in bold in the revision) makes the paragraph more clearly focused and therefore easier for the writer to revise further. Note also that the writer deleted the underlined ideas because they did not directly relate to the paragraph's main point:

FIRST DRAFT

Germany is ranked first on worldwide production levels. Automobiles, aircraft, and electronic equipment are among Germany's most important products for export. As the standard of living of the citizens of what was formerly East Germany increases due to reunification, their purchasing power and productivity will increase. A major problem is that east Germany is not as productive or efficient as west Germany, and so it would be better if less money were invested in the east. Germany is involved in most global treaties that protect business interests, and intellectual property is well protected. A plus for potential ventures and production plans is its highly skilled workforce. Another factor that indicates that Germany will remain strong in the arena of productivity and trade is its physical location in the world. "Its terrain and geographical position have combined to make Germany an important crossroads for traffic between the North Sea, the Baltic, and the Mediterranean. International transportation routes pass through all of Germany," thus utilizing a comprehensive and efficient network of transportation, both on land and over water ("Germany," 1995, p. 185). Businesses can operate plants in Germany and have no difficulties transporting goods and services to other parts of the country. Generally, private enterprise, government, banks, and unions cooperate, making the country more amenable to negotiations for business entry or joint ventures.

REVISION

For many reasons, Germany is attractive both as a market for other nations and as a location for production. As the standard of living of the citizens of what was formerly East Germany increases due to reunification, their purchasing power and productivity will increase. Intellectual property is well protected, and

Germany is involved in most global treaties that protect business interests. Germany's highly skilled workforce is another plus for potential ventures and production plans. Generally, private enterprise, government, banks, and unions cooperate, making the country amenable to negotiations for business entry or joint ventures. Germany also has an excellent physical location that makes it an "important crossroads for traffic between the North Sea, the Baltic, and the Mediterranean" ("Germany," 1995, p. 185). Equally important, a comprehensive and efficient transportation system allows businesses to operate plants in Germany and easily transport their goods and services to other parts of the country and the world.

—JENNIFER KOEHLER, "Germany's Path to Continuing Prosperity," student paper

3. Coherence

A coherent paragraph flows smoothly, with an organization that is easy to follow and each sentence clearly related to the next. (*See Chapter 6, pp. 58–68, for tips on how to develop well-organized paragraphs.*) You can improve coherence both within and among the paragraphs in your draft by using repetition, pronouns, parallel structure, synonyms, and transitions. Maintaining grammatical consistency will also help.

www.mhhe.com/
awr3
For help with coherence, go to
**Writing >
Paragraph/Essay
Development >
Coherence**

- Repeat key words to emphasize the main idea:

  A photograph displays a unique *moment*. To capture that *moment* . . .

- Use pronouns and antecedents to form connections between sentences and avoid unnecessary repetition. In the following example, *it* refers back to *Germany* and connects the two sentences:

  Germany imports raw materials, energy sources, and food products. *It* exports a wide range of industrial products, including automobiles, aircraft, and machine tools.

- Repeat sentence structures to emphasize connections:

  Because the former West Germany lived through a generation of prosperity, its people developed high expectations of material comfort. *Because the former East Germany* lived through a generation of deprivation, its people developed disdain for material values.

- Use **synonyms**—words that are close in meaning to words or phrases that have preceded them:

  In the world of photography, critics *argue* for either a scientific or an artistic approach. This *controversy* . . .

- Use transitional words and phrases. One-word transitions and **transitional expressions** link one idea with another, showing the relationship between them. (*See the list of common transitional expressions in the box on p. 84.*) Compare the

TRANSITIONAL EXPRESSIONS

- **To show relationships in space:** above, adjacent to, against, alongside, around, at a distance from, at the . . . , below, beside, beyond, encircling, far off, forward, from the . . . , in front of, in the rear, inside, near the end, nearby, next to, on, over, surrounding, there, through the, to the left, up front
- **To show relationships in time:** afterward, at last, before, earlier, first, former, formerly, immediately, in the first place, in the meantime, in the next place, in the last place, later on, meanwhile, next, now, often, once, previously, second, simultaneously, sometime later, subsequently, suddenly, then, third, today, tomorrow, until now, when, years ago, yesterday
- **To show addition or to compare:** again, also, and, and then, besides, further, furthermore, in addition, last, likewise, moreover, next, too
- **To give examples that intensify points:** after all, as an example, certainly, clearly, for example, for instance, indeed, in fact, in truth, it is true, of course, specifically, that is
- **To show similarities:** alike, in the same way, like, likewise, resembling, similarly
- **To show contrasts:** after all, although, but, conversely, differ(s) from, difference, different, dissimilar, even though, granted, however, in contrast, in spite of, nevertheless, notwithstanding, on the contrary, on the other hand, otherwise, still, though, unlike, while this may be true, yet
- **To indicate cause and effect:** accordingly, as a result, because, consequently, hence, since, then, therefore, thus
- **To conclude or summarize:** finally, in brief, in conclusion, in other words, in short, in summary, that is, to summarize

following two paragraphs, the first version without transitions and the second, revised version with transitions (in bold type) that connect one thought to another:

FIRST DRAFT

Glaser was in a position to powerfully affect Armstrong's career and his life. There is little evidence that the musician submitted to whatever his business manager wanted or demanded. Armstrong seemed to recognize that he gave Glaser whatever power the manager enjoyed over him. Armstrong could and did resist Glaser's control when he wanted to. That may be one reason why he liked and trusted Glaser as much as he did.

REVISION

Clearly, Glaser was in a position to affect powerfully Armstrong's career and his life . **However,** there is little evidence that the musician submitted to whatever his business manager wanted or demanded. **In fact,** Armstrong seemed to recognize that he gave Glaser whatever power the manager enjoyed over him. When he wanted to, Armstrong could and did resist Glaser's control, and that may be one reason why he liked and trusted Glaser as much as he did.

—Esther Hoffman, "Louis Armstrong and Joe Glaser"

- Use repetition, pronouns, parallelism, transitions, and **transitional sentences,** which refer back to the previous paragraph and move your essay on to the next point, to show how paragraphs in an essay are related to one another:

  The vertical black and white stripes of the blanket direct our eyes to the infants' faces and hands, which are framed by a horizontal white stripe. The whites of their eyes in particular stand out against the darkness created by the shell of the blankets. The camera's lens also seems to be in sharper focus on the faces than on the blankets, again focusing our attention on the babies' expressions.

  Each baby has a different response to the camera. The baby on the left returns our gaze with a heart-wrenching look. . . .

- Avoid confusing shifts between person and number of verbs and pronouns, as well as verb tenses. (*See Tab 9: Editing for Clarity, Chapter 41: Confusing Shifts, pp. 399–403.*)

👁 7h Revise visuals.

If you have used visuals to display data in your paper, you should return to them during the revision stage to eliminate what scholar Edward Tufte calls **chartjunk,** or distracting visual elements. The box on page 85 contains Tufte's suggestions for editing visuals so that your readers will focus on your data rather than your "data containers."

7i Edit sentences.

www.mhhe.com/awr3
For additional help with editing, go to
Editing

When you are satisfied with the overall placement and development of your ideas, you can turn your attention to individual sentences, phrases, and words. Tabs 9 and 10 of this handbook address the many specific questions that writers have when they are editing for clarity, word choice, and grammar conventions.

1. Editing for clarity

As you edit, concentrate on sentence style, aiming for clearly focused and interestingly varied writing. A volley of short, choppy sentences, for example, will probably distract readers from what you have to say,

CHECKLIST

Revising Visuals

☐ 1. **Are grid lines needed in tables?** Eliminate grid lines or, if the lines are needed for clarity, lighten them. Tables should not look like nets with every number enclosed. Vertical rules are needed only when space is extremely tight between columns.

☐ 2. **Are there any unnecessary 3D renderings?** Cubes and shadows can distort the information in a visual. For most charts, including pie charts, a flat image makes it easier for readers to compare parts.

☐ 3. **Are data labeled clearly,** avoiding abbreviations and legends if possible? Does each visual have an informative title?

☐ 4. **Do bright colors focus attention on the key data?** For example, if you are including a map, use muted colors over large areas and save strong colors for areas you want to emphasize.

☐ 5. **Do pictures distract from the visual's purpose?** Clip art and other decorative elements seldom make data more interesting or appear more substantial.

☐ 6. **Are data distorted?** In the first graph in Figure 7.3 on page 87, each month gets its own point, except for January, February, March, and April. This creates a misleading impression of hurricane activity by month. The revision corrects this distortion and also eliminates other elements of chartjunk.

while an unbroken stream of long, complicated sentences is likely to dull their senses. Also vary sentence openings and structure. In the example that follows, notice how the revised version connects ideas for readers and, consequently, is easier to read:

DRAFT

My father was a zealous fisherman. He took his fishing rod on every family outing. He often spent the whole outing staring at the water, waiting for a nibble. He went to the kitchen as soon as he got home. He usually cleaned and cooked the fish the same day he caught them.

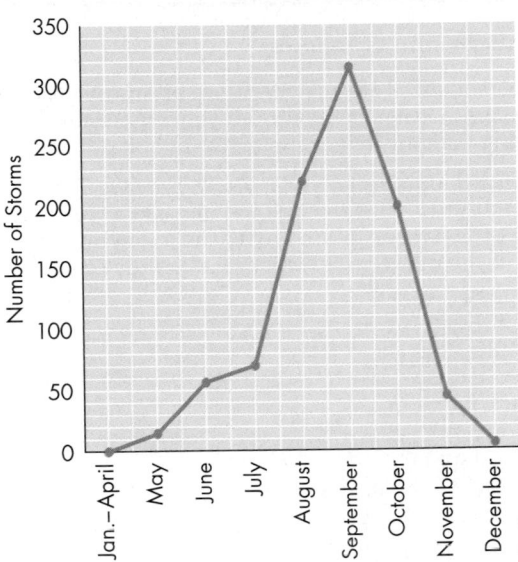

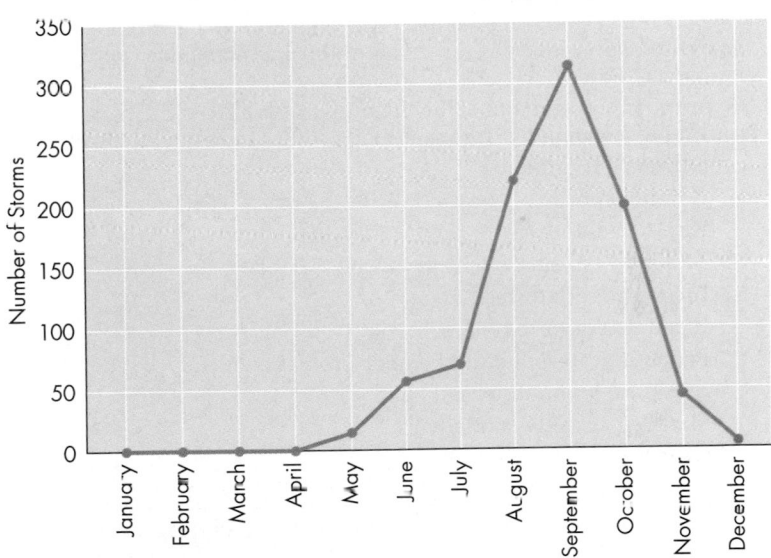

FIGURE 7.3 Misleading (top) and revised graphs. In the graph at the top, the activity in the first part of the year is combined into one point on the axis, misleading readers. The graph at the bottom has been revised to correct this problem.

CHECKLIST

Editing for Style and Grammar

To create a personalized editing checklist, fill in the boxes next to your trouble spots, as determined from your instructor's comments on your writing and any diagnostic tests you have taken.

1. **Clarity** (*Tab 9, Chapters 38–46, pp. 389–418*): Does every sentence communicate the intended meaning in a clear, direct style? Does the paper contain any of the following common causes of unclear sentences? Note sections that could be clearer.
   - ☐ Wordiness
   - ☐ Missing words
   - ☐ Mixed constructions
   - ☐ Confusing shifts
   - ☐ Faulty parallelism
   - ☐ Misplaced and dangling modifiers
   - ☐ Problem with coordination and subordination
   - ☐ Other: _____

2. **Word choice** (*Tab 9, Chapters 47–50, pp. 419–42*): How could the choice of words be more precise? Does the text include slang, biased language, clichés, or other inappropriate usages? Does it misuse any commonly confused words (for example, *advice* vs. *advise*) or use any nonstandard expressions (for example, *could of*)?

3. **Grammar conventions** (*Tab 10, pp. 443–95*): Does the paper contain any common errors that may confuse or distract readers?
   - ☐ Sentence fragments
   - ☐ Comma splices
   - ☐ Run-on sentences
   - ☐ Subject-verb agreement problems
   - ☐ Incorrect verb forms
   - ☐ Inconsistent verb tenses
   - ☐ Pronoun-antecedent agreement problems
   - ☐ Incorrect pronoun forms
   - ☐ Misused adjectives or adverbs
   - ☐ Other: _____

If you are in the process of developing fluency in English, consult Tab 12: Basic Grammar Review for more editing advice.

REVISED

A zealous fisherman, my father took his fishing rod on every family outing. He would often spend the whole afternoon by the shore, waiting for a nibble, and then hurry straight to the kitchen to clean and cook his catch.

You should also condense and focus sentences that are wordy and lack a clear subject and vivid verb:

DRAFT

Although both vertebral and wrist fractures cause deformity and impair movement, hip fractures, which are one of the most devastating consequences of osteoporosis, significantly increase the risk of death, since 12%–30% of patients with a hip fracture die within one year after the fracture, while the mortality rate climbs to 40% for the first two years post fracture.

REVISED

Hip fractures are one of the most devastating consequences of osteoporosis. Although vertebral and wrist fractures cause deformity and impair movement, hip fractures significantly increase the risk of death. Within one year after a hip fracture, 12%–20% of the injured die. The mortality rate climbs to 40% after two years.

More often than not, sentences beginning with *it is* or *there is* or *there are* (*it was* or *there was*)—called **expletive constructions**—are weak and indirect. Using a clear subject and a vivid verb usually makes such sentences more powerful:

DRAFT

There are stereotypes from the days of a divided Germany.

REVISED

Stereotypes formed in the days of a divided Germany persist.

2. Editing for word choice

Different disciplines and occupations have their own terminology. The word *significant,* for example, has a mathematical meaning for the statistician and a different meaning for the literary critic. When taking courses in a discipline, you should use its terminology accurately.

As you review your draft, look for general terms that might need to be made more specific:

DRAFT

Foreign direct investment (FDI) in Germany will probably remain low because of several *factors.* [Factors *is a general word. To get specific, answer the question* "What *factors?"*]

REVISED

Foreign direct investment (FDI) in Germany will probably remain low because of *high labor costs, high taxation, and government regulation.*

Your search for more specific words can lead you to a dictionary and thesaurus, two essential tools for choosing precise words. (*For more on using a dictionary and a thesaurus, see Chapter 49.*)

3. Editing for grammar conventions

Sometimes, writers will construct a sentence or choose a word form that does not follow the rules of standard written English:

DRAFT

Photographs of illegal immigrants being captured by the U.S. border patrol, of emotional immigrants on the plane to their new country, and of villagers fleeing rebel gangs. [*This is a sentence fragment because it lacks a verb and omits the writer's point about these images.*]

EDITED SENTENCE

Photographs of illegal immigrants being captured by the U.S. border patrol, of emotional immigrants on the plane to their new country, and of villagers fleeing rebel gangs exemplify the range of migration stories.

A list of common abbreviations and symbols used to note errors in a manuscript can be found at the end of this text. Your instructor and other readers may use these.

TextConnex

You Know More than Grammar and Spell Checkers

Grammar and spell checkers can help you spot some errors, but they miss many others and may even flag a correct sentence. Consider the following example:

Thee neighbors puts there cats' outsider.

A spelling and grammar checker did not catch the five errors in the sentence. (Correct version: *The neighbors put their cats outside.*)

If you are aware of your program's limitations, then you can make some use of it as you edit your document. Be sure, however, to review your writing carefully yourself.

7j Proofread carefully.

Once you have revised your paper at the essay, paragraph, and sentence levels, it is time to give your work one last check to make sure that it is free of typos and other mechanical errors.

Proofread a printout of your paper even if you are submitting an electronic version. A ruler placed under each line as you are proofing can make it easier to focus. Another proofreading technique is to start at the end of the paper and proofread your way backward to the beginning, sentence by sentence. Some students read their drafts aloud. Do not read for content, but look at each word.

CHECKLIST

Proofreading

☐ Have you included your name, the date, your professor's name, and the paper title? (*See Tabs 6–8 for the formats to use for MLA, APA, Chicago, or CSE style.*)

☐ Are all words spelled correctly? Be sure to check the spelling of titles and headings. (*See Chapter 68, pp. 555–59.*)

☐ Have you used the words you intended, or have you substituted words that sound like the ones you want but have a different spelling and meaning, such as *too* for *to, their* for *there,* or *it's* for *its*? (*See Chapter 50, pp. 432–40.*)

☐ Are all proper names capitalized? Have you capitalized titles of works correctly and either italicized them or put them in quotation marks as required? (*See Chapter 63, pp. 538–43, and Chapter 66, pp. 549–52.*)

☐ Have you punctuated your sentences correctly? (*See Tab 12.*)

☐ Are sources cited correctly? Is the works-cited or references list in the correct format? (*See Tabs 6 8.*)

☐ Have you checked anything you retyped—for example, quotations and tables—against the original?

👁 **7k** Learn from one student's revisions.

In the second draft of Diane Chen's paper on an exhibit of photographs by Sebastião Salgado, you can see how she revised her draft to tighten the focus of her descriptive paragraphs and edited to improve clarity, word choice, and grammar. The photograph Chen focuses on appears on p. 93.

The Caring Eye of Sebastião Salgado

Photographer Sebastiao Salgado spent seven years ~~of his life~~traveling along migration routes to city slums ~~and~~ refugee camps~~, and migration routes~~ in order to document the lives of people uprooted from their homelands. A selection of his photographs can be seen in the exhibit, "*Migrations: Humanity in Transition.*" Like a photojournalist, Salgado brings

Diane Chen 4/24/08 5:32 PM
Deleted: of his life ...,..., and migration routes.   ... [1]

Diane Chen 4/24/08 5:33 PM
Deleted: "..."   ... [2]

us images of newsworthy events, but he goes beyond objective reporting, imparting his compassion for refugees and migrants to the viewer.

So mMany of the photographs in Salgado's show are certain to impress and touch the viewers with their subject matter and sheer beauty. Whether capturing the thousandsmillions of refugee tents in Africa that seem to stretch on for miles or the disheartened faces of small immigrant children, Salgado brings an artistic element to his pictures thatthe images in *Migrations* suggests that he Salgado does so much more with his camera than just point and shoot.

Salgado's photograph of the most vulnerable of these refugees illustrates the power of his work. "Orphanage attached to the hospital at Kibumba, Number One Camp, Goma Zaire," (fig. 1) depicts three apparently newborn or several month old babiesinfants, who are victims of the genocidal war in neighboring Rwanda. The label for the photograph reveals tells us that there were 4,000 orphans at this camp and an estimated 100,000 Rwandan orphans overall. Those numbers are mind-numbing abstractions, but this picture is not.

The orphanage photograph is shot in black and white, as are the others in the show, and provides the audience withgiving it a very documentary, newspaper type of feel that emphasizes that this is a real, newsworthy situation that we need to be aware of deserving our attention. But Salgado's choice of black-and-white photography is also an artistic decision. He uses the contrasts of light and dark to create a dramatic image of the three babies.

The vertical black-and-white stripes of the blanket direct our eyes to the infants' faces and hands, which are framed by a horizontal white stripe. The whites of their eyes in particular stand out against the darkness created by the shell of the blankets. The camera's lens also seems to be in sharper focus on the faces than on the blankets, again focusing our attention on the babies' expressions. Each baby has a different response to the camera. The center baby, with his or her extra-wide eyes, appears startled and in need of comforting. The baby to the right is oblivious to the camera and in fact seems to be starving or ill. The healthy baby on the left returns our gaze.

The vantage point ofthat this photograph was taken from is one of a mother or fatherparent directly standing directly over his or herthe child. In this sense the infants become our own. Salgado also makes an interesting point with the framing offrames this picture strategically. The babies in their blanket consumes the entire space, so that their innocence and vulnerability consume~~s~~ the viewer.

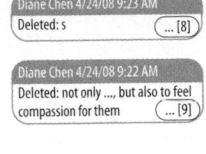
Diane Chen 4/24/08 9:23 AM
Deleted: s ... [8]

Salgado uses his skills as an artist to get us ~~not only~~ to look at these difficult subjects~~, but also to feel compassion for them~~. He is able to bring a story as big and complex as the epic displacement of the world's people to us through a collection of intimate and intensely moving images. As he says in his introduction to the exhibit catalog, "We hold the key to humanity's future, but for that we must understand the present. We cannot afford to look away (15)."

Diane Chen 4/24/08 9:22 AM
Deleted: not only ..., but also to feel compassion for them ... [9]

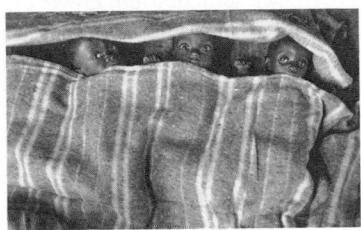

Fig. 1. Sebastião Salgado, *Migrations*, "Orphanage attached to the hospital at Kibumba, Number One Camp, Goma, Zaire."

------------------------------------[new page]------------------------------------

Work Cited

Salgado, Sebastião. *Migrations*. New York: Aperture, 2000. Print.

8 Designing Academic Papers and Portfolios

One of your final writing tasks is to format your text so that readers can "see" your ideas clearly. In this chapter, our main focus is on designing academic papers. (*Multimedia presentations, posters, and Web sites can be found in Chapters 13 and 14, and brochures, newsletters, résumés, and other documents in Chapters 15 and 17.*)

In your writing course, as well as in other courses and in your professional life, you may be called on to compile a print or electronic **portfolio**—a collection of your writings. This chapter offers guidelines for designing portfolios that showcase your work effectively.

www.mhhe.com/
awr3

For links to information
on document and Web
design, go to

Writing > Writing
Web Links >
Annotated Links
on Design

8a Consider audience and purpose.

As you plan your document, consider your purpose as well as the needs of your audience. If you are writing an informative paper for a psychology class, your instructor—your primary audience—will probably prefer that you follow the guidelines provided by the American Psychological Association (APA). If you are writing a lab report for a biology or chemistry course, you will likely need to follow a well-established format and use the documentation style recommended by the Council of Science Editors (CSE) to cite any sources you use. A history assignment might call for the use of the Chicago style. Interpretive essays for language and literature courses usually use the style recommended by the Modern Language Association (MLA). In any composition, however, ensure your source citations enhance the content of your text, rather than decorating it. (*For help with these documentation styles, see Tabs 6–8.*)

8b Use the tools available in your word-processing program.

Most word-processing programs give you a range of options for editing, sharing, and, especially, designing your document. For example, if you are using Microsoft Word 2007, you can access groups of commands by clicking on the various tabs at the top of the screen. Figure 8.1 shows the Home tab, which contains basic formatting and editing commands. You can choose different typefaces; add bold, italic, or underlined type; insert numbered or bulleted lists, and so on. Other tabs allow you to add boxes and drawings into your text, make comments, and change the page layout.

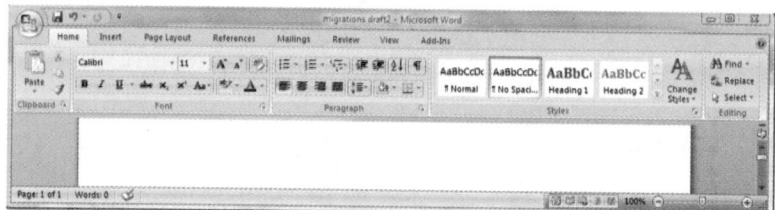

FIGURE 8.1 The Home Tab in Microsoft Word 2007.

Many word-processing programs are organized differently. Some include menus of commands on toolbars instead of on tabs. Take some time to learn the different formatting options available in your program.

👁 **8c** Think intentionally about design.

For any document that you create in print or online, whether for an academic course or for a purpose and an audience outside of college, you should apply the same basic design principles:

- Organize information for readers.
- Use type style, lists, and other graphic elements to make your text readable and to emphasize key material.
- Format related design elements consistently.
- Include headings to organize long papers.
- Show restraint.
- Meet the needs of readers with disabilities.

A sample page from a student's report on a local food bank, which includes information that she gathered while serving as a volunteer, illustrates these principles. The content in the sample on page 98 is at a disadvantage because the author has not adhered to these principles. In contrast, the same content on page 99 is clearer and easier for readers to understand because of its design.

1. Organizing information for readers

Organize information visually and topically by grouping related items, using boxes, indents, headings, spacing, and lists. For example, in this book, headings help to group information for readers, and bulleted and numbered lists such as the bulleted list in the Tips box on page 96 present related points. These variations in text appearance help readers scan, locate information, and dive in when they need to know more about a topic. If a color printer is available to you and your instructor allows you to use color in your paper, then it can help you create visual variety. For instance, in this text, headings are in red type and subheadings are in blue type. Use color with restraint, and remember that colors may look different on screen and on paper. Consider readers with disabilities (*pp. 100–01*).

You can also use **white space**—the areas of your document that do not contain type or graphics—to help organize information for your readers. Allowing generous margins and plenty of white space above headings and around other elements makes text easier to read.

You should also introduce any visuals within your text and position them so that they appear near—but never before—this text reference. Strive for a pleasing balance between visuals and other text elements; for example, don't try to cram too many visuals onto one page.

2. Using type style and lists for readability and emphasis

Typefaces are designs that have been established by printers for the letters in the alphabet, numbers, punctuation marks, and special

Tips

LEARNING in COLLEGE

The Basics: Margins, Spacing, Type, and Page Numbers

Here are a few basic guidelines for formatting academic papers:

- **First page:** In a paper that is no longer than five pages, you can usually place a header with your name, your professor's name, your course and section number, and the date on the first page, above the text. (*See the first page of Esther Hoffman's paper on p. 313.*) If your paper exceeds five pages, page 1 is often a title page. (*See the first page of Audrey Galeano's paper, which is in APA style, on p. 349.*)

- **Type:** Select a common typeface and choose an 11- or 12-point size.

- **Margins:** Use one-inch margins on all four sides of your text. Adequate margins make your paper easier to read and give your instructor room to write comments and suggestions.

- **Margin justification:** Line up, or justify, the lines of your document along the left margin but not along the right margin. Leaving a "ragged-right"—or uneven—right margin, as in this box, enables you to avoid odd spacing between words.

- **Spacing:** Always double-space your paper unless you are instructed to do otherwise, and indent the first line of each paragraph five spaces. (Many business documents are single-spaced, with an extra line space between paragraphs, which are not indented.)

- **Page numbers:** Place page numbers in the upper or lower right-hand corner of the page. Some documentation styles require a header next to the page number. (*See Tabs 6–8.*)

characters. For most academic papers, you should choose a standard, easy-to-read typeface and use an 11- or 12-point size. **Fonts** are all of the variations available in a certain typeface and size (for example, 12-point Times New Roman is available in **bold** and *italics*). **Serif** typefaces have tiny lines (serifs) at the ends of letters such as *n* and *y;* **sans serif** typefaces do not have these lines. Standard serif typefaces such as the following have traditionally been used for printed text because they are easy to read.

Times New Roman   Courier
Bookman Old Style   Palatino

Sans serif typefaces such as the following are sometimes used for headings because they offer a contrast, or for Web documents because they are more readable on screen. Norms may be changing. Calibri, the default typeface in Microsoft Word 2007, is a sans serif typeface.

Calibri   Arial   Verdana

Many typefaces available on your computer are known as **display fonts,** for example:

Curlz   Old English

These should be used rarely, if ever, in academic papers, on the screen, or in presentations. They can be used effectively in other kinds of documents, however, such as brochures, fliers, and posters.

You can emphasize a word or phrase in your text by selecting it and making it **bold,** *italicized,* or underlined. Numbered or bulleted lists help you cluster large amounts of information, making the information easier for readers to reference and understand. Because they stand out from your text visually, lists also help readers see that ideas are related. You can use a numbered list to display steps in a sequence, present checklists, or suggest recommendations for action.

Format text as a numbered or bulleted list by choosing the option you want from your word-processing program's formatting commands. Introduce the list with a complete sentence followed by a colon, use parallel structure in your list items, and put a period at the end of each item only if the entries are complete sentences.

Putting information in a box emphasizes it and also makes it easier for readers to find if they need to refer to it again. Most word-processing programs offer several ways to enclose text within a border or box.

3. Formatting related design elements

In design, simplicity, contrast, and consistency matter. If you emphasize an item by putting it in italic or bold type or in color, or if you use a graphic element such as a box to set it off, consider repeating this effect for similar items so that your document has a unified look. Even a simple horizontal line can be a purposeful element in a long document when used consistently to help organize information.

4. Using headings to organize long papers

In short papers, headings can disrupt the text and are usually not necessary. In longer papers, though, they can help you organize complex information. (For headings in APA style, see Chapter 33.)

Effective headings are brief and descriptive. The headings in academic papers are usually in the form of phrases, although they might be in the form of questions or even imperative sentences. Make sure that your headings are consistent in grammatical structure as well as formatting:

PHRASES BEGINNING WITH *-ING* WORDS

Fielding Inquiries

Handling Complaints

EXAMPLE OF A POORLY DESIGNED REPORT

Emphasis wrong: title of report is not as prominent as heading within report.

Margins are not wide enough, making page look crowded.

Bar chart is not introduced in text and does not have caption.

The Caring Express Food Bank

The Caring Express Food Bank serves a varied population of clients, including chronically homeless people, temporarily homeless people, recent immigrants, elderly people on fixed incomes, and people in need of temporary services.

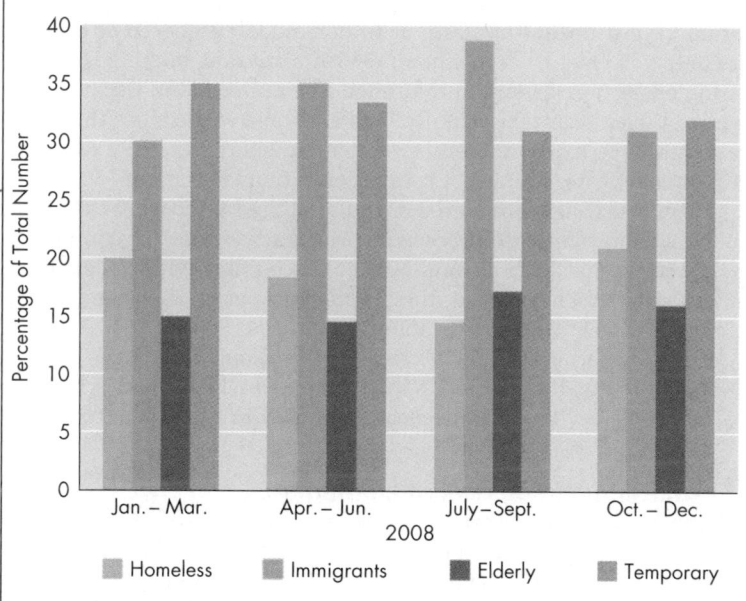

While the number of homeless, both temporary and permanent, that Caring Express assisted in 2008 decreased during the summer months, the number of immigrant workers increased. The percentage of elderly people and people in need of temporary services remained fairly stable throughout the year.

How Caring Express Helps Clients

Description of procedure is dense, hard to follow.

Use of bold type and different typeface for no reason.

When new clients come to Caring Express, a volunteer fills out a **form** with their **address** (if they have one), their **phone number,** their **income,** their **employment situation,** and the help they are receiving, if any, from the local department of human services. Clients who do not live in Maple Valley are referred to a food bank or outreach program in their area. Clients who qualify check off the food they need from a list, and then that food is packed and distributed to them.

EXAMPLE OF A WELL-DESIGNED REPORT

The Caring Express Food Bank

The Caring Express Food Bank serves a varied population of clients, including chronically homeless people, temporarily homeless people, recent immigrants, elderly people on fixed incomes, and people in need of temporary services. As Figure 1 shows, while the number of homeless, both temporary and permanent, that Caring Express assisted in 2008 decreased during the summer months, the number of immigrant workers increased. The percentage of elderly people and people in need of temporary services remained fairly stable throughout the year.

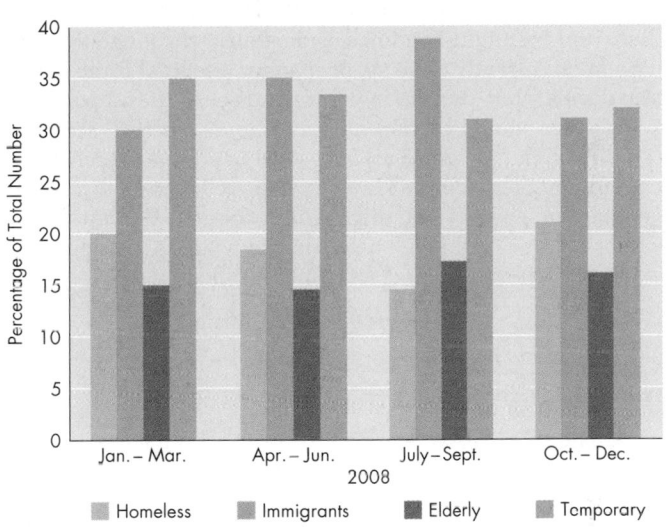

Figure 1. Percentage of clients in each group during 2008

How Caring Express Helps Clients

When new clients come to Caring Express, the volunteers follow this procedure:

1. The volunteer fills out a form with the client's address (if he or she has one), phone number, income, and employment situation.
2. Clients who do not live in Maple Valley are referred to a food bank or outreach program in their area.
3. Clients who qualify check off the food they need from a list.
4. The food is packed and distributed to them.

Title is centered and in larger type than text and heading.

Bar chart is introduced and explained.

White space above and below figure.

Caption explains figure.

Heading is subordinate to title.

Procedure is explained in numbered list. Parallel structure used for list entries.

NOUNS AND NOUN PHRASES

Customer Inquiries

Complaints

QUESTIONS

How Do I Field Inquiries?

How Do I Handle Complaints?

IMPERATIVE SENTENCES

Field Inquiries Efficiently

Handle Complaints Calmly and Politely

Headings at different levels can be in different forms. For example, the first-level headings in a book might be imperative sentences, while the second-level headings might begin with *-ing* words.

Place and highlight headings consistently throughout your paper. If you have not already done so, preparing a formal topic outline will help you decide what your main points and second-level points are and where headings should go. (*For help with topic outlines, see Chapter 5, pp. 50–54.*) You might center all first-level headings, which correspond to the main points in your outline. If you have second-level headings—your supporting points—you might align them at the left margin and underline them. Third-level headings, if you have them, could be aligned at the left margin and set in plain type:

First-Level Heading

<u>Second-Level Heading</u>

Third-Level Heading

A heading should never appear at the very bottom of a page. If a heading falls in this position, move it to the top of the next page.

5. Using restraint

If you use too many graphics, headings, bullets, boxes, or other elements in a document, you risk making it as "noisy" as a loud radio. Standard typefaces and fonts have become standard because they are easy on the eye. Variations from these standard fonts jar the eye. Bold or italic type, underlining, or any other graphic effect should not continue for more than one sentence at a time.

6. Meeting the needs of readers with disabilities

If your potential audience might include the visually- or hearing-impaired, take these principles into account:

- **Use a large, easily readable font:** The font should be 14 point or larger. Use a sans serif font such as Arial, as readers with poor vision find these fonts easier to read. Make head-

Tips   LEARNING in COLLEGE

Standard Headings and Templates

Some types of papers, such as lab reports and case studies, have standard headings, such as "Introduction," "Abstract," and "Methods and Materials" for a lab report. (*See Chapter 12, pp. 142–45.*)

Word-processing programs allow you to create **templates,** preformatted styles that establish the structure and settings for a document and apply them automatically. If you will need to produce a certain kind of assignment that requires a specific kind of formatting—such as a lab report—on a regular basis, consider creating a template for it.

ings larger than the surrounding text (rather than relying on a change in font, bold, italics, or color to set them apart).

- **Use ample spacing between lines:** The American Council of the Blind recommends a line space of 1.5.

- **Use appropriate, high-contrast colors:** Black text on a white background is best. If you use color for text or visuals, put light material on a dark background and dark material on a light background. Use colors from different families (such as yellow on purple). Also, avoid red and green because color-blind readers may have trouble distinguishing them. Do not use glossy paper.

- **Include narrative descriptions of all visuals:** Describe each chart, map, photograph, or other visual in your paper. Indicate the key information and the point the visual makes. (This is more important when writing for the Web because individuals may use screen-reader software [pp. 169–70].)

- **If you include audio or video files in an electronic document, provide transcripts:** Also include narrative description of what is happening in the video.

For further information, consult the American Council of the Blind (<http://acb.org/accessible-formats.html>), Lighthouse International (<http://www.lighthouse.org/print_leg.htm>), and the American Printing House for the Blind (<http://www.aph.org/edresearch/lpguide.htm>).

👁 8d Compile an effective print or electronic portfolio.

When presenting their written work for final submission, students are often asked to collect it in a portfolio. Likewise, when applying for a position that calls for a great deal of writing, job candidates are often asked to provide a portfolio of their writing. Although most portfolios consist of a collection of papers in print form, many students create writing portfolios that are available electronically (e-portfolios).

Portfolios, regardless of medium, share at least three common features:

- They are a *collection* of work.
- They offer a *selection*—or subset—of a larger body of work.
- They are introduced, narrated, or commented on by a document that offers the writer's *reflection* on her or his work.

As with any type of writing, portfolios serve a purpose and address an audience—to demonstrate your progress in a course for your instructor, for example, or to present your best work for a prospective employer. Portfolios allow writers to assess their own work and set new writing goals.

1. Assembling a print portfolio

Course requirements vary, so always follow the guidelines your instructor provides. You will usually engage in the five activities mentioned in the box below.

Gathering your writing Create a list, or inventory, of the items that you might include. For a writing course, you may need to provide your exploratory writing, notes, and comments from peer reviewers as well as all your drafts for one or more of the papers you include. Make sure all of your materials have your name on them and that your final draft does not include any errors.

Reviewing written work and making appropriate selections As you review your work, keep the purpose of the portfolio in mind as well

CHECKLIST

Assembling a Print Portfolio

- ☐ Gather all your written work.
- ☐ Make appropriate selections.
- ☐ Arrange the selections.
- ☐ Include a reflective essay or letter.
- ☐ Polish your portfolio.

as the criteria that will be used to evaluate it. If you are assembling a presentation portfolio, you want to select your very best work. If you are demonstrating your improvement as a writer in a process portfolio, you want to select papers that show your development and creativity.

If no criteria have been provided, consider the audience for the portfolio when deciding which selections will be most appropriate. Who will read it and what qualities will they be looking for?

Arranging the selections deliberately If you have not been told how to organize your portfolio—for instance, in the order in which you wrote the pieces—think of it as if it were a single text and decide on an arrangement that will serve your purpose: from weakest item to strongest? from a less important paper to a more important paper? How will you determine importance?

Explain your rationale for this arrangement in a letter to the reader, in a brief introduction, or in annotations in the table of contents.

Writing a reflective essay or letter The reflective statement may take the form of an essay or a letter, depending on your purpose or the requirements you have been given. Sometimes, the reflective essay will be the last one in a portfolio so that the reader can review all of the work first and then read the writer's interpretation at the end. Or a reflective letter can open the portfolio. Regardless of its genre or placement, the reflective text gives you an opportunity to explain something about your writing or about yourself as a writer. Common topics in the reflective text include

- How you developed various projects
- Which texts you believe are particularly strong and why
- What you learned as you worked on these assignments
- Who you are now as a writer

Follow the stages of the writing process in preparing your reflective essay or letter. Then assemble all of the components of your portfolio in a folder or three-ring binder.

Polishing your portfolio In the process of writing the reflective letter or essay, you might discover a better way to arrange your work, or as you arrange your portfolio, you might want to review all your work again. Do not be surprised if you find yourself repeating some of these tasks. As with any writing, a portfolio will also improve if it is revised based on peer review.

Most students learn about themselves and their writing as they compile their portfolios and write reflections on their work. The process not only makes them better writers, but it also helps them learn how to demonstrate their strengths as well.

2. Preparing an electronic portfolio

For some courses or professional purposes, you will need to present your work in an electronic format. For example, an education student might be required to provide an electronic portfolio of lesson plans, class handouts, and other instructional materials. Electronic portfolios can be saved on a CD or DVD, or they can be published on the Web.

Digital portfolios allow you to include different kinds of texts, such as audio files and video clips; they can be connected to other texts using hyperlinks; and their success depends on the use of visual elements. The process of creating an electronic portfolio differs somewhat from that of creating a print portfolio. See the box below for the essential steps.

Gathering your written work as well as your audio, video, and visual texts   Depending on your assignment, you may need to collect exploratory writing, peer comments, and all drafts. You will need to make up to four inventories:

- A verbal inventory, consisting of your written work (be sure to scan in any handwritten work that you will not be providing as a digital text)
- An audio inventory (examples: speeches, music, podcasts)
- A video inventory (examples: movie clips, videos you have created)
- A visual inventory (examples: photographs, drawings)

The most important—and typical—components of an electronic portfolio tend to be the verbal and visual texts. Think about the images you will want to use to describe your work visually. One writer, for instance, might use images of everyday life in two countries to show that she has included texts in two languages in her portfolio.

CHECKLIST

Creating an Electronic Portfolio

☐ Gather all your written work and audio, video, and visual texts.

☐ Make selections and consider connections.

☐ Decide on an arrangement, navigation, and presentation.

☐ Include a reflective essay or letter.

☐ Test your portfolio for usability.

Selecting appropriate texts and making connections among them Choose works from your inventory based on your portfolio's purpose and criteria for evaluation. Consider the relationships among your selections as well as external materials. These connections should reveal something about you and your writing. They will become the links that help the reader navigate your digital portfolio. *Internal links* connect items within the portfolio. For instance, a writer might link an earlier draft to a later one. *External links* connect the reader to related files external to the portfolio. For instance, if you collaborated with a colleague or a classmate on a project, you might link to that person's electronic portfolio. (*See Chapter 14: Multimedia Writing, pp. 160–61.*)

Deciding on an arrangement, navigation, and presentation As in a print portfolio, your work can be arranged in a variety of ways, such as chronological order. Once you have decided on an arrangement, help your reader navigate the portfolio. Create a storyboard or chart that shows each item in your portfolio and how it is linked to others. (*See Chapter 14: Multimedia Writing, p. 165.*) After you have planned your site's structure, add hyperlinks to your documents. The link text should be clearly descriptive (a link reading "Résumé" should lead to your résumé).

One method for helping readers navigate the portfolio is to provide a table of contents with links to the text for each item. Each final draft might link to exploratory writing, drafts in progress, and comments from peer reviewers. Alternatively, you might open with a reflective letter embedded with links that take readers to your written work and other texts. The portfolio in Figure 8.2 on page 106 features a menu of links that appears on each page, as well as links in the reflective text.

Consider how the opening screen will establish your purpose and appeal to your audience. Choose colors, images for the front page and successive pages, and typefaces that visually suggest who you are as a writer and establish a tone appropriate for your purpose.

Writing a reflective text As in a print portfolio, the reflective text explains the selections to readers. A digital environment, however, offers more possibilities for presenting this reflection. You can make it highly visual; for example, you might have it cascade across a series of screens. Another option would be to link to an audio or video file in which you talk directly to the reader.

Testing your electronic portfolio Before releasing your portfolio, you should navigate all the way through it yourself and ask a friend to do so from a different machine. Sometimes links fail to work, or files stored on one machine don't open on another. In addition, another person may have suggestions about the portfolio's structure or the content of your reflective text. Ultimately, this feedback will help you make the portfolio easy for others to navigate and understand.

Process & Product
Reflections

Home

Essays

Reflections

Process & Product

Audience & Genre

Evidence & Analysis

Who is Ken Tinnes?

External Links

Throughout this semester, one of my main goals for this course was to be able to learn how to effectively create and utilize a detailed outline to assist with my writing process in order to ensure good organizational skills. The essay from this semester in which I was best able to achieve this goal was the research project. Due to the abundance of sources, as well as the mere size of the assignment, I knew I would need any organizational help I could get.

Before I could begin writing my paper, or even working on an outline for it, I needed to decide what exactly I wanted to write about, and how I would approach that topic specifically. To do this, I created a thesis statement for my essay. I read and revised my thesis numerous times on my own. I also looked to some of my peers from my dorm floor to revise my thesis as well. After establishing an accurate and detailed thesis summarizing and introducing the content of my essay, I was ready to research and prewrite.

Throughout the entire writing process for the research paper, I was focused on the structure of my essay. When I would find new sources, I would try to automatically classify the topic of that source, and cite it in my outline wherever I found it to be most appropriate. I tried to establish some of my transitions, and extract the exact quotes or information I would be using in my essay. By doing this, I was able to see the progression of my paper before it was even written. I didn't have to worry about rearranging my essay after it had already been written. That was extremely helpful, as there is nothing I find to be more difficult than rearranging full paragraphs, while trying to maintain a rhythmic flow to my paper.

As I wrote my paper, I tried my best to stick to the outline. If I came up with fresh ideas as I was writing, I would put them into my outline first, so that I would know where they would best fit inside my paper. By doing this, I was able to avoid many of the problems I experienced in some of my earlier writings. By filtering everything through my outline first, I was able to think of an intelligent way to convey my information. I would write my main arguments for each source and thought contained in my paper, so that I was able to reconstruct them until they were perfect. In doing this, I created what I like to think of as the most elaborate and detailed passages that I have ever written.

By writing these passages in my outline first, rather than my essay, I was able to avoid the disorganization that comes with a rush of thoughts, and focus on the sole goal of establishing thorough theses and arguments that would have a greater chance of being fully and accurately conveyed by my audience.

Home > Reflections > Process & Product >

© 2006 Ken Tinnes Contact Me

FIGURE 8.2 A screen from a student's electronic portfolio. Note the many links for easy navigation.

Auguste Rodin's sculpture The Thinker evokes the psychological complexity of human thought and suggests the spirit of critical inquiry common to all disciplines across the curriculum.

Anybody who is involved in working across
the disciplines is much more likely to have
a lively mind and a lively life.

—MARY FIELD BELENKY

Common
Assignments
across the
Curriculum

3 Common Assignments

Section dealing with visual rhetoric. For a complete listing, see the Quick Guide to Key Resources at the back of this book.

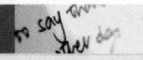
Tab 3: Common Assignments across the Curriculum
This section will help you answer the following questions about your writing:

Rhetorical Knowledge
How can I argue persuasively? **(11b)**
How can I keep my audience interested in my oral presentation? **(13b)**
What should I *not* put on my blog or social networking page? **(14f)**

Critical Thinking, Reading, and Writing
How do I analyze a literary work? **(10b)**
How can I defend my thesis against counterarguments? **(11b)**

Processes
What is the best way to prepare for essay exams? **(12d)**
How can I use presentation software (such as PowerPoint) effectively? **(13b, 14d)**
What steps should I take in planning my Web site? **(14e)**

Knowledge of Conventions
What is a review of the literature, and where do such reviews appear? **(9d, 12c)**
Which disciplines use lab reports and case studies? **(12b, c)**

Most college courses require writing—from the lab report in chemistry to the policy proposal in economics. This section gives you tips on writing the most common kinds of college assignments and explains the distinctive features of each kind.

9 Informative Reports

Imagine what the world would be like if each person had to learn everything from scratch, by trial and error, with no recipes, no encyclopedias, no textbooks, no newspapers— nothing that records what others have learned. Fortunately, we have many sources of information to draw on, including informative reports.

9a Understand the assignment.

An **informative report** passes on what someone has learned about a topic or issue; it teaches. When your instructor assigns an informative report, he or she expects you to find out what is currently known about some specific topic and to present what you discover in a clear, unbiased way.

An informative report gives you a chance to

- Learn more about an issue that interests you.
- Make sense of what you have read, heard, and seen.
- Teach others what you have learned.

www.mhhe.com/
awr3
For an interactive tutorial on writing informative reports, go to

Writing >
Writing Tutors >
Informative
Reports

9b Approach writing an informative report as a process.

1. Selecting a topic that interests you

The major challenge in writing informative reports is engaging readers' interest. Selecting a topic that interests you makes it more likely that your report will interest your readers.

Connect what you are learning in one course with a topic you are studying in another course or with your personal experience. For example, student John Terrell, a political science major, aspired to a career in international relations. For his topic, he decided to investigate how one Muslim organization was pursuing human rights for women. (*Terrell's paper begins on p. 113.*)

2. Considering what your readers know about the topic

Unless the assignment designates a different group, consider your classmates and instructor as your audience. In other words, assume that your readers have some familiarity with the topic but that most of

CHARTING the TERRITORY

Informative Reports

Informative reports are commonly written by members of humanities, social sciences, and natural sciences disciplines, as these examples indicate:

- In a published article, an anthropologist surveys and summarizes a large body of material on indigenous warfare among the Pueblos before the arrival of the Spanish explorers.
- For an encyclopedia of British women writers, a professor of literature briefly recounts the life and work of Eliza Fenwick, a recently rediscovered eighteenth-century author.
- In an academic journal, two biochemists summarize the findings of more than two hundred recently published articles on defense mechanisms in plants.

them do not have clear, specific knowledge of it. In his paper on Sisters in Islam, Terrell assumes that his readers probably have seen images of Afghan women in burqas.

3. Developing an objective stance
A commitment to objectivity gives your report its authority. Present differing views fairly and do not take sides in a debate.

4. Composing a thesis that summarizes your knowledge of the topic
An informative thesis typically reports the results of the writer's study. Before you decide on a thesis, review the information you have collected. Compose a thesis statement that presents the goal of your paper and forecasts its content. (*For more on thesis statements, see Tab 2: Writing and Designing Texts, pp. 48–50.*)

www.mhhe.com/
awr3
For more help with developing a thesis, go to
Writing >
Paragraph/Essay Development >
Thesis/Central Idea

In the paper about Sisters in Islam (SIS), Terrell develops a general thesis that he supports in the body of his paper with information about how the group does its work:

> Based in Malaysia, SIS has developed three key ways to promote women's rights within the context of the Muslim religion and its holy book, the Qur'an.

Notice how the phrase "three key ways" forecasts the body of Terrell's report. We expect to learn something about each of the three key ways, and the report is structured to give us that information, subtopic by subtopic.

5. Providing context in your introduction
Informative reports usually begin with a simple introduction to the topic and a straightforward statement of the thesis. Provide some relevant context or background, but get to your specific topic as quickly as possible and keep it in the foreground. (*For more on introductions, see Tab 2: Writing and Designing Texts, pp. 71–72.*)

6. Organizing your report by classifying and dividing information
Develop ideas in an organized way by classifying and dividing information into categories, subtopics, or the stages of a process. (*For more on developing your ideas, see Tab 2: Writing and Designing Texts, pp. 58–68.*)

www.mhhe.com/
awr3
For more on using patterns of development, go to
Writing >
Paragraph Patterns

7. Illustrating key ideas with examples
Use specific examples to help readers understand your ideas. In his paper on Sisters in Islam, Terrell provides many specific examples, including pertinent quotations from the Qur'an, a discussion of the attempt to establish the Domestic Violence Act, and descriptions of

SIS educational programs. Examples make his report interesting as well as educational. (*For more on using examples, see Tab 2: Writing and Designing Texts, p. 59.*)

8. Defining specialized terms and spelling out unfamiliar abbreviations

Specialized terms (such as foreign words or discipline-specific terminology) will probably not be familiar to most readers. Explain these terms with a synonym or a brief definition. For example, Terrell provides a synonym and a brief description of the term *sharia* in the third paragraph of his informative report on Sisters in Islam. (*For more on definition, see Tab 2: Writing and Designing Texts, p. 63.*) Unfamiliar abbreviations like SIS (Sisters in Islam) and NGO (non-governmental organization) are spelled out the first time they are used, with the abbreviation in parentheses.

9. Concluding by answering "so what?"

www.mhhe.com/
awr3
For more information on conclusions, go to

Writing >
Paragraph/Essay
Development >
Conclusions

Conclude with an image that suggests the information's value. The conclusion reminds readers of the topic and thesis. It then answers the "so what?" question.

At the end of his report on Sisters in Islam, Terrell answers the "so what?" question by contrasting press stereotypes of the status of women in Islam with the more encouraging view his paper presents:

> But their efforts show that the situation of women in Islamic countries is actually much more complex and encouraging than many recent newspaper images and stories have led us to believe.

(*For more on conclusions, see Tab 2: Writing and Designing Texts, p. 72.*)

9c Student paper: Informative report

In the informative paper that follows, John Terrell reports what he has learned about a Muslim nongovernmental organization dedicated to promoting women's rights. As you read his report, notice how Terrell provides a context for his topic, cites various sources (using APA documentation style), divides the information into subtopics, and illustrates his ideas with examples, all hallmarks of a clear, carefully developed paper. The annotations in the margin of this paper point out specific features of the informative report.

> *Note:* For details on the proper formatting of a paper in APA style, see Chapter 33 and the sample paper that begins on page 349.

SAMPLE STUDENT INFORMATIVE REPORT

Sisters Redefining the Divine

John Terrell

Political Science 252 Contemporary Issues: Human Rights

Professor Paul

December 20, 2008

----------------------------------[new page]----------------------------------

Sisters Redefining the Divine

The rights of women in Islamist and majority-Muslim nations
have recently become an issue of concern and contention. Images
of women in burqas, along with news stories describing forced
marriages, public executions by flogging, and virtual house arrest
for women without chaperones have led many Americans to
assume that Muslim women have no rights and no way to change
that situation. But that is not the whole picture. In many parts of
the Islamic world, non-governmental organizations (NGOs) are
working hard to make sure that women and their interests have a
political voice. Sisters in Islam (SIS) is just such an organization.
Based in Malaysia, SIS has developed three key ways to promote
women's rights within the context of the Muslim religion and its
holy book, the Qur'an.

One way that SIS works to promote women's rights is to show
how those rights are rooted in the origins of Islam and the Qur'an.
Members note that women fought side by side with the prophet
Muhammad in the early struggle to establish Islam's rule and point
out that allowing some degree of choice in marriage, permitting
divorce, and granting inheritance rights for women were
revolutionary concepts when Muslims first introduced them to the
world 1,400 years ago (Othman, 1997). Furthermore, they argue
that the Qur'an mandates "the principles of equality, justice and
freedom" and does not specifically prohibit women from assuming
leadership roles or contributing to public service. But they also

Marginal notes:

Following APA style, Terrell includes a separate title page. He does not include an abstract, because his instructor did not require one for this assignment.

Topic introduced.

First use of unfamiliar abbreviation spelled out.

Thesis stated.

First way— introduces a subtopic.

Source information summarized.

recognize that the revolutionary possibilities of Islam were curtailed when a small group of men claimed "exclusive control over the interpretation of the Qur'an" (Sisters in Islam, 2007).

Source named in signal phrase.

According to Coleman (2006), the Qur'an contains almost 80 sections on legal issues, but neither it nor the secondary texts and oral traditions of Islam contain instruction on everyday matters. To make matters even more complex, the Qur'an includes many seemingly contradictory passages. Its statements on polygamy are a prime example. One verse in the text says, "Marry those women who are lawful for you, up to two, three, or four, but only if you can treat them equally," while a later verse reads, "No matter how you try you will never be able to treat your wives equally." In the early years following the death of the prophet Muhammad, legal scholars were called upon to examine issues in need of clarification. They were also encouraged to apply independent thinking and then make non-binding rulings. This practice lasted until the 11th century, at which time Sunni religious scholars consolidated legal judgments into strict schools of thought and placed a ban on independent interpretation. The result was *sharia,* or Muslim law. Over the next nine hundred years, this approach to the law changed little. In application, however, sharia does vary according to regional traditions. In Tunisia, for example, taking more than one wife is banned altogether, while India provides few restrictions upon polygamy (Women Living under Muslim Laws, 2003). Likewise, rules concerning dress and moral codes vary from state to state, with headscarves for women being obligatory in Iran and optional in Egypt.

Example given for clarity and interest.

Unfamiliar term defined.

National diversity in applying sharia accounts for the second way that SIS promotes women's rights within the framework of Islam: it focuses its work for change on one country, Malaysia. Before 1957, Malaysia was a British colony with a court system divided between the federal and the local levels. Local Islamic leaders were allowed to establish courts to preside over cases of family law, while most other legal matters went to the federal courts. After

Second way— introduces subtopic.

Malaysia gained independence, Article 3 of its constitution named Islam as the state religion, although a clause in the same article guaranteed non-Muslims the right to practice their faiths (Mohamad, 1988). The court system, however, remained the same, meaning that the 60 percent of the population who are Muslim are still subject to local Islamic family courts, while the 40 percent who do not follow Islam are not (U.S. Department of State, 2005).

Malaysia's legal system complicates the work of SIS, as the 1995 campaign to pass a Domestic Violence Act shows. In matters of violence against women, Muslim family law provides little legal recourse. The usual response by Islamic judges is to send the woman home to reconcile with her husband. So in 1995 the SIS campaigned to pass the Domestic Violence Act, which aimed to provide basic legal protections for women. After a vigorous lobbying campaign, the law was passed. Yet the response from Malaysia's Islamic religious establishment was to say that the law would apply only to non-Muslims (Othman, 1997). Even though this interpretation of the law has not been successfully reversed, SIS continues to work on family law reform, submitting to the government memoranda and reports on such issues as divorce, guardianship, and polygamy. In 2005, for example, SIS and five other NGOs formed a Joint Action Group on Gender Equality (JAG) and prepared a memorandum requesting a review and withdrawal of parts of a bill that was intended to improve the Islamic Family Law Act of 1984. While praising the new requirement that in cases of contracting polygamous marriages, both the existing and future wives must be present in the court, JAG (2005) objected to other parts of the bill such as a change in wording that would make it easier for men to practice polygamy; instead of having to show that the new marriage was both "just and necessary," the men would only have to show that it was "just or necessary."

Although advocating for changes in the law is certainly important, SIS has developed another key way of promoting women's rights: public research and education. Using surveys and

Source given for specific data.

Objective stance.

Example given for clarity and interest.

Third way— introduces subtopic.

interviews, the group began a pilot research project in 2004, the "Impact of Polygamy on the Family Institution"; that research project has recently gone national. As its Web site documents, SIS also sponsors numerous public lectures and forums on such issues as Islam and the political participation of women, the challenges of modernity, the use of fatwa, and the emergence of genetic engineering. There are also seminars and workshops for specific groups such as single parents, study sessions with visiting writers, and a rich array of printed material, including newspaper columns that answer women's questions as well as pamphlets on such concerns as family planning, Qur'an interpretation, and domestic violence. Clearly SIS takes a very public approach to reform, an approach that their executive director, Zainah Anwar (2004), contends is necessary to ensure that Islam does not "remain the exclusive preserve of the *ulama* [traditionally trained religious scholars]."

Instead of waiting patiently for Islamic scholars and judges to work issues out in closed sessions, SIS has developed an activist approach to reform. So it is not surprising that the group's key ways of effecting change sometimes get as much criticism from conservative Islamists as the proposed changes themselves do (Anwar, 2004). It remains to be seen whether SIS, along with other NGOs working for human rights in Muslim countries, will succeed in moderating what they see as harmful expressions of their faith. But the efforts of SIS show that the situation of women in Islamic countries is actually much more complex and encouraging than many recent newspaper images and stories have led us to believe.

----------------------------------[new page]----------------------------------

References

Anwar, Z. (2004, September-October). Sisters in Islam: A voice for everyone. *Fellowship Magazine.* Retrieved from http://www .forusa.org/fellowship/sept-oct-04/anwar.html

Margin notes:

Examples given for clarity and interest.

Quotaton integrated into writer's sentence.

Interpretation provided without biased opinion.

Point and purpose restated in conclusion.

References list follows APA style and begins on a new page.

Coleman, I. (2006, January-February). Women, Islam, and
the new Iraq. *Foreign Affairs.* Retrieved from http://www
.foreignaffairs.org/20060101faessay85104/isobel-coleman/
women-islam-and-the-new-iraq.html

Joint Action Group on Gender Equality. (2005, December).
Memorandum to Ahli Dewan Negara to review the Islamic
Family Law (Federal Territories) (Amendment) Bill 2005.
Retrieved from http://www.sistersinislam.org.my/memo/
08122005.htm

Mohamad, M. (1988). Islam, the secular state, and Muslim women
in Malaysia. Retrieved December 11, 2008, from http://www
.wluml.org/english/pubsfulltst.shtml?cmd[87]=i-87-2615

Othman, N. (1997). Implementing women's human rights in
Malaysia. *Human Rights Dialogue, 1*(9). Retrieved from
http://www.cceia.org/resources/publications/dialogue/
1_09/articles/567.html

Sisters in Islam. (2007). Mission. Retrieved December 10, 2008,
from http://sistersinislam.org.my/mission.htm

U.S. Department of State. Bureau of Democracy, Human Rights,
and Labor. (2005, November 8). *Malaysia: International
Religious Freedom Report 2005.* Retrieved from http://www
.state.gov/g/drl/rls/irf/2005/51518.htm

Women Living under Muslim Laws. (2003). Knowing our rights:
Women, family, laws, and customs in the Muslim world.
Retrieved December 12, 2008, from http://www.wluml.org/
english/pubsfulltst.shtml?cmd[87]=i-87-16766

9d Write reviews of the literature to survey ideas.

In upper-division courses instructors sometimes assign a special kind of informative report called a **review of the literature.** Here the term *literature* refers to published research reports, and the term *review* means that you need to survey others' ideas, not evaluate them or argue for your opinion. A review presents an organized account of the current state of knowledge in a specific area that you and other researchers can use to help determine new projects and new directions for research. The review of the literature may also be a subsection within a research report.

The following paragraph is an excerpt from the review of the literature section in an article by psychologists investigating the motivations for suicide:

> One source of information about suicide motives is suicide notes. International studies of suicide notes suggest that women and men do not differ with regard to love versus achievement motives. For example, in a study of German suicide notes, Linn and Lester (1997) found that women and men did not differ with regard to relationship versus financial or work motives. In a study of Hong Kong suicide notes, Ho, Yip, Chiu, and Halliday (1998) reported no gender or age differences with regard to interpersonal problems or financial/job problems. Similarly, in a UK study, McClelland, Reicher, and Booth (2000) found that men's suicide notes did not differ from women's notes in terms of mentioning career failures. In fact, in the UK study, relationship losses were reported more often in men's than in women's suicide notes.
>
> —SILVIA SARA CANETTO AND DAVID LESTER,
> "Love and Achievement Motives in
> Women's and Men's Suicide Notes"

10 Interpretive Analyses and Writing about Literature

Interpretation involves figuring out a way of understanding a written document, literary work, cultural artifact, social situation, or natural event and presenting it to readers in a meaningful way.

10a Understand the assignment.

When an assignment asks you to compare, explain, analyze, or discuss something, you are expected to study that subject closely. An **interpretive analysis** moves beyond simple description and examines or compares particular items for a reason: to enhance your readers' understanding of people's conditions, actions, beliefs, or desires.

www.mhhe.com/
awr3

For an interactive tutorial on writing interpretive analyses, go to

Writing >
Writing Tutors >
Interpretive
Analyses

10b Approach writing an interpretive analysis as a process.

Writing an interpretive analysis typically begins with critical reading. (*See Chapter 4: Reading, Thinking, Writing: The Critical Connection.*)

1. Discovering an aspect of the subject that is meaningful to you

Think about your own feelings and experiences while you read, listen, or observe. Connecting your own thoughts and experiences to what you are studying can help you develop fresh interpretations.

2. Developing a thoughtful stance

Think of yourself as an explorer. Be thoughtful, inquisitive, and open-minded. You are exploring the possible meaning of something. When you write your paper, invite your readers to join you on an intellectual journey, saying, in effect, "Come, think this through with me."

3. Using an intellectual framework

To interpret your subject effectively, use a relevant perspective or an intellectual framework. For example, the elements of a work of fiction, such as plot, character, and setting, are often used to analyze stories. Sigmund Freud's theory of conscious and unconscious forces in conflict might be applied to various subjects. In his analysis of Flannery O'Connor's story "Everything That Rises Must Converge," Rajeev Bector uses sociologist Erving Goffman's ideas about "character contests" to interpret the conflict between a son and his mother. (*Bector's analysis begins on p. 124.*)

No matter what framework you use, analysis often entails taking something apart and then putting it back together by figuring out how its parts contribute to a meaningful whole. Because the goal of analysis is to create a meaningful interpretation, you need to treat the whole as more than the sum of its parts and recognize that finding meaning is a complex problem with multiple solutions.

 WRITING AFTER COLLEGE

Interpretive Analyses

You can find interpretive analyses like the following in professional journals like *PMLA* (*Publications of the Modern Language Association*) as well as popular publications like the *New Yorker* and the *Atlantic Monthly.* Consider these examples:

- A cultural critic contrasts the way AIDS and cancer are talked about, imagined, and therefore treated.
- Two geologists analyze photos of an arctic coastal plain taken from an airplane and infer that the effects of seismic exploration vary according to the type of vegetation.
- A musicologist compares the revised endings of two pieces by Beethoven to figure out what makes a work complete and finished.

CHARTING the TERRITORY

Student Analyses across the Disciplines

Students are often called on to write interpretive analyses such as the following:

- Rajeev Bector, a student in a literature course, asserts that Flannery O'Connor's story "Everything That Rises Must Converge" can be understood as a character contest.

- A student majoring in music spells out the emotional implications of the tempo and harmonic progression in Schubert's *Der Atlas*.

- A student in an economics course demonstrates that, according to an econometric model of nine variables, deregulation has not decreased the level of airline safety.

www.mhhe.com/
awr3
For more help with
developing a thesis,
go to

Writing >
Paragraph/Essay
Development >
Thesis/Central
Idea

4. Listing, comparing, questioning, and classifying to discover your thesis

To figure out your thesis, you may find it useful to explore distinctive features of your subject. If you are analyzing literature, you might consider the plot, the characters, the setting, and the tone before deciding to focus your thesis on one character's personality.

Try one or more of the following strategies:

- Take notes about what you see or read, and if it helps, write a summary.

- Ask yourself questions about the subject you are analyzing, and write down any interesting answers. Imagine what kinds of questions your instructor or classmates might ask about the artifact, document, or performance you are considering. In answering these questions, try to figure out the thesis you will present and support.

- Name the class of things to which the item you are analyzing belongs (for example, memoirs), and then identify important parts or features of that class (for example, scene, point of view, helpers, and turning points).

5. Making your thesis focused and purposeful

To make a point about your subject, focus your paper on one or two questions that are key to understanding it. Resist the temptation to describe everything you see. Consider this example of a focused, purposeful thesis:

> In O'Connor's short story, plot, setting, and characterization work together to reinforce the impression that racism is a complex and pervasive problem.

QUESTIONS FOR ANALYZING LITERATURE

Plot and Structure

What events take place over the course of the work? What did you think and feel at different places? How do the parts of the work relate to one another?

Characters

What are the relationships among the people portrayed? How do they change? What does dialogue reveal about their motivations?

Setting

What is the significance of the time and place? What associations does the writer make with the location?

Point of View

Is there a first-person narrator ("I"), or is the story told by a third-person narrator who reveals what one, all, or none of the characters are thinking?

Tone

Is the work's tone stern or playful, melancholy, or something else?

Language

Does the work conjure images that appeal to the senses? Does it use simile to directly compare two things using *like* or *as*? Does it use metaphor to implicitly link two things? What feelings or ideas do individual words suggest?

Theme

What is at issue in the work? What statement does the author seem to be making about the issue?

Although you want your point to be clear, you also want to make sure that your thesis anticipates the "so what?" question and sets up an interesting context for your interpretation. Unless you relate your specific thesis to some more general issue, idea, or problem, your interpretive analysis may seem pointless to readers. (*For more on developing your thesis, see Tab 2: Writing and Designing Texts, pp. 48–50.*)

www.mhhe.com/
awr3

For more on crafting
introductions, go to

Writing >
Paragraph/Essay
Development >
Introductions

6. Introducing the general issue, a clear thesis or question, and relevant context

In interpretive analyses, it often takes more than one paragraph to do what an introduction needs to do:

- Identify the general issue, concept, or problem at stake. You can also present the intellectual framework that you are applying.
- Provide relevant background information.
- Name the specific item or items you will focus on.
- State the thesis you will support and develop or the main question(s) your analysis will answer.

You need not do these things in the order listed. Sometimes it is a good idea to introduce the specific focus of your analysis before presenting either the issue or the background information. Even though you may begin with a provocative statement or an example designed to capture your readers' attention, make sure that your introduction does the four things it needs to do. (*For more on introductions, see Tab 2: Writing and Designing Texts, pp. 71–72.*)

7. Planning your paper so that each point supports your thesis

After you pose a key question or state your thesis, you need to organize your points to answer the question or support your thesis. Readers must be able to follow your train of thought and see how each point you make is related to your thesis. (*For more on developing your ideas, see Tab 2: Writing and Designing Texts, pp. 58–68.*)

For example, if Bector had simply described the events in O'Connor's story or presented a random list of insights, his paper would not have shed any light on what the story means. Instead, Bector ends his introduction with a compelling question about one character's motives:

> **QUESTION** But why would Julian want to hurt his mother, a woman who is already suffering from high blood pressure?

Bector answers this interpretive question in the body of his paper by pointing out and explaining three features of the character contest between mother and son.

www.mhhe.com/
awr3

For more information
on conclusions, go to

Writing >
Paragraph/Essay
Development >
Conclusions

8. Concluding by answering "so what?"

The conclusion of an interpretive analysis needs to answer the "so what?" question by saying why your thesis—as well as the analysis that supports and develops it—is relevant to the larger issue identified in the introduction. What does your interpretation reveal about that issue? (*For information about conclusions, see Tab 2: Writing and Designing Texts, p. 72.*)

CHARTING the TERRITORY

Ideas and Practices for Writing in the Humanities

- **Base your analysis on the work itself.** Works of art affect each of us differently, and any interpretation has a subjective element. There are numerous critical theories about the significance of art. However, the possibility of different interpretations does not mean that any one interpretation is as valid as any other. Your reading of the work needs to be grounded in details from the work itself.

- **Consider how the concepts you are learning in your course apply to the work you are analyzing.** If your course focuses on the formal elements of art, for example, you might look at how those elements function in the painting you have chosen. If your course focuses on the social context of a work, you might look at how it shares or subverts the belief system and worldview that was common in its time.

- **Use the present tense when writing about the work and the past tense when writing about its history.** Use the present tense to talk about the events that happen within a work: "In Aristophanes' plays, characters frequently *step* out of the scene and *address* the audience directly." Use the past tense, however, to relate historical information about the work or creator: "Kant *wrote* about science, history, criminal justice, and politics as well as philosophical ideas."

10c Student paper: Interpretive analysis

In the following paper, Rajeev Bector uses Erving Goffman's ideas to analyze and interpret the actions of two characters in Flannery O'Connor's short story "Everything That Rises Must Converge." What provoked Bector's interpretation in the first place is this question: How can we understand the mean ways Julian and his mother treat each other? As he helps us better understand Julian and his mother, Bector raises the larger issue of racism. To what extent does Bector's interpretive analysis of O'Connor's story also illuminate the workings of racism in our society?

Note: For details on the proper formatting of a paper in MLA style, see Chapter 29 and the sample paper that begins on page 313.

**www.mhhe.com/
awr3**
For another sample
of interpretive
writing, go to

**Writing >
Writing Samples >
Interpretive Paper**

SAMPLE STUDENT ANALYSIS OF A SHORT STORY

The Character Contest in Flannery O'Connor's
"Everything That Rises Must Converge"

Sociologist Erving Goffman believes that every social
interaction establishes our identity and preserves our image,
honor, and credibility in the hearts and minds of others. Social
interactions, he says, are in essence "character contests" that occur
not only in games and sports but also in our everyday dealings
with strangers, peers, friends, and even family members. Goffman
defines character contests as "disputes [that] are sought out and
indulged in (often with glee) as a means of establishing where
one's boundaries are" (29). Just such a contest occurs in Flannery
O'Connor's short story "Everything That Rises Must Converge."

As they travel from home to the Y, Julian and his mother,
Mrs. Chestny, engage in a character contest, a dispute we must
understand in order to figure out the story's theme. Julian is so
frustrated with his mother that he virtually "declare[s] war on
her," "allow[s] no glimmer of sympathy to show on his face," and
"imagine[s] various unlikely ways by which he could teach her a
lesson" (O'Connor 185, 186). But why would Julian want to hurt
his mother, a woman who is already suffering from high blood
pressure?

Julian's conflict with Mrs. Chestny results from pent-up
hostility and tension. As Goffman explains, character contests are
a way of living that often leaves a "residue": "Every day in many
ways we can try to score points and every day we can be shot
down" (29). For many years, Julian has had to live under his racist
mother's authority, and every time he protested her racist views he
was probably shot down because of his "radical ideas" and "lack
of practical experience" (O'Connor 184). As a result, a residue of
defeat and shame has accumulated that fuels a fire of rebellion
against his mother. But even though Julian rebels against his
mother's racist views, it doesn't mean that he isn't a racist himself.

Marginal notes:

Key idea that
provides
intellectual
framework.

Question
posed.

Interpretation
organized point
by point—first
point.

Julian doesn't realize that in his own way, he is as prejudiced as his mother. He makes it "a point" to sit next to blacks, in contrast to his mother, who purposely sits next to whites (182). They are two extremes, each biased, for if Julian were truly fair to all, he would not care whom he sat next to.

When we look at the situation from Mrs. Chestny's viewpoint, we realize that she must maintain her values and beliefs for two important reasons: to uphold her character as Julian's mother and to act out her prescribed role in society. Even if she finds Julian's arguments on race relations and integration valid and plausible, Mrs. Chestny must still refute them. If she didn't, she would lose face as Julian's mother—that image of herself as the one with authority. By preserving her self-image, Mrs. Chestny shows that she has what Goffman sees as key to "character": some quality that seems "essential and unchanging" (28).

"We" indicates thoughtful stance, not Bector's personal feelings.

Second point.

Besides upholding her character as Julian's mother, Mrs. Chestny wants to preserve the honor and dignity of her family tradition. Like an actor performing before an audience, she must play the role prescribed for her—the role of a white supremacist. But her situation is hopeless, for the role she must play fails to acknowledge the racial realities that have transformed her world. According to Goffman, when a "situation" is "hopeless," a character "can gamely give everything . . . and then go down bravely, or proudly, or insolently, or gracefully or with an ironic smile on his lips" (32). For Mrs. Chestny, being game means trying to preserve her honor and dignity as she goes down to physical defeat in the face of hopeless odds.

Third point.

Given the differences between Mrs. Chestny's and her son's values, as well as the oppressiveness of Mrs. Chestny's racist views, we can understand why Julian struggles to "teach" his mother "a lesson" (185) throughout the entire bus ride. Goffman would point out that "each individual is engaged in providing evidence to establish a definition of himself at the expense of what can remain for the other" (29). But in the end, neither character wins the

Thesis.

contest. Julian's mother loses her sense of self when she is pushed down to the ground by a "colored woman" wearing a hat identical to hers (187). Faced with his mother's breakdown, Julian feels his own identity being overwhelmed by "the world of guilt and sorrow" (191).

Conclusion—main point about Julian and his mother related to larger issue of racism.

------------------------------------[new page]------------------------------------

Works Cited

"Works Cited" list follows MLA style and begins on a new page.

Goffman, Erving. "Character Contests." *Text Book: An Introduction to Literary Language.* Ed. Robert Scholes, Nancy Comley, and Gregory Ulmer. New York: St. Martin's, 1988. 27–33. Print.

O'Connor, Flannery. "Everything That Rises Must Converge." *Fiction.* Ed. R. S. Gwynn. 2nd ed. New York: Addison, 1998. 179–91. Print.

11 Arguments

Writing arguments is a way to form reasoned positions on debatable issues. Bearing in mind that reasonable people can see things differently, always strive to write well-informed, thoughtful arguments.

11a Understand the assignment.

When you write an **argument paper,** your purpose is not to win but to take part in a discussion by stating and supporting your position on an issue. Written arguments appear in various forms, including critiques, reviews, and proposals.

- **Critiques:** Critiques address the question "What is true?" A critique fairly summarizes someone's position before either refuting or defending it. Refutations use one of two basic strate-

Arguments

Arguments are central to American democracy and its institutions of higher learning because they help create the common ground that is sometimes called public space. Fields inside and outside of the academy value reason and welcome arguments such as the following:

- The board of a national dietetic association publishes a position statement identifying obesity as a growing health problem that dieticians should be involved in preventing and treating.
- An art critic praises a museum's special exhibition of modern American paintings for its diversity and thematic coherence.
- A sociologist proposes four policies that he claims will improve the prospects of people living in inner-city neighborhoods.

gies: either exposing the reasoning of the position as inadequate or presenting evidence that contradicts the position. Matt Shadwell's "Person of the Year" refutes *Time* magazine's choice of "you" for this distinction. (*Shadwell's critique begins on p. 134.*) Defenses make use of three strategies: clarifying the author's key terms and reasoning, presenting new arguments to support the position, and showing that criticisms of the position are unconvincing.

- **Reviews:** Reviews address the question "What is good?" The writer evaluates an event, artifact, practice, or institution, judging by reasonable principles and criteria.

- **Proposals, or policy papers:** Proposals, sometimes called policy papers, address the question "What should be done?" They are designed to cause change. Readers are encouraged to see a situation in a specific way and to take action.

👁 11b Approach writing an argument as a process.

www.mhhe.com/ awr3

For an interactive tutorial on writing arguments, go to

Writing > Writing Tutors > Arguments

In every course you take, you will gain practice in addressing issues that are important in the larger community. Selecting a topic that you care about will give you the impetus to think matters through and make cogent arguments. Of course, you will have to go beyond your personal emotions about an issue to make the most convincing case. You will also have to empathize with potential readers who may disagree with you about a subject that is important to you.

TextConnex

Blogs

Blogs frequently function as vehicles for public debate. For example, online editions of many newspapers include blogs, which invite readers to comment on the news of the day and to present dissenting opinions. While online debate can be freewheeling, it's important to search for common ground with your readers when writing persuasive formal arguments. (*For more on blogs, see Chapter 14, pp. 170–72.*)

1. Figuring out what is at issue

Before you can take a position on a topic like air pollution or population growth, you must figure out what is at issue. Ask questions about your topic. Are there indications that all is not as it should be? Have things always been this way, or have they changed for the worse? From what different perspectives—economic, social, political, cultural, medical, geographic—can problems like world food shortages be understood? Do people interested in the topic disagree about what is true, what is good, or what should be done?

Based on your answers to such questions, identify the issues your topic raises, and decide which of these issues you think is most important, interesting, and appropriate to write about.

2. Developing a reasonable stance that negotiates differences

When writing arguments, you want your readers to respect your intelligence and trust your judgment. By getting readers to trust your character, you build **ethos** or credibility. Conducting research on your issue can make you well informed; reading and thinking critically about other views can enhance your thoughtfulness. Find out what others have to say about the issue, and make it part of your purpose to negotiate the differences between your position and theirs. Pay attention to the places where you disagree with other people's views, but also note what you have in common—interests, key questions, or underlying values. (*For more on ethos and other appeals to your audience, see Tab 2: Writing and Designing Texts, p. 32.*)

Avoid language that may promote prejudice or fear. Misrepresentations of other people's ideas are out of place as are personal attacks on their character. Write arguments to open minds, not to slam doors shut. (*See the box on blogs above.*)

Trying out different perspectives can also help you figure out where you stand on an issue. (*Also see the next section on stating your position.*) Make lists of the arguments for and against a specific position; then compare the lists and decide where you stand. Does one set of arguments seem stronger than the other? Do you want to change or qualify your initial position?

3. Composing a thesis that states your position

A successful argument requires a strong, engaging, arguable thesis. As noted in the section on the Toulmin model of argument, personal feelings and accepted facts cannot serve as an argument's thesis because they are not debatable (*see 4b, pp. 30–31*).

www.mhhe.com/ awr3
For more help with developing a thesis, go to
Writing > Paragraph/Essay Development > Thesis/Central Idea

PERSONAL FEELING, NOT A DEBATABLE THESIS

I feel that developing nations should not suffer food shortages.

ACCEPTED FACT, NOT A DEBATABLE THESIS

Food shortages are growing in many developing nations.

DEBATABLE THESIS

Current food shortages in developing nations are in large part caused by climate change and the use of food crops in biofuels.

In proposals and policy papers, the thesis presents a solution in terms of the writer's definition of the problem. The logic behind a thesis for a proposal can be stated like this:

Given these key variables and their underlying cause, one solution to the problem would be . . .

Because this kind of thesis is both complex and qualified, you will often need more than one sentence to state it clearly. You will also need numerous well-supported arguments to make it credible. Readers ultimately want to know that the proposed solution will not cause more problems than it solves; they realize that policy papers and proposals call for actions, and actions have consequences.

4. Identifying key points to support and develop your thesis

A strong, debatable thesis needs to be supported and developed with sound reasoning and carefully documented evidence. You can think of an argument as a dialogue between writer and readers. The writer states a debatable thesis, and one reader wonders, "Why do you believe that?" Another reader wants to know, "But what about this factor?" The writer should anticipate questions such as those and answer them by presenting claims (reasons) that are substantiated with evidence and by refuting opposing views. (*For more on claims and evidence, see Tab 2: Writing and Designing Texts, pp. 30–31.*)

Usually, a well-developed argument paper includes more than one type of claim and one kind of evidence. In addition to generalizations based on empirical data, it often includes authoritative claims based on the opinions of experts and ethical claims based on the application of principle. In his critique of *Time* magazine's choice for Person of the Year, Matt Shadwell presents facts about the passivity of YouTube users, citing the percentage who contribute information at only 0.07 percent. He also quotes an expert commentator, Frank Rich, who points out that Internet users prefer sites about celebrities to sites that focus on world events (*see p. 137*). In addition, Shadwell presents the anecdotal example of an average user, whose actions are far from revolutionary. As you conduct research, note evidence—facts, examples or anecdotes, and expert testimony—that can be used to support each argument for or against your position. You will want to demonstrate your trustworthiness by properly quoting and documenting the information you have gathered from your sources.

In developing your argument, you will build your credibility by paying attention to **counterarguments,** substantiated claims that do not support your position. Consider whether a reader could reasonably draw different conclusions from your evidence or disagree with your assumptions. Use one of the following strategies to take the most important counterarguments into account:

- Qualify your thesis in light of the counterargument by including a word such as *most, some, usually,* or *likely:* "Students with credit cards *usually* have trouble with debt" recognizes that some do not.

- Add to the thesis a statement of the conditions for or exceptions to your position: "Businesses *with over five hundred employees* saved money using the new process."

- Choose at least one or two counterarguments and refute their truth or their importance. Introduce a counterargument with a signal phrase like "Others might contend . . ." (*See Tab 5: Researching, p. 262 for a discussion of signal phrases.*) You can refute a counterargument's truth by questioning the author's interpretation of the evidence or the validity of the author's assumptions. Shadwell, for example, refutes the counterargument that passive users of the Internet are an appropriate choice for Person of the Year. He suggests that the editors of *Time* have assumed that all Internet users also create content, and he shows this is not the case.

www.mhhe.com/
awr3

For more help with creating an outline, go to

Writing >
Paragraph/Essay
Development >
Outlines

5. Creating an outline that includes a linked set of reasons

Arguments are most effective when they present a chain—a linked set—of reasons, so it is a good idea to begin drafting by writing down your thesis and outlining the way you will support and develop it. Shadwell presents evidence first and builds to his thesis at the end of his critique. While there are multiple ways to order an argument, your outline should include the following parts (arranged below following **classical structure**):

- An introduction to the topic and the debatable issue, establishing your credibility
- A thesis stating your position on the issue
- A point-by-point account of the reasons for your position, including the evidence (facts, examples, authorities) you will use to substantiate each major reason
- A fair presentation and refutation of one or two key counterarguments
- A response to the "so what?" question. Why does your argument matter?

If you expect your audience to disagree with you, consider using a **Rogerian structure:**

- An introduction to the topic and the debatable issue
- An attempt to reach common ground by naming values you share and providing a sympathetic portrayal of your readers' (opposing) position
- A statement of your position and presentation of supporting evidence
- A conclusion that restates your view and suggests a compromise or synthesis

6. Emphasizing your commitment to dialogue in the introduction

Look for common ground with readers: beliefs, concerns, and values you share with those who disagree with you and those who are undecided. Sometimes called **Rogerian argument** after the psychologist Carl Rogers, the common-ground approach is particularly important in your introduction, where it can build bridges with readers who might otherwise become too defensive or annoyed to read further. For example, Shadwell begins his essay with a review of previous choices for Person of the Year. He invites readers to consider their accomplishments in order to establish a contrast with the lack of achievement by "you." If possible, return to that common ground at the end of your argument.

You want readers to see you as reasonable, ethical, and empathetic. Giving reasons and supplying evidence for your position and avoiding fallacies establish your **logos.** You also need to show readers that you are sincere (ethos) and that you care about your readers' feelings **(pathos).** When you read your argument, pay attention to how

www.mhhe.com/
awr3
For more help on crafting introductions, go to
Writing >
Paragraph/Essay Development >
Introductions

you are coming across. (*For more on fallacies and the three appeals, see Tab 2: Writing and Designing Texts, pp. 32–35.*)

7. Concluding by restating your position and emphasizing its importance

After presenting your reasoning in detail, remind readers of your thesis. The version of your thesis that you present in your conclusion should be more complex and qualified than the version in your introduction. Readers may not agree with you, but they should know why the issue and your argument matter.

8. Using visuals in your argument

Consider including visuals that support your argument's purpose. Each should relate directly to your argument as a whole or a point within it. Matt Shadwell takes the cover of *Time* magazine as the subject of his argument, refuting its message (*see pp. 134–39*). Visuals also may provide evidence: a photograph can illustrate an example, and a graph can present statistics that support an argument.

Visual evidence makes emotional, logical, and ethical appeals. The Absolute AA ad in Chapter 4 (*p. 36*) makes an emotional appeal by substituting a warning against alcoholism for the expected commercial message. The graph of Amazon deforestation rates in Audrey Galeano's paper (*Tab 7: APA Documentation Style, p. 351*) makes a logical appeal by presenting evidence that supports her claim. It also demonstrates the depth of her research (building her ethos).

Consider how your audience is likely to react to your visuals. Help them interpret your visuals with specific captions. Each caption should describe the visual, indicating how it supports your argument. Also mention each image in your text. Make sure charts and graphs are free of distortion or chartjunk (*pp. 85–86*). Acknowledge any data from other sources, and obtain permission when necessary. (*See also Tab 5: Researching, pp. 219–26 and Tab 2: Writing and Designing Texts, pp. 85–87.*)

9. Reexamining your reasoning

After you have completed the first draft of your paper, take time to re-examine your reasoning for errors. Having peers review your work is especially important.

👁 11c Student paper: Argument

In the following critique, Matt Shadwell argues that the editors of *Time* magazine made a poor choice in designating "you" as Person of the Year. As you read Shadwell's argument, notice how he defines criteria of ac-

CHECKLIST

Self/Peer Review of an Argument

Ask yourself and your peer reviewers the following questions:

- ☐ What makes the thesis strong and arguable?

- ☐ Does the argument contain any mistakes in logic? (*See the list of common logical fallacies, Tab 2: Writing and Designing Texts, pp. 32–35.*)

- ☐ How does the argument develop each claim presented in support of the thesis? Is the supporting evidence sufficient? Does the argument quote or paraphrase from sources accurately and document them properly? (*For more on quoting, paraphrasing, and documenting sources, see Tab 5: Researching, pp. 252–65, and Tabs 6–8.*)

- ☐ How does the essay address counterarguments?

- ☐ How do the visuals fit the purpose and audience?

For MULTILINGUAL STUDENTS

Learning about Cultural Differences through Peer Review

U.S. culture encourages direct and explicit argument, while some other cultures do not. When you share your work with peers raised in the United States, you may learn that the vocabulary or the style of presentation you have used to express your ideas makes it difficult for them to understand your point. They may want you to be more direct. Ask your peers to suggest different words and approaches, and then decide whether their suggestions would really make your ideas more accessible to others.

complishment and then shows that "you" do not fit those standards. In critiquing the *Time* magazine cover, he is also criticizing the passivity of Internet users, refuting the cover's basic claim that "you" are actively engaged in a "flat" world through surfing and blogging.

> *Note:* For details on the proper formatting of a paper in MLA style, see Chapter 29 and the sample paper that begins on page 313.

SAMPLE STUDENT ARGUMENT

Person of the Year

Time's Persons of the Year have ranged from celebrities, politicians, religious leaders, and humanitarians to more inclusive or abstract selections such as "the American Soldier," "the Peacemakers," and "Endangered Earth." The rationale for selection has varied as widely as the character of its "persons." The Man of the Year in 1938, Adolf Hitler, was chosen for the singular power of his personality and the scale of his terrifying accomplishments; on the other hand, "U.S. Scientists" were named collectively in 1960 for affecting "the life of every human presently inhabiting the planet" through a long list of breakthroughs including the discovery of DNA. In its eighty-year retrospective of this annual cover story, *Time* states that the recognition is "bestowed by the editors on the person or persons who most affected the news and our lives, for good or ill, and embodied what was important about the year." It is therefore baffling to consider *Time*'s 2006 honoree, "you" (see fig. 1).

According to the 2006 Person of the Year cover story, the world's boundaries have been broken and its people have united via the Internet. People are flocking to social networking and content-sharing sites like MySpace and YouTube to broadcast programming and information to millions worldwide. Access to potentially enormous audiences is simpler and more widely available than ever, and *Time*'s editors admiringly note that people are finding more uses for this broad public forum every day. Lev Grossman, author of the cover story, writes:

> [W]ho are these people? Seriously, who actually sits down after a long day at work and says, I'm not going to watch *Lost*

Marginal annotations:

Lively beginning inviting readers to consider other Person of the Year choices, including those selected for evil accomplishments.

Topic introduced.

Fig. 1. Cover of *Time* announcing Person of the Year, December 25, 2006. *Note:* Hochstein, Arthur, and Spencer Jones-Glasshouse. *Time* cover. 13 Dec. 2006. *Time.com*. Web. 2 Mar. 2008.

tonight. I'm going to turn on my computer and make a movie starring my pet iguana. I'm going to mash up 50 Cent's vocals with Queen's instrumentals? I'm going to blog about my state of mind or the state of the nation or the steak-frites at the new bistro down the street? Who has that time and energy and passion? The answer is, you do.

Since *Time* is honoring "you" for this achievement, it seems worthwhile to question whom precisely the magazine's editors are referring to. In conferring responsibility for this revolution in the control and flow of information, does *Time* mean to honor each and every person in the world who surfed the Internet in 2006,

Presents *Time* magazine's position fairly via an engaging quote.

Poses key question about article's claim.

or just the comparatively small number of computer-savvy individuals who produce mass quantities of text, film, music, etc. online? At the beginning of "What Is the 1% Rule," Charles Arthur writes that "If you get a group of 100 people online, then one will create content, 10 will 'interact' with it (commenting or offering improvements) and the other 89 will just view it." To illustrate the "One Percent Rule," examine the statistics of uploading and downloading content on YouTube. According to Antony Mayfield, YouTube's hundreds of millions of daily downloads (passive viewings) outnumber its uploads (posting of content) by a margin of 1,538 to 1. That means that the percentage of users on YouTube who contribute information is about 0.07 percent—a good deal less than the One Percent Rule would predict . "You" would therefore seem a rather generous way to describe a relatively small number of people.

Alternatively, one might suppose the magazine truly wishes to honor the vast numbers of passive users as well. This, too, seems ill-conceived. Consider a typical Internet user. He or she accesses the Web daily, visiting sites such as YouTube on a regular basis. On social networking sites such as MySpace and Facebook, the user maintains a profile to stay in touch with friends, occasionally adding photos, sending out notices, or posting entries on a blog. Sites like these offer a degree of self-expression through personalized page designs (including music, images, and sometimes video); they also typically allow users to control access to their sites, enabling them to designate certain features or their profile at large as either public, private, or selectively public (meaning only visitors designated as "friends" can look at the features).

As novel as such activities may seem to the tens of millions of people who visit such sites daily, it is difficult to see how pasting a YouTube video on a MySpace profile deserves recognition for "seizing the reins of the global media, for founding and framing the new digital democracy, for working for nothing and beating the pros at their own game" (Grossman). If *Time* means to include everyone who uses the Internet in their profile, then the editors are simply congratulating people for becoming more eager consumers of an emerging technological market. This is like honoring "Cable TV Viewers" for changing the face of television, or "Hybrid Car Buyers" for revolutionizing the auto industry.

One wonders if the magazine isn't actually expressing wonder over the technology itself, much as it did when it honored "the Computer" in 1982. Since the Internet itself is nothing new, one can only assume *Time*'s editors are terrifically impressed by new applications of existing technology. Web sites such as YouTube or Google Video, which essentially are do-it-yourself video outlets, are visited by millions of viewers every day; but is their content as significant or groundbreaking as the *Time* article seems to claim, or do such sites and their content exist mostly to entertain? Some have argued that the availability of footage from the Iraq war typifies the potential informative power of online video sites. Certainly, in an era in which the Pentagon limits media access to military funerals (Tapper), and official reports of civilian casualties remain haphazard (and often contradictory), one can argue for the value of access to footage taken by American soldiers and Iraqi civilians in the war zone. Unfortunately, access to information does not necessarily equal interest. *New York Times* columnist Frank Rich wrote that a typical Internet search showed that "Britney Spears Nude on Beach" received over a million hits by YouTube's visitors, while "Iraq" clips were viewed by a little over twenty thousand users. It would seem, then, that online media exists primarily for entertainment. And it is difficult to see how watching fifteen-second clips of *I Love Lucy* or montages of Rocky Marciano's knockout punches changes the world for better or worse.

Likewise, *Time*'s assertion that YouTube serves as a powerful mirror into the life of the typical American seems overstated. Grossman claimed that "[y]ou can learn more about how Americans live just by looking at the backgrounds of YouTube videos—those rumpled bedrooms and toy-strewn basement

> Compelling critique of *Time*'s editors for being swayed by novelty of new Internet applications.

> Uses expert testimony to support critique.

> Refutes *Time*'s secondary argument that YouTube videos reveal 21st century lives.

recreation rooms—than you could from 1,000 hours of network television." Is it revelatory to learn that many people keep messy homes? Also, it must be remembered that an individual's control over content can prevent these glimpses into people's everyday lives from being truly spontaneous or accurate. The person behind the camcorder controls what he or she wants us to see.

Refutes claim that "you" are in control of information.

Finally, it should be noted that while the Internet has certainly made more information instantly available than ever before, in many countries this access falls under government control. In China, for example, search engines such as Google have been forced to purge links to any Web sites disapproved of by the government. As a result, it is difficult for the typical Chinese Internet user to find information about Tibet, student protests, or dissident groups such as Falun Gong (Thompson). In the United States, legislation such as the Child Online Protection Act of 1998 has sought to punish online providers of sexually explicit material (ACLU). Though such laws have been repeatedly struck down by the Supreme Court due to First Amendment concerns, many Web sites, including MySpace and YouTube, voluntarily police content that its administrators or users identify as sexually explicit or otherwise objectionable. How can one accept the claim that "you" have taken control of the flow of information when governments and service providers still have ultimate power over what is and isn't seen?

Establishes common ground with reader by acknowledging the difficulty of selecting a Person of the Year.

It would be difficult to identify single figures who dominated the events of 2006; rather, the continuing conflicts in Iraq and Afghanistan, the deepening diplomatic crises surrounding the nuclear ambitions of North Korea and Iran, and the sudden reversals of political fortunes in Washington involved numerous individuals, many of them anonymous, slogging through complex issues that are difficult to characterize in a simple way. Perhaps this complexity is the best explanation for *Time*'s baffling choice for Person of the Year. It does seem, however, that the rationale for the selection lacks reason, clarity, or meaning. For good or ill, a Person

Full statement of thesis refuting the choice of Person of the Year.

of the Year should actually have accomplished something significant. *Time*'s "you" has not really done so.

----------------------------------[new page]----------------------------------

Works Cited

American Civil Liberties Union. "ACLU Victorious in Defense of Online Free Speech." *American Civil Liberties Union*. American Civil Liberties Union, 22 Mar. 2007. Web. 5 Mar. 2008.

Arthur, Charles. "What Is the 1% Rule?" *guardian.co.uk*. Guardian News and Media Ltd., 20 Jul. 2006. Web. 5 Mar. 2008.

Grossman, Lev. "Time's Person of the Year: You." *Time.com*. Time Warner, 13 Dec. 2006. Web. 2 Mar. 2008.

Hochstein, Arthur, and Spencer Jones-Glasshouse. *Time* cover. *Time.com*. Time Warner, 13 Dec. 2006. Web. 2 Mar. 2008.

Mayfield, Antony. (2006, July 17). "0-60% in under 18 Months: YouTube Dominates Online Video." *Open*. N.p., 17 Jul. 2006. Web. 6 Mar. 2008.

Rich, Frank. "Yes, You Are the Person of the Year." *New York Times*. New York Times, 24 Dec. 2006. Web. 4 Mar. 2008.

Tapper, Jake. "Pentagon Limits Media Coverage of Funerals." *ABC News Online*. ABC News, 14 Nov. 2006. Web. 4 Mar. 2008.

Thompson, Clive. "Google's China Problem (and China's Google Problem)." *New York Times*. New York Times, 23 Apr. 2006. Web. 4 Mar. 2008.

"*Time*'s Person of the Year, 1927–2006." *Time.com*. Time Warner, 27 Nov. 2007. Web. 5 Mar. 2008.

Underlines the critique's importance by emphasizing that *Time*'s choice misleads readers into thinking that passive Internet users are accomplishing something.

Works Cited list begins on new page and is formatted according to MLA style.

12 Other Kinds of Assignments

12a Personal essays

The **personal essay** is literary, like a poem, a play, or a story. It feels meaningful to readers and relevant to their lives. It speaks in a distinctive voice. It is both compelling and memorable.

1. Making connections between your experiences and those of your readers

When you write a personal essay, you are exploring your experiences, clarifying your values, and composing a public self. The focus, however, does not need to be on you. You might write a personal essay about a tree in autumn, an encounter with a stranger, or an athletic event. The real topic is how these objects and experiences have become meaningful to you.

When we read a personal essay, we expect to learn more than the details of the writer's experience; we expect to see the connections between that experience and our own.

 TEXTCONNEX

Personal Writing and Social Networking Web Sites

In addition to writing personal essays for class, you may use the Web sites Facebook and MySpace for personal writing. Remember that these sites are networked so that you do not always know who is reading your information. Strangers, including prospective employers, often view people's profiles and make judgments.

2. Turning your essay into a conversation

Personal essayists usually use the first person (*I* and *we*) to create a sense that the writer and reader are engaged in the open-ended give-and-take of conversation. How you appear in this conversation—shy, belligerent, or friendly, for example—will be determined by the details you include in your essay as well as the connotations of the words you use. Consider how Meghan Daum represents herself in relation to both computer-literate and computer-phobic readers in the following excerpt from her personal essay "Virtual Love," which appeared in a 1997 issue of the *New Yorker:*

> The kindness pouring forth from my computer screen was bizarrely exhilarating, and I logged off and thought about it

for a few hours before writing back to express how flattered and "touched"—this was probably the first time I had ever used that word in earnest—I was by his message.

I am not what most people would call a computer person. I have no interest in chat rooms, news groups, or most Web sites. I derive a palpable thrill from sticking a letter in the United States mail.

Besides Daum's conversational stance, notice the emotional effect of her remark on the word *touched* and her choice of words connoting excitement: *pouring forth, exhilarating,* and *palpable thrill.*

3. Structuring your essay like a story

There are three common ways to narrate events and reflections:

- **Chronological sequence:** uses an order determined by clock time; what happened first is presented first, followed by what happened second, then third, and so on.

- **Emphatic sequence:** uses an order determined by the point you want to make; for emphasis, events and reflections are arranged from either least to most or most to least important.

- **Suspenseful sequence:** uses an order determined by the emotional effect the writer wants the essay to have on readers. To keep readers hanging, the essay may begin in the middle of things with a puzzling event, then flash back or go forward to clear things up. Some essays may even begin with the end and then flash back to recount how the writer came to that insight.

4. Letting details tell your story

It is in the details that the story takes shape. The details you emphasize, the words you choose, and the characters you create communicate the point of your essay. Often, it is not even necessary to state your thesis.

Consider, for example, the following passage by Gloria Ladson-Billings:

Mrs. Harris, my third-grade teacher, was quite a sharp dresser. She wore beautiful high-heeled shoes. Sometimes she switched to flats in the afternoon if her feet got tired, but every morning began with the click, click, click of her high heels as she greeted us up and down the rows. I wanted to dress the way Mrs. Harris did. I didn't want to wear old-lady comforters like Mrs. Benn's, and I certainly didn't want to wear worn-out loafers like those of my first-grade teacher, Miss Schwartz. I wanted to wear beautiful, shiny, high-heeled shoes like Mrs. Harris's. That was the way a teacher should look, I thought.

—GLORIA LADSON-BILLINGS, *The Dreamkeepers: Successful Teachers of African-American Children*

Ladson-Billings uses details to make her idea of a good teacher come alive for the reader. At one level—the literal—the "click, click, click" refers to the sound of Mrs. Harris's shoes. At another level, it represents the glamorous teacher. And at the most figurative level, the "click, click, click" evokes the kind of feminine power that the narrator both longs for and admires.

5. Connecting your experience to a larger issue

To demonstrate the significance of a personal essay to readers, writers usually connect their individual experience to a larger issue. Here, for example, are the closing lines of Daum's essay "Virtual Love":

> The world had proved to be too cluttered and too fast for us, too polluted to allow the thing we'd attempted through technology ever to grow on the earth. PFSlider and I had joined the angry and exhausted living. Even if we met on the street, we wouldn't recognize each other, our particular version of intimacy now obscured by the branches and bodies and falling debris that make up the physical world.

Notice how Daum relates the disappointment of her failed Internet romance with "PFSlider" to a larger social issue: the general contrast between cyberspace and material realities. Her point, however, is surprising; most people do not think of cyberspace as more "intimate"—or touching—than their everyday world of "branches and bodies."

👁 **12b** Lab reports in the experimental sciences

Scientists form hypotheses and plan new experiments as they observe, read, and write. When they work in the laboratory, they keep detailed notebooks. They also write and publish lab reports to share their discoveries with other scientists.

Lab reports usually include the following sections: Abstract, Introduction, Methods and Materials, Results, Discussion, Acknowledgments, and References. Start writing your report by drafting the methods and materials and results sections; then draft your introduction and discussion sections. Include a clearly stated hypothesis in your introduction. Finally, prepare the references section, the acknowledgments, and the abstract.

Follow the scientific conventions for abbreviations, symbols, and numbers. See if your textbook includes a list of acceptable abbreviations and symbols, or ask your professor where you might find such a list. Use numerals for dates, time, pages, figures, tables, and standard units of measurement. Spell out numbers between one and nine that are not part of a series of larger numbers.

1. Abstract

An **abstract** is a one-paragraph summary of your lab report. It answers these questions:

WRITING AFTER COLLEGE

Scientific Research

Research reports by professional scientists are published in journals such as *Science.* Here are some examples of scientific research:

- A biochemist tests the hypothesis that THC (the major active ingredient in marijuana) acts as an estrogen (a female hormone).
- A mechanical engineer tests the hypothesis that 50 pounds of force is sufficient to overcome the thermal contact resistance in the coupling joint of a mechanical switch designed for use on a rocket-borne telescope.

- What methods were used in the experiment?
- What variables were measured?
- What were the findings?
- What do the findings imply?

2. Introduction

In the introduction, state your topic, summarize prior research, and present your hypothesis.

Employ precise scientific terminology (*α-amylase*), and spell out the terms that you will later abbreviate (*gibbelleric acid [GA]*). Use the passive voice when describing objects of study that are more important than the experimenter. When appropriate, choose the active voice. (*For a discussion of active and passive voices, see Tab 9: Editing for Clarity, pp. 418–19.*) Use the present tense to state established knowledge ("the rye seed *produces*"); use the past tense to summarize the work of prior researchers ("Haberlandt *reported*"). The writer of the excerpt below cites sources using a superscript number system. (*For information on CSE style, see pp. 380–88.*)

www.mhhe.com/ awr3

For more on crafting introductions, go to

Writing > Paragraph/Essay Development > Introductions

> According to studies by Yomo,[1] Paleg,[2] and others,[3,4] barley seed embryos produce a gibbelleric acid (GA) which stimulates the release of hydrolytic enzymes, especially α-amylase. It is evident that these enzymes break down the endosperm, thereby making stored energy sources available to the germinating plant. What is not evident, however, is how GA actually works on the molecular level to stimulate the production of hydrolytic enzymes. As several experiments[5–8] have documented, GA has an RNA-enhancing effect. Is this general enhancement of RNA synthesis just a side effect of GA's action, or is it directly involved in the stimulation of α-amylase?

The first sentence names both a general topic, barley seed embryos, and a specific issue, GA's stimulation of hydrolytic enzymes. The last sentence poses a question that prepares readers for the hypothesis by focusing their attention on the role enhanced RNA synthesis plays in barley seed germination.

3. Methods and materials

Select the details that other scientists will need to replicate the experiment. Using the past tense, recount in chronological order what was done with specific materials.

4. Results

In this section, tell readers about the results that are relevant to your hypothesis, especially those that are statistically significant. Results may be relevant even if they are different from what you expected.

You might summarize results in a table or graph. For example, the graph in Figure 12.1, which plots the distance (in centimeters, y-axis) covered by a glider over a period of time (in seconds, x-axis), was used to summarize the results of an engineering assignment.

Every table and figure you include in a lab report must be referred to in the text. Point out relevant patterns the table or figure reveals. If you run statistical tests on your findings, do not make the tests themselves the focus of your writing. Refrain from interpreting why things happened the way they did.

> **Note:** Like the terms *correlated* and *random,* the term *significant* has a specific statistical meaning for scientists and should therefore be used in a lab report only in relation to the appropriate statistical tests.

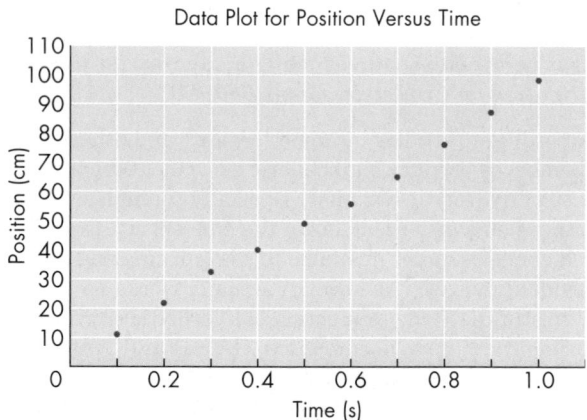

FIGURE 12.1 A graph used to summarize the results of an engineering assignment.

5. Discussion

In discussing your results, interpret your major findings by explaining how and why each finding does or does not confirm the original hypothesis. Connect your research with prior scientific research, and look ahead to potential future research.

6. Acknowledgments

In professional journals, most reports of experimental findings include a brief statement acknowledging those who assisted the author(s).

7. References

Include at the end of your report a listing of all manuals, books, and journal articles you consulted during the research and writing process. Use one of the citation formats developed by the Council of Science Editors (CSE style), unless your instructor prefers another format. (*See Tab 8: Other Documentation Styles.*)

12c Case studies in the social sciences

Social scientists are trained observers and recorders of individual and group behavior. Accurate observations are essential starting points for a case study, and writing helps researchers make clear and precise observations.

www.mhhe.com/ awr3

For online resources in various disciplines, go to

Learning > Links across the Curriculum

1. Choosing a topic that raises a question

In doing a case study, your purpose is to connect what you see and hear with issues and concepts in the social sciences. Choose a topic and turn it into a research question. Before engaging in field research, write down your hypothesis—a tentative answer to your research question—as well as some categories of behavior or other things to look for.

2. Collecting data

Make a detailed and accurate record of what you observe and when and how you observe it. Whenever you can, count or measure, and take down word-for-word what is said. Use frequency counts—the number of occurrences of specific, narrowly defined instances of behavior. If you are observing a classroom, for example, you might count the number of teacher-directed questions asked by several children. Your research methodologies course will introduce you to many ways to quantify data.

3. Assuming an unbiased stance

In a case study, you are presenting empirical findings, based on careful observation. Avoid value-laden terms and unsupported generalizations.

4. Discovering meaning in your data

As you review your notes, try to uncover connections, identify inconsistencies, and draw inferences. For example, ask yourself why a subject

Case Studies

Social scientists publish their findings in such journals as the *American Sociological Review, Harvard Business Review,* and *Journal of Marriage and the Family.* Take a look at these journals to see the work of professional social scientists:

- A developmental psychologist studies conflict resolution in children by observing a group of four-year-olds in a day care center.
- A sociologist studies how the state enforces gender stereotypes by observing and interviewing women in the juvenile justice system.

behaved in a specific way, and consider different explanations for the behavior. You will also need to draw on the techniques for quantitative analysis that you learn in a statistics course.

5. Presenting your findings in an organized way

There are two basic ways to present your findings in the body of a case study: as stages of a process and in analytic categories. Using stages of a process, a student studying gang initiation organized her observations chronologically into appropriate stages. If you organize your study this way, be sure to transform the minute-by-minute history of your observations into a pattern with distinct stages. Using analytic categories, a student observing the behavior of a preschool child organized his findings according to three categories from his textbook: motor coordination, cognition, and socialization.

> ***Note:*** Develop stages or categories while you are making your observations. In your paper, be sure to illustrate your stages or categories with material drawn from your observations—with descriptions of people, places, and behavior, as well as with well-chosen quotations.

6. Including a review of the literature, a statement of your hypothesis, and a description of your methodology in your introduction

The introduction presents the framework, background, and rationale for your study. Begin with the topic, and review related research, working your way to the specific question that your study addresses. Follow that with a statement of your hypothesis, accompanied by a de-

CHARTING the TERRITORY

Case Studies

You will find case studies used in a number of social science disciplines.

- **In sociology:** You may be asked to analyze a small group to which you have belonged or belong now. Your study will address such issues as the group's norms and values, cultural characteristics, and stratification and roles. Your audience will be your professor, who wants to see how your observations reflect current theories on group norms.

- **In nursing:** For a nursing class, you will note details of your care for a patient that corroborate or complicate what you have been taught to expect. Your audience will be the supervising nurse, who is interested in your interactions with the patient.

- **In education:** As a student teacher, you may closely observe and write about one student in the context of his or her socioeconomic and family background. Your audience will be the cooperating teacher, who seeks greater insight into the behavior of class members.

scription of your **methodology**—how, when, and where you made your observations and how you recorded them.

7. Discussing your findings in the conclusion

The conclusion of your case study should answer these three questions: (1) Did you find what you expected? (2) What do your findings show, or what is the bigger picture? and (3) What should researchers explore further?

👁 **12d** Essay exams

When you take an essay exam, you are pressed for time and uninterested in thinking about how to approach test-taking. If you spend some of your study time thinking about what you are expected to do on these tests, you may feel more confident during the test itself.

1. Preparing with the course and your instructor in mind

Consider the specific course as your writing context and the course's instructor as your audience:

- What questions or problems did your instructor explicitly or implicitly address?

Essay Exam Questions across the Curriculum

During finals week, you may be asked to respond to essay questions like the following:

1. Discuss the power of the contemporary presidency as well as the limits of that power. [*from a political science course*]

2. Compare and contrast the treatment of labor supply decisions in the economic models proposed by Greg Lewis and Gary Becker. [*from an economics course*]

3. Describe the observations that would be made in an alpha-particle scattering experiment if (a) the nucleus of an atom were negatively charged and the protons occupied the empty space outside the nucleus and (b) the electrons were embedded in a positively charged sphere. [*from a chemistry course*]

4. Examine the uses of caesura and enjambment in the following poem, and analyze their effect on the poem's rhythm. [*from a literature course*]

5. In 1800, was Thomas Jefferson a "dangerous radical"? Define your key terms and support your position with evidence from specific events, documents, and so on. [*from an American history course*]

- What frameworks did your instructor use to analyze topics?
- What key terms did your instructor repeatedly use during lectures and discussions?

2. Understanding your assignment

Essay exams are designed to test your knowledge, not just your memory. To study, create some essay questions that require you to do the following:

- **Explain** what you have learned in a clear, well-organized way. (*See question 1 in the box above.*)
- **Connect** what you know about one topic with what you know about another topic. (*See question 2 in the box above.*)
- **Apply** what you have learned to a new situation. (*See question 3 in the box above.*)
- **Interpret** the causes, effects, meanings, value, or potential of something. (*See question 4 in the box above.*)
- **Argue** for or against some controversial statement about what you have learned. (*See question 5 in the box above.*)

3. Planning your time

At the beginning of the exam, quickly look through the whole exam, and determine how much time you will spend on each part or question. You will want to move as quickly as possible through the questions with lower point values so that you can spend the bulk of your time responding to the questions that are worth the greatest number of points.

4. Responding to short-answer questions by showing the significance of the information

The most common type of short-answer question is the identification question: Who or what is X? In answering questions of this sort, present just enough information to show that you understand X's significance within the context of the course. For example, if you are asked to identify "Judith Loftus" on an American literature exam, don't just write, "character who knows Huckleberry Finn is a boy." Instead, craft one or two sentences that identify Loftus as a character Huckleberry Finn encounters while he is disguised as a girl; by telling Huck how she knows that he is not a girl, Loftus compels readers to think in complex ways about gender.

5. Being tactical in responding to essay questions

Keep in mind that essay questions usually ask you to do something specific. Begin by determining precisely what you are being asked to do. Before you write anything, read the question—all of it—and circle key words.

> Explain two ways in which Picasso's *Guernica* evokes war's terrifying destructiveness.

To answer this question, you need to focus on two of the painting's features, such as coloring and composition, not on Picasso's life.

6. Using the essay question to structure your response

Usually, you will be able to transform the question itself into the thesis of your answer. If you are asked to agree/disagree with the Federalists' characterization of Thomas Jefferson in the election of 1800, you might begin with this thesis:

> In the election of 1800, the Federalists characterized Jefferson as a dangerous radical. Although Jefferson's ideas were radical for the times, they were not dangerous to the republic.

Take a minute or two to list evidence for each of your main points, and then write the essay.

7. Checking your work

Save a few minutes to read through your completed answer, looking for words you might have omitted or key sentences that make no sense. Make corrections neatly.

SAMPLE ESSAY TEST RESPONSE

A student's response to an essay question in an art appreciation course appears below. Both the question and the student's notes are provided.

QUESTION

Both of these buildings (Figure 1 and Figure 2) feature dome construction. Identify the buildings, and discuss the differences in the visual effects created by the different dome styles.

STUDENT'S NOTES

Fig 1: Pantheon. Plain outside—concrete, can barely see dome. Dramatic inside—dome opens up huge interior space. Oculus to sky: light, air, rain. Coffered ceiling.

Fig 2: Taj Mahal. Dramatic exterior—dome set high, marble, reflecting pool, exterior lines go up. Inside not meant to be visited.

STUDENT'S ANSWER

Answers identification question and states thesis.

Key points supported by details.

The Pantheon (Figure 1) and the Taj Mahal (Figure 2) are famous for their dome construction. The styles of the domes are dramatically different, however, resulting in dramatically different visual effects.

The Pantheon, which was built by the Romans as a temple to the gods, looks very plain on the exterior. The dome is barely visible from the outside, and it is made of a dull grey concrete. Inside the building, however, the dome produces an amazing effect. It opens up a huge space within the building, unobstructed by interior supports. The sides of the dome are coffered, and those recessed rectangles both lessen the weight of the dome and add to its visual beauty. Most dramatically, the top of the dome is open to

FIGURE 1

FIGURE 2

the sky, allowing sun or rain to pour into the building. This opening is called the oculus, meaning "eye" (to or of Heaven).

The Taj Mahal, which was built by a Muslim emperor of India as a tomb for his wife, is the opposite of the Pantheon—dazzling on the outside and plain on the inside. The large central dome is set up high on the base so that it can be seen from far away. It is made of white marble, which reflects light beautifully. The dome is surrounded by other structures that frame it and draw attention to its exterior—a long reflecting pond and four minarets. Arches and smaller domes on the outside of the building repeat the large dome's shape. Because the Taj Mahal's dome is tall and narrow, however, it does not produce the kind of vast interior space of the shorter, squatter Pantheon dome. Indeed, the inside of the Taj Mahal is not meant to be visited. Unlike the Pantheon, the dome of the Taj Mahal is intended to be admired from the outside.

Uses specialized terms from course.

Sets up comparison.

Key point supported by details.

Overall comparison as a brief conclusion.

12e Coauthored projects

A project is coauthored when more than one person is responsible for producing it. In many fields, working collaboratively is essential. Here are some suggestions to help you make the most of this challenge:

- Working with your partners, decide on some ground rules, including meeting times, deadlines, and ways of reconciling differences. Will the majority rule, or will some other principle prevail? Is there an interested and respected third party who can be consulted if the group's dynamics break down?

- Will the group meet primarily online or in person? See the box below for guidelines for online communication.

- Divide the work fairly so that everyone has a part to contribute to the project. Keep in mind that each group member should do some researching, drafting, revising, and editing. Responsibility for taking notes at meetings should rotate.

- In your personal journal, record, analyze, and evaluate the intellectual and interpersonal workings of the group as you see and experience them. If the group's dynamics begin to break down, seek the assistance of a third party.

- After each group member has completed his or her assigned part or subtopic, gather the whole group to weave the parts together and create a focused piece of writing with a consistent voice. This is the point at which group members usually need to negotiate with one another. Although healthy debate is good for a project, tact is essential.

TEXTCONNEX

For Coauthoring Online

Computer networks make it easy for two or more writers to co-author texts. Wikis allow writers to contribute to a common structure and edit one another's work. Most courseware (such as Blackboard) includes chat rooms and public space for posting and commenting on drafts. Word-processing software also allows writers to make tracked changes in files.

If your group meets online, make sure a transcript of the discussion is saved. If you exchange ideas via e-mail, you automatically will have a record of how the piece developed and how well the group worked together. Archive these transcripts and e-mails into designated folders. In all online communications, be especially careful with your tone. Without the benefit of facial expression and other cues, the writer can easily misinterpret even the most constructive criticism.

13 Oral Presentations

Preparing an oral presentation, like preparing any text, is a process. Consider your audience and purpose as you choose the focus and level of your topic. Gather information; decide on the main idea of your presentation; think through the organization; and choose visuals that support your points.

13a Plan and shape your oral presentation.

1. Considering the interests, background knowledge, and attitudes of your audience

If your audience is composed of your classmates, you will have the advantage of knowing how much background knowledge they have and what their intellectual interests are. Do you want to intensify your audience's commitment to what they already think, provide new and clarifying information, provoke more analysis and understanding of the issue, or change what the audience believes about something?

If you are addressing an unfamiliar audience, ask the people who invited you to speak to fill you in on the audience's interests and expectations. You also can adjust your speech once you get in front of the actual audience, making your language more or less technical, for example, or offering additional examples to illustrate points.

2. Working within the time allotted to your presentation

Gauge how many words you speak per minute by reading a passage aloud at a conversational pace (about 120–150 words per minute is ideal). Be sure to time your presentation when you practice it.

13b Draft your presentation with the rhetorical situation in mind.

www.mhhe.com/awr3

For more on crafting introductions, go to

Writing >
Paragraph/Essay
Development >
Introductions

1. Making your opening interesting

A strong opening both sets the speaker at ease and gains the audience's confidence and attention. Try out several approaches to your introduction to see what gets the best reactions during rehearsal. Stories, brief quotations, striking statistics, and surprising statements are good attention getters. Craft an introduction that lets your listeners know what they have to gain from your presentation—for example, new information or new perspectives on a subject of common interest.

2. Making the focus and organization of your presentation explicit

Select two or three ideas that you most want your audience to hear—and remember. Make these ideas the focus of your presentation, and

153

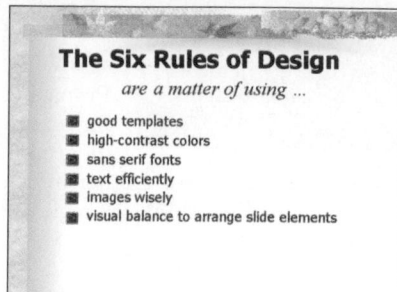

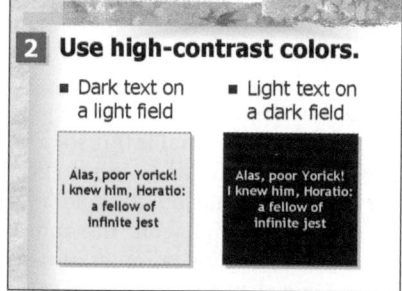

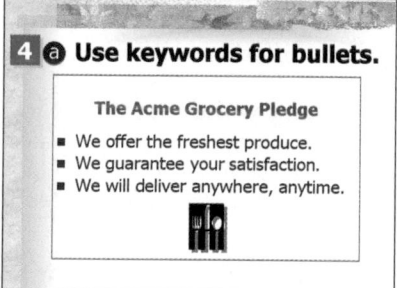

FIGURE 13.1 Guidelines for preparing effective PowerPoint slides.

let your audience know what to expect by previewing the content of your presentation—"I intend to make three points about fraternities on campus"—and then listing the three points.

The phrase "to make three points" signals a topical organization. Other common organizational patterns, include chronological (*at first . . . later . . . in the end*), causal (*because of that . . . then this follows*), and problem-solution (*given the situation . . . then this set of proposals*). A question-answer format also works well, either as an overall strategy or as part of another organizational pattern.

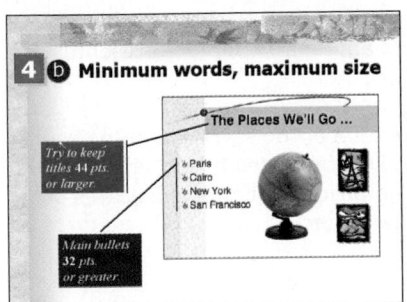

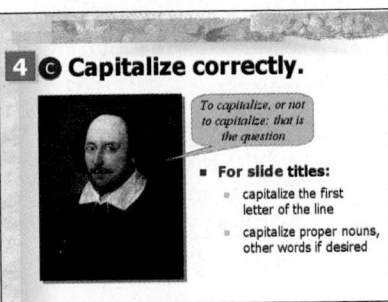

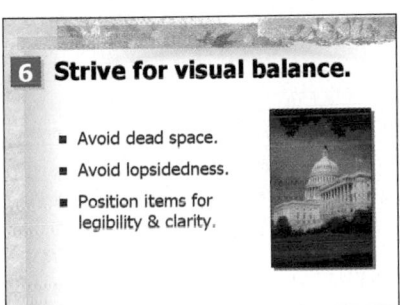

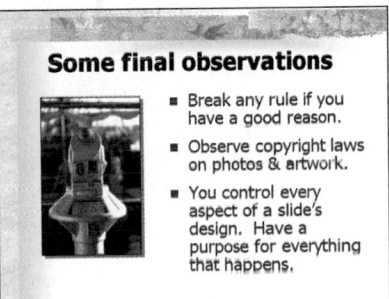

3. Being direct

What your audience hears and remembers has as much to do with how you communicate your message as it does with what you say. Use a direct, simple style:

- Choose basic sentence structures.
- Repeat key terms.
- Pay attention to the pace and rhythm of your speech.
- Don't be afraid to use the pronouns *I, you,* and *we.*

Notice how applying these principles transforms the following written sentence into a group of sentences appropriate for oral presentation:

WRITTEN

Although the claim that the position of the stars can help people predict the future has yet to be substantiated by either an ample body or an exemplary piece of empirical research, advocates of astrology persist in pressing the claim.

ORAL

Your sign says a lot about you. So say advocates of astrology. But what evidence do we have that the position of the stars helps people predict the future? Do we have lots of empirical research or even one really good study? The answer is, "Not yet."

4. Using visual aids

www.mhhe.com/
awr3

For an interactive tutorial on using PowerPoint, go to

Writing >
PowerPoint
Tutorial

Slides, posters, objects, video clips, and music help make your focus explicit. Avoid oversimplifying your ideas, and be sure any multimedia elements fit your purpose and audience.

Presentation software such as PowerPoint can help you stay focused while you are speaking. The twelve PowerPoint slides in Figure 13.1 on pages 154–55 offer advice on how to design effective slides for a presentation. (*For more on using presentation software to incorporate multimedia elements into a presentation, see Chapter 14: Multimedia Writing, pp. 161–63.*)

5. Concluding memorably

www.mhhe.com/
awr3

For more information on conclusions, go to

Writing >
Paragraph/Essay
Development >
Conclusions

Try to make your ending truly memorable: return to that surprising opener, play with the words of your opening quotation, look at the initial image from another angle, or reflect on the story you have told. Make sure your listeners are aware that you are about to end your presentation, using such signal phrases as "in conclusion" or "let me end by saying," if necessary. Keep your conclusion short to hold the audience's attention.

13c Prepare for your presentation.

1. Deciding whether to use notes or a written script

When giving your talk, make eye contact with your listeners to monitor their responses and adjust your message accordingly. For most occasions, it is inappropriate to write out everything you want to say and then read it word for word. Write out only those parts of your presentation where precise wording counts, such as quotations.

In some scholarly or formal settings, precise wording may be necessary, especially if your oral presentation is to be published or if your remarks will be quoted by others. Sometimes the setting for your presentation may be so formal or the audience may be so large that a script feels necessary. In such instances, do the following:

- Triple-space the typescript of your text.
- Avoid carrying sentences over from one page to another.
- Mark your manuscript for pauses, emphasis, and the pronunciation of proper names.

2. Rehearsing, revising, and polishing

Whether you are using an outline or a script, practice your presentation aloud. Adjust transitions that don't work, points that need further development, and sections that are too long. After you have settled on the content of your speech and can project it comfortably, focus on polishing the style of your delivery. Ask your friends to watch and listen to your rehearsal. Check that your body posture is straight but relaxed, that your voice is loud and clear, and that you are making eye contact around the room. Time your final rehearsals, adding and cutting material as necessary.

3. Accepting nervousness as normal

The adrenaline surge you feel before a presentation can actually invest your talk with positive energy. Practice and revise your presentation until it flows smoothly, and make sure that you have a strong opener to get you through the first, most difficult moments of the speech. Remember that other people cannot always tell that you are nervous.

14 Multimedia Writing

Multimedia writing combines words with images, video, or audio into a single composition. The most common form of multimedia writing is the combination of words and still visuals—such as photographs, maps, charts, or graphs—discussed in many chapters of this handbook. Another form is an oral presentation with any kind of visual support, from a diagram on a blackboard to a PowerPoint slide show (*see Chapter 13, Oral Presentations*). Digital technology also allows writers to create works that combine written words with sound, video, and animation. You probably have used social networking Web sites such as Facebook and MySpace, which let users integrate text, images, and other multimedia elements.

Like any form of writing, multimedia writing allows you to convey a message to a particular audience for a particular purpose—to inform, to interpret, or to persuade. A video or audio segment—like a photograph, map, or chart—must support this purpose in a way that is appropriate to the situation.

14a   Learn about tools for creating multimedia texts.

Multimedia writing can take a variety of forms and can be created with a variety of software tools. Here are a few options:

- Most word processors allow you to integrate still visuals with text in a single document, and many also make it possible to write text that permits readers to connect to various files—including audio, image, and video files (*see 14b and 14c*).

- Most presentation software packages similarly allow you to accompany a presentation with audio and video files as well as still visuals (*see 14d*).

- A variety of programs and Web-based tools allow you to create your own **Web pages** and **Web sites,** which can include a wide range of multimedia features (*see 14e*).

- You can create a **Weblog (blog),** on which, in addition to your written entries, you can post visuals and other multimedia files and link to files on other blogs and Web sites (*see 14f*). You also can collaborate with other writers on a **wiki.**

👁 14b   Combine text and image using a word-processing program to analyze images.

Two types of multimedia assignments you might be called on to write are image analyses and imaginary stories.

1. Composing image analyses

You may be called on to analyze a single image such as an intriguing painting from a museum (possibly viewed online). In this case, your two tasks are to describe the picture as fully as possible, using adjectives, comparisons, and words that help readers focus on the picture and the details that compose it; and, most importantly, to analyze the argument the picture seems to be making.

2. Imagining narratives

Sometimes a writer tries to imagine the story behind an evocative photograph. Often this is as much an expression of the writer as it is a statement about the photograph.

Some photographs, like the one in Figure 14.1, taken by photojournalist Thomas Hoepker on September 11, 2001, connect private life and public events. On the morning of the catastrophe, Hoepker drove across

FIGURE 14.1 New York City, September 11, 2001.

SOURCE: © Thomas Hoepker/Magnum.

New York City's East River from Manhattan to Brooklyn, with the intention of shooting a panoramic view of the burning World Trade Center towers. He took this photo of five young people who, in the photographer's opinion, "didn't seem to care." When David Plotz, deputy editor of the online magazine *Slate,* saw the photo, he disagreed and called for a response from any of the people in the photograph <http://www.slate.com/id/2149508>. Walter Sipser, one of the photograph's subjects, wrote to *Slate,* saying that "we were in a profound state of shock" <http://www.slate.com/id/2149578/>. What do you think this photograph indicates?

If you have read W. H. Auden's poem "Musée des Beaux Arts," or seen the painting described in the poem, Pieter Breughel's "Fall of Icarus" (Figure 14.2 on p. 160), you may see a telling comparison between Hoepker's interpretation of the reaction of the photographic subjects to 9/11 and the response of those who observed "a boy falling out of the sky." Compare the composition of Hoepker's photo with Breughel's painting. Hoepker himself has wondered about "the devious lie of a snapshot" <http://www.slate.com/id/2149675>. In light of Sipser's remarks, what might Hoepker mean by that?

Musée des Beaux Arts
by W. H. Auden

About suffering they were never wrong,
The Old Masters; how well, they understood
Its human position; how it takes place
While someone else is eating or opening a window or just walking
    dully along;

FIGURE 14.2 "Fall of Icarus" by Pieter Breughel. Only Icarus's leg can be seen in the water between the closest boat and the shore.

How, when the aged are reverently, passionately waiting
For the miraculous birth, there always must be
Children who did not specially want it to happen, skating
On a pond at the edge of the wood:
They never forgot
That even the dreadful martyrdom must run its course
Anyhow in a corner, some untidy spot
Where the dogs go on with their doggy life and the torturer's horse
Scratches its innocent behind on a tree.
In Breughel's Icarus, for instance: how everything turns away
Quite leisurely from the disaster; the ploughman may
Have heard the splash, the forsaken cry,
But for him it was not an important failure; the sun shone
As it had to on the white legs disappearing into the green
Water; and the expensive delicate ship that must have seen
Something amazing, a boy falling out of the sky,
had somewhere to get to and sailed calmly on.

14c Use a word-processing program to create a hypertext essay.

Writers create multimedia hypertext essays using word processors, Web development software, blogs, or wikis. Links in the document take readers to other files, including text, image, audio, and video files. Links can take several forms:

- **Internal links** connect from one place in a document to another place in the same document, or to other files stored on the writer's computer or storage device (CD, DVD, or flash drive).

- **External links** connect to Web sites or files on the Internet.

As with any evidence, you must show the relevance of multimedia files to the audience and purpose of the essay. The files can either complement the essay's verbal claims or, like a good chart or graph, support the claims directly. For example, you might include links to video files of several presidents delivering their inaugural addresses for a political science project. These links might simply complement your thesis, or they might provide direct evidence for an important point about, say, a particular president's delivery. However, unless your assignment includes specific directions to emphasize linked material as evidence, think of it as supplemental to your written claims.

If you have never created a hypertext essay, start with a limited set of links that you connect to your audience and purpose. You can create internal links to the full information about works on your works-cited page, to any assignments that are related to your current topic, to tangential material that you collected while working on the essay, or to a file in which you raise additional questions about your topic. You can create external links to works on your topic written by your classmates or to background material on the Web.

> *Caution:* When you revise your hypertext essay, be sure to check all links to make sure they are relevant and functioning correctly. Also, if your essay includes internal links to files on your computer, be sure to include those files with the file for the essay when you submit it to your instructor.

👁 14d Use presentation software to create multimedia presentations.

www.mhhe.com/ awr3

For an interactive tutorial on using PowerPoint, go to

Writing > PowerPoint Tutorial

Presentation software makes it possible to incorporate audio, video, and animation into a talk. It can also be used to create a multimedia composition that viewers can go through on their own.

1. Using presentation software for an oral presentation

Presentation slides that accompany a talk should identify major points and display information in a visually effective way. Remember that slides support your talk, but they do not replace it (nor should you simply read them aloud). Limit the amount of information on each slide, and plan to show each slide for about one minute. Use bulleted lists and phrases rather than full sentences. Make fonts large enough to be seen by your audience: titles should be in 44-point type or larger, subheads in 32-point type or larger. High-contrast color schemes and sufficient blank space between slide elements will also increase the visibility of your presentation. (*See Chapter 13: Oral Presentations, pp. 153–57.*)

2. Using presentation software to create an independent composition

With presentation software, you can also create compositions that run on their own or at the prompting of viewers. This capability is especially useful in distance-learning settings, in which students attend class and share information electronically.

3. Preparing a slide presentation

Begin thinking about slides while you plan what you are going to say. As you decide on the words for the talk or composition, you will think of visuals that support your points; and, as you work out the visuals, you are likely to see additional points you can make and adjust your presentation accordingly. Every aspect of your slides—such as fonts, images, and animations—should support your purpose and appeal to your audience. Never use multimedia elements for mere decoration. The following guidelines apply:

- **Decide on a slide format.** Before you create your slides, establish their basic appearance. What background color will they have? What typeface or typefaces? What design elements such as borders and rules? Will the templates provided by the software fit your talk? If not, modify them or start from scratch, using the templates as a basis for comparison as you develop your design.

www.mhhe.com/ awr3

For more on designing documents, go to

Writing > Writing Web Links > Document and Web Design

- **Incorporate visuals into your presentation when appropriate.** Select visuals to support your purpose. For example, you might use a chart or graph to summarize quantitative information. (*For more on choosing visuals, see Chapter 5, pp. 54–56.*)

- **Incorporate other multimedia elements.** Slides can also include audio files. You might record interviews and other background information for some slides in an independent composition. Or, for a presentation on music, you might insert audio files to show how a type of music has developed over time. Presentation slides can also include video files and **animation**—visuals that have moving parts or that change over time. An animated diagram of the process of cell division, for example, could help illustrate a presentation on cellular biology. As you would for any other source, provide documentation if you are using files that belong to others. If you plan to make your presentation publicly available online, obtain permission from the copyright holder to use these items. (*For more on finding and citing multimedia, see Tab 5: Researching, pp. 219–26.*)

■ **Incorporate hypertext links.** You might use an internal link within a slide sequence to jump to another slide that illustrates or explains a particular point, enlivening the presentation and helping the audience remember the information. External links to files on the Web can allow you to showcase resources for your audience. Be careful not to overload your presentation with external links, however, because they can undermine the coherence of a presentation. They can also take a long time to load. If you use them, run through your presentation on site so that your links are cached.

> *Caution:* If you plan to make external links part of your presentation, make sure that you have a functioning Web browser on your computer and that a fast connection to the Internet is available where you will be giving the presentation. Bring a backup copy of the files, if possible.

4. Reviewing the presentation

Carefully review your slides to make sure they work together coherently:

■ **Check how slides in your software's slide sorter window proceed one to the next.** Do you have an introductory slide? Do you need to include transitional effects, such as fades or animation, that reveal the content of a slide item by item? Some of these transitional effects permit audio—would that support your purpose? (Use transitional effects to support your rhetorical situation.) Do you have a concluding slide?

■ **Check to make sure the slides are consistent with the script of your talk.** If the slides are intended as an independent document, do they include enough explanation and an adequate introduction and conclusion?

■ **Check the arrangement of your slides.** You might try printing them as paper handouts and spreading them out over a large surface, rearranging them if necessary. You can then return to the computer to implement needed changes.

■ **Check the slides to be sure they have a unified look.** Make sure, for example, that all the slides have the same background and that each uses the same typeface(s) in the same way. Are headers and bullets consistent?

👁 **14e** Create a Web site.

Thanks to Web editing software, it is now almost as easy to create a Web site and post it on the Internet as it is to write and print a paper. Web-based businesses like Google provide server space for hosting sites and

www.mhhe.com/ awr3

For more on designing Web sites, go to

Writing > Writing Web Links > Document and Web Design

CHECKLIST

Planning a Web Site

When you begin your Web composition, consider these questions:

- [ ] What is your purpose?

- [ ] Who are your viewers, and what are their needs? Will the site be limited by password protection to a specific group of viewers, or should you plan for a broader audience?

- [ ] What type of content will you include on your site: images, audio files, video files?

- [ ] Will you need to get permission to use any visuals or other files that you obtain from other sources?

- [ ] What design elements will appeal to your audience and complement your purpose and content?

- [ ] Given your technical knowledge, amount of content, and deadline, how much time should you allot to each stage of building your site?

- [ ] Will the site be updated and, if so, how frequently?

offer tools for creating Web pages. Many schools also make server space available for student Web sites.

To be effective, a Web site must be well designed and serve a well-defined purpose for its audience. In creating a Web site, you will need to plan your site, draft content, select visuals, revise, and edit, just as you would for any kind of composition. (*See Tab 2: Writing and Designing Texts.*) The following sections offer guidelines for making some of the unique decisions you will encounter when composing for the Web.

1. Planning a structure for your site

Like most paper documents, a Web site can have a linear structure, where one page leads to the next. Because of the hyperlinked nature of this medium, however, a site can also be organized in a hierarchy or with a number of pages that connect to a central page, or hub, like the spokes of a wheel. The diagrams in Figure 14.3 illustrate these two possible structures.

To choose the structure that will work best for your site, consider how you expect visitors to use it. For the site about historic buildings, visitors intrigued by this topic will probably want to explore. For the site about resources for caregivers, visitors will probably want to find

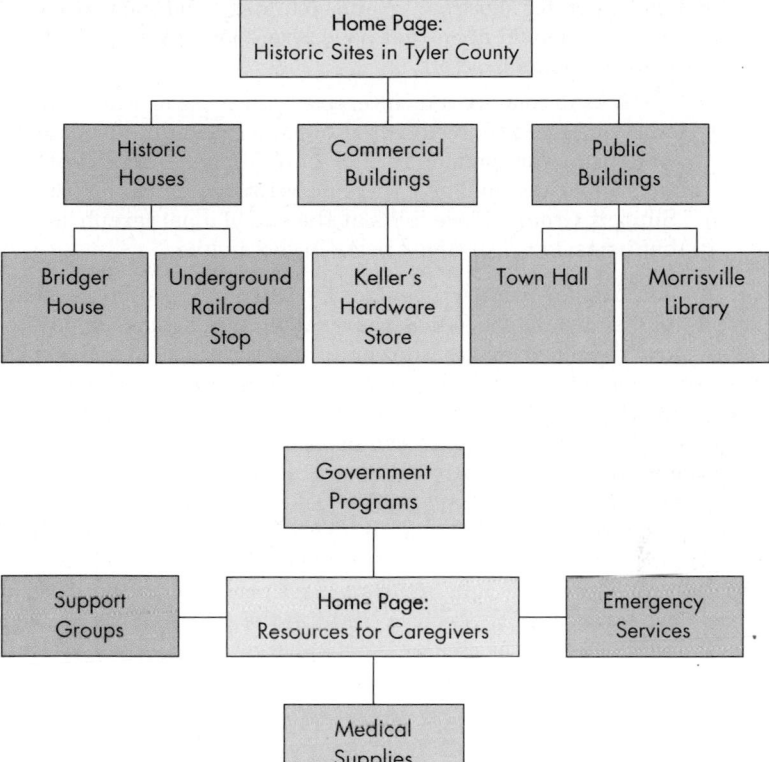

FIGURE 14.3 Hierarchical (top) and hub structure (bottom).

specific information quickly. The structure of each site accommodates its users' needs.

To determine your site's structure, try mapping out the connections among its pages by arranging them in a storyboard. Represent each page with an index card, and experiment with different possible configurations. How will readers navigate through the site?

2. Gathering content for your site

The content for a Web site will usually consist of written work along with links and graphics. Depending on your topic and purpose, you might also provide audio files, video files, and even animation.

There are some special requirements for written content that appears on a Web site:

- Readers neither expect nor want lengthy text explanations. Instead, they want to find the link or information they are looking for quickly.

- Readers prefer short paragraphs (chunks), and the text for each page should fit on that page. Avoid long passages that require readers to scroll.

- Use links to connect your interests with those of others and to provide extra sources of credible and relevant information. Avoid using the command "Click here." Instead, make links part of your text and give them descriptive names such as "Support Group." Place links at the end of a paragraph so that users do not navigate away in the middle.

As you prepare your written text, gather any graphics, photographs, and audio and video files that you plan to include. Some sites allow you to download images, and some images, such as historical photographs available through the Library of Congress, are in the public domain. Another useful site for visual, audio, and video files is Creative Commons <http://search.creativecommons.org>. This site directs you to material licensed with Creative Commons so that certain blanket uses are permitted. Check the license of the material to see how it may be used. Be sure to cite any material that you do not generate yourself. If your Web text will be public, request permission for use of any material not in the public domain unless the site says permission is not needed. To request permission, check for a credit in the source. If the name or contact information of the creator is not apparent, e-mail the sponsor of the site and ask. (*For information on citing visual and multimedia material, see Tabs 6–8.*).

3. Designing Web pages to capture and hold interest
On helpful Web sites, you will find such easy-to-follow links as "what you'll find here," FAQs (frequently asked questions), or "list of those involved." In planning the structure and content of your site, keep your readers' convenience in mind.

4. Designing a readable site with a unified look
The design of your site should suit its purpose and intended audience: a government site to inform users about copyright law will present a basic, uncluttered design that focuses attention on the text. Readers generally appreciate a site with a unified look. "Sets" or "themes" are readily available at free graphics sites offering banners, navigation buttons, and other design elements. You also can create visuals with a graphics program or scan your personal art and photographs. Design your home page to complement your other pages, or your readers may lose track of where they are in the site—and lose their interest in staying.

- Consider including a site map—a Web page that serves as a table of contents for your entire site.

Understanding Web Jargon

- **Browser:** software that allows you to access and view material on the Web. When you identify a site you want to see on the Web by typing in a URL (see below), your browser (*Microsoft Internet Explorer, Mozilla Firefox,* or *Safari,* for example) tells a distant computer—a **server**—to send that site to you.

- **JPEG and GIF:** formats for photographs and other visuals that are recognized by browsers. Photographs that appear on a Web site should be saved in JPEG format (Joint Photographic Experts Group, pronounced *jay-peg.*) The file extension is .jpg or .jpeg. Clip art should be saved as GIF files (Graphics Interchange Format, pronounced like *gift* without the *t.*)

- **HTML/XML:** hypertext markup language/extensible markup language. These languages tag or code text so that your browser can rebuild a document from the compressed files that are sent through the Internet. Instead of working directly in HTML or XML, many people use programs such as *FrontPage, PageMill, Dreamweaver, Nvue,* and *Mozilla* that provide a WYSIWYG (What You See Is What You Get) interface for creating Web pages. Most word processors have a "Save as HTML" option.

- **URL:** uniform resource locator or Web address. When you type or paste a URL into your Web browser, you are sending a request through your browser to another computer, asking it to transfer data to your computer.

- Establish a design template, including background color and fonts. Choose a uniform location for material that will appear on each page.

- Select elements such as buttons, signs, animations, sounds, and backgrounds with a consistent design suited to your purpose and audience.

- Use colors that provide adequate contrast, white space, and sans serif fonts to make text easy to read. Pages that are too busy are not visually compelling. (*For more on design, see Tab 2: Writing and Designing Texts, pp. 95–101.*)

- Leave time to find appropriate image, audio, and video files created by others, and to obtain permission to use them.

- Avoid using overly wide lines of text; readers find them difficult to process.

The home page and interior page shown in Figure 14.4 on the next page illustrate some of these design considerations.

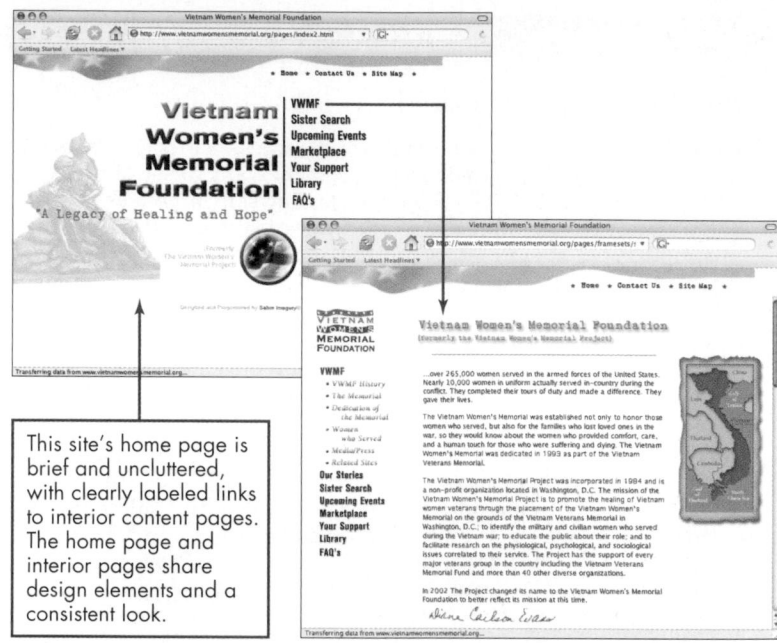

The text box within the figure reads:

This site's home page is brief and uncluttered, with clearly labeled links to interior content pages. The home page and interior pages share design elements and a consistent look.

FIGURE 14.4 Home page and an interior page from the Web site of the Vietnam Women's Memorial Foundation.

5. Designing a Web site that is easy to access and navigate

Help readers find their way to the areas of the site they want to visit. Make it easy for them to take interesting side trips without wasting their time or losing their way. Here are some guidelines to help you accomplish this:

- **Identify your Web site on each page, and provide a link to the home page.** Remember that readers will not always enter your Web site through the home page. Give the title of the site on each page and provide an easy-to-spot link to your home page.

- **Provide a navigation bar on each page.** A **navigation bar** can be a simple line of links that you copy and paste at the top or bottom of each page. A navigation bar on each page makes it easy for visitors to move from the site's home page to other pages and back again.

- **Use graphics that load quickly.** Limit the size of your images to no more than 40 kilobytes so that they will load faster.

TEXTCONNEX

Web Resources for Site Design and Construction

- *Webmonkey:* <http://www.webmonkey.com>
- *American Council of the Blind*—information about creating Web pages for people with disabilities <http://acb.org/accessible-formats.html>

- **Use graphics judiciously.** Your Web site should not depend on graphics alone to make its message clear and interesting. Graphics should be used to reinforce your purpose. The designers of the Library of Congress Web site (*Figure 14.5*) use icons such as musical notation and a map to help visitors navigate the site. Avoid clip art, which often looks unprofessional.

- **Be aware of the needs of visitors with disabilities.** Provide alternate ways of accessing any visual or auditory information.

FIGURE 14.5 The home page of the Web site of the Library of Congress.

Designing a Web Site Collaboratively

If you are asked to create a Web site as part of a class assignment, try to make arrangements to work with a partner or a small group. Periodically, you can invite peers to look over the writing you contribute and make suggestions. At the same time, you will be able to provide the project with the benefit of your multicultural viewpoint.

Include text descriptions of visuals, media files, and tables (for users of screen-reader software or text-only browsers). All audio files should have captions and full transcriptions. (*See Tab 2: Writing and Designing Texts, pp. 100–01.*)

6. Using peer feedback to revise your Web site

Before publishing your site, to be read by anyone in the world, proofread your text carefully, and ask friends to look at your site in different browsers and share their responses with you. Make sure your site reflects favorably on your abilities.

14f   Create and interact with Weblogs.

Weblogs (blogs) are part of Web 2.0, a term applied to Web sites that facilitate creativity and interaction among users. Blogs are Web sites that can be continually updated. Readers usually can post comments to entries. Some blogs provide a space where a group of writers can discuss each other's work and ideas.

In schools, classes have used blogs to discuss issues, organize work, compile portfolios, and gather and store material and commentary. Figure 14.6 depicts a blog for an English class at Queens College. Here, instructor Jason Tougow and his students discuss the title of their upcoming conference.

In general, blogs have become important as vehicles for public discussion and commentary. For example, most presidential campaigns in

TEXTCONNEX

Blog Resources

Blogs 101—The New York Times—directory of blogs by topic
<http://www.nytimes.com/ref/technology/blogs_101.html>
Technorati—search engine for blogs <http://www.technorati.com>

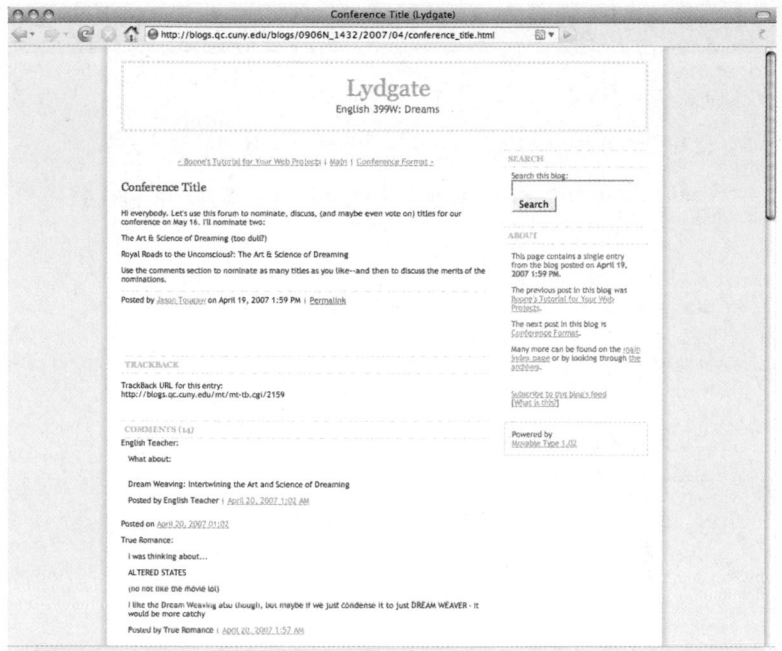

FIGURE 14.6 The blog for Jason Tougow's English course. Here, a student comments on the instructor's post.

2008 maintained blogs on their Web sites, and many "conventional" news sources, like the *New York Times,* link to their own blogs on their Web sites. Compared to other types of publications and academic writing, blogs have an informal tone that combines information, entertainment, and personal opinion.

To begin blogging, set up a blog site with a server such as blogger .com or wordpress.com. You may at first want to confine yourself to a very specific purpose before launching into wide-ranging commentary.

Some social networking sites such as MySpace also allow users to create blogs. Social networking sites sometimes can be used to explore a topic via discussion groups, find an expert on a particular subject, or conduct an informal poll (if campus policy permits).

CHECKLIST

Setting up a Blog

When you begin your blog, consider these questions:

- [ ] What is your purpose? How will your blog's visual design reflect that purpose?

- [ ] To whom will you give access? Should the blog be public for all to see or be limited to a specific group of viewers?

- [ ] Do you want to allow others to post to your blog and/or comment on your posts?

- [ ] Do you want to set up a schedule of postings or a series of reminders that will cue you to post?

- [ ] Do you know others with blogs? Do you want to link to their sites? Should they link to yours and comment on it?

Caution: Blogs and profiles on social networking sites are more or less public depending on the level of access they allow. Do not post anything (including photographs and videos) that you would not want parents, teachers, and prospective employers to view.

TEXTCONNEX

Wikis

A wiki is another kind of Web-interfaced database that can be updated easily. While a blog typically is managed by one person, a wiki allows multiple writers to post and edit content. Thus, wikis are useful spaces for collaborative authoring and often are used to compile research.

One well-known wiki is the online encyclopedia Wikipedia (*see Chapter 19, p. 207*). Many instructors do not consider Wikipedia a credible source for papers because almost anyone can create or edit its content. Changes are not immediately or always reviewed by experts before appearing on the site. Since the information provided isn't always correct, confirm it with another source. Some other wikis, such as Citizendium, rely on experts in a discipline to write and edit articles.

The aim of education must be the
training of independently acting and
thinking individuals, who, however, see in
the service of the community their
highest life problem.

—ALBERT EINSTEIN

Writing beyond College

4 Writing beyond College

 Section dealing with visual rhetoric. For a complete listing, see the Quick Guide to Key Resources at the back of this book.

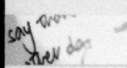

WRITING OUTCOMES

Tab 4: Writing beyond College
This section will help you answer questions such as:

Rhetorical Knowledge
How can I design brochures and newsletters to reach a particular community? **(15b)**
What do I need to consider when writing professional e-mail? **(17e)**

Critical Thinking, Reading, and Writing
What is the best way to make my voice heard on an issue in the community? **(16a)**
How can I write a letter of complaint that will help me as a consumer? **(16b)**

Processes
How do I apply for a job? **(17b, c, d)**
What are some online resources for job-hunting? **(17e)**

Knowledge of Conventions
What should go on my résumé? **(17b)**
How should I format my résumé and cover letter? **(17b, c)**
How do I organize a business memo? **(17e)**

Although college may be unfamiliar territory to the newcomer, it is part of the larger world. Writing represents an access road—a way of connecting classroom, workplace, and community.

15 Service Learning and Community-Service Writing

Your ability to research and write can be of great value to organizations that serve the community. Courses at every level of the university, as well as extracurricular activities, offer opportunities to work with organizations such as homeless shelters, tutoring centers, and environmental groups.

15a Address the community to effect change.

Your work with community organizations may involve writing newsletters, press releases, or funding proposals. When you are writing for a community group, consider these questions:

- What do community members talk about?
- How do they talk about these issues, and why?
- Who is an outsider (member of the community), and who is an insider (member of the organization)?
- How can you best write from the inside to the outside?

Your answers will help you shape your writing so that it reaches its intended audience and moves that audience to action.

Writing on behalf of a community organization almost always involves negotiation and collaboration. A community organization may revise your draft to fit its needs, and you will have to live with those revisions. In these situations, having a cooperative attitude is as important as having strong writing skills.

Even if you are not writing on behalf of a group, you can still do community-service writing. You can write in your own name to raise an issue of concern in a public forum—for example, a newspaper editorial or a letter to a public official. Any time you address readers as fellow citizens with the purpose of educating them or advocating change, you are doing community-service writing.

15b Design brochures, posters, and newsletters with an eye to purpose and audience.

If you are participating in a service learning program or an internship, you may have opportunities to design brochures and newsletters for

www.mhhe.com/
awr3
For interactive help
with design, go to
**Writing > Visual
Rhetoric**

wide distribution, as well as posters to create awareness and promote events. To create an effective brochure, newsletter, or poster, you will need to integrate your skills in document design with what you have learned about purpose and audience.

Here are a few tips:

- Consider how readers will access and review the brochure or newsletter. How will it be mailed or distributed? What are the implications for the overall design?

- It may be a good idea to sketch the design in pencil before using the computer so that you have a plan.

- In making decisions about photographs, illustrations, type fonts, and the design in general, think about the overall image you wish to convey about the sponsoring organization.

- If the organization has a logo, include it; if not, suggest designing one. A **logo** is a small visual symbol, like the Nike "swoosh" or the distinctive font used for Coca-Cola.

- Create a template for the brochure, poster, or newsletter so that you can easily produce future editions. In word-processing and document design programs, a **template** is a blank document that includes all of the formatting and codes. When you use a template, you just plug in new content and visuals—the format and design are already done.

Notice, for example, how the brochure for the PSFS Building in Philadelphia, Pennsylvania (*Figure 15.1*) purposefully connects the history and importance of an architectural landmark with the prestige of the Loews Philadelphia Hotel, into which "the world's first Modernist skyscraper" has been renovated. The brochure has an informative and also a subtly persuasive purpose. Readers are meant to feel that by staying at this Loews they are participating in a great tradition. The front cover is divided in half, with a striking photo of the building on the left side and an account of its history on the right. The interior page places a photo of the bank above an image of hotel comfort. On both pages, quotations running vertically beside the photographs reinforce the building's architectural significance.

The newsletter from the Harvard Medical School titled "Women's Health Watch" (*Figure 15.2 on p. 178*) has a simple, clear design. The designer keeps in mind the purpose and audience, which are explicitly stated in the title and the headline below the title. The shaded area on the right lists the topics that are covered on the interior pages so that readers can get to the information they need quickly and easily. The Web address is prominently displayed in blue so that readers can find further information. The lead article, "Does Excess Vitamin A Cause Hip Fracture?" is simply designed in two columns, with the headline in bold type, subheadings in blue, a readable typeface, and a graphic

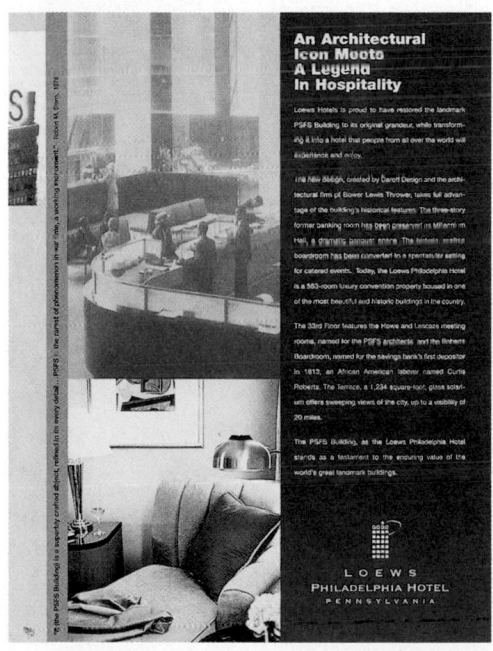

FIGURE 15.1 Example of a brochure.

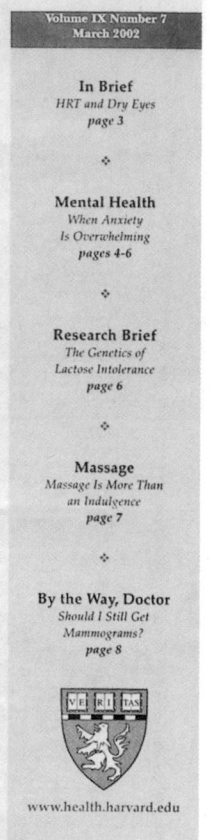

HARVARD
Women's Health Watch
INFORMATION FOR ENLIGHTENED CHOICES FROM HARVARD MEDICAL SCHOOL

Does Excess Vitamin A Cause Hip Fracture?

Hip fracture is one of the most dreaded risks of aging. More than 350,000 hip fractures occur annually in the United States, mostly in women over 65. Half of these women never regain the ability to live independently. About 20% die within a year. Many others suffer chronic pain, anxiety, and depression. The consequences are so grim that many older women contacted in surveys on this subject say they'd rather die than suffer a hip fracture that would send them to a nursing home.

Current recommendations on reducing fracture risk advise women to exercise, make sure they get enough calcium and vitamin D, and, if necessary, take medications that help preserve bone strength. Some women also learn strategies for preventing falls or take classes such as tai chi to improve their balance. Now, a new study suggests that we should also pay attention to vitamin A. At high levels, this essential nutrient may actually increase our risk for hip fracture.

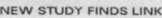

15% of women age 50 will suffer a hip fracture before age 80.

NEW STUDY FINDS LINK

Researchers at Harvard Medical School reported in the Jan. 2, 2002, *Journal of the American Medical Association* on the relationship between postmenopausal hip fracture and vitamin A intake. The data came from 72,337 women enrolled in the Nurses' Health Study. The women were divided into five groups according to their average daily consumption, over an 18-year period, of vitamin A from food and supplements.

Researchers then correlated vitamin A intake with hip fracture incidence. They found that women with the highest intake—3,000 micrograms (mcg) or more per day—had a 48% greater risk for hip fractures, compared to women with the lowest intake (1,250 mcg or less per day).

The increased risk was mainly due to *retinol*, a particular form of vitamin A. In fact, women consuming 2,000 mcg of retinol or more daily had a hip fracture risk almost *double* that of women whose daily intake was under 500 mcg. In contrast, consuming high levels of *beta-carotene*, also a source of vitamin A, had a negligible impact on hip fracture risk. Participants taking hormone replacement therapy (HRT) were somewhat protected from the effects of too much retinol.

ABOUT VITAMIN A

Vitamin A is important for vision, the immune system, and the growth of bone, hair, and skin cells. Retinol, also called "preformed vitamin A," is the active form of the vitamin. It occurs naturally in animal products such as eggs, whole milk, cheese, and liver. Other food sources of vitamin A are *carotenoids*, which are found in green leafy vegetables and in dark yellow or orange fruits and vegetables. The body can convert these plant compounds to retinol. Beta-carotene is the most plentiful carotenoid and it converts most efficiently. For now, you need about 12 times as much beta-carotene as retinol to get the same amount of vitamin A.

Because vitamin A is lost in the process of removing fat, many fat-free dairy products are fortified with retinol. So are some margarines and ready-to-eat cereals. The vitamin A in supplements and multivitamins may come from retinol, beta-carotene, or both. Beta-carotene is preferable because it's also an antioxidant.

Although vitamin A deficiency is a leading cause of blindness in developing countries, it's not a major problem in the United States. The main concern here is excess vitamin A, which can produce birth defects, liver damage, and reduced bone mineral density (BMD).

Volume IX Number 7
March 2002

In Brief
HRT and Dry Eyes
page 3

❖

Mental Health
*When Anxiety
Is Overwhelming*
pages 4–6

❖

Research Brief
*The Genetics of
Lactose Intolerance*
page 6

❖

Massage
*Massage Is More Than
an Indulgence*
page 7

❖

By the Way, Doctor
*Should I Still Get
Mammograms?*
page 8

www.health.harvard.edu

FIGURE 15.2 Example of a well-designed newsletter.

strategically placed to break up the text and add visual interest. In all of these ways, the design supports the Harvard Medical School's purpose of helping the general public get reliable information about the latest advances in medical research. (*For more information on document design, see pp. 95–101.*)

16 Letters to Raise Awareness and Share Concern

Your ability to write and your willingness to share your opinions and insight can influence community actions and affect the way a corporation treats you. A letter to a local politician regarding a current issue or to an organization regarding customer service can accomplish much if clearly argued, concisely phrased, and appropriately directed.

16a Write about a public issue.

Your task in writing to a newspaper, community organization, or public figure is to present yourself as a polite, engaged, and reasonable person who is invested in a particular issue and who can offer a compelling case for a particular course of action.

Most publications, corporations, and nonprofit organizations include forms, links, or e-mail addresses on their Web sites for submitting letters or comments. Whenever possible, use online options instead of writing a print letter. Here are some guidelines for e-mails and online comments:

- Address the appropriate person or department by name. Consult the organization's Web site for this information.
- Concisely state your area of concern in the subject line.
- Never include an attachment to your e-mail: an organization's server may screen out your message as spam.
- Keep it brief. Many community organizations and corporations receive millions of e-mails each week. Most publications post specific word-count limits for letters to the editor or comments.
- Follow the conventions of professional e-mail (*see pp. 189–90*). Use capital letters and standard punctuation.
- Keep your tone polite and professional (neither combative nor overly chatty).

If you send a print letter, use the following guidelines:

- Address the appropriate person(s). If you are writing to a newspaper or magazine's editorial pages, see how published letters are addressed ("To the editors," for example), and whether guidelines are available. If you are writing to an organization, consult its Web site or call the main number to find out the preferred means of address and submission. It is always best to address your letter to a specific person or department.
- Use the format for a business letter. (*See the business letter in block format on p. 187.*)

- Write no more than three or four paragraphs (e-mails should be shorter).

Regardless of medium, follow this format:

- In the first paragraph, clearly and briefly state your area of concern and why the issue is important to you. For example, if you are writing to your local school board, you might state that you are the parent of a child at the local school.

- In the second paragraph, provide clear and compelling evidence for your concern. If relevant, propose a solution.

- In your conclusion, thank the reader for considering your thoughts. Repeat any request for specific action, such as having an item added to the agenda of the next school board meeting. If you want a specific response, politely request an e-mail or telephone call. If you intend to follow up on your letter, note that you will be calling or writing again within a week (or however long is appropriate).

16b Write as a consumer.

1. Writing a letter of complaint

Suppose you had ordered a product from an online store as a gift, only to find your purchase delayed in transit so that it arrived too late. Following the Customer Service link on the Web site, you compose an e-mail letter of complaint like the one in Figure 16.1. In writing such a letter, present yourself as a reasonable person who has experienced unfair treatment. If you are writing on behalf of your company or as a representative of your company, state that fact calmly and propose a resolution.

Here are some guidelines for writing a letter of complaint:

- If possible, send the complaint via e-mail unless you must submit supporting documentation (such as receipts).

- If you are sending a print letter, use the business format on page 187.

- Follow any procedures for submitting a complaint specified on the company's Web site.

- Address the letter to the person in charge by name. (If you do not know the correct name and title, consult the corporate Web site or call the company.)

- Increase your credibility by proposing reasonable recompense and enclosing copies of receipts, if appropriate. Do *not* send scans of receipts as e-mail attachments.

- Mention previous positive experiences with the organization, if you can. Your protest will have more credibility if you come

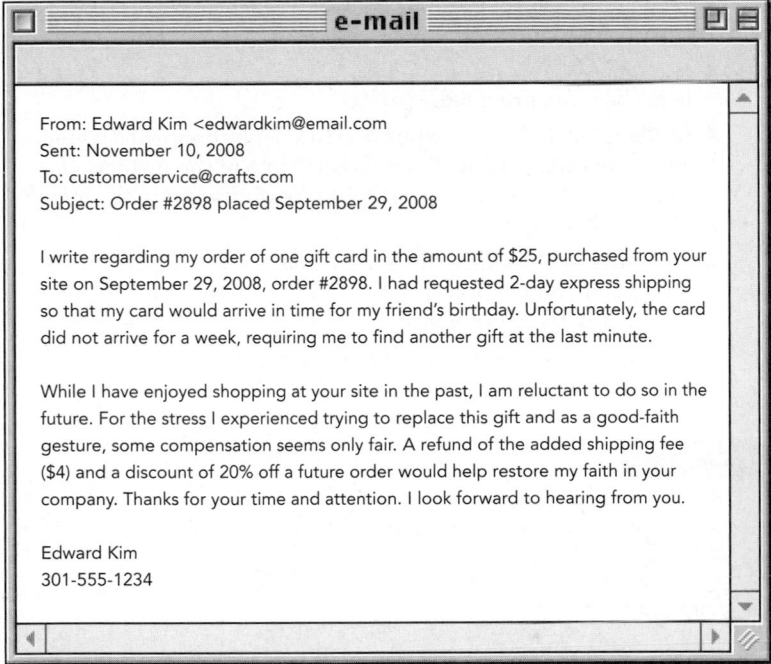

FIGURE 16.1 Sample letter of complaint.

> across as a person who does not usually complain but is forced to do so in this instance.
>
> - Conclude by expressing thanks and the hope that the company's response will enable you to continue as a customer.
> - Send copies to the people whom you mention and, if appropriate, to the individual's supervisor.
> - Keep copies of all correspondence for your records.

Consider, for example, the e-mail in Figure 16.1 by Edward Kim. Notice how Kim's letter adheres to the guidelines just presented.

2. Writing a letter of praise

Suppose that you wish to thank an airline employee who has been exceptionally helpful to you. In the workplace, you might write a letter of praise to a colleague who worked long hours to complete a project, or to congratulate a team for bringing in new clients.

Here are some guidelines for writing a letter of praise:

> - Address the letter to the person in charge by name. (If you do not know the correct name and title to use, call the corporate headquarters.)

- If you are sending a print letter, use the format for a business letter.

- In the first paragraph, concisely state the situation and the help that was provided.

- In the following paragraphs, narrate what happened, referring to details such as the date and time of the incident so that the person you are writing to can follow up with the person who helped you.

- Conclude by thanking the person you are writing to for his or her time and expressing your intention to continue doing business with the company.

- Send copies to the people whom you mention.

17 Writing to Get and Keep a Job

Many students work on or off campus in jobs, as interns, or as volunteers for community organizations. Writing is one way to connect your work, your other activities, and your studies. Strong writing skills will also help you find a good job once you leave college and advance in your chosen career.

www.mhhe.com/ awr3

For more on professional writing, go to

Learning > College to Career

17a Explore internship possibilities, and keep a portfolio of career-related writing.

An internship, in which you do actual work in your chosen field, is a vital connection between the classroom and the workplace. You gain academic credit for what you learn from the job. Writing and learning go together. Keep a journal to record and analyze your experiences, as well as a file of any writing you do on the job. Your final project for the internship credit may require that you analyze the file of writing you have produced.

Files of writing from internships, clippings of articles and editorials you have written for the school newspaper, writing you have done for a community organization—these and other documents demonstrate your ability to apply intellectual concepts to real-world demands. Organized into a portfolio, this material displays your marketable skills. (*For more on preparing a portfolio, see Tab 2: Writing and Designing Texts, pp. 101–06.*) Your campus career center can help you assess your skills and determine what kind of internship would best suit your career goals. It may also assist you in compiling a portfolio, keep it on file, and help you send it to potential employers or graduate schools.

17b Keep your résumé up-to-date and available on a computer disk.

A **résumé** is a brief summary of your education and your work experience that you send to prospective employers. Expect the person reviewing your résumé to give it no more than sixty seconds. Make that first impression count. Design a document that is easy to read, attractively formatted, and flawlessly edited.

Guidelines for writing a résumé

Always include the following *necessary* categories in a résumé:

- Heading (name, address, phone number, e-mail address)
- Education (in reverse chronological order; do not include high school)
- Work experience (in reverse chronological order)
- References (often included on a separate sheet; for many situations, you can add the line "References available on request" instead)

Include the following *optional* categories in your résumé as appropriate:

- Objective
- Honors and awards
- Internships
- Activities and service
- Special skills

Sometimes career counselors recommend that you list a career objective right under the heading of your résumé. If you do so, be sure you know what the prospective employer is looking for and tailor your résumé accordingly.

Laura Amabisca has organized the information in her résumé (*p. 184*) by time and by categories. Within each category, she has listed items from the most to least recent. This reverse chronological order gives appropriate emphasis to what she is doing now and has just done. Because she was applying for jobs in public relations, she has highlighted her internship in that field by placing it at the top of her experience section.

The résumé on page 184 reflects appropriate formatting for print. Note the use of a line rule, alignment of text, bullet points, and bold and italic type. These elements organize the information visually, directing the reader's eye appropriately.

Laura's entire résumé is just one page. A brief, well-organized résumé is more attractive to potential employers than a multi-page, rambling résumé.

The résumé features active verbs such as "researched."

Laura Amabisca
20650 North 58th Avenue, Apt. 15A
Glendale, AZ 85308
623-555-7310
lamabisca@peoplelink.com

Objective To obtain a position as public relations assistant at a nonprofit organization

Education **Arizona State University West,** Phoenix
- Bachelor of Arts, History, Minor in Global Management (May 2008)
- Senior Thesis: Picturing the Hopi, 1920–1940: A Historical Analysis

Glendale Community College, Glendale, AZ (2004–2006)

Experience **Public Relations Office, Arizona State University West**
Intern (Summer 2007)
- Researched and reported on university external publications.
- Created original content for print and Web.
- Assisted in planning fundraising campaigns and events.

Sears, Bell Road, Phoenix, AZ
Assistant Manager, Sporting Goods Department (2006–present)
- Supervised team of sales associates.
- Ensured quality customer service.

Sales Associate, Sporting Goods Department (2003–2006)
- Recommended products to meet customer needs.
- Processed sales and returns.

Stock Clerk, Sporting Goods Department (2000–2003)
- Received, sorted, and tracked incoming merchandise.
- Stocked shelves to ensure appropriate supply on sales floor.

Special Skills *Language:* Bilingual: Spanish/English
Computer: Windows, Mac OS, MS Office, HTML

Activities **America Reads**
Tutor, Public-Relations Consultant (2007)
- Taught reading to first-grade students.
- Created brochure to recruit tutors.

Multicultural Festival, Arizona State University West
Student Coordinator (2007)
Organized festival of international performances, crafts, and community organizations.

Writing Center, Glendale Community College
Tutor (2004–2006)
Met with peers to help them with writing assignments.

References Available on request to Career Services, Arizona State University West

LAURA AMABISCA
20650 North 58th Avenue, Apt. 15A
Glendale, AZ 85308
623-555-7310
lamabisca@peoplelink.com

OBJECTIVE
To obtain a position as public relations assistant at a nonprofit organization

EDUCATION
Arizona State University West, Phoenix
*Bachelor of Arts, History, Minor in Global Management (May 2008)
*Senior Thesis: Picturing the Hopi, 1920-1940: A Historical Analysis

Glendale Community College, Glendale, AZ (2004–2006)

EXPERIENCE
Public Relations Office, Arizona State University West (Summer 2007)
Intern
*Researched and reported on university external publications.
*Created original content for print and Web.
*Assisted in planning fundraising campaigns and events.

Sears, Bell Road, Phoenix, AZ
Assistant Manager, Sporting Goods Department (2006–present)
*Supervise team of sales associates.
*Ensure quality customer service.

Sales Associate, Sporting Goods Department (2003–2006)
*Recommended products to meet customer needs.
*Processed sales and returns.

Stock Clerk, Sporting Goods Department (2000–2003)
*Received, sorted, and tracked incoming merchandise.
*Stocked shelves to ensure appropriate supply on sales floor.

SPECIAL SKILLS
Language: Bilingual: Spanish/English
Computer: Windows, Mac OS, MS Office, HTML

ACTIVITIES
America Reads (2007)
Tutor, Public-Relations Consultant
*Taught reading to first-grade students.
*Created brochure to recruit tutors.

Multicultural Festival, Arizona State University West (2007)
Student Coordinator
Organized festival of international performances, crafts, and community organizations.

Writing Center, Glendale Community College (2004–2006)
Tutor
Met with peers to help them with writing assignments.

REFERENCES
Available on request to Career Services, Arizona State University West

Laura uses a simple font and no bold or italic type, ensuring that the résumé will be scannable.

Asterisks replace bullets.

Laura includes keywords (highlighted in blue here) that will be most likely to catch the eye of a potential employer or match desired positions in a database. Laura knows that a position in public relations requires computer skills, communication skills, and experience working with diverse groups of people. Key words such as "sales," "bilingual," "HTML," and "public relations" are critical to her résumé.

Electronic and Scannable Résumés

Many employers now request résumés by e-mail and electronically scan print résumés. Here are some tips for using electronic technology to submit your résumé:

■ Contact the human resource department of a potential employer and ask whether your résumé should be scannable.

■ If so, be sure to use a clear, common typeface in an easy-to read size. Do not include any unusual symbols or characters.

■ If the employer expects the résumé as an e-mail attachment, save it in a widely readable form such as rich text format (RTF) or PDF. Use minimal formatting and no colors, unusual fonts, or decorative flourishes.

■ Configure your e-mail program to send you an automated reply when your e-mail has been successfully received.

■ Include specific keywords that allow employers to locate your electronic résumé in a database. See the résumé section of Monster.com at http://resume.monster.com for industry-specific advice on appropriate keywords and other step-by-step advice.

Laura's scannable résumé (*p. 185*) contains no italics, bold, or other formatting so that it may be submitted electronically or entered into an employer's database (*see the box above*).

17c Write a tailored application letter.

A clear and concise **application letter** should always accompany a résumé. Before drafting a job application letter, do some research about the organization you are contacting. For example, even though Laura Amabisca was already familiar with the Heard Museum, she found out the name of the director of public relations. (*Amabisca's application letter appears on p. 187.*) If you are unable to identify an appropriate name, it is better to direct the letter to "Dear Director of Public Relations" than to "Dear Sir or Madam."

Here are some additional guidelines:

■ **Tailor your letter.** A form letter accompanied by a generic résumé is not an effective way of getting a job interview. Before writing an application letter or preparing a résumé, you should try to find out precisely what the employer is looking for. You can then tailor your documents to those precise requirements.

■ **Use business style.** Use the block form shown on page 187. Type your address at the top of the page, with each line starting

20650 North 58th Avenue, Apt. 15A
Glendale, AZ 85308
August 17, 2008

Ms. Jaclyn Abel
Director of Public Relations
Heard Museum
2301 North Central Avenue
Phoenix, AZ 85004

Dear Ms. Abel:

I am writing to apply for the position of Public Relations Assistant that you recently advertised in the *Arizona Republic*. I believe that my experience and qualifications fit well with your needs at the Heard, a museum that I have visited and loved all my life.

As the enclosed résumé indicates, I have experience in the public relations field. While at Arizona State University West, I worked as an intern in the Public Relations Office, where I was responsible for analyzing and reporting on the image projected by the university's external publications. I also had a hand in creating the brochure for the University-College Center and participated in planning ASU West's "Dream Big" campaign. In addition I assisted in organizing an opening convocation attended by 800 people. This work in the not-for-profit sector has prepared me well for employment at the Heard.

My undergraduate major in American history has also helped me understand the rich heritage of Native Americans. In my senior thesis, which received the Westmarc Writing Award, I studied the history of the relationship between the Hopis and the Anglo population as reflected in photographs taken from 1920 to 1940. Although my thesis focuses on a specific tribe, I have been interested for many years in Native American culture and have often made use of resources in the Heard. I think that I would do a superior job of presenting the Heard as the premier museum of Native American culture.

Confidential reference letters are available from ASU West Career Services. I sincerely hope that we will have an opportunity to talk further about the Heard Museum and its outstanding cultural contributions to the Phoenix metropolitan area. Please contact me at 623-555-7310.

Sincerely,

Laura Amabisca

Laura Amabisca

Enc.

Laura writes to a specific person and uses the correct salutation (*Mr., Ms., Dr.,* etc.). Never use only a first name in an application letter, even if you are writing to an acquaintance.

Laura briefly sums up her work experience. This information is also available on her résumé, but she makes evident in her cover letter why she is applying for the job. Without this explanation, a potential employer might not even look at her résumé.

Laura mentions her familiarity with the museum to which she is applying. This demonstrates her genuine interest in joining the organization.

at the left margin; place the date at the left margin two lines above the recipient's name and address; use a colon (:) after the greeting; double-space between single-spaced paragraphs; use a traditional closing (*Sincerely, Sincerely yours, Yours truly*); and make sure that the inside address and the address on the envelope match exactly.

■ **Be professional.** Your letter should be crisp and to the point. Be direct as well as objective in presenting your qualifications, and maintain a courteous tone toward the prospective employer. Your résumé should contain only education and work-related information. It is better not to include personal information (such as ethnicity, age, or marital status).

■ **Limit your letter to three or four paragraphs.** Focus clearly and concisely on what the employer needs to know. In the first paragraph, identify the position you are applying for, mention how you heard about it, and briefly state that you are qualified. In the following one or two paragraphs, explain your qualifications, elaborating on the most pertinent items in your résumé. Because Amabisca was applying for a public relations job at a museum of Native American culture, she chose to highlight her internship and her thesis. In another application letter, however, this time for a management position at American Express, she made different choices. In that letter, she emphasized her work experience at Sears, including the fact that she had moved up in the organization through positions of increasing responsibility.

■ **State your expectation for future contact.** Conclude with a one- or two-sentence paragraph informing the reader that you are anticipating a follow-up to your letter.

■ **Use *Enc.* if you are enclosing additional materials.** Decide whether it is appropriate to enclose supporting materials other than your résumé, such as samples of your writing. Amabisca decided to do so because she was applying for her ideal job and had highly relevant materials to send. If you have been instructed to send a cover letter and résumé by e-mail as attachments, include the word "Attachments" after your e-mail "signature."

17d Prepare in advance for the job interview.

Many campus career centers offer free seminars on interviewing skills and can also arrange for you to role-play an interview with a career guidance counselor.

Here are some additional guidelines for job interviews:

For MULTILINGUAL STUDENTS

Applying for a Job

Before applying for an internship or a job in the United States, be sure that you have the appropriate visa or work permits. American employers are required by law to confirm such documentation before they can hire anyone. (American citizens must prove their citizenship as well.) For more information, visit your campus international student center and the campus career resource center.

- Call to confirm your interview the day before it is scheduled. Determine how much time you will need to get there. A late appearance at an interview can count heavily against you.
- Dress professionally.
- Bring an additional copy of your résumé and cover letter.
- Expect to speak with several people—perhaps someone from human resources as well as the person for whom you would actually be working and other people in his or her department.
- *Always* send a personalized thank-you note or e-mail to everyone who took the time to meet you. In each, mention an interesting point that the person made and your interest in working with him or her. Send these notes within twenty-four hours of your interview.

17e Apply what you learn in college to your on-the-job writing.

Once you get a job, writing is a way to establish and maintain lines of communication with your colleagues and other contacts. When you write in the workplace, you should imagine a reader who is pressed for time and wants you to get to the point immediately.

1. Writing e-mail and memos in the workplace

In the workplace, you will do much of your writing online, in the form of e-mail. (*For more on e-mail, see Tab 1: Learning across the Curriculum, pp. 9–11.*) Most e-mail programs set up messages in memo format, with "To," "From," "Date," and "Subject" lines, as in Figure 17.1 on page 190.

E-mail in the workplace requires a more formal style than the e-mail you send to family and friends. In an e-mail for a business occasion—communication with colleagues, a request for information, or a thank-you note after an interview—you should observe the same

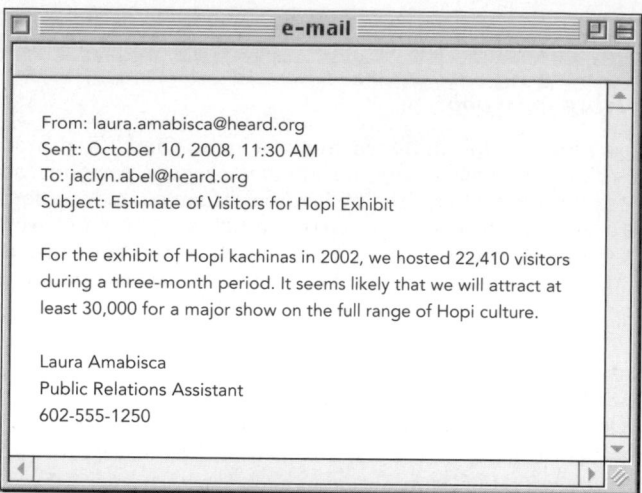

FIGURE 17.1 Sample workplace e-mail.

care with organization, spelling, and tone that you would in a business letter. More specifically:

- Use a concise subject line to cue the reader as to the intent of the e-mail. When replying to messages, replace subject lines that do not clearly reflect the topic.
- Maintain a courteous tone. Use joking, informality, and sarcasm cautiously, as they can cause the recipient to misunderstand your intent.
- Make sentences brief and to the point. Use short paragraphs.
- Use special formatting such as italics sparingly, as not all readers will be able to view it.
- Use standard punctuation and capitalization.
- Close with your name and contact information. (*See the example above.*)
- Particularly when you do not know the recipient, use the conventions of letter-writing such as opening with "Dear" and ending with "Sincerely."

Business memos are used for communication with others within an organization. Like business e-mails, they are concise and formal. Memos may establish meetings, summarize information, or make announcements. (*See the example on p. 191.*) They generally contain the following elements and characteristics:

To: Sonia Gonzalez, Grace Kim, Jonathan Jones
From: Jennifer Richer, Design Team Manager   JR
Date: March 3, 2009
Re: Meeting on Monday

Please plan to attend a meeting on Monday at 9:00 a.m. in Room 401. At that time, we'll review our progress on the library project as well as outline future activities to ensure the following:

• Client satisfaction
• Maintenance of the current schedule
• Operation within budget constraints

In addition, we will discuss assignments related to other upcoming projects, such as the renovation of the gymnasium and science lab. Please bring design ideas and be prepared to brainstorm. Thanks.

cc: Michael Garcia, Director, Worldwide Design

■ A header at the top that identifies recipient, author, date, and subject
■ Block paragraphs that are single-spaced within the paragraph and double-spaced between paragraphs
■ Bulleted lists and other design elements (such as headers) to set off sections of longer memos
■ A section at the bottom that indicates other members of the organization who have received copies of the memo
■ A professional tone

Whether you are writing an e-mail message or a conventional memo, you need to consider not only what your workplace document says but also how it looks. Various strategies can make your document easier to read. For example, presenting your information as a numbered or bulleted list surrounded by white space aids readability and allows you to highlight important points and to emphasize crucial ideas. (*For more help with document design, see Tab 2: Writing and Designing Texts, pp. 95–101.*)

2. Writing in other business genres

Conventional forms of business writing also increase readability because readers have built-in expectations for the genre and therefore

www.mhhe.com/
awr3
For help with
PowerPoint, go to
**Writing >
PowerPoint Tutorial**

E-mail in the Workplace

Anything you write using a company's or an organization's computers or computer systems is considered company property. If you want to gossip with a coworker, do so over lunch. If you want to e-mail your best friend about your personal life, do so from your home computer. The following guidelines will help you use e-mail wisely:

- When you are replying to an e-mail that has been sent to several people (the term *cc* means "carbon copy"), determine whether your response needs to go to all of the original recipients or just to the original sender. Avoid cluttering other people's in-boxes.
- Open attachments from known senders only.
- File your e-mail as carefully as you would paper documents. Create separate folders in your e-mail program for each client, project, or coworker. Save any particularly important e-mails as separate files.
- While it may be acceptable for you to browse news and shopping sites during your breaks and lunchtime, do not visit any sites while in the workplace that would embarrass you if a colleague or your supervisor suddenly looked over your shoulder.

know what to look for. Besides the memo, there are a number of common business genres:

- **Business letters:** Use business letters to communicate formally with people outside an organization. Typically, letters in business format have single-spaced block paragraphs with double spacing between the paragraphs. (*See the example on p. 187.*)

- **Business reports and proposals:** Like college research papers, business reports and proposals can be used to inform, analyze, and interpret. An abstract, sometimes called an **executive summary,** is almost always required, as are tables and graphs. (*For more on these visual elements, see Tab 2: Writing and Designing Texts, pp. 54–56.*)

- **Evaluations and recommendations:** You might need to evaluate a person, or you might be called on to evaluate a product or a procedure and recommend whether the company should buy or use it. Like the reviews and critiques that college writers compose, workplace evaluations should be reasonable as well as convincing. Always support your account of both strengths and weaknesses with specific illustrations or examples.

- **Presentations:** In many professions, information is presented in ways both formal and informal to groups of people. You might suddenly be asked to offer an opinion in a group meeting; or you might be given a week to prepare a formal presentation, with visuals, on an ongoing project. (*For more information on oral presentations, see Tab 3: Common Assignments, pp. 153–57. To learn more about PowerPoint and other presentation tools, see pp. 161–63.*)

TEXTCONNEX

Writing Connections

- *Job Central* <http://jobstar.org/tools/resume/samples.cfm>: This site provides samples of résumés for many different situations, as well as sample cover letters.
- *Career Collection: Write a Résumé* <http://college.library.wisc.edu/collections/career/careerresume.html>: This site provides help with preparing cover letters and writing résumés.
- *Résumé services and tips from Monster:* <http://career-advice.monster.com/resume-tips/home.aspx>: This site includes sample résumés and cover letters in addition to career advice.

Interplanetary probes help astronomers research the far reaches of the solar system. Voyager 2 sent this image of Saturn's rings to Earth.

5

For all knowledge and wonder (which is the seed of knowledge) is an impression of pleasure in itself.

—FRANCIS BACON

Researching

5 Researching

Sections dealing with visual rhetoric. For a complete listing, see the Quick Guide to Key Resources at the back of this book.

Tab 5: Researching
This section will help you answer questions such as:

Rhetorical Knowledge
What writing situation does my assignment specify? **(18c)**

Critical Thinking, Reading, and Writing
What resources can I find in the library and online? **(19)**
How can I tell if sources are worth including? **(21)**
How do I present my ideas along with those of my sources? **(24c, e)**

Processes
How can I think of a topic for my research paper? **(18d)**
How should I plan my research project? **(18e)**
When and how should I use visuals in my paper? **(20)**

Knowledge of Conventions
What is an annotated bibliography, and how do I create one? **(24b)**
What is a documentation style? Which one should I use? **(25c)**

18 Understanding Research

Your campus or neighborhood library provides valuable resources for almost any kind of research. These libraries offer not just books, magazines, and journals but also specialized online databases and the expert guidance of research librarians.

Doing research in the twenty-first century includes the library but is not limited to it. The Internet now provides rapid, direct access to an abundance of information unimaginable to earlier generations of students. The results of Internet searches, however, can sometimes provide an overwhelming flood of sources, many of questionable legitimacy.

The goal of the research section of this book (*Chapters 18–25*) is to help you learn to navigate today's research landscape skillfully, manage the information you discover within it, and use that information to write research papers.

18a Understand primary and secondary research.

Primary research means working in a laboratory, in the field, or with an archive of raw data, original documents, and authentic artifacts to

197

TEXTCONNEX

Types of Sources

- *Primary or secondary?*
  <http://library.ucsc.edu/ref/howto/primarysecondary.html>:
  Discusses the difference between primary and secondary
  research sources.
- *Research papers: resources*
  <http://owl.english.purdue.edu/workshops/hypertext/
  ResearchW/resource.html>: provides guidelines for finding
  primary and secondary sources.

make firsthand discoveries. (*For more information on primary research,
see Chapter 22, pp. 235–40.*) **Secondary research** means looking to
see what other people have learned and written about a topic.

Knowing how to identify facts, interpretations, and evaluations
is key to good secondary research:

- **Facts** are objective. Like your body weight, facts can be measured, observed, or independently verified in some way.

- **Interpretations** spell out the implications of facts. Are you
  as thin as you are because of your genes, because you exercise
  every day, or because of both or other factors? The answer to
  this question is an interpretation.

- **Evaluations** are debatable judgments about a set of facts or
  a situation. The assertion attributed to Wallis Simpson that
  "one can never be too rich or too thin" is an evaluation.

Once you are up-to-date on the facts, interpretations, and evaluations in a particular area, you will be able to design a research project
that adds your *perspective* on the sources you found and read:

- Given all that you have learned about the topic, what strikes
  you as important or interesting?

- What patterns do you see, or what connections can you make
  between one person's work and another's?

- Where is the research going, and what problems still need
  to be explored?

18b Recognize the connection between research and college writing.

In many ways research informs all college writing. But some assignments require more rigorous and systematic research than others. **Research project** assignments offer you a chance to find and read both

CHARTING the TERRITORY

Classic and Current Sources

Classic sources are well-known and respected older works that made such an important contribution to a discipline or a particular area of research that contemporary researchers use them as touchstones for further research in that area. In many fields, sources published within the past five years are considered current. However, sources on topics related to medicine, recent scientific discoveries, or technological change must be much more recent to be considered current.

classic and current material on a specific issue. A research paper constitutes your contribution to the ongoing academic conversation about that issue.

18c Understand the research assignment.

Consider the rhetorical situation of the research project as you would any other piece of writing. Think about your paper's audience, purpose, and scope (*see Tab 2: Writing and Designing Texts, pp. 37–42*).

1. Audience

Although your *audience* will most likely include only your instructor and perhaps your classmates, thinking critically about the needs and expectations of practitioners of the discipline will help you to plan a research strategy.

Consider the following questions about the members of your audience:

- What do they already know about your subject? How much background information and context will you need to provide? (Your research should include **facts.**)
- Might they find your paper controversial or challenging? How should you accommodate and acknowledge different perspectives and viewpoints? (Your research should include **interpretations,** and you will need to balance opposing interpretations.)
- Will you expect the audience to take action based on your research? (Your research should include **evaluations,** carefully supported by facts and interpretations, that demonstrate clearly why readers should adopt a course of action or point of view.)

2. Purpose

Your *purpose* for writing a research paper depends on both the specifics of the assignment as set by your instructor and your own interest in the topic. Your purpose might be **informative**—to educate your audience about an unfamiliar subject or point of view (*see Chapter 9: Informative Reports, p. 109*). Your purpose might be **interpretive**—to reveal the meaning or significance of a work of art, a historical document, a literary work, or a scientific study (*see Chapter 10: Interpretive Analyses and Writing about Literature, p. 118*). Your purpose might be **persuasive**—to convince your audience, with logic and evidence, to accept your point of view on a controversial issue or to act on the information in your paper (*see Chapter 11: Arguments, p. 126*). Review your assignment for keywords that signal its purpose. Note, however, that some terms can signal more than one type of assignment, depending on the context. Here are some examples:

- **Informative:** Explain, describe, define, review
- **Interpretive:** Analyze, compare, explain, interpret
- **Persuasive:** Assess, justify, defend, refute, determine

3. Scope
A project's scope includes the expected length of the paper, the deadline, and any other requirements such as number and type of sources. Are primary sources appropriate? Should you include visuals, and is any type specified?

18d Choose an interesting research question for critical inquiry.

Approach your assignment in a spirit of critical inquiry. *Critical* in this sense does not mean "fault finding," "skeptical," "cynical," or even "urgent." Rather, it refers to a receptive, but reasonable and discerning, frame of mind. Choosing an interesting topic will help you make the results of your inquiry meaningful—to yourself and your readers.

1. Choosing a question with personal significance
Even though you are writing for an academic assignment, you can still get personally involved in your work. Begin with the wording of the assignment, analyzing the project's required audience, purpose, and scope (*see section 18c, pp. 199–200*). Then browse through the course texts and your class notes, looking for a match between your interests and topics, issues, or problems in the subject area.

For example, suppose you are assigned to write a report on a country's global economic prospects. If you have visited Mexico, you might find it interesting to explore that country's prospects.

2. Making your question specific
The more specific your question, the more your research will have direction and focus. To make a question more specific, use the "five *w*'s and

Typical Lines of Inquiry in Different Disciplines

Research topics and questions differ from one discipline to another, as the following examples show:

- **History:** How did India's experience of British imperialism affect its response to globalization?
- **Marketing:** How do corporations develop strategies for marketing their products to international consumers?
- **Political science:** Why did many nations of Europe agree to unite, creating a common currency and an essentially borderless state of Europe (the European Union, or EU)?
- **Anthropology:** What is the impact of globalization on the world's indigenous cultures?

an *h*" strategy by asking about the *who, what, where, why, when,* and *how* of a topic (*see Tab 2: Writing and Designing Texts, pp. 44–45*).

After you have compiled a list of possible research questions, choose one that is specific or rewrite a broad one to make it more specific and therefore answerable. For example, as Audrey Galeano developed a topic for a research paper on the impact of globalization for an anthropology course, she rewrote the following broad question to make it answerable:

www.mhhe.com/awr3

For more on narrowing your topic, go to

Writing > Paragraph/Essay Development > Thesis/Central Idea

TOO BROAD	How has globalization affected the Amazon River Basin?
ANSWERABLE	How has large-scale agriculture in the Amazon Basin affected the region's indigenous peoples?

(*Galeano's finished paper appears in Chapter 34, pp. 349–58.*)

3. Finding a challenging question

To be interesting, a research question must be challenging. If it can be answered with a yes or no, a dictionary-like definition, or a textbook presentation of information, you should choose another question or rework it to make it more challenging.

NOT CHALLENGING	Has economic globalization contributed to the destruction of the Amazon rain forest?
CHALLENGING	How can agricultural interests and indigenous peoples in the Amazon region work together to preserve the environment while creating a sustainable economy?

LEARNING in COLLEGE

Scheduling Your Research Project

Task	Date

Phase I:

- Complete general plan for research. _____
- Decide on topic and research question. _____
- Consult reference works and reference librarians. _____
- Make a list of relevant keywords for online searching (*see Chapter 19, p. 208*). _____
- Compile **working bibliography** (*see Chapter 24, p. 252*). _____
- Sample some items in bibliography. _____
- Make arrangements for primary research (if necessary). _____

Phase II

- Locate, read, and evaluate selected sources. _____
- Take notes, write summaries and paraphrases. _____
- Cross-check notes with working bibliography. _____
- Conduct primary research (if necessary). _____
- Find and create visuals. _____
- Confer with instructor or Writing Center (optional). _____
- Develop thesis and outline or plan organization of paper. _____

Phase III

- Write first draft, deciding which primary and secondary source materials to include. _____
- Have peer review (optional). _____
- Revise draft. _____
- Confer with instructor or Writing Center (optional). _____
- Do final revision and editing. _____
- Create Works Cited or References page. _____
- Proofread and check spelling. _____

Due date _____

4. Speculating about answers

Sometimes it can be useful to speculate on the answer to your research question so that you have a **hypothesis** to work with during the research process. Don't forget, though, that a hypothesis is a tentative answer that must be tested and revised based on the evidence you turn up in your research. Be aware of the assumptions embedded in your hypothesis or research question. Consider, for example, the following:

HYPOTHESIS The global demand for agricultural products will destroy the Amazon rain forest.

This hypothesis assumes that destructive farming practices in the Amazon region are the only possible response to global demand. But assumptions are always open to question. Researchers must be willing to adjust their ideas as they learn more about a topic.

As the above example demonstrates, your research question must allow you to generate testable hypotheses. Assertions about your personal beliefs and feelings cannot be tested.

18e Create a research plan.

Your research will be more productive if you create a general plan and a detailed schedule immediately after you receive your assignment. A general plan ensures that you understand the full scope of your assignment. A detailed schedule helps you set priorities and meet your deadlines. Use the box on the opposite page, which outlines the steps in a research project, as a starting point, adjusting the time allotments based on the amount of time you have to complete the assignment. Consider what you already know about your topic as well as what you must learn through your research.

SOURCE SMART

Planning Your Search

Your research plan should include where you expect to find your sources. For example, you may have to visit the library to view print material that predates 1980; you will need to consult a subscription database online or at the library for recent scientific discoveries; historical documents may require archival research; and you may need to conduct field research, such as interviewing fellow students. Set priorities to increase your efficiency in each location (library, archive, online).

19 Finding and Managing Print and Online Sources

The amount of information available is vast, so a search for useful sources entails three activities:

- Collecting keywords from reference works
- Using library databases
- Finding material in the library and on the Web

www.mhhe.com/ awr3

For more information on links, go to

Research > Using the Library

19a Use the library in person and online.

Librarians know what is available at your library and how to get material from other libraries. They can also show you how to access the library's computerized book catalog, periodical databases, and electronic resources or how to use the Internet to find information relevant to your project. At many schools, reference librarians are available for online chats, and some even take queries via text message. Your library's Web site may also have links to subscription databases or important reference works available on the Internet, as shown in Figure 19.1.

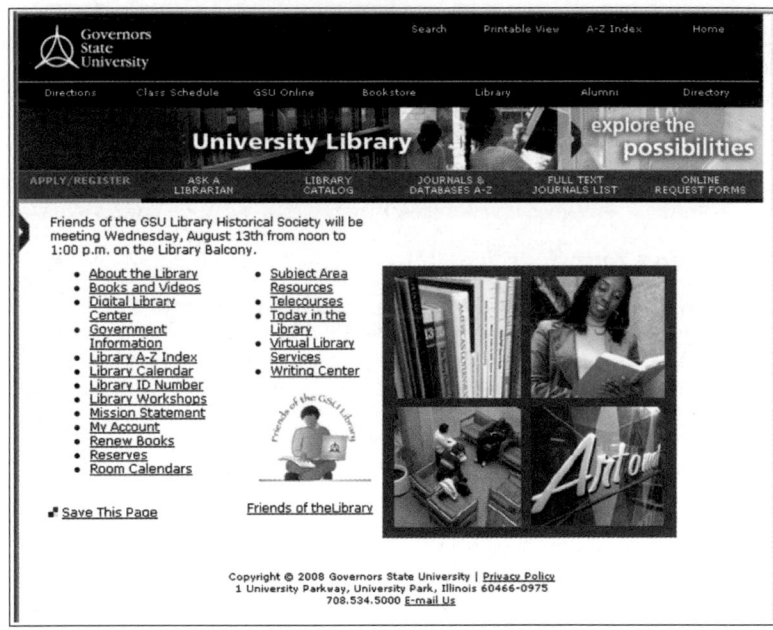

FIGURE 19.1 A page from the Web site of Governors State University. The Web page provides links to a variety of Web-based reference sources.

204

In addition, **help sheets** or online tutorials, found at most college libraries, list the location of both general and discipline-specific periodicals and noncirculating reference books, along with information about the book catalog, special databases, indexes, Web resources, and library policies.

19b Consult various kinds of sources.

Consult more than one source and more than one kind of source. Your assignment may specify how many print and electronic sources you are expected to consult and cite. These are some of the kinds of sources available to you:

- **General reference works (for overview and keywords)**

  Encyclopedias, annuals, almanacs

  Computer databases, bibliographies, abstracts

- **Specialized reference works (for overview and keywords)**

  Discipline-specific encyclopedias, almanacs, and dictionaries

- **Books**
- **Periodical articles**

  In newspapers

  In magazines

  In scholarly and technical journals

  On the Web

- **Specialized databases**
- **Web sites**
- **News groups, ListServs, and e-mail**
- **Virtual communities**

  MUDs (multiuser dimensions)

  MOOs (multiuser object-oriented dimensions)

- **Government documents, pamphlets, census data**
- **Primary sources**

  Original documents like literary works, art objects, performances, manuscripts, letters, and personal journals

  Museum collections; maps; photo, film, sound, and music archives

  Field notes, surveys, interviews

  Results of observation and lab experiments

LEARNING in COLLEGE

Popular or Scholarly?

The audience and purpose of a source, especially a publication, determine whether it should be considered *scholarly* or *popular*. You may begin your inquiry into a research topic with popular sources, but to become fully informed about your topic, you need to delve into scholarly sources.

Popular sources:

- If in print, are widely available on newsstands and in retail stores
- If in print, are printed on magazine paper with a color cover
- Accept advertising for a wide range of consumer goods or are themselves widely advertised (in the case of books)
- Are published by a commercial publishing house or media company (such as Time Warner)
- Include a wide range of topics in each issue, from international affairs to popular entertainment
- Usually do not contain bibliographic information.
- If online, have a URL that likely ends in .com

Scholarly sources:

- If in print, are usually found in libraries, not on newsstands
- If in print, list article titles and authors on the cover
- Have few advertisements
- Are published by a scholarly or nonprofit organization, often in association with a university press
- Focus on discipline-specific topics
- Include articles mostly by authors who are affiliated with colleges, museums, or other scholarly institutions
- Include articles with extensive citations and bibliographies
- If online, have a URL that likely ends in .edu or .org
- Are **refereed** (peer reviewed), which means that each article has been reviewed, commented on, and accepted for publication by other scholars in the field

www.mhhe.com/
awr3

For disciplinary
resources to begin
your search, go to

Research >
Discipline Specific
Resources

19c Use printed and online reference works for general information.

Reference works provide an overview of a subject area and typically are less up-to-date than the specialized knowledge found in academic journals and scholarly books. If your instructor approves, you may start your research by consulting a general or discipline-specific encyclopedia, but for college research, you need to explore your topic in more depth. Often, the list of references at the end of an encyclopedia article can lead you to useful sources on your topic.

Reference books do not circulate, so plan to take notes or make photocopies of the pages you may need to consult later. Many college libraries subscribe to services that provide access to online encyclopedias. Check your college library's home page for appropriate links.

Here is a list of some other kinds of reference materials available in print, on the Internet, or both:

ALMANACS	*Almanac of American Politics* *Information Please Almanac* *World Almanac*
BIBLIOGRAPHIES	*Bibliographic Index* *Bibliography of Asian Studies* *MLA International Bibliography*
BIOGRAPHIES	*African American Biographical Database* *American Men and Women of Science* *Dictionary of American Biography* *Dictionary of Literary Biography:* *Chicano Writers* *Dictionary of National Biography* *Webster's New Biographical Dictionary* *Who's Who*
DICTIONARIES	*American Heritage Dictionary of the* *English Language* *Concise Oxford Dictionary of Literary Terms* *Dictionary of American History* *Dictionary of Philosophy* *Dictionary of the Social Sciences* *Oxford English Dictionary (OED)*

TextConnex

Evaluating Wikipedia

The online encyclopedia Wikipedia offers information on almost any subject, and it can be a good starting place for research. However, you should evaluate its content critically. Volunteers (who may or may not be experts) write Wikipedia's articles, and almost any user may edit any article. While the site has some mechanisms to help it maintain the accuracy of its information, always check any findings with another source (and cite that source, if you use the information).

Tips   LEARNING in COLLEGE

Refining Keyword Searches

Although search engines vary, the following guidelines should work for many of the search engines you will use:

- **Group words together.** Put quotation marks or parentheses around the specific phrase you are looking for, for example, "Dixieland Jazz."
- **Use Boolean operators.**

AND (+)	Use AND or + when you need sites with both of two or more words: Armstrong + Glaser.
OR	Use OR when you want sites with either of two or more terms: jazz OR "musical improvisation".
NOT	Use NOT in front of words that you do not want to appear together in your results: Armstrong NOT Neil.

- **Use a "wildcard."** For more results, combine part of a keyword with an asterisk (*) used as a wildcard: music* (for "music," "musician," "musical," and so forth).
- **Search the fields.** Some search engines permit you to search within fields, such as the title field of Web pages or the author field of a library catalog. Thus, TITLE + "Louis Armstrong" will give you all pages that have "Louis Armstrong" in their title.

19d   Understand keywords and keyword searches.

Most online research—whether in your library's catalog, in a specialized database, or on the Web—requires an understanding of **keyword searches.** In this context, a **keyword** is a term (or terms) you enter into a **search engine** (searching software) to find sources that have information you need.

To home in on your subject, adjust your initial search term. The "Tips" box above describes a variety of techniques for doing so that work in most search engines. Many search engines also have an advanced search feature that can help with the refining process.

19e   Use print indexes and online databases to find articles in journals and other periodicals.

1. Periodicals

Newspapers, magazines, and scholarly journals that are published at regular intervals are classified as **periodicals.** The articles in scholarly and technical journals, written by experts and based on up-to-date research, are more reliable than articles in popular newspapers and

For MULTILINGUAL STUDENTS

Researching a Full Range of Sources

Your mastery of a language other than English can sometimes give you access to important sources. Do not limit yourself to sources in your first language, however. Even if you find researching in English challenging, it is important to broaden your search as soon as you can to include a range of print and Internet resources written in English.

magazines. Ask your instructor or librarian which periodicals are considered important in the discipline you are studying.

2. Indexes and databases

Articles published in periodicals are cataloged in general and specialized **indexes.** Indexes are available on subscription-only **databases** and as print volumes. If you are searching for articles that are more than twenty years old, you may use print indexes, or an appropriate electronic index. Print indexes can be searched by author, subject, or title. Electronic databases can also be searched by date and keyword and will provide you with a list of articles that meet your search criteria. Each entry in the list will include the information you need to find and cite the article.

You can find databases on your library's Web site (and on CD-ROMs in the library). When selecting a database, consult its description on your library's site (often labeled "Info") to see the types of sources included, subjects covered, and number of periodicals from each subject area. Would your topic be best served by a general database (such as EBSCO Academic Search Premier), or one that is discipline specific (such as PsycINFO)? Also consider the time period the database spans.

The "Tips" box on page 211 lists common formats for database information. The "TextConnex" box on pages 212–13 lists some of the major online databases, and the screen shots in Figure 19.2 on page 210 illustrate a search on one of them, ProQuest Research Library. Keep in mind that not all libraries subscribe to all databases.

19f Use search engines and subject directories to find Internet sources.

To find information that has been published in Web pages, use an Internet search engine. Because each search engine searches the Web in its own way, you will probably use more than one. (*See the box on*

www.mhhe.com/awr3

For more information on links, go to

Research > Using the Internet

A. The database will be searched for articles that mention both Armstrong and Glaser.

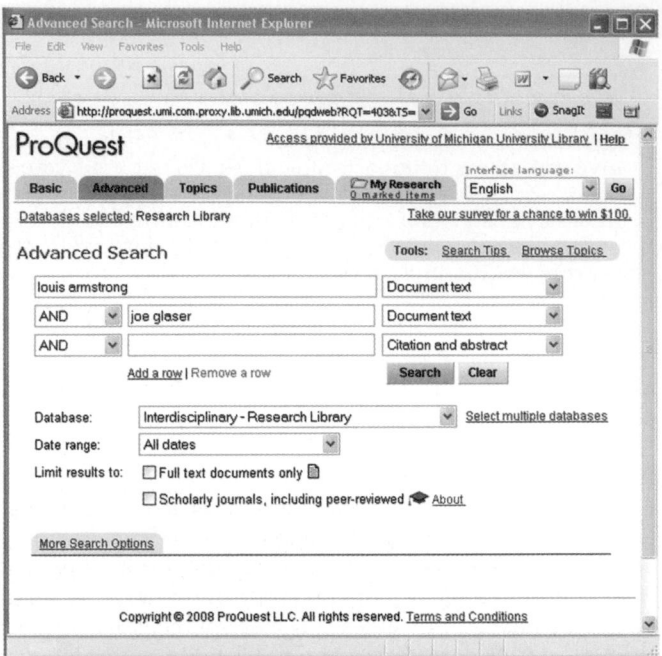

B. Entries include title, author, name of journal, viewing options (e.g., abstract).

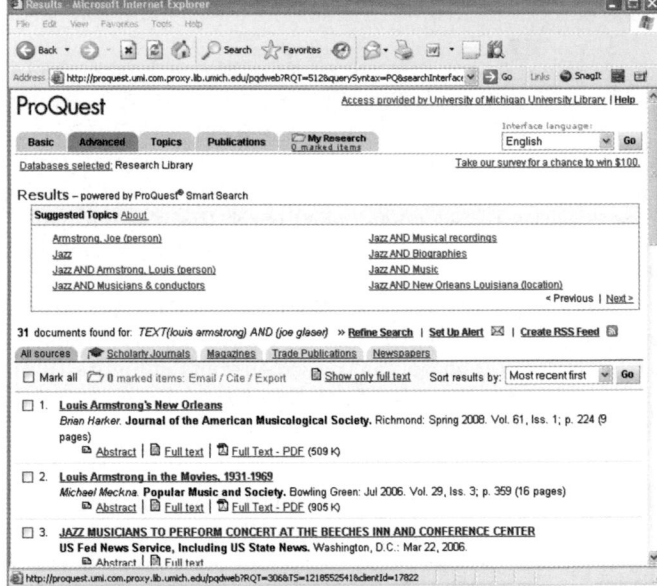

FIGURE 19.2 ProQuest's Advanced Search page (A) and partial results of search (B).

Tips LEARNING in COLLEGE

Formats for Database Information

When searching a database, you will encounter both abstracts and full-text articles, and full-text articles may be available in either PDF or HTML format.

- **Abstract:** An abstract is a brief summary of a full-text article. Abstracts appear at the beginning of articles in some scholarly journals and are used in databases to summarize complete articles. (Do not mistake an abstract for a full-text source.)
- **Full text:** When an article is listed as "full text," the database provides you with a link to the complete text. Full-text articles accessed through databases do not always include accompanying photographs or other illustrations, however.
- **PDF** and **HTML:** Articles in databases and other online sources may be in either PDF or HTML format (or both). Documents in HTML (hypertext markup language) have been formatted to read as Web pages. Documents in PDF (portable document format) appear as a facsimile of the original pages. To read a PDF document, download *Adobe Acrobat Reader* for free at <http://www.adobe.com>.

p. 218 for a list of popular Internet search engines.) To learn how a search engine can best serve your needs, look for a link labeled "search help," "about us," or something similar.

Some Internet search engines provide specialized searches—for images, for example (*see Chapter 20*). Google Book Search can help you find books on your topic. Google also offers a service called "Google Scholar" that locates only scholarly sources in response to a search term. At this point, it offers incomplete information, so you should not rely on it alone.

Many Internet search engines also include sponsored links—links that a commercial enterprise has paid to have appear in response to specific search terms. These are usually clearly identified.

Internet keyword searches should be carefully worded to provide relevant results. For example, a search of Google using the keywords *louis armstrong* yields a list of more than 3.8 *million* Web sites.

Refining the search by putting quotation marks around *louis armstrong* and linking that term to the term *jazz* with the Boolean operator AND (which will find all sites with the words *louis* and *armstrong* together and also the word *jazz*) reduces the number of hits to a still unmanageable 942,000. Altering the keywords to make them even more specific narrows the results significantly, as shown in Figure 19.3 on page 214.

Some Online Databases

- **ABC-CLIO:** This service offers access to two history-related databases: *America: History and Life* and *Historical Abstracts.*

- **EBSCOhost:** The *Academic Search Premier* database provides full-text coverage for more than 8,000 scholarly publications and indexes articles in all academic subject areas.

- **ERIC:** This database lists publications in the area of education.

- **Factiva:** This database offers access to the Dow Jones and Reuters news agencies, including newspapers, magazines, journals, newsletters, and Web sites.

- **General Science Index:** This index is general (rather than specialized). It lists articles by biologists, chemists, and other scientists.

- **GDCS:** Updated monthly, the Government Documents Catalog Service (GDCS) contains records of all publications printed by the United States Government Printing Office since 1976.

- **GPO Access:** This service of the U.S. Government Printing Office provides free electronic access to government documents.

- **Humanities Index:** This index lists articles from journals in language and literature, history, philosophy, and similar areas.

- **InfoTrac Web:** This Web-based service searches bibliographic and other databases such as the *General Reference Center Gold, General Business File ASAP,* and *Health Reference Center.*

- **JSTOR:** This archive provides full-text access to journals in the humanities, social sciences, and natural sciences.

- **LexisNexis Academic:** Updated daily, this online service provides full-text access to around 6,000 newspapers, professional publications, legal references, and congressional sources.

- **MLA Bibliography:** Covering 1963 to the present, the *MLA Bibliography* indexes journals, dissertations, and serials published worldwide in the fields of modern languages, literature, literary criticism, linguistics, and folklore.

Most search engines have an Advanced Search option. This allows you to search for exact phrases, to exclude a specific term, to search only for pages in a certain language, and to refine searches in other ways.

In addition to keyword searches, many Internet search engines offer a **subject directory**—a listing of broad categories. Clicking on a category brings you to a more specific array of choices. Clicking through this hierarchy of choices eventually brings you to a list of sites related to a specific topic.

Just as with online databases and print indexes, some Web sites provide content-specific subject directories designed for research in a

- *New York Times Index:* This index lists major articles published by the *Times* since 1913.
- *Newspaper Abstracts:* This database provides an index to fifty national and regional newspapers.
- *PAIS International:* Produced by the Public Affairs Information Service, this database indexes literature on public policy, social policy, and the social sciences from 1972 to the present.
- *Periodical Abstracts:* This database indexes more than 2,000 general and academic journals covering business, current affairs, economics, literature, religion, psychology, and women's studies from 1987 to the present.
- *ProQuest:* This database provides access to dissertations; newspapers and journals; information on sources in business, general reference, the social sciences, and humanities; and historical sources dating back to the nineteenth century.
- *PsycInfo:* Sponsored by the American Psychological Association (APA), this database indexes and abstracts books, scholarly articles, technical reports, and dissertations in psychology and related disciplines.
- *PubMed:* The National Library of Medicine publishes this database, which indexes and abstracts 15 million journal articles in biomedicine and provides links to related databases.
- *Sociological Abstracts:* This database indexes and abstracts articles from more than 2,600 journals, as well as books, conference papers, and dissertations.
- *Social Science Index:* This index lists articles from such fields as economics, psychology, political science, and sociology.
- *WorldCat:* This is a catalog of books and other resources available in libraries worldwide.

particular field. These sites are often reviewed or screened and are excellent starting points for academic research.

Other online tools can help you organize sources and keep track of your Web research. You should save the URLs of promising sites to your browser's bookmarks or favorites. Your browser's history function can allow you to retrace your steps if you forget how to find a particular site. The box on page 215 includes additional online resources.

19g Use your library's online catalog or card catalog to find books.

Books in most libraries are shelved by **call numbers** based on the Library of Congress classification system. The *Library of Congress*

Number of hits

Search terms

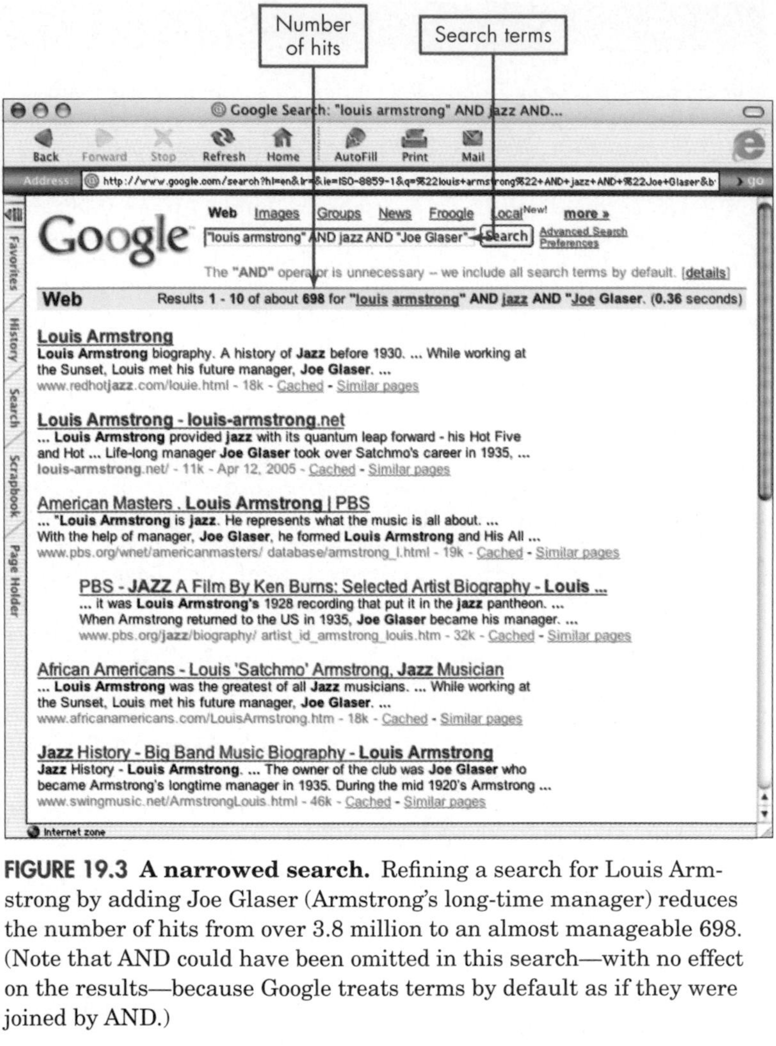

FIGURE 19.3 A narrowed search. Refining a search for Louis Armstrong by adding Joe Glaser (Armstrong's long-time manager) reduces the number of hits from over 3.8 million to an almost manageable 698. (Note that AND could have been omitted in this search—with no effect on the results—because Google treats terms by default as if they were joined by AND.)

Subject Headings (LCSH) shows you how your research topic is classified and provides you with a set of key terms that you can use in your search. In this system, books on the same topic have similar call numbers and are shelved together. You will need the call number to locate the actual book on the library's shelves. Therefore, when consulting a library catalog, be sure to jot down (or print out) the call numbers of books you want to consult.

You can conduct a keyword search of most online library catalogs by author, by title, or by subject. Many catalogs also search by pub-

TEXTCONNEX

Online Tools for Research

- *Zotero* <http://www.zotero.org>: Compatible with the *Mozilla Firefox* browser (version 2.0 and higher), this program automatically saves citation information for many types of online sources (text and images) via your browser. It creates formatted references in multiple styles and helps you organize your sources by assigning tags (categories based on keywords) to them.
- *Del.icio.us* <http://www.del.icio.us>: This site allows you to create an online collection of Web links that functions like a portable bookmarks or favorites list. You can access this list from any computer, and you can organize its entries by creating categories and assigning tags.
- *DiRT (Digital Research Tools)* <http://digitalresearchtools .pbwiki.com/>: This site links to online tools that help researchers in the humanities and social sciences perform many tasks, such as collaborating with others, finding sources, and visualizing data.

lisher, notes, and other fields. For example, a search of the term *Louis Armstrong* by author would produce a list of works by Louis Armstrong; a search by title would produce a list of works with "Louis Armstrong" in the title; and a search by subject would produce a list of works that are all or partly about Louis Armstrong.

Card catalogs are rarely used except by archives and specialized libraries. Cards are usually filed by author, title, and subject (based on the *Library of Congress Subject Headings*).

The results of a keyword search of a library's online catalog will provide a list composed mostly of books. In the examples in Figures 19.4 and 19.5 of a search of the City University of New York's online

SOURCE SMART

Organizing Your Sources

List your sources alphabetically. For each, include citation information *(see pp. 248–49)*, key points, and relevance. Does the source support or detract from your claim? Is it an early source or a later one? Does it agree or disagree with other sources you have read? Do other sources reference this one? You might color-code your list to indicate related ideas across sources. Include useful quotations and their page numbers.

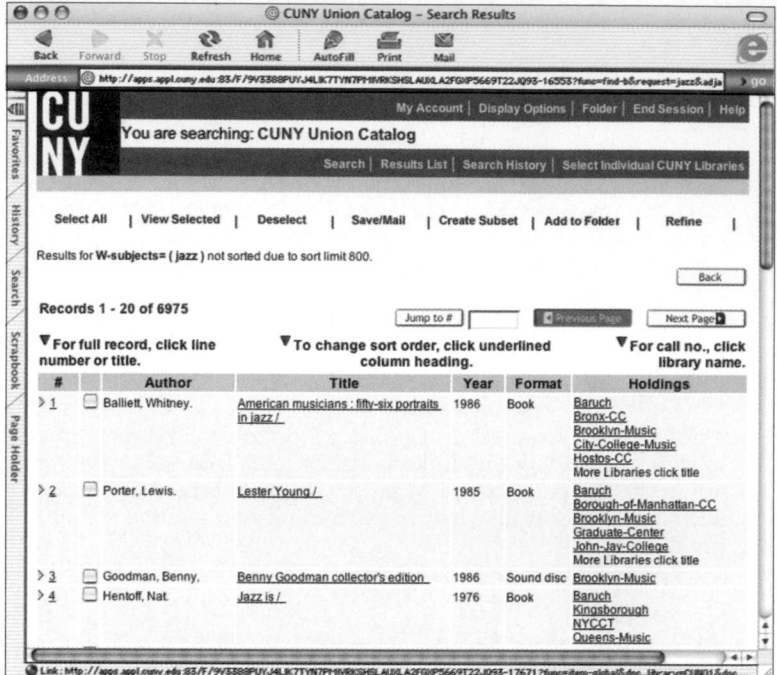

FIGURE 19.4 Initial search using the keyword *jazz*. Using the word *jazz* as a keyword in a subject search produces an unmanageable 6,975 sources. The "Holdings" column indicates which libraries in the CUNY system have the book. Clicking on a library name gives the book's call number at that library.

catalog (*above*), notice that under the column "Format" other kinds of media that match a keyword subject search are also listed; you can alter the terms of a search to restrict the formats to a specific medium.

As with any keyword search, whether you get what you really need—a manageable number of relevant sources—depends on your choice of keywords. If your search terms are too broad, you will get too many hits; if they are too narrow, you will get few or none.

19h Take advantage of printed and online government documents.

The U.S. government publishes an enormous amount of information and research every year, most of which is available online. The *Monthly Catalog of U.S. Government Publications* and the *U.S. Government Periodicals Index* are available as online databases. The Government

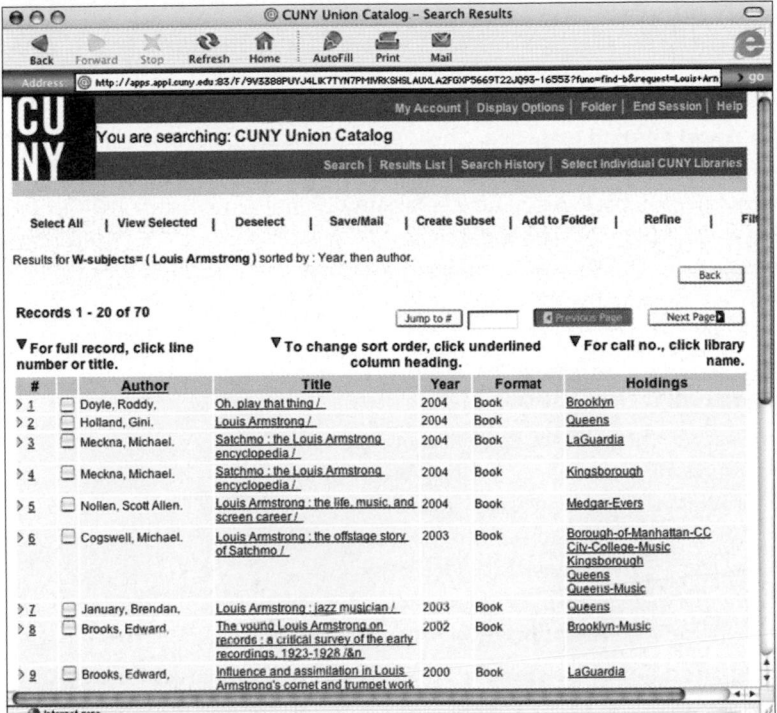

FIGURE 19.5 Second search with a narrower keyword. A keyword search using the term Louis Armstrong produces 70 results, a manageable number.

Printing Office's own Web site, *GPO Access* <http://www.gpoaccess .gov/>, is an excellent resource for identifying when federal government publications are available and where to find them. Other online government resources include the following:

- *FedWorld Information Network* (maintained by the National Technical Information Service) <http://www.fedworld.gov/>
- *FirstGov* (the U.S. government's "Official Web Portal") <http://firstgov.gov/>
- *The National Institutes of Health* <http://www.nih.gov>
- *U.S. Census Bureau* <http://www.census.gov>

19i Explore online communication.

The Internet provides access to communities with common interests and varying levels of expertise on different subjects. Information from

Popular Internet Search Engines

General search engines: These sites allow for both category and keyword searches.

- *AltaVista* <http://www.altavista.com>
- *Google* <http://www.google.com>
- *Live Search* (Microsoft) <http://www.msn.com>
- *Vivisimo* <http://vivisimo.com>
- *Yahoo!* <http://www.yahoo.com>

Meta search engines: These sites search several different search engines at once.

- *Dogpile* <http://www.dogpile.com>
- *Internet Public Library* <http://www.ipl.org>
- *Ixquick* <http://www.ixquick.com>
- *Librarian's Index to the Internet* <http://lii.org>
- *Library of Congress* <http://loc.gov>
- *MetaCrawler* <http://www.metacrawler.com>
- *WebCrawler* <http://www.webcrawler.com>

Mediated search engines: These sites have been assembled and reviewed by people who sometimes provide annotations and commentary about topic areas and specific sites.

- *About.com* <http://www.about.com>
- *Looksmart* <http://search.looksmart.com>

these sources must be evaluated carefully (*see Chapter 21, pp. 226–34*). Discussion lists (electronic mailing lists), Usenet news groups, social networking sites, and some Weblogs (blogs) are online forums for communities. Various forms of synchronous communication exist as well. Online forums can help you with research in the following ways:

- You can get an idea for a paper by finding out what topics interest and concern people.
- You can zero in on a very specific or current topic.
- You can query an expert in the field about your topic via e-mail or a social networking site.

Discussion lists (electronic mailing lists) are networked e-mail conversations on particular topics. Lists can be open (anyone can join) or closed (only certain people can join). If the list is open, you can subscribe by sending a message to a computer that has list-processing software installed on it.

> *Caution:* The level of expertise among the people who participate in online forums, as well as the scholarly seriousness of the forums themselves, varies widely. Look for reputable forums via your library or department site.

Unlike lists, **Usenet news groups** are posted to a **news server**—a computer that hosts the news group and distributes postings to participating servers. You must subscribe to read postings, and they are not automatically distributed by e-mail.

Podcasts are downloadable digital audio or video recordings, updated regularly. The Smithsonian produces reliable podcasts on many topics <http://www.si.edu/podcasts>.

RSS (Really Simple Syndication) **feeds** deliver the latest content from continuously updated Web sites to your browser or home page. You can use RSS feeds to keep up with information on your topic, once you identify relevant Web sites.

Interactively structured Web sites provide another medium for online communication. **Blogs,** for example (*see Chapter 14*), can be designed to allow readers to post their own comments and queries. **Wikis,** sites designed for online collaboration, go further, allowing people to both comment on and modify one another's contributions. **Social networking** sites help people form online communities (*see Chapter 14*).

Chat rooms permit one form of **synchronous communication,** which involves various types of real-time electronic exchanges between individuals. Chat rooms are usually organized by topic. **Instant messaging (IM)** is another medium for real-time communication, but it involves only people who have agreed to form a group. Other, less common, formats for synchronous communication include multiuser dimensions and multiuser object-oriented dimensions (MUDs and MOOs), as well as virtual worlds such as SecondLife.com, which can be used for collaborative projects.

20 Finding and Creating Effective Visuals

www.mhhe.com/awr3

For resources to begin your search, go to

Research > Discipline Specific Resources

Visuals are often included as support for a writer's thesis, sometimes to enhance an argument and other times to make the writer's own argument. A relief organization, for example, might post a series of compelling visuals on its Web site to persuade potential donors to contribute money following a catastrophic event. In some writing situations, you will be able to prepare or provide your own visuals. You may, for example, create bar graphs from data that you collected. In other situations, however, you may decide to create a visual from data that you found in a source or to search in your library or on the Internet for a visual to use.

◉ 20a Find quantitative data and display it visually.

Research writing in many disciplines, especially the sciences, social sciences, business, and other technical fields often requires reference to quantitative information, and quantitative information often has more impact when it is displayed visually in a chart, graph, or map. (*For examples of graphs and charts, and a discussion of what situations to use them in, see Tab 2: Writing and Designing Texts, pp. 54–56.*)

> ***Caution:*** Whether you are using data from a source to create an image or incorporating an image created by someone else into your paper, you must give credit to the source of the data or image. Furthermore, if you plan to publish a visual you selected from another source on a Web site or in another medium, you must obtain permission to use it from the copyright holder unless the source specifically states that such use is allowed.

www.mhhe.com/
awr3
For an interactive
tutorial, go to

Writing >
Visual Rhetoric

1. Finding existing graphs, charts, and maps
As you search for print and online sources (*see Chapter 19*), take notes on useful graphs, charts, or maps that you can incorporate (with proper acknowledgment) into your paper. If your source is available in print only, you may be able to use a scanner to capture and digitize it.

2. Creating visuals from quantitative data
Sometimes you may find data presented in writing or in tables that would be more effective as a chart or graph. Using the graphics tool available in spreadsheet or other software, you can create your own visual.

SOURCE SMART

Citing Data

Make citations of data specific. Indicate the report and page number or Web address(es) where you found the information, as well as any other elements required by your documentation style. If you analyze the data, refer to any analysis in the source before presenting your own interpretation.

For example, suppose you are writing about population trends in the United States in the nineteenth century and want to illustrate the country's population growth in that period with a line graph, using data from the U.S. Census Bureau, which is in the public domain. Most census data, however, appears in tables like the one shown in Figure 20.1 on page 222. If you transfer data from a table to a spreadsheet program or some word-processing programs, you can use it to create graphs that you can insert into a paper, as in Figure 20.1.

3. Displaying the right data

Display data in a way that is consistent with your purpose and not misleading to viewers. For example, Nancy Kaplan has pointed out distortions in a graph from a National Endowment for the Arts report on reading practices (Figure 20.2 on page 223). The NEA graph presents the years 1988 to 2004, showing a sharp decline in reading. However, the source for the graph, the National Center for Educational Statistics (NCES), presents a less alarming picture in Figure 20.3 on page 223. Here, reading levels are plotted over a longer period of time, from 1971 to 2004. In addition, the NEA graph is not consistent in its units: the period 1984 to 1988 takes up the same amount of space as 1988 to 1990. In selectively displaying and distorting data, the NEA graph stacks the deck to argue for the reality of a reading crisis.

Avoid intentionally or unintentionally distorting data. Never use photo-editing software to alter photographs in a way that misleads viewers. Plot the axes of line and bar graphs so that they do not misrepresent data. (*See Tab 2: Writing and Designing Texts, p. 55.*)

👁 20b Search for appropriate images in online and print sources.

Photographs, pictures of artwork, drawings, diagrams, and maps can provide visual support for many kinds of papers, particularly in subjects like history, English and other languages, philosophy, music, theater, and other performing arts. As with the display of quantitative data, you might *choose* an image from another source, or you might *create* one. If you were doing a report comparing the way different corporations are organized, for example, you might use organizational charts that appear in corporate reports. Alternatively, you might use your word processor's drawing feature to create your own organizational charts based on information you find in the corporate reports. When using an image from another source, be sure to cite it correctly. If the image will appear on a public Web site, consult the copyright holder for permission.

The following are three sources of images that you can draw on:

- **Online library and museum image collections and subscription databases:** Several libraries and other archives maintain collections of images online. See the TextConnex box

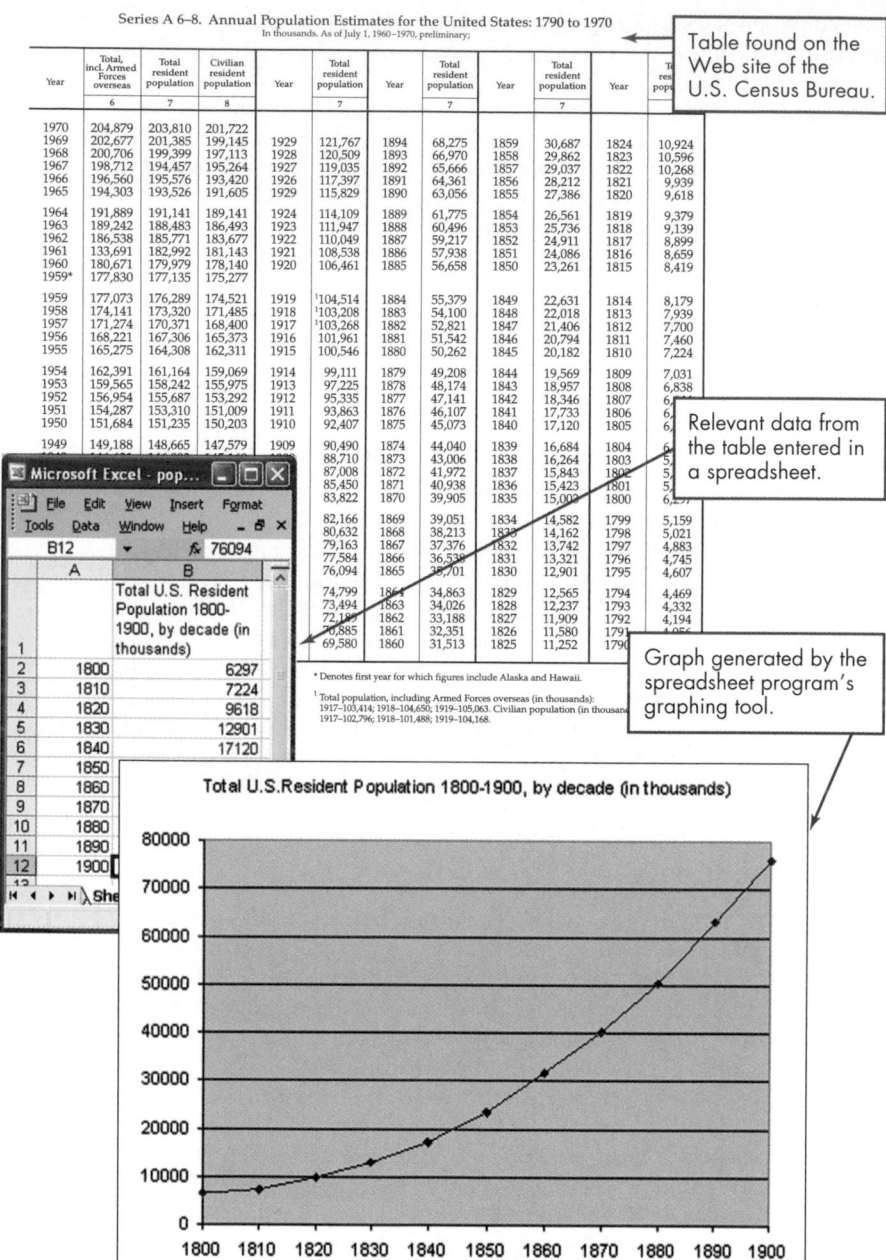

FIGURE 20.1 Using a spreadsheet program to create a graph from data in a table.

FIGURE 20.2 A distorted display of reading practices indicates a decline.

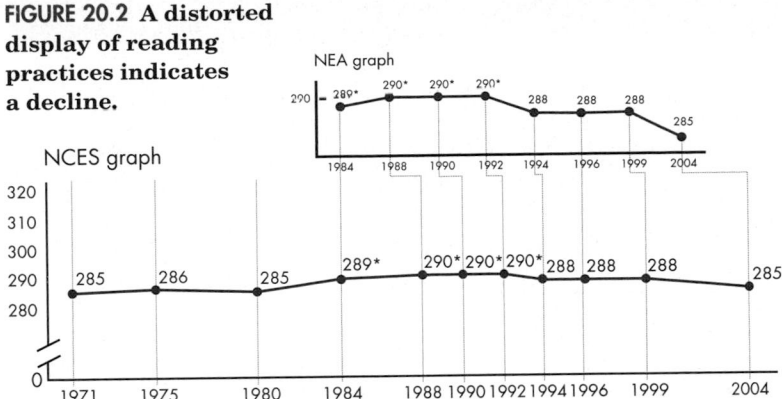

FIGURE 20.3 An accurate display of reading practices shows only mild fluctuations.

CHECKLIST

Deciding When to Use an Image in Your Paper

Regardless of the kind or number of images you use, there are several questions you will want to consider as you look for them:

- ☐ What contribution will each image make to the text?

- ☐ What contribution do the images taken as a whole make to the text?

- ☐ How many images do you need?

- ☐ Where will each image appear in the text?

- ☐ Does the audience have enough background information to interpret each image in the way you intend?

- ☐ If not, is there additional information that should be included in the text?

- ☐ What information needs to be in the caption?

- ☐ Have you reviewed your own text (and perhaps asked a friend to review it as well) to see how well the image is "working"— in terms of appropriateness, location, and context?

CHECKLIST

Deciding What Kind of Chart or Graph to Use

In deciding the kind of chart or graph you want to use, you will want to consider these questions:

- [ ] What information do you want to show, and why?

- [ ] What options do you have for displaying this information?

- [ ] How much context do you want to include, and why?

- [ ] How many graphs do you think you might need?

- [ ] How detailed should your graph be, and why?

- [ ] Will your visual be used as a tool of analysis for the future, or will it be used to report on what was?

- [ ] What information will be left out or minimized, and how important is that omission?

- [ ] What other information—an introduction, an explanation, a summary, an interpretation—will readers need to make sense of the graphed information?

on page 226 for the URLs of image collections. Follow the guidelines for usage posted on these sites. Your library also may subscribe to an image database such as the Associated Press *AP Multimedia Archive.*

www.mhhe.com/
awr3
For a selection of
search engines, go to

Research >
Additional Links
on Research

- ■ **Images on the Internet:** Many search engines have the ability to search the Web for images alone. You can conduct an image search on Google, for example, by clicking on the "images" option, entering the key term, and then clicking "search." Image- and media-sharing sites such as Flickr and YouTube can serve as sources as well. Read the information on the site carefully to see what uses of the material are permitted. The Creative Commons site (www.creativecommons .org) lets you search for material with a Creative Commons license. Such a license, shown in Figure 20.4, describes allowed uses of the content. The material shown can be used or altered for noncommercial purposes, as long as it is cited.

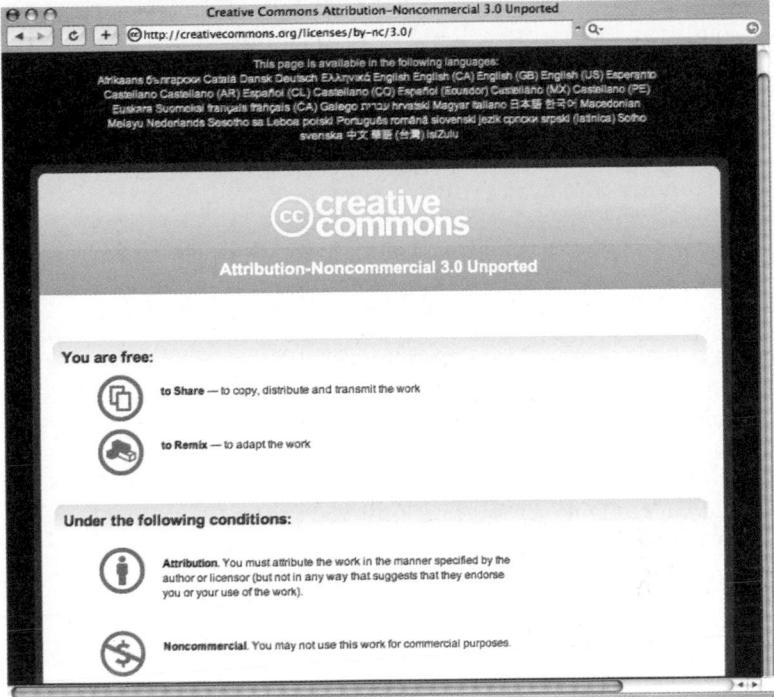

FIGURE 20.4 Creative Commons license. This page shows the terms of use for a particular online work.

Assume that copyright applies to material on the Web unless the site says otherwise. If your project will be published or placed on a public Web site, you must obtain permission to use this material. (*See Chapter 23: Plagiarism, Copyright, and Intellectual Property, pp. 241–47.*)

■ **Images scanned from a book or journal:** You can use a scanner to scan some images from books and journals into a paper, but, as always, only if you are sure your use is within fair-use guidelines. Also, be sure to credit the source.

Caution: The results of Internet image searches, like those of any Internet search, must be carefully evaluated for relevance and reliability. (*See Chapter 21: Evaluating Sources, pp. 226–34.*) Make sure you have proper source information for any images you use that you find in this way.

TEXTCONNEX

Some Online Image Collections

- *Art Institute of Chicago* (selected works from the museum's collection) <http://www.artic.edu/aic/index.html>
- *The Library of Congress* <http://www.loc.gov/>
- *National Archives Digital Classroom* (documents and photographs from American history) <http://www.archives.gov/digital_classroom/index.html>
- *National Aeronautics and Space Administration* (images and multimedia features on space exploration) <http://www.nasa.gov/vision/universe/features/index.html>
- *National Park Service Digital Image Archive* (thousands of public domain photographs of U.S. national parks) <http://photo.itc.nps.gov/storage/images/index.html>
- *New York Public Library* <www.nypl.org/digital/>
- *Schomburg Center for Research in Black Culture* <www.nypl.org/research/sc/sc.html>
- *VRoma: A Virtual Community for Teaching and Learning Classics* (images and other resources related to ancient Rome) <http://www.vroma.org/>

21 Evaluating Sources

It is up to you to evaluate each potential source to determine whether it is both *relevant* and *reliable*. A source is relevant if it pertains to your research topic. A source is reliable if it provides trustworthy information.

Evaluating sources requires you to think critically and make judgments about which sources will be useful for answering your research question. This process helps you manage your research and focus your time on those sources that deserve close scrutiny.

21a Question print sources.

Just because something is in print does not make it relevant or true. How can you determine whether a print source is likely to be both re-

For MULTILINGUAL WRITERS

Questioning Sources

While some cultures emphasize respect for established authors, the intellectual tradition of American universities values careful questioning. Consider the pertinence and reliability of all potential sources.

liable and useful? The Checklist box (*pp. 228–29*) contains some questions to ask about any source you are considering.

Relevance can be a tricky matter. For example, your sociology instructor will expect you to give special preference to sociological sources in a project on the organization of the workplace. Your business management instructor will expect you to use material from that field in a project on the same topic. Be prepared to find that some promising sources turn out to be less relevant than you first thought.

21b Question Internet sources.

Web resources require specific methods of ensuring the credibility of information presented. Most of the material in the library has been evaluated to some extent for credibility. Editors and publishers have reviewed the content of books, magazines, journals, and newspapers. At the same time, some presses and publications are more reputable than others. Subscription databases generally compile articles that originally

SOURCE SMART

Evaluating Citations

When you look for sources using a database or library catalog, you can save yourself time by eliminating inappropriate search results. Some of the techniques used to evaluate a source's relevance and reliability also work with only the citation. You still can judge

- the author's level of expertise (with a simple Web, catalog, or database search),
- the title's relevance to your research question,
- the source's currency, and
- the publisher's or publication's reputation.

CHECKLIST

Relevance and Reliability of Sources

Relevance

☐ **Do the source's title and subtitle indicate that it addresses your specific research question?**

☐ **What is the publication date?** Is the material up-to-date, classic, or historic? The concept of "up-to-date" depends on discipline and topic. Ask your instructor how recent sources should be for your paper.

☐ **Does the table of contents indicate that a book covers useful information?**

☐ **If the source is a book, does it have an index?** Scan the index for keywords related to your topic.

☐ **Does the abstract at the beginning or the summary at the end of an article suggest it will be useful?** An abstract or a summary presents the main points made in the article.

☐ **Does the work contain headings?** Skim the headings to see whether they indicate that the source covers useful information.

appeared in print, and librarians try to purchase the most reliable databases. While you can have some confidence that most of the material you find in the library is credible, you must evaluate all sources.

In contrast, anyone can choose a subject and create a Web site that looks attractive but contains nonsense. Similarly, the people who post to blogs, discussion lists, and news groups may not be experts or even marginally well informed. So, while information on the Web may be valuable and timely, you must assess its credibility carefully. Consult the Checklist box on pages 233–34 and consider the following questions when determining whether online information is reliable:

1. Who is hosting the site? Is the site hosted by a university or by a government agency (like the National Science Foundation or the National Endowment for the Humanities)? In general, sites hosted by institutions with scholarly credentials are more likely to be trustworthy. They remain open to critical inquiry (as exemplified by the NEA graph on page 223).

Reliability

☐ **What information can you find about the writer's credentials?** Obtain biographical information about the writer by checking the source itself, consulting a biographical dictionary, or conducting an Internet search of the writer's name. Is the writer affiliated with a research institution that contributes knowledge about an issue? Is the writer an expert on the topic? Is the writer cited frequently in other sources about the topic?

☐ **Who is the publisher?** University presses and academic publishers are considered more scholarly than the popular press.

☐ **Does the work include a bibliography of works consulted or cited?** Trustworthy writers cite a variety of sources and document their citations properly. Does this source do so? Does the source include a variety of citations?

☐ **Does the work argue reasonably for its position and treat opposing views fairly?** What kind of tone does the author use? Is the work objective or subjective? Are the writer's arguments clear and logical? What is the author's point of view? Does he or she present other views fairly? (*For more on evaluating arguments, see Tab 2, Writing and Designing Texts, pp. 27–37.*)

2. Who is speaking on the site? A nationally recognized biologist is likely to be more credible on biological topics than a graduate student in biology. Do not use a source if you cannot identify the author.

3. What links does the site provide? If it is networked to sites with obviously unreasonable or inaccurate content, you must question the credibility of the original site.

4. Is the information on the site supported with documentation from scholarly or otherwise reliable sources? Reliable sources of information could include government reports, for example. Do other sources cite this one?

Consider these factors as well:

▪ **Authority and credibility:** Are the author and sponsor of the Web site identifiable? Does the author include biographical information? Is there any indication that the author has relevant expertise on the subject? Look for information about the individual or organization sponsoring the site. The following extensions in the Web address, or uniform resource locator (URL), can help you determine the type of site (which often tells you something about its purpose):

.com	commercial (business)	**.edu**	educational	**.mil**	military
.org	nonprofit organization	**.gov**	U.S. government	**.net**	network

A tilde (~) followed by a name in a URL usually means the site is a personal home page not affiliated with any organization.

- **Audience and purpose:** Does the appearance of the site and the tone of any written material suggest an audience? A site's purpose also influences the way it presents information and the reliability of that information. Is the site's main purpose to promote a cause, raise money, advertise a product or service, provide factual information, present research results, provide news, share personal information, or offer entertainment? Always try to view the site's home page; you may need to delete everything after the first slash in the URL to do so.

- **Objectivity and reasonableness:** Look carefully at the purpose and tone of the text. Nearly all sources express a point of view or bias. You should consult sources that represent a range of opinions on your topic. However, unreasonable sources have no place in academic debate. Clues that indicate a lack of reasonableness include an intemperate tone, broad claims, exaggerated statements of significance, conflicts of interest, no recognition of opposing views, and strident attacks on opposing views. (*For more on evaluating arguments, see Tab 2: Writing and Designing Texts, pp. 27–37.*)

- **Relevance and timeliness:** In what ways does the information from an online source specifically support (or refute) your thesis or topic? Do the site's intended audience and purpose include an academic audience? Does the site indicate how recently it has been updated, and are most of the included links still working?

- **Context:** Do others' comments on a blog or posts to a discussion list make your source appear more credible?

Consider a student writing a paper on the reintroduction of gray wolves in the western United States following their near-extinction. Many environmentalists have favored this program, while farmers and ranchers have worried about the impact of wolves on livestock.

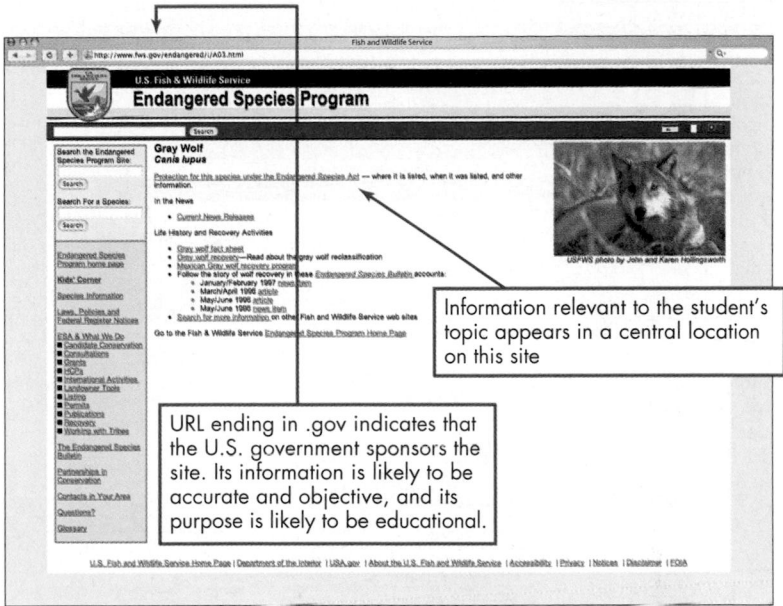

FIGURE 21.1 U.S. Fish & Wildlife Service Endangered Species Program site on the gray wolf. This goverment site provides information on the efforts to preserve and rebuild the gray wolf population in the United States.

The student conducts an online keyword search and finds the site in Figure 21.1. This site focuses on the gray wolf population in America and its status under the Endangered Species Act, making it relevant to the student's topic. The URL indicates that the site belongs to a U.S. government agency, suggesting its reliability (although such sites are not immune from politics and bias). Information on the site appears in a simple, easy-to-follow format, indicating an educational purpose. It links to other government sites. Scrolling down, the student sees the site has been updated recently. This site's apparent authority, credibility, and purpose make it a good candidate for use as a source.

Next, the student finds the site in Figure 21.2 on page 232. Following the link that says "About us," the student learns that the site is sponsored by the WWF (formerly World Wildlife Fund), a nonprofit organization that advocates for environmental conservation. The site includes policy papers with clearly documented sources for the data cited, suggesting its reliability. However, it deals only with the reintroduction of wolves in Europe, not the United States. It would

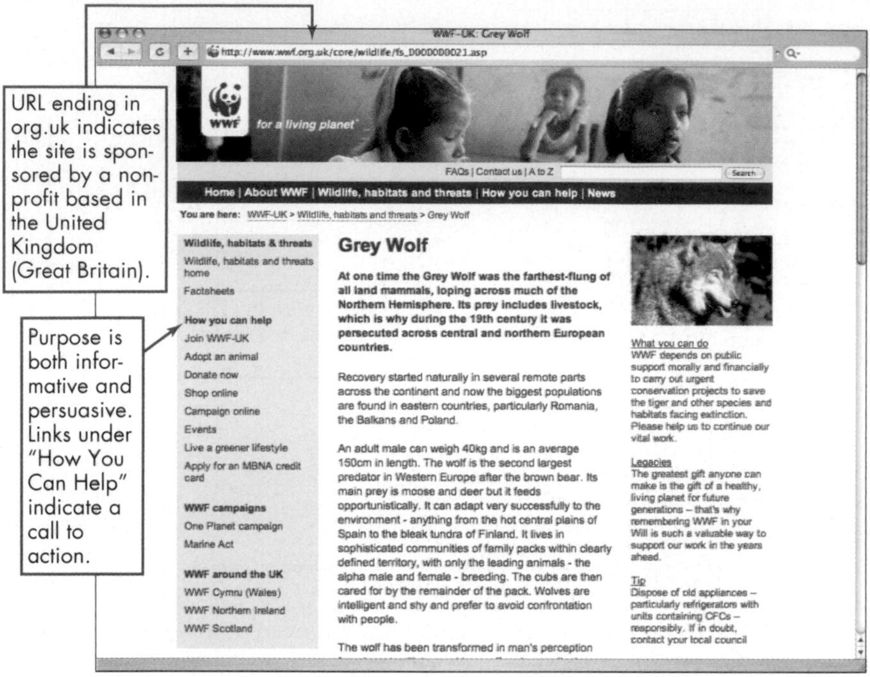

URL ending in org.uk indicates the site is sponsored by a nonprofit based in the United Kingdom (Great Britain).

Purpose is both informative and persuasive. Links under "How You Can Help" indicate a call to action.

FIGURE 21.2 WWF (formerly World Wildlife Fund) page about Europe's grey wolf. This advocacy site describes efforts to preserve a wolf population in Europe.

be a relevant source if the student used the European program as an example.

Finally the student reaches the site in Figure 21.3. This site gives apparently accurate information about wolves in an impartial way. Scrolling down, the student sees that the site also features advertisements, which do not appear in most scholarly sources. The site does not state the author's credentials, nor does it include documentation for its information. The student should confirm its statements with another source.

www.mhhe.com/ awr3

For an interactive tutorial using the CARS checklist, go to

Research > CARS Source Evaluation Tutor

21c Evaluate a source's arguments.

As you read the sources you have selected, you should continue to assess their reliability. Look for arguments that are qualified, supported with evidence, and well documented. Avoid sources that appeal mostly to emotions or promote one-sided agendas instead of inquiry and discussion. A fair-minded researcher needs to read and evaluate sources on many sides of an issue.

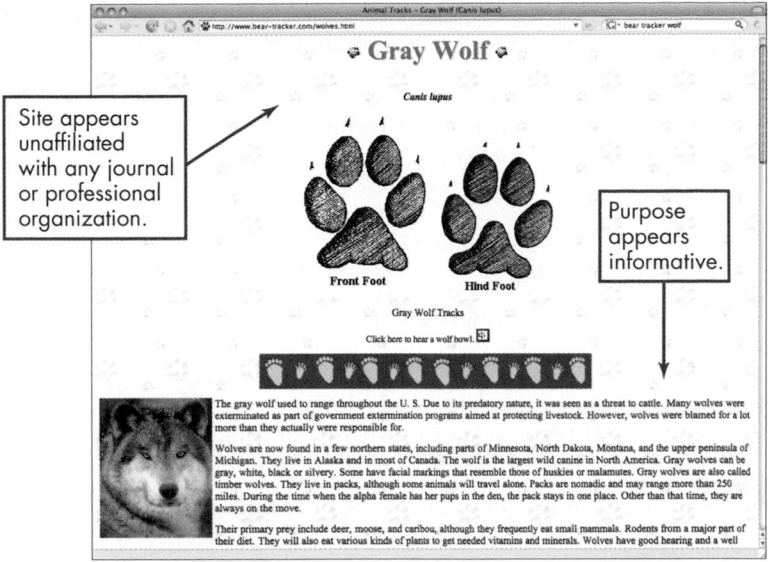

FIGURE 21.3 Animal Tracks gray wolf site. This site's information appears to be accurate, but it does not document its sources or present the author's credentials.

CHECKLIST

Using the CARS Checklist to Evaluate Web Sites

A Web site that is Credible, Accurate, Reasonable, and Supported (CARS) should meet the following criteria:

Credibility

☐ The source is trustworthy; you would consider a print version to be authoritative (for example, an online edition of a major newspaper or news magazine).

☐ The argument and use of evidence are clear and logical.

☐ The author's or sponsor's credentials are available. (Visit the home page and look for a link that says "About Us.")

☐ Quality control is evident (for example, spelling and grammar are correct, and links are functional).

(continued)

☐ The source is a known or respected authority; it has organizational support (such as a university, a research institution, or a major news publication).

Accuracy

☐ The site is updated frequently, if not daily (and includes "last updated" information).

☐ The site provides evidence for its assertions.

☐ The site is detailed; text appears in full paragraphs.

☐ The site is comprehensive, including archives, links, and additional resources. A search feature and table of contents or tabs allow you to quickly find the information you need.

☐ The site's purpose includes completeness and accuracy.

Reasonableness

☐ The site is fair, balanced, and objective. (Look at responses on a blog or related messages on a news group.)

☐ The site makes its purpose clear. (Is it selling something? Prompting site visitors to sign a petition? Promoting a new film?)

☐ The site contains no conflict of interest.

☐ The site does not include fallacies or a slanted tone. (*For more on fallacies, see Chapter 4, pp. 32–35*).

Support

☐ The site lists sources for its information, providing links where available.

☐ The site clarifies which content it is responsible for and which links are created by unrelated authors or sponsors.

☐ The site provides contact information for its authors and/or sponsors.

☐ If the site is an academic resource, it follows the conventions of a specific citation style (MLA, APA, or another accepted style).

22 Doing Research in the Archive, Field, and Lab

Research involves more than **secondary research**—finding answers to questions in books and other print and online resources. When you conduct **primary research**—looking up old maps, consulting census records, polling community members about a current issue—you participate in the discovery of knowledge.

The three kinds of primary research discussed in this chapter are archival research, field research, and laboratory research.

- **Archival research:** An **archive** is a cataloged collection of documents, manuscripts, and other materials, possibly including receipts, wills, photographs, sound recordings, and other kinds of media.

- **Field research:** Field research takes you out into the world to gather and record information.

- **Laboratory research:** Every science course you take will most likely involve a laboratory component. In the laboratory, you work individually or as a team to carefully record each step of an experiment.

22a Adhere to ethical principles when doing primary research.

In the archive, field, or lab, you are working directly with something precious and immediate: an original record, a group of people, or special materials. An ethical researcher shows respect for materials, experimental subjects, fellow researchers, and readers. Here are some guidelines for ethical research:

- Handle original documents and materials with great care, always leaving sources and data available for other researchers.

- Accurately report your sources and results.

- Follow proper procedures when working with human participants.

Research with human participants should also adhere to the following basic principles:

- **Confidentiality:** People who fill out surveys, participate in focus groups, or respond to interviews should be assured that their names will not be used without their permission.

Primary Research in the Disciplines

Different disciplines engage in characteristically different forms of primary research. Here are some examples:

- **Archival research:** languages and literature; education; music and the performing arts; visual arts; media and popular culture; social sciences
- **Field research:** social sciences; marketing and advertising; media and communication
- **Laboratory research:** life sciences; physical sciences; computer science; engineering

- **Informed consent:** Before participating in an experiment, all participants must sign a statement affirming that they understand the general purpose of the research.
- **Minimal risk:** Participants in experiments should not incur any risks greater than they do in everyday life.
- **Protection of vulnerable groups:** Researchers must be held strictly accountable for research done with the physically disabled, prisoners, people who are mentally impaired or incompetent, minors, the elderly, and pregnant women.

22b Prepare yourself for archival research.

Archives are found in libraries, museums, other institutions and private collections, and on video and audiotape. Your own attic may contain family archives—letters, diaries, and photographs that could have value to a researcher. Some archival collections are accessible through the Internet; others you must visit in person (*see the TextConnex box*). The more you know about your area of study, the more likely you will be to see the significance of an item in an archival collection.

Archives generally require that you call or e-mail to arrange a time for your visit, and some are restricted. If you find an archive on the Internet that you would like to visit, phone or e-mail well in advance to find out if you will need references, a letter of introduction, or other qualifying papers. Archives also generally require you to present a photo ID and to leave personal items in a locker or at a coat check. They have strict policies about reproducing materials and rarely allow anything to leave the premises. The more you know about

Online Information about Archives

Here are some Internet sites that will help you find and understand a wide range of archival sources:

- *American Memory* <http://memory.loc.gov>: This site offers access to more than seven million digital items from over a hundred collections of material on U.S. history and culture.
- *ArchivesUSA* <http://archives.chadwyck.com>: This subscription service is available via ProQuest. It provides information about 80,000 manuscript collections, more than 50,000 document collections, and more than 5,000 other archival repositories.
- *U.S. National Archives and Record Administration (NARA)* <http://www.nara.gov>: Learn how to use the National Archives in this site's research room, and then search the site for the documents you want.
- *Radio Program Archive* <http://www.people.memphis.edu/ ~mbensman>: This site lists radio archives available from the University of Memphis and explains how to obtain cassettes of programs.
- *Repositories of Primary Sources* <http://www.uidaho.edu/ special-collections/OtherRepositories.html>: This site lists more than 4,800 Web sites describing holdings of manuscripts, rare books, historical photographs, and other archival materials.
- *Television News Archive* <http://tvnews.vanderbilt.edu>: This site provides summaries of television news broadcasts and information on how to order videocassettes.
- *Virtual Library Museums Page* <http://icom.org/vlmp>: This site lists online museums throughout the world.
- *Women Writers Project* <http://www.wwp.brown.edu/texts/ wwoentry.html>: This site lists archived texts by pre-Victorian women writers that are available through the project.

the archive's policies and procedures before you visit, the more productive your visit will be.

22c Plan your field research carefully.

Field research involves recording observations, conducting interviews, and administering surveys. To conduct field research at a particular site, such as a place of business or a school, you will need to obtain permission. Explain the nature of your project, the date and time you would like to visit, and how much time you will need. Will you be observing? Interviewing people? Taking photographs? Also ask for a confirming letter or e-mail. Always write a thank-you note after you have concluded your research. Do *not* attempt to conduct your research without first obtaining permission. To do so is unethical and may constitute illegal trespassing.

1. Observing and writing field notes

When you use direct observation, keep careful records in order to retain the information you gather. Figure 22.1 shows a scientist taking field notes. Here are some guidelines to follow:

- Be systematic in your observations, but be alert to unexpected behavior.
- Record what you see and hear as objectively as possible.
- Take more notes than you think you will need.
- When appropriate, categorize the types of behavior you are looking for, and devise a system for counting instances of each type.
- When you have recorded data over a significant period of time, group your observations into categories for careful study.

FIGURE 22.1 Archaeologist Anna Roosevelt taking notes during the excavation of a site in the Amazon region of South America. Systematic, purposeful observation and careful note taking are crucial to the success of all fieldwork.

Quoting from Interviews

Before an interview, obtain permission to quote the interviewee. If the interview is not being recorded (or captured on a transcript if online), use oversized quotation marks to enclose direct quotations in your notes. Record the interviewee's name and the location and date of the interview in your research notebook. Afterward, verify quotations with your interviewee.

(For advice on conducting direct observations for a case study, see Tab 3: Common Assignments across the Curriculum, pp. 145–47.)

2. Conducting interviews

To be useful as research tools, interviews require systematic preparation and implementation:

- Identify appropriate people for your interviews.
- Do background research, and plan a list of open-ended questions.
- Take careful notes and, if possible, tape-record the interview (but be sure to obtain your subject's permission if you use audiotape or videotape). Verify quotations.
- Follow up on vague responses with questions that get at specific information. Do not rush interviewees.
- Politely probe inconsistencies and contradictions.
- Write thank-you notes to interviewees, and later send them copies of your report.

3. Taking surveys

Conducted either orally or in writing, **surveys** are made up of structured questions. Written surveys are called **questionnaires.** Many colleges have offices that must review and approve student surveys. Check to see what guidelines your school may have. The following suggestions will help you prepare informal surveys:

- Define your purpose and your target population.
- Write clear directions and questions. For example, if you are asking multiple-choice questions, make sure that you cover all possible options and that your options do not overlap.
- Make sure that your questions do not suggest a preference for one answer over another.
- Make the survey brief and easy to complete.

22d   Keep a notebook when doing lab research.

To provide a complete and accurate account of your laboratory work, keep careful records in a notebook. The following guidelines will help you take accurate notes on your research:

- Record immediate, on-the-spot, accurate notes on what happens in the lab. Write down as much detail as possible. Measure precisely; do not estimate. Identify major pieces of apparatus, unusual chemicals, and laboratory animals in enough detail so that, for example, a reader can determine the size or type of equipment you used. Use drawings, when appropriate, to illustrate complicated equipment setups. Include tables, when useful, to present results.

- Follow a basic format. Present your results in a format that allows you to communicate all the major features of an experiment. The five basic sections that must be included are title, purpose, materials and methods, results, and conclusions. (*For more advice on preparing a lab report, see Tab 3: Common Assignments across the Curriculum, pp. 142–45.*)

- Write in complete sentences, even if you are filling in answers to questions in a lab manual. Resist the temptation to use shorthand to record your notes. Later, the complete sentences will provide a clear record of your procedures and results. Highlight connections in your sentences by using the following transitions: *then, next, consequently, because,* and *therefore.* Cause-effect relationships should be clear.

- When necessary, revise and correct your laboratory notebook in visible ways. If you make a mistake in recording laboratory results, correct it as clearly as possible, either by erasing or by crossing out and rewriting on the original sheet. If you make an uncorrectable mistake in your notebook, simply fold the sheet lengthwise and mark *omit* on the face side. Unanticipated results often occur in the lab, and you may find yourself jotting down notes on a convenient piece of scrap paper. Attach these notes to your notebook.

23 Plagiarism, Copyright, and Intellectual Property

Integrity and honesty require us to acknowledge others, especially when we use their words or ideas. Researchers who fail to acknowledge their sources—either intentionally or unintentionally—commit **plagiarism.** Buying a term paper from an online paper mill or "borrowing" a friend's completed assignment are obvious forms of plagiarism. But plagiarism also involves paraphrasing or summarizing material without properly citing its source. (*See Chapter 24: Working with Sources and Avoiding Plagiarism, pp. 248–65, for more on paraphrasing and summarizing.*)

www.mhhe.com/
awr3
For information on
material that does not
need citing, go to
Research > Avoiding
Plagiarism >
Common Knowledge

Journalists who are caught plagiarizing are publicly exposed and often fired by the publications they write for. Those publications must then work hard to repair their credibility. Scholars who fail to acknowledge the words and ideas of others lose their professional credibility, and often their jobs. Students who plagiarize may receive a failing grade for an assignment or course and face other disciplinary action—including expulsion. Your campus probably has a written policy regarding plagiarism and its consequences.

The Internet has made many types of sources available, and it can be unclear what, when, and how to cite. For example, bloggers and other

SOURCE SMART

Determining What Is "Common Knowledge"

Information that an audience could be expected to know from many sources is considered common knowledge. You do not need to cite common knowledge if you use your own wording and sentence structure. Common knowledge can take various forms, including at least these four:

- Folktales with no particular author (e.g., Johnny Appleseed supposedly spread apple seeds across the USA)
- Common sense (e.g., property values in an area fall when crime rises)
- Historical facts and dates (e.g., the United States entered World War II in 1941)
- Information found in many general reference works (e.g., the heart drives the body's circulation system)

Maps, charts, graphs, and other visual displays of information are not considered common knowledge. Even though everyone knows that Paris is the capital of France, if you reproduce a map of France in your paper, you must credit the map's creator.

Learning More about Plagiarism, Copyright and Fair Use, and Intellectual Property

- **Plagiarism:** For more information about plagiarism, see the Council of Writing Program Administrator's "Defining and Avoiding Plagiarism: The WPA Statement on Best Practices" <www.wpacouncil.org/positions/plagiarism.html>. Educators at Indiana University offer tips on avoiding plagiarism at <www.Indiana.edu/~frick/plagiarism>. Georgetown University's Honor Council offers an example of a campus honor code pertaining to plagiarism and academic ethics at <gervaseprograms.georgetown.edu/hc/plagiarism.html>.

- **Copyright and fair use:** For information and discussion of fair use, see Copyright and Fair Use at <fairuse.stanford.edu>, and the U.S. Copyright Office at <www.loc.gov/copyright>. The University of Texas posts guidelines for fair use and multimedia projects at <www.utsystem.edu/OGC/IntellectualProperty/ccmcguide.htm>.

- **Intellectual property:** For information about what constitutes intellectual property and related issues, see the World Intellectual Property Organization Web site at <www.wipo.int/>. For a legal perspective, the American Intellectual Property Law Association offers information and overviews of recent cases at <www.aipla.org/>.

Web authors often reproduce material from other sites, while some musicians make their music available for free download. Although the line between "original" and "borrowed" appears to be blurring in our society, there are guidelines to help you credit sources appropriately.

23a Understand how plagiarism relates to copyright and intellectual property.

Related to plagiarism are copyright and intellectual property, which apply to *published* use of someone else's work. **Copyright** is the legal right to control the reproduction of any original work—a piece of writing, a musical composition, a play, a movie, a computer program, a photograph, a work of art. A copyrighted work is the **intellectual property** of the copyright holder, whether that entity is a publisher, a record company, an entertainment conglomerate, or the individual creator of the work. Here is some additional information on these important legal concepts:

- **Copyright:** A copyrighted text cannot be reprinted (in print or online) without the written permission of the copyright holder. The copyright protects the right of authors and publishers to make money from their productions.

- **Fair use:** The concept of **fair use** protects most academic use of copyrighted sources. Under this provision of copyright law, you can legally quote a brief passage from a copyrighted text without infringing on copyright. Of course, to avoid plagiarism you must identify the passage as a quotation and cite it properly. (*See page 247 for more information.*)

- **Intellectual property:** In addition to works protected by copyright, intellectual property includes patented inventions, trademarks, industrial designs, and similar intellectual creations that are protected by other laws.

SOURCE SMART

What Must Be Acknowledged?

You **do not** have to acknowledge

- common knowledge expressed in your words and sentence structure (*see the box on page 241*),
- your independent thinking, or
- your original field observations, surveys, or experimental results.

You **must** acknowledge

- any concepts you learned from a source, whether or not you copy the source's language,
- interviews other than surveys,
- abstracts,
- visuals,
- statistics, including those you use to create your own visuals (*see Chapter 20, p. 220*), and
- your own work for another assignment (use only with your instructor's permission).

Acknowledge the source each time you cite from the material, regardless of the length of the selection. If you use multiple sources in a paragraph, make clear which sentences are from which sources. (*See Tab 6: MLA Documentation Style, p. 282 and Tab 7: APA Documentation Style, p. 331 for examples.*)

23b Avoid inadvertent and deliberate plagiarism.

Students under the pressure of a deadline can sometimes make poor choices. Inadvertent plagiarism occurs when busy students take notes carelessly, forgetting to jot down the source of a paraphrase or accidentally inserting material downloaded from a Web site into a paper. Deliberate plagiarism occurs when students wait until the last minute and then "borrow" a paper from a friend or copy and paste large portions of an online article into their own work. No matter how tired or pressured you may be, there is no justification for plagiarism.

To avoid plagiarism, adhere to these guidelines:

- When you receive your assignment, write down your thoughts and questions before you begin looking at sources. Use this record to keep track of changes in your ideas.

- As you do research, record your ideas in one color and those of others in a different color.

- As you continue researching and taking notes, keep accurate records. If you do not know where you got an idea or a piece of information, do not use it in your paper until you find out.

- When you take notes, put quotation marks around words, phrases, or sentences taken verbatim from a source and note the pages. If you use any of those words, phrases, or sentences when summarizing or paraphrasing the source, put them in quotation marks. Changing a word here and there while keeping a source's sentence structure or phrasing constitutes plagiarism even if you credit the source for the ideas. (*See pp. 255–57 for examples.*)

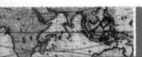

For MULTILINGUAL STUDENTS

Cultural Assumptions and Misunderstandings about Plagiarism

Respect for ownership of ideas is a core value in the United States. Your culture may consider the knowledge in classic texts a national heritage and, therefore, common property. As a result, you may have been encouraged to incorporate words and information from those texts into writing without citing their source. In the United States, academic culture requires you to identify any use you make of someone else's original work and to cite the work properly in an appropriate documentation style (*see Tabs 6–8*). You must similarly credit the source of ideas that are not considered common knowledge. You should accept these rules as nonnegotiable and apply them conscientiously to avoid plagiarism and its serious consequences. When in doubt about citation rules, ask your instructor.

CHECKLIST

Avoiding Plagiarism

Sources

☐ Is my thesis my own idea, not something I found in one of my sources?

☐ Have I used a variety of sources, not just one or two?

☐ Have I identified each source clearly?

☐ Do I fully understand and explain all words, phrases, and ideas in my paper?

☐ Have I acknowledged all ideas that are based on neither my original thinking nor common knowledge?

Quotations

☐ Have I enclosed in quotation marks any uncommon terms, distinctive phrases, or direct quotations from a source?

☐ Have I checked all quotations against the original source?

☐ Do I include ellipsis marks and brackets where I have altered the original wording and capitalization of quotations?

Paraphrases

☐ Have I used my own words and sentence structure for all paraphrases?

☐ Have I maintained the original meaning?

Summaries

☐ Do all my summaries include my own wording and sentence structure? Are they shorter than the original text?

☐ Do they accurately represent the content of the original?

Documentation

☐ Have I indicated my source for all quotations, paraphrases, summaries, statistics, and visuals either within the text or in a parenthetical citation?

☐ Have I included citations for all visuals from other sources (or visuals based on data from other sources)?

(continued)

CHECKLIST *(continued)*

☐ Have I included page numbers as required for all quotations, paraphrases, and summaries?

☐ Does every in-text citation have a corresponding entry in the list of works cited or references?

Permission

☐ If I am composing a public online text, have I received all needed permissions?

■ Do not rely too much on one source, or you may easily slip into using that person's thoughts as your own.

■ Cite the source of all ideas, opinions, facts, and statistics that are not common knowledge.

■ Choose an appropriate documentation style, and use it consistently and properly. (*See Tabs 6–8 for information about the most common documentation styles for academic writing.*)

When working with electronic sources, keep in mind the following guidelines:

■ Print or save to your computer any online source you consult. Note the date on which you viewed it, and be sure to keep the complete URL in case you need to view the source again or if your documentation style requires it (*see Tabs 6–8*).

■ If you copy and paste a passage from a Web site into a word-processing file, use a different font to identify that material as well as the URL and the access date.

■ Acknowledge all sites you use as sources, including those you access via links on another site.

■ As a courtesy, request the author's permission before quoting from blogs, news group postings, or e-mails.

■ Acknowledge any audio, video, or illustrated material that has informed your research.

While it's easy to copy and paste material from the Internet into an individual text without acknowledgment, it's ill-advised to do so. Instructors can detect such plagiarism by taking that copied text and using a search engine to locate the original.

Posting material on a publicly accessible Web site is usually considered the legal equivalent of publishing it in print format. (Password-protected sites generally are exempt.) When writing a text to be posted online and accessible to the general public, you must seek copyright permission from all your sources. (*See the guidelines for fair use below and the box on p. 241.*)

23c Use copyrighted materials fairly.

All original works, including student papers, graphics, and videos, are covered by copyright even if they do not bear an official copyright symbol. A copyright grants its owner—often the creator—exclusive rights to the use of a protected work, including reproducing, distributing, and displaying the work. The popularity of the Web as a venue for publication has led to increased concerns about the fair use of copyrighted material. Before you publish your paper on the Web or produce a multimedia presentation that includes audio, video, and graphic elements copied from a Web site, make sure that you have used copyrighted material fairly by considering these four questions:

- **What is the purpose of the use?** Educational, nonprofit, and personal use are more likely to be considered fair than is commercial use.
- **What is the nature of the work being used?** In most cases, imaginative and unpublished materials can be used only if you have the permission of the copyright holder.
- **How much of the copyrighted work is being used?** The use of a small portion of a text for academic purposes is more likely to be considered fair than the use of a whole work for commercial purposes. While no clear legal definition of "a small portion" exists, one conservative guideline is that you can quote up to fifty words from an article (print or online) and three hundred words from a book. It is safest to ask permission to quote an entire work or a substantial portion of a text (be cautious with poems, plays, and songs). Images and multimedia clips are considered entire works. Also, you may need permission to link your Web site to another.
- **What effect would this use have on the market for the original?** The use of a work is usually considered unfair if it would hurt sales of the original.
    When in doubt, always ask permission.

24 Working with Sources and Avoiding Plagiarism

Once you have a research question to answer, an idea about what the library and Internet have to offer, and some reliable, appropriate sources in hand, you are ready to begin working with your sources. Paying attention to detail and keeping careful records at this stage will help you integrate sources responsibly into your text.

www.mhhe.com/
awr3
For help with creating
a bibliography, go to

Research >
Bibliomaker

24a Maintain a working bibliography.

As you research, compile a **working bibliography**—a list of those books, articles, pamphlets, Web sites, and other sources that seem most likely to help you answer your research question. Maintain an accurate and complete record of all sources you consult so that you can find sources again and cite them accurately.

While the exact bibliographic information you will need depends on your documentation style, the following list includes the major elements of most systems. (*See Tabs 6–8 for the requirements of specific documentation styles.*)

Book
- Call number (so you can find the source again)
- All authors, editors, and translators
- Title of chapter
- Title and subtitle of book
- Edition (if not the first), volume number (if applicable)
- Publication information (city, publisher, date)
- Medium (print)

Periodical article
- Authors
- Title and subtitle of article
- Title and subtitle of periodical
- Date, edition or volume number, issue number
- Page numbers
- Medium (print)

Article from database (in addition to the above)
- Name of database
- Date you retrieved source
- URL of database's home page (if online)
- Medium (Web, CD-ROM, or DVD-ROM)

Internet source (including visual, audio, video)
- All authors, editors, or creators
- Title and subtitle of source

- Title of larger site, project, or database (if applicable)
- Version or edition, if any
- Publication information, if available, including any about a version in another medium (such as print, radio, or film)
- Date of electronic publication or latest update, if available
- Sponsor of site
- Date you accessed site
- URL of site
- Any other identifying numbers, such as a Digital Object Identifier (DOI)

Other type of source
- Author or creator
- Title
- Format (for example, photograph or lecture)
- Title of larger publication, if any
- Publisher, sponsor, or institution housing the source
- Date of creation or publication
- Any identifying numbers

(*See the foldouts following Tabs 6 and 7 for examples of these elements.*)

You can record bibliographic information on note cards or in a word-processing file; you can print out or e-mail to yourself bibliographic information obtained from online searches in databases and library catalogs; or you can record bibliographic information directly on photocopies of source material. You can also save most Web pages and other online sources to your own computer.

1. Using note cards or a word processor
Before computers became widely available, most researchers used 3-by-5-inch or 4-by-6-inch note cards to compile the working bibliography, with each potential source getting a separate card. This method

SOURCE SMART

The Uses and Limits of Bibliographic Software

Programs such as *Microsoft Word 2007* and *Bibliomaker* (from this book's companion *Catalyst* Web site) allow you to store source data, automatically insert citations in common documentation styles, and generate a list of references. While these features are useful, such programs often do not incorporate the most recent updates to documentation style. Talk to your instructor before using bibliographic software, and check your citations carefully against the models in Tabs 6–8. Also check references that a database creates for you.

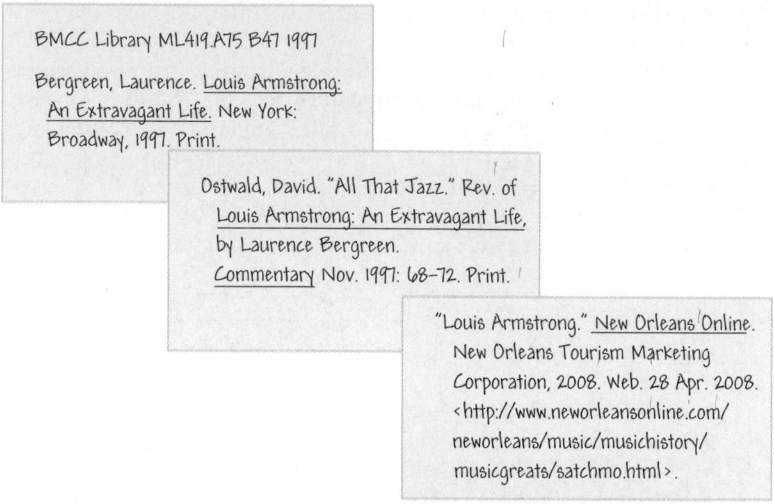

> BMCC Library ML419.A75 B47 1997
>
> Bergreen, Laurence. <u>Louis Armstrong:</u>
>   <u>An Extravagant Life.</u> New York:
>   Broadway, 1997. Print.

> Ostwald, David. "All That Jazz." Rev. of
>   <u>Louis Armstrong: An Extravagant Life,</u>
>   by Laurence Bergreen.
>   <u>Commentary</u> Nov. 1997: 68–72. Print.

> "Louis Armstrong." <u>New Orleans Online.</u>
>   New Orleans Tourism Marketing
>   Corporation, 2008. Web. 28 Apr. 2008.
>   <http://www.neworleansonline.com/
>   neworleans/music/musichistory/
>   musicgreats/satchmo.html>.

FIGURE 24.1 Three sample bibliography note cards. The cards are for a book (top), for a journal article (middle), and for a Web site (bottom).

allows you to rearrange information when you are deciding how to organize your paper (see Figure 24.1). You can use the cards to include all information necessary for documentation, to record brief quotations, and to note your own comments (carefully marked as yours).

Instead of handwriting on cards, you can also record bibliographic information in a word-processing file. Or you can combine the two methods, recording bibliographic information in a word-processing file, then printing it, cutting it out, and taping it on a note card.

2. Printing the results of online searches in databases and library catalogs

The results of searches in online indexes and databases usually include bibliographic information about the sources they list. (*See the example of a database search in Chapter 19, p. 210.*) You can print these results directly from your browser or, in some cases, save them to disk and

---

Caution: If you download the full text of an article from a database and refer to it in your paper, your citation may require information about the database (depending on your documentation style) as well as bibliographic information about the article itself. (*See Tabs 6–8.*)

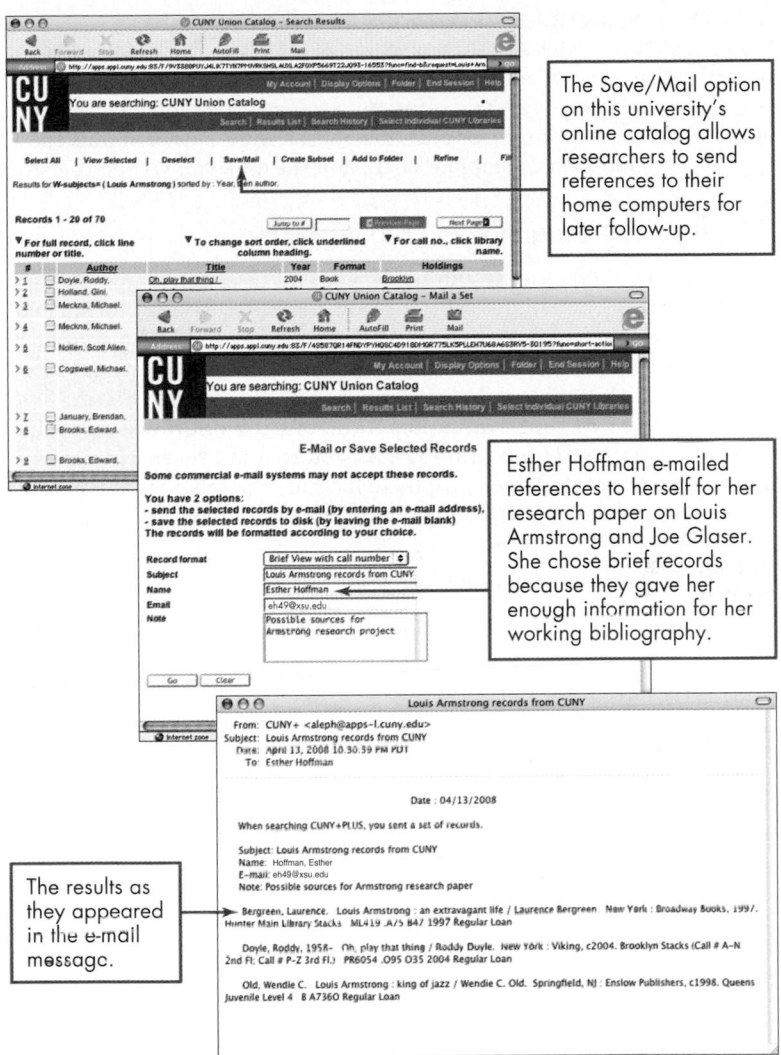

FIGURE 24.2 Three sample screens showing the results of an online search of a library database.

transfer them to a word-processing file. Be sure also to record the name of the database and the date of your search.

You can similarly print out or save bibliographic information from the results of searches in online library catalogs. Some college libraries make it possible for you to send your list of sources to yourself by e-mail as in Figure 24.2.

3. Using photocopies and printouts from Web sites

If you photocopy articles, essays, or pages of reference works from a print or a microfilm source, take time to note the bibliographic information on the photocopy. Similarly, if you print out a source you found on a Web site or copy it to your computer, be sure to note the site's author, name, sponsor, date of publication, complete URL, and the date you visited the site.

24b Create an annotated bibliography.

An annotated bibliography can be very useful to you in your research. The bibliography includes full citation details, correctly formatted, which you will need for your paper. The annotation provides a summary of major points for each source, including your own reactions and ideas about where this material might fit in your paper (*see Figure 24.3 below*). Also record your evaluation of the source's relevance and reliability (*see Chapter 21, pp. 226–34*). As you conduct research, you will find that an annotated bibliography helps you remember what you have found in your search, as well as helping you organize your findings.

24c Take notes on your sources.

www.mhhe.com/
awr3

For more information
and interactive
exercises, go to

Research >
Research
Techniques

Taking notes helps you think through the answer to your research question. You can take notes on the information you glean from your sources by annotating photocopies or printouts or by noting useful quotations and ideas on paper, on note cards, or in a computer file. See if categories emerge that can help you organize the paper.

Bergreen, Laurence. *Louis Armstrong: An Extravagant Life.* New York: Broadway, 1997. Print.
Aimed at a popular audience, Bergreen's book provides a detailed history of Armstrong's life as well as its social context. Bergreen also presents Armstrong's relationship with manager Glaser throughout the years and Glaser's own colorful background. Essentially the partnership provided benefits to both performer and manager. (Ostwald notes a few errors.)

Collier, James Lincoln. *Louis Armstrong, an American Genius.* New York: Oxford UP, 1983. Print.
This scholarly study of Armstrong's life and work presents his formative influence on American music. Collier includes numerous telling details that support my ideas about Armstrong and Glaser's relationship, such as the fact that Glaser paid Armstrong's personal expenses while acting as his manager.

FIGURE 24.3 Sample annotated bibliography. A section of Esther Hoffman's annotated bibliography.

1. Annotating

One way to take notes is to annotate photocopied articles and printouts from online information services or Web sites. See Figure 24.4 for an example. (Do this for sources you save to your computer by using the Comments feature in your word processor.) As you read, do the following:

FIGURE 24.4 An annotated Web page printout.

- On the first page, write down complete bibliographic information for the source.

- As you read, record questions, reactions, and ideas in the margins.

- Comment in the margins on ideas that agree with or differ from those you have already learned about.

- Put important and difficult passages into your own words by paraphrasing or summarizing them in the margins. (*For help with paraphrasing and summarizing, see pp. 255–60.*)

- Highlight statements that you may want to quote because they are key to your readers' understanding of the issue or are especially well expressed.

2. Taking notes in a research journal or log

A **research journal** or **research log** is a tool for keeping track of your research. It can be a spiral or loose-leaf notebook, a box of note cards, or a word-processing document on a laptop computer—whatever you are most comfortable with. Some use a blog. Use the journal to write down leads for sources to consult and to record ideas and observations about your topic as they occur to you. A blog can link to sources.

When you have finished annotating a photocopy, printout, or electronic version of an article, use your research journal to explore some of the comments, connections, and questions you recorded. If you do not have a copy of the material to annotate, take notes directly in your journal. Writing down each idea on a separate card, notebook page, word-processing page, or blog entry will make it easier to organize the material later. Whatever method you use, be sure to record the source's bibliographic information as well as the specific page number for each idea.

Enclose in quotation marks any exact words from a source. If you think you may forget that the phrasing, as well as the idea, came from someone else, label the passage a "quotation" and note the page number, as Esther Hoffman did in the following excerpt from her research notebook:

> Notes on Dan Morgenstern. "Louis Armstrong and the Development and Diffusion of Jazz." Louis Armstrong: A Cultural Legacy. Ed. Marc H. Miller. Seattle: U of Washington P and Queens Museum of Art, 1994. 95–145. Print.
>
> - Armstrong having trouble with managers. Fires Johnny Collins in London, 1933. Collins blocks Armstrong from playing with Chick Webb's band (pp. 124–5).
> - Armstrong turned to Glaser, an old Chicago acquaintance. Quotation: "Joe Glaser . . . proved to be the right man at the right time" (p. 128).

SOURCE SMART

Deciding to Quote, Paraphrase, or Summarize

Point is eloquently, memorably, or uniquely stated	→	Quote
Details important but not uniquely or eloquently expressed	→	Paraphrase
Long section of material (with many points), main ideas important, details not important	→	Summarize
Part of longer passage is uniquely stated	→	Use quotation inside paraphrased or summarized passage

Unless you think you might use a particular quotation in your paper, it is usually better to express the author's ideas in your own words by using a paraphrase or a summary.

3. Paraphrasing

Paraphrase when a passage's details are important to your topic but its exact words are not memorable. When you paraphrase, you put someone else's statements into your words and sentence structures. A paraphrase should be about the same length and level of detail as the original. Paraphrase when you need to reorder a source's ideas or clarify complicated information. Cite the original writer and put quotation marks around any exact phrasing from the source. See the Source Smart box on page 256 for advice on approaching the task.

www.mhhe.com/
awr3
For more information
and interactive
exercises, go to
**Research > Avoiding
Plagiarism >
Summarize/
Paraphrase**

In the first unacceptable paraphrase that follows, the writer has done a word-for-word translation, using synonyms for some terms but retaining phrases from the original and failing to enclose them in quotation marks ("nonsense syllables," "free invention of rhythm, melody, and syllables"). The borrowed phrases are highlighted. Notice also how close the sentence structures in the first faulty paraphrase are to the original.

SOURCE

Scat singing. A technique of jazz singing in which onomatopoeic or nonsense syllables are sung to improvised melodies. Some writers have traced scat singing back to the practice, common in West African musics, of translating percussion patterns into vocal

Guidelines for Writing a Paraphrase

- **Read the passage carefully.** Focus on its sequence of ideas and important details.
- **Be sure you understand the material.** Look up any unfamiliar words.
- **Imagine addressing an audience that has not read the material.**
- **Without looking at the original passage, write down its main ideas and key details.**
- **Use clear, direct language.** Express complicated ideas as a series of simple ones.
- **Check your paraphrase against the original.** Make sure your text conveys the source's ideas accurately without copying its words or sentence structures. Add quotes around any phrases from the source or rewrite them.
- **Note the citation information.** List author and page number after every important point.

lines by assigning syllables to characteristic rhythms. However, since this allows little scope for melodic improvisation and the earliest recorded examples of jazz scat singing involved the free invention of rhythm, melody, and syllables, it is more likely that the technique began in the USA as singers imitated the sounds of jazz instrumentalists.

—J. BRADFORD ROBINSON,
The New Grove Dictionary of Jazz

UNACCEPTABLE PARAPHRASE: PLAGIARISM

Scat is a way of singing that uses nonsense syllables and extemporaneous melodies. Some people think that scat goes back to the custom in West African music of turning drum rhythms into vocal lines. But that doesn't explain the free invention of rhythm, melody, and syllables of the first recorded instances of scat singing. It is more likely that scat was started in the U.S. by singers imitating the way instrumental jazz sounded (Robinson 515).

In the next example of a faulty paraphrase, the writer has merely substituted synonyms for the original author's words (such as "meaningless vocalization" instead of "nonsense syllables") and kept the source's sentence structure. Because it relies on the sentence structure of the original source, the paraphrase constitutes plagiarism.

UNACCEPTABLE PARAPHRASE (SENTENCE STRUCTURE OF SOURCE): PLAGIARISM

Scat is a way of singing that uses meaningless vocalization and extemporaneous melodies. One theory is that scat originated from the West African custom of turning drum rhythms into singing. But that doesn't explain the loose improvisation of pulse, pitch, and sound of the first recorded instances of scat singing. Scat more probably was started in the United States by singers imitating the way instrumental jazz sounded (Robinson 515).

The third unacceptable paraphrase alters the sentence structure of the source but plagiarizes by using some of the original wording (highlighted below) without quotation marks.

UNACCEPTABLE PARAPHRASE (WORDING FROM SOURCE): PLAGIARISM

Scat, a highly inventive type of jazz singing, combines onomatopoetic or nonsense syllables with improvised melodies (Robinson 515).

In contrast, the acceptable paraphrase expresses all ideas from the original using different wording and phrasing. Although it quotes a few words from the source, the writer has used quotation marks and expressed the definition in a new and different way. The author's name indicates where the paraphrase begins.

ACCEPTABLE PARAPHRASE

According to Robinson, scat is a highly inventive type of jazz singing that combines "nonsense syllables [with] improvised melodies." Although syllabic singing of drum rhythms occurs in West Africa, scat probably owes more to the early attempts of American singers to mimic both the sound and the inventive musical style of instrumental jazz (Robinson 515).

An acceptable paraphrase that does not include a direct quotation still requires a citation.

In the following two paraphrases of a podcast, note that the unacceptable version copies words and phrasing from the source.

SOURCE

Two of the greatest all-time performers in the history of popular music are coupled on this exciting and entertaining album. The Groaner and Satchmo team up for a great bash that has been arranged for and constructed by the talented Billy May.

—FRESH SOUNDS. "Bing Crosby Meets Louis Armstrong." *Jazzarific: Jazz Vinyl Podcast.* 26 Dec. 2006. Web. 25 Feb. 2008. <http://jazzvinyl.podomatic.com/>.

UNACCEPTABLE PARAPHRASE: PLAGIARISM

The Groaner and Satchmo are coupled on this exciting album in a great bash that the talented Billy May has arranged.

ACCEPTABLE PARAPHRASE

The Fresh Sounds podcast describes this thrilling album that brings together two consummate performers, Bing Crosby and Louis Armstrong, with arrangements by Billy May (Fresh Sounds).

www.mhhe.com/
awr3
For more information
and interactive
exercises, go to

Research >
Avoiding
Plagiarism >
Summarize/
Paraphrase

4. Summarizing

When you **summarize,** you state the main point of a piece, condensing paragraphs into sentences, pages into paragraphs, or a book into a few pages. As you take notes on sources, you will summarize more frequently than you will quote or paraphrase. Summarizing works best for very long passages or when the central idea of a passage is important but the details are not. See the box below for advice.

Here is a passage by John Ephland followed by two summaries. The first, unacceptable, summary is simply a restatement of Ephland's

SOURCE SMART

Guidelines for Writing a Summary

- **Read the material carefully.** Locate relevant sections.
- **Be sure you understand the material.**
- **Imagine addressing an audience that has not read the material.**
- **Identify the main point of the source, in your words.** Compose a sentence that names the text, the writer, what the writer does (reports, argues), and the most important point.
- **Note any other points that relate to your topic.** State each one (in your own words) in one sentence or less. Simplify complex language.
- **If the text is longer than a few paragraphs, divide it into sections, and in one or two sentences sum up each section.** Compose a topic sentence for each of these sections.
- **Combine your sentence stating the writer's main point with your sentences about secondary points or those summarizing the text's sections.**
- **Check your summary against the original** to see if it makes sense, expresses the source's meaning, and does not copy any wording or sentence structure.
- **Note all the citation information for the source.**

Tips LEARNING in COLLEGE

Using Sources to Establish Your Credibility

As noted in Chapter 4, effective writers appeal to their audience by demonstrating that they are *reasonable, ethical,* and *empathetic (see p. 32)*. When you present relevant evidence from reliable sources, you demonstrate that you are reasonable. When you put other writers' ideas into your own words and indicate the sources of all ideas and quotations that are not your own and that are not common knowledge *(see p. 241)*, you demonstrate that you are ethical. When you follow the citation formats required by your discipline, you demonstrate your empathy for your readers by making it easier for them to consult your sources.

thesis, using much of his phrasing (highlighted). The second, acceptable, summary states Ephland's main point in the writer's own words.

SOURCE

The origins of jazz, an urban music, stemmed from the countryside of the South as well as the streets of America's cities. It resulted from two distinct musical traditions, those of West Africa and Europe. West Africa gave jazz its incessant rhythmic drive, the need to move and the emotional urgency that has served the music so well. The European ingredients had more to do with classical qualities pertaining to harmony and melody.

The blending of these two traditions resulted in a music that played around with meter and reinterpreted the use of notes in new combinations, creating blue notes that expressed feelings both sad and joyous. The field hollers of Southern sharecropping slaves combined with the more urban, stylized sounds of musicians from New Orleans, creating a new music. Gospel music from the church melded with what became known in the 20th century as the blues offered a vocal ingredient that translated well to instruments.

—JOHN EPHLAND, "Down Beat's Jazz 101:
The Very Beginning" (from downbeat.com)

UNACCEPTABLE SUMMARY: PLAGIARISM

The origins of jazz are two distinct musical traditions, those of West Africa and Europe. New meters and new note combinations capable of expressing both sad and joyous feelings resulted from the blending of these two traditions.

ACCEPTABLE SUMMARY

According to Ephland, jazz has its roots in the musical traditions of both West Africa and Europe. It combines rhythmic, harmonic, and melodic features of both traditions in new and emotionally expressive ways (Ephland).

Note that the acceptable summary still requires a citation.

www.mhhe.com/
awr3

For more information
and interactive
exercises, go to

Research >
Avoiding
Plagiarism >
Using Quotations

5. Quoting directly

Sometimes the writer of a source will say something highly relevant so eloquently and perceptively that you will want to include that writer's words as a **direct quotation.** In general, quote the following:

- Primary sources (for example, in a paper about Louis Armstrong, a direct quotation from Armstrong or an associate)
- Sources containing very technical language that cannot be paraphrased
- Literary sources, when you analyze the wording
- An authority in the field whose words support your thesis
- Debaters explaining their different positions on an issue

To avoid inadvertent plagiarism, be careful to indicate that the content is a direct quotation when you copy it onto your note cards, and place quotation marks around it. You might copy quotations in a different color, or deliberately make quotation marks oversized.

When referring to most secondary sources, paraphrase or summarize instead of quoting. Your readers will have difficulty following a paper with too many quotes, and they may think you lack original ideas. In some instances you may use paraphrase, summary, and quotation together. You might summarize a long passage, paraphrase an important section of it, and directly paraphrase a short part of that section.

Note: If you have used more than one quotation every two or three paragraphs, convert most of the quotations into paraphrases (*see pp. 255–58*).

24d Take stock of and synthesize what you have learned.

When you take stock, you review the research you have done to see how your sources compare to each other: where do they agree, and where do they disagree? Where do you stand relative to these sources? Which do you agree with, which do you disagree with, and why? Did anything you read surprise or disturb you? Conducting this review allows you to synthesize what you have learned from the sources you have consulted. As you review your research, you may want to write down your responses to the questions listed above, since this process can help you clarify what you have learned.

The credibility of your work depends on the relevance and reliability of your sources as well as the scope and depth of your reading and observation. College research projects tend to require multiple sources and viewpoints. A paper on Louis Armstrong is unlikely to be credible if it relies on only one source of information. A report about an issue in the social sciences will not be taken seriously if it cites research on only one side of the debate.

As the context and kind of writing change, so too do the requirements for types and numbers of sources. As a general rule, however, you should consult more than two sources and use only sources that are both reliable and respected by people working in the field. To determine whether you have located appropriate and sufficient sources, ask yourself the following questions:

- Are your sources trustworthy? (*See Chapter 21, pp. 226–34, for more on evaluating sources.*)

- If you have started to develop a tentative answer to your research question, have your sources provided you with a sufficient number of facts, examples, and ideas to support that answer?

- Have you used sources that examine the issues from several different perspectives?

24e Integrate quotations, paraphrases, and summaries properly and effectively.

www.mhhe.com/ awr3
For more information and interactive exercises, go to
Research > Avoiding Plagiarism > Using Sources Accurately

Ultimately, you will use some of the paraphrases, summaries, and quotations you have collected during the course of your research to support and develop the ideas you present in your paper. Here are some guidelines for integrating them properly and effectively. (Examples in this section represent MLA format for in-text citations and block quotations.)

1. Integrating quotations

Short quotations should be enclosed in quotation marks and well integrated into your sentence structure. Set off longer quotations in blocks (*see p. 263*). The following example from Esther Hoffman's paper on Louis Armstrong and Joe Glaser shows the use of a short quotation:

> In his dedication to the unpublished manuscript "Louis Armstrong and the Jewish Family in New Orleans, the Year of 1907," Armstrong calls Glaser "the best friend that I ever had," while in a letter to Max Jones, he writes, "I did not get

> really happy until I got with my man—my dearest friend—
> Joe Glaser" (qtd. in Jones and Chilton 16).

When you are integrating someone else's words into your writing, use a **signal phrase** that indicates whom you are quoting. The signal phrases "Armstrong calls Glaser" and "he writes" identify Armstrong as the source of the two quotations in the preceding passage.

A signal phrase clearly indicates where your words end and the source's words begin. The first time you quote a source, include the author's full name and credentials (or authority to describe a topic), such as "literary scholar Jacob Miller" or "Armstrong's wife, Lucille." Instead of introducing a quotation, the signal phrase can follow or interrupt it:

FOLLOWS

> "I did not get really happy until I got with my man—my dearest friend—Joe Glaser," writes Armstrong.

INTERRUPTS

> "I did not get really happy," writes Armstrong, "until I got with my man—my dearest friend—Joe Glaser."

The particular verb you use in a signal phrase, such as *refutes* or *summarizes,* should show how you are using the quotation in your paper. If your source provides an example that strengthens your argument, you could say, "Mann *supports* this line of reasoning." (*For more on varying signal phrases, see the box on p. 264.*) Note that MLA style places signal phrase verbs in present tense (*Johnson writes*) while APA uses past tense (*Johnson wrote*). (*See Chapter 25, p. 268, for more on these documentation styles.*)

When a quotation, paraphrase, or summary in MLA or APA style begins with a signal phrase, the ending citation includes the page number (unless the work lacks page numbers). You can quote directly without a signal phrase, as long as you provide the author's name as part of the parenthetical citation (in MLA and APA style).

Brackets within quotations Sentences that include quotations must make sense grammatically. Sometimes you may have to adjust a quotation to make it fit your sentence. Use brackets to indicate any such minor adjustments. For example, *my* has been changed to *his* to make the quotation fit in the following sentence:

> Armstrong confided to a friend that Glaser's death "broke [his] heart" (Bergreen 490).

Ellipses within quotations Use **ellipses** (. . .) to indicate that words have been omitted from the body of a quotation, but be sure that what you omit does not significantly alter the source's meaning.

As Morgenstern puts it, "Joe Glaser . . . proved to be the right man at the right time" (128).

(For more on using ellipses, see Tab 11: Editing for Correctness, pp. 536–37.)

Quotations in block format   Quotations longer than four lines should be used rarely. Tell your readers why you want them to read a long quotation, and, afterward, comment on it.

If you use a verse quotation longer than three lines or a prose quotation longer than four typed lines, set the quotation off on a new line and indent each line one inch (ten spaces) from the left margin. (This is MLA style; APA and Chicago have different conventions.) Double-space above and below the quotation. If the quotation is more than one paragraph, indent the first line of each new paragraph a quarter inch. Do not use quotation marks. Writers often introduce a block quotation with a sentence ending in a colon.

As Carl Schorske points out, the young Freud was passionately interested in

classical archeology:

> He cultivated a new friendship in the Viennese professional elite--
>
> especially rare in those days of withdrawal--with Emanuel Loewy,
>
> a professor of archeology. "He keeps me up till three o'clock in the
>
> morning," Freud wrote appreciatively to Fliess. "He tells me about
>
> Rome." (273)

Longer verse quotations (four lines or more) are indented block style. *(For short quotations of poetry, see Tab 11: Editing for Correctness, pp. 526 and 537.)* If you cannot fit an entire line of poetry on a single line of your typescript, indent the turned line an extra quarter inch.

In the following lines from "Crossing Brooklyn Ferry," Walt Whitman celebrates

the beauty of the Manhattan skyline and his love for the city:

> Ah, what can ever be more stately and
>
> admirable to me than mast-hemm'd
>
> Manhattan?
>
> River and sunset and scallop-edg'd waves of
>
> flood-tide? (lines 92–93)

2. Integrating paraphrases and summaries

The principles for integrating paraphrases and summaries into your text are similar to those for including direct quotations. Provide a smooth transition between a source's point and your own voice, and give credit to the source. Use signal phrases to introduce ideas you

Tips

LEARNING in COLLEGE

Varying Signal Phrases

To keep your work interesting, to show the original writer's purpose (*Martinez describes* or *Lin argues*), and to connect the quote to your reasoning (*Johnson refutes . . .*), use appropriate signal phrases. Instead of using the verbs *says* and *writes* again and again, consider including some of the following:

acknowledges	denies	points out
adds	describes	proposes
admits	emphasizes	proves
argues	explains	refutes
asks	expresses	rejects
asserts	finds	remarks
charges	holds	reports
claims	implies	responds
comments	insists	shows
complains	interprets	speculates
concedes	maintains	states
concludes	notes	suggests
considers	observes	warns
contends		

have borrowed from your sources. Besides crediting others for their work, signal phrases make ideas more interesting by giving them a human face. Include a citation after the paraphrase or summary. Here are some examples:

> As biographer Laurence Bergreen points out, Armstrong easily reached difficult high notes, the F's and G's that stymied other trumpeters (248).

In this passage, Esther Hoffman uses the signal phrase "As biographer Laurence Bergreen points out" to identify Bergreen as the source of the paraphrased information about Louis Armstrong's extraordinary technical abilities.

> According to Howard Mandel in his blog entry "International Jazz at IA JE," young people today listen not only to pop music but also to jazz, especially its current eclectic styles.

This passage in a student paper by Roger Hart uses the signal phrase "According to Howard Mandel" to lead into a summary of Mandel's blog entry. No citation is needed because the signal phrase names the author and the source lacks page numbers.

A 1960 letter from Glaser to Lucille Armstrong corroborates Gold's account; it shows that Glaser assumed responsibility for buying the musician and his wife a new car as well as for filing the paperwork needed to retain the old license plate number.

In this passage, Esther Hoffman uses "corroborates" to signal her paraphrase of an original letter she found in the Louis Armstrong archives. She names the source (the author of the letter), so she does not need additional parenthetical documentation.

25 Writing the Paper

You have chosen a challenging research question and have located, read, and evaluated a variety of relevant sources. Now you need a thesis that will allow you to share what you have learned as well as your perspective on the issue.

25a Plan and draft your paper.

Begin by recalling the context and the purpose of your paper. If you have an assignment, review it to see if the paper is supposed to be primarily informative, interpretive, or argumentative. Consider how much your audience is likely to know about your topic. Keep your purpose, audience, and context in mind as you decide on your thesis.

1. Gathering and evaluating your information

Your note-taking strategies will determine how you collect and organize your information. If you have taken notes on index cards, group them according to topic and subtopic. For example, Esther Hoffman could have used the following categories to organize her notes:

Biography – Armstrong
Biography – Glaser
Glaser as manager
Conflict – A & G
Armstrong – media image
Jazz – general info

Sorting index cards into stacks that match up topics and subtopics allows you to see what you have gathered. A small stack of cards for a particular subtopic might mean that the subtopic is not as important as you originally thought—or that you need to do additional research focused on that specific subtopic.

If your notes are primarily on your computer, you can create a new category heading for each topic and subtopic, and then copy and paste to move information to the appropriate category.

www.mhhe.com/ awr3

For help with developing a thesis, go to

Writing > Paragraph/Essay Development > Thesis/Central Idea

2. Deciding on a thesis

Consider the question that guided your research as well as others provoked by what you have learned during your research. Revise the wording of these questions and summarize them in a central question that is interesting and relevant to your audience (*see Chapter 18, pp. 197–203*). After you write down this question, compose an answer that you can use as your working thesis, as Esther Hoffman did in the following example:

HOFFMAN'S FOCAL QUESTION

What kind of relationship did Louis Armstrong and Joe Glaser actually have?

HOFFMAN'S WORKING THESIS

Armstrong and Glaser enjoyed not only a successful business partnership but also a complex friendship based on mutual respect and caring.

(*For more on devising a thesis, see Tab 2: Writing and Designing Texts, pp. 48–50.*)

www.mhhe.com/ awr3

For interactive help with outlines, go to

Writing > Outlining Tutor

3. Outlining a plan for supporting and developing your thesis

Guided by your tentative thesis, outline a plan that uses your sources in a purposeful way. Decide on the kind of structure you will use— explanatory, exploratory, or persuasive—and choose facts, examples, and ideas drawn from a variety of sources to support your thesis. (*See Chapters 9–11 in Tab 3 for more on these structures.*)

For her interpretive paper on Armstrong and Glaser, Hoffman decided on an exploratory structure, an approach organized around raising and answering a central question:

- State the question: what kind of relationship did Armstrong and Glaser have?
- State the thesis: Armstrong and Glaser enjoyed a mutual business and personal relationship.
- Background information on jazz age
- Introduce Armstrong
- Introduce Glaser
- Discuss Glaser as Armstrong's business manager—support for idea that it was Glaser who made Armstrong a star.

- Discuss Armstrong's resistance to being controlled by Glaser.
- Conclude: Armstrong and Glaser worked well together as friends who respected and cared for each other.

To develop this outline, Hoffman would need to list supporting facts, examples, or ideas for each point, as well as indicate the sources of this information. Each section centers on her original thinking, backed by her analysis of sources. (*For more on developing an outline, see Tab 2: Writing and Designing Texts, pp. 51–54.*)

4. Writing a draft that you can revise, share, and edit

www.mhhe.com/
awr3

For more information
and interactive
exercises, go to

Writing >
Paragraph/Essay
Development >
Drafting and
Revising

When you have a tentative thesis and a plan, you are ready to write a draft. Many writers present their thesis or focal question at the end of an introductory paragraph or two. Regardless, the introduction should interest readers.

As you write beyond the introduction, be prepared to reexamine and refine your thesis. When drawing on ideas from your sources, be sure to quote and paraphrase properly. (*For advice on quoting and paraphrasing, see Chapter 24, pp. 255–65.*)

Make your conclusion as memorable as possible. You may need to review the paper as a whole before writing the conclusion. In the final version of Hoffman's paper, on pages 313–23, note how she uses a visual and a play on words—"more than meets the eye"—to end her paper. In doing so, she enhances her concluding point—that the two men were different, yet complementary, and that their relationship was complex.

Hoffman came up with the last line of her paper as she revised her first draft. Often writers will come up with fresh ideas at this stage—a good reason to spend time revising and editing your paper. (*For more on revising, see Tab 2, pp. 73–93. For help with editing, see Tabs 9–12.*)

5. Integrating visuals

When appropriate for the assignment, well-chosen visuals help illustrate your argument. Hoffman found two images in her archival research about Louis Armstrong. She described both of them in her paper and was able to include a reproduction of one of them. Two additional items to consider when integrating a visual into your paper are figure numbers and captions.

- **Figure numbers:** Both MLA and APA style require writers to number each image in a research paper. In MLA style, the word "figure" is abbreviated to "Fig." In APA style, the full word "Figure" is written out.
- **Captions:** Each visual that you include in your paper must be followed by a caption that includes the title of the visual

(if given; otherwise, a brief description will do) and its source. In MLA style, each caption begins with the figure number and a period after the number (*Fig. 1.*); in APA style, use italics for the figure number (*Figure 1.*).

25b Revise your draft.

You may prefer to revise a hard copy of your draft by hand, or you might find it easier to use the Track Changes feature in your word-processing program. Either way, be sure to keep previous versions of your drafts. It is useful to have a record of how your paper evolved—especially if you need to track down a particular source or want to reincorporate something that you used earlier in the process. The Checklist box can help you revise your paper.

www.mhhe.com/ awr3

For help with documenting sources, go to

Research > Avoiding Plagiarism > Citing Sources

25c Document your sources.

Whenever you use information, ideas, or words from someone else's work, you must acknowledge that person. As noted in the box on page 241, the only exception to this principle is when you use information that is common knowledge, such as the chemical composition of water or the names of the thirteen original states. When you tell readers what sources you have consulted, they can more readily understand your paper as well as the conversation you are participating in by writing it.

How sources are documented varies by field and discipline. Choose a documentation style that is appropriate for the particular course you are taking, and use it properly and consistently.

Specific documentation styles meet the needs of different disciplines. Literature and some other humanities disciplines use MLA style. Researchers in these disciplines use many historic texts including multiple editions of certain sources. The author's name and page number, but not the year, appear in the in-text citation. The edition of the source appears in the works-cited list. The author's full name appears at the first mention of the work, and sources are referred to in present tense (because writing exists in the present).

APA style, used by practitioners of the social sciences, places the date of a work in the in-text citation. The currency of sources matters in these disciplines. References to past research appear in the past tense, and researchers are referred to by last name only.

Chicago, or CMS, style, used by other humanities disciplines, has two forms. The first minimizes the in-text references to sources by using footnotes or endnotes indicated by superscript numerals. Disciplines that use it, such as history, tend to use many sources. An alternative form of CMS resembles APA style.

CSE style, used by the sciences, has different forms. Name-year style shares important features with APA style, while citation-sequence

CHECKLIST

Revising and Editing a Research Paper

Consider these questions as you read your draft and gather feedback from your instructor and peers (*see also Checklist for Avoiding Plagiarism, Chapter 23, pp. 245–46*):

Thesis and structure

☐ How does my paper address the topic and purpose given in the assignment?

☐ How well does my thesis fit my evidence and reasoning?

☐ Is the central idea of each section based on my own thinking and backed with evidence from my sources?

☐ How have I dealt with the most likely critiques of my thesis?

☐ Do the transitions from section to section assist the reader in moving from one topic to the next?

☐ What evidence do I use to support each point? Is it sufficient?

Editing: Use of sources

☐ Do my paraphrases and summaries alter the wording and sentence structure, but not the meaning, of the original text?

☐ Have I checked all quotations for accuracy and used ellipses or brackets where necessary?

☐ Do signal phrases set off and establish context for quotations, paraphrases, and summaries?

☐ Have I provided adequate in-text citation for each source? Do my in-text citations match my list of works cited or references?

☐ Do all of my illustrations have complete and accurate captions?

(*See also the checklists Revising Content and Organization, p. 79, Editing for Style and Grammar, p. 86, and Proofreading, p. 91.*)

and citation-name style use endnotes. The prevalence of abbreviations in CSE style indicates that researchers are expected to know the major texts in their fields.

If you are not sure which of the four styles covered in this handbook to use, ask your instructor. If you are required to use an alternative, discipline-specific documentation style, consult the list of manuals on page 271.

For her paper on Louis Armstrong and Joe Glaser, Esther Hoffman used the MLA documentation style. (*The final draft of the paper appears in Tab 6: MLA Documentation, on pp. 313–23.*)

CHARTING the TERRITORY

Documentation Styles Covered in This Text

TYPE OF COURSE	DOCUMENTATION STYLE MOST COMMONLY USED	WHERE TO FIND THIS STYLE IN THE HANDBOOK
Humanities (English, religion, music, art, philosophy)	MLA (Modern Language Association) or Chicago (*Chicago Manual of Style*)	MLA: *pp. 273–324* Chicago: *pp. 361–79*
Social sciences (anthropology, psychology, sociology, education, business)	APA (American Psychological Association)	*pp. 325–58*
Sciences (mathematics, natural sciences, engineering, computer science)	CSE (Council of Science Editors)	*pp. 380–88*

CHARTING the TERRITORY

Style Manuals for Specific Disciplines

SPECIFIC DISCIPLINE	POSSIBLE STYLE MANUAL
Chemistry	Coghill, Anne M. and Lorrin R. Garson, eds. *The ACS Style Guide: A Manual for Authors and Editors.* 3rd ed. Washington: American Chemical Society, 2006.
Geology	Bates, Robert L., Rex Buchanan, and Marla Adkins-Heljeson, eds. *Geowriting: A Guide to Writing, Editing, and Printing in Earth Science.* 5th ed. Alexandria: American Geological Institute, 1995.
Government and law	Garner, Diane L., and Diane H. Smith, eds. *The Complete Guide to Citing Government Information Resources: A Manual for Writers and Librarians.* Rev. ed. Bethesda: Congressional Information Service, 1993.
	Harvard Law Review et al. *The Bluebook: A Uniform System of Citation.* 18th ed. Cambridge: Harvard Law Review Assn., 2005.
Journalism	Goldstein, Norm, ed. *Associated Press Stylebook, 2008.* Revised and updated ed. New York: Associated Press, 2008.
Linguistics	Linguistic Society of America. "LSA Style Sheet." *LSA Bulletin.* Published annually in the December issue.
Mathematics	American Mathematical Society. *AMS Author Handbook: General Instructions for Preparing Manuscripts.* Providence: AMS, 2007.
Medicine	Iverson, Cheryl, ed. *American Medical Association Manual of Style: A Guide for Authors and Editors.* 10th ed. New York: Oxford University Press, 2007.
Political science	American Political Science Association. *Style Manual for Political Science.* Rev. ed. Washington: APSA, 2006.

The Library of Congress houses the largest collection of books and documents in the world, and all U.S. libraries use its cataloguing systems. The Library's architectural design suggests the Italian Renaissance; its interior features work by American artists.

6

Next to the originator of a good sentence is the first quoter of it.

—RALPH WALDO EMERSON

MLA
Documentation
Style

6 MLA Documentation Style

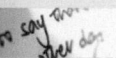
MLA style requires writers to provide bibliographic information about their sources in a works-cited list at the end of a paper. In order to format works-cited entries correctly, know first of all what kind of source you are citing. The directory on pages 284–85 will help you find the appropriate sample to use as your model. As an alternative, you can use the charts on the foldout pages that follow. Answering the questions provided in the charts will usually lead you to the sample entry you need. If you cannot find what you are looking for consult your instructor for help.

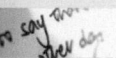 Sections dealing with visual rhetoric. For a complete listing, see the Quick Guide to Key Resources at the back of this book.

WRITING OUTCOMES

Tab 6: MLA Documentation Style
This section will help you answer questions such as:

Rhetorical Knowledge
Which disciplines use MLA style? **(26)**
When should I use explanatory notes in MLA style? **(28)**

Critical Thinking, Reading, and Writing
Why do I need to document my sources? **(26)**

Processes
How do I create a works-cited list? **(27)**
How should I position and label visuals? **(29)**

Knowledge of Conventions
What are correct formats for in-text citations **(26)**, works-cited list entries **(27)** and notes **(28)**?
How do I cite electronic sources such as databases, Web sites, and podcasts? **(27)**
What kind of spacing and margins should my paper have? **(29)**

Self-Assessment: *Take an online quiz at www.mhhe.com/awr3 to test your familiarity with the topics covered in Chapters 26–27. As you consult the following chapters, pay special attention to the sections that correspond to any questions you answer incorrectly.*

The documentation style developed by the Modern Language Association (MLA) is used by many researchers in the arts and humanities, especially by those who write about language and literature. The guidelines presented here are based on the seventh edition of the *MLA Handbook for Writers of Research Papers* (New York: MLA, 2009).

College papers include information, ideas, and quotations from sources that must be accurately documented. Documentation allows others to see the path you have taken in researching and writing your paper. (*For more on what to document, see Tab 5: Researching, pp. 241–47.*)

MLA documentation style has three parts:

- In-text citations
- List of works cited
- Explanatory notes and acknowledgments

In-text citations and a list of works cited are mandatory; explanatory notes are optional.

26 MLA Style: In-Text Citations

In-text citations let readers know that they can find full bibliographical information about your sources in the works-cited list at the end of your paper.

www.mhhe.com/
awr3
For links to Web sites for documentation styles used in various disciplines, go to

Research > Links to Documentation Sites

1. Author named in sentence

In your first reference, give the author's full name as the source gives it. Afterward, use the last name only, unless two or more of your sources have the same last name (*no. 6.*), or unless two or more works by the same author appear in your works-cited list (*no. 3*).

signal phrase
As Thomas J. Hennessey explains, record deals were usually negotiated by "white

middlemen" (127).

The parenthetical page citation comes after the closing quotation mark but before the period.

MLA IN-TEXT CITATIONS: DIRECTORY to SAMPLE TYPES

(See pp. 283–309 for works-cited examples.)

2. Author named in parentheses

If you do not name the source's author in your sentence, provide the last name in the parentheses. (Give the full name if the author of another source has the same last name.)

> Armstrong easily reached difficult high notes, the F's and G's that stymied other
> *no comma after author's name*
> trumpeters (Bergreen 248).

There is no comma between the author's name and the page number. If you cite two or more distinct pages, however, separate the numbers with a comma: (Bergreen 450, 457).

3. Two or more works by the same author

If you use two or more works by the same author, you must identify which work you are citing, either in your sentence or in an abbreviated form in parentheses: (Collier, *Louis Armstrong* 330).

MLA IN-TEXT CITATIONS

- Name the author, either in a signal phrase such as "Laurence Bergreen maintains" or in a parenthetical citation.
- Include a page reference in parentheses. No "p." precedes the page number, and if the author is named in the parentheses, there is no punctuation between the author's name and the page number.
- Place the citation as close to the material being cited as possible and before any punctuation marks that divide or end the sentence, except in a block quotation, where the citation comes one space after the period or final punctuation mark. See no. 12 for quotations ending with a question mark or an exclamation point.
- Italicize the titles of books, magazines, and plays. Place quotation marks around the titles of articles and short poems.
- For Internet sources, follow the same general guidelines as for print sources. Keep the parenthetical citation simple, providing enough information for your reader to find the full citation in your works-cited list. Cite either the author's name or the title of the site or article. Begin the parenthetical citation with the first word of the corresponding works-cited list entry.
- For works without page or paragraph numbers, give the author or title only. Often it is best to mention them in your sentence, in which case no parenthetical citation is needed.

book title is italicized

In *Louis Armstrong: An American Genius,* James Lincoln Collier reports that Glaser

paid Armstrong's mortgage, taxes, and basic living expenses (330).

4. Two or three authors of the same work

If a source has up to three authors, name them all either in your text, as shown below, or in parentheses: (Jones and Chilton 160, 220).

According to Max Jones and John Chilton, Glaser's responsibilities included

booking appearances, making travel arrangements, and paying the band

members' salaries (160, 220).

5. More than three authors

If a source has more than three authors, either list all the authors or give the first author's last name followed by "et al.," meaning "and others." Do the same in your works-cited list.

Changes in social regulations are bound to produce new forms of subjectivity

(Henriques et al. 275).

6. Authors with the same last name

If the authors of two or more of your sources have the same last name, include the first initial of the author you are citing (R. Campbell 63); if the first initial is also shared, use the full first name, as shown below.

> In the late nineteenth century, the sale of sheet music spread rapidly in a
>
> Manhattan area along Broadway known as Tin Pan Alley (Richard Campbell 63).

7. Organization as author

Treat the organization as the author. If the name is long, put it in a signal phrase.

> The Centre for Contemporary Cultural Studies claims that "there is nothing
>
> inherently concrete about historiography" (10).

8. Unknown author

When no author is given, cite a work by its title, using either the full title in a signal phrase or an abbreviated version in the parentheses. When abbreviating the title, begin with the word by which it is alphabetized in your works-cited list.

title of article
> "Squaresville, USA vs. Beatsville" makes the Midwestern small-town home seem
>
> boring compared with the West Coast artist's "pad" (31).

> The Midwestern small-town home seems boring compared with the West Coast
>
> artist's "pad" ("Squaresville" 31).

9. Entire work

Acknowledge an entire work in your text, not in a parenthetical citation. Include the work in your list of works cited, and include in the text the word by which the entry is alphabetized.

> Sidney J. Furie's film *Lady Sings the Blues* presents Billie Holiday as a beautiful
>
> woman in pain rather than as the great jazz artist she was.

10. Paraphrased or summarized source

If you include the author's name in your paraphrase or summary, include only the page number(s) in your parenthetical citation. Signal phrases clarify that you are paraphrasing or summarizing.

signal phrase
> Bergreen recounts how in Southern states, where blacks were prohibited from
>
> entering many stores, Glaser sometimes had to shop for the band's food and
>
> other supplies (378, 381).

11. Source of a long quotation

For a quotation of more than four typed lines of prose or three of poetry, do not use quotation marks. Instead, indent the material you are quoting by one inch. Following the final punctuation mark of the quotation, allow one space before the parenthetical information.

> Glaser managed the Sunset Café, a club where Armstrong often performed:
>
> > There was a pronounced gangster element at the Sunset, but Louis, accustomed to being employed and protected by mobsters, didn't think twice about that. Mr. Capone's men ensured the flow of alcohol, and their presence reassured many whites. (Bergreen 279)

12. Source of a short quotation

Close the quotation before the parenthetical citation. If the quotation concludes with an exclamation point or a question mark, place the closing quotation mark after that punctuation mark and place the sentence period after the parenthetical citation.

> His innovative singing style also featured "scat," a technique that combines
> brackets enclose a word that substitutes for omitted text
> "nonsense syllables [with] improvised melodies" (Robinson 515).

> Shakespeare's Sonnet XVIII asks, "Shall I compare thee to a summer's day?" (line 1).

13. One-page source

You need not include a page number in the parenthetical citation for a one-page printed source.

14. Government publication

To avoid an overly long parenthetical citation, give the name of the government agency that published the source within your text.

> According to a report issued by the Bureau of National Affairs, many employers in 1964 needed guidance to apply new workplace rules that ensured fairness and complied with the Civil Rights Act of 1964 (32).

15. Photograph, map, graph, chart, or other visual

VISUAL APPEARS IN YOUR PAPER

> An aerial photograph of Manhattan (Fig. 3), taken by the United States Geographical Survey, demonstrates how creative city planning can introduce parks and green spaces within even the most densely populated urban areas.

If the caption you write for a visual appearing in your paper includes all the information found in a works-cited list entry, you need not include it in your works-cited list. See page 320 for an example.

VISUAL DOES NOT APPEAR IN YOUR PAPER

An aerial photograph of Manhattan taken by the United States Geographical

Survey demonstrates how creative city planning can introduce parks and green

spaces within even the most densely populated urban areas (TerraServer-USA).

Provide a parenthetical citation that directs your reader to information about the source of the image in your works-cited list.

16. Web site or other online electronic source

If you cannot find the author of an online source, then identify the source by title, either in your text or in a parenthetical citation. Because most online sources do not have set page, section, or paragraph numbers, they must usually be cited as entire works.

Peter Davis gave [Armstrong] "basic musical training on the cornet"

("Louis Armstrong").

17. Work with numbered paragraphs or sections instead of pages

Give the paragraph or section number(s) after the author's name and a comma. To distinguish them from page numbers, use the abbreviation *par(s).* or type of division such as *section(s).*

Many German Romantic musical techniques may have originated in Italian opera

(Rothstein, par. 9).

18. Work with no page or paragraph numbers

When citing an online or print source without page, paragraph, or other reference numbers, try to include the author's name in your text instead of in a parenthetical citation.

author's name
Crouch argues that Armstrong remains a driving force in present-day music,

from country and western music to the chanted doggerel of rap.

19. Multivolume work

When citing more than one volume of a multivolume work in your project, include with each citation the volume number, followed by a colon, a space, and the page number.

Schuller argues that even though jazz's traditional framework appears European,

its musical essence is African (1: 62).

If you consult only one volume of a multivolume work, then specify that volume in the works-cited list (*see p. 289*) but not in the parenthetical citation.

20. Literary work

Novels and literary nonfiction books   Include the relevant page number, followed by a semicolon, a space, and the chapter number.

> Louis Armstrong figures throughout Ellison's *Invisible Man,* including in the
>
> narrator's penultimate decision to become a "yes" man who "undermine[s] them
>
> with grins" (384; ch. 23).

If the author is not named in your sentence, add the name in front of the page number: (Ellison 384; ch. 23).

Poems   Use line numbers, not page numbers.

> In "Trumpet Player," Hughes says that the music "Is honey / Mixed with liquid fire"
>
> (lines 19-20). This image returns at the end of the poem, when Hughes concludes
>
> that "Trouble / Mellows to a golden note" (43-44).

Note that the word *lines* (not *l.* or *ll.*) is used in the first citation to establish what the numbers in parentheses refer to; subsequent citations need not use the word *lines* (which is not italicized).

Plays and long, multisection poems   Use division (act, scene, canto, book, part) and lines, not page numbers. In the following example, notice that arabic numerals are used for act and scene divisions as well as for line numbers: (*Ham.* 2.3.22-27). The same is true for canto, verse, and lines in the following citation of Byron's *Don Juan:* (*DJ* 1.37.4-8). (The *MLA Handbook* lists abbreviations for titles of certain literary works.)

21. Religious text

Cite material in the Bible, Upanishads, or Koran by book, chapter, and verse, using an appropriate abbreviation when the name of the book is in parentheses rather than in your sentence. Name the edition from which you are citing.

> As the Bible says, "The wise man knows there will be a time of judgment"
>
> (*Holy Bible, Rev. Stand. Vers.,* Eccles. 1.9).

Note that titles of biblical books are not italicized.

22. Historical document

For familiar documents such as the Constitution and the Declaration of Independence, provide the document's name and the numbers of the parts you are citing.

Judges are allowed to remain in office "during good behavior," a vague standard

that has had various interpretations (US Const., art. 3, sec. 1).

23. Indirect source

When you use or paraphrase a quotation you found in someone else's work, put *qtd. in* (not italicized, meaning "quoted in") before the name of your source.

Armstrong confided to a friend that Glaser's death "broke [his] heart" (qtd. in

Bergreen 490).

In your list of works cited, list only the work you consulted, in this case the indirect source by Bergreen.

24. Two or more sources in one citation

When you credit two or more sources, use a semicolon to separate the citations.

Giving up his other business ventures, Glaser now became Armstrong's exclusive

agent (Bergreen 376-78; Collier 273-76; Morgenstern 124-28).

25. Two or more sources in one sentence

Include a parenthetical reference after each idea or quotation you have borrowed.

Ironically, Americans lavish more money each year on their pets than they

spend on children's toys (Merkin 21), but the feral cat population—consisting

of abandoned pets and their offspring—is at an estimated 70 million and

growing (Mott).

26. Work in an anthology

When citing a work in a collection, give the name of the specific work's author, not the name of the editor of the whole collection.

When Dexter Gordon threatened to quit, Armstrong offered him

a raise—without consulting with Glaser (Morgenstern 132).

Here, Morgenstern is cited as the source even though his work appears in a collection edited by Marc Miller. Note that the list of works cited must include an entry for Morgenstern (*see p. 323*).

27. E-mail, letter, or personal interview

Cite by name the person you communicated with, using either a signal phrase or parentheses.

Much to Glaser's surprise, both "Hello, Dolly" and "What a Wonderful World" became big hits after the rights had been sold (Jacobs).

In the works-cited list, after giving the person's name you will need to identify the kind of communication and its date (*see pp. 295, 305, and 308*).

27 MLA Style: List of Works Cited

MLA documentation style requires a works-cited page with full bibliographic information about your sources. The list of works cited should appear at the end of your paper, beginning on a new page titled "Works Cited." Include only those sources you cite in your paper, unless your instructor tells you to prepare a "Works Consulted" list.

www.mhhe.com/awr3

To download Bibliomaker software for MLA, go to

Research > Bibliomaker

Books

1. Book with one author

Italicize the book's title. Generally, only the city, not the state, is included in the publication data. Conclude with the medium (Print). Notice that in the example the publisher's name, *Wayne State University Press*, is abbreviated to *Wayne State UP* (not italicized).

> Hennessey, Thomas J. *From Jazz to Swing: African-Americans and Their Music 1890-1935*. Detroit: Wayne State UP, 1984. Print.

2. Two or more works by the same author(s)

Give the author's name in the first entry only. For subsequent works authored by that person, replace the name with three hyphens and a period. Alphabetize by title.

> Collier, James Lincoln. *Jazz: The American Theme Song*. New York: Oxford UP, 1993. Print.
>
> ---. *Louis Armstrong: An American Genius*. New York: Oxford UP, 1983. Print.

MLA WORKS-CITED ENTRIES: DIRECTORY to SAMPLE TYPES

(See pp. 275–83 for examples of in-text citations.)

3. Book with two or three authors

Name the two or three authors in the order in which they appear on the title page, putting the last name first for the first author only.

> Davis, Miles, and Quincy Troupe. *Miles: The Autobiography*. New York: Simon,
>
> 1989. Print.

4. Book with four or more authors

When a work has more than three authors, you may list them all or use the abbreviation *et al.* (meaning "and others") to replace the names of all authors except the first.

> Henriques, Julian, et al. *Changing the Subject: Psychology, Social Regulation,*
>
> *and Subjectivity*. New York: Methuen, 1984. Print.

5. Organization as author

Consider as an organization any group, commission, association, or corporation whose members are not identified on the title page.

> Centre for Contemporary Cultural Studies. *Making Histories: Studies*
>
> *in History Writing and Politics*. London: Hutchinson, 1982. Print.

6. Book by an editor or editors

If the title page lists an editor instead of an author, begin with the editor's name followed by the abbreviation *ed.* (not italicized). Use *eds.* when more than one editor is listed. Only the first editor's name should appear in reverse order.

> Miller, Paul Eduard, ed. *Esquire's Jazz Book*. New York: Smith, 1944. Print.

7. Book with an author and an editor

Put the author and title first, followed by *Ed.* (not italicized) and the name of the editor. However, if you cited something written by the editor, see no. 15.

> editor's name not in reverse order
> Armstrong, Louis. *Louis Armstrong: A Self-Portrait*. Ed. Richard Meryman. New York:
>
> Eakins, 1971. Print.

8. Work in an anthology or chapter in an edited book

List the author and title of the selection, followed by the title of the anthology, the abbreviation *Ed.* (not italicized) for "edited by," the editor's name, publication data, page numbers of the selection, and medium.

> Smith, Hale. "Here I Stand." *Readings in Black American Music*.
>
> Ed. Eileen Southern. New York: Norton, 1971. 286-89. Print.

MLA LIST of WORKS CITED

- Begin on a new page with the centered title "Works Cited."
- Include an entry for every source cited in your text.
- Include author, title, publication data, and medium (such as print, Web, radio) for each entry, if available. Use a period to set off each of these elements from the others. Leave one space after the periods.
- Do not number the entries.
- Put entries in alphabetical order by author's or editor's last name. If the work has more than one author, see nos. 3 and 4 (*p. 286*). (If the author is unknown, use the first word of the title, excluding the articles *a, an,* or *the*).
- Italicize titles of books, periodicals, long poems, and plays. Put quotation marks around titles of articles, short stories, and short poems.
- Capitalize the first and last and all important words in all titles and subtitles. Do not capitalize articles, prepositions, coordinating conjunctions, and the *to* in infinitives unless they appear first or last in the title. Place a colon between title and subtitle unless the title ends in a question mark or an exclamation point.
- In the publication data, abbreviate months and publishers' names (*Dec.* rather than December; Oxford UP instead of Oxford University Press), and include the name of the city in which the publisher is located but not the state (unless the city is obscure or ambiguous): Ithaca: Cornell UP. Use n.p. in place of publisher or location information if none is available. If the date of publication is not given, provide the approximate date, enclosed in brackets: [c. 1975]. If you cannot approximate the date, use n.d. for "no date."
- Do not use p., pp., or page(s). Use n. pag. if the source lacks page or paragraph numbers or other divisions. When page spans over 100 have the same first digit, do not repeat it for the second number: 243–47.
- Abbreviate all months except May, June, and July.
- For articles and other print sources that skip pages, provide the page number for the beginning of the article followed by a plus (+) sign.
- Use a hanging indent: Start the first line of each entry at the left margin, and indent all subsequent lines of the entry five spaces (or one-half inch on the computer).
- Double-space within entries and between them.

9. Two or more items from one anthology

Include a complete entry for the anthology beginning with the name of the editor(s). Each selection should have its own entry in the alphabetical list that includes only the author, title of the selection, editor, and page numbers.

entry for a selection from the anthology
Johnson, Hall. "Notes on the Negro Spiritual." Southern 268-75.
entry for the anthology
Southern, Eileen, ed. *Readings in Black American Music.* New York:

Norton, 1971. Print.

entry for a selection from the anthology
Still, William Grant. "The Structure of Music." Southern 276-79.

10. Signed article in an encyclopedia or another reference work

Cite the author's name, title of the entry (in quotation marks), title of the reference work (italicized), editor if the work is not well known, publication information, and medium. If entries appear in alphabetical order, omit page numbers.

Robinson, J. Bradford. "Scat Singing." *The New Grove Dictionary of Jazz.*

Ed. Barry Kernfeld. Vol. 3. London: Macmillan, 2002. Print.

11. Unsigned entry in an encyclopedia or another reference work

Start the entry with the title. For well-known reference works, omit the place and publisher.

"Scat." *Merriam-Webster's Collegiate Dictionary.* 11th ed. 2003. Print.

12. Article from a collection of reprinted articles

Haney-Peritz, Janice. "Monumental Feminism and Literature's Ancestral House:

Another Look at 'The Yellow Wallpaper.'" *Women's Studies* 12.2 (1986):
abbreviation for "reprinted"
113-28. Rpt. in *The Captive Imagination: A Casebook on "The Yellow Wallpaper."*

Ed. Catherine Golden. New York: Feminist, 1992. 261-76. Print.

13. Anthology

Eggers, Dave, ed. *The Best American Nonrequired Reading 2007.* Boston: Houghton,

2007. Print.

14. Publisher's imprint

For books published by a division within a publishing company, known as an *imprint,* put a hyphen between the imprint and publisher.

title in title
Wells, Ken, ed. *Floating off the Page: The Best Stories from* The Wall Street Journal's

"*Middle Column.*" New York: Wall Street Journal-Simon, 2002. Print.

15. Preface, foreword, introduction, or afterword

When the writer of the part is different from the author of the book, use the word *By* after the book's title and cite the author's full name. If the book's sole author wrote the part and the book has an editor, use only the author's last name after *By*. If there is no editor and the author wrote the part, cite the complete book.

name of part of book
Crawford, Richard. Foreword. *The Jazz Tradition.* By Martin Williams. New York:

Oxford UP, 1993. v-xiii. Print.

16. Translation

The translator's name goes after the title, with the abbreviation *Trans.*

Goffin, Robert. *Horn of Plenty: The Story of Louis Armstrong.* Trans. James F. Bezov.

New York: Da Capo, 1977. Print.

17. Edition other than the first

Include the number of the edition: *2nd ed.*, *3rd ed.* (not italicized), and so on. Place the number after the title, or if there is an editor, after that person's name.

Panassie, Hugues. *Louis Armstrong.* 2nd ed. New York: Da Capo, 1980. Print.

18. Religious text

Give the version, italicized, the editor's or translator's name (if any); and the publication information including medium.

New American Standard Bible. La Habra: Lockman Foundation, 1995. Print.

The Upanishads. Trans. Eknath Easwaran. Tomales, CA: Nilgiri, 1987. Print.

19. Multivolume work

The first example indicates that the researcher used more than one volume of the work; the second shows that only the second volume was used.

Lissauer, Robert. *Lissauer's Encyclopedia of Popular Music in America.* 3 vols.

New York: Facts on File, 1996. Print.

Lissauer, Robert. *Lissauer's Encyclopedia of Popular Music in America.* Vol. 2.

New York: Facts on File, 1996. Print.

20. Book in a series

After the medium, put the name of the series and, if available on the title page, the number of the work.

> Floyd, Samuel A., Jr., ed. *Black Music in the Harlem Renaissance*. New York:
>
> name of series not italicized
> Greenwood, 1990. Print. Contributions in Afro-American and African
>
> Studies 128.

21. Republished book

Put the original date of publication, followed by a period, before the current publication data.

> original publication date
> Cuney-Hare, Maud. *Negro Musicians and Their Music*. 1936. New York: Da Capo,
>
> 1974. Print.

22. Title in a title

When a book's title contains the title of another book, do not italicize the second title. For the novel *Invisible Man:*

> O'Meally, Robert, ed. *New Essays on* Invisible Man. Cambridge: Cambridge UP,
>
> 1988. Print.

23. Unknown author

The citation begins with the title. In the list of works cited, alphabetize the citation by the first important word, not by articles like *A, An,* or *The.*

> *Webster's College Dictionary*. New York: Random; New York: McGraw, 1991. Print.

Note that this entry includes both of the publishers listed on the dictionary's title page; they are separated by a semicolon.

24. Book with illustrator

List the illustrator after the title with the abbreviation *illus.* (not italicized). If you refer primarily to the illustrator, put the name before the title instead of the author's. (For a graphic novel or comic book, see no. 25.)

> Carroll, Lewis. *Alice's Adventures in Wonderland and through the Looking-Glass*.
>
> Introd. A. S. Byatt. Illus. John Tenniel. New York: Modern Library-Random,
>
> 2002. Print.

> Tenniel, John, illus. *Alice's Adventures in Wonderland and through the Looking-*
>
> *Glass*. By Lewis Carroll. Introd. A. S. Byatt. New York: Modern Library-Random,
>
> 2002. Print.

25. Graphic novel or comic book

Cite graphic narratives created by one person as you would any other book or multivolume work. For collaborations, begin with the person whose work you refer to most and list others in the order in which they appear on the title page. Indicate each person's contribution. (If the work is part of a series, see no. 20.)

Satrapi, Marjane. *Persepolis.* 2 vols. New York: Pantheon-Random, 2004-05. Print.

Moore, Alan, writer. *Watchmen.* Illus. David Gibbons. Color by John Higgins.

New York: DC Comics, 1987. Print.

Periodicals

Periodicals are published at set intervals, usually four times a year for scholarly journals, monthly or weekly for magazines, and daily or weekly for newspapers. Between the author and the publication data are two titles: the title of the article, in quotation marks, and the title of the periodical, italicized. (*For online versions of print periodicals and periodicals published only online, see pp. 298–99 and 303–05.*)

26. Article in a journal with volume numbers

Most journals have a volume number corresponding to the year and an issue number for each publication that year. The issue may be indicated by a month or season. Put the volume number after the title. Follow it with a period and the issue number. Give the year of publication in parentheses, followed by a colon, a space, and the page numbers of the article. End with the medium.

Tirro, Frank. "Constructive Elements in Jazz Improvisation." *Journal of the American*

Musicological Society 27.2 (1974): 285-305. Print.

27. Article in a journal with issue numbers only

Give only the issue number.

Lousley, Cheryl. "Knowledge, Power and Place." *Canadian Literature* 195 (2007):

11-30. Print.

28. Article in a monthly magazine

Provide the month and year, abbreviating the names of all months except May, June, and July.

Walker, Malcolm. "Discography: Bill Evans." *Jazz Monthly* June 1965: 20-22. Print.

29. Article in a weekly magazine

Include the complete date of publication: day, month, and year.

Taylor, J. R. "Jazz History: The Incompleted Past." *Village Voice* 3 July 1978:

65-67. Print.

30. Article in a newspaper

Provide the day, month, and year. If an edition is named on the top of the first page, specify the edition (*natl. ed.* or *late ed.* [without italics], for example) after the date. If the section letter is part of the page number, see the first example. Give the title of an unnumbered section with *sec.* (not italicized). If the article appears on nonconsecutive pages, put a plus (+) sign after the first page number.

Blumenthal, Ralph. "Satchmo with His Tape Recorder Running." *New York Times*

3 Aug. 1999, natl. ed.: E1+. Print.

Just, Julie. "Children's Bookshelf." *New York Times* 15 Mar. 2009, natl. ed., Book

Review sec.:13. Print.

31. Unsigned article

The citation begins with the title and is alphabetized by the first word excluding articles such as *A, An,* or *The.*

"Squaresville, USA vs. Beatsville." *Life* 21 Sept. 1959: 31. Print.

32. Review

Begin with the name of the reviewer and, if there is one, the title of the review. Add *Rev. of* (meaning "review of," not italicized) and the title plus the author or performer of the work being reviewed.

Ostwald, David. "All That Jazz." Rev. of *Louis Armstrong: An Extravagant Life,*

by Laurence Bergreen. *Commentary* Nov. 1997: 68-72. Print.

33. Editorial

Treat editorials as articles, but add the word *Editorial* (not italicized) after the title. If the editorial is unsigned, begin with the title.

Shaw, Theodore M. "The Debate over Race Needs Minority Students' Voices."

Editorial. *Chronicle of Higher Education* 25 Feb. 2000: A72. Print.

34. Abstract of a journal article

Include the publication information for the original article, followed by the title of the publication that provides the abstract, the volume, the year in parentheses, the item or the page number, and the medium.

Theiler, Anne M., and Louise G. Lippman. "Effects of Mental Practice and Modeling

on Guitar and Vocal Performance." *Journal of General Psychology* 122.4 (1995):

329-43. *Psychological Abstracts* 83.1 (1996): item 30039. Print.

35. Letter to the editor

> Tyler, Steve. Letter. *National Geographic Adventure* Apr. 2004: 11. Print.

Other Print Sources

36. Government document

Either the name of the government and agency or the document's author's name comes first. If the government and agency name come first, follow the title of the document with the word *By* for a writer, *Ed.* for an editor, or *Comp.* for a compiler (if any), and give the name. Publication information and medium come last.

> United States. Bureau of Natl. Affairs. *The Civil Rights Act of 1964: Text, Analysis,*
>
> *Legislative History; What It Means to Employers, Businessmen, Unions,*
>
> *Employees, Minority Groups.* Washington: BNA, 1964. Print.

For the format to use when citing the *Congressional Record,* see no. 75.

37. Pamphlet or brochure

Treat as a book. If the pamphlet or brochure has an author, list his or her name first; otherwise, begin with the title.

> *All Music Guide to Jazz.* 2nd ed. San Francisco: Miller Freeman, 1996. Print.

38. Conference proceedings

Cite as you would a book, but include information about the conference if it is not in the title.

> Mendel, Arthur, Gustave Reese, and Gilbert Chase, eds. *Papers Read at the International*
>
> *Congress of Musicology Held at New York September 11th to 16th, 1939.* New York:
>
> Music Educators' Natl. Conf. for the American Musicological Soc., 1944. Print.

39. Published dissertation

Cite as you would a book. After the title, add *Diss.* (not italicized) for "dissertation," the name of the institution, the year the dissertation was written, and the medium.

> Fraser, Wilmot Alfred. *Jazzology: A Study of the Tradition in Which Jazz Musicians*
>
> *Learn to Improvise.* Diss. U of Pennsylvania, 1983. Ann Arbor: UMI, 1987. Print.

40. Unpublished dissertation

Begin with the author's name, followed by the title in quotation marks, the abbreviation *Diss.* (not italicized), the name of the institution, the year the dissertation was written, and the medium.

Reyes-Schramm, Adelaida. "The Role of Music in the Interaction of Black Americans

and Hispanos in New York City's East Harlem." Diss. Columbia U, 1975. Print.

41. Abstract of a dissertation

Use the format for an unpublished dissertation. After the dissertation date, give the abbreviation *DA* or *DAI* (for *Dissertation Abstracts* or *Dissertation Abstracts International*), then the volume number, the issue number, the date of publication, the page number, and the medium.

Quinn, Richard Allen. "Playing Together: Improvisation in Postwar American

Literature and Culture." Diss. U of Iowa, 2000. *DAI* 61.6 (2001): 2305A. Print.

42. Published interview

Name the person interviewed and give the title of the interview or the descriptive term *Interview* (not italicized), the name of the interviewer (if known and relevant), the publication information, and the medium.

Armstrong, Louis. Interview by Richard Meryman. "Authentic American Genius."

Life 15 Apr. 1966: 92-102. Print.

43. Map or chart

Cite as you would a book with an unknown author. Italicize the title of the map or chart, and add the word *Map* or *Chart* (not italicized) following the title.

Let's Go Map Guide to New Orleans. Map. New York: St. Martin's, 1997. Print.

44. Cartoon

Include the cartoonist's name, the title of the cartoon (if any) in quotation marks, the word *Cartoon* (not italicized), the publication information, and the medium.

Myller, Jorgen. "Louis Armstrong's First Lesson." Cartoon. *Melody Maker*

Mar. 1931: 12. Print.

45. Reproduction of artwork

Treat a reproduction of a work of art in another source like a work in an anthology (*no. 8*). Italicize the titles of both the artwork and the source. Include the institution or collection and city where the work can be found, prior to information about the source in which it appears.

Da Vinci, Leonardo. *Mona Lisa.* N.d. Louvre, Paris. *Gardner's Art through the Ages:*

A Concise History of Western Art. By Fred S. Kleiner and Christin J. Mamiya.

Belmont, CA: Thomson, 2008. 253. Print.

46. Advertisement

Name the item or organization being advertised, include the word *Advertisement* (not italicized), and indicate where the ad appeared.

> Hartwick College Summer Music Festival and Institute. Advertisement. *New York*
>
> *Times Magazine* 3 Jan. 1999: 54. Print.

47. Published letter

Treat like a work in an anthology, but include the date. Include the number, if one was assigned by the editor. If you use more than one letter from a published collection, follow the instructions for cross-referencing in no. 9.

> Hughes, Langston. "To Arna Bontemps." 17 Jan. 1938. *Arna Bontemps--Langston*
>
> *Hughes Letters 1925-1967*. Ed. Charles H. Nichols. New York: Dodd, 1980.
>
> 27-28. Print.

48. Personal letter

To cite a letter you received, start with the writer's name, followed by the descriptive phrase *Letter to the author* (not italicized), the date, and MS (*manuscript*).

> Cogswell, Michael. Letter to the author. 15 Mar. 2008. MS.

To cite someone else's unpublished personal letter, see no. 49.

49. Manuscripts, typescripts, and material in archives

Give the author, a title or description (*Letter, Notebook*), the form (*MS.* if handwritten, *TS.* if typed), any identifying number, and the name and location of the institution housing the material. (Do not italicize any part of the citation.)

> Glaser, Joe. Letter to Lucille Armstrong. 28 Sept. 1960. MS. Box 3. Louis Armstrong
>
> Archives. Queens College City U of New York, Flushing.

> Pollack, Bracha. "A Man ahead of His Time." 1997. TS.

50. Legal source (print or online)

To cite a specific act, give its name, Public Law number, its Statutes at Large number, page range, the date it was enacted, and the medium.

> Energy Policy Act of 2005. Pub. L. 109-58. 119 Stat. 594-1143. 8 Aug. 2005. Print.

To cite a law case, provide the names of the plaintiff and defendant, the case number, the court that decided the case, the date of the decision, and the medium.

PRINT

Ashcroft v. the Free Speech Coalition. 535 US 234-73. Supreme Court of the US.

2002. Print.

WEB

Ashcroft v. the Free Speech Coalition. 535 US 234-73. Supreme Court of the US.

2002. *Supreme Court Collection.* Legal Information Inst., Cornell U Law School,

n.d. Web. 20 May 2008.

For more information about citing legal documents or case law, the MLA recommends consulting *The Bluebook: A Uniform System of Citation,* published by the Harvard Law Review Association.

Online Sources

The examples that follow are based on the guidelines for the citation of electronic sources in the seventh edition of the *MLA Handbook for Writers of Research Papers* (2009).

For scholarly journals published online, see no. 88. For periodical articles from an online database, see no. 92. Cite most other Web sources according to nos. 51 and 52. For works that also exist in another medium (e.g., print), your citation may include information about the other version. See nos. 76–87. (The MLA recommends giving this information if possible.)

Basic Web sources

51. Web site or independent online work

Begin with the author, editor (*ed.*), compiler (*comp.*), director (*dir.*), performer (*perf.*), or translator (*trans.*), if any. Give the title (italicized), the version or edition (if any), the publisher or sponsor (or *n.p.*), publication date (or last update, or *n.d.*), medium, and your access date. (Use italics for the title only.) (Citations 51–74 follow this format.)

Raeburn, Bruce Boyd, ed. *William Ransom Hogan Archive of New Orleans Jazz.*

Tulane U, 13 Apr. 2006. Web. 11 May 2008.

52. Part of a Web site or larger online work

Give the title of the part in quotation marks.

Oliver, Rachel. "All About: Forests and Carbon Trading." *CNN.com.* Cable News

Network, 11 Feb. 2008. Web. 14 Mar. 2008.

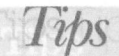 **Tips** LEARNING in COLLEGE

Web Addresses in MLA Citations

Include the URL (Web address) of an online source in a citation only if your reader would be unable to find the source without it (via a seach engine). For example, basic citation information might not sufficiently identify your source if multiple versions of a document exist online without version numbers. Place a URL at the end of your citation in angle brackets and end with a period. This example (also used in no. 51) shows the format:

> Raeburn, Bruce Boyd, ed. *William Ransom Hogan Archive of New Orleans Jazz.*
>
> Tulane U, 13 Apr. 2006. Web. 11 May 2008. <http://www.tulane.edu/
>
> ~lmiller/JazzHome.html>.

If you need to divide a URL between lines, do so after a slash and do not insert a hyphen. If the URL is long (more than one line of your text), give the URL of the site's search page. Do not make the URL a hyperlink.

53. Personal Web site

If no title is available, use a descriptive term such as "Home page."

no publisher
Henson, Keith. *The Keith Henson Jazzpage.* N.p. 1996. Web. 11 May 2008.

54. Home page for a course

After the instructor's name, list the course title, then the department and school names.

course title
Hea, Kimme. *Spatial and Visual Rhetorics.* Dept. of English, U of Arizona, 4 Jan. 2003.

Web. 11 May 2008.

55. Home page for an academic department

Department of English. U of Arizona, 14 May 2008. Web. 19 May 2008.

56. Personal page on a social networking site

Xiu Xiu. "Xiu Xiu." *Myspace.com.* MySpace, 26 Apr. 2008. Web. 11 May 2008.

57. Entire blog

McLennan, Doug. *Diacritical.* ArtsJournal, 20 Feb. 2008. Web. 11 May 2008.

CITING ELECTRONIC SOURCES IN MLA STYLE

- Begin with the name of the writer, editor, compiler, translator, director, or performer.
- Put the title of a short work in quotation marks.
- If there is no title, use a descriptive term such as *editorial* or *comment* (not italicized).
- Italicize the name of the publication or Web site. The online versions of some print magazines and newspapers have different titles than the print versions.
- Cite the date of publication or last update.
- For an online magazine or newspaper article or a Web original source, give the source (in quotation marks), the site title (italicized), version (if any), publisher or sponsor, date of publication, medium (Web), and access date (*See p. 296.*)
- You may cite online sources that also appear in another medium with information about the other version (*see p. 301*). Do not cite online versions of print newspapers and magazines in this way.
- For a journal article, include the article title (in quotation marks), periodical title (italicized), volume and issue numbers, and inclusive page numbers or *n. pag.* Conclude with the medium (Web) and access date. (*See p. 303*).
- To cite a periodical article from an online database, provide the print publication information, the database title (italicized), the medium, and your access date.
- If the source is not divided into sections or pages, include *n. pag.* (no pagination).
- Give the medium (Web). Include your most recent date of access to the specific source (not the general site).
- Conclude the citation with a URL only if readers may have difficulty finding the source without it (*see the box on p. 297*).

58. Blog entry

McLennan, Doug. "The Rise of Arts Culture." *Diacritical.* ArtsJournal, 21 Nov. 2007.

Web. 11 May 2008.

59. Article in an online magazine

Borushko, Matthew. "The Reinvention of Jazz." *The Atlantic.com.* Atlantic Monthly

Group, 18 Apr. 2007. Web. 13 May 2008.

60. Article in an online newspaper

> Howard, Hilary. "A Cruise for Jazz Fans with a Soft Side." *New York Times*. New York
>
> Times, 11 May 2008. Web. 11 May 2008.

61. Editorial in an online newspaper

Include the word *Editorial* (not italicized) after the published title of the editorial.

> "Schwarzenegger's Bad-News Budget." Editorial. *SFGate*. San Francisco Chronicle,
>
> 14 Jan. 2008. Web. 12 May 2008.

62. Letter to the editor in an online newspaper

Include the name of the letter writer, as well as the word *Letter* (not italicized).

> Dow, Roger. Letter. *SFGate*. San Francisco Chronicle, 10 Jan. 2008. Web.
>
> 12 May 2008.

63. Online review

> Kot, Greg. "The Roots Fuel Their Rage into 'Rising Down.'" Rev. of *Rising Down*,
>
> by the Roots. *chicagotribune.com*. Chicago Tribune, 11 May 2008. Web.
>
> 12 May 2008.

64. Online interview

See no. 42 for a print interview.

> Haddon, Mark. Interview by Dave Welch. *Powells.com*. Powell's Books, 24 June 2003.
>
> Web. 15 May 2008.

65. Article in an online encyclopedia or another reference work

Begin with the author's name if any is given.

> "Louis Armstrong." *Encyclopaedia Britannica Online*. Encyclopaedia Britannica,
>
> 2008. Web. 12 May 2008.

66. Entry in a wiki

List the title of the entry, the wiki name, the sponsor, the date of latest update, the medium, and your access date. Check with your instructor before using a wiki as a source.

> "Symphony." *Citizendium*. Citizendium Foundation, 1 Nov. 2007. Web. 12 May 2008.

67. Online map (Web only)
Include the descriptive word *Map.*

> "Denver, Colorado." Map. *Google Maps.* Google, 12 May 2008. Web. 12 May 2008.

68. Audio podcast

> Fresh Sounds. "Jazzarific: Bing Crosby Meets Louis Armstrong." *JazzVinyl.com.*
> no publisher
> N.p., 26 Dec. 2007. Web. 12 May 2008.

69. Video podcast

> Mahr, Krista. "Saving China's Grasslands." *Time.com.* Time, Inc., 10 Oct. 2007. Web.
>
> 12 May 2008.

70. Online video (Web original)
For material posted online from a film, TV series, or other non-Web source, see nos. 83 and 85.

> Wesch, Michael. "The Machine Is Us/ing Us." *Digital Ethnography.* Kansas State U,
>
> 31 Jan. 2007. Web. 12 May 2008.

71. Posting to a news group or an electronic forum
Treat an archived posting as a Web source. Use the subject line as the title of the posting and give the name of the Web site. If there is no subject, substitute *Online posting.*

> Pomeroy, Leslie K., Jr. "Racing with the Moon." *rec.music.bluenote.* N.p., 4 May 2008.
>
> Web. 12 May 2008.

72. Posting to an e-mail discussion list
Include the author and use the subject line as the title.

> Harbin, David. "Furtwangler's Beethoven 9 Bayreuth." *Opera-L Archives.* City U of
>
> New York, 3 Jan. 2008. Web. 12 May 2008.

73. Synchronous (real-time) communication
Cite the online transcript of a synchronous communication as you would a Web site. Include a description, the date of the event, the title of the forum, the medium, and the date of access. If relevant, the speaker's name can begin the citation.

> Curran, Stuart, and Harry Rusche. "Discussion: Plenary Log 6. Third Annual Graduate
>
> Student Conference in Romanticism." *Prometheus Unplugged: Emory MOO.*
>
> Emory U, 20 Apr. 1996. Web. 4 Jan. 1999.

74. Online government publication except the *Congressional Record*

Begin with the name of the country, followed by the name of the sponsoring department, the title of the document, and the names (if listed) of the authors.

> United States. National Commission on Terrorist Attacks upon the United States.
>
> > *The 9/11 Commission Report.* By Thomas H. Kean, et al. 5 Aug. 2004. Web.
>
> 12 May 2008.

75. *Congressional Record* (online or print)

The *Congressional Record* has its own citation format, which is the same for print and online (apart from the medium). Abbreviate the title and include the date and page numbers. Give the medium (print or Web).

> *Cong. Rec.* 28 Apr. 2005: D419-D428. Web. 12 May 2008.

Web sources also available in another medium

If an online work also appears in another medium (e.g., print), the MLA recommends (but does not require) that your citation include information about the other version of the work. (Information about the editor or sponsor of the Web site or database is optional in this model.) If the facts about the other version of the source are not available, cite as a basic Web source (*see nos. 51 and 52*). (Articles on the Web sites of newspapers and magazines are never cited with print publication information. For academic journals, see nos. 88–91).

76. Online book

Cite as a print book (*no. 1*). Instead of ending with "Print," give the Web site or database, the medium (Web), and your access date. Optional information about the site's sponsor, publisher, or editor follows the site name.

> Arter, Jared Maurice. *Echoes from a Pioneer Life.* Atlanta: Caldwell, 1922.
>
> > optional name and location of Web publisher
> > *Documenting the American South.* U of North Carolina, Chapel Hill. Web.
>
> 21 May 2008.

77. Selection from an online book

Add the title of the selection after the author. If the online version of the work lacks page numbers, use *n. pag.*

> Sandburg, Carl. "Chicago." *Chicago Poems.* New York, Holt: 1916.
>
> > N. pag. *Bartleby.com.* Web. 12 May 2008.

78. Online dissertation

Give the Web site or database, the medium (Web), and your access date. Or cite as a basic Web source (*see nos. 51 and 52*).

> Kosiba, Sara A. "A Successful Revolt? The Redefinition of Midwestern Literary
>
> Culture in the 1920s and 1930s." Diss. Kent State U, 2007. *OhioLINK*. Web.
>
> 12 May 2008.

79. Online pamphlet or brochure (also in print)

Cite as a book. Give the title of the Web site or database, the medium (Web), and your access date. Or cite as a basic Web source (*see no. 51*).

> United States. Securities and Exchange Commission. Division of Corporate Finance.
>
> *International Investing: Get the Facts.* Washington: GPO, 1999. *US Securities*
>
> *and Exchange Commission.* Web. 12 May 2008.

80. Online map or chart (also in print)

See no. 43 for a print map. Remove the medium; add the title of the database or Web site, the medium (Web), and your access date. (See no. 67 for a Web-only map.) Or cite as a basic Web source (*see nos. 51 and 52*).

> *MTA New York City Subway.* New York: Metropolitan Transit Authority, 2008.
>
> *MTA New York City Transit.* Web. 12 May 2008.

81. Online cartoon (also in print)

See no. 44 for a cartoon. Remove the medium; add the database or site, the medium (Web), and your access date. Or cite as a basic Web source (*see nos. 51 and 52*).

> Ziegler, Jack. "A Viking Funeral for My Goldfish." *New Yorker* 19 May 2008: 65.
>
> *Cartoonbank.com.* Web. 20 May 2008.

82. Online rendering of visual artwork

Cite as you would the original (*no. 115*). Remove the original medium; add the database or Web site, the medium (Web), and your access date. Or cite as a basic Web source (*see nos. 51 and 52*).

> Seurat, Georges-Pierre. *Evening, Honfleur.* 1886. Museum of Mod. Art, New York.
>
> *MoMA.org.* Web. 8 May 2008.

83. Online video/film (also on film, DVD, or videocassette)

See nos. 107–08 for a film or video. Remove the medium; add the database or site, the medium (Web), and your access date. Or cite as a basic Web source (*see nos. 51 and 52*).

Night of the Living Dead. Dir. George A. Romero. Image Ten, 1968. *Internet Archive.*

Web. 12 May 2008.

84. Online radio program

See no. 110 for a radio program. Remove the medium; add the database or site, the medium (Web), and your access date. Or cite as a basic Web source (*see nos. 51 and 52*).

"Bill Evans: 'Piano Impressionism.' " *Jazz Profiles.* Narr. Nancy Wilson. Natl. Public

Radio. WGBH, Boston, 27 Feb. 2008. *NPR.org.* Web. 16 Mar. 2008.

85. Online TV program

See no. 111 for a TV program. Remove the medium; add the database or site, the medium (Web), and your access date. Or cite as a basic Web source (*see nos. 51 and 52*).

episode   director of episode (not series) series   performer in series
"Local Ad." Dir. Jason Reitman. *The Office.* Perf. Steve Carrell. NBC. WNBC,

New York, 12 Dec. 2007. *NBC.com.* Web. 12 May 2008.

86. Online broadcast interview

See no. 112 for a broadcast interview. Remove the medium, add the site and "Web," and give your access date. Or cite as a basic Web source (*see nos. 51 and 52*).

Jones, Sharon. Interview by Terry Gross. *Fresh Air.* Natl. Public Radio. WNYC,

New York, 28 Nov. 2007. *NPR.org.* Web. 12 May 2008.

87. Online archival material

Provide the information for the original. Add the Web site or database, the medium (Web), and your access date. Otherwise, cite as a basic Web source (*see nos. 51 and 52*).

date uncertain
Whitman, Walt. "After the Argument." [c. 1890]. The Charles E. Feinberg Collection

of the Papers of Walt Whitman, Lib. of Cong. *The Walt Whitman Archive.* Web.

13 May 2008.

Works in online scholarly journals

Use the same format for all online journals, including those with print editions.

88. Article in an online journal

Give the author, the article title (in quotation marks) or a term such as *Editorial* (not italicized), the journal title (italicized), the volume number, issue number, date, and the inclusive page range (or n. pag. if the source lacks page numbers). Conclude with the medium (Web) and your access date.

Parla, Jale. "The Wounded Tongue: Turkey's Language Reform and the Canonicity of the Novel." *PMLA* 123.1 (2008): 27-40. Web. 7 May 2008.

89. Review in an online journal

Friedman, Edward H. Rev. of *Transnational Cervantes,* by William Childers. *Cervantes: Bulletin of the Cervantes Society of America* 27.2 (2007): 41-43. Web. 13 May 2008.

90. Editorial in an online journal

Heitmeyer, Wilhelm, et al. "Letter from the Editors." Editorial. *International Journal of Conflict and Violence* 1.1 (2007): n. pag. Web. 14 May 2008.

91. Letter to the editor in an online journal

Destaillats, Frédéric, Julie Moulin, and Jean-Baptiste Bezelgues. Letter. *Nutrition & Metabolism* 4.10 (2007): n. pag. Web. 14 May 2008.

Works from online databases

In addition to information about the print version of the source, provide the title of the database (in italics), the medium (Web), and your access date.

92. Newspaper article from an online database

Blumenfeld, Larry. "House of Blues." *New York Times* 11 Nov. 2007: A33. *Academic Universe.* Web. 31 Dec. 2007.

93. Magazine article from an online database

Farley, Christopher John. "Music Goes Global." *Time* 15 Sept. 2001: 4+. *General OneFile.* Web. 31 Dec. 2007.

94. Journal article from an online database

Nielson, Aldon Lynn. "A Hard Rain." *Callaloo* 25.1 (2002): 135-45. *Academic Search Premier.* Web. 17 Mar. 2008.

95. Journal abstract from an online database

Dempsey, Nicholas P. "Hook-Ups and Train Wrecks: Contextual Parameters and the

Coordination of Jazz Interactions." *Symbolic Interaction* 31.1 (2008): 57-75.

Abstract. *Academic Search Premier.* Web. 17 Mar. 2008.

96. Work from a subscription service

Cite the database but not the library subscription service (e.g., EBSCO, InfoTrac) or the subscribing library. Follow the format of nos. 92–95.

In the past, America Online offered personal database subscriptions. However, it has stopped doing so, and most subscription databases can be accessed at the library.

Other Electronic (Non-Web) Sources

97. E-mail

Include the author, the subject line (if any) in quotation marks, the descriptive term *Message to* (not italicized), the name of the recipient, the date of the message, and the medium.

Hoffman, Esther. "Re: My Louis Armstrong Paper." Message to J. Peritz.

14 Apr. 2008. E-mail.

98. A text file stored on your computer

Cite local word-processor documents as manuscripts (*see no. 49*) and if you wish to cite a specific draft or version, note the date last modified. Record the file format as the medium.

McNutt, Lea. "The Origination of Avian Flight." 2008. *Microsoft Word* file.

Hoffman, Esther. "Louis Armstrong and Joe Glaser: More than Meets the Eye."

File last modified on 9 May 2008. *Microsoft Word* file.

99. A PDF file

Treat local PDF files as published and follow the closest print model.

United States. US Copyright Office. *Report on Orphan Works.* Washington: US

Copyright Office, 2006. PDF file.

100. An audio file

Use the format for a sound recording (*see no. 113*). Record the file format as the medium.

Holiday, Billie. "God Bless the Child." *God Bless the Child.* Columbia, 1936.

MP3 file.

101. A visual file

Cite local image files as works of visual art (*see no. 115*). Record the file format as the medium.

> Gursky, Andreas. *Times Square, New York.* 1997. Museum of Mod. Art, New York.
>
>> JPEG file.

102. Other digital files

Record the file format as the medium (for example, *XML file*). If the format is unclear, use the designation *Digital file* (not italicized). Use the citation format of the most closely related print or nonprint source.

103. CD-ROM or DVD-ROM published periodically

If a CD-ROM or DVD-ROM is revised on a regular basis, include in its citation the author, title of the work, any print publication information, medium, title of the CD-ROM or DVD-ROM (if different from the original title), vendor, and date of electronic publication.

> Ross, Alex. "Separate Worlds, Linked Electronically." *New York Times* 29 Apr. 1996,
>
>> late ed.: A22. CD-ROM. *New York Times Ondisc.* UMI-ProQuest. Dec. 1996.

104. CD-ROM or DVD-ROM not published periodically

Works on CD-ROM or DVD-ROM are usually cited like books or parts of books if they are not revised periodically. The medium and the name of the vendor (if different from the publisher) appear after the publication data. For a work that also exists in print, give the print publication information (as in the example) followed by the medium, electronic publisher, and date of electronic publication.

> print publisher omitted for pre-1900 work
> Jones, Owen. *The Grammar of Ornament.* London, 1856. CD-ROM. Octavo, 1998.

105. CD-ROM or DVD-ROM with multiple discs

List the total number of discs at the end of the entry, or give the number of the disc you reviewed if you used only one.

> American Educational Research Association. *AERA Journals Collection.* Washington:
>
>> AERA, 2007. CD-ROM. 10 discs.

106. Computer software

Include the title, version, publisher, and date in your text or in an explanatory note. Do not include an entry in your works-cited list.

Audiovisual and Other Nonprint Sources

107. Film

Begin with the title (italicized), unless you want to highlight a particular contributor. For a film, cite the director and the featured performers or narrator (*Perf.* or *Narr.*), followed by the distributor and year. Conclude with the medium.

> *Artists and Models.* Dir. Raoul Walsh. Perf. Jack Benny, Ida Lupino, and Alan
>> Townsend. Paramount, 1937. Film.

108. DVD or videotape

See no. 107. Include the original film's release date if relevant. Conclude with the medium (*DVD* or *Videocassette*). (Do not italicize the medium.)

> *Casablanca.* Dir. Michael Curtiz. Perf. Humphrey Bogart and Ingrid Bergman. 1942.
>> Warner Home Video, 2000. DVD.

109. Personal/archival video or audio recording

Give the date recorded and the location of the recording.

> Adderley, Nat. Interview by Jimmy Owens. Rec. 2 Apr. 1993. Videocassette.
>> Schomburg Center for Research in Black Culture, New York Public Lib.

110. Radio program

Give the episode title (in quotation marks), the program title (italicized), the name of the series (if any), the network (call letters), the city, the broadcast date, and the medium. Name individuals if relevant.

> "Legends Play 'Jazz in Our Time.'" *Jazz Set.* Narr. DeeDee Bridgewater.
>> WBGO-FM, New York, 17 Jan. 2008. Radio.

111. TV program

Cite as you would a radio program (*see no. 110*), but give *Television* (not italicized) as the medium.

> episode   director of episode   series   performer in series
> "Local Ad." Dir. Jason Reitman. *The Office.* Perf. Steve Carrell. NBC. WNBC, New York,
>> 12 Dec. 2007. Television.

112. Broadcast interview

Give the name of the person interviewed, followed by the word *Interview* and the name of the interviewer if you know it. End with information about the broadcast and the medium.

> Knox, Shelby. Interview by David Brancaccio. *NOW.* PBS. WNET, New York,
>> 17 June 2005. Television.

113. Sound recording

Start with the composer, conductor, or performer, depending on your focus. Include the following information: the work's title (italicized); the artist(s), if not already mentioned; the manufacturer; the date of release; and the medium.

> Armstrong, Louis. *Town Hall Concert Plus*. RCA Victor, 1957. LP.

114. Musical composition

Include only the composer and title, unless you are referring to a published score. Published scores are treated like books except that the date of composition appears after the title. Titles of instrumental pieces are not italicized when known only by form and number, unless the reference is to a published score.

> Ellington, Duke. *Satin Doll*.

> Haydn, Franz Josef. Symphony no. 94 in G Major.
> reference to a published score
> Haydn, Franz Josef. *Symphony No. 94 in G Major*. 1791. Ed. H. C. Robbins Landon.
>
> Salzburg: Haydn-Mozart, 1965. Print.

115. Artwork

Provide the artist's name, the title of the artwork (italicized), the date (if unknown, write n.d.), the medium, the institution or private collection, and city (or n.p.) in which the artwork can be found. For anonymous collectors, write *Private collection* (not italicized) and omit the city information.

> Leonard, Herman. *Louis Armstrong: Birdland 1949*. 1949. Photograph. Barbara
>
> Gillman Gallery, Miami.

116. Personal, telephone, or e-mail interview

Begin with the person interviewed, followed by *Personal interview, Telephone interview,* or *E-mail interview* (not italicized) and the date of the interview. (*See no. 42 for a published interview.*)

> Jacobs, Phoebe. Personal interview. 5 May 2008.

117. Lecture or speech

Give the speaker, the title (in quotation marks), the name of the forum or sponsor, the location, and the date. Conclude with *Address* or *Lecture* (not italicized).

> Taylor, Billy. "What Is Jazz?" John F. Kennedy Center for the Performing Arts,
>
> Washington. 14 Feb. 1995. Lecture.

118. Live performance

To cite a play, opera, dance performance, or concert, begin with the title; followed by the authors (*By*); information about the performance, such as the director (*Dir.*) and major performers; the site; the city; the performance date; and *Performance* (not italicized).

Ragtime. By Terrence McNally, Lynn Athrens, and Stephen Flaherty. Dir. Frank

Galati. Ford Performing Arts Center, New York. 11 Nov. 1998. Performance.

119. Microfiche/microform/microfilm

Cite as you would the print version. Include the medium, followed by the name of the microform and any identifying numbers.

Johnson, Charles S. "A Southern Negro's View of the South." *Journal of Negro*

Education 26.1 (1957): 4-9. Microform. *The Schomburg Collection of the*

New York Public Library 167 (1970): 101405.

120. Publication in more than one medium

If you are citing a publication that consists of several different media, list alphabetically all of the media you consulted. Follow the citation format of the medium you used primarily (print in the example).

Sadker, David M., and Karen Zittleman. *Teachers, Schools, and Society: A Brief*

Introduction to Education. New York: McGraw, 2007. CD-ROM, print, Web.

28 MLA Style: Explanatory Notes and Acknowledgments

Explanatory notes are used to cite multiple sources for borrowed material or to give readers supplemental information. You can also use notes to acknowledge people who helped you with research and writing. Acknowledgments are a courteous gesture. If you acknowledge someone's assistance in your explanatory notes, be sure to send that person a copy of your text.

TEXT

One answer to these questions is suggested by a large (24-by-36-inch) painting

discovered in Armstrong's house.[2]

NOTE

[2] I want to thank George Arevalo of the Louis Armstrong Archives for his help

on this project. George showed me the two pictures I describe in this paper. Seeing those pictures helped me figure out what I wanted to say—and why I wanted to say it. For introducing me to archival research and to the art of Louis Armstrong, I also want to thank the head of the Louis Armstrong Archives, Michael Cogswell, and my English teacher, Professor Amy Tucker.

29 MLA Style: Paper Format

The following format guidelines are recommended by the seventh edition of the *MLA Handbook for Writers of Research Papers.* For an example of a research paper that has been prepared using MLA style, see pages 313–23.

Materials   Back up your final draft on a flash drive, CD, or DVD. Use a high-quality printer and high-quality, white 8½-by-11-inch paper. Put the printed pages together with a paper clip.

Heading and title   In the upper left-hand corner of the first page, one inch from the top and side, type on separate, double-spaced lines your name, your instructor's name, the course number, and the date. Double-space between the date and the paper's title and the title and the first line of text, as well as throughout your paper. The title should be centered and properly capitalized (*see p. 313*). Do not italicize the title or put it in quotation marks or bold type.

Margins and spacing   Use one-inch margins all around, except for the top right-hand corner, where the page number goes. Your right margin should be ragged (not "justified," or even).

Double-space lines throughout the paper, including in quotations, notes, and the works-cited list. Indent the first word of each paragraph one-half inch (or five spaces) from the left margin. For block quotations, indent one inch (or ten spaces) from the left.

Page numbers   Put your last name and the page number in the upper right-hand corner of the page, one-half inch from the top and flush with the right margin.

👁 **Visuals**   Place visuals (tables, charts, graphs, and images) close to the place in your text where you refer to them. Label and number tables consecutively (*Table 1, Table 2*) and give each one an explanatory

TextConnex

Electronic Submission of Papers

Some instructors may request that you submit your paper electronically. Keep these tips in mind:

- Confirm the appropriate procedure for submission.
- Find out in advance the preferred format for the submission of documents. *Always ask permission before sending an attached document to anyone.*
- If you are asked to send a document as an attachment, save your document as a "rich text format" (.rtf) file or in PDF format.
- As a courtesy, run a virus scan on your file before sending it electronically or submitting it on a CD-ROM.

caption; put this information above the table. The term *Figure* (abbreviated *Fig.*) is used to label all other kinds of visuals, except for musical illustrations, which are labeled *Example* (abbreviated *Ex.*). Place figure or example captions below the visual. Below all visuals, cite the source of the material and provide explanatory notes as needed. *(For more on using visuals effectively, see Tab 2: Writing and Designing Texts.)*

30 Student Paper in MLA Style

As a first-year college student, Esther Hoffman wrote the following paper for her composition course. She knew little about Louis Armstrong and jazz before her class visited the Louis Armstrong Archives. She did archival research based on what she had learned from consulting online and print sources.

www.mhhe.com/ awr3

For another sample of a paper in MLA style, go to

Research > Sample Research Papers > MLA Style

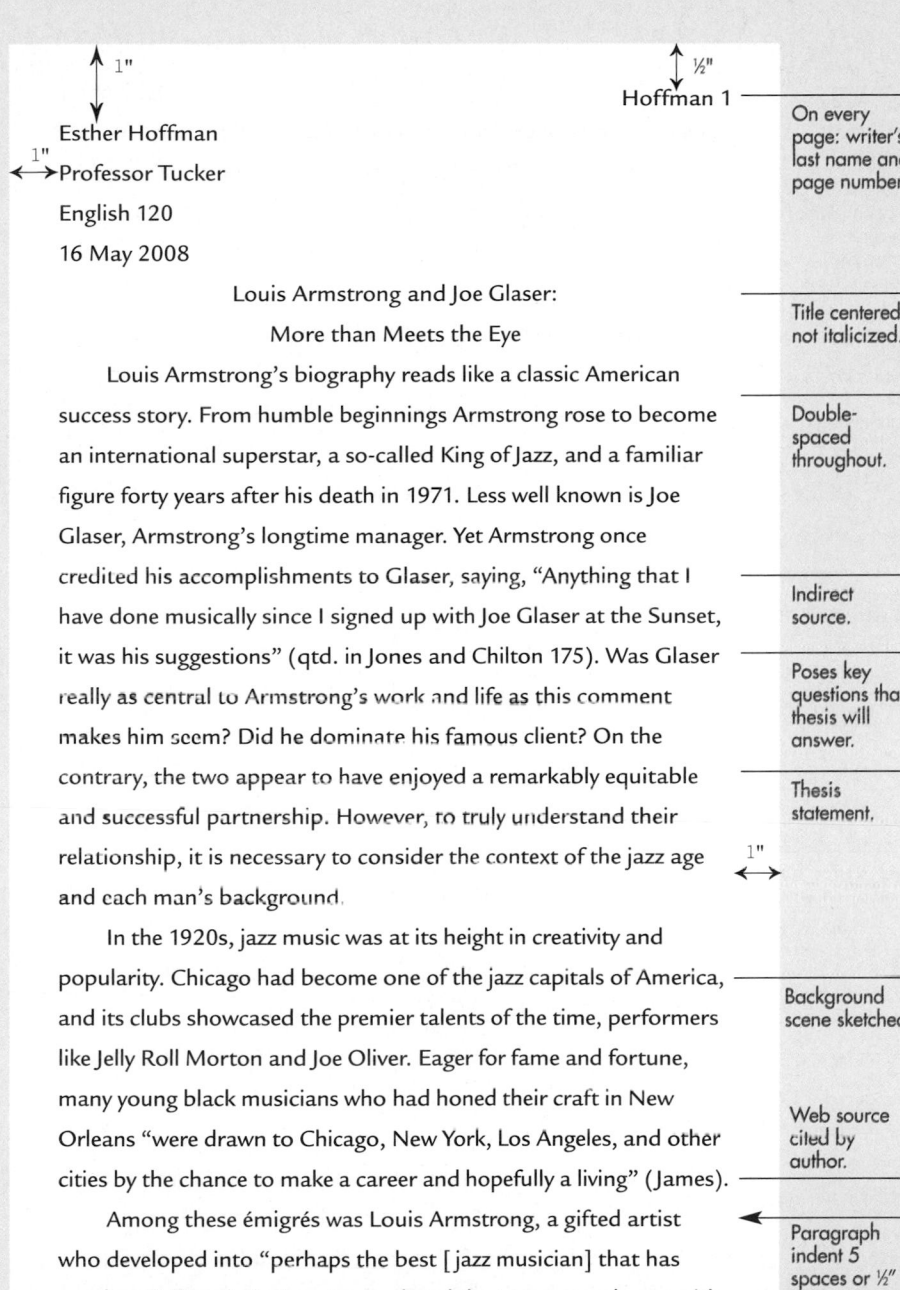

Hoffman 1

Esther Hoffman

Professor Tucker

English 120

16 May 2008

Louis Armstrong and Joe Glaser:

More than Meets the Eye

Louis Armstrong's biography reads like a classic American success story. From humble beginnings Armstrong rose to become an international superstar, a so-called King of Jazz, and a familiar figure forty years after his death in 1971. Less well known is Joe Glaser, Armstrong's longtime manager. Yet Armstrong once credited his accomplishments to Glaser, saying, "Anything that I have done musically since I signed up with Joe Glaser at the Sunset, it was his suggestions" (qtd. in Jones and Chilton 175). Was Glaser really as central to Armstrong's work and life as this comment makes him seem? Did he dominate his famous client? On the contrary, the two appear to have enjoyed a remarkably equitable and successful partnership. However, to truly understand their relationship, it is necessary to consider the context of the jazz age and each man's background.

In the 1920s, jazz music was at its height in creativity and popularity. Chicago had become one of the jazz capitals of America, and its clubs showcased the premier talents of the time, performers like Jelly Roll Morton and Joe Oliver. Eager for fame and fortune, many young black musicians who had honed their craft in New Orleans "were drawn to Chicago, New York, Los Angeles, and other cities by the chance to make a career and hopefully a living" (James).

Among these émigrés was Louis Armstrong, a gifted artist who developed into "perhaps the best [jazz musician] that has ever been" ("Louis"). Armstrong played the trumpet and sang with

Annotations (right margin):

On every page: writer's last name and page number.

Title centered, not italicized.

Double-spaced throughout.

Indirect source.

Poses key questions that thesis will answer.

Thesis statement.

Background scene sketched.

Web source cited by author.

Paragraph indent 5 spaces or ½"

Topic introduced.

Hoffman 2

unusual improvisational ability as well as technical mastery. As

biographer Laurence Bergreen points out, Armstrong easily reached

difficult high notes, the F's and G's that stymied other trumpeters

(248). His innovative singing style also featured "scat," a technique

that "place[s] emphasis on the human voice as an additionally

important component in jazz music" (Anderson 329). According to

one popular anecdote, Armstrong invented scat during a recording

session; mid-song, he dropped his lyrics sheet and--not wanting to

disrupt a great take--began to improvise (Edwards 619). Eventually

Armstrong's innovations became the standard, as more and more

jazz musicians took their cue from his style.

Armstrong's beginnings give no hint of the greatness that

he would achieve. In New Orleans, he was born into poverty and

received little formal education. As a youngster, Armstrong had

to take odd jobs like delivering coal and selling newspapers so that he

could earn money to help his family. At the age of twelve, Armstrong

was placed in the Colored Waifs' Home to serve an eighteen-month

sentence for firing a gun in a public place. There "Captain" Peter

Davis gave him "basic musical training on the cornet" ("Louis

Armstrong"). Older, more established musicians soon noticed

Armstrong's talent and offered him opportunities to play with them.

In 1922, Joe Oliver invited Armstrong to join his band in Chicago,

and the twenty-one-year-old trumpeter headed north.

It was in Chicago that Armstrong met Joe Glaser. According

to Bergreen, Glaser had a reputation for being a tough but

trustworthy guy who could handle any situation. He was raised in

a middle-class home by parents who were Jewish immigrants from

Russia. As a young man, Glaser got caught up in the Chicago

underworld and soon had a rap sheet that included indictments

for running a brothel as well as for statutory rape.[1] Glaser's mob

---

Margin annotations:

MLA in-text citation: author [Bergreen] named in signal phrase.

MLA in-text citation: author named in parentheses.

Development by narration (*see p. 60*).

Web source cited by title.

Focus introduced.

Superscript number indicating explanatory note.

Hoffman 3

connections also led to his involvement in Chicago's club scene, a business almost completely controlled by gangsters like Al Capone. During the era of Prohibition, Glaser managed the Sunset Cafe, a club where Armstrong often performed:

> There was a pronounced gangster element at the Sunset, but Louis, accustomed to being employed and protected by mobsters, didn't think twice about that. Mr. Capone's men ensured the flow of alcohol, and their presence reassured many whites. (Bergreen 279)

By the early thirties, Armstrong had become one of the most popular musicians in the world. He attracted thousands of fans during his 1930 European tour, and his "Hot Five" and "Hot Seven" recordings were considered some of the best jazz ever played. Financially, Armstrong should have been doing very well, but instead he was having business difficulties. He owed money to Johnny Collins, his former manager, and Lil' Hardin, his ex-wife, was suing him for a share of the royalties on the song "Struttin' with Some Barbecue." At this point, Armstrong asked Glaser to be his business manager. Glaser quickly paid off Collins and settled with Lil' Hardin. Giving up his other business ventures, Glaser now became Armstrong's exclusive agent (Morgenstern 124-28; Collier 273-76; Bergreen 376-78). For the next thirty-four years, his responsibilities included booking appearances, organizing the bands, making travel arrangements, and paying the band members' salaries (Jones and Chilton 160, 220).

Some might posit that Glaser controlled all aspects of Armstrong's work and life. This view is suggested by a large (24-by-36-inch) oil painting discovered in Armstrong's house.[2] Joe Glaser is pictured in the middle of the canvas. Four black-and-white quadrants surround the central image of Glaser. One quadrant

Block quotation indented 10 spaces or 1".

Summary of material from a number of sources.

Citation of multiple sources.

Use of information from two separate pages in one source.

Hoffman 4

Development
by description
(*see p. 61*).

depicts a city scene, the scene in which Glaser thrived. The bottom two quadrants picture dogs, a reminder that Glaser raised show dogs. The remaining quadrant presents an image of Louis Armstrong. By placing Glaser in the center and Armstrong off in a corner, the unknown artist seems to suggest that even though Armstrong was the star, it was Glaser who made him one.

Presents a
claim plus
supporting
evidence.

In fact, Glaser did advance Armstrong's career in numerous important ways. In 1935, he negotiated the lucrative record contract with Decca that led to the production of hits like "I'm in the Mood for Love" and "You Are My Lucky Star" (Bergreen 380). Glaser also decided when to sell the rights to Armstrong's songs. Determined to make as much money as possible, he sometimes sold the rights to a song as soon as it was released, especially when he thought the song might not turn out to be a big hit. However, in at least two instances, this money-making strategy backfired: much to Glaser's surprise, both "Hello, Dolly" and "What a Wonderful World" became big hits after the rights had been sold (Jacobs).

Development
by illustration
(*see p. 59*).

To expand Armstrong's popularity, Glaser increased his exposure to white audiences in the United States. In 1935, articles on Armstrong appeared in *Vanity Fair* and *Esquire,* two magazines with a predominantly white readership (Bergreen 385). Glaser also promoted Armstrong's movie career. At a time when only a handful of black performers were accepted in Hollywood, Armstrong had roles in a number of films, including *Pennies from Heaven* (1936) with Bing Crosby. Moreover, "Jeepers Creepers," a song Armstrong sang in *Going Places* (1938), received an Academy Award nomination (Bogle 149, 157). Of course, more exposure sometimes meant more discomfort, if not danger, especially when

Note use of
transitional
expressions
(*see pp.
83–86*).

Hoffman 5

Armstrong and his band members were touring in the South. Bergreen recounts how in Southern states, where blacks were prohibited from entering many stores, Glaser sometimes had to shop for the band's food and other supplies (378, 381).

As Armstrong's manager, Glaser also exerted some control over the musician's personal finances and habits. According to Dave Gold, an accountant who worked for Associated Booking, it was Glaser who paid Armstrong's mortgage, taxes, and basic living expenses (Collier 330). A 1960 letter from Glaser to Lucille Armstrong corroborates Gold's account; it shows that Glaser assumed responsibility for buying the musician and his wife a new car as well as for filing the paperwork needed to retain the old license plate number. More personal were Glaser's attempts to control Armstrong's habitual use of marijuana. In 1931, Armstrong received a suspended sentence after his arrest for marijuana possession. He continued to use the drug, however, especially during performances, and told Glaser that he wanted to write a book about marijuana's positive effects. Glaser flatly rejected the book idea and, fearful of a scandal, also forbade Armstrong's smoking any marijuana while on tour in Europe (Pollack).

Clearly, Glaser was in a position to affect powerfully Armstrong's career and his life. However, Armstrong seemed to recognize that he gave Glaser whatever power over him the manager enjoyed. When he wanted to, Armstrong could and did resist Glaser's control, and that may be one reason why he liked and trusted Glaser as much as he did.

After Glaser became his manager, Armstrong no longer had to worry about the behind-the-scenes details of his career. He was free to concentrate on creating music and making the most of the

Support by expert opinion (*see p. 31*).

Support by key fact (*see p. 31*).

Support by anecdote (*see p. 31*).

Restatement of thesis.

Hoffman 6

opportunities his manager worked out for him. Glaser booked
Armstrong into engagements with legendary performers like Benny
Goodman, Ella Fitzgerald, and Duke Ellington. He also worked
with the record companies to ensure that Armstrong would make
the best and most profitable recordings possible (Bergreen 457).
During the thirty-four years they worked together, both Armstrong
and Glaser made lots of money. More important, their relationship
freed Armstrong to make extraordinary music.

If Armstrong acquiesced to most of Glaser's business
decisions, it may have been because he had no reason to resist
them. However, when he deemed it necessary, Armstrong acted on
his own. For example, in 1944 a talented band member named
Dexter Gordon threatened to quit, so Armstrong offered him a
raise--without consulting first with Glaser (Morgenstern 132).
In 1957, when Armstrong wanted to put a stop to backstage
crowding, he not only directed Glaser to make a sign prohibiting
guests from going backstage but also told him exactly what to
say on the sign (Armstrong, "Backstage Instructions"). As these
incidents suggest, when Armstrong was displeased with the way
his career was being handled, he acted to amend the situation.

Armstrong also knew how to resist Glaser's attempts to
control the more personal aspects of his life. In a recent interview,
Phoebe Jacobs, formerly one of Glaser's employees, sheds new
light on the relationship between the manager and the musician.
Armstrong's legendary generosity was tough on his pocketbook.
It was well known that if someone needed money, Armstrong
would readily hand over some bills. At one point, Glaser asked
Jacobs to give Armstrong smaller denominations so that he would
not give away so much money. The trumpeter soon figured out

Source cited:
archival
material.

Source cited:
personal
interview.

what was going on and admonished Jacobs for following Glaser's
orders about money that belonged to him, not Glaser. On another
occasion, Armstrong declined an invitation to join Glaser for
dinner at a Chinese restaurant, saying, "I want to eat what I want
to eat" (qtd. by Jacobs).

Even though he sometimes pushed Glaser away, Armstrong
obviously loved and trusted his manager. In all the years of their
association, the two men signed only one contract and, in the
musician's words, "after that we didn't bother" (qtd. in Jones
and Chilton 240). A picture of Joe Glaser in one of Armstrong's
scrapbooks bears the following label in the star's handwriting:
"the greatest." In his dedication to the unpublished manuscript
"Louis Armstrong and the Jewish Family in New Orleans, the year
of 1907," Armstrong calls Glaser "the best friend that I ever had,"
while in a letter to Max Jones, he writes, "I did not get really happy
until I got with my man--my dearest friend--Joe Glaser" (qtd. in
Jones and Chilton 16). In 1969, Joe Glaser died. Referring to him
again as "the greatest," Armstrong confided to a friend that
Glaser's death "broke [his] heart" (qtd. in Bergreen 490).

Although there are hints of a struggle for the upper hand, the
relationship between Louis Armstrong and Joe Glaser seems to
have been genuinely friendly and trusting. Armstrong gave Glaser
a good deal of authority over his career, and Glaser used that
authority to make Armstrong a musical and monetary success.
Armstrong was happy to take the opportunities that Glaser
provided for him, but he was not submissive. This equitable and
friendly relationship is depicted by another picture found in
Armstrong's house. The 25-by-21-inch picture, shown in fig. 1,
is a caricature that may seem jarring to contemporary viewers, but

Authoritative
quotation
(see p. 31).

Memorable
quotation
(see p. 260).

Wording
of quotation
adjusted (see
pp. 261–63).

Concludes
with qualified
version of
thesis.

Memorable
illustration.

Hoffman 8

Effective visual
(p. 56).

Fig. 1 An anonymous watercolor
caricature of Armstrong with his
manager, Joe Glaser, c. 1950. Louis
Armstrong Archives, Queens College,
City U of New York, Flushing.

when seen in its historical context it implies a mutual relationship
between Armstrong and Glaser. The pair stand side by side, and
Glaser has his hand on Armstrong's shoulder. Armstrong, who is
dressed for a performance, looks and smiles at us as if he were
facing an audience. But Glaser looks only at Armstrong, the
musician who was his main concern from 1935 to the day he died.
In appearance alone, the men are clearly different. But seen in their
longstanding partnership, the two make up a whole--one picture
that offers us more than meets the eye.

Hoffman 10

Notes

[1]Bergreen 372-76. Even though Ostwald points out a few mistakes in Bergreen's *Louis Armstrong: An Extravagant Life,* I think the book's new information about Glaser is useful and trustworthy.

[2]I want to thank George Arevalo of the Louis Armstrong Archives for his help on this project. George showed me the two pictures I describe in this paper. Seeing those pictures helped me figure out what I wanted to say--and why I wanted to say it. For introducing me to archival research and to the art of Louis Armstrong, I also want to thank the head of the Louis Armstrong Archives, Michael Cogswell, and my English teacher, Professor Amy Tucker.

New page, title centered.

Gives supplemental information about key source.

Indent first line 5 spaces or ½".

Acknowledges others who helped.

Works Cited

Anderson, T. J. "Body and Soul: Bob Kaufman's *Golden Sardine*."
    African American Review 34.2 (2000): 329-46. *Academic Search
    Complete*. Web. 11 Apr. 2008.

Armstrong, Louis. "Backstage Instructions to Glaser." Apr. 1957.
    MS. Accessions 1997-26. Louis Armstrong Archives. Queens
    College, City U of New York, Flushing.

---. "Louis Armstrong and the Jewish Family in New Orleans, the
    Year of 1907." 31 Mar. 1969. MS. Box 1. Louis Armstrong
    Archives. Queens College, City U of New York, Flushing.

Bergreen, Laurence. *Louis Armstrong: An Extravagant Life*. New York:
    Broadway, 1997. Print.

Bogle, Donald. "Louis Armstrong: The Films." Miller 147-79.

Collier, James Lincoln. *Louis Armstrong: An American Genius*. New
    York: Oxford UP, 1983. Print.

Edwards, Brent Hayes. "Louis Armstrong and the Syntax of Scat."
    Critical Inquiry 28.3 (2002): 618-49. Print.

Glaser, Joe. Letter to Lucille Armstrong. 28 Sept. 1960. MS. Box 3.
    Louis Armstrong Archives. Queens College, City U of New
    York, Flushing.

Jacobs, Phoebe. Personal interview. 5 May 2008.

James, Gregory N. *The Southern Diaspora: How the Great Migrations
    of Black and White Southerners Transformed America*. Chapel
    Hill: U of North Carolina P, 2007. *Blues, Jazz, and the Great
    Migration*. Web. 7 May 2008.

Jones, Max, and John Chilton. *Louis: The Louis Armstrong Story,
    1900-1971*. Boston: Little, 1971. Print.

"Louis Armstrong." *New Orleans Online*. New Orleans Tourism
    Marketing Corporation, 2008. Web. 7 May 2008.

New page,
title centered.

Source: journal
article from
database.

Source:
archival
material.

3 hyphens
used instead
of repeating
author's name.

Source:
whole book.

Source:
journal.

Hanging indent
5 spaces or ½".

Source:
personal
interview.

Entries in
alphabetical
order.

Miller, Marc, ed. *Louis Armstrong: A Cultural Legacy.* Seattle: U of
Washington P and Queens Museum of Art, 1994. Print.

Morgenstern, Dan. "Louis Armstrong and the Development and
Diffusion of Jazz." Miller 95-145.

Ostwald, David. "All That Jazz." Rev. of *Louis Armstrong: An
Extravagant Life,* by Laurence Bergreen. *Commentary* Nov. 1997:
68-72. Print.

Pollack, Bracha. "A Man ahead of His Time." 1997. TS.

Robinson, J. Bradford. "Scat Singing." *The New Grove Dictionary of
Jazz.* Ed. Barry Kernfeld. Vol. 3. London: Macmillan, 2002.
515-16. Print.

Source: work
in edited
book cross-
referenced
to Miller.

Source:
review in a
monthly
magazine.

7

Take the whole range of imaginative
literature, and we are all wholesale
borrowers. In every matter that relates to
invention, to use, or beauty or form,
we are borrowers.

—WENDELL PHILLIPS

APA
Documentation
Style

APA style requires writers to provide bibliographic information about their sources in a list of references at the end of a paper. In order to format entries for the list of references correctly, it is important to know what kind of source you are citing. The directory on pages 332–33 will help you find the appropriate sample to use as a model. Alternatively, you can use the charts on the foldout pages that follow. Answering the questions in the charts will usually lead you to the sample entry you need. If you cannot find what you are looking for, consult your instructor.

Sections dealing with visual rhetoric. For a complete listing, see the Quick Guide to Key Resources at the back of this book.

WRITING OUTCOMES

Tab 7: APA Documentation Style
This section will help you answer questions such as:

Rhetorical Knowledge
Which disciplines use APA style? **(31)**

Critical Thinking, Reading, and Writing
Why do I need to document my sources? **(31, 32)**

Processes
What is a Digital Object Identifier (DOI) and how is it used? **(32)**
How should I position and label visuals? **(33)**
What information should an abstract contain? **(33)**

Knowledge of Conventions
How do I cite sources in the text of my paper? **(31)**
How do I create a list of references? **(32)**
How do I cite electronic sources, such as Web sites, podcasts, and online articles with DOIs? **(32)**
What kind of spacing and margins should my paper have? **(33)**

Self-Assessment: *Take an online quiz at www.mhhe.com/awr3 to test your familiarity with the topics covered in Chapters 31–32. As you consult the following chapters, pay special attention to the sections that correspond to any questions you answer incorrectly.*

Instructors of courses in psychology, sociology, political science, communications, education, and business usually prefer a documentation style that emphasizes the author and the year of publication.

The information in Chapters 31–34 is based on the fifth edition of the American Psychological Association's *Publication Manual* (Washington: APA, 2001) and the *APA Style Guide to Electronic References* (Washington: APA, 2007). For updates, check the APA-sponsored Web site at <http://www.apastyle.org>.

APA documentation style has two mandatory parts:

- In-text citations
- List of references

www.mhhe.com/
awr3
For links to Web sites
for documentation
styles used in various
disciplines, go to
**Research > Links to
Documentation Sites**

31 | APA Style: In-Text Citations

In-text citations let readers know that they can find full information about the source of an idea you have paraphrased or summarized, or the source of a quotation, in the list of references at the end of your paper.

1. Author named in your sentence

Follow the author's name with the year of publication (in parentheses).

signal phrase

According to Brookfield (2001), nearly 12% of the Amazonian rain forest in

Brazil has been shaped or influenced by thousands of years of indigenous

human culture.

2. Author named in parentheses

If you do not name the source's author in your sentence, you must include the name in parentheses, followed by the date and, if you are giving a quotation or a specific piece of information, the page number. The name, date, and page number are separated by commas.

The Organization of Indigenous Peoples of the Colombian Amazon attempted

in 2001 to take legal action to ban such fumigation over indigenous lands. Their

ampersand used within parentheses

efforts were not supported by the Colombian government (Lloyd & Soltani,

2001, p. 5).

3. Two to five authors

If a source has five or fewer authors, name all of them the first time you cite the source.

APA IN-TEXT CITATIONS: DIRECTORY to SAMPLE TYPES

(See pp. 332–47 for examples of reference entries.)

As Kaimowitz, Mertens, Wunder, and Pacheco (2004) report in "Hamburger Connection Fuels Amazon Destruction," there are three key factors behind the burgeoning demand for Brazilian beef and the resulting burning of the Amazon rain forest for pasture land.

If you put the names of the authors in parentheses, use an ampersand (&) instead of *and*.

There are three key factors behind the burgeoning demand for Brazilian beef and the resulting burning of the Amazon rain forest for pasture land (Kaimowitz, Mertens, Wunder, & Pacheco, 2004, p. 3).

After the first time you cite a work by three or more authors, use the first author's name plus *et al.* Always use both names when citing a work by two authors.

Another key factor is concern over livestock diseases in other countries (Kaimowitz et al., 2004, p. 4).

4. Six or more authors

For in-text citations of a work by six or more authors, always give the first author's name plus *et al.* In the reference list, however, list the first six authors' names, followed by *et al.*

APA IN-TEXT CITATIONS

- Identify the author(s) of the source, either in the sentence or in a parenthetical citation.
- Indicate the year of publication of the source following the author's name, either in parentheses if the author's name is part of the sentence or, if the author is not named in the sentence, after the author's name and a comma in a parenthetical citation.
- Include a page reference for a quotation or a specific piece of information. Put a *p.* before the page number. If the author is named in the text, the page number appears in the parenthetical citation following the borrowed material. Page numbers are not necessary when you are summarizing the source as a whole or paraphrasing an idea found throughout a work. (*For more on summary, paraphrase, and quotation, see Tab 5: Researching, pp. 255–65.*)
- If the source does not have page numbers (as with many online sources), do your best to direct readers toward the specific part of the text you are citing. If the source has no page or paragraph numbering or easily identifiable headings, just use the source name and date.

As Barbre et al. (1989) have argued, using personal narratives enables researchers to connect the individual and the social.

5. Organization as author

Treat the organization as the author, and spell out its name the first time the source is cited. If the organization is well known, you may use an abbreviation thereafter.

According to a report issued by the Inter-American Association for Environmental Defense (2004), a significant population of Colombia's indigenous peoples live within these protected parklands.

Public service announcements were used to inform parents of these findings (National Institute of Mental Health [NIMH], 1991).

In subsequent citations, only the abbreviation and the date need to be given: (*NIMH, 1991*).

6. Unknown author

Give the first one or two important words of the title. Use quotation marks for titles of articles or chapters and italics for titles of books or reports.

The transformation of women's lives has been hailed as "the single most important

change of the past 1,000 years" ("Reflections," 1999, p. 77).

7. Two or more authors with the same last name

If the authors of two or more sources have the same last name, always include their first initial, even if the year of publication differs.

M. Smith (1988) showed how globalization has restructured both cities and states.

8. Two or more works by the same author in the same year

Alphabetize the works by their titles in your reference list and assign a letter in alphabetical order (for example, 2006a, 2006b). Use that same year-letter designation in your in-text citation.

J. P. Agarwal described the relationship between trade and foreign direct

investment (1996b).

9. Two or more sources cited at one time

Cite the authors in the order in which they appear in the list of references, separated by a semicolon.

Other years see greater destruction from large-scale economic and industrial

initiatives, such as logging (Geographical, 2000; Kaimowitz et al., 2004, p. 2).

10. E-mail, letters, conversations

To cite information received from unpublished forms of personal communication, such as conversations, letters, notes, and e-mail messages, give the source's initials and last name, and provide as precise a date as possible. Because readers do not have access to them, do not include personal communications in your reference list.

According to ethnobotanist G. Freid (personal communication, May 4, 2008),

the work of research scientists in the Brazilian Amazon has been greatly impeded

within the last 10 years because of the destruction of potentially unrecorded plant

species.

11. Specific part of a source

Include the chapter (*chap.*), page (*p.*), or figure or table number.

Despite the new law, the state saw no drop in car fatalities involving drivers

ages 16-21 (Johnson, 2006, chap. 4).

12. Indirect source

When referring to a source that you know only from reading another source, use the phrase *as cited in,* followed by the author of the source you actually read and its year of publication.

According to the Center for International Forestry Research, an Indonesia-based

NGO (as cited in Prugh, 2004), an area of land the size of Uruguay was deforested

in the years 2002 and 2003 alone.

The work by the Center for International Forestry Research would not be included in the reference list, but the work by Prugh would be included.

13. Electronic source

Cite the author's last name and the publication date. If the document is a PDF (portable document format) file with stable page numbers, cite the page number. If the source has paragraph numbers instead of page numbers, use *para.* or ¶ instead of *p.* (*see no. 14*).

Applications of herbicides have caused widespread damage to biodiversity,

livestock, and crops, and have caused "thousands" of peasants and indigenous

peoples to flee these lands (Amazon Alliance, 2004).

> ***Note:*** If the specific part lacks page or paragraph numbering, cite the heading and the number of the paragraph under that heading where the information can be found. If you cannot determine the date, use the abbreviation "n.d." in its place: (*Wilson, n.d.*).

14. Two or more sources in one sentence

Include a parenthetical reference after each fact, idea, or quotation you have borrowed.

By one estimate, nearly 12 percent of the Amazonian rain forest in Brazil has

been shaped or influenced by thousands of years of indigenous human culture

(Brookfield, 2001); the evidence is as basic as the *terra preta do Indio,* or "Indian

Black Earth," for which the Brazilian region of Santarem is known (Glick, 2007,

para. 4).

15. Sacred or classical text

Cite within your text only, and include the version you consulted as well as any standard book, part, or section numbers.

The famous song sets forth a series of opposites, culminating in "a time to

love, and a time to hate; a time of war, and a time of peace" (Eccles. 3:8, King

James Bible).

32 APA Style: References

APA documentation style requires a list of references where readers can find complete bibliographical information about the sources referred to in your paper. The list of references should appear at the end of your paper, beginning on a new page titled "References."

www.mhhe.com/ awr3

To download Bibliomaker software for APA, go to

Research > Bibliomaker

APA REFERENCE ENTRIES: DIRECTORY to SAMPLE TYPES

(See pp. 327–31 for examples of in-text citations.)

APA REFERENCE ENTRIES: DIRECTORY to SAMPLE TYPES

Books

1. Book with one author

Brookfield, H. (2001). *Exploring agrodiversity*. New York: Columbia University Press.

2. Book with two or more authors

Goulding, M., Mahar, D., & Smith, N. (1996). *Floods of fortune: Ecology and economy along the Amazon*. New York: Columbia University Press.

3. Organization as author

When the publisher is the author, use *Author* instead of repeating the organization's name as the publisher.

APA LIST OF REFERENCES

- Begin on a new page.
- Begin with the centered title "References."
- Include a reference for every in-text citation except personal communications (*see in-text citations no. 10 on p. 330*).
- Put references in alphabetical order by author's last name.
- Give the last name and first or first and second initials for each author. If the work has more than one author, see no. 2.
- Put the publication year in parentheses following the author's or authors' names.
- Capitalize only the first word and proper nouns in titles. Also capitalize the first word following the colon in a subtitle.
- Use italics for titles of books but not articles. Do not enclose titles of articles in quotation marks.
- Include the city and publisher for books. If the city is not well known, include the state, using its two-letter postal abbreviation.
- Include the periodical name and volume number (both in italics) as well as the page numbers for an article.
- Separate the author's or authors' names, date (in parentheses), title, and publication information with periods.
- Use a hanging indent: Begin the first line of each entry at the left margin, and indent all subsequent lines of an entry one-half inch (five spaces).
- Double-space within and between entries.

Deutsche Bank, Economics Department. (1991). *Rebuilding Eastern Europe.*

Frankfurt, Germany: Author.

4. Two or more works by the same author

List the works in publication order, with the earliest one first.

Wilson, S. (Ed.). (1997). *The indigenous people of the Caribbean.* Gainesville:

University Press of Florida.

Wilson, S. (1999). *The emperor's giraffe and other stories of cultures*

in contact. Boulder, CO: Westview Press.

If the works were published in the same year, put them in alphabetical order by title and add a letter (*a, b, c*) to the year to distinguish each entry in your in-text citations (*see no. 18*).

5. Book with editor(s)

Add (*Ed.*) or (*Eds.*) after the name. If a book lists an author and an editor, treat the editor like a translator (*see no. 8*).

> Lifton, K. (Ed.). (1998). *The greening of sovereignty in world politics.* Cambridge, MA:
>
> MIT Press.

6. Selection in an edited book or anthology

The selection's author, year of publication, and title come first, followed by the word *In* and information about the edited book. The page numbers of the selection go in parentheses after the book's title.

> Wilmer, F. (1998). Taking indigenous critiques seriously: The enemy 'r' us.
>
> In K. Lifton (Ed.), *The greening of sovereignty in world politics* (pp. 55-60).
>
> Cambridge, MA: MIT Press.

7. Introduction, preface, foreword, or afterword

List the author and the section cited. If the book has a different author, next write *In,* followed by the book's author and the title.

> Bellow, S. (1987). Foreword. In A. Bloom, *The closing of the American mind: How*
>
> *higher education has failed democracy and impoverished the souls of today's*
>
> *students.* New York: Simon & Schuster.

8. Translation

After the title of the translation, put the name(s) of the translator(s) in parentheses, followed by the abbreviation *Trans.*

> Jarausch, K. H., & Gransow, V. (1994). *Uniting Germany: Documents and debates,*
>
> *1944-1993* (A. Brown & B. Cooper, Trans.). Providence, RI: Berg.

9. Article in a reference work

Begin with the author of the selection, if given. If no author is given, begin with the selection's title.

> title of the selection
> Arawak. (2000). In *The Columbia encyclopedia* (p. 2533). New York: Columbia
>
> University Press.

10. Entire dictionary or reference work

Unless an author is indicated on the title page, list dictionaries by title, with the edition number in parentheses. (The in-text citation should include the title or a portion of the title.) (*See no. 9 on listing an article in a reference book and no. 11 on alphabetizing a work listed by title.*)

The American Heritage dictionary of the English language (4th ed.). (2000). Boston:

Houghton Mifflin.

Hinson, M. (2004). *The pianist's dictionary.* Bloomington: Indiana University Press.

11. Unknown author or editor

Start with the title. When alphabetizing, use the first important word of the title (excluding articles such as *The, A,* or *An*).

Give me liberty. (1960). New York: World.

12. Edition other than the first

Smyser, W. R. (1993). *The German economy: Colossus at crossroads* (2nd ed.).

New York: St. Martin's Press.

13. One volume of a multivolume work

If the volume has its own title, put it before the title of the whole work. No period separates the title and parenthetical volume number.

Handl, G. (1990). The Mesoamerican biodiversity legal project. In *Yearbook of*

international environmental law (Vol. 4). London: Graham & Trotman.

14. Republished book

In-text citations should give both years: "As Le Bon (1895/1960) pointed out . . ."

Le Bon, G. (1960). *The crowd: A study of the popular mind.* New York: Viking.

(Original work published 1895)

Periodicals

15. Article in a journal paginated by volume

Do not use *pp.* before the page numbers. Italicize the title of the periodical and the volume number.

da Cunha, M. C., & de Almeida, M. (2000). Indigenous people, traditional people

and conservation in the Amazon. *Daedalus, 129,* 315.

16. Article in a journal paginated by issue

Include the issue number (in parentheses). The issue number is not italicized.

Epstein, J. (2002). A voice in the wilderness. *Latin Trade, 10*(12), 26.

17. Abstract

For an abstract that appears in the original source, add the word *Abstract* in brackets after the title. If the abstract appears in a printed source that is different from the original publication, include the publication information for the complete article and original publication, followed by the publication information for the source of the abstract. If the dates of the publications differ, cite them both, with a slash between them, in the in-text citation: *Murphy (2003/2004).*

> Burnby, J. G. L. (1985, June). Pharmaceutical connections: The Maw family
>
> [Abstract]. *Pharmaceutical Historian, 15*(2), 9-11.

> Murphy, M. (2003). Getting carbon out of thin air. *Chemistry & Industry, 6,* 14-16.
>
> Abstract obtained from *Fuel and Energy Abstracts,* 2004, *45*(6), 389.

18. Two or more works in one year by the same author

Alphabetize by title, and attach a letter to each entry's year of publication, beginning with *a*. In-text citations must use the letter as well as the year.

> Agarwal, J. P. (1996a). *Does foreign direct investment contribute to unemployment*
>
> *in home countries?—An empirical survey* (Discussion Paper No. 765). Kiel,
>
> Germany: Institute of World Economics.

> Agarwal, J. P. (1996b). Impact of Europe agreements on FDI in developing
>
> countries. *International Journal of Social Economics, 23*(10/11), 150-163.

19. Article in a magazine

After the year, add the month for magazines published monthly or the month and day for magazines published weekly. Note that the volume number is also included.

> Gross, P. (2001, February). Exorcising sociobiology. *New Criterion, 19,* 24.

20. Article in a newspaper

Use *p.* or *pp.* with the section and page number. List all page numbers, separated by commas, if the article appears on discontinuous pages: *pp. C1, C4, C6.* If there is no identified author, begin with the title of the article.

> Smith, T. (2003, October 8). Grass is green for Amazon farmers. *The New York Times,*
>
> p. W1.

21. Editorial or letter to the editor

> Krugman, P. (2000, July 16). Who's acquiring whom? [Editorial]. *The New York*
>
> *Times,* Sec. 4, p. 15.

> Deren, C. (2005, May 5). The last days of LI potatoes? [Letter to the editor].
>
> *Newsday,* p. A49.

22. Unsigned article

Begin the entry with the title, and alphabetize it by the first important word (excluding articles such as *The, A,* or *An*).

> Reflection on a thousand years: Introduction. (1999, April 18). *The New York Times*
>
> *Magazine,* p. 77.

23. Review

If the review is untitled, use the bracketed description in place of a title.

> Kaimowitz, D. (2002). Amazon deforestation revisited [Review of the book *Brazil,*
>
> *forests in the balance: Challenges of conservation with development*]. *Latin*
>
> *American Research Review, 37,* 221-236.

> Scott, A. O. (2002, May 10). Kicking up cosmic dust [Review of the motion picture
>
> *Star wars: Episode II—Attack of the clones*]. *The New York Times,* p. B1.

Other Print and Audiovisual Sources

24. Government document

When no author is listed, use the government agency as the author.

> U.S. Bureau of the Census. (1976). *Historical statistics of the United States: Colonial*
>
> *times to 1970.* Washington, DC: U.S. Government Printing Office.

For an enacted resolution or piece of legislation, see no. 57.

25. Report or working paper

If the issuing agency numbered the report, include that number in parentheses after the title. For reports from a deposit service like the Educational Resources Information Center (ERIC), put the document number in parentheses at the end of the entry.

Agarwal, J. P. (1996a). *Does foreign direct investment contribute to unemployment in home countries?--An empirical survey* (Discussion Paper No. 765). Kiel, Germany: Institute of World Economics.

26. Conference presentation

Treat published conference presentations as a selection in a book (*no. 6*), as a periodical article (*no. 15 or 16*), or as a report (*no. 25*), whatever applies. For unpublished conference presentations, provide the author, the year and month of the conference, the title of the presentation, and the presentation's form, forum, and place.

Markusen, J. (1998, June). *The role of multinationals in global economic analysis.* Paper presented at the First Annual Conference in Global Economic Analysis, West Lafayette, IN.

Desantis, R. (1998, June). *Optimal export taxes, welfare, industry concentration and firm size: A general equilibrium analysis.* Poster session presented at the First Annual Conference in Global Economic Analysis, West Lafayette, IN.

27. Unpublished dissertation or dissertation abstract

Weinbaum, A. E. (1998). Genealogies of "race" and reproduction in transatlantic modern thought (Doctoral dissertation, Columbia University, 1998). *Dissertation Abstracts International, 58,* 229.

If you used the abstract but not the actual dissertation, treat the entry like a periodical article.

Weinbaum, A. E. (1998). Genealogies of "race" and reproduction in transatlantic modern thought. *Dissertation Abstracts International, 58,* 229.

28. Brochure, pamphlet, fact sheet, press release

If there is no date of publication, put *n.d.* in place of the date. If the publisher is an organization, list it first, and name the publisher as *Author.*

United States Postal Service. (1995, January). *A consumer's guide to postal services and products* [Brochure]. Washington, DC: Author.

Union College. (n.d.). *The Nott Memorial: A national historic landmark at Union College* [Pamphlet]. Schenectady, NY: Author.

29. Film, DVD, videotape

Begin with the cited person's name and, if appropriate, a parenthetical notation of his or her role. After the title, identify the medium as [Motion picture], followed by the country and name of the distributor. (*For online video, see no. 68.*)

> Rowling, J. K., Goldenberg, M. (Writers), Yates, D. (Director), & Barron, D. (Producer).
>
> (2007). *Harry Potter and the order of the phoenix* [Motion picture]. United
>
> States: Warner Brothers Pictures.

For films and videotapes that might be hard to find, add the name and address of the distributor in parentheses after the bracketed medium information.

30. CD, audio recording

See no. 65 for an MP3 or no. 66 for an audio podcast.

> Corigliano, J. (2007). Red violin concerto [Recorded by J. Bell]. On *Red violin*
>
> *concerto* [CD]. New York: Sony Classics.

31. Radio broadcast

See no. 66 for an audio podcast.

> Adamski, G., & Conti, K. (Hosts). (2007, January 16). *Legally speaking* [Radio
>
> broadcast]. Chicago: WGN Radio.

32. TV series

For an entire TV series or specific news broadcast, treat the producer as author.

> Simon, D. & Noble, N. K. (Producers). (2002). *The wire* [Television series].
>
> New York: HBO.

33. Episode from a TV series

Treat the writer as the author and the producer as the editor of the series. See no. 67 for a podcast TV series episode.

> Burns, E., Simon, D. (Writers), & Johnson, C. (Director). (2002). The target
>
> [Television series episode]. In D. Simon & N. K. Noble (Producers), *The wire.*
>
> New York: HBO.

34. Advertisement

> Geek Squad. (2007, December 10). [Advertisement]. Minneapolis/St. Paul:
>
> WCCO-TV.

35. Image, photograph, or work of art

If you have reproduced a visual, give the source information with the caption. See no. 51 for online visuals.

> Smith, W. E. (1950). *Guardia civil, Spain* [Photograph]. Minneapolis: Minneapolis
>
> Institute of Arts.

36. Map or chart

If you have reproduced a visual, give the source information with the caption (*for an example, see p. 351*). See no. 51 for online visuals.

> *Colonial Virginia.* (1960). [Map]. Chapel Hill, VA: Virginia Historical Society.

37. Live performance

> Ibsen, H. (Author), Bly, R. (Translator), & Carroll, T. (Director). (2008, January 12).
>
> *Peer Gynt* [Theatrical performance]. Guthrie Theater, Minneapolis, MN.

38. Musical composition

> Rachmaninoff, S. (1900). *Piano concerto no. 2, opus 18* [Musical composition].

39. Lecture, speech, address

List the speaker, the year and month, and the title of the presentation (in italics). Include location information when available. (For online versions, add "Retrieved from" and the URL.)

> Cicerone, R. (2007, September 22). *Climate change in the U.S.* George S. Benton
>
> Lecture given at Johns Hopkins University, Baltimore, MD.

40. Personal interview

Like other unpublished personal communications, personal interviews are not listed in the reference list. See in-text citation entry 10 (*p. 330*).

Electronic Sources

41. Online journal article with Digital Object Identifier (DOI)

If your source has a DOI, include it at the end of the entry; URL and access date are not needed. Always include the issue number.

> Ray, R., Wilhelm, F., & Gross, J. (2008). All in the mind's eye? Anger rumination and
>
> reappraisal. *Journal of Personality and Social Psychology, 94*(1), 133-145.
>
> doi:10.1037/0022-3514.94.1.133

APA ELECTRONIC REFERENCES

From **APA Style Guide for Electronic References** *(2007)*

Cite online works as you would the same works in another medium, apart from these concerns:

- Many online journal articles have a Digital Object Identifier (DOI), a unique alphanumeric string. Citations of online documents with DOIs do not require the URL or retrieval date.
- Only include a retrieval date for items that lack a publication date, items that probably will change (such as an in-press article), and reference sources (such as an encyclopedia article).
- Do not include information about a database or library subscription service in the citation unless the work is only in a few databases or difficult to find in print.
- For online journal articles, always include the issue number.
- Include the URL of the home page for items that require a subscription, appear in reference works, or appear on frames.
- Include the full URL for all other items, except those with a DOI.

42. Online journal article without DOI

Include the complete URL unless the source is available only via subscription or search, in which case include the home page URL. If your source is not likely to change (such as the final version of an article), no access date is needed. Always include the issue number. Place page numbers (if available) after the issue number.

> Chan, L. (2004, November 3). Supporting and enhancing scholarship in the digital
>
> age: The role of open access institutional repository. *Canadian Journal*
>
> *of Communication, 29*(3), 277-300. Retrieved from http://www.cjc-online.ca
>
> /viewarticle.php?id=850

43. Journal article from an online, subscription, or library database

Include database information only if the article is rare or found in just a few databases. If you include the database name, omit the URL.

> Epstein, J. (2002). A voice in the wilderness. *Latin Trade, 10*(12), 26.

> Gore, W. C. (1916). Memory, concept, judgment, logic (theory). *Psychological*
>
> *Bulletin, 13*(9), 355-358. Retrieved from PsycARTICLES database.

44. Abstract as original source

Welsh, W. (2003). *Evaluation of prison-based therapeutic community drug treatment*

programs in Pennsylvania (NCJ No. 221276) [Abstract]. Retrieved from

National Criminal Justice Reference Service abstracts database.

45. Published dissertation from a database

Include the dissertation file number (AAT) at the end of the entry, if available.

Gorski, A. (2007). *The environmental aesthetic appreciation of cultural landscapes.*

Retrieved from ProQuest Digital Dissertations. (AAT 1443335)

46. Newspaper or magazine article from a database

Include database information only if the article is rare or found in just a few databases. Omit the URL.

Culnan, J. (1927, November 20). Madison to celebrate arrival of first air mail

plane. *Wisconsin State Journal,* p. A1. Retrieved from Wisconsin Historical

Society database.

47. Article in an online newspaper

Rohter, L. (2004, December 12). South America seeks to fill the world's table.

The New York Times. Retrieved from http://www.nytimes.com

48. Article in an online magazine

Include the volume number after the magazine title if available (not shown below).

Biello, D. (2007, December 5). Thunder, hail, fire: What does climate change mean

for the U.S.? *Scientific American.* Retrieved from http://www.sciam.com

49. Online exclusive magazine content

Francis, A. (2006, March 24). Fighting for the rainforest [Online exclusive]. *Newsweek*

International. Retrieved from http://www.newsweek.com/id/47178

50. Article in an online newsletter

Use volume, issue, and page numbers if available. Often they are not, as below.

Gray, L. (2008, February). Corn gluten meal. *Shenandoah Chapter Newsletter,*

Virginia Native Plant Society. Retrieved from http://www.vnps.org/chapters

/shenandoah/Feb2008.pdf

51. Document or visual on a Web site

If the document is an entire article or report, include the basic information for an online document. If you have used a graph, chart, map, or image, give the source information following the figure caption (*for an example, see p. 351*).

> *Seattle.* (2008). [Map]. Retrieved from http://www.mapquest.com

52. Article or report from a secondary source's Web site

Include information about the host organization's Web site in the retrieval statement.

> World Health Organization. (1992). *ICD-10 criteria for borderline personality disorder.*
>
> Retrieved from BPD Sanctuary Web site: http://www.mhsanctuary.com
>
> /borderline/icd10.htm

53. Document on a university's Web site

Include relevant information about the university and department after the retrieval date.

> Tugal, C. (2002, February). Islamism in Turkey: Beyond instrument and meaning.
>
> *Economy and Society, 31(1),* 85–111. Retrieved November 7, 2008, from
>
> University of California-Berkeley, Department of Sociology Web site:
>
> http://sociology.berkeley.edu/public_sociology_pdf/tugal.pps05.pdf

54. Section of an Internet document

> United States Bureau of Oceans and International Environmental and Scientific
>
> Affairs (2007, July 27). Projected greenhouse gas emissions. In *Fourth United*
>
> *States climate action report* (chap. 4). Retrieved from http://www.state.gov
>
> /g/oes/rls/rpts/car/90312.htm

55. Online book

Give information about the online source if the book exists only in electronic format or is difficult to locate in print.

> Münsterberg, H. (1913). *Psychology and industrial efficiency.* Retrieved from
>
> http://www.gutenberg.org/etext/15154

56. Online government document except the *Congressional Record*

> National Commission on Terrorist Attacks upon the United States. (2004, August 5).
>
> *The 9/11 Commission report.* Retrieved from http://www.gpoaccess.gov/911
>
> /index.html

57. *Congressional Record* (online or in print)

For enacted resolutions or legislation, give the number of the congress after the number of the resolution or legislation, the volume number for the *Congressional Record,* the page number(s), and the year, followed by *(enacted).*

> H. Res. 2408, 108th Cong., 150 Cong. Rec. 1331-1332 (2004)(enacted).

Give the full name of the resolution or legislation when citing it within your sentence, but abbreviate it when it appears in a parenthetical in-text citation: *(H. Res. 2408, 2004).*

58. Online document lacking either date or author

Place the title before the date if no author is given. Use the abbreviation *n.d.* (no date) for any undated document and give the retrieval date.

> Center for Science in the Public Interest. (n.d.). *Food additives to avoid.* Retrieved
>
> March 4, 2008, from http://www.mindfully.org/Food/Food-Additives-
>
> Avoid.htm

59. Article in online reference work

Begin with the author's name if given followed by the publication date. If no author is given, place the title before the date. Include the date you accessed the article and the home page URL.

> Special Olympics. (2008). In *Encyclopaedia Britannica online.* Retrieved February 15,
>
> 2008, from http://www.britannica.com

60. Wiki article

Wikis are collaboratively written Web sites. Most are updated regularly, so include the access date in your citation. Check with your instructor before using a wiki article as a source.

> Demographic transition. (2007, October 8). Retrieved March 3, 2008, from
>
> Citizendium: http://en.citizendium.org/wiki/Demographic_transition

Tips APA EXPLANATORY NOTES

APA discourages the use of explanatory content notes. If you do include notes, put superscript numbers at appropriate points in your text. Type the notes, double spaced, on a separate page with the centered title "Footnotes." Indent the first line of each note five spaces, and type the appropriate superscript number followed by the note, with all lines after the first flush with the left margin.

61. Blog posting

Ben. (2008, February 18). Re: Opening the government's books at fedspending.org.

Message posted to http://www.iq.harvard.edu/blog/sss/

62. Post to a newsgroup or discussion forum

Provide the message's author, its date, and its subject line as the title. Give identifying information in brackets. After the phrase *Message posted to*, give the name of the newsgroup or forum, followed by the address of the archived message.

Jones, D. (2001, February 3). California solar power [Msg. 1]. Message posted

to sci.space.policy, archived at http://yarchive.net/space/politics/

california_power.html

63. Post to an electronic mailing list

Provide the message's author, its date, and its subject line as the title. After the phrase *Message posted to*, give the name of the mailing list, followed by the address of the archived message.

Glick, D. (2007, February 10). Bio-char sequestration in terrestrial ecosystems--a

review. Message posted to Terrapreta electronic mailing list, archived

at http://bioenergylists.org/pipermail/terrapreta_bioenergylists.org

/2007-February/000023.html

64. E-mail or instant message (IM)

E-mail, instant messages, or other nonarchived personal communication should be cited in the body of your paper but not listed in the references list (*see in-text citation entry 10, on p. 330*).

65. MP3

Hansard, G., & Irglova, M. (2006). Falling slowly. On *The swell season* [MP3].

Chicago: Overcoat Recordings.

66. Audio podcast:

Glass I. (Host). (2008, June 30). Social engineering [Show 358]. *This American Life.*

Podcast retrieved from http://www.thisamericanlife.org

67. Podcast TV series episode

Reitman, J. (Director), & Novak, B. J. (Writer). (2007, December 12). Local ad

[Television series episode]. In S. Carrell, M. Kaling, L. Eisenberg, &

G. Stupnitsky (Producers), *The office*. Podcast retrieved from NBC:

http://www.nbc.com/the_office/video/episodes.shtml

68. Online video
For an online speech, see no. 39.

Wesch, M. (2007). The machine is us/ing us [Video file]. Video posted to

http://mediatedcultures.net/ksudigg/?p=84

69. Computer software
Cite only specialized software.

Buscemi, S. (2003). AllWrite! 2.1 with Online Handbook [Software]. New York:

McGraw-Hill.

33 APA Style: Paper Format

The following guidelines are recommended by the *Publication Manual of the American Psychological Association,* fifth edition. For an example of a research paper that has been prepared using APA style, see pages 349–58.

Materials. Before printing your paper, make sure that you have backed up your final draft. Use a high-quality printer and high-quality, white 8½-by-11-inch paper. Do not justify your text or hyphenate words at the right margin; it should be ragged.

Title page. The first page of your paper should be a title page. Center the title between the left and right margins in the upper half of the page, and put your name a few lines below the title. Most instructors will also want you to include the course number and title, the instructor's name, and the date. (*See p. 349 for an example.*)

Margins and spacing. Use one-inch margins all around, except for the upper right-hand corner, where the page number goes.

Double-space lines throughout the paper, including in the abstract, within any notes, and in the list of references. Indent the first word of each paragraph one-half inch (or five spaces).

For quotations of more than forty words, use block format and indent five spaces from the left margin. Double-space the quoted lines.

Page numbers and abbreviated titles. All pages, including the title page, should have a number preceded by a short (one- or two-word) version of your title. Put this information in the upper right-hand corner of each page, one-half inch from the top.

Abstract. Instructors sometimes require an abstract—a 75- to 120-word summary of your paper's thesis, major points or lines of development, and conclusions. The abstract appears on its own numbered page, entitled "Abstract," and is placed right after the title page.

Headings. Primary headings should be centered, and all keywords in the heading should be capitalized.

Secondary headings should be italicized and appear flush against the left-hand margin. Do not use a heading for your introduction, however. (*For more on headings, see Tab 2: Writing and Designing Texts, pp. 97–100.*)

👁 Visuals. Place visuals (tables, charts, graphs, and images) close to the place in your text where you refer to them. Label each visual as a table or a figure, and number each kind consecutively (Table 1, Table 2). Provide an informative caption for each visual. Cite the source of the material, preceded by the word *Note* and a period, and provide explanatory notes as needed. (*For more on using visuals effectively, see Tab 2: Writing and Designing Texts, pp. 54–56.*)

34 Student Paper in APA Style

Audrey Galeano researched and wrote a report on the indigenous peoples of the Amazon for her anthropology course Indigenous Peoples and Globalization. Her sources included books, journal articles, and Web sites.

www.mhhe.com/ awr3

For another sample of a paper in APA style, go to

Research > Sample Research Papers > APA Style

Saving the Amazon:

Globalization and Deforestation

Audrey Galeano

Anthropology 314: Indigenous Peoples and Globalization

Professor Mura

May 3, 2008

All pages: short title and page number.

ull title, entered.

Title appears on separate page, centered, with course information, and date.

Abstract

The impact of globalization on fragile ecosystems is a complex problem. In the Amazon River basin, globalization has led to massive deforestation as multinational corporations exploit the rain forest's natural resources. In particular, large-scale industrial agriculture has caused significant damage to the local environment. In an effort to resist the loss of this ecosystem, indigenous peoples in the Amazon basin are reaching out to each other, to nongovernmental organizations (NGOs), and to other interest groups to combat industrial agriculture and promote sustainable regional agriculture. Although these efforts have had mixed success, it is hoped that the native peoples of this region can continue to live on their homelands without feeling intense pressure to acquiesce to industrialization or to relocate.

Abstract appears on new page after title page. First line is not indented.

Objective stance used, with no reference to essay. Essay concisely summarized—key points included, but not details or statistics.

Paragraph should be no longer than 120 words.

↑ 1"
↕

Saving the Amazon:

Globalization and Deforestation

For thousands of years, the indigenous peoples of the Amazon

River basin have practiced forms of sustainable agriculture. These

peoples developed ways of farming and hunting that enabled   1"

them to provide food and trade goods for their communities with   ↔

minimal impact on the environment. These methods have endured

despite colonization and industrialization. Today, the greatest

threat to indigenous peoples in the Amazon River basin is posed by

the massive deforestation caused by industrial-scale farming and

ranching, as revealed in satellite images taken since 1988 by Brazil's

National Institute of Space Research. (See graph in Figure 1.)

Because of the injury to ecosystems and native ways of life,

indigenous peoples and antiglobalization activists have joined

forces to promote sustainable agriculture and the rights of native

peoples throughout the Amazon river basin.

Sustainable Lifeways, Endangered Lives

Recent work in historical ecology has altered our

understanding of how humans have shaped what is romantically

called "virgin forest." As anthropologist Anna Roosevelt (as cited

in Society for California Archaeology, 2000) observes, "People

adapt to environments but they also change them. There are no

virgin environments on earth in areas where people lived." By one

estimate, nearly 12 percent of the Amazonian rain forest in Brazil

has been shaped or influenced by thousands of years of indigenous

human culture (Brookfield, 2001); the evidence is as basic as the

terra preta do Indio, or "Indian Black Earth," for which the Brazilian

region of Santarem is known (Glick, 2007, para. 4).

Full title
repeated on
first page
only.

Figure
introduced
and
commented
on.

Thesis
statement.

Primary
heading,
centered,
subtly reveals
writer's
stance.

Parenthetical
citation of
source with
organization
as author.

Information
from two dif-
ferent sources
combined in
one sentence.

Saving the Amazon   4

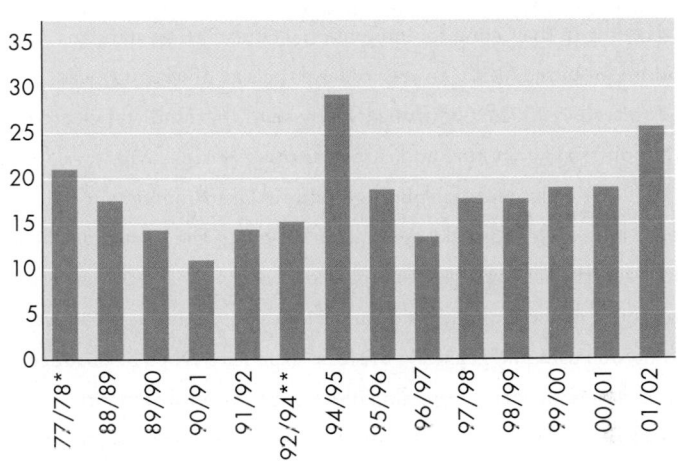

Figure 1. Annual deforestation rates in the Brazilian Amazon, 1988-2002 (thousands of square kilometers). *Note.* From National Institute of Space Research. (2002). In D. Kaimowitz, B. Mertens, S. Wunder, & P. Pacheco, *Hamburger connection fuels Amazon destruction: Cattle ranching and deforestation in Brazil's Amazon.* Retrieved April 16, 2008, from http://www.cifor.cgiar.org/publications/pdf_files/media/Amazon.pdf

The previous thousands of years of human influence on the Amazon is slight, however, compared with the modern-day destruction of rain forests around the globe, and in the Amazon River basin in particular. The sources of this destruction vary from country to country and year to year, with certain years affected more by climate change and other years seeing greater destruction from human initiatives, such as logging (Walker, Moran, & Anselin, 2000).

Graph presents statistics in visual form for readers.

Informative caption and source note appear below figure.

Support by key facts (see p. 31).

According to the Center for International Forestry Research, an Indonesia-based NGO, an area of land the size of Uruguay was deforested in 2002-2003 alone. Nearly all of this land was cleared for industrial agriculture and cattle ranching (Prugh, 2004).

Globalization and Agricultural Destruction

Large-scale industrial agriculture seeks out the least expensive ways to produce the highest number of crops. Perhaps the largest cash crop of the late 20th and early 21st centuries is soy, which has numerous uses and is among the least expensive crops to produce. According to Roberto Smeraldi, director of the environmental action group Friends of the Earth, "soybeans are the single biggest driver for deforestation" in the Brazilian Amazon; in the 12 months ending in August 2003, 9,169 square miles of rain forest had been cleared by soy farmers, ranchers, and loggers in Brazil (as cited in Stewart, 2004, paras. 4-5). Although Brazilian officials have attempted to regulate the depredations of the rain forest by multinational soy producers, Stewart notes that, in 2003, soybean production brought nearly $8 billion to the Brazilian economy, forcing indigenous and small-scale farmers off their lands and damaging local climate.

An Associated Press (AP) report reprinted on the Organic Consumer's Association Web site describes the impact of soy production on Brazil's Xingu National Park, a protected rain forest reserve that is home to 14 indigenous tribes. "The soy is arriving very fast. Every time I leave the reservation I don't recognize anything anymore because the forest keeps disappearing," a director of the Xingu Indian Land Association is quoted as observing (AP, 2003, para. 11). Although the industrial soy farms have not crossed the borders of the Xingu National Park, they

---

Paragraph expands on introductory paragraph.

Discussion of details begun and linked to broader issue of globalization.

Abbreviation given at first mention of organization.

Abbreviation for organization used in parenthetical citation.

surround the protected lands and have raised fears that chemical pesticides and deforestation will dry up rivers and kill fish. "Our Xingu is not just what's here. It's a very long thread, and when it rains the soy brings venom down the same river that passes by our door," says Capivara chief Jywapan Kayabi (para. 24).

Cattle ranching has also led to the deforestation of the Amazon. The cattle population of the Amazon nations increased from 26 million in 1990 to 57 million in 2002 (Prugh, 2004). Attention to the destruction caused by industrial cattle-ranching began in the late 1980s. Barrett (2001) points out that ranchers were using lands already depleted of fertility and biodiversity by logging, road building, and colonization of the Brazilian Amazon in the 1960s and 1970s. Ranching, Barrett observes, "doesn't require nutrient-rich soil" and therefore "took the place vacated by other activities, along with the blame for soil erosion and loss of biodiversity" (p. 1).

Indigenous Peoples and Regional Activism

Depopulation of these lands as a result of colonization meant that traditional agricultural practices were no longer sustained. In recent years, antiglobalization NGOs, the international movement for indigenous peoples' rights, and increased understanding of the consequences of deforestation are helping native peoples reclaim lands and reestablish traditional agricultural practices. However, some kinds of alliances and interventions are not as productive as others.

Anthropologists da Cunha and de Almeida ask a provocative question: "Can traditional peoples be described as 'cultural conservationists'?" (2000, p. 315). Although as many as 50 indigenous groups in Amazonia still have no contact with the

---

First main cause of deforestation discussed.

Second main cause of deforestation discussed.

Page number given for quotation.

Contributing factor in problem of deforestation shows complexity of situation.

outside world, other indigenous peoples have secured their land
rights through international efforts over the past 20 years. Some
of these efforts, da Cunha and de Almeida argue, are influenced by
romantic ideas about "noble savages" and fail to acknowledge the
ways in which indigenous peoples in contemporary Brazil make a
living from rain forest resources.

Barham and Coomes (1997) also note that a better
understanding of how indigenous peoples live is necessary if
the efforts of international groups such as Amazon Alliance are to
succeed. Indigenous peoples need to see some material benefit
from conservationist practices. After all, as da Cunha and de
Almeida write, "Traditional peoples are neither outside the central
economy nor any longer simply in the periphery of the world
system" (2000).

Franke Wilmer (1998) suggests that "human action and its
impact in the world are directed by a view that is dangerously out
of touch with natural laws which, according to indigenous peoples,
govern all life on this planet" (p. 57). For instance, although the
Kayapo people of south-central Amazonia have been devastated
by colonization, they still "used their knowledge to manipulate
ecosystems in remarkable ways . . . to maximize biological
diversity" (Brookfield, 2001, p. 141). Among the Kayapo's
sustainable practices are crop rotation, the use of ash to fertilize
fields, and the transition of older fields back to secondary forest
(Brookfield, 2001).

Some socially conscious global corporations have attempted
to assist indigenous Amazonian farmers in developing sustainable,
profitable crops. Two of the best-known efforts, described in a
2003 *New York Times* article by Tony Smith, provide a cautionary

---

Local culture,
history, and
economics
shown to be
linked to
global
systems.

Ellipses
indicate
omission in
quotation.

Saving the Amazon 8

tale. In the 1990s, the British multinational "green" cosmetics company The Body Shop and American ice cream manufacturer Ben and Jerry's both developed "eco-friendly" products from the Amazon. Ben and Jerry's Rainforest Crunch ice cream used Brazil nuts that were harvested in a sustainable fashion by an Amazonian cooperative, and The Body Shop also used the oils from Brazil nuts in some of its cosmetics. But Rainforest Crunch proved so popular that the cooperative couldn't meet the demand, and Ben and Jerry's had to turn to other suppliers, "some notorious for their antilabor practices" (Smith, 2003, p. W1). The Body Shop wound up being sued by a chief of the Kayapo tribe, whose image was used in Body Shop advertising without permission (Smith).

Problems caused by one solution discussed.

The best solution might be for Brazilian businesses, developers, government officials, and indigenous peoples to work together. One new initiative described in the *Times* article is the cultivation of the sweet-scented native Amazon grass called priprioca, on which the Sao Paulo cosmetics company Natura is basing a new fragrance. Farmer Jose Mateus, who has grown watermelons and manioc on his small farm near the Amazon city of Belem, has agreed to grow priprioca instead--and he expects to get twice the price for the grass than he would for his usual crop (Smith, 2003). Eduardo Luppi, director of innovation for Natura, comments, "We do have the advantage that we are Brazilian and we are in Brazil. If you are in England or America and want to manage something like this in the Amazon by remote control, you can forget it" (as cited in Smith, 2003, p. W1).

Solutions described, backed up with quotations from experts, which come from secondary source.

Although indigenous peoples face extraordinary obstacles in their quest for environmental justice, some political officials support their struggles. In the Acre state of Brazil, Governor Jorge

Saving the Amazon   9

Viana was inspired by the example of martyred environmental activist Chico Mendes to secure financing from Brazil's federal development bank for sustainable development in his impoverished Amazonian state (Epstein, 2002). Viana, who holds a degree in forest engineering, told the journal *Latin Trade* that "we want to bring local populations into the policy of forest management. . . . We have to show them how to exploit without destroying" (as cited in Epstein, p. 26).

Conclusion

Essay concludes on optimistic note, balancing writer's and sources' concerns.

The social, economic, climate-related, and political pressures on the Amazonian ecosystem may prove insurmountable; report after report describes the enormous annual loss of rain forest habitat. The best hope for saving the rain forest is public pressure on multinational agricultural corporations to practice accountable, safe, and sustainable methods. In addition, it is important to encourage indigenous peoples to practice their age-old sustainable agriculture and land-management strategies while guaranteeing their rights and safety. Much in the Amazon has been ruined, but cooperative efforts like those discussed in this paper can nurture and sustain what remains for future generations.

References

Associated Press. (2003, December 18). *Soybeans: The new threat to Brazilian rainforest.* Retrieved April 8, 2008, from http://www.organicconsumers.org/corp/soy121903.cfm

Barham, B. L., & Coomes, O. T. (1997). Rain forest extraction and conservation in Amazonia. *The Geographical Journal, 163*(2), 180.

Barrett, J. R. (2001). Livestock farming: Eating up the environment? *Environmental Health Perspectives, 109*(7), A312.

Brookfield, H. (2001). *Exploring agrodiversity.* New York: Columbia University Press.

da Cunha, M. C., & de Almeida, M. (2000). Indigenous people, traditional people and conservation in the Amazon. *Daedalus, 129*(2), 315.

Epstein, J. (2002). A voice in the wilderness. *Latin Trade, 10*(12), 26.

Glick, D. (2007, February 10). Bio-char sequestration in terrestrial ecosystems--a review. Message posted to Terrapreta electronic mailing list, archived at http://bioenergylists.org/pipermail /newsgroup-archive/terrapreta_bioenergylists.org/2007 -February/000023.html

Prugh, T. (2004). Ranching accelerates Amazon deforestation. *World Watch, 17*(4), 8.

Smith, T. (2003, October 8). Grass is green for Amazon farmers. *The New York Times,* p. W1.

Society for California Archaeology. (2000). *Interview with Dr. Anna Roosevelt.* Retrieved April 20, 2008, from http://www.scahome .org/about_california_archaeology/2000_Roosevelt.htm

New page, heading centered.

Entries in alphabetical order and double-spaced.

◄— Hanging indent 5 spaces or ½".

Stewart, A. (2004, July 14). Brazil's soy success brings
environmental challenges. *Dow Jones.* Retrieved from
http://www.amazonia.org.br/English/noticias/
noticia.cfm?id=116059

Walker, R., Moran, E., & Anselin, L. (2000). Deforestation and
cattle ranching in the Brazilian Amazon: External capital and
household processes. *World Development, 28*(4), 683-699.

Wilmer, F. (1998). Taking indigenous critiques seriously: The
enemy 'r' us. In K. Lifton (Ed.), *The greening of sovereignty in
world politics* (pp. 55-60). Cambridge, MA: MIT Press.

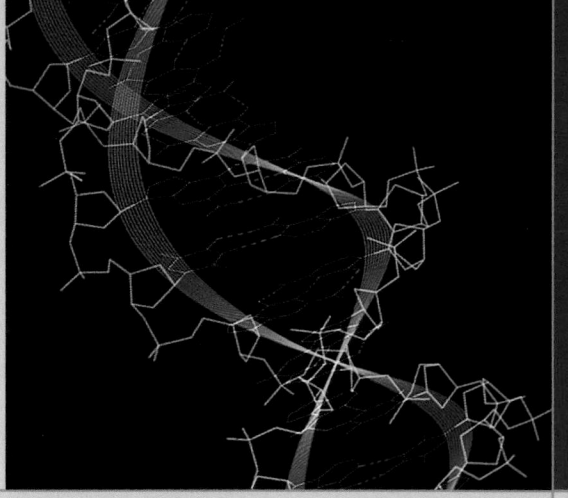

8

Nothing gives an author so much pleasure as to find his works respectfully quoted by other learned authors.

—BENJAMIN FRANKLIN

Other Documentation Styles
Chicago and CSE

8 Other Documentation Styles

WRITING OUTCOMES

Tab 8: Other Documentation Styles
This section will help you answer questions such as:

Rhetorical Knowledge
Which disciplines use Chicago style? **(35)**
Which disciplines use CSE style? **(37)**
What are the three forms of CSE style? **(37)**

Critical Thinking, Reading, and Writing
Why do I need to document my sources? **(35, 37)**

Knowledge of Conventions
How do I cite sources in the text of my paper in Chicago and CSE style? **(35, 36, 37)**
What formats are used for a bibliography or works-cited list in Chicago style? **(35, 36)**
What is appropriate formatting for a list of references in CSE style? **(37)**

There are many documentation styles besides those developed by the Modern Language Association (*see Tab 6*) and the American Psychological Association (*see Tab 7*). In this section, we cover the *Chicago Manual* style and the three styles developed by the Council of Science Editors. To find out where you can learn about other style types, consult the list of style manuals on page 271. If you are not sure which style to use, ask your instructor.

www.mhhe.com/
awr3

For links to Web sites for documentation styles used in various disciplines, go to

Research > Links to Documentation Sites

35 Chicago Documentation Style: Elements

The note and bibliography style presented in the fifteenth edition of *The Chicago Manual of Style* (Chicago: University of Chicago Press, 2003) is used in many disciplines, including history, art, philosophy, business, and communications. This style has three parts:

- Numbered in-text citations
- Numbered footnotes or endnotes
- A bibliography of works consulted

The first two parts are necessary; the third is optional, unless your instructor requires it. (The *Chicago Manual* also has an alternative author-date system that is similar to APA style.) For more information on this style, consult the *Chicago Manual* or *A Manual for Writers of Research Papers, Theses, and Dissertations*, seventh edition, by Kate L. Turabian (Chicago: University of Chicago Press, 2007). For updates and answers to frequently asked questions about this style, go to the *Chicago Manual*'s Web site at <http://www.press.uchicago.edu> and click on "*Chicago Manual of Style* Web site."

35a Use numbered in-text citations and notes.

Whenever you use information or ideas from a source, you need to indicate what you have borrowed by putting a superscript number in the text ([1]) at the end of the borrowed material. These superscript numbers are placed after all punctuation marks except for the dash.

As biographer Laurence Bergreen points out, Armstrong easily reached difficult high notes, the F's and G's that stymied other trumpeters.[3] And his innovative singing style featured "scat," a technique that "place[s] emphasis on the human voice as an additionally important component in jazz music."[4]

361

TEXTCONNEX

Superscript Numbers

Most computer word-processing programs allow you to insert superscript numbers. Get to know your program's options.

If a quotation is fairly long, you can set it off as a block quotation. Indent it five spaces or one-half inch from the left margin, and double-space the quotation, leaving an extra space above and below it. Place the superscript number after the period that ends the quotation. (*See p. 377 for an example.*)

Each in-text superscript number must have a corresponding note either at the foot of the page or at the end of the text. Indent the first line of each footnote like a paragraph. Footnotes begin with the number and are single-spaced, with a double space between notes.

If you are using endnotes instead of footnotes, they should begin after the last page of your text on a new numbered page titled "Notes." Single-space within and double-space between endnotes.

The first time you cite a source in either a footnote or an endnote, you should include a full citation. Subsequent citations require less information.

FIRST REFERENCE TO SOURCE

3. Laurence Bergreen, *Louis Armstrong: An Extravagant Life* (New York: Broadway Books, 1997), 248.

ENTRY FOR SOURCE ALREADY CITED

6. Bergreen, 370.

If several pages pass between references to the same title, include a brief version of the title to clarify the reference.

ENTRY FOR SOURCE ALREADY CITED IN LONGER PAPER

7. Bergreen, *Louis Armstrong,* 370.

If you quote from the same work immediately after providing a full footnote, use the abbreviation *Ibid.* (Latin for "in the same place"), followed by the page number.

8. Ibid., 370.

35b Prepare a separate bibliography if your instructor requires one.

Some instructors require a separate list of works cited or of works consulted. If you are asked to provide a works-cited list, do so on a separate, numbered page titled "Works Cited." If the list should include all works you consulted, title it "Bibliography."

Bergreen, Laurence. *Louis Armstrong: An Extravagant Life.* New York: Broadway Books, 1997.

35c Use the correct Chicago style for notes and bibliography entries.

CHICAGO STYLE: DIRECTORY TO SAMPLE TYPES

Books

1. Book with one author

NOTE

    1. James Lincoln Collier, *Louis Armstrong: An American Genius* (New York: Oxford University Press, 1983), 82.

BIBLIOGRAPHY ENTRY

Collier, James Lincoln. *Louis Armstrong: An American Genius.* New York: Oxford University Press, 1983.

2. Multiple works by the same author

After providing complete information in the first footnote, include only a shortened version of the title with the author's last name and the page number in any subsequent footnotes. In the bibliography, list entries either in alphabetical order by title or from earliest to most recent. After the first listing, replace the author's name with a "3-em" dash (type three hyphens in a row).

NOTES

    7. Collier, *Jazz,* 154.

    12. Collier, *Louis Armstrong,* 32.

BIBLIOGRAPHY ENTRIES

Collier, James Lincoln. *Jazz: The American Theme Song.* New York: Oxford University Press, 1993.

———. *Louis Armstrong: An American Genius.* New York: Oxford University Press, 1983.

3. Book with two or more authors

In notes, you can name up to three authors. When there are three authors, put a comma after the first name and a comma plus *and* after the second.

NOTE

    2. Miles Davis and Quincy Troupe, *Miles: The Autobiography* (New York: Simon & Schuster, 1989), 15.

BIBLIOGRAPHY ENTRY

Davis, Miles, and Quincy Troupe. *Miles: The Autobiography.* New York: Simon & Schuster, 1989.

BIBLIOGRAPHY or WORKS-CITED LIST in CHICAGO STYLE

- Begin on a new page.
- Begin with the centered title "Works Cited" if you are including only works referred to in your paper. Use the title "Bibliography" if you are including every work you consulted.
- List sources alphabetically by author's (or editor's) last name.
- Capitalize the first and last words in titles as well as all important words and words that follow colons.
- Indent all lines five spaces except the first of each entry, using your word processor's hanging indent feature.
- Use periods between author and title as well as between title and publication data.
- Single-space each entry; double-space between entries.

When more than three authors are listed on the title page, use *and others* or *et al.* after the first author's name in the note.

NOTE

3. Julian Henriques and others, *Changing the Subject: Psychology, Social Regulation and Subjectivity* (New York: Methuen, 1984), 275.

BIBLIOGRAPHY ENTRY

Henriques, Julian, Wendy Holloway, Cathy Urwin, Couze Venn, and Valerie Walkerdine. *Changing the Subject: Psychology, Social Regulation and Subjectivity.* New York: Methuen, 1984.

Give all author names in bibliography entries.

4. Book with an author and an editor or a translator

Put the author's name first and add the editor's (*ed.*) or translator's (*trans.*) name after the title. Spell out *Edited* or *Translated* in the bibliography entry.

NOTE

4. Louis Armstrong, *Louis Armstrong: A Self-Portrait,* ed. Richard Meryman (New York: Eakins Press, 1971), 54.

BIBLIOGRAPHY ENTRIES

Armstrong, Louis. *Louis Armstrong: A Self-Portrait.* Edited by Richard Meryman. New York: Eakins Press, 1971.

Goffin, Robert. *Horn of Plenty: The Story of Louis Armstrong.* Translated by James F. Bezov. New York: Da Capo Press, 1977.

5. Book with editor(s)

NOTE

5. Paul Eduard Miller, ed., *Esquire's Jazz Book* (New York: Smith & Durrell, 1944), 31.

BIBLIOGRAPHY ENTRY

Miller, Paul Eduard, ed. *Esquire's Jazz Book.* New York: Smith & Durrell, 1944.

6. Organization as author

NOTE

6. Centre for Contemporary Cultural Studies, *Making Histories: Studies in History Writing and Politics* (London: Hutchinson, 1982), 10.

BIBLIOGRAPHY ENTRY

Centre for Contemporary Cultural Studies. *Making Histories: Studies in History Writing and Politics.* London: Hutchinson, 1982.

7. Work in an anthology or part of an edited book
Begin with the author and title of the specific work or part.

NOTES

7. Hale Smith, "Here I Stand," in *Readings in Black American Music,* ed. Eileen Southern (New York: Norton, 1971), 287.

8. Richard Crawford, foreword to *The Jazz Tradition,* by Martin Williams (New York: Oxford University Press, 1993).

BIBLIOGRAPHY ENTRIES

Smith, Hale. "Here I Stand." In *Readings in Black American Music,* edited by Eileen Southern, 286-89. New York: Norton, 1971.

Crawford, Richard. Foreword to *The Jazz Tradition,* by Martin Williams. New York: Oxford University Press, 1993.

In notes, descriptive terms such as *foreword* are not capitalized. In bibliography entries, these descriptive terms are capitalized.

8. Article in an encyclopedia or a dictionary
For well-known reference works, publication data can be omitted from a note, but the edition or copyright date should be included. There is

no need to include page numbers for entries in reference works that are arranged alphabetically; the abbreviation *s.v.* (meaning "under the word") plus the entry's title can be used instead.

NOTES

> 9. J. Bradford Robinson, "Scat Singing," in *The New Grove Dictionary of Jazz* (2002).

> 10. *Encyclopaedia Britannica,* 15th ed., s.v. "Jazz."

Reference works are not listed in the bibliography unless they are unusual or crucial to your paper.

BIBLIOGRAPHY ENTRY

Robinson, J. Bradford. "Scat Singing." In *The New Grove Dictionary of Jazz.* Edited by Barry Kernfeld. Vol. 3. London: Macmillan, 2002.

9. The Bible

Abbreviate the name of the book, and use arabic numbers for chapter and verse, separated by a colon. Name the version of the Bible cited, and do not include the Bible in your bibliography.

NOTE

> 11. Eccles. 8:5 (Jerusalem Bible).

10. Edition other than the first

Include the number of the edition after the title or, if there is an editor, after that person's name.

NOTE

> 12. Hugues Panassie, *Louis Armstrong,* 2d ed. (New York: Da Capo Press, 1980), 12.

BIBLIOGRAPHY ENTRY

Panassie, Hugues. *Louis Armstrong.* 2d ed. New York: Da Capo Press, 1980.

11. Multivolume work

Put the volume number in arabic numerals followed by a colon, before the page number.

NOTE

> 13. Robert Lissauer, *Lissauer's Encyclopedia of Popular Music in America* (New York: Facts on File, 1996), 2:33-34.

BIBLIOGRAPHY ENTRY

Lissauer, Robert. *Lissauer's Encyclopedia of Popular Music in America.* Vol. 2. New York: Facts on File, 1996.

12. Work in a series

Include the name of the series as well as the book's series number if any. The series name should not be italicized or underlined.

NOTE

> 14. Samuel A. Floyd, ed., *Black Music in the Harlem Renaissance,* Contributions in Afro-American and African Studies, no. 128 (New York: Greenwood Press, 1990), 2.

BIBLIOGRAPHY ENTRY

> Floyd, Samuel A., ed. *Black Music in the Harlem Renaissance.* Contributions in Afro-American and African Studies, no. 128. New York: Greenwood Press, 1990.

13. Unknown author

Cite anonymous works by title, and alphabetize them by the first word, ignoring *A, An,* or *The.*

NOTE

> 15. *The British Album* (London: John Bell, 1790), 2:43-47.

BIBLIOGRAPHY ENTRY

> *The British Album.* Vol. 2. London: John Bell, 1790.

14. Source quoted in another source

Quote a source within a source only if you are unable to find the original source. List both sources in the entry.

NOTE

> 16. Peter Gay, *Modernism: The Lure of Heresy* (New York: Norton, 2007), 262, quoted in Terry Teachout, "The Cult of the Difficult," *Commentary* 124, no. 5 (2007): 66-69.

BIBLIOGRAPHY ENTRY

> Gay, Peter. *Modernism: The Lure of Heresy.* New York: Norton, 2007. Quoted in Terry Teachout. "The Cult of the Difficult." *Commentary* 124, no. 5 (2007): 66-69.

Periodicals

15. Article in a journal paginated by volume

When journals are paginated by yearly volume, your citation should include the following: author, title of article in quotation marks, title of journal, volume number and year, and page number(s).

NOTE

> 17. Frank Tirro, "Constructive Elements in Jazz Improvisation," *Journal of the American Musicological Society* 27 (1974): 300.

BIBLIOGRAPHY ENTRY

Tirro, Frank. "Constructive Elements in Jazz Improvisation." *Journal of the American Musicological Society* 27 (1974): 285-305.

16. Article in a journal paginated by issue

If the periodical is paginated by issue rather than by volume, add the issue number, preceded by the abbreviation *no.*

NOTE

18. Sarah Appleton Aguiar, "'Everywhere and Nowhere': Beloved's 'Wild' Legacy in Toni Morrison's *Jazz,*" *Notes on Contemporary Literature* 25, no. 4 (1995): 11.

BIBLIOGRAPHY ENTRY

Aguiar, Sarah Appleton. "'Everywhere and Nowhere': Beloved's 'Wild' Legacy in Toni Morrison's *Jazz.*" *Notes on Contemporary Literature* 25, no. 4 (1995): 11-12.

17. Article in a magazine

Identify magazines by week (if available) and month of publication. In the note, give only the specific page cited; in the bibliography, give the full range of pages.

NOTE

19. Malcolm Walker, "Discography: Bill Evans," *Jazz Monthly,* June 1965, 22.

BIBLIOGRAPHY ENTRY

Walker, Malcolm. "Discography: Bill Evans." *Jazz Monthly,* June 1965, 20-22.

If the article cited does not appear on consecutive pages, do not put any page numbers in the bibliography entry. You can, however, give specific pages in the note. In Chicago style, the month precedes the date, and months are not abbreviated.

NOTE

20. J. R. Taylor, "Jazz History: The Incompleted Past," *Village Voice,* July 3, 1978, 65.

BIBLIOGRAPHY ENTRY

Taylor, J. R. "Jazz History: The Incompleted Past." *Village Voice,* July 3, 1978.

18. Article in a newspaper

Provide the author's name (if known), the title of the article, the name of the newspaper, and the date of publication. Do not give a page number. Instead, give the section number or title if it is indicated. If applicable, indicate the edition (for example, *national edition*) before the section number.

NOTE

> 21. Ralph Blumenthal, "Satchmo with His Tape Recorder Running," *New York Times*, August 3, 1999, sec. E.

Newspaper articles cited in the text of your paper do not need to be included in a bibliography or reference list. However, if you are asked to include newspaper articles in the bibliography or reference list, or if you did not provide full citation information in the essay or the note, format the entry as follows.

BIBLIOGRAPHY ENTRY

> Blumenthal, Ralph. "Satchmo with His Tape Recorder Running." *New York Times*, August 3, 1999, sec. E.

19. Unsigned article or editorial in a newspaper

Begin the note and the bibliography or reference list entry with the name of the newspaper.

NOTE

> 22. *New York Times*, "A Promising Cloning Proposal," October 15, 2004.

BIBLIOGRAPHY ENTRY

> *New York Times*, "A Promising Cloning Proposal." October 15, 2004.

Other Sources

20. Review

If the review is untitled, start with the author's name (if any) and *review of* for a note or *Review of* for a bibliography entry.

NOTE

> 23. David Ostwald, "All That Jazz," review of *Louis Armstrong: An Extravagant Life*, by Laurence Bergreen, *Commentary*, November 1997, 72.

BIBLIOGRAPHY ENTRY

> Ostwald, David. "All That Jazz." Review of *Louis Armstrong: An Extravagant Life*, by Laurence Bergreen. *Commentary*, November 1997, 68-72.

21. Interview

Start with the name of the person interviewed. If a record of an unpublished interview exists, note the medium and where it may be found. Only interviews accessible to your readers are listed in the bibliography. Treat published interviews like articles.

NOTES

24. Louis Armstrong, "Authentic American Genius," interview by Richard Meryman, *Life,* April 15, 1966, 92.

25. Michael Cogswell, interview by author, May 3, 2008, tape recording, Louis Armstrong Archives, Queens College CUNY, Flushing, NY.

BIBLIOGRAPHY ENTRY

Armstrong, Louis. "Authentic American Genius." Interview by Richard Meryman. *Life,* April 15, 1966, 92-102.

22. Personal letter or e-mail
Do not list in your bibliography.

NOTES

26. Jorge Ramados, letter to author, November 30, 2007.

27. George Hermanson, e-mail message to author, November 15, 2007.

23. Government document
If it is not already obvious in your text, name the country first.

NOTE

28. Bureau of National Affairs, *The Civil Rights Act of 1964: Text, Analysis, Legislative History; What It Means to Employers, Businessmen, Unions, Employees, Minority Groups* (Washington, DC: BNA, 1964), 22-23.

BIBLIOGRAPHY ENTRY

U.S. Bureau of National Affairs. *The Civil Rights Act of 1964. Text, Analysis, Legislative History; What It Means to Employers, Businessmen, Unions, Employees, Minority Groups.* Washington, DC: BNA, 1964.

24. Unpublished dissertation or document
Include a description of the document as well as information about where it is available. If more than one item from an archive is cited, include only one entry for the archive in your bibliography (*see p. 379*).

NOTES

29. Adelaida Reyes-Schramm, "The Role of Music in the Interaction of Black Americans and Hispanos in New York City's East Harlem" (Ph.D. diss., Columbia University, 1975), 34-37.

30. Joe Glaser to Lucille Armstrong, September 28, 1960, Louis Armstrong Archives, Rosenthal Library, Queens College CUNY, Flushing, NY.

BIBLIOGRAPHY ENTRIES

Reyes-Schramm, Adelaida. "The Role of Music in the Interaction of Black Americans and Hispanos in New York City's East Harlem." Ph.D. diss., Columbia University, 1975.

Glaser, Joe. Letter to Lucille Armstrong. Louis Armstrong Archives. Rosenthal Library, Queens College CUNY, Flushing, NY.

25. DVD or videocassette

Include the original release date before the publication information if it differs from the release date for the DVD or videocassette.

NOTE

31. *Wit,* DVD, directed by Mike Nichols (New York: HBO Home Video, 2001).

BIBLIOGRAPHY

Wit. DVD. Directed by Mike Nichols. New York: HBO Home Video, 2001.

26. Sound recording

Begin with the composer or other person responsible for the content.

NOTE

32. Louis Armstrong, *Town Hall Concert Plus,* RCA INTS 5070.

BIBLIOGRAPHY ENTRY

Armstrong, Louis. *Town Hall Concert Plus.* RCA INTS 5070.

27. Artwork

Begin with the artist's name, and include both the name and the location of the institution holding the work. Works of art are usually not included in the bibliography.

NOTE

33. Herman Leonard, *Louis Armstrong: Birdland 1949,* black-and-white photograph, 1949, Barbara Gillman Gallery, Miami.

28. CD-ROM or other electronic non-Internet source

Indicate the format after the publication information.

NOTE

34. *Microsoft Encarta Multimedia Encyclopedia,* s.v. "Armstrong, (Daniel) Louis 'Satchmo' " (Redmond, WA: Microsoft, 1994), CD-ROM.

BIBLIOGRAPHY ENTRY

Microsoft Encarta Multimedia Encyclopedia. "Armstrong, (Daniel) Louis 'Satchmo.' " Redmond, WA: Microsoft, 1994. CD-ROM.

Online Sources

The fifteenth edition of *The Chicago Manual of Style* specifically addresses the documentation of electronic and online sources. In general, citations for electronic sources include all of the information required for print sources, in addition to a URL and, in some cases, the date of access. There are three key differences between Chicago- and MLA-style online citations:

- Chicago requires URLs for all online sources, without angle brackets.
- Months are not abbreviated, and the date is usually given in the following order: month, day, year (September 13, 2008).
- Dates of access are necessary only for sites that are frequently updated (such as news media sites or blogs) and for books.

29. Online book

Include the date of access in parentheses.

NOTE

> 35. Carl Sandburg, *Chicago Poems* (New York: Henry Holt, 1916), http://www.bartleby.com/165/index.html (accessed March 18, 2008).

BIBLIOGRAPHY ENTRY

> Sandburg, Carl. *Chicago Poems*. New York: Henry Holt, 1916. http:// www.bartleby.com/165/index.html (accessed March 18, 2008).

30. Partial or entire Web site

Identify as many of the following as you can: author (if any), title of short work or page (if applicable), title or sponsor of site, and URL.

NOTES

> 36. Bruce Boyd Raeburn, "An Introduction to New Orleans Jazz," *William Ransom Hogan Archive of New Orleans Jazz* , http://www.tulane.edu/~lmiller/ BeginnersIntro.html.

> 37. Tulane University, *William Ransom Hogan Archive of New Orleans Jazz*, http://www.tulane.edu/~lmiller /JazzHome.html.

BIBLIOGRAPHY ENTRIES

> Raeburn, Bruce Boyd. "An Introduction to New Orleans Jazz." *William Ransom Hogan Archive of New Orleans Jazz*. http://www.tulane.edu/~lmiller/ BeginnersIntro.html.

> Tulane University. *William Ransom Hogan Archive of New Orleans Jazz*. http://www.tulane.edu/~lmiller /JazzHome.html.

31. Article from an online journal, magazine, or newspaper

Include the date of access if required or if the material is time sensitive.

NOTES

38. Janet Schmalfeldt, "On Keeping the Score," *Music Theory Online* 4, no. 2 (1998), http://www.societymusictheory.org/mto/issues/mto.98.4.2/mto.98.4.2 .schmalfeldt_frames.html.

39. Michael E. Ross, "The New Sultans of Swing," *Salon*, April 18, 1996, http://www.salon.com/weekly/music1.html.

40. Don Heckman, "Jazz, Pop in Spirited Harmony," *Los Angeles Times*, August 10, 2005, http://articles.latimes.com/2005/08/10/calendar/et-hancock10 (accessed August 12, 2008).

BIBLIOGRAPHY ENTRIES

Schmalfeldt, Janet. "On Keeping the Score." *Music Theory Online* 4, no. 2 (1998). http://www.societymusictheory.org/mto/issues/mto.98.4.2/mto.98.4.2 .schmalfeldt_frames.html.

Ross, Michael E. "The New Sultans of Swing." *Salon*, April 18, 1996. http://www .salon.com/weekly/music1.html.

Heckman, Don. "Jazz, Pop in Spirited Harmony." *Los Angeles Times*, August 10, 2005. http://articles.latimes.com/2005/08/10/calendar/et-hancock10 (accessed August 12, 2008).

32. Journal, magazine, or newspaper article from a library subscription database

Give the home page URL. Access date is optional.

NOTE

41. T. J. Anderson, "Body and Soul: Bob Kaufman's *Golden Sardine*,"*African American Review* 34, no. 2 (Summer 2000): 329-46, http://www.ebsco.com (accessed April 11, 2008).

BIBLIOGRAPHY ENTRY

Anderson, T. J. "Body and Soul: Bob Kaufman's *Golden Sardine*."*African American Review* 34, no. 2 (Summer 2000): 329-46. http://www.ebsco.com (accessed April 11, 2008).

33. Blog posting

NOTE

42. Rich Copley, "Major Universities Can Have a Major Impact on Local Arts," *Flyover*, March 15, 2008, http://www.artsjournal.com/flyover/2008/03/ major_universities_can_have_a.html (accessed March 18, 2008).

BIBLIOGRAPHY ENTRY

Copley, Rich. "Major Universities Can Have a Major Impact on Local Arts."
Flyover. March 15, 2008. http://www.artsjournal.com/flyover/2008/03/
major_universities_can_have_a.html (accessed March 18, 2008).

34. E-mail to discussion list

Give the URL if the posting is archived. Do not create a bibliography
entry.

NOTE

43. Roland Kayser, e-mail to Opera-L mailing list, January 3, 2008,
http://listserv.bccls.org/cgi-bin/wa?A2=ind0801A&L=OPERA-L&D=0&P=57634.

35. Podcast

NOTE

44. Fresh Sounds [pseud.], "Bing Crosby Meets Louis Armstrong," *Jazzarific:
Jazz Vinyl Podcast,* http://jazzvinyl.podomatic.com/entry/2006-12-26T10_29_
06-08_00 (accessed January 15, 2008).

BIBLIOGRAPHY ENTRY

Fresh Sounds [pseud.]. "Bing Crosby Meets Louis Armstrong." *Jazzarific: Jazz Vinyl
Podcast.* http://jazzvinyl.podomatic.com/entry/2006-12-26T10_29_06-08_00
(accessed January 15, 2008).

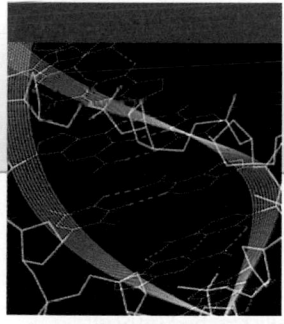

36 Chicago Documentation Style: Sample Paper Excerpt

The following excerpt from Esther Hoffman's paper on Louis Armstrong has been
adapted and put into Chicago style so that
you can see how citation numbers, end-
notes, and bibliography work together. (Hoffman's entire paper, in
MLA style, can be found on pages 313–23.)

www.mhhe.com/
awr3
For another sample of
a paper in Chicago
style, go to

Research > Sample
Research Papers >
CMS Style

Chicago style allows you the option of including a title page. If you
do provide a title page, count it as page 1, but do not include the number on the page. Put page numbers in the upper right-hand corner of
the remaining pages, except for the pages with the titles "Notes" and
"Bibliography" or "Works Cited"; on these pages, the number should be
centered at the bottom of the page.

2

Louis Armstrong's life seems like a classic American success story. From humble beginnings Armstrong rose to become an international superstar, a so-called King of Jazz, and a familiar figure forty years after his death in 1971. Less well known is Joe Glaser, Armstrong's longtime manager. Yet Armstrong once credited his accomplishments to Glaser, saying, "Anything that I have done musically since I signed up with Joe Glaser at the Sunset, it was his suggestions."[1] Was Glaser really as central to Armstrong's work and life as this comment makes him seem? Did he dominate his famous client? Considered in the context of the Jazz Age and each man's background, the relationship between Armstrong and Glaser actually appears to have been a remarkably equitable and successful partnership.

In the 1920s, jazz music was at its height in creativity and popularity. Chicago had become one of the jazz capitals of America, and its clubs showcased the premier talents of the time, performers like Jelly Roll Morton and Joe Oliver. Eager for fame and fortune, many young black musicians who had honed their craft in New Orleans "were drawn to Chicago, New York, Los Angeles, and other cities by the chance to make a career and . . . a living."[2]

Among these émigrés was Louis Armstrong, a gifted musician who developed into "perhaps the best [jazz musician] that has ever been."[3] Armstrong played the trumpet and sang with unusual improvisational ability as well as technical mastery. As biographer Laurence Bergreen points out, Armstrong easily reached difficult high notes, the F's and G's that stymied other trumpeters.[4] His innovative singing style featured "scat," a technique that "place[s] emphasis on the human voice as an additionally important component in jazz music."[5] Eventually, Armstrong's innovations became the standard, as more and more jazz musicians took their cue from his style.

3

Armstrong's beginnings give no hint of the greatness that he would achieve. In New Orleans, he was born into poverty and received little formal education. As a youngster, Armstrong had to take odd jobs like delivering coal and selling newspapers so that he could earn money to help his family. At the age of twelve, Armstrong was placed in the Colored Waifs' Home to serve an eighteen-month sentence for firing a gun in a public place. There "Captain" Peter Davis gave him "basic musical training on the cornet."[6] Older, more established musicians soon noticed Armstrong's talent and offered him opportunities to play with them. In 1922, Joe Oliver invited Armstrong to join his band in Chicago, and the twenty-one-year-old trumpeter headed north.

It was in Chicago that Armstrong met Joe Glaser. According to Bergreen, Glaser had a reputation for being a tough but trustworthy guy who could handle any situation. He was raised in a middle-class home by parents who were Jewish immigrants from Russia. As a young man, Glaser got caught up in the Chicago underworld and soon had a rap sheet that included indictments for running a brothel as well as for statutory rape.[7] Glaser's mob connections also led to his involvement in Chicago's club scene, a business almost completely controlled by gangsters like Al Capone. During the era of Prohibition, Glaser managed the Sunset Café, a club where Armstrong often performed:

> There was a pronounced gangster element at the Sunset, but Louis, accustomed to being employed and protected by mobsters, didn't think twice about that. Mr. Capone's men ensured the flow of alcohol, and their presence reassured many whites.[8]

Notes

1. Max Jones and John Chilton, *Louis: The Louis Armstrong Story, 1900-1971* (Boston: Little, Brown, 1971), 175.

2. James N. Gregory, *The Southern Diaspora: How the Great Migrations of Black and White Southerners Transformed America* (Chapel Hill: University of North Carolina Press, 2007), 139.

3. New Orleans Tourism Marketing Corporation, "Louis Armstrong," *New Orleans Online,* http://www.neworleansonline.com/neworleans/music/musichistory/musicgreats/satchmo.html.

4. Laurence Bergreen, *Louis Armstrong: An Extravagant Life* (New York: Broadway Books, 1997), 248.

5. T. J. Anderson, "Body and Soul: Bob Kaufman's *Golden Sardine*," *African American Review* 34, no. 2 (2000): 329-46, http://www.ebsco.com (accessed April 11, 2008).

6. New Orleans Tourism Marketing Corporation, "Louis Armstrong."

7. Bergreen, 372-76.

8. Ibid., 279.

Bibliography

Anderson, T. J. "Body and Soul: Bob Kaufman's *Golden Sardine." African American Review* 34, no. 2 (2000): 329-46. http://www.ebsco.com (accessed April 11, 2008).

Armstrong, Louis. "Authentic American Genius." Interview by Richard Meryman. *Life,* April 15, 1966, 92-102.

——. Louis Armstrong Archives. Rosenthal Library, Queens College, CUNY, Flushing, NY.

——. *Town Hall Concert Plus.* RCA INTS 5070.

Bergreen, Laurence. *Louis Armstrong: An Extravagant Life.* New York: Broadway Books, 1997.

Bogle, Donald. "Louis Armstrong: The Films." In *Louis Armstrong: A Cultural Legacy,* edited by Marc H. Miller, 147-79. Seattle: University of Washington Press and Queens Museum of Art, 1994.

Collier, James Lincoln. *Jazz: The American Theme Song.* New York: Oxford University Press, 1993.

——. *Louis Armstrong: An American Genius.* New York: Oxford University Press, 1983.

Crawford, Richard. Foreword to *The Jazz Tradition,* by Martin Williams. New York: Oxford University Press, 1993.

Davis, Miles, and Quincy Troupe. *Miles: The Autobiography.* New York: Simon & Schuster, 1989.

Gregory, James N. *The Southern Diaspora: How the Great Migrations of Black and White Southerners Transformed America.* Chapel Hill: University of North Carolina Press, 2007.

Jones, Max, and John Chilton. *Louis: The Louis Armstrong Story, 1900-1971.* Boston: Little, Brown, 1971.

Morgenstern, Dan. "Louis Armstrong and the Development and Diffusion of Jazz." In *Louis Armstrong: A Cultural Legacy,* edited by Marc H. Miller, 95-145. Seattle: University of Washington Press and Queens Museum of Art, 1994.

Writer includes *all* sources she consulted, not just those she cited in body of paper.

12

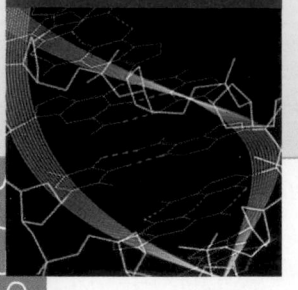

37 CSE Documentation Style

The Council of Science Editors (CSE) endorses three documentation styles in the seventh edition of *Scientific Style and Format: The CSE Manual for Authors, Editors, and Publishers* (Reston, VA: CSE, 2006):

- The **name-year style** includes the last name of the author and year of publication in the text. In the list of references, sources are in alphabetical order and unnumbered.
- The **citation-sequence style** includes a superscript number or a number in parentheses in the text. In the list of references, sources are numbered and appear in order of citation.
- The **citation-name style** also uses a superscript number or a number in parentheses in the text. In the list of references, however, sources are numbered and arranged in alphabetical order.

Learn your instructor's preferred style and use it consistently within a paper. Also, ask your instructor about line spacing, headings, and other design elements, which the CSE manual does not specify.

www.mhhe.com/ awr3

For links to Web sites for documentation styles used in various disciplines, go to

Research > Links to Documentation Sites

37a CSE in-text citations

Name-Year Style

Include the author's last name and the year of publication.

> According to Gleeson (1993), a woman loses 35% of cortical bone and 50% of trabecular bone during her lifetime.

> In epidemiologic studies, small increases in BMD and decreases in fracture risk have been reported in individuals using NSAIDS (Raisz 2001; Carbone et al. 2003).

Citation-Sequence or Citation-Name Style

Insert a superscript number immediately after the relevant name, word, or phrase, and before any punctuation. Put a space before and after the superscript unless a punctuation mark follows.

> As a group, American women over 45 years of age sustain approximately 1 million fractures each year, 70% of which are due to osteoporosis[1].

That number now belongs to that source, and you should use it if you refer to that source again in your paper.

> According to Gleeson[6], a woman loses 35% of cortical bone and 50% of trabecular bone over her lifetime.

Credit more than one source at a time by referring to each source's number. Separate the numbers with a comma.

> According to studies by Yomo[2], Paleg[3], and others[1,4], barley seed embryos produce a substance that stimulates the release of hydrolytic enzymes.

If more than two numbers are in sequence, however, separate them with a hyphen.

> As several others[1-4] have documented, GA has an RNA-enhancing effect.

37b CSE list of references

www.mhhe.com/awr3
To download Bibliomaker software for CSE style, go to
Research > Bibliomaker

Every source cited in your paper must correspond to an entry in your list of references, which should be prepared according to the guidelines in the box on page 382.

Books, Reports, and Papers

In *name-year style*, include the author(s), last name first; publication year; title; place; and publisher. In *citation-sequence* or *citation-name*

CSE STYLE: DIRECTORY to SAMPLE TYPES

CSE LIST OF REFERENCES

- Begin on a new page after your text but before any appendices, tables, and figures.
- Use the centered title "References."
- Include only references that are cited in your paper.
- Start each entry with the author's last name, followed by initials for first and middle names. Add no spaces or periods between initials.
- Abbreviate periodical titles as per the CSE manual, and capitalize major words.
- Use complete book or article titles; capitalize the first word and any proper nouns or proper adjectives.
- Do not use italics, underlining, or quotation marks to set off any kind of title.
- List the extent of a source (number of pages or screens) at the end of the entry if your instructor requires it.

Name-Year Style
- Always put the date after the author's name.
- List the references in alphabetical order, but do not number them.

Citation-Sequence Style
- Put the date after the name of the book publisher or periodical.
- List and number the references in the order they first appear in the text.

Citation-Name Style
- Put the date after the name of the book publisher or periodical.
- List and number the references in alphabetical order. Make the numbering of your in-text citations match.

style, include the same information, but put the year after the publisher.

1. Book with one author

NAME-YEAR

Bailey C. 1991. The new fit or fat. Boston (MA): Houghton Mifflin.

CITATION-SEQUENCE OR CITATION-NAME

1. Bailey C. The new fit or fat. Boston (MA): Houghton Mifflin; 1991.

2. Book with two or more authors

List up to ten authors; if there are more than ten, use the first ten names with the phrase *and others* or *et al.* (not italicized).

NAME-YEAR

Begon M, Harper JL, Townsend CR. 1990. Ecology: individuals, populations, and communities. 2nd ed. Boston (MA): Blackwell.

CITATION-SEQUENCE OR CITATION-NAME

2. Begon M, Harper JL, Townsend CR. Ecology: individuals, populations, and communities. 2nd ed. Boston (MA): Blackwell; 1990.

3. Book with organization as author

In name-year style, start the entry with the organization's abbreviation, but alphabetize by the full name.

NAME-YEAR

[NIH] National Institutes of Health (US). 1993. Clinical trials supported by the National Eye Institute (US): celebrating vision research. Bethesda (MD): US Dept. of Health and Human Services.

CITATION-SEQUENCE OR CITATION-NAME

3. National Institutes of Health (US). Clinical trials supported by the National Eye Institute (US): celebrating vision research. Bethesda (MD): US Dept. of Health and Human Services; 1993.

4. Chapter in a book

NAME-YEAR

O'Connell C. 2007. The elephant's secret sense: the hidden life of the wild herds of Africa. New York: Free Press. Chapter 9, Cracking elephant Morse code; p. 119-126.

CITATION-SEQUENCE OR CITATION-NAME

4. O'Connell C. The elephant's secret sense: the hidden life of the wild herds of Africa. New York: Free Press; 2007. Chapter 9, Cracking elephant Morse code; p. 119-126.

5. Book with editor(s)

NAME-YEAR

Wilder E, editor. 1988. Obstetric and gynecologic physical therapy. New York: Churchill Livingstone.

CITATION-SEQUENCE OR CITATION-NAME

5. Wilder E, editor. Obstetric and gynecologic physical therapy. New York: Churchill Livingstone; 1988.

6. Selection in an edited book

NAME-YEAR

Bohus B, Koolhaas JM. 1993. Psychoimmunology of social factors in rodents and other subprimate vertebrates. In: Ader R, Felten DL, Cohen N, editors. Psychoneuroimmunology. San Diego (CA): Academic Press. p. 807-830.

CITATION-SEQUENCE OR CITATION-NAME

6. Bohus B, Koolhaas JM. Psychoimmunology of social factors in rodents and other subprimate vertebrates. In: Ader R, Felten DL, Cohen N, editors. Psychoneuroimmunology. San Diego (CA): Academic Press; 1993. p. 807-830.

7. Technical report or government document

Include the name of the sponsoring organization or agency as well as any report or contract number.

NAME-YEAR

Bolen S, Wilson L, Vassy J, Feldman L, Yeh J, Marinopoulos S, Wilson R, Cheng D, Wiley C, Selvin E, et al. (Johns Hopkins University Evidence-based Practice Center, Baltimore, MD). 2007. Comparative effectiveness and safety of oral diabetes medications for adults with type 2 diabetes. Comparative effectiveness review No. 8. Rockville (MD): Agency for Healthcare Research and Quality (US). Contract No.: 290-02-0018. Available from: AHRQ, Rockville, MD; AHRQ Pub. No. 07-EHC010-1.

CITATION-SEQUENCE OR CITATION-NAME

7. Bolen S, Wilson L, Vassy J, Feldman L, Yeh J, Marinopoulos S, Wilson R, Cheng D, Wiley C, Selvin E, et al. (Johns Hopkins University Evidence-based Practice Center, Baltimore, MD). Comparative effectiveness and safety of oral diabetes medications for adults with type 2 diabetes. Comparative effectiveness review No. 8. Rockville (MD): Agency for Healthcare Research and Quality (US); 2007. Contract No.: 290-02-0018. Available from: AHRQ, Rockville, MD; AHRQ Pub. No. 07-EHC010-1.

8. Paper in conference proceedings

NAME-YEAR

De Jong E, Franke L, Siebes A. 2007. On the measurement of genetic interactions. In: Berthold MR, Glen RC, Feelders AJ, editors. Proceedings of the AIP 940. 3rd International Symposium on Computational Life Science; 2007 Oct 4-5; Utretcht (Netherlands). Melville (NY): American Institute of Physics. p. 16-25.

CITATION-SEQUENCE OR CITATION-NAME

8. De Jong E, Franke L, Siebes A. On the measurement of genetic interactions. In: Berthold MR, Glen RC, Feelders AJ, editors. Proceedings of the AIP 940. 3rd International Symposium on Computational Life Science; 2007 Oct 4-5; Utretcht (Netherlands). Melville (NY): American Institute of Physics; c2007. p. 16-25.

9. Dissertation

NAME-YEAR

Bertrand KN. 2007. Fishes and floods: stream ecosystem drivers in the Great Plains [dissertation]. [Manhattan (KS)]: Kansas State University.

CITATION-SEQUENCE OR CITATION-NAME

9. Bertrand KN. Fishes and floods: stream ecosystem drivers in the Great Plains [dissertation]. [Manhattan (KS)]: Kansas State University; 2007.

Periodicals

When listing most periodical articles, include the author(s); year; title of article; title of journal (abbreviated); number of the volume; number of the issue, if available (in parentheses); and page numbers. In *name-year style,* put the year after the author(s). In *citation-sequence* or *citation-name style,* put the year after the journal title.

Up to ten authors can be listed by name. If you cannot determine the article's author, begin with the title.

10. Article in a journal that uses only volume numbers

NAME-YEAR

Devine A, Prince RL, Bell R. 1996. Nutritional effect of calcium supplementation by skim milk powder or calcium tablets on total nutrient intake in postmenopausal women. Am J Clin Nutr. 64:731-737.

CITATION-SEQUENCE OR CITATION-NAME

10. Devine A, Prince RL, Bell R. Nutritional effect of calcium supplementation by skim milk powder or calcium tablets on total nutrient intake in postmenopausal women. Am J Clin Nutr.1996;64:731-737.

11. Article in a journal that uses volume and issue numbers

NAME-YEAR

Hummel-Berry K. 1990. Obstetric low back pain, a comprehensive review, part 2: evaluation and treatment. J Ob Gyn PT. 14(2):9-11.

CITATION-SEQUENCE OR CITATION-NAME

11. Hummel-Berry K. Obstetric low back pain, a comprehensive review, part 2: evaluation and treatment. J Ob Gyn PT. 1990;14(2):9-11.

12. Article in a magazine

Indicate the year, month, and day (if available) of publication.

NAME-YEAR

Sternfeld B. 1997 Jan 1. Physical activity and pregnancy outcome. Review and recommendations. Sports Med. 33-47.

CITATION-SEQUENCE OR CITATION-NAME

12. Sternfeld B. Physical activity and pregnancy outcome. Review and recommendations. Sports Med. 1997 Jan 1:33-47.

Online Sources

Include information on author, title, and so forth as with print works. Follow these special guidelines:

- Indicate the medium in brackets ([Internet]).
- Include in brackets the date of the most recent update (if any) and date you viewed the source.
- List the publisher or sponsor, or use the bracketed phrase [publisher unknown].
- To indicate length of a document without page numbers, use designations such as [16 paragraphs] or [4 screens].
- List the URL at the end of the reference, preceded by the phrase *Available from.* Do not put a period after a URL unless it ends with a slash.

The following examples are in the citation-sequence or citation-name style. For name-year style, list the publication date after the author's name and do not number your references.

13. Article in an online journal

13. Krieger D, Onodipe S, Charles PJ, Sclabassi RJ. Real time signal processing in the clinical setting. Ann Biomed Engn [Internet]. 1998 [cited 2007 Oct 19];26(3);462-472. Available from: http://www.springerlink.com/content/n31828q461h54282

14. Online book (monograph)

14. Kohn LT, Corrigan JM, Donaldson MS, editors. To err is human: building a safer health system [Internet]. Washington (DC): National Academy Press;

c2000 [cited 2007 Oct 19]. Available from: http://www.nap.edu/books/
0309068371/html

15. Material from a Web site

15. Hutchinson JR. Vertebrate flight [Internet]. Berkeley (CA): University of
California; c1994-2008 [modified 2005 Sept 29; cited 2008 Jan 15]. Available
from: http://www.ucmp.berkeley.edu/vertebrates/flight/flightintro.html

16. Material from a library subscription database

CSE does not specify a format. Give the information for an online journal article with database title and publication information.

16. Baccarelli A, Zanobetti A, Martinelli I, Grillo P, Lifang H, Lanzani G, Mannucci
PM, Bertazzi PA, Schwartz J. Air pollution, smoking, and plasma homocysteine.
Environ Health Perspect [Internet]. 2007 Feb [cited 2007 Oct 23];115(2):
176-181. Health Source: Nursing/Academic Edition. Birmingham (AL): EBSCO.
Available from: http://www.ebsco.com

37c Sample reference list: CSE name-year style

www.mhhe.com/
awr3

For the complete sample
paper that includes
these, go to

Research > Sample
Research Papers >
CSE Style

References

Anderson A. 1991. Early bird threatens archaeopteryx's perch. Science.
253(5015):35.

Geist N, Feduccia A. 2000. Gravity-defying behaviors: identifying
models for protoaves. Am Zoologist. 40(4):664-675.

Goslow GE, Dial KP, Jenkins FA. 1990. Bird flight: insights and
complications. Bioscience. 40(2):108-116.

Hinchcliffe R. 1997. Evolution: the forward march of the bird-
dinosaurs halted? Science. 278(5338):597-599.

Hutchinson JR. Vertebrate flight [Internet]. c1994-2008. Berkeley (CA):
University of California; [modified 2005 Sept 29; cited 2008 Jan 15].
Available from:
http://www.ucmp.berkeley.edu/vertebrates/flight/flightintro.html

Liem K, Bernis W, Walker W, Grande L. 2001. Functional anatomy
of the vertebrates: an evolutionary perspective. New York: Harcourt
College Publishers.

Padian K. 2001. Cross testing adaptive hypothesis: phylogenetic
analysis and the origin of bird flight. Am Zoologist. 41(30):598-607.

(Read the complete student paper on the *Catalyst* Web site that accompanies this book, as noted in the margin.)

www.mhhe.com/
awr3
For the complete
sample paper that
includes these, go to
**Research > Sample
Research Papers >
CSE Style**

37d Sample reference list: CSE citation-name style

Here are the same references in citation-name style, listed and numbered in alphabetical order. Citation-sequence style would look the same, but entries would be in the order in which they were cited in the paper.

References

1. Anderson A. Early bird threatens archaeopteryx's perch. Science. 1991; 253(5015):35.

2. Geist N, Feduccia A. Gravity-defying behaviors: identifying models for protoaves. Am Zoologist. 2000;40(4):664-675.

3. Goslow GE, Dial KP, Jenkins FA. Bird flight: insights and complications. Bioscience. 1990;40(2):108-116.

4. Hinchcliffe R. Evolution: the forward march of the bird-dinosaurs halted? Science. 1997;278(5338):597-599.

5. Hutchinson JR. Vertebrate flight [Internet]. Berkeley (CA): University of California; c1994-2008 [modified 2005 Sept 29; cited 2008 Jan 15]. Available from: http://www.ucmp.berkeley.edu/vertebrates/flight/flightintro.html

6. Liem K, Bernis W, Walker W, Grande L. Functional anatomy of the vertebrates: an evolutionary perspective. New York: Harcourt College Publishers; 2001.

7. Padian K. Cross testing adaptive hypothesis: phylogenetic analysis and the origin of bird flight. Am Zoologist. 2001;41(30): 598-607.

Frank Lloyd Wright's Robie House features 174 stained-glass windows. Sunlight brings out the clarity of each window's design; in turn, the designs—a variety of geometric, colorful patterns—transform the light.

9

I ... believe that words can help us move or keep us paralyzed, and that our choices of language and verbal tone have something—a great deal—to do with how we live our lives and whom we end up speaking with and hearing.

—ADRIENNE RICH

Editing
for Clarity

9 Editing for Clarity

✓ Sections referenced in Resources for Writers: Identifying and Editing Common Problems pullout section.

WRITING OUTCOMES

Tab 9: Editing for Clarity
This section will help you answer questions such as:

Rhetorical Knowledge
Is my writing too informal or formal for college assignments? **(47b)**
How can I avoid sexist language such as *mankind* and the general use of *he*? **(47e)**

Critical Thinking, Reading, and Writing
How can subordination clarify relationships between ideas? **(44b)**
How can I choose between two words with similar meanings? **(48a, 49a, b)**

Processes
Can my word processor's grammar checker help me edit for clarity? **(38–46)**

Knowledge of Conventions
What's wrong with the comparison *I like manga more than John*? **(39c)**
What's wrong with saying *the reason . . . is because*? **(40c)**
Should I use *their, there,* or *they're*? **(50)**

Self-Assessment: Take an online quiz at www.mhhe.com/awr3 to test your familiarity with the topics covered in Chapters 38–50. As you consult the following chapters, pay special attention to the sections that correspond to any questions you answer incorrectly.

38 Wordy Sentences

A sentence does not have to be short and simple to be concise. Instead, every word in it must count.

Wordiness and Grammar Checkers

Most computer grammar checkers recognize wordy structures inconsistently. One style checker flagged most passive verbs and some *it is* and *there are* (expletive) constructions, but not others. It also flagged the redundant expression *true fact,* but missed *round circle* and the empty phrase *it is a fact that.*

www.mhhe.com/awr3

For more information on and practice eliminating redundancies, go to

Editing > Wordiness

38a Eliminate redundancies.

Redundancies are meaningless repetitions that result in wordiness. Look out for such commonplace redundancies as *first and foremost, full and complete, final result, past histories, round in shape,* and *refer back.*

▶ Students living ~~in close proximity~~ in the dorms need to cooperate ~~together if they want~~ to live in harmony.

Sometimes, modifiers such as *very, rather,* and *really* and intensifiers such as *absolutely, definitely,* and *incredibly* do not add meaning to a sentence but are redundant.

▶ That film was ~~really~~ hard to watch, but ~~absolutely~~ worth seeing.

▶ The ending ~~definitely~~ shocked us ~~very much~~.

38b Do not repeat words unnecessarily.

Although repetition is sometimes used for emphasis, unnecessary repetitions weaken sentences and should be removed.

▶ The children enjoyed watching television more than ~~they enjoyed~~ reading books.

▶ They watched cartoons in the morning and ~~cartoons~~ in the late afternoon.

38c Avoid wordy phrases.

Make your sentences more concise by replacing wordy phrases with appropriate one-word alternatives or eliminating them.

ALTERNATIVES for WORDY PHRASES

Wordy Phrases	Concise Alternatives
at this point in time	now
at the present time	now
in the not-too-distant future	soon
in close proximity to	near
is necessary that	must
is able to	can
has the ability to	can
due to the fact that	because
for the reason that	because
in spite of the fact that	although
in the event that	if
in the final analysis	finally
in order to	to
for the purpose(s) of	to

► ~~It is necessary at this point in time that tests~~ *Tests must now* be run ~~for the purposes of~~

    ~~measuring~~ *to measure* the switch's strength.

► What ~~I mean to say~~ is that Wordsworth's poetry inspired many other

    writers of the Romantic period.

38d Reduce clauses and phrases.

For conciseness and clarity, simplify your sentence structure by turning modifying clauses into phrases.

► The film *Dirty Pretty Things,* ~~which was~~ directed by Stephen Frears,

    portrays the struggles of illegal immigrants in London.

Also look for opportunities to reduce phrases to single words.

► Stephen Frears's film *Dirty Pretty Things* portrays the struggles of illegal

    immigrants in London.

38e Combine sentences.

Sometimes, you can combine several short, repetitive sentences into a single, more concise, sentence.

► Hurricane Ike ~~had a devastating effect on~~ our town~~.~~/~~, The destruction~~

 's torrential rains devastated

~~resulted from torrential rains. Flooding~~ submerged Main Street under

 ing

eight feet of water~~. The rain also~~ trigger~~ed~~ mudslides that destroyed two

 and *ing*

nearby towns.

IDENTIFY AND EDIT
Wordy Sentences

W

To make your writing concise, ask yourself these questions as you edit:

❓ 1. *Do any sentences contain wordy or empty phrases such as at this point in time? Do any of them contain redundancies or other unnecessary repetitions?*

> ◆ ~~The fact is that at this point in time more~~ women than men~~
> *More* *now*
> attend college.

> ◆ Total college enrollments have increased steadily ~~upward~~ since the 1940s, but since the 1970s women have enrolled in greater numbers than men ~~have~~.

❓ 2. *Can any clauses be reduced to phrases, or phrases to single words? Can any sentences be combined to reduce repetitive information?*

> ◆ ~~Reports that come from college~~ officials ~~indicate~~ that
> *College* *report*
> applications from women exceed those from men/~~This~~
> ~~pattern indicates~~ that women will continue to outnumber
> *, indicating*
> men in college for some time to come.

❓ 3. *Do any sentences include* there is, *or* there are, *or* it is *expressions; weak verbs; or nouns derived from verbs?*

> ◆ In 1970,~~there were~~ more than 1.5 million. ~~more men in~~
> *men outnumbered women in college by*
> ~~college than women.~~

> ◆ This trend~~is a reflection of~~ broad changes in gender roles
> *reflects*
> throughout American society.

38f Make your sentences straightforward.

Concise sentences get to the point quickly. Eliminate expletive constructions like *there is, there are,* and *it is,* and replace the static verbs *to be* and *to have* with active verbs. (*For more on active verbs, see pp. 417–18.*) Change passive voice constructions (*The book was read by Miguel*) to the active voice (*Miguel read the book*).

ROUNDABOUT

There are stylistic similarities between "This Lime-Tree Bower" and "Tintern Abbey," which are indications of the influence that Coleridge had on Wordsworth.

STRAIGHTFORWARD

The stylistic similarities between "This Lime-Tree Bower" and "Tintern Abbey" indicate that Coleridge influenced Wordsworth.

Eliminating the expletive *There are* makes the main subject of the sentence—*similarities*—clearer. To find the action in the sentence, ask what *similarities* do here; they *indicate*. Find the noun (*indications*) that can become the verb (*indicate*). Do the same for the sentence's other subject, *Coleridge,* by asking what he did. *Coleridge . . . influenced.*

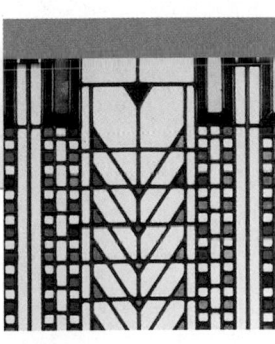

39 Missing Words

When editing, make sure you have not omitted any words readers need to understand your meaning.

✓ 39a Add words needed to make compound structures complete and clear.

www.mhhe.com/ awr3

For information and exercises on missing words, go to

Editing > Word Choice

For conciseness, words can sometimes be omitted from compound structures (which then are called *elliptical structures*): *His anger is extreme and his behavior* [*is*] *violent.*

Do not leave out part of a compound structure unless both parts of the compound are the same, however.

► The gang members neither cooperated nor listened to the authorities.

with

39b Include *that* when it is needed for clarity.

The subordinator *that* should be omitted only when the clause it introduces is short and the sentence's meaning is clear: *Carrie Underwood sings the kind of songs many women love.* Usually, *that* should be included.

► The attorney argued *that* men and women should receive equal pay for

   equal work.

39c Make comparisons clear.

To be clear, comparisons must be complete. If you have just said "Peanut butter sandwiches are boring," you can say immediately afterward "Curried chicken sandwiches are more interesting." Saying "Curried chicken sandwiches are more interesting" in isolation does not give your audience enough information, however. Name who or what completes the comparison.

   Sometimes, what is being compared can be unclear. To clarify, add the missing words.

► I loved my grandmother more than my sister *did*.

► I loved my grandmother more than *I loved* my sister.

When you use *as* to compare people or things, be sure to use it twice.

► Napoleon's temper was *as* volatile as a volcano.

Include *other* or *else* to indicate that people or things belong to the group with which the subject is being compared.

► High schools and colleges stage *The Laramie Project* more than any *other* play.

► Professor Koonig wrote more books than anyone *else* in the department.

Use a possessive form when comparing attributes or possessions.

► Plato's philosophy is easier to read than ~~that of Aristotle.~~ *Aristotle's.*

39d Add articles (*a, an, the*) where necessary.

In English, omitting an article usually makes an expression sound odd, unless the omission occurs in a series of nouns.

▶ A dog that bites should be kept on *a* leash.

▶ He gave me *the* books he liked best.

▶ The classroom contained *a* fish tank, birdcage, and rabbit hutch.

Note: If the articles in a series are not the same, each one must be included.

▶ The classroom contained an aquarium, *a* birdcage, and *a* rabbit hutch.

(*For more information about the use of articles, multilingual writers should consult Tab 12: Basic Grammar Review, pp. 574–76.*)

40 Mixed Constructions

Sentence parts that do not fit together either grammatically or logically confuse readers and must be revised to make meaning clear.

✓ 40a Untangle mixed-up sentence structures.

www.mhhe.com/awr3
For information and exercises on mixed constructions, go to
Editing > Mixed Constructions

Mixed constructions occur when writers start a sentence one way and then, midway through, change grammatical direction. The following sentence begins with a prepositional phrase (a phrase introduced by a preposition such as *at, by, for, in,* or *of*), which the writer then tries to make into the subject. A prepositional phrase cannot be the subject of a sentence, however. Eliminating the preposition *for* makes it clear that *family members* is the subject of the verb *decide.*

▶ ~~For family~~ *Family* members who enjoy one another's company often decide on a

vacation spot together.

In the following example, the dependent clause *when a Curandero is consulted* cannot serve as the subject of the sentence. Transforming the dependent clause into an independent clause with a subject and predicate (a complete verb) solves the problem.

> ▶ In Mexican culture, ~~when~~ a Curandero ~~is~~ consulted ~~can address~~ spiritual
> *can be* *for*
>
> or physical illness.

Sometimes you may have to separate your ideas into more than one sentence to clarify your point. The following sentence is trying to do two things at one time: to contrast England and France in 1805 and to define the difference between an oligarchy and a dictatorship. Using two sentences instead of one makes both ideas clear.

MIXED UP

In an oligarchy like England was in 1805, a few people had the power rather than a dictatorship like France, which was ruled by Napoleon.

REVISED

In 1805, England was an oligarchy, a state ruled by the few. In contrast, France was a dictatorship, a state ruled by one man: Napoleon.

Mixed Constructions and Grammar Checkers

Computer grammar checkers are unreliable at detecting mixed constructions. For example, a grammar checker failed to highlight the three examples of mixed-up sentences in section 40a.

40b Make sure predicates fit their subjects.

A **predicate** (the verb plus its object or complement) must connect logically to a sentence's subject. When it does not, the result is faulty predication.

> ▶ ~~The best kind of education for me would be~~ a university with both
> *A*
>
> a school of music and a school of government./
> *would be best for me.*

A university is an institution, not a type of education.

40c Edit sentences with *is when*, *is where*, and *the reason . . . is because* to make the subject clear.

The phrases *is where* and *is when* may sound logical, but they usually result in faulty predication.

► Photosynthesis is ~~where~~ carbon dioxide, water, and chlorophyll ~~interact~~ in
  the production of carbohydrates from the interaction of
  the presence of sunlight. ~~to form carbohydrates.~~

Photosynthesis is not a place, so *is where* is illogical.

Although *the reason . . . is because* may seem logical, it creates an awkward sentence. To fix this kind of faulty predication, change *because* to *that,* or change the subject of the sentence.

► The reason the joint did not hold is ~~because~~ the coupling bolt broke.
  that

or

► ~~The reason the~~ joint did not hold ~~is~~ because the coupling bolt broke.
  The

41 Confusing Shifts

When you are editing, look for jarring shifts and revise to make your sentences consistent.

Confusing Shifts and Grammar Checkers

Computer grammar checkers rarely flag sentences with confusing shifts like the following:

► The teacher entered the room and then roll is called.

Although it shifts confusingly from past to present tense and from active to passive voice, at least one grammar checker failed to highlight it.

✓ 41a Make your point of view consistent.

Once you choose a point of view, use it consistently. Writers have three points of view to choose from:

- First person (*I* or *we*) emphasizes the writer and is used in personal writing.
- Second person (*you*) focuses attention on readers and is used to give orders, directions, or advice.
- Third person (*he, she, it, one,* or *they*) is topic oriented, so is prevalent in academic writing.

Writers sometimes make jarring shifts in point of view when they compose generalizations. For example, the writer of the following sentence initially shifted from the third person (*students*) to the second person (*you*), a common kind of confusing shift.

▶ Students will have no trouble getting access to a computer if ~~you~~ arrive *they*

at the lab before noon.

Do not switch from singular to plural or plural to singular for no reason. When editing such shifts, choose the plural to avoid using *his or her* or introducing gender bias. (*See Tab 10: Editing for Grammar Conventions, p. 481.*)

▶ ~~A person is~~ often assumed to be dumb if they are attractive and smart if *People are*

they are unattractive.

✓ **41b** Keep your verb tenses consistent.

www.mhhe.com/
awr3
For information and
exercises on shifts and
verb tense and voice,
go to
Editing > Verb
and Voice Shifts

Verb tenses show the time of an action in relation to other actions. Choose a time frame—present, past, or future—and use it consistently, changing tense only when the meaning requires it.

Confusing shifts in time from past to present may occur when you are narrating events that are still vivid in your mind.

▶ The wind was blowing a hundred miles an hour when suddenly there

~~is~~ a big crash, and a tree ~~falls~~ into the living room. *was* *fell*

You may also introduce inconsistencies when you are using the present perfect tense, perhaps because the past participle causes you to slip from present tense to past tense.

▶ She has admired many strange buildings at the university but ~~thought~~ that *thinks*

the new Science Center ~~looked~~ out of place. *looks*

Present Tense and Literary Works

By convention, the present tense is used to write about the content of literary works. When you write about literary works, be careful to maintain the present tense throughout.

► David Copperfield describes villains such as Mr. Murdstone and heroes

   is
such as Mr. Micawber in unforgettable detail. But Copperfield ~~was~~ not
            ^

himself an especially interesting person.

41c Avoid unnecessary shifts in mood and voice.

Besides tense, verbs in a sentence have a mood and a voice. There are three basic moods: (1) the **indicative,** used to state or question facts, acts, and opinions; (2) the **imperative,** used to give commands or advice; and (3) the **subjunctive,** used to express wishes, conjectures, and hypothetical conditions. Unnecessary shifts in mood can confuse and distract readers. Look out for shifts between the indicative and the subjunctive and between the indicative and the imperative.

   could go
► If he ~~goes~~ to night school, he would take a course in accounting.
     ^

► The sign says that in case of emergency passengers should follow the

                     should not
instructions of the train crew and ~~don't~~ leave the train unless instructed
                     ^

to do so.

Most verbs have two voices. In the **active voice,** the subject does the acting; in the **passive voice,** the subject is acted upon. Abrupt shifts in voice often indicate sudden and awkward changes in subject.

                    They favored violet,
► The Impressionist painters hated black. ~~Violet,~~ green, blue, pink, and red.
                    ^   ^

~~were favored by them.~~

The revision uses *they* to make "the Impressionist painters" the subject of the second sentence as well as the first.

IDENTIFY AND EDIT
Confusing Shifts

shift

To avoid confusing shifts, ask yourself these questions as you edit your writing:

❓ 1. *Does the sentence shift from one point of view to another? For example, does it shift from third person to second?*

> ◆ Over the centuries, millions of laborers helped build and
> maintain the Great Wall of China, and ~~if you were one, you~~ ^{most of them}
> ~~probably~~ suffered great hardship as a result.

❓ 2. *Are the verbs in your sentence consistent in the following ways:*

> *In tense (past, present, or future)?*
>
> ◆ Historians call the period before the unification of China the
> Warring States period. It ~~ends~~ ^{ended} when the ruler of the Ch'in
> state conquered the last of his independent neighbors.
>
> *In mood (statements vs. commands or hypothetical conditions)?*
>
> ◆ If a similar wall ~~is~~ ^{were} built today, it would cost untold amounts
> of time and money.
>
> *In voice (active vs. passive)?*
>
> ◆ The purpose of the wall was to protect against invasion, but ,
> ^{it also promoted.} commerce ~~was promoted by it also.~~

❓ 3. *Are quotations and questions clearly phrased in either direct or indirect form?*

> ◆ The visitor asked the guide ^{, "When} ~~when~~ did construction of the
> Great Wall begin?"
>
> ◆ The visitor asked the guide when ~~did~~ construction of the
> Great Wall ~~begin?~~ ^{began.}

41d Avoid awkward shifts between direct and indirect quotations and questions.

Indirect quotations report what others wrote or said without repeating their words exactly. **Direct quotations** report the words of others exactly and should be enclosed in quotation marks. (*For more on punctuating quotations, see Tab 11: Editing for Correctness, pp. 527–31.*) Do not shift from one form of quotation to the other within a sentence.

► In his inaugural speech, President Kennedy called on Americans not to

ask what their country could do for them but instead *to* ask what ~~you can~~ *they could*

do for ~~your~~ *their* country.~~/~~

The writer could have included the quotation in its entirety: *In his inaugural speech, President Kennedy said, "My fellow Americans, ask not what your country can do for you; ask what you can do for your country."*

Similarly, do not shift from an indirect to a direct question.

► The performance was so bad the audience wondered ~~had~~ *whether* the performers

had ever rehearsed.

As an alternative, the writer could ask the question directly: *Had the performers ever rehearsed? The performance was so bad the audience wasn't sure.*

42 Faulty Parallelism

Parallel constructions present equally important ideas in the same grammatical form. The following sentence presents three prepositional phrases.

► At Gettysburg in 1863, Lincoln said that the Civil War was being fought to make sure that government *of the people, by the people,* and *for the people* might not perish from the earth.

If items in a series or paired ideas do not have the same grammatical form, edit to make them parallel. Put items at the same level in an outline or items in a list in parallel form.

www.mhhe.com/
awr3

For information
and exercises on
parallelism, go to

Editing >
Parallelism

42a Edit items in a series to make them parallel. ✓

A list or series of equally important items should be parallel in grammatical structure.

► The Census Bureau classifies people as employed if they receive payment

for any kind of labor, are temporarily absent from their jobs, or ~~working~~ *work* at

least fifteen hours as unpaid laborers in a family business.

In the next example, the writer changed a noun to an adjective. Notice that the writer also decided to repeat the word *too* to make the sentence more forceful and memorable.

► My sister obviously thought that I was too young, *too* ignorant, and ~~a~~

too troublesome.
~~troublemaker.~~

42b Edit paired ideas to make them parallel.

Paired ideas connected with a coordinating conjunction (*and, but, or, nor, for, so, yet*), a correlative conjunction (*not only . . . but also, both . . . and, either . . . or, neither . . . nor*), or a comparative expression (*as much as, more than, less than*) must have parallel grammatical form.

► Successful teachers must inspire ~~students~~ *both* and ~~challenging them is also~~ *challenge their students.*

~~important.~~

► I dreamed not only of getting the girl but also of *winning* the gold medal.

► Many people find that having meaningful work is more important

than high pay. *earning*

42c Repeat function words as needed to keep parallel structures clear.

Function words give information about a word or indicate the relationships among words in a sentence. Function words include:

IDENTIFY AND EDIT
Faulty Parallelism

//

To avoid faulty parallelism, ask yourself these questions as you edit your writing:

? *1. Are the items in a series in parallel form?*

> ◆ The senator stepped to the podium, ~~an angry glance~~
>   *glanced angrily at*
>   ~~shooting toward~~ her challenger, and began to refute his
>   charges.

? *2. Are paired items in parallel form?*

> ◆ Her challenger, she claimed, ~~had~~ not only accused her
>   *had*
>   falsely of accepting illegal campaign contributions, but ~~his~~
>   *also had accepted illegal contributions himself.*
>   ~~contributions were from illegal sources also.~~

? *3. Are the items in outlines and lists in parallel form?*

> FAULTY PARALLELISM
>
> She listed four reasons for voters to send her back to Washington:
> 1. Ability to protect the state's interests
> 2. Her senority on important committees
> 3. Works with members of both parties to get things done
> 4. Has a close working relationship with the President
>
> REVISED
>
> She listed four reasons for voters to send her back to Washington:
> 1. *Her ability* to protect the state's interests
> 2. *Her seniority* on important committees
> 3. *Her ability* to work with members of both parties to get things done
> 4. *Her* close working *relationship* with the President

- Articles (*the, a, an*)
- Prepositions (for example, *to, for,* and *by*)
- Subordinating conjunctions (for example, *although* and *that*)
- The word *to* in infinitives

You can omit repeated function words whenever the parallel structure is clear without them, as in the first example. Otherwise, you should include them, as in the second example.

▶ Her goals for retirement were to travel, ~~to~~ study art history, and ~~to~~

write a book about Michelangelo.

▶ The project has three goals: to survey the valley for Inca-period sites,

to
excavate a test trench at each site, and *to* excavate one of those sites
  ^   ^

completely.

The writer added *to* to make it clear where one goal ends and the next begins.

43 Misplaced and Dangling Modifiers

For a sentence to make sense, its parts must be arranged appropriately. When a modifying word, phrase, or clause is misplaced or dangling, readers get confused.

www.mhhe.com/
awr3

For information and exercises on misplaced modifiers, go to

Editing > Misplaced Modifiers

43a Put modifiers close to the words they modify.

For clarity, modifiers should come immediately before or after the words they modify. In the following sentence, the clause *after the police arrested them* modifies *protesters,* not *destroying.* Putting the clause before the word it modifies makes it clear that if any property destruction occurred, it occurred before—not after—the arrest.

After the police arrested them, the
▶ ~~The~~ protesters were charged with destroying college property. ~~after the~~
  ^   ^

~~police had arrested them.~~

Misplaced Modifiers and Grammar Checkers

Some grammar checkers will reliably highlight split infinitives (*see 43d*) but only occasionally highlight other types of misplaced modifiers. One grammar checker, for example, missed the misplaced modifier *with a loud crash* in this sentence.

► The valuable vase *with a loud crash* fell to the floor and broke into hundreds of pieces.

The following sentence was revised to make it clear that the hikers were watching the storm from the porch:

► *From the cabin's porch, the* ~~The~~ hikers watched the storm gathering force. ~~from the cabin's porch.~~

43b Clarify ambiguous modifiers.

Adverbs can modify what precedes or follows them. Make sure the adverbs you use are not ambiguously placed (such modifiers are called **squinting modifiers**). The following revision clarifies that it is the objection that is vehement, not the argument.

► *vehemently* Historians who object to this account ~~vehemently~~ argue that the

presidency was never endangered.

Problems occur with **limiting modifiers** such as *only, even, almost, nearly,* and *just.* Check every sentence that includes one of these modifiers. In the following sentence, does the writer mean that vegetarian dishes are the only dishes served at dinner or that dinner is the only time when vegetarian dishes are available? Place the modifier immediately before the modified word or phrase.

AMBIGUOUS

The restaurant *only offers* vegetarian dishes for dinner.

REVISED

The restaurant *offers only* vegetarian dishes for dinner.

or

The restaurant *offers* vegetarian dishes *only* at dinner.

Misplacing *not,* another limiting modifier, can result in an inaccurate sentence.

► *Not all* ~~All~~ of the vegetarian dishes are ~~not~~ low in fat and calories.

43c Move disruptive modifiers.

When you separate grammatical elements that belong together with a lengthy modifying phrase or clause, the resulting sentence can be difficult to read. In the following sentence, the phrase beginning with *despite* initially came between the subject and verb, disrupting the flow of the sentence. With the modifying phrase at the beginning of the sentence, the edited version restores the connection between subject and verb.

Despite their similar conceptions of the self,
► Descartes and Hume, ~~despite their similar conceptions of the self,~~

deal with the issue of personal identity in different ways.

43d Check split infinitives for ambiguity.

An **infinitive** couples the word *to* with the present tense of a verb. In a **split infinitive,** one or more words intervene between *to* and the verb form. Avoid separating the parts of an infinitive with a modifier unless keeping them together results in an awkward or ambiguous construction.

In the following example, the modifier *successfully* should be moved. The modifier *carefully* should probably stay where it is, however, even though it splits the infinitive *to assess. Carefully* needs to be close to the verb it modifies, and putting it after *assess* would cause ambiguity because readers might think it modifies *projected economic benefits.*

successfully,
► To ~~successfully~~ complete this assignment students have to carefully

assess projected economic benefits in relation to potential social

problems.

✓ 43e Fix dangling modifiers.

www.mhhe.com/
awr3
For information and
exercises on dangling
modifiers, go to
Editing > Dangling
Modifiers

A **dangling modifier** is a descriptive phrase that implies an actor different from the sentence's subject. When readers try to connect the modifying phrase with the actual subject, the results may be humorous as well as confusing. To fix a dangling modifier, you must name its implied actor explicitly, either as the subject of the sentence or in the modifier itself.

DANGLING MODIFIER   *Swimming toward the boat on the horizon,* the crowded beach felt as if it were miles away.

REVISED   Swimming toward the boat on the horizon, *I* felt as if the crowded beach were miles away.

or

IDENTIFY AND EDIT
Misplaced Modifiers

| mm |

To avoid misplaced modifiers, ask yourself these questions as you edit your writing:

? 1. *Are all the modifiers close to the expressions they modify?*

> *At the beginning of the Great Depression, people*
> ◆ ~~People~~ panicked and all tried to get their money out of the
>   ^
> banks at the same time, forcing many banks to close. ~~at the~~
>   ^
> ~~beginning of the Great Depression.~~

? 2. *Are any modifiers placed in such a way that they modify more than one expression? Pay particular attention to limiting modifiers such as only, even, and just.*

> *quickly*
> ◆ President Roosevelt declared a bank holiday, ~~quickly~~ helping
>   ^   ^
>   to restore confidence in the nation's financial system.
>
> ◆ Congress enacted many programs to combat the Depression
>   *only*
>   ~~only~~ within the first one hundred days of Roosevelt's
>   ^
>   presidency.

? 3. *Do any modifiers disrupt the relationships among the grammatical elements of the sentence?*

> *Given how entrenched segregation was at the time, the*
> ◆ ~~The~~ president's wife, Eleanor, was a surprisingly
>   ^
> strong, ~~given how entrenched segregation was at the time,~~
>
> advocate for racial justice in Roosevelt's administration.

> As *I swam* toward the boat on the horizon, the
> crowded beach seemed miles away.

Simply moving a dangling modifier will not fix the problem. To make the meaning clear, you must make the implied actor in the modifying phrase explicit.

DANGLING MODIFIER   *After struggling for weeks in the wilderness,* the town pleased them mightily.

REVISED   After struggling for weeks in the wilderness, *they* were pleased to come upon the town.

or

After *they had struggled* for weeks in the wilderness, the town was a pleasing sight.

Dangling Modifiers and Grammar Checkers

Computer grammar checkers cannot distinguish a descriptive phrase that properly modifies the subject of the sentence from one that implies a different actor. As a result, they do not flag dangling modifiers.

IDENTIFY AND EDIT
Dangling Modifiers

dm

To avoid dangling modifiers, ask yourself these questions when you see a descriptive phase at the beginning of a sentence:

? *1. What is the subject of the sentence?*

- Snorkeling in Hawaii, ancient sea turtles were an amazing sight.

  The subject of the sentence is *sea turtles.*

? *2. Could the phrase at the beginning of the sentence possibly describe this subject?*

- Snorkeling in Hawaii, ancient sea turtles were an amazing sight.

  No, sea turtles do not snorkel in Hawaii or anywhere else.

? *3. Who or what is the phrase really describing? Either make that person or thing the subject of the main clause, or add a subject to the modifier.*

- Snorkeling in Hawaii, *we saw* ancient sea turtles, ~~were~~ an amazing sight.
- *While we were snorkeling* ~~Snorkeling~~ in Hawaii, ancient sea turtles *amazed us.* ~~were an amazing sight.~~

44 Coordination and Subordination

Coordination and subordination allow you to combine and develop ideas in ways that readers can follow and understand. Coordination should be used only when two or more ideas deserve equal emphasis. Subordination should be used to indicate that information is of secondary importance and to show its logical relation to the main idea.

www.mhhe.com/
awr3
For information
and exercises on
coordination and
subordination, go to

Editing >
Coordination and
Subordination

44a Use coordination to express equal ideas.

Coordination gives two or more ideas equal weight. To coordinate parts within a sentence, join them with a coordinating conjunction (*and, but, or, for, nor, yet,* or *so*) or a correlative conjunction (*either . . . or, both . . . and*). To coordinate two or more sentences, use a comma plus a coordinating conjunction, or insert a semicolon. A semicolon is often followed by a conjunctive adverb such as *moreover, nevertheless, however, therefore,* or *subsequently.* (*For more on conjunctive adverbs and correlative conjunctions, see Tab 12: Basic Grammar Review, pp. 587–89.*)

▶ The auditorium was huge, *and* the acoustics were terrible.

▶ The tenor bellowed loudly, *but* no one in the back could hear him.

▶ The student was *both* late for class *and* unprepared.

▶ Jones did not agree with her position on health care; *nevertheless,* he supported her campaign for office.

44b Use subordination to express unequal ideas.

Subordination makes one idea depend on another and is therefore used to combine ideas that are not of equal importance. The main idea is expressed in an independent clause, and the secondary ideas are expressed in subordinate clauses or phrases. Subordinate clauses start with a relative pronoun (*who, whom, that, which, whoever, whomever, whose*) or a subordinating conjunction such as *after, although, because, if, since, when,* or *where.*

▶ The blue liquid, *which will be added to the beaker later,* must be kept at room temperature.

▶ Christopher Columbus discovered the New World in 1492, *although he never understood just what he had found.*

▶ *After writing the opening four sections,* Wordsworth put the work aside for two years.

411

> **Note:** Commas often set off subordinate ideas, especially when the subordinate clause or phrase opens the sentence. (*For more on using commas, see Tab 11: Editing for Correctness, pp. 501–14.*)

44c Do not subordinate major ideas.

Major ideas belong in main clauses, not in subordinate clauses or phrases. The writer revised the following sentence because the subject of the paper was definitions of literacy, not people who value literacy.

INEFFECTIVE SUBORDINATION

Literacy, which has been defined as the ability to talk intelligently about many topics, is highly valued by businesspeople as well as academics.

REVISION

Highly valued by businesspeople as well as academics, literacy has been defined as the ability to talk intelligently about many topics.

44d Combine short, choppy sentences.

Short sentences are easy to read, but several of them in a row can become so monotonous that meaning gets lost.

CHOPPY

My cousin Jim is not an accountant. But he does my taxes every year. He suggests various deductions. These deductions reduce my tax bill considerably.

Use subordination to combine a series of short, choppy sentences into a longer, more meaningful sentence. Put the idea you want to emphasize in the main clause, and use subordinate clauses and phrases for the other ideas. In the following revision, the main clause is italicized.

REVISED

Even though he is not an accountant, *my cousin Jim does my taxes every year,* suggesting various deductions that reduce my tax bill considerably.

If a series of short sentences includes two major ideas of equal importance, use coordination for the two major ideas and subordinate the secondary information.

CHOPPY

Bilingual education is designed for children. The native language of these children is not English. Smith supports expanding bilingual education. Johnson does not support expanding bilingual education.

REVISED

Smith supports bilingual education for children whose native language is not English; Johnson, however, does not support bilingual education.

44e Avoid overloading sentences with excessive subordination.

Separate an overloaded sentence into two or more sentences.

OVERLOADED

Big-city mayors, who are supported by public funds, should be cautious about spending taxpayers' money for personal needs, such as home furnishings, especially when municipal budget shortfalls have caused extensive job layoffs, angering city workers and the general public.

REVISED

Big-city mayors should be cautious about spending taxpayers' money for personal needs, especially when municipal budget shortfalls have caused extensive job layoffs. They risk angering city workers and the general public by using public funds for home furnishings.

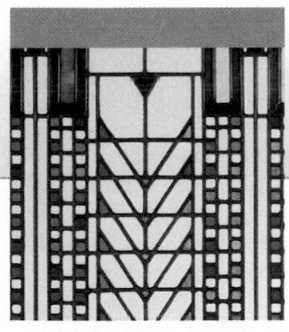

45 Sentence Variety

Enliven your prose and keep your readers interested by using a variety of sentence patterns.

Sentence Variety and Grammar Checkers

Monotony is not a grammatical error; sentence variety is an issue of style, not syntax. A computer grammar checker might flag a very long sentence, but it cannot decide whether the sentence is too long.

www.mhhe.com/
awr3
For information and
exercises on sentence
variety, go to
Editing > Sentence
Variety

45a Vary your sentence openings.

When all the sentences in a passage begin with the subject, you risk losing your readers' attention. Vary your sentences by moving a modifier to the beginning. The modifier may be a single word, a phrase, or a clause.

> *Eventually,*
> ► Armstrong's innovations ~~eventually~~ became the standard.
>   ^

> *In at least two instances, this*
> ► ~~This~~ money-making strategy backfired. ~~in at least two instances.~~
>   ^   ^

> *After Glaser became his manager,*
> ► Armstrong no longer had to worry about business. ~~after Glaser became~~
>   ^   ^
>
> ~~his manager.~~

A **participial phrase** begins with an *-ing* verb (*driving*) or a past participle (*moved, driven*) and is used as a modifier. You can often move it to the beginning of a sentence for variety, but if you move it, make sure that the phrase describes the explicit subject of the sentence or you will end up with a dangling modifier (*see pp. 408–10*).

> *Pushing the other children aside,*
> ► Joseph~~, pushing the other children aside,~~ demanded that the teacher
>   ^
>
> give him a cookie first.

> *Stunned by the stock market crash, many*
> ► ~~Many~~ brokers~~, stunned by the stock market crash,~~ committed suicide.
>   ^

45b Vary the length and structure of your sentences.

Short, simple sentences (under ten words) will keep your readers alert, but only if these sentences occur in a context that also includes longer, complex sentences.

As you edit your work, check to see if you have overused one kind of sentence structure. Are most of your sentences short and simple? If so, use subordination to combine some of them (*see p. 411*). But if most of your sentences are long and complex, put at least one of your ideas into a short, simple sentence. The goal is to achieve a good mix.

DRAFT

I dived quickly into the sea. I peered through my mask at the watery world. It turned darker. A school of fish went by. The distant light glittered on their bodies, and I stopped swimming. I waited to see if the fish might be chased by a shark. I was satisfied that there was no shark and continued down.

Adverbial Modifiers and Subject-Verb Order

In standard English word order, the subject of a sentence precedes the verb. When certain adverbs come at the beginning of a sentence, however, they force changes in this order, usually requiring the subject to fall between a helping verb and the main verb. Adverbs that have this effect include *never, not since, seldom, rarely, in no case,* and *not until.*

	helping main
	subject verb verb
FAULTY	Rarely Simon has tried harder at work than he did today.
	helping main
	verb subject verb
REVISED	Rarely has Simon tried harder at work than he did today.

REVISED

I dived quickly into the sea, peering through my mask at a watery world that turned darker as I descended. A school of fish went by, the distant light glittering on their bodies. I stopped swimming and waited. Perhaps the fish were being chased by a shark? Satisfied that there was no shark, I continued down.

(For more information on sentence types, see Tab 12: Basic Grammar Review, pp. 600–01. For more on sentence variety, see Tab 2: Writing and Designing Texts, pp. 86–89.)

45c Include a few cumulative and periodic sentences and rhetorical questions.

Cumulative sentences add a series of descriptive participial or absolute phrases to the basic subject-plus-verb pattern, making your writing forceful and detailed. (*See Tab 12: Basic Grammar Review, pp. 596–97 for more on these phrases.*) They can also be used to add details, as the following example shows.

▶ The motorcycle spun out of control, *plunging down the ravine, crashing through the fence,* and *coming to rest on its side.*

Another way to increase the force of your writing is to use a few **periodic sentences,** in which the key word, phrase, or idea appears at the end, where readers are most likely to remember it.

▶ *In 1946 and 1947, young people*
~~Young people fell in love with the jukebox in 1946 and 1947 and~~ turned

and fell in love—with the jukebox.
away from the horrors of World War II./

To get your readers to participate more actively in your work, you can ask a question. Because you do not expect an answer, this kind of question is called a **rhetorical question.**

▶ Players injured at an early age too often find themselves without a job, a college degree, and their health. Is it any wonder that a few turn to drugs and alcohol?

Rhetorical questions work best in the middle or at the end of a long, complicated passage. They can also help you make a transition from one topic to another. Avoid using them more than a few times in a text, however, and do not begin an essay with a broad rhetorical question such as "How did the Peace Corps begin?"

45d Try an occasional inversion.

Occasionally try using an inverted sentence pattern or another sentence type, such as a rhetorical question or an exclamation, to vary the normal sentence pattern of subject plus verb plus object. (*For more on sentence types, see Tab 12: Basic Grammar Review, pp. 600–01.*)

You can create an **inversion** by putting the verb before the subject. Because many inversions sound odd, they should be used infrequently and carefully. In a passage on the qualities of various contemporary artists, the following inversion makes sense and adds interest.

▶ Characteristic of Smith's work are bold design and original thinking.

CHARTING the TERRITORY

Exclamation Points in Academic Writing

In academic writing, exclamations are rare, perhaps because they seem immature. If you decide to use one for special effect, be sure that you want to express strong emotion about the idea and can do so without losing credibility.

▶ Wordsworth completed the thirteen-book *Prelude* in 1805, after seven years of hard work. Instead of publishing his masterpiece, however, he devoted himself to revising it—for more than thirty years! The poem, in a fourteen-book version, was finally published in 1850, after he had died.

46 Active Verbs

Active verbs such as *run, shout, write,* and *think* are more direct and forceful than forms of the *be* verb (*am, are, is, was, were, been, being*) or passive-voice constructions. The more active verbs you use, the stronger and clearer your writing will be.

www.mhhe.com/awr3
For information and exercises on active verbs, go to
Editing > Verbs and Verbals

Active Verbs and Grammar Checkers

Computer grammar checkers generally do not flag weak uses of the *be* verb. A grammar checker did not flag the sentence *The paper was an argument for a stronger police presence* because it is grammatically correct. The writer would need to notice the weak *be* verb and change the sentence to *The paper argued . . . .*

Some grammar checkers do flag most passive-voice sentences (*see 46b*), but their suggestions for revising them can sometimes make the sentence worse.

46a Consider alternatives to some *be* verbs.

Although it is not a strong verb, *be* does a lot of work in English.

As a linking verb:

► Germany *is* relatively poor in natural resources.

► Decent health care *is* a necessity, not a luxury.

As a helping verb:

► Macbeth *was* returning from battle when he met the three witches.

Be verbs are so useful that they get overworked. Consider using active verbs in place of *be* verbs, and clunky, abstract nouns made from verbs (like *is a demonstration of*). (*See also Chapter 38: Wordy Sentences, pp. 392–95.*)

► The mayor's refusal to meet with our group ~~is a demonstration of~~ *demonstrates* his

lack of respect for us, as well as for the environment.

46b Prefer the active voice.

Transitive verbs, which connect an actor with something that receives the action, can be in the active or passive voice. In the **active voice,**

417

the subject of the sentence acts; in the **passive voice,** the subject is acted upon.

| **ACTIVE** | The Senate finally passed the bill. |
| **PASSIVE** | The bill was finally passed by the Senate. |

The passive voice downplays the actors as well as the action, so much so that the actors are often left out of the sentence.

| **PASSIVE** | The bill was finally passed. |

CHARTING the TERRITORY

Passive Voice in Scientific Writing

The passive voice is often used in scientific reports to keep the focus on the experiment and its results rather than on the experimenters.

▶ **The bacteria were treated carefully with nicotine and were observed to stop reproducing.**

The active voice is more forceful, and readers usually want to know who or what does the acting.

| **PASSIVE** | Polluting chemicals were dumped into the river. |
| **ACTIVE** | Industrial Products Corporation dumped polluting chemicals into the river. |

When the recipient of the action is more important than the doer of the action, however, the passive voice is the more appropriate choice.

▶ **After her heart attack, my mother was taken to the hospital.**

Mother and the fact that she was taken to the hospital are more important than who took her to the hospital.

47 Appropriate Language

Language is appropriate when it fits your topic, purpose, and audience. Whether you are preparing to write about literature or natural science or history, take some time to read how writers in the field have handled your topic.

www.mhhe.com/
awr3
For information
and exercises on
appropriate language,
go to

Editing >
Word Choice

47a In college writing, avoid slang, regional expressions, and nonstandard English.

Slang, regional sayings, and nonstandard English appear often in conversation but are too informal for college writing—unless that writing is literary or reporting conversation.

Slang words change frequently. (Remember *phat*?). In college writing, slang terms and the hip tone that goes with them should be avoided.

SLANG In *Heart of Darkness,* we hear a lot about a *dude* named Kurtz, but we don't see the *guy* much.

REVISED In *Heart of Darkness,* Marlow, the narrator, talks continually about Kurtz, but we meet Kurtz himself only at the end.

Like slang, regional and nonstandard expressions such as *y'all, hisself,* and *don't be doing that* work fine in conversation but not in formal college writing. In American colleges, professions, and businesses, the dominant dialect is standard written English. Most of your instructors will expect you to write in this dialect, unless you have a good reason not to. (*See the Glossary of Usage for common nonstandard expressions, pp. 432–40.*)

47b Use an appropriate level of formality.

College writing assignments usually call for a style that avoids the extremes of the stuffy and the casual, the pretentious and the chatty. Revise passages that veer toward one extreme or the other.

PRETENTIOUS Romantic lovers are characterized by a preoccupation with a deliberately restricted set of qualities in the love object that are viewed as means to some ideal end.

REVISED People in love see what they want to see, usually by idealizing the beloved.

419

Prefer clear, concise language to overinflated words.

Pretentious	Simple
ascertain	find out
commence	begin
endeavor	try
factor	cause
finalize	finish
impact (as verb)	affect
optimal	best
parameters	limits
prior to	before
reside	live
utilize	use

47c Avoid jargon.

When specialists communicate with each other, they often use technical language. **Jargon** is the inappropriate use of specialized or technical language. You should not use discourse that is appropriate for specialists when you are writing for a general audience.

JARGON   Pegasus Technologies developed a Web-based PSP system to support standard off-line brands in meeting their loyalty-driven marketing objectives via the Internet space.

REVISED   Pegasus Technologies developed a system that helps businesses create Web sites to run promotions for their customers.

If you need to use technical terms when writing for nonspecialists, be sure to define them.

▶ Armstrong's innovative singing style featured "scat," a technique that combines "nonsense syllables [with] improvised melodies" (Robinson 515).

47d Avoid most euphemisms and all doublespeak.

Euphemisms and doublespeak have one goal: to cover up the truth. **Euphemisms** substitute words like *correctional facility* and *passing away* for such harsh realities as *prison* and *death*.

Doublespeak is used to obscure facts and evade responsibility.

▶ Pursuant to the environmental protection regulations enforcement policy of the Bureau of Natural Resources, special management area land use permit issuance procedures have been instituted.

Avoid using words that evade or deceive.

Discourse Communities

People who share certain interests, knowledge, and customary ways of communicating constitute a **discourse community.** Baseball fans, for example, talk and write about *switch-hitters, batting averages,* and *earned run averages*—terms that are probably unfamiliar to people outside the community. The more familiar you are with a discourse community, the more you will know about the language that is appropriate in that community.

47e Do not use biased or sexist language.

1. Recognizing biased language

Be on the lookout for stereotypes that demean, ignore, or patronize people on the basis of gender, race, religion, national origin, ethnicity, physical ability, sexual orientation, occupation, age, or any other human condition. Revise for inclusiveness.

For example, do not assume that Irish Catholics have large families.

► ~~Although the~~ *The* Browns ~~are~~ *an* Irish ~~Catholics, there are~~ *Catholic family with* only two children. ~~in~~

~~the family.~~

In addition, remember that a positive stereotype is still a stereotype.

► ~~Because Asian students are whizzes at math, we~~ *We* all wanted ~~them~~ *math whizzes* in our

study group.

Do not assume that readers will share your background. Be careful about using *we* and *they.*

Refer to groups as they refer to themselves (for example, *Asian,* not *Oriental*). Do not refer unnecessarily to someone's ethnicity, religion, age, or other circumstances.

Avoid language that demeans or stereotypes women and men. Many labels and clichés imply that women are not as able or as mature as men. Consider the meaning of words and phrases like *the fair sex, acting like a girl, poetess,* and *coed.*

2. Revising sexist language

Avoiding bias means avoiding subtle stereotypes. For example, not all heads of state are or have to be men.

CHARTING the TERRITORY

Biased Language

The American Psychological Association recommends this test: Substitute your own group for the group you are discussing. If you are offended by the resulting statement, revise your phrasing to eliminate bias.

BIASED   Wives of heads of state typically choose to promote a charity that benefits a cause they care about.

REVISED   Spouses of heads of state typically choose to promote a charity that benefits a cause they care about.

Traditionally, the pronoun *he* has been used to represent either gender. Today, however, the use of *he* or *man* or any other masculine noun to represent people in general is considered offensive.

BIASED   Everybody had his way.

REVISED   We all had our way.

BIASED   It's every man for himself.

REVISED   All of us have to save ourselves.

Follow these simple principles to eliminate gender bias from your writing.

■ Replace terms that indicate gender with their genderless equivalents:

No	Yes
chairman	chair, chairperson
congressman	representative, member of Congress
forefathers	ancestors
male nurse	nurse
man, mankind	people, humans
manmade	artificial
policeman	police officer
spokesman	spokesperson
woman doctor	doctor

■ Refer to men and women in parallel ways: *ladies and gentlemen* [not *ladies and men*], *men and women, husband and wife.*

BIASED   D. H. Lawrence and Mrs. Woolf met each other, but Lawrence did not like the Bloomsbury circle that revolved around Virginia.

REVISED   D. H. Lawrence and Virginia Woolf met each other, but Lawrence did not like the Bloomsbury circle that revolved around Woolf.

- Replace the masculine pronouns *he, him, his,* and *himself* when they are being used generically to refer to both women and men. One way to replace masculine pronouns is to use the plural.

>   *Senators*   *their districts*
> ► ~~Each senator~~ returned to ~~his district~~ during the break.

Some writers alternate *he* and *she,* and *him* and *her.* This strategy may be effective in some writing situations, but switching back and forth can also be distracting. The constructions *his or her* and *he or she* are acceptable as long as they are not used excessively or more than once in a sentence.

AWKWARD   Each student in the psychology class was to choose a different book according to *his or her* interests, to read the book overnight, to do without *his or her* normal sleep, to write a short summary of what *he or she* had read, and then to see if *he or she* dreamed about the book the following night.

REVISED   Every student was to choose a book, read it overnight, do without sleep, write a short summary of the book the next morning, and then see if *he or she* dreamed about the book the following night.

The constructions *his/her* and *s/he* are not acceptable.

Note: Using the neuter impersonal pronoun *one* can sometimes help you avoid masculine pronouns, but *one* can make your writing sound stuffy.

STUFFY   The American creed holds that if *one* works hard, *one* will succeed in life.

REVISED   The American creed holds that those who work hard will succeed in life.

(*For more on editing to avoid the generic use of* he, him, his, *or* himself, *see Tab 10: Editing for Grammar Conventions, pp. 480–81.*)

48 Exact Language

To convey your meaning clearly, you need to choose the right words. As you revise, look for problems with diction: Is your choice of words as precise as it should be?

www.mhhe.com/awr3

For information and exercises on exact language, go to

Editing > Word Choice

48a Choose words with suitable connotations.

Words have denotations and connotations. **Denotations** are the primary meanings of the word. **Connotations** are the feelings and images associated with a word.

Consider, for example, the following three statements:

Murdock *ignored* the no-smoking rule.
Murdock *disobeyed* the no-smoking rule.
Murdock *flouted* the no-smoking rule.

Even though the three sentences depict the same event, each sentence describes Murdock's action somewhat differently. If Murdock *ignored* the rule, it may simply have been because he did not know or care about it. If he *disobeyed* the rule, he must have known about it and consciously decided not to follow it, but what if he *flouted* the rule? Well, there was probably a look of disdain on his face as he made sure that others would see him puffing away at a cigarette.

As you revise, consider replacing any word whose connotations do not exactly fit what you want to say.

► The players' union should ~~request~~ *demand* that the NFL amend its pension plan.

If you cannot think of a more suitable word, consult a thesaurus (*see p. 431*) for **synonyms**—words with similar meanings. Keep in mind, however, that most words have connotations that allow them to work in some contexts but not in others. To find out more about a synonym's connotations, look up the word in a dictionary.

48b Include specific and concrete words.

In addition to general and abstract terms, clear writers use specific and concrete words.

General words name broad categories of things, such as *trees, books, politicians,* and *students.* **Specific words** name particular kinds of things or items, such as *pines* and *college sophomores.*

Abstract words name qualities and ideas that do not have physical properties, such as *charity, beauty, hope,* and *radical.* **Concrete words** name things we can sense by touch, taste, smell, hearing, and sight, such as *velvet, vinegar, smoke, screech,* and *sweater.*

For MULTILINGUAL STUDENTS

Usage Problems

Most students whose first language is not English consider vocabulary use a major challenge. Even though they learn the meaning of a word, they may have trouble using it correctly in their speaking and writing. Certain types of word combinations are determined by conventional use rather than by their literal meaning (for example, *you do homework* but *you make a plan*).

Study English words and phrases in context, with sensitivity to their connotations. It helps to keep a dictionary close by (*see Chapter 49, pp. 427–31*).

By creating images that appeal to the senses, specific and concrete words make writing more precise.

VAGUE   The trees were affected by the bad weather.

PRECISE   The tall pines shook in the gale.

As you edit, make sure that you have developed your ideas with specific and concrete details. Also check for overused, vague terms—such as *factor, thing, good, nice,* and *interesting*—and replace them with specific and concrete alternatives.

► The protesters were charged with ~~things~~ they never ~~did.~~
                                    crimes   *committed.*

48c Use standard idioms.

Idioms are habitual ways of expressing ideas. They are not always logical and can be hard to translate. Often they involve selecting the right preposition: we do not go *with* the car but *in* the car or simply *by* car; we do not abide *with* a rule but *by* a rule. If you are not sure which preposition to use, look up the main word in a dictionary. (*For more on idioms and multilingual writers, see Tab 12: Basic Grammar Review, pp. 584–85, 585–86.*)

Some verbs, called **phrasal verbs,** include a preposition to make their idiomatic meaning complete:

Henry *made up* with Gloria.
Henry *made off* with Gloria.
Henry *made out* with Gloria.

(*For more on phrasal verbs, see p. 586.*)

48d Avoid clichés.

A **cliché** is an overworked expression. If someone says, "She was as mad as a ———," we expect the next word to be *hornet*. We have heard this expression so often that it no longer creates a vivid picture in our imagination. It is usually best to rephrase clichés in plain language.

> **CLICHÉ**   When John turned his papers in three weeks late, he had to *face the music*.

> **BETTER**   When John turned his papers in three weeks late, he had to *accept the consequences*.

The list that follows gives some common clichés to avoid.

COMMON CLICHÉS

agony of suspense	flat as a pancake	rise to the occasion
beat a hasty retreat	give 110 percent	sadder but wiser
beyond a shadow of a doubt	green with envy	sink or swim
blind as a bat	heave a sigh of relief	smart as a whip
calm, cool, and collected	hit the nail on the head	sneaking suspicion
cold, hard facts	last but not least	straight and narrow
cool as a cucumber	the other side of the coin	tired but happy
crazy as a loon	pale as a ghost	tried and true
dead as a doornail	pass the buck	ugly as sin
deep, dark secret	pretty as a picture	untimely death
depths of despair	quick as a flash	white as a sheet
few and far between		worth its weight in gold

48e Create suitable figures of speech.

Figures of speech make writing vivid, most often by using a comparison to supplement the literal meaning of words. A **simile** is a comparison that contains the word *like* or *as*.

> ▶   His smile was like sunshine after a rainstorm.

A **metaphor** is an implied comparison. It treats one thing or action, such as a critic's review, as if it were something else.

> ▶   The critic's slash-and-burn review devastated the cast.

Because it is compressed, a metaphor is often more forceful than a simile.

Comparisons can make your prose more vivid, but only if they suit your subject and purpose. Do not mix metaphors; if you use two or more comparisons together, make sure they are compatible.

MIXED His presentation of the plan was so *crystal clear* that in a *burst of speed* we decided *to come aboard*.

REVISED His clear presentation immediately convinced us to support the plan.

✓ 48f Avoid misusing words.

Avoid mistakes in your use of new terms and unfamiliar words by consulting a dictionary whenever you include an unfamiliar word in your writing.

> The aristocracy ~~exuded~~ *exhibited* numerous vices, including greed and ~~license.~~ *licentiousness.*

Think critically about the suggestions made by your word-processing program's spell checker. In the example, the writer mistyped the word *instate* as *enstate* and received the incorrect suggestion *estate*.

> We needed approval to ~~estate~~ *instate* the change.

As you edit, read carefully to make sure that you have the right word in the right place.

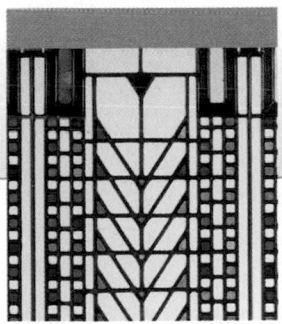

49 The Dictionary and the Thesaurus

A dictionary and a thesaurus are essential tools for all writers.

49a Make using the dictionary a habit.

A standard desk dictionary—such as the *Random House Webster's College Dictionary* or the *American Heritage College Dictionary*—contains 140,000 to 180,000 entries. These dictionaries also provide information such as the correct spellings of important place names, the official names of countries, correct forms of address, and conversion tables for weights and measures. Dictionaries of varying size also appear in most word-processing software and on Web sites (*see Figure 49.1 on p. 430*).

CHARTING the TERRITORY

Dictionaries

In the library's reference section, you can find specialized dictionaries such as biographical and geographical dictionaries; foreign language dictionaries; dictionaries of first lines of poems and of famous quotations; dictionaries of legal and medical terms; and dictionaries of philosophy, sociology, engineering, and other disciplines.

All dictionaries include guides to their use. The guides explain the terms and abbreviations that appear in the entries as well as special notations such as *slang, nonstandard,* and *vulgar.*

An entry from the *Random House Webster's College Dictionary* follows. The labels point to the kinds of information discussed in the following sections.

	Phonetic symbols showing pronunciation.	Word endings and grammatical abbreviations.

Dictionary entry.

com•pare (kəmpâr´), *v.,* **-pared, -par • ing,** *n.* —*v.t.* **1.** to examine (two or more objects, ideas, people, etc.) in order to note similarities and differences. **2.** to consider or describe as similar; liken: *"Shall I compare thee to a summer's day?"* **3.** to form or display the degrees of comparison of (an adjective or adverb). — *v.i.* **4.** to be worthy of comparison: *Whose plays can compare with Shakespeare's?* **5.** to be in similar standing; be alike: *This recital compares with the one he gave last year.* **6.** to appear in quality, progress, etc., as specified: *Their development compares poorly with that of neighbor nations.* **7.** to make comparisons. —*n.* **8.** comparison: *a beauty beyond compare.* —**Idiom. 9. compare notes,** to exchange views, ideas, or impressions. [1375–1425; late ME < OF *comperer* < L *comparāre* to place together, match, v. der. of *compar* alike, matching (see COM-, PAR)] —**com•par´er,** *n.* —**Usage.** A traditional rule states that COMPARE should be followed by *to* when it points out likenesses between unlike persons or things: *she compared his handwriting to knotted string.* It should be followed by *with,* the rule says, when it examines two entities of the same general class for similarities or differences: *She compared his handwriting with mine.* This rule, though sensible, is not always followed, even in formal speech and writing. Common practice is to use *to* for likeness between members of different classes: *to compare a language to a living organism.* Between members of the same category, both *to* and *with* are used: *Compare the Chicago of today with* (or *to*) *the Chicago of the 1890s.* After the past participle COMPARED, either *to* or *with* is used regardless of the type of comparison.

Definition as noun (n.).

Etymology (word origin)

Definitions as transitive verb (*v.t.*).

Definitions as intransitive verb (*v.i.*).

Special meaning.

Usage note.

1. Spelling, word division, and pronunciation

Entries in a dictionary are listed in alphabetical order according to their standard spelling. In the *Random House Webster's College Dictionary,* the verb *compare* is entered as **com•pare.** The dot separates the word into its two syllables. If you had to divide the word *compare* at the end of a line, you would place a hyphen where the dot appears.

Phonetic symbols in parentheses following the entry show its correct pronunciation. The second syllable of *compare* receives the greater stress when you pronounce the word correctly: you say "comPARE." In this dictionary, an accent mark (´) appears after the syllable that receives the primary stress. Online dictionaries often include a recording of the pronunciation.

Plurals of nouns are usually not given if they are formed by adding an *s,* unless the word is foreign (*gondolas, dashikis*). Irregular plurals—such as *children* for *child*—are noted.

Note: Some dictionaries list alternate spellings, always giving the preferred spelling first or placing the full entry under the preferred spelling only.

CHECKLIST

Using a Dictionary

☐ **Use the guide words.** Guide words at the top of each dictionary page tell you the first and last words on the page. Locate a word by looking for guide words that would appear before and after it.

☐ **Try alternate spellings** if you cannot find a word.

☐ **Use the pronunciation key.** The letters and symbols that indicate each word's pronunciation are explained in a separate section at the front or back of a dictionary.

☐ **Pay attention to the parts of speech in a definition.** A word's meaning may depend on how it is used in a sentence.

☐ **Always test the meaning you find.** Substitute the meaning for the word in your sentence and see if it makes sense.

2. Word endings and grammatical labels

The abbreviation *v.* immediately after the pronunciation tells you that *compare* is most frequently used as a verb. The next abbreviation, *n.,* indicates that *compare* can sometimes function as a noun, as in the phrase *beyond compare.*

Here is a list of common abbreviations for grammatical terms:

adj.	adjective	*prep.*	preposition
adv.	adverb	*pron.*	pronoun
conj.	conjunction	*sing.*	singular
interj.	interjection	*v.*	verb
n.	noun	*v.i.*	intransitive verb
pl.	plural	*v.t.*	transitive verb
poss.	possessive		

The *-pared* shows the simple past and past participle form of the verb; the present participle form, *-paring,* follows, indicating that *compare* drops the final *e* when *-ing* is added.

3. Definitions and word origins

In the sample entry on page 428, the definitions begin after the abbreviation *v.t.,* which indicates that the first three meanings relate to *compare* as a transitive verb. A little further down in the entry, *v.i.* introduces definitions of *compare* as an intransitive verb. Next, after *n.,* comes the definition of *compare* as a noun. Finally, the word *Idiom* signals a special meaning not included in the previous definitions.

Included in most dictionary entries is an **etymology**—a brief history of the word's origins—set off in brackets. *Compare* came into En-

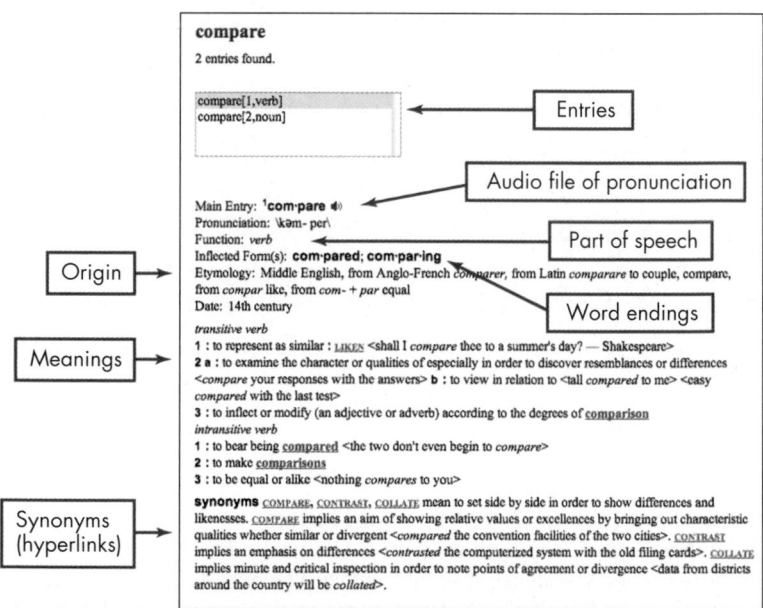

FIGURE 49.1 Online dictionary from Merriam-Webster.

glish between 1375 and 1425 and was derived from the Old French word *comperer,* which came from Latin.

4. Usage

Some main entries in the dictionary conclude with examples of and comments about the common usage of the word. These might include labels like *slang* (very informal), *nonstandard, regional,* and *obsolete* (out-of-date).

49b Consult a thesaurus for words that have similar meanings.

A **thesaurus** is a dictionary of synonyms. Several kinds of thesauruses are available, many called *Roget's* after Peter Mark Roget (pronounced ro-ZHAY), who published the first one in 1852. Today, thesauruses are included in most word-processing software packages.

Consider the connotations as well as the denotations of the words you find in the thesaurus. Do not choose a word just because it sounds smart or fancy.

CHECKLIST

Using a Thesaurus

☐ Use a thesaurus to find a more precise word, not a fancier one.

☐ Become familiar with how the words in your thesaurus are arranged. In *Roget's International Thesaurus,* the words are listed in numbered categories. In other thesauruses, the words are arranged in alphabetical order. Usually, a thesaurus in a word processor will provide synonyms for words that you highlight in your text.

☐ Never use an unfamiliar word from a thesaurus without first looking it up in the dictionary.

☐ Make sure that your replacement word has appropriate connotations as well as the correct denotation.

50 Glossary of Usage

The following words and expressions are often confused (such as *advice* and *advise*), misused (such as *etc.*), or considered nonstandard (such as *could of*). Consulting this list will help you use these words precisely.

www.mhhe.com/
awr3

For an online glossary of usage and exercises, go to

Editing > Word Choice

a, an Use *a* with a word that begins with a consonant sound: *a cat, a dog, a one-sided argument* (*one* begins with consonant sound) *a house* (pronounced *h*). Use *an* with a word that begins with a vowel sound: *an apple, an X-ray, an honor* (silent *h*).

accept, except *Accept* is a verb meaning "to receive willingly": *Please accept my apologies. Except* usually is a preposition meaning "but": *Everyone except Julie saw the film.* Except can be a verb meaning "to exclude": *We must except present company from the contest.*

adapt, adopt *Adapt* means "to adjust or become accustomed to": *They adapted to the customs of their new country. Adopt* means "to take as one's own": *We adopted a puppy.*

advice, advise *Advice* is a noun meaning "suggestion"; *advise* is a verb meaning "suggest": *I took his advice and deeply regretted it. I advise you to disregard it, too.*

affect, effect As a verb, *affect* means "to influence": *Inflation affects our sense of security.* As a noun, *affect* means "a feeling or an emotion": *To study affect, psychologists probe the unconscious.* As a noun, *effect* means "result": *Inflation is one of the many effects of war.* As a verb, *effect* means "to make or accomplish": *Inflation has effected many changes in the way we spend money.*

aggravate While *aggravate* colloquially means "irritate," in formal writing it means "intensify" or "worsen": *The need to refuel the plane aggravated the delay, which irritated the passengers.*

agree to, agree with *Agree to* means "consent to"; *agree with* means "be in accord with": *They will agree to a peace treaty, even though they do not agree with each other on all points.*

ain't A slang contraction for *is not, am not,* or *are not, ain't* should not be used in formal writing or speech.

all ready, already *All ready* means "fully prepared"; *already* means "previously": *We were all ready to go out when we discovered that Jack had already ordered a pizza.*

all right, alright *Alright* is nonstandard. Use *all right. He told me it was all right to miss class tomorrow.*

all together, altogether *All together* expresses unity or common location; *altogether* means "completely," often in a tone of ironic understatement: *At the casino, it was altogether startling to see so many kinds of gambling all together in one place.*

allude, elude, refer to *Allude* means "to refer indirectly": *He alluded to his miserable adolescence. Elude* means "to avoid" or "to escape from": *She eluded the police for nearly two days.* Do not use *allude* to mean "to refer directly": *The teacher referred* [not *alluded*] *to page 468 in the text.*

almost, most *Almost* means "nearly." *Most* means "the greater part of." Do not use *most* when you mean *almost: He wrote to me about almost* [not *most*] *everything he did. He told his mother about most things he did.*

a lot *A lot* is always two words. Do not use *alot.*

A.M., AM, a.m. These abbreviations mean "before noon" when used with numbers: 6 A.M., 6 a.m. Be consistent, and do not use the abbreviations as a synonym for *morning: In the morning* [not *a.m.*], *the train is full.*

among, between Generally, use *among* with three or more nouns, and *between* with two: *The distance between Boston and Knoxville is a thousand miles. The desire to quit smoking is common among those who have smoked for a long time.*

amoral, immoral *Amoral* means "neither moral nor immoral" and "not caring about moral judgments"; *immoral* means "morally wrong": *Unlike such amoral natural disasters as earthquakes and hurricanes, war is intentionally violent and therefore immoral.*

amount, number Use *amount* for quantities you cannot count; use *number* for quantities you can count: *The amount of oil left underground in the United States is a matter of dispute, but the number of oil companies losing money is tiny.*

an *See* a, an.

anxious, eager *Anxious* means "fearful": *I am anxious before a test. Eager* signals strong interest or desire: *I am eager to be done with that exam.*

anymore, any more *Anymore* means "no longer." *Any more* means "no more." Both are used in negative contexts: *I do not enjoy dancing anymore. I do not want any more peanut butter.*

anyone/any one, anybody/any body, everyone/every one, everybody/ every body *Anyone, anybody, everyone,* and *everybody* are singular indefinite pronouns: *Anybody can make a mistake.* When the pronoun *one* or the noun *body* is modified by the adjective *any* or *every,* the words should be separated by a space: *A good mystery writer accounts for every body that turns up in the story.*

as Do not use *as* as a synonym for *since, when,* or *because: I told him he should visit Alcatraz since* [not *as*] *he was going to San Francisco. When* [not *as*] *I complained about the meal, the cook said he did not like to eat there himself. Because* [not *as*] *we asked her nicely, our teacher decided to cancel the exam.*

as, like In formal writing, avoid the use of *like* as a conjunction: *He sneezed as if* [not *like*] *he had a cold. Like* is perfectly acceptable as a preposition that introduces a comparison: *She handled the reins like an expert.*

at Avoid the use of *at* to complete the notion of *where:* not *Where is Michael at?* but *Where is Michael?*

awful, awfully Use *awful* and *awfully* to convey terror or wonder (awe-full): *The vampire flew out the window with an awful shriek.* In formal writing, do not use *awful* to mean "bad" or *awfully* to mean "very" or "extremely."

awhile, a while *Awhile* is an adverb: *Stay awhile with me. A while* is an article and a noun; always use *a while* after a preposition: *Many authors are unable to write anything else for a while after they publish their first novel.*

bad, badly *Bad* is an adjective used after a linking verb such as feel; *badly* is an adverb: *She felt bad about playing the piano badly at the recital.*

being as, being that Do not use *being as* or *being that* as synonyms for *since* or *because: Because* [not *being as*] *the mountain was there, we had to climb it.*

belief, believe *Belief* is a noun meaning "conviction"; *believe* is a verb meaning "to have confidence in the truth of": *Her belief that lying was often justified made it hard for us to believe her story.*

beside, besides *Beside* is a preposition meaning "next to" or "apart from": *The ski slope was beside the lodge. She was beside herself with joy. Besides* is both a preposition and an adverb meaning "in addition to" or "except for": *Besides a bicycle, he will need a tent and a pack.*

better Avoid using *better* in expressions of quantity: *Crossing the continent by train took more than* [not *better than*] *four days.*

between *See* among, between.

bring, take Use *bring* when an object is being moved toward you, and *take* when it is being moved away: *Please bring me a new disk and take the old one home with you.*

but that, but what In expressions of doubt, avoid writing *but that* or *but what* when you mean *that: I have no doubt that* [not *but that*] *you can learn to write well.*

can, may *Can* refers to ability; *may* refers to possibility or permission: *I see that you can rollerblade without crashing into people, but nevertheless you may not rollerblade on the promenade.*

can't hardly This double negative is ungrammatical and self-contradictory: *I can* [not *can't*] *hardly understand algebra. I can't understand algebra.*

capital, capitol *Capital* can refer to wealth or resources or to a city; *capitol* refers to a building where lawmakers meet: *Protesters traveled to the state capital to converge on the capitol steps.*

censor, censure *Censor* means "to remove or suppress material"; *censure* means "to reprimand formally." (Both also can be nouns.) *The Chinese government has been censured by the U.S. Congress for censoring newspapers.*

cite, sight, site The verb *cite* means "to quote or mention": *Be sure to cite all your sources in your bibliography.* As a noun, the word *sight* means "view": *It was love at first sight. Site* is a noun meaning "a particular place" as well as "a location on the Internet."

compare to, compare with Use *compare to* to point out similarities between two things: *She compared his singing to the croaking of a wounded frog.* Use *compare with* to assess differences or likenesses: *Compare Shakespeare's* Antony and Cleopatra *with Dryden's* All for Love.

complement, compliment *Complement* is a verb or noun meaning "to go well with" or "something that goes well with or completes something else": *I consider sauerkraut the perfect complement to sausages. Compliment* is a noun or verb meaning "praise": *She received many compliments on her thesis.*

conscience, conscious The noun *conscience* means "a sense of right and wrong": *His conscience bothered him.* The adjective *conscious* means "awake" or "aware": *I was conscious of a presence in the room.*

continual, continuous *Continual* means "repeated regularly and frequently": *She continually checked her computer for new e-mail. Continuous* means "extended or prolonged without interruption": *The car alarm made a continuous wail in the night.*

could care less *Could care less* is nonstandard; use *does not care at all* instead: *She does not care at all about her physics homework.*

could of, should of, would of Avoid these nonstandard forms of *could have, should have,* and *would have.*

criteria, criterion *Criteria* is the plural form of the Latin word *criterion,* meaning "standard of judgment": *The criteria are not very strict. The most important criterion is whether you can do the work.*

data *Data* is the plural form of the Latin word *datum,* meaning "fact." Although informally used as a singular noun, *data* should be treated as a plural noun in writing: *The data indicate that recycling has gained popularity.*

differ from, differ with *Differ from* expresses a lack of similarity: *The ancient Greeks differed greatly from the Persians. Differ with* expresses disagreement: *Aristotle differed with Plato on some important issues.*

different from, different than Use *different from: The east coast of Florida is very different from the west coast.*

discreet, discrete *Discreet* means "tactful" or "prudent." *Discrete* means "separate" or "distinct." *What's a discreet way of telling them that these are two discrete issues?*

disinterested, uninterested *Disinterested* means "impartial": *We expect members of a jury to be disinterested. Uninterested* means "indifferent": *Most people today are uninterested in alchemy.*

don't, doesn't *Don't* is the contraction for *do not* and is used with *I, you, we, they,* and plural nouns; *doesn't* is the contraction for *does not* and is used with *he, she, it,* and singular nouns: *You don't know what you're talking about. He doesn't know what you're talking about either.*

due to *Due to* is an overworked and often confusing expression when it is used for *because of.* Use *due to* only in expressions of time in infinitive constructions or in other contexts where the meaning is "scheduled": *The plane is due to arrive in one hour. He missed the train because of a car accident.*

each and every Use one of these words or the other but not both: *Every cow came in at feeding time. Each one had to be watered.*

each other, one another Use *each other* in sentences involving two subjects and *one another* in sentences involving more than two: *Husbands and wives should help each other. Classmates should share ideas with one another.*

eager *See* anxious, eager.

effect *See* affect, effect.

e.g., i.e. The abbreviation *e.g.* stands for the Latin words meaning "for example." The abbreviation *i.e.* stands for the Latin for "that is." *Come as soon as you can, i.e., today or tomorrow. Bring fruit with you, e.g., apples and peaches.* In formal writing, replace the abbreviations with the English words: *Keats wrote many different kinds of lyrics, for example, odes, sonnets, and songs.*

either, neither Both *either* and *neither* are singular: *Neither of the two boys has played the game. Either of the two girls is willing to show you the way home.* When used as an intensive, *either* is always negative: *She told him she would not go either.* (For either . . . or and neither . . . nor *constructions, see p. 162.*)

elicit, illicit The verb *elicit* means "to draw out"; the adjective *illicit* means "unlawful": *The detective was unable to elicit any information about other illicit activity.*

elude *See* allude, elude, refer to.

emigrate, immigrate *Emigrate from* means "to move away from one's country": *My grandfather emigrated from Greece in 1905. Immigrate to* means "to move to another country and settle there": *Grandpa immigrated to the United States.*

eminent, imminent, immanent *Eminent* means "celebrated" or "well known": *Many eminent Victorians were melancholy. Imminent* means "about to happen" or "about to come": *In August 1939, many Europeans sensed that war was imminent. Immanent* refers to something invisible but dwelling throughout the world: *Medieval Christians believed that God's power was immanent through the universe.*

etc. The abbreviation *etc.* stands for the Latin *et cetera,* meaning "and others" or "and other things." Because *and* is included in the abbreviation, do not write *and etc.* In a series, a comma comes before *etc.,* just as it would before the coordinating conjunction that closes a series: *He brought string, wax, paper, etc.* In most college writing, it is better to end a series of examples with a final example or the words *and so on.*

everybody/every body, everyone/every one *See* anyone/any one.

except, accept *See* accept, except.

expect *Expect* means "to hope" or "to anticipate": *I expect a good grade on my final paper. Suppose* means "to presume": *I suppose you did not win the lottery on Saturday.*

explicit, implicit *Explicit* means "stated outright"; *Implicit* means "implied, unstated": *Her explicit instructions were to go to the party without her, but the implicit message she conveyed was disapproval.*

farther, further *Farther* describes geographical distances: *Ten miles farther on is a hotel. Further* means "in addition" when geography is not involved: *He said further that he didn't like my attitude.*

fewer, less *Fewer* refers to items that can be counted individually; *less* refers to general amounts: *Fewer people signed up for indoor soccer this year than last. Your argument has less substance than you think.*

firstly *Firstly* is common in British English but not in the United States. *First, second, third,* and so on are the accepted forms.

flaunt, flout *Flaunt* means "to wave" or "to show publicly" with delight or even arrogance: *He flaunted his wealth by wearing overalls lined with mink. Flout* means "to scorn" or "to defy," especially publicly, without concern for the consequences: *She flouted the traffic laws by running through red lights.*

former, latter *Former* refers to the first and *latter* to the second of two things mentioned previously: *Mario and Alice are both good cooks; the former is fonder of Chinese cooking, the latter of Mexican.*

further *See* farther, further.

get In formal writing, avoid colloquial uses of *get,* as in *get with it, get it all together, get-up-and-go, get it,* and *that gets me.*

good, well *Good* is an adjective and should not be used in place of the adverb *well*: *He felt good about doing well on the exam.*

hanged, hung People are *hanged* by the neck until dead. Pictures and all other things that can be suspended are *hung*.

hopefully *Hopefully* means "with hope." It is often misused to mean "it is hoped": *We waited hopefully for our ship to come in* [not *Hopefully, our ship will come in*].

i.e. *See* e.g., i.e.

if, whether Use *whether* instead of *if* when expressing options: *If we go to the movies, we don't know whether we'll see a comedy or a drama.*

illicit *See* elicit, illicit.

imminent *See* eminent, imminent, immanent.

immigrate *See* emigrate, immigrate.

immoral *See* amoral, immoral.

implicit *See* explicit, implicit.

imply, infer *Imply* means "to suggest without stating directly": *By putting his fingers in his ears, he implied that she should stop singing. Infer* means "to draw a conclusion": *When she dozed off during his declaration of love, he inferred that she did not feel the same way about him.*

in, in to, into *In* refers to a location inside something: *Charles kept a snake in his room. In to* refers to motion with a purpose: *The resident manager came in to capture it. Into* refers to movement from outside to inside or from separation to contact: *The snake escaped by crawling into a drain. The manager ran into the wall, and Charles got into big trouble.*

incredible, incredulous *Incredible* stories and events cannot be believed; *incredulous* people do not believe: *Nancy told an incredible story of being abducted by a UFO over the weekend. We were all incredulous.*

inside of, outside of The "of" is unnecessary in these phrases: *He was outside the house.*

ironically *Ironically* means "contrary to what was or might have been expected" in a sense that implies the unintentional or foolish: *Ironically, the peace activists were planning a "War Against Hate" campaign.* It should not be confused with *surprisingly* ("unexpectedly") or with *coincidentally* ("occurring at the same time or place").

irregardless This construction is a double negative because both the prefix *ir-* and the suffix *-less* are negatives. Use *regardless* instead.

it's, its *It's* is a contraction, usually for *it is* but sometimes for *it has*: *It's often been said that English is a difficult language to learn. Its* is a possessive pronoun: *The dog sat down and scratched its fleas.*

kind(s) *Kind* is singular: *This kind of house is easy to build. Kinds* is plural and should be used only to indicate more than one kind: *These three kinds of toys are better than those two kinds.*

kind of, sort of These constructions should not be used to mean *somewhat* or *a little: I was somewhat tired after the party.*

lay, lie *Lay* means "to place." Its main forms are *lay, laid,* and *laid.* It generally has a direct object, specifying what has been placed: *She laid her book on the steps and left it there. Lie* means "to recline" and does not take a direct object. Its main forms are *lie, lay,* and *lain: She often lay awake at night.*

less *See* fewer, less.

like *See* as, like.

literally *Literally* means "actually" or "exactly as written": *Literally thousands gathered along the parade route.* Do not use *literally* as an intensive adverb when it can be misleading or even ridiculous, as here: *His blood literally boiled.*

loose, lose *Loose* is an adjective that means "not securely attached." *Lose* is a verb that means "to misplace." *Better tighten that loose screw before you lose the whole structure.*

may *See* can, may.

maybe, may be *Maybe* is an adverb meaning "perhaps": *Maybe he can get a summer job as a lifeguard. May be* is a verb phrase meaning "is possible": *It may be that I can get a job as a lifeguard, too.*

moral, morale *Moral* means "lesson," especially a lesson about standards of behavior or the nature of life: *The moral of the story is do not drink and drive. Morale* means "attitude" or "mental condition": *Office morale dropped sharply after the dean was arrested.*

more important, more importantly Use *more important.*

most *See* almost, most.

myself (himself, herself, etc.) Pronouns ending with *-self* refer to or intensify other words: *Jack hurt himself. Standing in the doorway was the man himself.* When you are unsure whether to use *I* or *me, she* or *her, he* or *him* in a compound subject or object, you may be tempted to substitute one of the *-self* pronouns. Don't do it: *The quarrel was between her and me* [not *myself*]. (*Also see Tab 10: Problems with Pronouns, beginning on p. 478.*)

neither *See* either, neither

nohow, nowheres These words are nonstandard for *anyway, in no way, in any way, in any place,* and *in no place.* Do not use them in formal writing.

number *See* amount, number.

off of Omit the *of: She took the painting off the wall.*

one another *See* each other, one another.

outside of *See* inside of, outside of.

plus Avoid using *plus* as a coordinating conjunction (use *and*) or a transitional expression (use *moreover*): *He had to walk the dog, empty the garbage, and* [not *plus*] *write a term paper.*

precede, proceed *Precede* means "come before;" *proceed* means "go forward": *Despite the heavy snows that preceded us, we managed to proceed up the hiking trail.*

previous to, prior to Avoid these wordy and pompous substitutions for *before.*

principal, principle   *Principal* is an adjective meaning "most important" or a noun meaning "the head of an organization" or "a sum of money": *Our principal objections to the school's principal are that he is a liar and a cheat. Principle* is a noun meaning "a basic standard or law": *We believe in the principles of honesty and fair play.*

proceed   *See* precede, proceed.

raise, rise   *Raise* means "to lift or cause to move upward." It takes a direct object—someone raises something: *I raised the windows in the classroom. Rise* means "to go upward." It does not take a direct object—something rises by itself: *We watched the balloon rise to the ceiling.*

real, really   Do not use the word *real* when you mean *very: The cake was very* [not *real*] *good.*

reason . . . is because, reason why   These are redundant expressions. Use either *the reason is that* or *because: The reason he fell on the ice is that he cannot skate. He fell on the ice because he cannot skate.*

refer to   *See* allude, elude, refer to.

relation, relationship   *Relation* describes a connection between things: *There is a relation between smoking and lung cancer. Relationship* describes a connection between people: *The brothers have always had a close relationship.*

respectfully, respectively   *Respectfully* means "with respect": *Treat your partners respectfully. Respectively* means "in the given order": *The three Williams she referred to were Shakespeare, Wordsworth, and Yeats, respectively.*

rise   *See* raise, rise.

set, sit   *Set* is usually a transitive verb meaning "to establish" or "to place." It takes a direct object, and its principal parts are *set, set,* and *set: DiMaggio set the standard of excellence in fielding. She set the box down in the corner. Sit* is usually intransitive, meaning "to place oneself in a sitting position." Its principal parts are *sit, sat,* and *sat: The dog sat on command.*

shall, will   Today, most writers use *will* instead of *shall* in the ordinary future tense for the first person: *I will celebrate my birthday by throwing a big party. Shall* is still used in questions. *Shall we dance?*

should of   *See* could of, should of, would of.

site   *See* cite, sight, site.

sort of   *See* kind of, sort of.

stationary, stationery   *Stationary* means "standing still": *I worked out on my stationary bicycle. Stationery* is writing paper: *That stationery smells like a rose garden.*

suppose   *See* expect, suppose.

sure   Avoid confusing the adjective *sure* with the adverb *surely: The dress she wore to the party was surely bizarre.*

sure and   *Sure and* is often used colloquially. In formal writing, *sure to* is preferred: *Be sure to* [not *be sure and*] *get to the wedding on time.*

take   *See* bring, take.

than, then   *Than* is a conjunction used in comparisons: *I am taller than you. Then* is an adverb referring to a point in time: *We will sing and then dance.*

that, which Many writers use *that* for restrictive (i.e., essential) clauses and *which* for nonrestrictive (i.e., nonessential) clauses: *The bull that escaped from the ring ran through my china shop, which was located in the square.* (*Also see Commas, pp. 501–14, in Tab 11.*)

their, there, they're *Their* is a possessive pronoun: *They gave their lives. There* is an adverb of place: *She was standing there. They're* is a contraction of *they are: They're reading more poetry this semester.*

theirself, theirselves, themself Use *themselves.*

this here, these here, that there, them there When writing, avoid these nonstandard forms.

to, too, two *To* is a preposition; *too* is an adverb; *two* is a number: *The two of us got lost too many times on our way to his house.*

try and *Try to* is the standard form: *Try to* [not *try and*] *understand.*

uninterested *See* disinterested, uninterested.

unique *Unique* means "one of a kind." Do not use any qualifiers with it.

utilize *Use* is preferable because it is simpler: *Use five sources in your paper.*

verbally, orally To say something *orally* is to say it aloud: *We agreed orally to share credit for the work, but when I asked her to confirm it in writing, she refused.* To say something *verbally* is to use words: *His eyes flashed anger, but he did not express his feelings verbally.*

wait for, wait on People *wait for* those who are late; they *wait on* tables.

weather, whether The noun *weather* refers to the atmosphere: *She worried that the weather would not clear up in time for the victory celebration. Whether* is a conjunction referring to a choice between options: *I can't decide whether to go now or next week.*

well *See* good, well.

whether *See* if, whether, *and* weather, whether.

which, who, whose, that *Which* is used for things, and *who* and *whose* for people: *My fountain pen, which I had lost last week, was found by a child who had never seen one before, whose whole life had been spent with ballpoints.* Use *that* for things and groups of people: *The committee that makes hiring decisions meets on Friday.*

who, whom Use *who* with subjects and their complements. Use *whom* with objects of verbs: *The person who will fill the position is Jane, whom you met last week.* (*Also see Problems with Pronouns in Tab 10, pp. 488–89.*)

will *See* shall, will.

would of *See* could of, should of, would of.

your, you're *Your* is a possessive pronoun: *Is that your new car? You're* is a contraction of *you are: You're a lucky guy.*

CHECKLIST

Editing for Clarity

As you revise, check your writing for clarity by asking yourself these questions:

☐ Are all sentences concise and straightforward? (*See Chapter 38: Wordy Sentences, pp. 392–95.*)

☐ Are all sentences complete? Are any necessary words missing from compounds or comparisons? (*See Chapter 39: Missing Words, pp. 395–97.*)

☐ Do the parts of each sentence fit together in a way that makes sense, or is the sentence mixed up? (*See Chapter 40: Mixed Constructions, pp. 397–99.*)

☐ Do the key parts of each sentence fit together well, or are there disturbing mismatches in person, number, or grammatical structure? (*See Chapter 41: Confusing Shifts, pp. 399–403, and Chapter 42: Faulty Parallelism, pp. 403–06.*)

☐ Are the parts of each sentence clearly and closely connected, or are some modifiers separated from what they modify? (*See Chapter 43: Misplaced and Dangling Modifiers, pp. 406–10.*)

☐ Are the focus, flow, and voice of the sentences clear, or do some sentences have confusing shifts or ineffective coordination and subordination? (*See Chapter 41: Confusing Shifts, pp. 399–403, and Chapter 44: Coordination and Subordination, pp. 411–13.*)

☐ Do sentence patterns vary sufficiently? Is there a mixture of long and short sentences? (*See Chapter 45: Sentence Variety, pp. 413–16.*)

☐ Are all verbs strong and emphatic, or are the passive voice, the verb *to be*, or other weak or too-common verbs overused? (*See Chapter 46: Active Verbs, pp. 417–18.*)

CHECKLIST

Editing for Word Choice

Keep the following questions in mind to be sure that you understand words in your reading and use them appropriately in your writing:

☐ Do you have a dictionary at hand for unfamiliar words you encounter in your reading? Do you have a thesaurus at hand while writing to find the most appropriate word to convey your meaning? Can you infer the meaning of unfamiliar words from contextual clues? (*See Chapter 49: The Dictionary and the Thesaurus, pp. 427–31.*)

☐ Is your language appropriate to the assignment? Does it include any euphemisms, doublespeak, inappropriate slang expressions, regionalisms, or jargon? Have you used any stereotyping, biased, or sexist expressions? (*See Chapter 47: Appropriate Language, pp. 419–23.*)

☐ Have you chosen words with the appropriate connotations? Have you confused words that have similar denotations? (*See Chapter 48: Exact Language, pp. 424–27 and Chapter 50: Glossary of Usage, pp. 432–40.*)

☐ Have you used specific and concrete words and suitable figures of speech? Have you avoided clichés? (*See Chapter 48: Exact Language, pp. 424–27.*)

This detail from a first century CE wall painting in the ancient Roman city of Pompeii shows a woman writing on a wax covered tablet. Working on tablets like this, Roman writers could smooth over words and make corrections with ease.

10

There is a core simplicity to the English language and its American variant, but it's a slippery core.

—STEPHEN KING

Editing
for Grammar
Conventions

✓ Sections referenced in Resources for Writers: Identifying and Editing
Common Problems pullout section (following Tab 9).

Tab 10: Editing for Grammar Conventions
This section will help you answer questions such as:

Rhetorical Knowledge
Are sentence fragments ever acceptable in any kind of writing? **(51b)**

Critical Thinking, Reading, and Writing
What's wrong with *A student should enjoy their college experience*?
How can I fix it without introducing sexism? **(55a)**

Processes
Can my word processor's grammar checker help me edit for grammar conventions? **(51–56)**
How can I recognize and fix sentence fragments when I edit? **(51a)**

Knowledge of Conventions
When should I use *lie* or *lay*? **(54b)**
Is it ever correct to say *I feel good*? **(56b)**

Self-Assessment: *Take an online quiz at www.mhhe.com/awr3 to test your familiarity with the topics covered in Chapters 51–56. As you read the following chapters, pay special attention to the sections that correspond to any questions you answer incorrectly.*

When you edit, your purpose is to make the sentences in your text both clear and strong. The previous section of the handbook focused on editing for clarity. This section focuses on editing for common grammatical problems.

 For MULTILINGUAL STUDENTS

Sections of Special Interest to Multilingual Students

Using correct grammar involves more than just making sure the mechanics of the language are correct. You may wish to pay special attention to the following sections:

- **54f:** Use verb tenses accurately.
- **55a:** Make pronouns agree with their antecedents.
- **55b:** Make pronoun references clear.

(For help with areas that are especially troublesome for multilingual writers, see Tab 12.)

51 Sentence Fragments

A **sentence fragment** is an incomplete sentence treated as if it were complete. It may begin with a capital letter and end with a period, a question mark, or an exclamation point, but it lacks one or more of the following:

www.mhhe.com/ awr3

For information and exercises on sentence fragments, go to

Editing > Sentence Fragments

- A complete verb
- A subject
- An independent clause

Although writers sometimes use them intentionally (*see "Charting the Territory: Intentional Fragments" on p. 449*), fragments are rarely appropriate for college assignments.

✓ 51a Learn how to identify sentence fragments.

Identify fragments in your work by asking three questions:

- Do you see a complete verb?
- Do you see a subject?
- Do you see *only* a dependent clause?

1. Do you see a complete verb?

A **complete verb** consists of a main verb and any helping verbs needed to indicate tense, person, and number. (*See Chapter 54: Problems with Verbs, p. 41.*) A group of related words without a complete verb is a phrase fragment, not a sentence.

FRAGMENT	The ancient Mayas were among the first to develop many mathematical concepts. *For example, the concept of zero.* [no verb]
SENTENCE	The ancient Mayas were among the first to develop many mathematical concepts. *For example, they developed the concept of zero.*

2. Do you see a subject?

The **subject** is the *who* or *what* that a sentence is about. (*See Tab 12: Basic Grammar Review, p. 590.*) A group of related words without a subject or complete verb is a phrase fragment, not a sentence.

FRAGMENT	The ancient Mayas were accomplished mathematicians. *Developed the concept of zero, for example.* [no subject]
SENTENCE	The ancient Mayas were accomplished mathematicians. *They developed the concept of zero, for example.*

3. Do you see *only* a dependent clause?

An **independent clause** has a subject and complete verb and can stand on its own as a sentence. A **dependent** or **subordinate clause** also has a subject and complete verb, but it begins with a subordinating word such as *although, because, since, that, unless, which,* or *while.* Dependent clauses function within sentences as modifiers or nouns, but they cannot stand as sentences on their own. (*See Tab 12: Basic Grammar Review, p. 597.*)

> **FRAGMENT** The ancient Mayas deserve a place in the history of mathematics. *Because they were among the earliest people to develop the concept of zero.*

> **SENTENCE** The ancient Mayas deserve a place in the history of mathematics *because they were among the earliest people to develop the concept of zero.*

Fragments and Grammar Checkers

Grammar checkers identify some fragments, but they will not tell you what the fragment is missing or how to edit it. Grammar checkers can also miss fragments without subjects that could be interpreted as commands. Consider the following sentence: *Develop the concept of zero, for example.* As a command to the reader, this sentence is complete but does not make sense.

51b Learn how to edit sentence fragments.

You can repair sentence fragments by editing them in one of two ways:

- Transform them into sentences.

  > Many people feel threatened by globalization. ~~Because they~~ *They*
  >
  > think it will undermine their cultural traditions.

- Attach them to a nearby independent clause.

  > Many people feel threatened by globalization,/ ~~Because~~ *because* they
  >
  > think it will undermine their cultural traditions.

The approach to take in any particular case is a stylistic decision. Sometimes one approach may be clearly preferable to the other, and sometimes both approaches may seem equally effective.

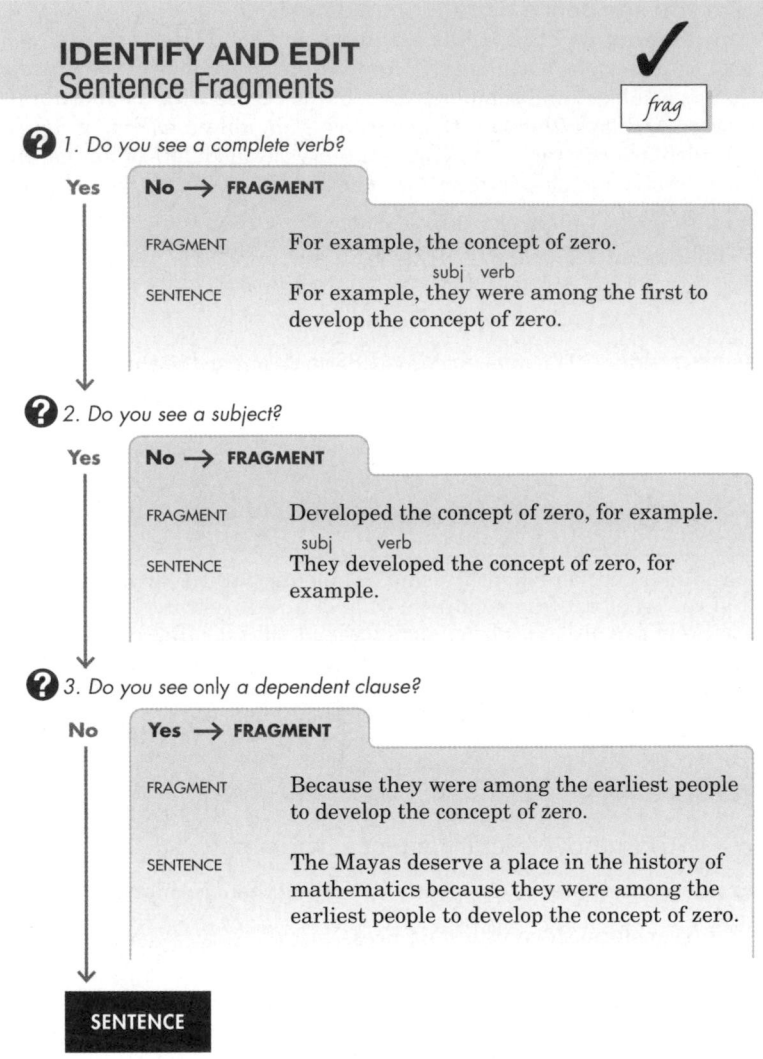

IDENTIFY AND EDIT
Sentence Fragments

✓ *frag*

? *1. Do you see a complete verb?*

Yes | **No → FRAGMENT**

FRAGMENT | For example, the concept of zero.

SENTENCE | subj verb
For example, they were among the first to develop the concept of zero.

? *2. Do you see a subject?*

Yes | **No → FRAGMENT**

FRAGMENT | Developed the concept of zero, for example.

SENTENCE | subj   verb
They developed the concept of zero, for example.

? *3. Do you see only a dependent clause?*

No | **Yes → FRAGMENT**

FRAGMENT | Because they were among the earliest people to develop the concept of zero.

SENTENCE | The Mayas deserve a place in the history of mathematics because they were among the earliest people to develop the concept of zero.

SENTENCE

You may, for example, choose to rewrite a fragment as a sentence for emphasis.

► The ambulance crew gave us tips on handling emergencies. ~~Stressing~~ the *They stressed*
importance of staying calm.

Rewriting long fragments as separate sentences can help keep your writing direct and concise.

Intentional Fragments

Advertisers often use attention-getting fragments: "Hot deal! Big savings! Because you're worth it." In everyday life, we often speak in fragments: "You okay?" "Fine." As a result, people who write fiction and drama use fragments to create realistic dialogue. Keep in mind, however, that advertising, literary writing, and college writing have different contexts and purposes. In formal writing, use intentional sentence fragments sparingly, if at all.

► Students with good time management habits start studying right away

Others,
in the evening. ~~Whereas others,~~ of the procrastinating variety, may go
^

running first, or make phone calls, or clean their rooms, or surf the

Internet, or watch television—anything to avoid getting to work.

Attaching a fragment to a related sentence, on the other hand, can highlight the relationship between ideas.

even
► The Mayas built great cities. / ~~Even~~ though they lacked metal tools.
^

51c Connect a phrase fragment to another sentence, or add the missing elements.

Often unintentional fragments are **phrases**—word groups that lack a subject or a complete verb or both and usually function as modifiers or nouns.

Avoiding Fragments

Many languages other than English permit constructions that, transferred literally into English, would result in fragments. For example, some languages—Russian and Chinese, to name two—permit the omission of the auxiliary or linking verb *be*. Transferred directly into English, this pattern can result in fragments like *He very happy with the news,* instead of the correct *He is very happy with the news.*

1. Watching for verbals

Phrase fragments frequently begin with **verbals**—words derived from verbs, such as *putting* or *to put*. They do not change form to reflect tense and number. (*For more on verbals, see p. 596.*)

> **FRAGMENT**   That summer, we had the time of our lives. *Fishing in the early morning hours, splashing in the lake after lunch, exploring the woods before dinner, and playing Scrabble until it was time for bed.*

One way to fix this fragment is to transform it into an independent clause with its own subject and verb.

> ▶   That summer, we had the time of our lives. ~~Fishing~~ ^{We fished} in the early morning
>
> hours, ~~splashing~~ ^{splashed} in the lake after lunch, ~~exploring~~ ^{explored} the woods before
>
> dinner, and ~~playing~~ ^{played} Scrabble until it was time for bed.

Notice that all of the *-ing* verbals in the fragment need to be changed to keep the phrases in the new sentence parallel. (*For more on parallelism, see Tab 9: Editing for Clarity, pp. 403–06.*)

Another way to fix the problem is to attach the fragment to the part of the previous sentence that it modifies (in this case, *the time of our lives*).

> ▶   That summer, we had the time of our lives/, ~~Fishing~~ ^{fishing} in the early morning
>
> hours, splashing in the lake after lunch, exploring the woods before
>
> dinner, and playing Scrabble until it was time for bed.

2. Watching for preposition fragments

Phrase fragments can also begin with one-word prepositions such as *as, at, by, for, from, in, of, on,* or *to.* To correct these types of fragments, you will often find it easiest to attach them to a nearby sentence.

> ▶   Impressionist painters often depicted their subjects in everyday
>
> situations/, ~~At~~ ^{at} a restaurant, perhaps, or by the seashore.

3. Watching for transitional phrases

Some fragments start with two- or three-word prepositions that function as transitions, such as *as well as, as compared with, except for, in addition to, in contrast with, in spite of,* or *instead of.*

▶ For the past sixty-five years, the growth in consumer spending has been

both steep and steady.~~/, As~~ *as* compared with the growth in gross domestic

product (GDP), which fluctuated significantly between 1929 and 1950.

4. Watching for words and phrases that introduce examples

Check word groups beginning with expressions that introduce examples—such as *for example, specifically,* or *such as*—to make sure they are complete sentences. If they are fragments, edit to make them into sentences or attach them to an independent clause.

▶ Elizabeth I of England faced many dangers as a princess. For example,

~~falling~~ *she fell* out of favor with her sister, Queen Mary, and ~~being~~ *was* imprisoned in

the Tower of London.

5. Watching for appositives

An **appositive** is a noun or noun phrase that renames a noun or pronoun.

▶ In 1965, Lyndon Johnson increased the number of troops in Vietnam.~~/, A~~ *a*

former French colony in southeast Asia.

6. Watching for fragments that consist of lists

Usually, you can connect a list to the preceding sentence using a colon. If you want to emphasize the list, consider using a dash instead.

▶ In the 1930s, three great band leaders helped popularize jazz.~~/: Louis~~

Armstrong, Benny Goodman, and Duke Ellington.

7. Watching for fragments that are parts of compound predicates

A **compound predicate** is made up of at least two verbs as well as their objects and modifiers, connected by a coordinating conjunction such as *and, but,* or *or.* The parts of a compound predicate have the same subject and should be together in one sentence.

▶ The group gathered at dawn at the base of the mountain.~~/ And~~ *and* assembled

their gear in preparation for the morning's climb.

51d Connect fragments that begin with a subordinating word (*although, because, since*) to another sentence, or eliminate the subordinating word.

Fragments often begin with a subordinating word such as *although, because, even though, since, so that, whenever,* or *whereas.* Usually, a fragment that begins with a subordinating word can be attached to a nearby independent clause.

► On the questionnaire, none of the thirty-three subjects indicated any

concern about the amount or kind of fruit the institution served/, ~~Even~~ *even*

though all of them identified diet as an important issue for those with

diabetes.

> ***Punctuation tip:*** A comma usually follows a dependent clause that begins a sentence. If the clause appears at the end of a sentence, it is usually not preceded by a comma unless it is a contrasting thought, as in the example above. (*See Tab 11: Editing for Correctness, p. 513.*)

It is sometimes better to transform such a fragment into a complete sentence by deleting the subordinating word.

► The solidarity of our group was undermined in two ways. ~~When~~

Participants
~~participants~~ either disagreed about priorities or advocated significantly

different political strategies.

For MULTILINGUAL STUDENTS

Adding a Subject Pronoun to a Dependent Clause

In English, a dependent clause needs a subject, even if it repeats the subject of the main clause. *The tire lost air because was punctured* should be changed to *The tire lost air because it was punctured.* In a dependent clause that begins with a relative pronoun, however, the pronoun *is* the subject. For example, *that* is the subject of the dependent clause in this sentence: *We replaced the tire that was punctured.*

52 Comma Splices and Run-on Sentences

Comma splices and run-on sentences are sentences with improperly joined independent clauses. While used in advertising and literature, they are not appropriate for college writing. Recall that an independent clause has a subject and a complete verb and can stand on its own as a sentence. (*See page 447.*)

✓ **52a** Learn how to identify comma splices and run-on sentences.

www.mhhe.com/
awr3
For information and
exercises on comma
splices, go to
Editing >
Comma Splices

A **comma splice** is a sentence with two independent clauses joined by only a comma.

COMMA SPLICE Dogs that compete in the annual Westminster Dog Show are already champions, they have each won at least one dog show before arriving at Madison Square Garden.

A **run-on sentence,** sometimes called a **fused sentence,** does not have even a comma between the independent clauses.

RUN-ON Sometimes new breeds enter the ring the Border Collie is a recent addition to the show.

Writers may mistakenly join two independent clauses with only a comma or create a run-on sentence in three situations:

- When a transitional expression like *as a result* or *for example* or a conjunctive adverb like *however* links the second clause to the first. (*A list of conjunctive adverbs and transitional expressions appears on p. 457.*)

COMMA SPLICE Rare books can be extremely valuable, *for example,* an original edition of Audubon's *Birds of America* is worth over a million dollars.

RUN-ON Most students complied with the new policy *however* a few refused to do so.

- When the second clause specifies or explains the first.

RUN-ON The economy changed in 1991 corporate bankruptcies increased by 40 percent.

- When the second clause begins with a pronoun.

COMMA SPLICE President Garfield was assassinated, he served only six months in office.

453

IDENTIFY AND EDIT
Comma Splices and Run-ons

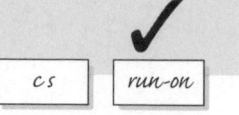

These questions can help you spot comma splices and run-on sentences:

? 1. Does the sentence contain only one independent clause?

No   **Yes →Not a run-on or comma splice**
↓

? 2. Does it contain two independent clauses joined by a comma and a coordinating conjunction (and, but, or, not, for, so, or yet)?

No   **Yes →Not a run-on or comma splice**
↓

? 3. Does it contain two independent clauses joined by a semicolon, a semicolon and a transitional expression, a colon, or a dash?

No   **Yes →Not a run-on or comma splice**
↓

RUN-ON	├──────── independent clause ────────┤ Football and most other team sports have a time limit ├── independent clause ──┤ baseball has no time limit.
COMMA SPLICE	Football and most other team sports have a time limit, baseball has no time limit.
REVISED: COMMA AND COORDINATING CONJUNCTION	Football and most other team sports have a time limit, but baseball has no time limit. [See 52c.]
REVISED: SEMICOLON	Football and most other team sports have a time limit; baseball has no time limit. [See 52d.]
REVISED: TWO SENTENCES	Football and most other team sports have a time limit. Baseball has no time limit. [See 52e.]
REVISED: SUBORDINATION	Although football and most other team sports have a time limit, baseball has no time limit. [See 52f.]
REVISED: ONE INDEPENDENT CLAUSE	Baseball, unlike football and most other team sports, has no time limit. [See 52g.]

1. Checking for transitional expressions and conjunctive adverbs

Check those sentences that include transitional expressions or conjunctive adverbs like *however* (*see p. 457*). If a comma precedes one of these words or phrases, you may have found a comma splice. If no punctuation precedes one of them, you may have found a run-on sentence. Can the word groups that precede and follow the conjunctive adverb or transitional expression both stand alone as sentences? If so, you have found a comma splice or a run-on sentence.

2. Reviewing sentences with commas

Check sentences that contain commas. Can the word groups that appear on both sides of the comma stand alone as sentences? If so, you have found a comma splice.

Comma Splices, Run-on Sentences, and Grammar Checkers

Computer grammar checkers are unreliable at distinguishing properly from improperly joined independent clauses. One grammar checker, for example, correctly flagged this sentence for incorrect comma usage: *Many history textbooks are clear, some are hard to follow.* It failed, however, to flag this longer alternative: *Many history textbooks are clear and easy to read, some are dense and hard to follow.*

52b Learn five ways to edit comma splices and run-on sentences.

www.mhhe.com/
awr3
For information and
exercises on run on
sentences, go to
Editing > Fused
Sentences

- Join the two clauses with a comma and a coordinating conjunction (*and, but, or, nor, for, so, yet*) (*52c, p. 456*).

  ▶ Dogs that compete in the annual Westminster Dog Show are

  for
  already champions, they have each won at least one dog show
       ^

  before arriving at Madison Square Garden.

- Join the two clauses with a semicolon (*52d, p. 456*).

  ▶ Sometimes new breeds enter the ring; the Border Collie is
                                      ^

  a recent addition to the show.

You can also add an appropriate conjunctive adverb or transitional expression, followed by a comma.

> ► Sometimes new breeds enter the ring *; for instance,* the Border Collie is
>
> a recent addition to the show.

- Separate the clauses into two sentences (*52e, p. 458*).

> ► Salt air corrodes metal easily *. Therefore,* ~~therefore~~ automobiles in coastal
>
> regions require frequent washing.

- Turn one of the independent clauses into a dependent clause (*52f, p. 458*). *For more on dependent clauses, see page 597.*

> ► Treasure hunters shopping in thrift stores and at garage sales
>
> should be realistic/ *because* valuable finds are extremely rare.

- Transform the two clauses into a single independent clause (*52g, p. 458*).

> ► The best history books are clear/ *and* ~~they also~~ tell a compelling story.

52c Join the two clauses with a comma and a coordinating conjunction such as *and, but, or, nor, for, so,* or *yet.*

If you decide to correct a comma splice or run-on by joining the two clauses, make sure the two ideas are equally important. Choose the coordinating conjunction that most clearly expresses the logical relationship between the clauses. A comma *must* precede the conjunction, or the sentence remains a run-on.

> ► John is a very stubborn person, *so* I had a hard time convincing him to let me
>
> take the wheel.

> ► My mother teaches at Central State *, but* I go to Eastern Tech.

52d Join the two clauses with a semicolon (or a colon or dash).

A semicolon tells readers that two closely related clauses are logically connected. However, a semicolon does not spell out the logic of the connection.

▶ Most students complied with the new policy/; a few refused to do so.
    ^

To show the logic of the connection, you can add a conjunctive adverb or transitional expression.

                                                    ; however,
▶ Most students complied with the new policy/ a few refused to do so.
    ^

Note: The conjunctive adverb or transitional expression is usually followed by a comma when it appears at the beginning of the second clause (as above). It can also appear in the middle of a clause, set off by two commas, or at the end, preceded by a comma.

                                                    , however,
▶ Most students complied with the new policy/; a few refused to do so.
    ^   ^

▶ Most students complied with the new policy/; a few refused to
    ^

    , however
    do so.
    ^

CONJUNCTIVE ADVERBS and TRANSITIONAL EXPRESSIONS

also	incidentally	now
as a result	indeed	nonetheless
besides	in fact	of course
certainly	in other words	on the contrary
consequently	instead	otherwise
finally	in the meantime	similarly
for example	likewise	still
for instance	meanwhile	then
furthermore	moreover	therefore
however	nevertheless	thus
in addition	next	undoubtedly

When the first independent clause introduces the second one, use a colon instead of a semicolon. A colon is also appropriate if the second clause expands on the first one in some way or introduces a quote. (*See Tab 11: Editing for Correctness, pp. 518–20.*) A dash may be appropriate for informal writing situations to highlight a list, explanation, or shift in tone. (*See Tab 11: Editing for Correctness, pp. 533–34.*)

▶ Professor Johnson then revealed his most important point: the paper
                                                              ^

    would count for half my grade.

52e Separate the clauses into two sentences.

The simplest way to correct comma splices and run-on sentences is to turn the clauses into separate sentences. The simplest solution is not always the best solution, however, especially if the result is one short, simple sentence followed by another. The simplest solution works well in this example because the second sentence is a compound sentence.

▶ I realized that it was time to choose,/ ~~either~~ *. Either* I had to learn how to drive, or I

had to move back to the city.

When the two independent clauses are part of a quotation, with a phrase such as *he said* or *she noted* between them, each clause should be a separate sentence.

▶ "This was the longest day of my life," she said,/. ~~"unfortunately,~~ *"Unfortunately,* it's not

over yet."

52f Turn one of the independent clauses into a dependent clause.

In editing the following sentence, the writer chose to make the clause about *a few* her main point and the clause about *most* a subordinate idea. Readers will expect subsequent sentences to tell them more about the subject of the main clause.

▶ *Although most* ~~Most~~ students complied with the new policy, ~~however~~ a few refused

to do so.

52g Transform the two clauses into one independent clause.

It is seldom easy, but transforming two clauses into one clear and correct independent clause is often worth the work.

▶ I realized that it was time ~~to choose, either I~~ had to learn how to drive or

~~I had~~ to move back to the city.

Sometimes you can change one of the clauses to a phrase and place it next to the word it modifies.

▶ Baseball cards are an obsession among some collectors,/. ~~the cards were~~ , *first printed in the nineteenth century,*

~~first printed in the nineteenth century.~~

53 Subject-Verb Agreement

All verbs must agree with their subjects in person (first, second, or third—*I, we; you; he, she, it, they*) and number (singular or plural).

✓ **53a** Learn the standard subject-verb combinations.

www.mhhe.com/
awr3

For information and exercises on subject-verb agreement, go to

Editing >
Subject-Verb
Agreement

For regular verbs, the present tense *-s* or *-es* ending is added to the verb if its subject is third-person singular; otherwise, the verb has no ending. Most verbs have one past-tense form, Note, however, that the verb *be* has irregular forms in both the present and the past tense. The irregular verbs *be, have,* and *do* have the following forms in the present and past tenses.

Verb Tenses (Present and *Past*)

	READ (REGULAR)	BE	HAS	DO
SINGULAR				
First person (I)	read (*read*)	am (*was*)	have (*had*)	do/don't (*did/didn't*)
Second person (you)	read (*read*)	are (*were*)	have (*had*)	do/don't (*did/didn't*)
Third person (he, she, it)	reads (*reads*)	is (*was*)	has (*had*)	does/doesn't (*did/didn't*)
PLURAL				
First person (we)	read (*read*)	am (*were*)	have (*had*)	do/don't (*did/didn't*)
Second person (you)	read (*read*)	are (*were*)	have (*had*)	do/don't (*did/didn't*)
Third person (they)	read (*read*)	are (*were*)	have (*had*)	do/don't (*did/didn't*)

Problems with subject-verb agreement tend to occur when writers do the following:

- Lose sight of the subject (*53b, p. 460*)
- Use compound, collective, or indefinite subjects (*53c–e, pp. 462–65*)
- Have a subject that follows the verb (*53f, p. 465*)
- Confuse a subject complement with the subject (*53g, p. 465*)
- Use a relative pronoun as the subject of a dependent clause (*53h, pp. 465–66*)
- Use a phrase beginning with an *-ing* verb or infinitive (*to* followed by the base form of the verb) as the subject (*53i, p. 466*)
- Use titles, company names, or words considered by themselves (*53j, p. 466*)

53b Do not lose sight of the subject when a word group separates it from the verb.

To locate the subject of a sentence, find the verb, and then ask the *who* or *what* question about it ("Who is?" "What is?"). Does that subject match the verb in number?

► The leaders of the trade union ~~opposes~~ *oppose* the new law.

The answer to the question "Who opposes?" is *leaders,* a plural noun, so the verb should be in the plural form: *oppose.*

Note: If a word group beginning with *as well as, along with,* or *in addition to* follows a singular subject, the subject does not become plural.

► My teacher, as well as other faculty members, ~~oppose~~ *opposes* the new

school policy.

Subject-Verb Agreement and Grammar Checkers

A grammar checker failed to flag this sentence for correction: *The candidate's position on foreign policy issues trouble some voters.* The subject is the singular noun *position,* so the verb should be *troubles.* Apparently, however, the grammar checker interpreted the word *issues* as the subject.

IDENTIFY AND EDIT
Subject-Verb Agreement

agr

✱ 1. Find the verb.

> verb
> PROBLEM SENTENCE Hamlet and Claudius *brings* down the Danish royal family.
>
> Verbs are words that specify action, condition, or state of being.

✱ 2. Ask the who or what question to identify the subject.

> |—— subject ——| |–verb–|
> PROBLEM SENTENCE *Hamlet and Claudius brings* down the Danish royal family.
>
> The answer to the question "What brings" is *Hamlet and Claudius*.

✱ 3. Determine the person (first, second, or third) and number (singular or plural) of the subject.

> |—— subject ——|
> PROBLEM SENTENCE *Hamlet and Claudius* brings down the Danish royal family.
>
> The subject of the sentence—*Hamlet and Claudius*—is a compound joined by *and* and is third-person plural.

✱ 4. If necessary, change the verb to agree with the subject.

> bring
> EDITED PROBLEM SENTENCE Hamlet and Claudius ~~brings~~ down the Danish royal family.
> ^
>
> *Bring* is the third-person plural form of the verb.

53c Treat most compound subjects—subjects connected by *and, or, nor, both . . . and, either . . . or,* or *neither . . . nor*—as plural.

Compound subjects are made up of two or more parts joined by either a coordinating conjunction (*and, or, nor*) or a correlative conjunction (*both . . . and, either . . . or, neither . . . nor*).

1. Treating most compound subjects as plural

Most subjects that are joined by *and* should be treated as plural.

► *The king and his advisers were* shocked by this turn of events.

► This poem's *first line and last word have* a powerful effect on the reader.

2. Treating some compound subjects as singular

There are exceptions to the rule that subjects joined by *and* are plural.

- The two subjects refer to the same entity.

  ► *My best girlfriend and most dependable advisor is* my mother.

- The two subjects are considered as a single unit.

  ► *Forty acres and a mule continues* to be what is needed.

- The two subjects are preceded by the word *each* or *every*.

  ► *Each* man, woman, and child *deserves* respect.

3. Treating some compound subjects as either plural or singular

Compound subjects connected by *or, nor, either . . . or,* or *neither . . . nor* can take either a singular or a plural verb, depending on the subject that is closest to the verb.

SINGULAR   Either the children or *their mother is* to blame.

PLURAL   Neither the experimenter nor *her subjects were* aware of

the takeover.

Sentences often sound less awkward with the plural subject closer to the verb.

53d Treat most collective subjects—subjects like *audience, family,* and *committee*—as singular.

A **collective noun** names a unit made up of many persons or things, treating it as an entity. Other examples are *group* and *team.*

1. Treating most collective nouns as singular *News, athletics, physics, statistics,* and other words like these are usually singular as well, despite their *-s* endings, because they function as collective subjects. (When a word like *statistics* refers to a collection of items, it is plural: *The statistics on car accidents worry me.*) Units of measurement used collectively, such as *six inches* or *20%,* are also singular.

► The *audience is* restless.

► That *news leaves* me speechless.

► *One-fourth* of the liquid *was* poured into test tube 1.

2. Treating some collective subjects as plural

When the members of a group are acting as individuals, the collective subject can be considered plural.

► The *group were* passing around a bottle of beer.

You may want to add a modifying phrase that contains a plural noun to make the sentence clearer and avoid awkwardness.

► The *group of troublemakers were* passing around a bottle of beer.

The modifying phrase *of troublemakers* makes the sentence less awkward.

When units of measurement refer to people or things, they are plural.

► *One-fourth* of the students in the class *are* failing the course.

3. Distinguishing between *a number* and *the number*

A number takes a plural verb while *the number* takes a singular verb.

► *A number* of shoppers *prefer* Brand X.

► *The number* of people who shop online *is* growing.

53e Treat most indefinite subjects—subjects like *everybody, no one, each, all,* and *none*—as singular.

Indefinite pronouns such as *everybody* and *no one* do not refer to a specific person or item.

1. Recognizing that most indefinite pronouns are singular

The following indefinite pronouns are always singular: *anybody, anyone, anything, each, either, everybody, everyone, everything, neither, nobody, none, no one, nothing, one, somebody, someone,* and *something.*

▶ *Everyone* in my hiking club *is* an experienced climber.

None and *neither* are singular when they appear by themselves.

▶ In the movie, five men set out on an expedition, but *none returns.*

▶ *Neither sees* a way out of this predicament.

If a prepositional phrase that includes a plural noun or pronoun follows *none* or *neither,* the indefinite pronoun seems to have a plural meaning. Although some writers treat *none* or *neither* as plural in such situations, others maintain that these two pronouns are always singular. It is a safe bet to consider them singular.

▶ In the movie, five men set out on an expedition, but *none* of them *returns.*

▶ *Neither* of the hikers *sees* a way out of this cave.

2. Recognizing that some indefinite pronouns are always plural

A handful of indefinite pronouns (*both, few, many, several*) are always plural because they mean more than one by definition. *Both,* for example, always indicates two.

▶ *Both* of us *want* to go to the rally for the environment.

▶ *Several* of my friends *were* very happy about the outcome of the election.

3. Recognizing that some indefinite pronouns can be either plural or singular

Some indefinite pronouns (*some, any, all, most*) may be either plural or singular, depending on whether they refer to a plural or singular noun in the context of the sentence.

▶ *Some* of the *book is* missing, but *all* of the *papers are* here.

4. Treating phrases beginning with question words as singular or revising to avoid awkwardness

► *How you do on the exam counts* for half your grade.

AWKWARD	*What we need is* new clothes.
BETTER	*We need* new clothes.

53f Make sure the subject and verb agree when the subject comes after the verb.

In most English sentences, the verb comes after the subject. Sometimes, however, a writer will switch this order. In the following sentence, you can locate the subject by asking, "Who or what stand?" The answer is the sentence's subject: *an oak and a weeping willow.* Because the subject is a compound subject (two subjects joined by *and*), the verb must be plural.

► Out back behind the lean-to *stand an old oak tree and a weeping willow.*

In sentences that begin with *there is* or *there are,* the subject always follows the verb.

► There *is* a worn wooden *bench* in the shade of the two trees.

In questions, the helping verb agrees with the subject.

► *Do you* understand her?

53g Make sure the verb agrees with its subject, not the subject complement.

A **subject complement** renames and specifies the sentence's subject. It follows a **linking verb**—a verb, often a form of *be,* that joins the subject to its description or definition: *children are innocent.* In the following sentence, the singular noun *gift* is the subject. *Books* is the subject complement. Therefore, *are* has been changed to *is* to agree in number with *gift.*

► One gift that gives her pleasure ~~are~~ *is* books.

53h *Who, which,* and *that* (relative pronouns) take verbs that agree with the subject they replace.

When a relative pronoun such as *who, which,* or *that* is the subject of a dependent clause, it is taking the place of a noun that appears earlier in the sentence—its **antecedent.** The verb that goes with *who, which,* or *that* needs to agree with this antecedent. In the following sentence, the relative pronoun *that* is the subject of the dependent clause *that has dangerous side effects. Disease,* a singular noun, is the antecedent of *that;* therefore, the verb in the dependent clause is singular.

► Measles is a childhood *disease that has* dangerous side effects.

The phrase *one of the* implies more than one and so is plural. *Only one of the* implies just one, however, and is singular. Generally, use the plural form of the verb when the phrase *one of the* comes before the antecedent. Use the singular form of the verb when *only one of the* comes before the plural noun.

PLURAL   Tuberculosis is *one of the* diseases *that have* long, tragic histories in many parts of the world.

SINGULAR   Barbara is the *only one of the* scientists *who has* a degree in physics.

53i Phrases beginning with *-ing* verbs or infinitives take the singular form of the verb when they are subjects.

A **gerund phrase** is an *-ing* verb form followed by objects, complements, or modifiers. When a gerund phrase is the subject in a sentence, it is singular.

► *Experimenting with drugs is* a dangerous practice.

Infinitive phrases (*see Tab 12: Basic Grammar Review, p. 597*) are singular subjects.

► *To win medals is* every competitor's dream.

53j Titles, company names, and words considered as words are singular.

► The Two Gentlemen of Verona ~~are~~ *is* considered the weakest of

Shakespeare's comedies.

► The McGraw-Hill Companies ~~include~~ *includes* many different divisions.

► In today's highly partisan politics, *moderates* ~~have~~ *has* come to mean

"wishy-washy people."

54 Problems with Verbs

Verbs report action and show time. They change form to indicate person, number, voice, and mood.

www.mhhe.com/
awr3

For information and exercises on verbs, go to

Editing > Verbs and Verbals

54a Learn the principal forms of regular and irregular verbs.

All English verbs have five main forms, except for the *be* verb, which has eight. (*For examples, see p. 459 and pp. 566–67.*)

- The **base form** is the form you find if you look up the verb in a dictionary. (*For irregular verbs, other forms are given as well. See p. 468 for a list.*)

- The **present tense** form is used to indicate an action occurring at the moment, habitually, or at a set future time, as well as to introduce quotations, literary events, and scientific facts (*54f, pp. 471–74, and 54h, p. 475*). The third-person singular present tense is the *-s* form.

- The **past tense** is used to indicate an action completed at a specific time in the past (*54f, pp. 471–74*).

- The **past participle** is used with *have, has,* or *had* to form the perfect tenses (*54f, pp. 471–74*); with a form of the *be* verb to form the passive voice; and as an adjective (the *polished* silver).

- The **present participle** is used with a form of the *be* verb to form the progressive tenses (*54f, pp. 471–74*). It can also be used as a noun (the *writing* is finished) and as an adjective (the *smiling* man).

1. Learning about common irregular verbs

Regular verbs always add *-d* or *-ed* to the base verb to form the past tense and past participle. **Irregular verbs,** in contrast, do not form the past tense or past participle in a consistent way. The box on page 468 lists the principal forms of common irregular verbs, which you can find in the dictionary.

2. Using the correct forms of irregular verbs that end in *-en*

The forms of irregular verbs with past tenses that end in *-e* and past participles that end in *-n* or *-en,* such as *ate / eaten* and *rode / ridden,* are sometimes confused.

▶ He had ~~ate~~ the apple.
eaten

▶ They had ~~rode~~ the whole way on the bus.
ridden

467

COMMON IRREGULAR VERBS

Base	Past tense	Past participle	Base	Past tense	Past participle
awake	awoke	awoke/ awakened	hang	hanged	hanged (for people)
arise	arose	arisen	have	had	had
be	was/were	been	hear	heard	heard
beat	beat	beaten	know	knew	known
become	became	become	lose	lost	lost
begin	began	begun	pay	paid	paid
blow	blew	blown	raise	raised	raised
break	broke	broken	ride	rode	ridden
bring	brought	brought	ring	rang	rung
buy	bought	bought	rise	rose	risen
catch	caught	caught	say	said	said
choose	chose	chosen	see	saw	seen
cling	clung	clung	set	set	set
come	came	come	shake	shook	shaken
do	did	done	sit	sat	sat
draw	drew	drawn	spin	spun	spun
drink	drank	drunk	steal	stole	stolen
drive	drove	driven	spend	spent	spent
eat	ate	eaten	strive	strove/ strived	striven/ strived
fall	fell	fallen			
fight	fought	fought	swear	swore	sworn
fly	flew	flown	swim	swam	swum
forget	forgot	forgotten/ forgot	swing	swung	swung
			take	took	taken
forgive	forgave	forgiven	tear	tore	torn
freeze	froze	frozen	tread	trod	trod/ trodden
get	got	gotten/got			
give	gave	given	wear	wore	worn
go	went	gone	weave	wove	woven
grow	grew	grown	wring	wrung	wrung
hang	hung	hung (for things)	write	wrote	written

3. Using the correct forms of *went* and *gone*, and *saw* and *seen*

Went and *saw* are the past tense forms of the irregular verbs *go* and *see*. *Gone* and *seen* are the past participle forms.

> ▶ I had ~~went~~ **gone** there yesterday.

> ▶ We ~~seen~~ **saw** the rabid dog and called for help.

For MULTILINGUAL STUDENTS

Nonstandard Irregular Verb Forms

In many dialects of English, the forms of some irregular verbs vary from those of standard English. In academic writing, however, always use the standard forms. When in doubt, consult the list of irregular verbs on the opposite page.

▶ The neighborhood gardeners ~~growed~~ *grew* their own vegetables in the

empty lot.

▶ The Sistine Chapel frescos ~~be~~ *were* cleaned in the 1980s.

▶ Achilles ~~drug~~ *dragged* Hector's body three times around the walls of Troy.

54b Distinguish between *lay* and *lie, rise* and *raise,* and *sit* and *set.*

Even experienced writers confuse the verbs *lay* and *lie, rise* and *raise,* and *sit* and *set.* The correct forms are given below.

Often-Confused Verbs and Their Principal Forms

BASE	-S FORM	PAST	PAST PARTICIPLE	PRESENT PARTICIPLE
lay (to place)	lays	laid	laid	laying
lie (to recline)	lies	lay	lain	lying
lie (to speak an untruth)	lies	lied	lied	lying
rise (to go/get up)	rises	rose	risen	rising
raise (to lift up)	raises	raised	raised	raising
sit (to be seated)	sits	sat	sat	sitting
set (to put on a surface)	sets	sat	set	setting

One verb in each of these groups (*lay, raise, set*) is **transitive:** an object receives the action of the verb. The other verbs (*lie, rise, sit*) are **intransitive** and cannot take an object. You should use a form of *lay, raise,* or *set,* if you can replace the verb with *place* or *put.* (*See Tab 12: Basic Grammar Review, pp. 593–95 for more on transitive and intransitive verbs.*)

direct object
► The dog *lays a bone* at your feet, then *lies* down and closes his eyes.

direct object
► As the flames *rise,* the heat *raises the temperature* of the room.

direct object
► The technician *sits* down and *sets the samples* in front of her.

Lay (to place) and *lie* (to recline) are also confusing because the past tense of the irregular verb *lie* is *lay* (*lie, lay, lain*). Always double-check the verb *lay* when it appears in your writing.

laid
► He washed the dishes carefully, then lay them on a clean towel.

54c Add an -s or -es ending when necessary.

In the present tense, almost all verbs add an *-s* or *-es* ending if the subject is third-person singular. (*See p. 459 for more on standard subject-verb combinations.*) Third-person singular subjects can be nouns (*woman, Benjamin, desk*), pronouns (*he, she, it*), or indefinite pronouns (*everyone*).

rises
► The stock market rise when economic news is good.

If the subject is in the first person (*I*), the second person (*you*), or the third-person plural (*people, they*), the verb does *not* add an *-s* or *-es* ending.

► You invests your money wisely.

► People needs to invest wisely.

54d Add a -d or an -ed ending when necessary.

When speaking, people sometimes leave the *-d* or *-ed* ending off certain verbs such as *asked, fixed, mixed, supposed to,* and *used to.* However, in writing, the endings should be included on all regular verbs in the past tense and all past participles of regular verbs.

asked
► The driving instructor ask the student driver to pull over to the curb.

mixed
► After we had mix the formula, we let it cool.

Also check for missing *-d* or *-ed* endings on past participles used as adjectives.

concerned
► The concern parents met with the school board.

> ## Verb Forms and Grammar and Spelling Checkers
>
> A grammar checker flagged the incorrect form in this sentence: *She had chose to go to the state college.* It also suggested the correct form: *chosen.* However, the checker missed the misuse of *set* in this sentence: *I am going to set down for a while.*
>
> Spelling checkers will not highlight a verb form that is used incorrectly in a sentence.

54e Make sure your verbs are complete.

A **complete verb** consists of the main verb and any helping verbs that are needed to express the tense (*see pp. 471–74*) or voice (*see p. 570*). **Helping verbs** include forms of *be, have,* and *do* and the modal verbs *can, could, may, might, shall, should, will, ought to, must* and *would.* (*For more on modals, see Tab 12: Basic Grammar Review, p. 570.*) Helping verbs can be part of contractions (*He's running, we'd better go*), but they cannot be left out of the sentence entirely.

►   *will*
► They be going on a field trip next week.

Do not use *of* in place of *have.*

►   *have*
► I could of finished earlier.

A **linking verb,** often a form of *be,* connects the subject to a description or definition of it: *Cats <u>are</u> mammals.* Linking verbs can be part of contractions (*She's a student*), but they should not be left out entirely.

►   *is*
► Montreal a major Canadian city.

54f Use verb tenses accurately.

Tenses show the time of a verb's action. English has three basic time frames—present, past, and future—and each tense has simple, perfect, progressive, and perfect progressive verb forms to indicate the time span of the actions that are taking place. (*For a review of the present tense forms of a typical verb and of the verbs* be, have, *and* do, *see 53a, p. 459; for a review of the principal forms of regular and irregular verbs, which are used to form tenses, see 54a, pp. 467–69.*)

1. The simple present and past tenses These two tenses do not use a helping verb or verbs. The **simple present tense** is used for actions occurring at the moment, habitually, or at a set future time.

The **simple past tense** is used for actions completed at a specific time in the past.

SIMPLE PRESENT

Every May, she *plans* next year's marketing strategy.

SIMPLE PAST

In the early morning hours before the office opened, she *planned* her marketing strategy.

2. The simple future tense

The **simple future tense** takes *will* plus the verb. It is used for actions that have not yet begun.

SIMPLE FUTURE

In May, I *will plan* next year's marketing strategy.

3. Perfect tenses

The **perfect tenses** take a form of *have* (*has, had*) plus the past participle. They are used to indicate actions that were or will be completed by the time of another action or a specific time. The present perfect also describes actions that continue into the present. (*For more on the past participle, see p. 467.*)

PRESENT PERFECT

She *has* already *planned* next year's marketing strategy. She *has planned* the marketing strategy for the past five years.

PAST PERFECT

By the time she resigned, Mary *had* already *planned* next year's marketing strategy.

FUTURE PERFECT

By May 31, she *will have planned* next year's marketing strategy.

When the verb in the past perfect is irregular, be sure to use the proper form of the past participle.

► By the time the week was over, both plants had g̶r̶e̶w̶ *grown* five inches.

4. Progressive tenses

The **progressive tenses** take a form of *be* (*am, are, was, were*) plus the present participle. The progressive forms of the simple and perfect tenses are used to indicate ongoing action.

PRESENT PROGRESSIVE

She *is planning* next year's marketing strategy now.

PAST PROGRESSIVE

She *was planning* next year's marketing strategy when she started to look for another job.

References to planned events that didn't happen take *was / were going to* plus the base form.

She *was going to plan* the marketing strategy, but she left the company.

FUTURE PROGRESSIVE

During the month of May, she *will be planning* next year's marketing strategy.

For MULTILINGUAL STUDENTS

When Not to Use the Progressive Tenses

Some verbs are not usually used in the progressive tenses, even when they relate to a continuous state or action. Typically, these verbs are about thoughts, preferences, and ownership.

► I ~~was understanding~~ *understood* the lecture until the last ten minutes.

► The manager ~~is wanting~~ *wants* the report by the end of the day.

► They ~~are owning~~ *own* the house they are renovating.

5. Perfect progressive tenses The **perfect progressive tenses** take *have* plus *be* plus the verb. These tenses indicate an action that takes place over a specific period of time. The present perfect progressive tense is used for actions that start in the past and continue to the present; the past and future perfect progressive tenses are used for actions that ended or will end at a specified time or before another action.

PRESENT PERFECT PROGRESSIVE

She *has been planning* next year's marketing strategy since the beginning of May.

PAST PERFECT PROGRESSIVE

She *had been planning* next year's marketing strategy when she was offered another job.

FUTURE PERFECT PROGRESSIVE

By May 18, she *will have been planning* next year's marketing strategy for more than two weeks.

54g Use the past perfect tense to indicate an action completed at a specific time or before another event.

When a past event was ongoing but ended before a particular time or another past event, use the past perfect rather than the simple past.

▶ Before the Johnstown Flood occurred in 1889, people in the

had
area expressed their concern about the safety of the dam on the
^

Conemaugh River.

People expressed their concern before the flood occurred.

If two past events happened simultaneously, however, use the simple past, not the past perfect.

▶ When the Conemaugh flooded, many people in the area ~~had~~ lost

their lives.

CHARTING the TERRITORY

Reporting Research Findings

Although a written work may be seen as always present, research findings are thought of as having been collected at one time in the past. Use the past or present perfect tense to report the results of research:

responded
▶ Three of the compounds (nos. 2, 3, and 6) ~~respond~~ positively by
^

turning purple.

has reviewed
▶ Clegg (1990) ~~reviews~~ studies of workplace organization focused on
^

struggles for control of the labor process.

Do not use *would have* in *if* (conditional) clauses.

► If the students ~~would have~~ *had* come to class, they would have known

the material.

54h Use the present tense for literary events, scientific facts, and introductions to quotations.

If the conventions of a discipline require you to state what your paper does, do so in the present, not the future, tense.

► In this paper, I *describe* the effects of increasing NaCl concentrations on the germination of radish seeds.

Here are some other special uses of the present tense:

- By convention, events in a novel, short story, poem, or other literary work are described in the present tense.

  ► Even though Huck's journey down the river ~~was~~ *is* an escape from

  society, his relationship with Jim ~~was~~ *is* a form of community.

- Like events in a literary work, scientific facts are considered to be perpetually present, even though they were discovered in the past. (Theories proven false should appear in the past tense.)

  ► Mendel discovered that genes ~~had~~ *have* different forms, or alleles.

- The present tense is also used to introduce a quotation, paraphrase, or summary of someone else's writing.

  ► William Julius Wilson ~~wrote~~ *writes* that "the disappearance of work has

  become a characteristic feature of the inner-city ghetto" (31).

Note: When using APA style, introduce others' writing or research findings with the past tense (for example, Wilson *wrote*) or past perfect tense (Johnson *has found*).

54i Make sure infinitives and participles fit with the tense of the main verb.

Infinitives and participles are **verbals**—words formed from verbs that have various functions within a sentence. Verbals can form phrases by taking objects, modifiers, or complements. Because they express time, verbals need to fit with the main verb in a sentence.

1. Using the correct tense for infinitives

An **infinitive** has the word *to* plus the base verb (*to breathe, to sing, to dance*). The perfect form of the infinitive is *to have* plus the past participle (*to have breathed, to have sung, to have danced*). If the action of the infinitive happens at the same time as or after the action of the main verb, use the present tense.

▶ I hope *to sing and dance* on Broadway next summer.

If the action of the infinitive happened before the action of the main verb, use the perfect form.

▶ My talented mother would like *to have sung and danced* on Broadway as a young woman, but she never had the chance.

2. Using the correct tense for participles that are part of phrases

Participial phrases can begin with the present participle (*breathing, dancing, singing*), the present perfect participle (*having breathed, having danced, having sung*), or the past participle (*breathed, danced, sung*). If the action of the participle happens simultaneously with the action of the sentence's verb, use the present participle.

▶ *Singing one hour a day together,* the chorus developed perfect harmony.

If the action of the participle happened before the action of the main verb, use the present perfect or past participle form.

▶ *Having breathed* the air of New York, I exulted in the possibilities for my life in the city.

▶ *Tinted* with a strange green light, the western sky looked threatening.

54j Use the subjunctive mood for wishes, requests, and conjecture.

The **mood** of a verb indicates the writer's attitude. Use the **indicative mood** to state or question facts, acts, and opinions (*Our collection is on display. Did you see it?*). Use the **imperative mood** for commands, directions, and entreaties. The subject of an imperative sentence is always *you,* but the *you* is usually understood, not written out (*Shut the door!*). Use the **subjunctive mood** to express a wish or a demand or to make a statement contrary to fact (*I wish I were a millionaire*). The mood that writers have the most trouble with is the subjunctive.

Verbs in the subjunctive mood may be in the present tense, past tense, or perfect tense. Present tense subjunctive verbs do not change form to signal person or number. The only form used is the verb's base form: *accompany* or *be,* not *accompanies* or *am, are, is.* Also, the verb *be* has only one past tense form in the subjunctive mood: *were.*

1. Using the subjunctive mood to express a wish

WISH

I wish I *were* more prepared for this test.

> *Note:* In everyday conversation, most speakers use the indicative rather than the subjunctive when expressing wishes (*I wish I was more prepared for this test*).

2. Using the subjunctive mood for requests, recommendations, and demands

Because requests, recommendations, and demands have not yet happened, they—like wishes—are expressed in the subjunctive mood. Words such as *ask, insist, recommend, request,* and *suggest* indicate the subjunctive mood; the verb in the *that* clause that follows should be in the subjunctive.

DEMAND

I insist that all applicants *find* their seats by 8:00 a.m.

3. Using the subjunctive in statements that are contrary to fact

Often such statements contain a subordinate clause that begins with *if:* the verb in the *if* clause should be in the subjunctive mood.

CONTRARY-TO-FACT STATEMENT

He would not be so irresponsible if his father *were* [not *was*] still alive.

> *Note:* Some common expressions of conjecture are in the subjunctive mood, including *as it were, come rain or shine, far be it from me,* and *be that as it may.*

55 Problems with Pronouns

A **pronoun** (*he* / *him, it* / *its, they* / *their*) takes the place of a noun. The noun that the pronoun replaces is called its **antecedent.** In the following sentence, *snow* is the antecedent of the pronoun *it*.

www.mhhe.com/
awr3

For information
and exercises on
pronouns, go to

Editing > Pronouns

▶ The *snow* fell all day long, and by nightfall *it* was three feet deep.

Like nouns, pronouns are singular or plural.

SINGULAR   The *house* was dark and gloomy, and *it* sat in a grove

of tall cedars.

PLURAL   The *cars* swept by on the highway, all of *them* doing

more than sixty-five miles per hour.

A pronoun needs an antecedent to refer to and agree with, and a pronoun must match its antecedent in number (*plural* / *singular*) and gender (*he* / *his, she* / *her, it* / *its*). A pronoun must also be in a form, or case, that matches its function in the sentence.

www.mhhe.com/
awr3

For information
and exercises on
pronoun-antecedent
agreement, go to

Editing > Pronoun-
Antecedent
Agreement

55a Make pronouns agree with their antecedents. ✓

Problems with pronoun-antecedent agreement tend to occur when a pronoun's antecedent is an indefinite pronoun, a collective noun, or a

For MULTILINGUAL STUDENTS

Nouns and Gender

Most English nouns are neuter in gender apart from those that specifically name females or males, such as *woman, girl, sister, mother, man, boy, brother,* and *father,* and names like *Louis* and *Anna.*

The gender of a pronoun should match its antecedent, not the word it modifies.

▶ Penelope waited twenty years for *her* [not *his*] husband Odysseus

to return from Troy.

Pronoun Problems and Grammar Checkers

Do not rely on grammar checkers to alert you to problems in pronoun-antecedent agreement or pronoun reference. Some computer grammar checkers do reliably flag many errors in pronoun case, but by no means all. One grammar checker, for example, missed the case error in the following sentence: *Ford's son Edsel, who [should be whom] the auto magnate treated very cruelly, was a brilliant automotive designer. (See p. 488 for a discussion of the proper use of who and whom.)*

compound noun. Problems may also occur when writers are trying to avoid the generic use of *he.*

1. Indefinite pronouns Indefinite pronouns such as *someone, anybody,* and *nothing* refer to nonspecific people or things. They sometimes function as antecedents for other pronouns. Most indefinite pronouns are singular (*anybody, anyone, anything, each, either, everybody, everyone, everything, much, neither, nobody, none* (meaning *not one*), *no one, nothing, one, somebody, something*).

ALWAYS SINGULAR Did *either* of the boys lose *his* bicycle?

Some writers and instructors consider *none* plural in certain circumstances (*see p. 464*), but it is safest to use it as singular.

A few indefinite pronouns—*both, few, many,* and *several*—are plural.

ALWAYS PLURAL *Both* of the boys lost *their* bicycles.

The indefinite pronouns *all, any, more, most,* and *some* can be either singular or plural, depending on the noun to which the pronoun refers.

PLURAL The students debated, *some* arguing that *their* positions on the issue were in the mainstream.

SINGULAR The bread is on the counter, but *some* of *it* has already been eaten.

Problems arise when writers attempt to make indefinite pronouns agree with their antecedents without introducing gender bias. There are three ways to avoid gender bias when correcting a pronoun agreement problem such as the following.

> **FAULTY** None of the great Romantic writers believed that their achievements equaled their aspirations.

▪ If possible, change a singular indefinite pronoun to a plural pronoun, editing the sentence as necessary.

>   *All*
> ► ~~None~~ of the great Romantic writers believed that their
>
>   *fell short of*
> achievements ~~equaled~~ their aspirations.

▪ Reword the sentence to eliminate the indefinite pronoun.

>   *The*
> ► ~~None of the~~ great Romantic writers believed that their
>
>   *did not equal*
> achievements ~~equaled~~ their aspirations.

▪ Substitute *he or she* or *his or her* (but never *his/her*) for the singular pronoun. Change the sentence as necessary to avoid using this construction more than once.

> ► None of the great Romantic writers believed that ~~their~~
>
>   *his or her*   *had been realized*
> ~~achievements equaled their~~ aspirations.

2. Generic nouns

A **generic noun** represents anyone and everyone in a group—a typical doctor, the average voter. Because most groups consist of both males and females, using male pronouns to refer to generic nouns is usually considered sexist. To fix agreement problems with generic nouns, use one of the three options suggested above.

>   *College students*   *s*
> ► ~~A college student~~ should have a mind of their own.
>
>   *an independent point of view.*
> ► A college student should have ~~a mind of their own.~~
>
>   *his or her*
> ► A college student should have a mind of ~~their~~ own.

3. Collective nouns

Collective nouns such as *team, family, jury, committee,* and *crowd* are treated as singular unless the people in the group are acting as individuals.

> ► All together, the crowd surged through the palace gates, trampling over
>
>   *its*
> everything in ~~their~~ path.

IDENTIFY AND EDIT
Pronoun-Antecedent Agreement and Gender Bias

agr

Try these three strategies for avoiding gender bias when an indefinite pronoun or generic noun is the antecedent in a sentence:

★ 1. *If possible, change the antecedent to a plural indefinite pronoun or a plural noun.*

> ◆ ~~Each~~ *All* of us should decide ~~their~~ *our* vote on issues, not personality.
>
> ◆ *Responsible citizens decide* ~~The responsible citizen decides~~ their vote on issues, not personality.

★ 2. *Reword the sentence to eliminate the pronoun.*

> ◆ Each of us should ~~decide their~~ vote on issues, not personality.
>
> ◆ The responsible citizen ~~decides their vote~~ *votes* on issues, not personality.

★ 3. *Substitute* he or she *or* his or her *(but never* his/her*) for the singular pronoun to maintain pronoun-antecedent agreement.*

> ◆ Each of us should decide ~~their~~ *his or her* vote on issues, not personality.
>
> ◆ The responsible citizen decides ~~their~~ *his or her* vote on issues, not personality.
>
> **Caution:** Use this strategy sparingly. Using *he or she* or *his or her* several times in quick succession makes for tedious reading.

The phrase *all together* indicates that this crowd is acting as a collection of individuals.

▶ **The committee left the conference room and returned to ~~its~~ *their* offices.**

In this case, the members of the committee are acting as individuals: each is returning to an office.

If you are using a collective noun that has a plural meaning, consider adding a plural noun to clarify the meaning.

▶ The *committee members* left the conference room and returned to *their* offices.

4. Compound antecedents

Compound antecedents joined by *and* are almost always plural.

▶ To remove all traces of the crime, James put the book and the

                    their
  magnifying glass back in ~~its~~ place.

When a compound antecedent is joined by *or* or *nor,* the pronoun should agree with the closest part of the compound antecedent. If one part is singular and the other is plural, the sentence will be smoother and more effective if the plural antecedent is closest to the pronoun.

    PLURAL   Neither *the child nor the parents* shared *their* food.

If the compound antecedent consists of a male and a female, however, the rule does not apply. Revise the sentence to avoid this situation.

              and   *were late for their*   *s.*
▶ ~~Neither~~ José ~~nor~~ Laura ~~could make it to her~~ appointment ~~on time.~~

When the two parts of the compound antecedent refer to the same person, or when the word *each* or *every* precedes the compound antecedent, use a singular pronoun.

    SINGULAR   Being *a teacher and a mother* keeps *her* busy.

    SINGULAR   *Every* poem and letter by Keats has *its* own special power.

www.mhhe.com/ awr3

For information and exercises on pronoun reference, go to

Editing > Pronoun Reference

55b Make pronoun references clear. ✓

If a pronoun does not clearly refer to a specific antecedent, readers can become confused. Two common problems are ambiguous references and implied references.

1. Ambiguous pronoun references

If a pronoun can refer to more than one noun in a sentence, the reference is ambiguous.

VAGUE	The friendly banter between Hamlet and Horatio eventually provokes him to declare that his world-view has changed.

To clear up the ambiguity, eliminate the pronoun and use the appropriate noun.

CLEAR	The friendly banter between Hamlet and Horatio eventually provokes Hamlet to declare that his worldview has changed.

Sometimes the ambiguous reference can be cleared up by rewriting the sentence.

VAGUE	Jane Austen and Cassandra corresponded regularly when she was in London.

CLEAR	When Jane Austen was in London, she corresponded regularly with Cassandra.

2. Implied pronoun references

The antecedent that a pronoun refers to must be present in the sentence, and it must be a noun or another pronoun, not a word that modifies a noun. Possessives and verbs cannot be antecedents in college writing, although this usage is common in speech and informal contexts.

▶ In Wilson's essay "When Work Disappears," he proposes a four-point plan
his … *Wilson*

for the revitalization of blighted inner-city communities.

Replacing *he* with *Wilson* gives the pronoun *his* an antecedent that is stated explicitly, not just implied. Note that in the revised sentence, the antecedent follows the pronoun.

▶ Every weekday afternoon, my brothers skateboard home from school,

and then they leave them in the driveway.
their skateboards

In the original sentence, *skateboard* is a verb, not a noun, and cannot act as a pronoun antecedent.

3. References for *this, that,* and *which*

The pronouns *this, that,* and *which* are often used to refer to ideas expressed in preceding sentences. To make the sentence containing the pronoun clearer, either change the pronoun to a specific noun or add a specific antecedent or clarifying noun.

▶ As government funding for higher education decreases, tuition increases.

these higher costs
Are we students supposed to accept ~~this~~ without protest?
 ^

▶ As government funding for higher education decreases, tuition increases.

situation
Are we students supposed to accept this without protest?
 ^

4. References for *you, they,* and *it*

The pronouns *you, they,* and *it* should refer to definite, explicitly stated antecedents. If the antecedent is unclear, replace the pronoun with an appropriately specific noun, or rewrite the sentence to eliminate the pronoun.

the government pays
▶ In some countries, such as Canada, ~~they pay~~ for such medical procedures.
 ^

students
▶ According to college policy, ~~you~~ must have a permit to park a car on
 ^

campus.

The
▶ ~~In the~~ textbook, / ~~it~~ states that borrowing to fund the purchase of financial
 ^

assets results in a double-counting of debt.

In college writing, use *you* only to address the reader: *Turn left when you reach the corner.*

> *Note:* Writers sometimes use *one* as a generic pronoun. This practice usually seems pompous, however, and is best avoided.

55c Make your pronouns consistent within a sentence or passage.

Keep the same point of view (first, second, or third person) and number (singular or plural) within a sentence or series of related sentences.

▶ Once you discover how easy it can be to buy downloadable music, you

You   *as well as*
will be hooked. ~~One~~ can easily find any type of music, ~~and I have found~~
 ^   ^

a number of services that offer a good selection.

(For more on confusing shifts, see Tab 9: Editing for Clarity, p. 399.)

IDENTIFY AND EDIT
Pronoun Case

case

Follow these steps to decide on the proper form of pronouns in compound structures:

✱ 1. *Identify the compound structure (a pronoun and a noun or other pronoun joined by and, but, or, or nor) in the problem sentence.*

> compound structure
> PROBLEM SENTENCE [Her or her roommate] should call the campus technical support office and sign up for broadband Internet service.
>
> compound structure
> PROBLEM SENTENCE The director gave the leading roles to [my brother and I].

✱ 2. *Isolate the pronoun that you are unsure about, then read the sentence to yourself without the rest of the compound structure. If the result sounds wrong, change the case of the pronoun (subjective to objective, or vice versa), and read the sentence again.*

> PROBLEM SENTENCE [Her ~~or her roommate~~] should call the campus technical support office and sign up for broadband Internet service.
>
> *Her should call the campus technical support office* sounds wrong. The pronoun should be in the subjective case: *she.*
>
> PROBLEM SENTENCE The director gave the leading roles to [~~my brother and~~ I]
>
> *The director gave the leading roles to I* sounds wrong. The pronoun should be in the objective case: *me.*

✱ 3. *If necessary, correct the original sentence.*

> ♦ She
>   ~~Her~~ or her roommate should call the campus technical
>   ^
>   support office and sign up for broadband Internet service.
>
> ♦ me
>   The director gave the leading roles to my brother and ~~I~~.
>   ^

✓ **55d** Make pronoun cases match their function (for example, *I* vs. *me*).

When a pronoun's form, or **case,** does not match its function in a sentence, readers will feel that something is wrong.

- Pronouns in the subjective case are used as subjects or subject complements: *I, you, he, she, it, we, they, who, whoever.*
- Pronouns in the objective case are used as objects of verbs or prepositions: *me, you, him, her, it, us, them, whom, whomever.*
- Pronouns in the possessive case show ownership: *my, mine, your, yours, his, hers, its, our, ours, their, theirs, whose.* Adjective forms (*her* room, *our* office) appear before nouns. Noun forms stand alone (that room is *hers; mine* is on the left). When noun forms act as subjects, the verb agrees with the antecedent (*room*).

1. Compound structures
Compound structures (words or phrases joined by *and, or,* or *nor*) can appear as subjects or objects. If you are not sure which form of a pronoun to use in a compound structure, treat the pronoun as the only subject or object, and note how the sentence sounds.

SUBJECT   Angela and ~~me~~ *I* were cleaning up the kitchen.

If you treat the pronoun as the only subject, the original sentence is clearly wrong: *Me [was] cleaning up the kitchen.*

OBJECT   My parents waited for an answer from John and ~~I~~ *me.*

If you treat the pronoun as the only object, the original sentence is clearly wrong: *My parents waited for an answer from I.*

> ***Note:*** Do not substitute a reflexive pronoun for the pronoun you are unsure of: *Angela and I* [not *myself*] *were cleaning up the kitchen.* (*For more on reflexive and intensive pronouns, see Tab 12: Basic Grammar Review, pp. 576–77.*)

2. Subject complements
A **subject complement** renames and specifies the sentence's subject. It follows a **linking verb**—a verb, often a form of *be*, that links the subject to its description or definition: *Children <u>are</u> innocent.*

SUBJECT Mark's best friends are Jane and ~~me~~ *I*.

You can also switch the order to make the pronoun into the subject: *Jane and I are Mark's best friends.*

3. Appositives

Appositives are nouns or noun phrases that rename nouns or pronouns. They appear right after the word they rename and have the same function in the sentence that the word has.

SUBJECTIVE The two weary travelers, Ramon and ~~me~~ *I*, finally found

shelter.

OBJECTIVE The police arrested two protesters, Jane and ~~I~~ *me*.

4. *We* or *us*

When *we* or *us* comes before a noun, it has the same function in the sentence as the noun it precedes and renames.

SUBJECTIVE ~~Us~~ *We* students never get to decide such things.

OBJECTIVE Things were looking desperate for ~~we~~ *us* campers.

5. Comparisons with *than* or *as*

In comparisons, words are often left out of the sentence because the reader can guess what they would be. When a pronoun follows *than* or *as*, make sure you are using the correct form by mentally adding the missing word or words.

► Meg is quicker than she [is].

► We find ourselves remembering Maria as often as [we remember] her.

Sometimes the correct form depends on intended meaning:

► My brother likes our dog more than *I* [do].

► My brother likes our dog more than [he likes] *me*.

If a sentence with a comparison sounds too awkward or formal, add the missing words: *Meg is quicker than she is.*

6. Pronoun as the subject or the object of an infinitive

An infinitive has the word *to* plus the base verb (*to breathe, to sing, to dance*). Whether a pronoun functions as the subject or the object of an infinitive, it should be in the objective case.

► We wanted our lawyer and *her* (subject) to defend *us* (object) against this charge.

Note that in the example the subject of the infinitive is a compound noun. If a compound functioning as the subject or object of an infinitive has two pronouns, both should be in the objective case: *The nurse told her and me to go into the examining room.*

7. Noun or pronoun with an *-ing* noun (a gerund)

When a noun or pronoun appears before a **gerund** (an *-ing* verb form functioning as a noun), it should usually be treated as a possessive. Possessive nouns are formed by adding *'s* to singular nouns (*the teacher's desk*) or an apostrophe only (*'*) to plural nouns (*three teachers' rooms*). (*See Tab 11: Editing for Correctness, pp. 520–24.*)

► The ~~animals~~ **animals'** fighting disturbed the entire neighborhood.

► Because of ~~them~~ **their** screeching, no one could get any sleep.

Note: Possessive pronouns never contain an apostrophe and an *s*. Pronouns that appear with an apostrophe and an *s* are always part of a contraction. Be especially careful to use *its*, not *it's*, when the possessive form is called for: *The cat finally stopped its* [not *it's*] *screeching.*

55e Distinguish between *who* and *whom*.

The relative pronouns *who*, *whom*, *whoever*, and *whomever* are used to introduce dependent clauses and in questions. Their case depends on their function in the dependent clause or question.

- ▪ **Subjective:** *who, whoever*
- ▪ **Objective:** *whom, whomever*

1. Determining the pronoun's function in a clause   If the pronoun is functioning as a subject and is performing an action, use *who* or *whoever*. If the pronoun is the object of a verb or preposition, use *whom* or *whomever*. (Note that *whom* usually appears at the beginning of the clause.)

► Henry Ford, *who* started the Ford Motor Company, was autocratic and stubborn.

  Who, which refers to *Henry Ford,* is performing an action in the dependent clause: starting a company.

► Ford's son Edsel, *whom* the auto magnate treated cruelly, was a brilliant automobile designer.

Whom, which refers to *Edsel,* is the object of the verb *treated,* although it precedes the verb and the subject, *the auto magnate.* You can check the pronoun by changing the order within the clause: *The auto magnate treated whom* [*him*] *cruelly.*

Phrases such as *I think* or *they say* do not affect pronoun case.

▶ Ford, *who* many say was a visionary, pioneered use of the assembly line.

2. Determining the pronoun's function in a question
To choose the correct form for the pronoun, answer the question with a personal pronoun.

▶ *Who* founded the General Motors Corporation?

The answer could be *He founded it. He* is in the subjective case, so *who* is correct.

▶ *Whom* did Chrysler turn to for leadership in the 1980s?

The answer could be *It turned to him. Him* is in the objective case, so *whom* is correct.

Note: Infinitives take the objective case, *whom,* as a subject or object: *Ford could not decide whom* [not *who*] *to trust.*

56 Problems with Adjectives and Adverbs

Adjectives and **adverbs** are words that qualify—or modify—the meanings of other words. Adjectives modify nouns and pronouns. Adverbs modify verbs, adjectives, and other adverbs.

www.mhhe.com/ awr3

For information and exercises on adjectives and adverbs, go to

Editing > Adjectives and Adverbs

56a Use adverbs to modify verbs, adjectives, other adverbs, and whole clauses.

Adverbs tell where, when, why, how, how often, how much, or to what degree.

▶ The authenticity of the document is *hotly* contested.

▶ The water was *brilliant* blue and *icy* cold.

► Dickens mixed humor and pathos *better* than any other English writer after Shakespeare.

► *Consequently,* Dickens is still read by millions.

(For information on the placement of adverbs in sentences, see Tab 12: Basic Grammar Review, pp. 581–82.)

Adjectives, Adverbs, and Grammar Checkers

Computer grammar checkers are sensitive to some problems with adjectives and adverbs but miss far more than they catch. A grammar checker failed to flag the errors in the following sentences: *The price took a suddenly plunge* [should be *sudden*] and *The price plunged sudden* [should be *suddenly*].

56b Use adjectives to modify nouns or as subject complements.

Adjectives modify nouns and pronouns; they do not modify any other kind of word. Adjectives tell what kind or how many and may come before or after the noun or pronoun they modify.

► *Ominous gray* clouds loomed over the lake.

► The *looming* clouds, *ominous* and *gray,* frightened the children.

Some proper nouns have adjective forms. Proper adjectives, like the proper nouns they are derived from, are capitalized: *Victoria / Victorian, Britain / British, America / American, Shakespeare / Shakespearean.*

In some cases, a noun is used as an adjective without a change in form:

► *Cigarette* smoking harms the lungs and is banned in offices.

Occasionally, descriptive adjectives function as if they were nouns:

► The *unemployed* should not be equated with the *lazy.*

(For information on compound adjectives such as "well known," see Tab 11: Editing for Correctness, p. 553.)

For MULTILINGUAL STUDENTS

Using Adjectives

In English, adjectives do not change form to agree with plural nouns or pronouns. (However, *this* and *that* become *these* and *those* before a plural noun or pronoun: *this pot, those dishes.*)

► The recipe calls for one green pepper and two ~~reds~~ *red* peppers.

(*For more about adjectives in English, including rules about adjective order, see Tab 12: Basic Grammar Review, p. 580.*)

1. Avoiding incorrect use of adjectives

In common speech, we sometimes treat adjectives as adverbs. In writing, this informal usage should be avoided.

► He hit that ball ~~real good.~~ *really well.*

Both *real* and *good* are adjectives, but they are used as adverbs in the original sentence, with *real* modifying *good* and *good* modifying the verb *hit.*

Note that *well* can function as an adjective and subject complement with a linking verb to describe a person's health.

► After the treatment, the patient felt *well* again.

► She ~~sure~~ *certainly* made me work hard for my grade.

In the original sentence, the adjective *sure* tries to do the work of an adverb modifying the verb *made.*

2. Using adjectives after linking verbs

Linking verbs connect the subject of a sentence to its description. The most common linking verb is *be.* Descriptive adjectives that modify a sentence's subject but appear after a linking verb are called **subject complements.**

► During the winter, both Emily and Anne *were sick.*

► The road *is long, winding,* and *dangerous.*

Linking verbs are related to states of being and the five senses: *appear, become, feel, grow, make, prove, look, smell, sound,* and *taste.*

Verbs related to the senses can be either linking or action verbs, depending on the meaning of the sentence.

ADJECTIVE The dog smelled *bad.*

Bad modifies the noun *dog.* The sentence indicates that the dog needed a bath.

ADVERB The dog smelled *badly.*

Badly modifies the verb *smelled,* an action verb in this sentence. The sentence indicates that the dog had lost its sense of smell.

Good and *bad* appear after *feel* to describe emotional states.

► I feel *bad* [not *badly*] for her because she does not feel well.

3. Recognizing that some adjectives and adverbs are spelled alike

In most instances, *-ly* endings indicate adverbs; however, words with *-ly* endings can sometimes be adjectives (*the lovely girl*). In standard English, many adverbs do not require the *-ly* ending, and some words are both adjectives and adverbs: *fast, only, hard, right,* and *straight.* Note that *right* also has an *-ly* form as an adverb: *rightly.* When in doubt, consult a dictionary.

56c Use positive, comparative, and superlative adjectives and adverbs correctly.

Most adjectives and adverbs have three forms: positive (*dumb*), comparative (*dumber*), and superlative (*dumbest*). The simplest form of the adjective is the positive form.

1. Distinguishing between comparatives and superlatives

Use the comparative form to compare two things and the superlative form to compare three or more things.

► In total area, New York is a *larger* state than Pennsylvania.

► Texas is the *largest* state in the Southwest.

2. Learning when to use *-er/-est* endings and when to use *more/most,* or *less/least*

To form comparatives and superlatives of short adjectives, add the suffixes *-er* and *-est* (*brighter / brightest*). With longer adjectives (three or more syllables), use *more* or *less* and *most* or *least* (*more dangerous / most dangerous*). (A dictionary will tell you if an adjective takes *-er/-est.*)

                     nearest
► Mercury is the ~~most near~~ planet to the sun.
                        ^

A few short adverbs have *-er* and *-est* endings in their comparative and superlative forms (*harder / hardest*). Most adverbs, however, including all adverbs that end in *-ly,* use *more* and *most* in their comparative and superlative forms. Negative comparatives and superlatives are formed with *less* and *least: less funny / least funny.*

► She sings *more loudly* than we expected.

Two common adjectives—*good* and *bad*—form the comparative and superlative in an irregular way: *good, better, best* and *bad, worse, worst.*

► He felt ~~badder~~ *worse* as his illness progressed.

These and other irregular adjectives and adverbs are listed in the box on page 494. When in doubt, consult a dictionary.

3. Watching out for double comparatives and superlatives
Use either an *-er* or an *-est* ending or *more / most* to form the comparative or superlative, as appropriate; do not use both.

► Since World War II, Britain has been the ~~most~~ closest ally of the

United States.

4. Recognizing concepts that cannot be compared
Do not use comparative or superlative forms with adjectives such as *unique, infinite, impossible, perfect, round, square,* and *destroyed.* These concepts are *absolutes.* If something is unique, for example, it is the only one of its kind, making comparison impossible.

► You will never find ~~a more unique~~ *another* restaurant ~~than~~ *like* this one.

5. Making sure your comparison is complete
Unless the context of your sentence makes the comparison clear, be sure to include both items you are comparing.

► Charles Dickens had more popular successes. *than any other British writer of his time*

(*For more on making comparisons complete, see Tab 9, Editing for Clarity, p. 396.*)

56d Avoid double negatives.

The words *no, not,* and *never* can modify the meaning of nouns and pronouns as well as other sentence elements.

COMPARISON in ADJECTIVES and ADVERBS

Examples of Regular and Irregular Forms

Regular adjectives	Positive	Comparative	Superlative
One-syllable adjectives	red	redder, less red	reddest, least red
Two-syllable adjectives ending in –y	lonely	lonelier, less lonely	loneliest, least lonely
Other adjectives of two or more syllables	famous	more/less famous	most/least famous
Regular adverbs			
One-syllable	hard	harder, less hard	hardest, least hard
Most other adverbs	truthfully	more/less truthfully	most/least truthfully
Irregular adjectives			
	good	better	best
	bad	worse	worst
	little	less, littler	least, littlest
	many	more	most
	much	more	most
	some	more	most
Irregular adverbs			
	badly	worse	worst
	well	better	best

NOUN	You are *no* friend of mine.
ADJECTIVE	The red house was *not* large.
VERB	He *never* ran in a marathon.

However, it takes only one negative word to change the meaning of a sentence from positive to negative. When two negatives are used together, they cancel each other, resulting in a positive meaning. Unless you want your sentence to have a positive meaning (*I am not unaware of your feelings in this matter*), edit by changing or eliminating one of the negative words.

► They don't have ~~no~~ *any* reason to go there.

► He ~~can't~~ *can* hardly do that assignment.

Note that *hardly* has a negative meaning and cannot be used with *no, not,* or *never.*

CHECKLIST

Editing for Grammar Conventions

To detect grammatical problems in your writing, ask yourself the following questions:

☐ Is each sentence grammatically complete, or is some necessary part missing? Does each sentence include a subject, a complete verb, and an independent clause? (*See Chapter 51, Sentence Fragments, pp. 446–52.*)

☐ Does any sentence seem like two or more sentences jammed together without a break? If a sentence has more than one independent clause, are those clauses joined in an acceptable way? (*See Chapter 52, Comma Splices and Run-on Sentences, pp. 453–59.*)

☐ Do the key parts of each sentence fit together well, or are the subjects and verbs mismatched in person and number? (*See Chapter 53, Subject-Verb Agreement, pp. 459–66.*)

☐ Is the time frame of events represented accurately, conventionally, and consistently, or are there problems with verb form, tense, and sequence? (*See Chapter 54, Problems with Verbs, pp. 467–77.*)

☐ Do the pronouns in every sentence clearly refer to a specific noun or pronoun and agree with the nouns or pronouns they replace? (*See Chapter 55, Problems with Pronouns, pp. 478–89.*)

☐ Does the form of each modifier match its function in the sentence? (*See Chapter 56, Problems with Adjectives and Adverbs, pp. 489–95.*)

The great twelfth century inventor al-Jazari designed many innovative mechanical devices. This plan for a water-operated automaton documents the engineering behind one invention's design; each working part relies on the precise placement of others.

It wasn't a matter of rewriting but simply of tightening up all the bolts.
—MARGUERITE YOURCENAR

Editing
for Correctness

Punctuation, Mechanics, and Spelling

✓ Sections referenced in Resources for Writers: Identifying and Editing
Common Problems pullout section (following Tab 9).

WRITING OUTCOMES

Tab 11: Editing for Correctness
This section will help you answer questions such as:

Rhetorical Knowledge
Should I use contractions such as *can't* or *don't* in my college work? **(60b)**
Which numbers should be spelled out in my technical report? **(65c)**

Critical Thinking, Reading, and Writing
How should I set off words I have added to a quotation? **(62f)**
How do I use ellipses ethically to indicate omissions from quotations? **(62g)**

Processes
Can my word processor's grammar checker help me edit for punctuation and mechanics? **(57–59, 61–64)**
What are the strengths and limitations of my word processor's spelling checker? **(60, 68)**

Knowledge of Conventions
When should I set off a word or phrase with commas? **(57e)**
What is the difference between *its* and *it's*? **(60c)**

Self-Assessment: *Take an online quiz at www.mhhe.com/awr3 to test your familiarity with the topics covered in Chapters 57–68. As you read the following chapters, pay special attention to the sections that correspond to any questions you answer incorrectly.*

CHARTING the TERRITORY

Styles within Disciplines

The rules for capitalizing, abbreviating, and italicizing terms, as well as conventions for using numbers and hyphens, can vary from one course or discipline to another. If you are not sure about the conventions for a discipline, see what rules your course textbook follows. If you cannot figure out the accepted practice from your text, ask your instructor for help, use the general rules presented in this book, or consult a style manual from the list on page 271.

57 Commas

COMMON USES OF THE COMMA

You may have been told that commas are used to mark pauses, but that is not an accurate general principle. To clarify meaning, commas are used to set off sentence elements and in other conventional ways.

✓ **57a** Use a comma after an introductory word group that is *not* the subject of the sentence.

www.mhhe.com/awr3

For information and exercises on commas, go to

Editing > Commas

A comma both attaches an introductory word, phrase, or clause to and distinguishes it from the rest of the sentence.

► Finally, the speeding car careened to the right.

► Reflecting on her life experiences, Washburn attributed her successes to her own efforts.

► Until he noticed the handprint on the wall, the detective was frustrated by the lack of clues.

When the introductory phrase is less than five words long and there is no danger of confusion without a comma, the comma can be omitted.

► For several hours we rode on in silence.

Do not add a comma after a word group that functions as the subject of the sentence. Be especially careful with word groups that begin with *-ing* words.

► **Persuading constituents/ is one of a politician's most important tasks.**

Commas and Grammar Checkers

Computer grammar checkers usually will not highlight missing commas following introductory elements or between independent clauses joined by a coordinating conjunction such as *and,* and they cannot decide whether a sentence element is essential or nonessential.

57b Use commas between items in a series.

A comma should appear after each item in a series.

► **Three industries that have been important to New England are**

shipbuilding, tourism, and commercial fishing.

Commas clarify which items are part of the series. In the following example, the third comma clarifies that the hikers are packing lunch *and* snacks, not chocolate and trail mix for lunch.

CONFUSING   For the hiking trip, we needed to pack lunch, chocolate and trail mix.

CLEAR   For the hiking trip, we needed to pack lunch, chocolate, and trail mix.

If items in the series contain internal commas or other punctuation, separate them with a semicolon (*see Chapter 58, pp. 516–17*).

CHARTING the TERRITORY

Commas in Journalism

If you are writing for a journalism course, you may be required to leave out the final comma that precedes *and* in a series, just as magazines and newspapers sometimes do.

✓ **57c** Use a comma in front of a coordinating conjunction that joins independent clauses.

When a coordinating conjunction (*and, but, for, nor, or, so, yet*) joins clauses that could each stand alone as a sentence, put a comma before the coordinating conjunction.

► Injuries were so frequent that he began to worry, and his style of play

became more cautious.

If the word groups you are joining are not independent clauses, do not add a comma. (*See 57m on p. 512.*)

Exception: If you are joining two short clauses, you may leave out the comma unless it is needed for clarity.

► The running back caught the ball and the fans cheered.

57d Add a comma between coordinate adjectives not joined by *and,* but do not separate cumulative adjectives with a comma.

Use a comma between **coordinate** adjectives that precede a noun and modify it independently (*a brave, intelligent, persistent woman*). Adjectives are coordinate if they can be joined by *and* (brave *and* intelligent *and* persistent) or if their order can be changed (*a persistent, brave, intelligent woman*).

► This brave, intelligent, persistent woman was the first female to earn a

Ph.D. in psychology.

If you cannot add *and* between the adjectives or change their order, they are **cumulative,** with each one modifying the ones that follow it, and should not be separated with a comma or commas.

► Andrea Boccelli, the world-famous Italian tenor, has performed in concerts and operas.

World-famous modifies *Italian tenor,* not just the noun *tenor.* You could not add *and* between the adjectives (world-famous *and* Italian tenor) or change their order (*Italian world-famous tenor*).

✓ **57e** Use commas to set off nonessential additions to a sentence, but do not set off essential elements.

Nonessential, or **nonrestrictive,** words, phrases, and clauses add information to a sentence but are not required for its basic meaning to be understood. Nonrestrictive additions are set off with commas.

IDENTIFY AND EDIT
Commas with Coordinate Adjectives

Follow these steps if you have trouble determining whether commas should separate two or more adjectives that precede a noun:

✱ *1. Identify the adjectives.*

> PROBLEM SENTENCE
>
> Ann is an [excellent art] teacher and a [caring generous] mentor.
>
> Note that nouns such as *art* can also be used as adjectives.

✱ *2. Try changing the order of the adjectives or putting the word* and *between them. Then read the adjectives and noun to yourself. How do they sound?*

> PROBLEM SENTENCE
>
> Ann is an [art excellent] teacher and a [generous caring] mentor.
>
> We could say that Ann is a generous caring mentor, but it would be awkward to say that she is an art excellent teacher.

> PROBLEM SENTENCE
>
> Ann is an [excellent and art] teacher and a [caring and generous] mentor.
>
> We could say that Ann is a caring and generous mentor, but it would be awkward to say that she is an excellent and art teacher.

✱ *3. If the phrase sounds wrong, the adjectives are cumulative and don't need a comma between them. If the phrase sounds right, the adjectives are coordinate and require a comma. If need be, correct the original sentence.*

> Ann is an excellent art teacher and a caring, generous mentor.

NONRESTRICTIVE

Mary Shelley's best-known novel, *Frankenstein or the Modern Prometheus,* was first published in 1818.

The sentence would have the same basic meaning without the title (*Mary Shelley's best-known novel was first published in 1818*).

Restrictive words, phrases, and clauses are essential to a sentence because they identify exactly who or what the writer is talking about. Restrictive additions are not set off with commas.

RESTRICTIVE

Mary Shelley's novel *Frankenstein or the Modern Prometheus* was first published in 1818.

Without the title, the reader would not know which novel the sentence is referring to, so *Frankenstein or the Modern Prometheus* is restrictive.

Often, the context determines whether to enclose a word, phrase, or clause with commas. In the following examples, notice how a preceding sentence can affect the meaning and determine whether commas are needed around this participial phrase:

▶ Two customers with angry looks on their faces approached the check-out counter. The customers, demanding a refund, lined up by the register.

▶ The store opened at the usual time. The customers demanding a refund lined up by the register.

Three types of additions to sentences often cause problems: adjective clauses, adjective phrases, and appositives.

1. Adjective clauses

Adjective clauses begin with a relative pronoun or an adverb—*who, whom, whose, which, that, where,* or *when*—and modify a noun or pronoun within the sentence. Adjective clauses can be either nonrestrictive or restrictive.

NONRESTRICTIVE

With his tale of Odysseus, *whose journey can be traced on modern maps,* Homer brought accounts of alien and strange creatures to the ancient Greeks.

RESTRICTIVE

The contestant *whom he most wanted to beat* was his father.

Note: Use *that* only with restrictive clauses. Some writers prefer to use *which* only with nonrestrictive clauses.

---

2. Adjective phrases

Like an adjective clause, an adjective phrase also modifies a noun or pronoun in a sentence. Adjective phrases begin with a preposition (for example, *with, by, at,* or *for*) or a verbal (a word formed from a verb). Adjective phrases can be either nonrestrictive or restrictive.

IDENTIFY AND EDIT
Commas with Nonrestrictive Words
or Word Groups

Follow these steps if you have trouble deciding whether a
word or word group should be set off with a comma or commas:

⋆ 1. Identify the word or word group that may need to be set off with commas.
Pay special attention to words that appear between the subject and verb.

> subj
> PROBLEM   Dorothy Parker [a member of the famous Algonquin
> SENTENCE   verb
> Round Table] wrote humorous verse as well as short
>
> stories.
>
>   subj   verb
> PROBLEM   Her poem ["One Perfect Rose"] is a lament about a
> SENTENCE   well-intentioned gift that falls short.

⋆ 2. Read the sentence to yourself without the word or word group. Does the
basic meaning stay the same, or does it change? Can you tell what
person, place, or thing the sentence is about?

> SENTENCE   Dorothy Parker wrote humorous verse as well as
> WITHOUT
> THE WORD   short stories.
> GROUP
>   The subject of the sentence is identified by name, and the
>   basic meaning of the sentence does not change.
>
> SENTENCE   Her poem is a lament about a well-intentioned gift
> WITHOUT
> THE WORD   that falls short.
> GROUP
>   Without the words "One Perfect Rose," we cannot tell what
>   poem the sentence is describing.

⋆ 3. If the meaning of the sentence stays the same without the word or word
group, set it off with commas. If the meaning changes, the word or word
group should not be set off with commas.

> ⬥ Dorothy Parker, a member of the famous Algonquin Round
>   ∧
>   Table, wrote humorous verse as well as short stories.
>   ∧
>
> ⬥ Her poem "One Perfect Rose" is a lament about a well-
>
>   intentioned gift that falls short.
>
>   The sentence is correct. Commas are not needed to enclose "One
>   Perfect Rose."

NONRESTRICTIVE

Some people, *by their faith in human nature or their general good will,* bring out the best in others.

The phrase does not specify which people are being discussed. The sentence would have the same meaning without it.

RESTRICTIVE

People *fighting passionately for their rights* can inspire others to join a cause.

The phrase indicates which people the writer is talking about and therefore is restrictive. It is not set off with commas.

3. Appositives

Appositives are nouns or noun phrases that rename nouns or pronouns and appear right after the word they rename.

NONRESTRICTIVE

One researcher, *the widely respected R. S. Smith,* has shown that a child's performance on IQ tests can be very inconsistent.

Because the word *one* already restricts the word *researcher,* the researcher's name is not essential to the meaning of the sentence.

RESTRICTIVE

The researcher *R. S. Smith* has shown that a child's performance on IQ tests can be very inconsistent.

The name *R. S. Smith* tells readers which researcher is meant.

57f Use a comma or commas with transitional and parenthetical expressions, contrasting comments, and absolute phrases.

1. Transitional expressions

Transitional expressions show the relationship between ideas in a sentence. Conjunctive adverbs (*however, therefore, moreover*) and other transitional phrases (*for example, on the other hand*) are usually set off by commas when used at the beginning, in the middle, or at the end of a sentence. (*For a list of transitional expressions, see Tab 10: Editing for Grammar Conventions, p. 457.*)

► Brian Wilson, for example, was unable to cope with the pressures of touring with the Beach Boys.

► As a matter of fact, he had a nervous breakdown shortly after a tour.

▶ He is still considered one of the most important figures in rock and roll,
^
however.

When a transitional expression connects two independent clauses, use a semicolon before and a comma after it.

▶ The Beatles were a phenomenon when they toured the United States in

1964; subsequently, they became the most successful rock band of all time.
^   ^

> *Note:* Short expressions such as *also, at least, certainly, instead, of course, then, perhaps,* and *therefore* do not always need to be set off with commas.
>
> ▶ I found my notes and *also* got my story in on time.

2. Parenthetical expressions

The information that parenthetical expressions provide is relatively insignificant and could easily be left out. Therefore, they are set off with a comma or commas.

▶ Human cloning, so they say, will be possible within a decade.
^   ^

▶ The experiments would take a couple of weeks, more or less.
^

3. Contrasting comments

Contrasting comments beginning with words such as *not, unlike, while, although, even though,* or *in contrast to* should be set off with commas.

▶ Adam Sandler is famous as a comedian, not a tragedian.
^

▶ Comedy, unlike tragedy, often lacks critical respect.
^   ^

4. Absolute phrases

Absolute phrases usually include a noun (*sunlight*) followed by a participle (*shining*) and are used to modify whole sentences. Do not separate the noun and participle with a comma

▶ The snake slithered through the tall grass, the sunlight/ shining now and
^
then on its green skin.

57g Use a comma or commas to set off words of direct address, *yes* and *no*, mild interjections, and tag sentences.

Words that interrupt a sentence are set off by commas because they are not essential to the sentence's meaning.

► Thank you, Mr. Smith, for your help.

► Yes, I will meet you at noon.

► Of course, if that's what you want, we'll do it.

► We can do better, don't you think?

57h Use a comma or commas to separate a direct quotation from the rest of the sentence.

► Irving Howe declares, "Whitman is quite realistic about the place of the self in an urban world" (261).

► "Whitman is quite realistic about the place of the self in an urban world," declares Irving Howe (261).

Note that the comma appears inside the closing quotation mark.

Use commas to set off words that interrupt quotations.

► "When we interpret a poem," DiYanni says, "we explain it to ourselves in order to understand it."

If you are quoting more than one sentence and interrupting the quotation between sentences, the interrupting words should end with a period.

► "But it is not possible to give to each department an equal power of self defense," James Madison writes in *The Federalist No. 51*. "In republican government the legislative authority, necessarily, predominates."

A comma is not needed to separate an indirect quotation or a paraphrase from the words that identify its source. It is also not needed when a direct quotation is integrated into your sentence.

► Irving Howe notes, that Whitman realistically depicts the urban self as free to wander (261).

► Stanley Fish maintains that teaching content, "is a lure and a delusion."

(For more on quotations, see Chapter 61, pp. 525–31.)

57i Use commas with parts of dates, letters, and addresses; with people's titles; and in numbers.

▪ **Dates.** Use paired commas in dates when the month, day, and year are included. Do not use commas when the day of the month is omitted or when the day appears before the month.

> ► On March 4, 1931, she traveled to New York.

> ► She traveled to New York in March 1931.

> ► She traveled to New York on 4 March 1931.

▪ **Parts of letters.** Use a comma following the greeting in an informal letter and following the closing in any type of letter. (In a business letter, use a colon following the greeting.)

> ► Dear Martha,   Sincerely yours,

▪ **Addresses.** Use commas to set off the parts of an address or the name of a state, but do not use a comma preceding a zip code.

> ► At Cleveland, Ohio, the river changes direction.

> ► My address is 63 Oceanside Drive, Apt. 2A, Surf City, New Jersey 08008.

▪ **People's titles or degrees.** Put a comma between the person's name and the title or degree when it comes after the name, followed by another comma.

> ► Luis Mendez, MD, gave her the green light to resume her exercise regimen.

▪ **Numbers.** When a number has more than four digits, use commas to mark off the numerals by hundreds—that is, by groups of three, beginning at the right.

> ► Andrew Jackson received 647,276 votes in the 1828 election.

 **For MULTILINGUAL STUDENTS**

Long Numbers

In some other languages, periods, not commas, are used to mark off numerals by hundreds. However, in American English, periods are used for decimals only; commas are used in long numbers.

If the number is four digits long, the comma is optional.

> ► **The survey had 1856 [or 1,856] respondents.**

Exceptions: Street numbers, zip codes, telephone numbers, page numbers (p. 2304), and years (1828) do not include commas.

57j Use a comma to take the place of an omitted word or phrase or to prevent misreading.

When a writer omits one or more words from a sentence to create a special effect, a comma is often needed to make the meaning of the sentence clear for readers.

> ► **Under the tree he found his puppy, and under the car, his cat.**

The second comma substitutes for the phrase *he found.*

Commas are also used to keep readers from misunderstanding a writer's meaning when words are repeated or might be misread.

> ► **Many birds that sing, sing early in the morning, before the sun rises.**

> ► **Any items that can be, are sold at auction Web sites.**

COMMON MISUSES OF THE COMMA

Commas should *not* be used in the following situations.

57k Do not use commas to separate major elements in an independent clause.

Do not use a comma to separate a subject from a verb, a verb from its object, or a preposition from its object.

> ► **Reflecting on one's life,/ is necessary for emotional growth.**

The subject, *reflecting,* should not be separated from the verb, *is.*

> ► **Washburn decided,/ that her own efforts were the key to her success.**

The verb *decided* should not be separated from its direct object, the subordinate clause *that her own efforts were the key to her success.*

> ► **Although he is a famous actor he is in,/ emotional limbo.**

The preposition *in* should not be separated from its object, *emotional limbo.*

Note: If a nonessential phrase appears between the subject and verb, it should be set off with a pair of commas (*see 57e on p. 503*).

57l Do not add a comma before the first or after the final item in a series.

Use commas to separate items in a series but never before or after the series.

▶ **Americans work longer hours than,/ German, French, or British workers,/ are expected to work.**

Commas should never be used after *such as* or *like* (*see p. 514*).

57m Do not use commas to separate compound word groups unless they are independent clauses.

A comma should not be used between word groups joined with a coordinating conjunction such as *and* unless they are both full sentences.

▶ **Injuries were so frequent that he became worried,/ and started to play more cautiously.**

Here, *and* joins two verbs (*became* and *started*).

▶ **He is worried that injuries are more frequent,/ and that he will have to play more cautiously to avoid them.**

Here, *and* joins two subordinate clauses beginning with *that*.

57n Do not use commas to set off restrictive modifiers, appositives, or slightly parenthetical words or phrases.

If a word, phrase, or clause in a sentence is necessary to identify the noun or pronoun that precedes it, it is **restrictive** and should not be set off with commas. (*See pp. 503–07.*)

▶ **The applicants *who had studied for the admissions test* were restless and eager for the exam to begin.**

Because only those applicants who had studied were eager for the test to begin, the clause *who had studied for the admissions test* is restrictive and should not be set off with commas.

1. Appositives identifying nouns and pronouns
An **appositive** is a noun or noun phrase that renames a noun or pronoun and appears right after the word it renames.

▶ **The director,/ Michael Curtiz,/ was responsible for many great films in the 1930s and 1940s, including *Casablanca*.**

2. Concluding adverb clauses

Adverb clauses beginning with *after, as soon as, before, because, if, since, unless, until,* and *when* are usually essential to a sentence's meaning.

RESTRICTIVE

I am eager to test the children's IQ again *because significant variations in a child's test score indicate that the test itself may be flawed.*

Clauses beginning with *although, even though, though,* and *whereas* present a contrasting thought and are usually nonrestrictive.

NONRESTRICTIVE

IQ tests can be useful indicators of a child's abilities, *although they should not be taken as the definitive measurement of a child's intelligence.*

> *Note:* An adverb clause that appears at the beginning of a sentence is usually followed by a comma: *Until we meet, I'm continuing my work on the budget (see pp. 501–02).*

3. Words and phrases that are slightly parenthetical

If setting off a brief parenthetical remark with commas (*see p. 508*) would draw too much attention to the remark and interrupt the flow of the sentence, the commas can be left out.

► Science is *basically* the last frontier.

57o Correct other common comma errors.

- **Between cumulative adjectives:** (*see p. 503.*)

  ► Three,/ well-known,/ American writers visited the artist's studio.

- **Between adjectives and nouns:**

  ► An art review by a celebrated, powerful,/ writer would be guaranteed publication.

- **Between adverbs and adjectives:**

  ► The artist's studio was delightfully,/ chaotic.

- **Between a noun and participle in an absolute phrase:**

  ► My favorite singer,/ having lost the contest, I stopped paying attention.

- **After coordinating conjunctions** (*and, but, or, nor, for, so, yet*):

  ► The *duomo* in Siena was begun in the thirteenth century, and/ it was used as a model for other Italian cathedrals.

- **After *although, such as,* or *like:***

  ► Stage designers can achieve many unusual effects, such as/ the helicopter that landed in *Miss Saigon.*

- **Before *than:***

  ► An appointment to the Supreme Court has more long-range consequences/ than any other decision a President makes.

- **Before a parenthesis:**

  ► When in an office cubicle/ (a recent invention), workers need to be considerate of others.

- **With a question mark or an exclamation point that ends a quotation** (*also see Chapter 61, p. 528*):

  ► "Where are my glasses?/" she asked in a panic.

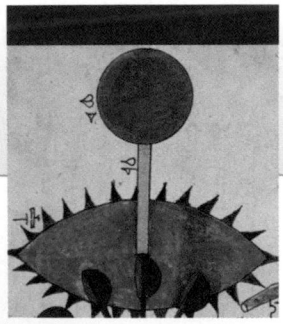

58 Semicolons

Semicolons are used to join ideas that are closely related and grammatically equivalent.

www.mhhe.com/
awr3
For information and
exercises on
semicolons, go to

Editing >
Semicolons

58a Use a semicolon to join independent clauses.

A semicolon should be used to join two related independent clauses when they are not joined by a comma and a coordinating conjunction

Semicolons and Grammar Checkers

Grammar checker programs will catch some comma splices that can be corrected by adding a semicolon between the two clauses. They will also catch some incorrect uses of the semicolon. They will not tell you when a semicolon *could* be used for clarity, however, nor will they tell you if the semicolon is the best choice.

(*and, but, or, nor, for, so, yet*). If the relationship between the two is clear without a coordinating conjunction, a semicolon is effective.

► Before 8000 BC wheat was not the luxuriant plant it is today; it was

merely a wild grass that spread throughout the Middle East.

Sometimes, the close relationship is a contrast.

► Philip had completed the assignment; Lucy had not.

> **Note:** When a semicolon appears next to a quotation mark, it is always placed outside of the quotation mark: *My doctor advised me to "get plenty of rest"; my supervisor had other ideas.*

An occasional semicolon adds variety to your writing, but too many can make it seem monotonous. If you have used three or more semicolons in a paragraph, revise to eliminate most of them.

> **Note:** If a comma is used between two clauses without a coordinating conjunction, the sentence is a comma splice, a serious error. One way to correct a comma splice is by changing the comma to a semicolon.
>
> ► Tracy Kidder wanted to write about architecture; House is the result.
>
> If no punctuation appears between the two clauses, the sentence is a run-on. One way to correct a run-on sentence is to add a semicolon between the two clauses.
>
> ► Magnolias bloom in the early spring; daffodils blossom at the
>
> same time.
>
> (*For more on comma splices and run-on sentences, see Tab 10: Editing for Grammar Conventions, pp. 453–59.*)

58b Use semicolons with transitional expressions that connect independent clauses.

Transitional expressions, including transitional phrases (*for example, in addition, on the contrary*) and conjunctive adverbs (*consequently, however, moreover, nevertheless, then, therefore*), indicate the relationship between two clauses. When a transitional expression appears between two clauses, it is preceded by a semicolon and usually followed by a comma. Using a comma instead of a semicolon creates a comma splice. (*For a list of transitional expressions, see Tab 10: Editing for Grammar Conventions, p. 457.)*

▶ Sheila had to wait until the plumber arrived; consequently, she was late
for the exam.

Coordinating conjunctions (*and, but, or, nor, for, so, yet*) also indicate the way clauses are related. Unlike transitional expressions, however, they are preceded by a comma, not a semicolon, when they join two independent clauses. (*For more on comma splices and run-on sentences, see Tab 10: Editing for Grammar Conventions, pp. 453–59.*)

Note: The semicolon always appears between the two clauses, even when the transitional expression is in another position within the second clause. Wherever it appears, the transitional expression is usually set off with a comma or commas.

▶ My friends are all taking golf lessons; my roommate and I, however, are more interested in tennis.

58c Use a semicolon to separate items in a series or clauses when the items or clauses contain commas.

Because the following sentence contains so many elements, the semicolons are needed for clarity.

▶ The committee included Dr. Curtis Youngblood, the county medical examiner; Roberta Collingwood, the director of the bureau's criminal division; and Darcy Coolidge, the chief of police.

Note: This rule is an exception to the general principle that there should be a full sentence (independent clause) on each side of a semicolon.

A comma is the correct punctuation before a coordinating conjunction (*and, but, for, nor, or, so, yet*) that joins independent clauses: *Forsythia blooms in the early spring, but azaleas bloom later.* However, if at least one independent clause already contains internal commas, a semicolon can help readers locate the point where the clauses are separated.

► The closing scenes return to the English countryside, recalling the opening; but these scenes are bathed in a different, cooler light, suggesting that memories of her marriage still haunt her.

58d Correct common semicolon errors.

- **Joining a dependent clause or a phrase to an independent clause:**

  ► Professional writers need to devote time every day to their

    writing;/, although doing so takes discipline.

  ► Seeming tame and lovable;/, housecats can actually be fierce

    hunters.

  ► Foremost among the German competition horses is the

    Hanoverian;/, a great show-jumping breed.

  The appositive phrase *a great show-jumping breed* should be set off with a comma, not a semicolon.

- **Joining independent clauses linked by a coordinating conjunction (*and, but, or, nor, for, so, yet*):** If the clauses contain commas, a semicolon is acceptable (*see p. 516*).

  ► Nineteenth-century women wore colorful clothes;/, but their

    clothes often look drab in the black-and-white photographs of

    the era.

- **Introducing a series, an explanation, or a quotation:** A colon should usually be used for this purpose.

  ► My day was planned;/: a morning walk, an afternoon in the

    library, dinner with friends, and a great horror movie.

  ► The doctor finally diagnosed the problem;/: a severe sinus

    infection.

  ► Boyd warns of the difficulty in describing Bach;/: "Even his physical

    appearance largely eludes us."

Note: Do not use a capital letter after a semicolon.

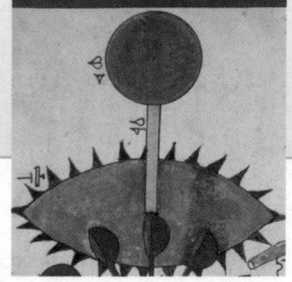

59 Colons

Colons draw attention to what they introduce. They also have other conventional uses. A colon always follows an independent clause, but unlike the semicolon (*see pp. 514–17*), the element that follows it need not be an independent clause.

www.mhhe.com/
awr3

For information and exercises on colons, go to

Editing > Colons

Colons and Grammar Checkers

A grammar checker may point out when you have used a colon incorrectly, but since colons are usually optional, most of the time you will need to decide whether a colon is your best choice in a sentence.

59a Use a colon after a complete sentence to introduce a list, an appositive, or a quotation.

A colon is used after a complete sentence (independent clause) to introduce lists, **appositives** (nouns or noun phrases that appear right after the word they rename), and quotations.

>   *independent clause*   *list*
> **Several majors interest me: biology, chemistry, and art.**

>   *independent clause*   *appositive*
> **She shared with me her favorite toys: a spatula and a pot lid.**

If you use *that is* or *namely* with an appositive, it should follow the colon.

>   *independent clause*   *quotation*
> **He said the dreaded words: "Let's just be friends."**

> *Note:* If you introduce a quotation with a signal phrase such as *he said* or *Morrison comments* instead of a complete sentence, you should use a comma, not a colon. (*For more on introducing quotations, see pp. 525–31.*)

When you use a colon to introduce a sentence element, make sure that it is preceded by an independent clause.

>   *are*
> **Three kinds of futility dealt with in the novel: pervasive poverty, lost love,**
>
> **and inescapable aging.**

The words *the following* or *as follows* often appear at the end of the introductory clause.

59b Use a colon when a second closely related independent clause elaborates on the first one.

Use a colon when you want to emphasize the second clause.

▶ I can predict tonight's sequence of events: my brother will arrive late, talk

loudly, and eat too much.

> *Note:* When a complete sentence follows a colon, the first word may begin with either a capital or a lowercase letter. Be consistent throughout your document.

59c Use colons in salutations in business documents, to indicate ratios, to indicate times of day, for city and publisher citations in bibliographies, and to separate titles and subtitles.

▶ Dear Mr. Worth: To:

▶ The ratio of armed to unarmed members of the gang was 3:1.

▶ He woke up at 6:30 in the morning.

▶ New York: McGraw-Hill, 2010

▶ *Possible Lives: The Promise of Public Education in America*

> *Note:* Colons are often used to separate biblical chapters and verses (John 3:16), but the Modern Language Association (MLA) recommends using a period instead (John 3.16).

59d Correct common colon errors.

■ **Between a verb and its object or complement:**

▶ The elements of a smoothie are: yogurt, fresh fruit, and honey.

■ **Between a preposition and its object or objects:**

▶ Many feel that cancer can be prevented by a diet of: fruit, nuts,

and vegetables.

- **After *such as*, *for example*, or *including*:**

  ► I am ready for a change, such as~~;~~ a vacation.

- **More than one colon in a sentence:**

  ► He was taken in by ~~a new con:~~ the Spanish lottery scam: victims

  are told they have won a prize and asked to send financial

  information to a fake Spanish company.

60 Apostrophes

Apostrophes show possession (*the dog's bone*) and indicate omitted letters in contractions (*don't*). Apostrophes are used in such a variety of ways that they can be confusing. The most common confusion is between plurals and possessives.

www.mhhe.com/
awr3
For information and
exercises on
apostrophes, go to

**Editing >
Apostrophes**

To tell whether a particular noun should be in the possessive form, reword the sentence using the word *of* (*the bone of the dog*) to make sure that the noun is not plural.

Apostrophes and Spelling Checkers

A spelling checker will sometimes highlight *its* used incorrectly (instead of *it's*) or an error in a possessive (for example, *Englands' glory*), but this identification is not consistent. You should double-check all words that end in *-s* in your work.

60a Use apostrophes with nouns and indefinite pronouns to indicate possession.

For a noun to be possessive, two elements are usually required: someone or something is the possessor; and someone, something, or some attribute or quality is possessed.

POSSESSOR	PERSON, THING, ATTRIBUTE, QUALITY, VALUE, OR FEATURE POSSESSED	POSSESSION
woman	son	the woman's son
Juanita	shovel	Juanita's shovel
child	bright smile	a child's bright smile

Sometimes the thing possessed precedes the possessor.

► **The motorcycle is the student's.**

Sometimes the sentence may not name the thing possessed, but its identity (in this case, *house*) is clearly understood by the reader.

► **I saw your cousin at Nick's.**

> *Note:* Possession can also be indicated using the preposition *of: the bright smile of a child.*

1. Deciding whether to use an apostrophe and an *s* or only an apostrophe

To form the possessive of all singular nouns, add an apostrophe plus -*s* to the ending: *baby's.* Even singular nouns that end in -*s* form the possessive by adding -*'s: bus's.*

If a singular noun with more than two syllables ends in -*s* and adding -*'s* would make the word sound awkward, it is acceptable to use only an apostrophe to form the possessive: *Socrates', Dickens'.* Be consistent.

- To form the possessive of a plural noun that ends in -*s,* add only an apostrophe: *subjects', babies'.*

- To form the possessive of a plural noun that does not end in -*s,* add an apostrophe plus -*s: men's, cattle's.*

- To form the possessive of most indefinite pronouns, such as *no one, everyone, everything,* or *something,* add an apostrophe plus -*s: no one's, anybody's.*

> *Note:* When adding -*'s* would make an indefinite pronoun sound awkward, use *of* to form the possessive: *the wishes of a few, the parents of both.*

Forming Possessives

IF THE WORD IS A(N)	ADD	EXAMPLE
singular noun	's	horse's Moore's
plural noun ending in -s	'	horses' Moores'
plural noun not ending in -s	's	children's
indefinite pronoun	's	everybody's

2. Using the apostrophe in tricky situations

■ To express joint ownership, use the possessive form for the last name only; to express individual ownership, use the possessive form for each name.

▶ **Felicia and Elias' report**

▶ **The city's and the state's finances**

■ To form the possessive of compound words, add an apostrophe plus *s* to the last word in the compound.

▶ **My father-in-law's job**

■ To form the possessive of proper names, follow the rules given above, with some exceptions. Some place or organizational names that include a possessive noun lack an apostrophe. In these cases, follow the established style rather than adding an apostrophe.

▶ **Kings Point**

▶ **Department of Veterans Affairs**

▶ **Pikes Peak**

> **Note:** To form the possessive of buildings, machines, and other inanimate objects, use *of* if adding *'s* sounds awkward: *the window of the house* (not *the house's window*).

60b Use apostrophes to form contractions.

In a contraction, the apostrophe substitutes for omitted letters.

we've	= we have	won't	= will not (irregular)
weren't	= were not	don't	= do not
here's	= here is	can't	= cannot

In informal writing, apostrophes can substitute for omitted numbers in a decade: *the '50s.* Spell out the name of the decade in formal writing: *the fifties.*

CHARTING the TERRITORY

Contractions in Academic Writing

Although the MLA and APA style manuals allow contractions in academic writing, some instructors think that they are too informal. Check with your instructor before using contractions.

✓ **60c** Distinguish between contractions and possessive pronouns.

The following pairs of **homonyms** (words that sound alike but have different meanings) often cause problems for writers. Note that the apostrophe is used only in the contraction.

CONTRACTION	POSSESSIVE PRONOUN
it's (it is or it has)	its
It's too hot.	The dog scratched *its* fleas.
you're (you are)	your
You're a lucky guy.	Is that *your* new car?
who's (who is)	whose
Who's there?	The man *whose* dog was lost called us.
they're (they are)	their*
They're reading poetry.	They gave *their* lives.

*The adverb *their* is also confused with *there: She was standing there.*

60d Using an apostrophe with *s* to form plural letters and words used as words is optional.

An apostrophe plus *s* (*'s*) can be used to show the plural of a letter. Underline or italicize single letters but not the apostrophe or the *s*. (Do not italicize letter grades.)

▶ *Committee* has two *m*'s, two *t*'s, and two *e*'s.

If a word is used as a word rather than as a symbol of the meaning it conveys, it can be made plural by adding an apostrophe plus *s*. The word should be italicized or underlined, but the *'s* should not be. If the word is in quotation marks, you should always use *'s* when you are forming the plural.

▶ There are twenty-five *no's* [or "no's"] in the first paragraph.

60e Watch out for common misuses of the apostrophe.

Never use an apostrophe with *s* to form a plural noun.

▶ The ~~teacher's~~ *teachers* asked the girls and boys for their attention.

(*See pp. 557–58 for more on forming plural nouns.*)

Never use an apostrophe with *s* to form the present tense of a verb used with a third-person singular subject (*he, she, it,* or a singular noun).

▶ A professional singer ~~need's~~ *needs* to practice a lot.

Never use an apostrophe with the possessive form of a pronoun such as *hers, ours,* or *theirs.*

▶ That cat of ~~our's~~ *ours* is always sleeping!

(*See 60c for advice on distinguishing contractions* [it's] *from possessive pronouns* [its].)

Never use an apostrophe with *s* to form the plural of a surname.

▶ The ~~Clinton's~~ *Clintons* made history when Hillary was elected to the Senate during

the same year Bill left the White House.

MLA and APA style recommend against using an apostrophe to form plurals of numbers and abbreviations. You may see that usage elsewhere.

▶ He makes his ~~2's~~ *2s* look like ~~5's~~ *5s*.

▶ Professor Morris has two ~~PhD's~~ *PhDs*.

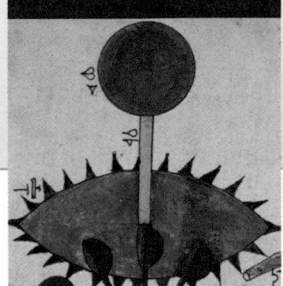

61 Quotation Marks

Quotation marks enclose words, phrases, and sentences that are quoted directly; titles of short works such as poems, articles, songs, and short stories; and words and phrases used in a special sense.

www.mhhe.com/ awr3

For information and exercises on quotation marks, go to

Editing > Quotation Marks

Note: Citations and formatting instructions in this chapter follow MLA style. See Tabs 7 and 8 for examples of APA, Chicago, and CSE styles.

Quotation Marks and Grammar Checkers

A grammar checker cannot determine where a quotation should begin and end, but it can alert you to the lack of an opening or closing mark. Grammar checkers may not point out errors in the use of quotation marks with other marks of punctuation, however. For example, a grammar checker did not highlight the error in the placement of the period at the end of the following sentence.

▶ Barbara Ehrenreich observes, "There are no Palm Pilots, cable channels, or Web sites to advise the low-wage job seeker".

61a Use quotation marks to indicate the exact words of a speaker or writer.

Direct quotations from written material may include whole sentences or only a few words or phrases. They can lend immediacy to your writing.

▶ In *Angela's Ashes,* Frank McCourt writes, "Worse than the ordinary miserable childhood is the miserable Irish childhood" (11).

▶ Frank McCourt believes that being Irish worsens what is all too "ordinary"—a "miserable childhood" (11).

Use quotation marks to enclose everything a speaker says in written dialogue. If the quoted sentence is interrupted by a phrase like *he said,* enclose just the quotation in quotation marks. When another person begins to speak, start a new paragraph to indicate a change in speaker.

> "I don't know what you're talking about," he said. "I did listen to everything you told me."
> "If you had been listening, you would know what I was talking about."

If a speaker continues for more than a paragraph, begin each subsequent paragraph with an opening quotation mark, but do not insert a closing quotation mark until the end of the quotation.

> *Note:* Do not use quotation marks to set off an indirect quotation, which reports what a speaker said but does not use the exact words.
>
> ► He said that ⁄ he didn't know what I was talking about ⁄

Two or three lines of poetry may be run in to your text, much like any other *short* quotation. Line breaks are shown with a slash. Leave a space before and after the slash. (*See also Chapter 62, p. 537.*)

► Wordsworth writes of the weary acquisitiveness of our modern age: "The world is too much with us; late and soon, / Getting and spending, we lay waste our powers" (lines 1–2).

> *Note:* In MLA style, line numbers appear in parentheses following the quotation. The word *lines* should precede the numbers the first time the poem is quoted.

61b Set off long quotations in indented blocks.

Set off a quotation that is longer than four typed lines as a block quotation. (*For detailed instructions on formatting block quotations and examples of block quotations, see Tab 5: Researching, p. 263.*) A block quotation is *not* surrounded by quotation marks. If the text you are quoting includes another direct quotation, however, use quotation marks to set that off.

61c Enclose a quotation within a quotation with single quotation marks.

Use single quotation marks to set off a quotation within a quotation.

► In response to the press, the president of the university said, "I know you're saying to me, 'We want a winning football team.' But I'm telling you this: 'I want an honest football team.' "

61d Use quotation marks to enclose titles of short works such as articles, poems, and stories.

The titles of long works, such as books, are usually put in italics (or underlined). (*See Chapter 66, pp. 549–51.*) The titles of book chapters, essays, most poems, and other short works are usually put in quotation marks. Quotation marks are also used for titles of unpublished works, including student papers, theses, and dissertations.

Works That Should Be Enclosed in Quotation Marks

- **Essays:** "Once More to the Lake"
- **Songs:** "Seven Nation Army"
- **Short poems:** "Daffodils"
- **Short stories:** "The Tell Tale Heart"
- **Articles in periodicals:** "Scotland Yard of the Wild" (from *American Way*)
- **Book chapters or sections:** "The Girl in Conflict" (Chapter 11 of *Coming of Age in Samoa*)
- **Episodes of radio and television programs:** "I Can't Remember" (on *48 Hours*)
- **Titles of unpublished works, including student papers, theses, and dissertations:** "Louis Armstrong and Joe Glaser: More than Meets the Eye" (Do not use quotation marks to enclose the title of your own paper on your title page.)

If quotation marks are needed within the title of a short work, use single quotation marks: "The 'Animal Rights' War on Medicine."

61e Use quotation marks to indicate that a word or phrase is being used in a special way.

Put quotation marks around a word or phrase that someone else has used in a way that you or your readers may not agree with. Quotation marks used in this way function like raised eyebrows do in conversation and should be used sparingly.

► The "worker's paradise" of Stalinist Russia included slave-labor camps.

Words cited as words can also be put in quotation marks, although the more common practice is to italicize them.

► The words "compliment" and "complement" sound alike but have different meanings.

Definitions and translations should appear in quotation marks.

► *Agua* means "water" in Spanish.

61f Place punctuation marks within or outside quotation marks, as convention and your meaning require.

As you edit, check all closing single and double quotation marks and the marks of punctuation that appear next to them to make sure that you have placed them in the right order.

1. Periods and commas

Always place the period or comma before the final quotation mark, even when the quotation is brief.

► "Instead of sharing an experience the spectator must come to grips with things," Brecht writes in "The Epic Theatre and Its Difficulties."

However, place the period or comma after a parenthetical reference.

► Brecht wants the spectator to "come to grips with things" (23).

2. Question marks and exclamation points

Place a question mark or an exclamation point after the final quotation mark if the quoted material is not itself a question or an exclamation.

► How does epic theatre make us "come to grips with things"?

Place a question mark or an exclamation point inside the final quotation mark when it is part of the quotation. No additional punctuation is needed, unless you are adding a parenthetical citation in MLA style (see the third example below).

► "Are we to see science in the theatre?" he was asked.

► Brecht was asked, "Are we to see science in the theatre?"

► Brecht was asked, "Are we to see science in the theatre?" (27).

3. Colons and semicolons

Place colons and semicolons after the final quotation mark.

► Dean Wilcox cited the items he called his "daily delights": a free parking space for his scooter at the faculty club, a special table in the club itself, and friends to laugh with after a day's work.

4. Dashes

Place a dash outside either an opening or a closing quotation mark, or both, if it precedes or follows the quotation or if two dashes are used to set off the quotation.

► One phrase—"time is running out"—haunted me.

Place a dash inside either an opening or a closing quotation mark if it is part of the quotation.

► "Where is the—" she called. "Oh, here it is. Never mind."

61g Integrate quotations smoothly into your sentences, using the correct punctuation.

1. Formal introductions

When you introduce a quotation with a complete sentence, use a colon.

► **Hamilton credits the Greeks with a shift in the portrayal of gods: "Until then, gods had no semblance of reality."**

2. *She said* and similar expressions

If you introduce a quotation with a signal phrase such as *he said* or *she noted,* add a comma after the phrase and use a capital letter to begin the quotation.

► **Hamilton says, "That is the miracle of Greek mythology—a humanized world."**

If the phrase follows the quotation, add a comma at the end of the quotation, before the closing quotation mark. (If the quotation ends in a question mark or an exclamation point, however, do not add a comma.)

Capitalize the first letter of the quotation even if the first word does not begin a sentence in the original source. If you change a lowercase letter to a capital letter, enclose the letter in brackets. (*See p. 535.*)

► **"The only white people who came to our house were welfare workers and bill collectors," James Baldwin wrote.**

> *Note:* Do not use a comma after expressions such as *he said* or *the researchers note* if an indirect quotation or a paraphrase follows.
>
> ► **He said/ that he believed he could do it.**

3. Interrupted quotations

If you interrupt a quoted sentence with a signal phrase such as *she said,* set the signal phrase off with commas. Note that the first word of the second part of the quoted sentence is not capitalized.

► **"The first thing that strikes one about Plath's journals," writes Katha Pollitt in *The Atlantic,* "is what they leave out."**

To interrupt a quotation of two or more sentences with a signal phrase, attach the signal phrase to the first sentence with a comma and a closing quotation mark, and put a period after it. The next sentence begins with an opening quotation mark and a capital letter.

▶ "There are at least four kinds of doublespeak," William Lutz observes. "The first is the euphemism, an inoffensive or positive word or phrase used to avoid a harsh, unpleasant, or distasteful reality."

4. Quotations that are integrated into a sentence

When a quotation is integrated into a sentence's structure, treat the quotation as you would any other sentence element, adding a comma or not as appropriate.

▶ Telling me that she wanted to "play hooky from her life," she set off on a three-week vacation.

▶ He said he had his "special reasons."

61h Edit to correct common errors in using quotation marks.

- **To distance yourself from slang, clichés, or trite expressions:** Avoid overused or slang expressions in college writing. If your writing situation permits slang, however, do not enclose it in quotation marks.

  ▶ Californians are so "laid back."

  Revising the sentence is usually a better solution.

  ▶ Many Californians have a carefree attitude.

- **For indirect quotations:** Do not use quotation marks for indirect quotations. Watch out for errors in pronoun reference as well. (*See Tab 10: Editing for Grammar Conventions, pp. 482–84.*)

  ▶ He told his boss that "the company lost its largest account."

  Another way to correct this sentence is to change to a direct quotation.

  ▶ He said to his boss, "We just lost our largest account."

- **In quotations that end with a question mark or exclamation point:** Do not add another question mark or exclamation point to the end of a quotation that already ends in one of these marks.

  ▶ What did Juliet mean when she cried, "O Romeo, Romeo! Wherefore art thou Romeo?"?

  If you quote a question within a sentence that makes a statement, place a question mark before the quotation mark and a period at the end of the sentence.

> ► "What was Henry Ford's greatest contribution to the Industrial Revolution?" he asked.

▪ **To enclose the title of your own paper on the title page or above the first line of the text:**

> ► ⸢Edgar Allan Poe and the Paradox of the Gothic⸥

If you use a quotation or a title of a short work in your title, though, put quotation marks around it.

> ► Edgar Allan Poe's "The Raven" and the Paradox of the Gothic

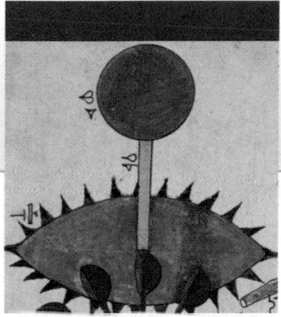

62 Other Punctuation Marks

Punctuation and Grammar Checkers

Your grammar checker might highlight a period used instead of a question mark at the end of a question. However, grammar checkers will not tell you when you might use a pair of dashes or parentheses to set material off in a sentence, or when you need a second dash or parenthesis to enclose parenthetical material.

62a Use a period to end sentences and with some abbreviations.

Use a period to end all sentences apart from direct questions or exclamations.

STATEMENT

There are more than one thousand periods in this book.

STATEMENT CONTAINING AN INDIRECT QUESTION

She asked me where I had gone to college.

POLITE REQUEST

Would you please read chapter 5 for next week.

A period or periods are conventionally used with the following common abbreviations, which end in lowercase letters.

www.mhhe.com/awr3
For information and exercises on other punctuation marks, go to
Editing > End Punctuation

| Mr. | Mrs. | i.e. | Mass. |
| Ms. | Dr. | e.g. | Jan. |

If the abbreviation is made up of capital letters, however, the periods are optional. Do not put a space after an internal period.

| RN (or R.N.) | BA (or B.A.) |
| MD (or M.D.) | PhD (or Ph.D.) |

Periods are omitted in abbreviations for organizations, famous people, states in mailing addresses, and acronyms (words made up of initials).

| FBI | JFK | MA | NATO |
| CIA | LBJ | TX | NAFTA |

When in doubt, consult a dictionary.

When an abbreviation ends a sentence, the period at the end of the abbreviation serves as the period for the sentence. If a question mark or an exclamation point ends the sentence, place it *after* the period in the abbreviation.

► When he was in the seventh grade, we called him "Stinky," but now he is William Percival Abernathy, Ph.D.!

62b Use a question mark after a direct question.

► Who wrote *The Old Man and the Sea*?

Occasionally, a question mark changes a statement into a question.

► You expect me to believe a story like that?

When questions follow one another in a series, each one can be followed by a question mark even if they are not complete sentences. Question fragments may begin with a capital or lowercase letter.

► What will you contribute? Your time? Your talent? Your money?

Use a question mark in parentheses to indicate a questionable date, number, or word, but do not use it to convey an ironic meaning.

► Chaucer was born in 1340 (?) and lived until 1400.

► His dog had graduated from obedience (?) training.

Do not use a question mark after an indirect question.

► He asked her if she would be at home later?.

Do not use a period or comma after a question mark that ends a direct quotation.

► She asked, "What is the word count?"/

62c Use exclamation points sparingly to convey shock, surprise, or some other strong emotion.

► **Stolen! The money was stolen! Right before our eyes, somebody snatched my purse and ran off with it.**

Using numerous exclamation points throughout a document actually weakens their force. Try to convey emotion with your choice of words and your sentence structure.

► **Jefferson and Adams both died on the same day in 1826, exactly fifty years after the signing of the Declaration of Independence!.**

The fact that the sentence reports is surprising enough without the addition of an exclamation point.

Do not use a period or comma after an exclamation point that ends a direct quotation.

62d Use the dash to emphasize the words that precede or follow.

www.mhhe.com/ awr3
For information and exercises on dashes, go to
Editing > Dashes

A typeset dash, sometimes called an *em dash*, is a single, unbroken line about as wide as a capital M. Make a dash with two hyphens in a row. Do not put a space before or after the dash.

1. Highlighting an explanation or a list
A dash indicates a strong pause and emphasizes what comes immediately before or after it.

► **Coca-Cola, potato chips, and brevity—these are the marks of a good study session in the dorm.**

► **I think the Comets will win the tournament for one reason—their goalie.**

A colon could also be used in the second example. (*See Chapter 59, p. 518.*)

If an appositive consists of a list of items, use dashes to set it off more clearly for readers.

► **The symptoms of hay fever/ sneezing, coughing, itchy eyes/ can be controlled with over-the-counter medications.**

Do not separate a subject and verb with a dash, however.

► **Haydn, Mozart, and Beethoven—are famous composers.**

2. Setting off a nonessential phrase or independent clause within a sentence

▶ All finite creations—including humans—are incomplete and contradictory.

▶ The first rotary gasoline engine—it was made by Mazda—burned 15 percent more fuel than conventional engines.

3. Indicating a sudden change in tone or idea

▶ Breathing heavily, the archaeologist opened the old chest in wild anticipation and found—an old pair of socks and an empty soda can.

Caution: The dash can make your writing disjointed if overused.

▶ After we found the puppy—⁄shivering under the porch—⁄, we brought

her into the house—into the entryway, actually—and wrapped her in

an old towel—⁄to warm her up.

www.mhhe.com/
awr3
For information and exercises on parentheses, go to

Editing >
Parentheses

62e Use parentheses for nonessential information.

Parentheses should be used infrequently and only to set off supplementary information, a digression, or a comment that interrupts the flow of thought within a sentence or paragraph.

▶ The tickets (ranging in price from $10 to $50) go on sale Monday.

When parentheses enclose a whole sentence, the sentence begins with a capital letter and ends with a period before the final parenthesis. A sentence that appears inside parentheses *within a sentence* should neither begin with a capital letter nor end with a period.

▶ Folktales and urban legends often reflect the concerns of a particular era. (The familiar tale of a cat accidentally caught in a microwave oven is an example.)

▶ John Henry (he was the man with the forty-pound hammer) was a hero to miners fearing the loss of their jobs to machines.

If the material in parentheses is at the end of an introductory or nonessential word group that is followed by a comma, the comma should be placed after the closing parenthesis. A comma should never appear before the opening parenthesis.

▶ As he walked past,⁄ (dressed, as always, in his Sunday best), I got ready to throw the spitball.

Parentheses enclose numbers or letters that label items in a list.

▶ He says the argument is nonsense because (1) university presidents don't work as well as machines, (2) university presidents don't do any real work at all, and (3) universities should be run by faculty committees.

Parentheses also enclose in-text citations in many systems of documenting sources. (*For more on documenting sources, see Tabs 6–8.*)

62f When quoting, use brackets to set off material that is not part of the original quotation.

Use brackets to set off information you add to a quotation that is not part of the quotation itself.

▶ Samuel Eliot Morison has written, "This passage has attracted a good deal of scorn to the Florentine mariner [Verrazzano], but without justice."

In this sentence, the writer places the name of the "Florentine mariner"—Verrazzano—in brackets so that readers will know his identity.

Brackets are also used around words that you insert within a quotation to make it fit the grammar or style of your own sentence. If you replace a word with your own word in brackets, ellipses are not needed.

▶ At the end of *Pygmalion,* Henry Higgins confesses to Eliza Doolittle that he has "grown accustomed to [her] voice and appearance."

To make the quotation fit properly into the sentence, the bracketed word *her* is inserted in place of *your.*

Use brackets to enclose the word *sic* (Latin for "thus") after a word in a quotation that was incorrect in the original. If you are following MLA style, the word *sic* should not be underlined or italicized.

▶ The critic noted that "the battle scenes in *The Patriot* are realistic, but the rest of the film is historically inacurate [sic]."

Sic should be used sparingly because it can appear condescending.

If you change the first letter or a word in a quotation to a capital or lowercase letter, enclose the letter in brackets: *Ackroyd writes, "[F]or half a million years there has been in London a pattern of habitation and hunting, if not settlement."*

If you need to set off words within material that is already in parentheses, use brackets: *(I found the information on a Web site published by the National Institutes of Health [NIH].)*

> **Note:** MLA style calls for brackets around ellipses that you insert to show omission from a source that already contains ellipses in the original.

62g Use ellipses to indicate that words have been omitted.

Use three spaced periods, called ellipses or an ellipsis mark, to show readers that you have omitted words from a passage you are quoting. Some instructors suggest that you use brackets to enclose any ellipses that you add. (See the note on page 535 regarding MLA style.)

FULL QUOTATION FROM A WORK BY WILKINS

In the nineteenth century, railroads, lacing their way across continents, reaching into the heart of every major city in Europe and America, and bringing a new romance to travel, added to the unity of nations and fueled the nationalist fires already set burning by the French Revolution and the wars of Napoleon.

EDITED QUOTATION

In his account of nineteenth-century society, Wilkins argues that "railroads . . . added to the unity of nations and fueled the nationalist fires already set burning by the French Revolution and the wars of Napoleon."

If you are leaving out the end of a quoted sentence, the three ellipsis points are preceded by a period to end the sentence.

EDITED QUOTATION

In describing the growth of railroads, Wilkins pictures them "lacing their way across continents, reaching into the heart of every major city in Europe and America. . . ."

When you need to add a parenthetical reference after the ellipses at the end of a sentence, place it after the quotation mark but before the final period: . . ." (253).

Ellipses are usually not needed to indicate an omission when only a word or phrase is being quoted.

▶ Railroads brought "a new romance to travel," according to Wilkins.

To indicate the omission of an entire line or more from the middle of a poem, insert a line of spaced periods.

> Shelley seems to be describing nature, but what's really at issue
>
> is the seductive nature of desire:
>
> > See the mountains kiss high Heaven,
> >
> > And the waves clasp one another;
> >
> > . . . .
> >
> > What is all this sweet work worth
> >
> > If thou kiss not me? (1-2, 7-8)

Ellipses should be used only as a means of shortening a quotation, never as a device for changing its fundamental meaning or emphasis.

Ellipses may be used at the end of a sentence if you mean to leave a thought hanging. In the following passage, Dick Gregory uses an ellipsis to suggest that there was no end to his worries.

► Oh God, I'm scared. I wish I could die right now with the feeling I have because I know Momma's gonna make me mad and I'm going to make her mad, and me and Presley's gonna fight ... "Richard, you get in here and put your coat on. Get in here or I'll whip you."

Ellipses also indicate pauses or interruptions in speech.

62h Use slashes according to convention.

Use the slash to show divisions between lines of poetry when you quote more than one line of a poem as part of a sentence. Add a space on either side of the slash. When you are quoting four or more lines of poetry, use a block quotation instead (*see p. 263 and above*).

► In "The Tower," Yeats makes his peace with "All those things whereof / Man makes a superhuman / Mirror-resembling dream" (163-165).

The slash is sometimes used between two words that represent choices or combinations. Do not add a space on either side of the slash when it is used in this way.

► The college offers three credit/noncredit courses.

Slashes are also used to mark divisions in online addresses (URLs): *http://www.georgetown.edu/crossroads/navigate.html.*

Some writers use the slash as a marker between the words *and* and *or* or between *he* and *she* or *his* and *her* to avoid sexism. Most writers, however, consider such usage awkward. It is usually better to rephrase the sentence. (*See also Tab 10: Editing for Grammar Conventions, pp. 479–81.*)

► A bill can originate in the House of Representatives, ~~and/or~~ the Senate.
   in ⌃   *, or both* ⌃

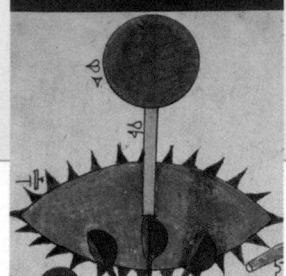

63 Capitalization

Many rules for the use of capital letters have been fixed by custom, such as the convention of beginning each sentence with a capital letter, but the rules change all the time. A recent dictionary is a good guide to capitalization.

www.mhhe.com/
awr3
For information
and exercises on
capitalization, go to

Editing >
Capitalization

63a Capitalize proper nouns (names), words derived from them, brand names, certain abbreviations, and call letters. ✓

Proper nouns are the names of specific people, places, or things. Capitalize proper nouns, words derived from proper nouns, brand names, abbreviations of capitalized words, and call letters of radio and television stations.

Capitalization and Grammar Checkers

Grammar checkers will flag words that should be capitalized or lowercased by convention, but they won't flag proper nouns unless the noun is stored in the program's dictionary, and they may not flag a noun that can be either proper or common, depending on the context. For example, a grammar checker flagged the error in the first sentence but not in the second:

► Maria is going to study the mammals of north America.

► The Darwin Martin House, designed by Frank Lloyd Wright, is located in buffalo, New York.

- **Proper nouns:** Ronald Reagan, the Sears Tower
- **Words derived from proper nouns:** Reaganomics, Siamese cat
- **Brand names:** Apple Computer, Kleenex, *but* eBay
- **Abbreviations:** FBI (government agency), A&E (cable television station)
- **Call letters:** WNBC (television), WMNR (radio)

Note: Seasons, such as *summer,* and the days of the month are not capitalized when they are spelled out.

► Why would *Valentine's Day,* the day representing love and romance, fall in *winter?*

► She can meet with you on Sunday, the *seventh* of March.

PROPER and COMMON NOUNS

- **People:** John F. Kennedy, Ruth Bader Ginsburg, Albert Einstein
- **Nationalities, ethnic groups, and languages:** English, Swiss, African Americans, Arabs, Chinese, Turkish
- **Places:** the United States of America, Tennessee, the Irunia Restaurant, the Great Lakes, *but* my state, the lake
- **Organizations and institutions:** Phi Beta Kappa, Republican Party (Republicans), Department of Defense, Cumberland College, the North Carolina Tarheels, *but* the department, this college, our hockey team
- **Religious bodies, books, and figures:** Jews, Christians, Baptists, Hindus, Roman Catholic Church, the Bible, the Koran *or* Qur'an, the Torah, God, Holy Spirit, Allah, *but* a Greek goddess, a biblical reference
- **Scientific names and terms:** *Homo sapiens, H. sapiens, Acer rubrum, A. rubrum,* Addison's disease, Cenozoic era, Newton's first law, *but* the law of gravity
- **Names of planets, stars, and other astronomical bodies:** Earth (as a planet) *but* the earth, Mercury, Polaris *or* the North Star, Whirlpool Galaxy, *but* a star, that galaxy, the solar system
- **Computer terms:** the Internet, the World Wide Web *or* the Web, *but* search engine, a network, my browser
- **Days, months, and holidays:** Monday, Veterans Day, August, the Fourth of July, *but* yesterday, spring and summer, the winter term, second-quarter earnings
- **Historical events, movements, periods, and documents:** World War II, Impressionism, the Renaissance, the Jazz Age, the Declaration of Independence, the Constitution of the United States, *but* the last war, a golden age, the twentieth century, the amendment
- **Academic subjects, and courses:** English 101, Psychology 221, a course in Italian, *but* a physics course, my art history class

63b Capitalize titles when they appear before a proper name but not when they are used alone or after the name.

TITLE USED BEFORE A NAME

Every Sunday, *Aunt Lou* tells fantastic stories.

TITLE USED BEFORE A NAME

Everyone knew that *Governor Grover Cleveland* of New York was the most likely candidate for the Democratic nomination.

TITLE USED ALONE

My *aunt* is arriving this afternoon.

TITLE USED AFTER A NAME

The most likely candidate for the Democratic nomination was Grover Cleveland, *governor* of New York.

> ***Exceptions:*** If the name for a family relationship is used alone (without a possessive such as *my* before it), it should be capitalized.
>
> ► **I saw *Father* infrequently during the summer months.**
>
> Most writers do not capitalize the title *president* unless they are referring to the President of the United States: "The *president* of this university has seventeen honorary degrees." Although usage varies, you should be consistent.

 For MULTILINGUAL STUDENTS

Capitalizing the Pronoun **I**

Unlike other languages, English requires you to capitalize the first-person singular pronoun (*I*). All other pronouns are lowercase, unless they start a sentence or are part of the title of a work.

► **When *I* get home, *I* will call my doctor for the test results and let you know what she says.**

63c Capitalize titles of works of literature, works of art, and musical compositions.

Capitalize the important words in titles and subtitles. Do not capitalize articles (*a, an,* and *the*), the *to* in infinitives, or prepositions and coordinating conjunctions unless they begin or end the title or subtitle. Capitalize both words in a hyphenated word. In MLA style, capitalize subordinating conjunctions (e.g., *because*). Capitalize the first word after a colon or semicolon in a title. Capitalize titles of major divisions of a work, such as chapters.

- ▪ **Book:** *Two Years before the Mast*
- ▪ **Play:** *The Taming of the Shrew*
- ▪ **Building:** the Eiffel Tower
- ▪ **Ships, aircraft:** the *Titanic,* the *Concorde*
- ▪ **Painting:** the *Mona Lisa*
- ▪ **Article or essay:** "On Old Age"
- ▪ **Poem:** "Ode on a Grecian Urn"

- **Music:** "The Star-Spangled Banner"
- **Chapter:** "Capitalization" in *A Writer's Resource*

63d Capitalize names of areas and regions.

Names of geographic regions are generally capitalized if they are well established, like *the Midwest* and *Central Europe*. Names of directions, as in the sentence *Turn south,* are not capitalized.

> **CORRECT**   *East* meets *West* at the summit.

> **CORRECT**   You will need to go *west* on Sunset.

The word *western,* when used as a general direction or the name of a genre, is not capitalized. It is capitalized when it is part of the name of a specific region.

> ► The ~~Western~~ *western* High Noon is one of my favorite movies.

> ► I visited ~~western~~ *Western* Europe last year.

63e Follow standard practice for capitalizing names of races, ethnic groups, and sacred things.

The words *black* and *white* are usually not capitalized when they are used to refer to members of racial groups because they are adjectives that substitute for the implied common nouns *black person* and *white person*. However, names of ethnic groups and races are capitalized: *African Americans, Italians, Asians, Caucasians.*

> *Note:* In accordance with current APA guidelines, most social scientists capitalize the terms *Black* and *White,* treating them as proper nouns.

TEXTCONNEX

Emphasis in E-Mail

Words or phrases in all capital letters are not always welcome in online chat rooms, e-mails, and electronic mailing list postings, where they are equivalent to shouting. Also, strings of words or sentences in capital letters can be difficult to read. If you want to emphasize a word or phrase in an online communication, put an asterisk before and after it:

> ►   That's a *very* interesting point.

Many religious terms, such as *sacrament, altar,* and *rabbi,* are not capitalized. The word *Bible* is capitalized (though *biblical* is not), but it is never capitalized when it is used as a metaphor for an essential book.

► His book *Winning at Stud Poker* used to be the *bible* of gamblers.

63f Capitalize the first word of a quoted sentence but not the first word of an indirect quotation.

► She cried, "Help!"

► He said that jazz was one of America's major art forms.

The first word of a quotation from a printed source is capitalized if the quotation is introduced with a phrase such as *she notes* or *he concludes.*

► Jim, the narrator of *My Ántonia,* concludes, "Whatever we had missed, we possessed together the precious, the incommunicable past" (324).

When a quotation from a printed source is treated as an element in your sentence and not as a sentence on its own, the first word is not capitalized.

► Jim took comfort in sharing with Ántonia "the precious, the incommunicable past" (324).

If you need to change the first letter of a quotation to fit your sentence, enclose the letter in brackets.

► The lawyer noted that "[t]he man seen leaving the area after the blast was not the same height as the defendant."

If you interrupt the sentence you are quoting with an expression such as *he said,* the first word of the rest of the quotation should not be capitalized.

► "When I come home an hour later," she explained, "the trains are usually less crowded."

When quoting a text directly, reproduce the capitalization used in the original source, whether or not it is correct by today's standards.

► Blake's marginalia include the following comment: "Paine is either a Devil or an Inspired Man" (603).

63g Capitalize the first word of a sentence.

A capital letter is used to signal the beginning of a new sentence.

► Robots reduce human error, so they produce uniform products.

Sentences in parentheses also begin with a capital letter unless they are embedded within another sentence:

► Although the week began with the news that he was hit by a car, by Thursday we knew he was going to be all right. (It was a terrible way to begin the week, though.)

► Although the week began with the news that he was hit by a car (it was a terrible way to begin the week), by Thursday we knew he was going to be all right.

63h Capitalizing the first word of an independent clause after a colon is optional.

If the word group that follows a colon is not a complete sentence, do not capitalize it. If it is a complete sentence, you can capitalize it or not, but be consistent throughout your document. (See if your instructor or style guide prefers one option.)

► The question is serious: do you think peace is possible?

or

► The question is serious: Do you think peace is possible?

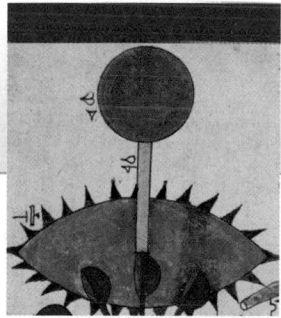

64 Abbreviations and Symbols

Unless you are writing a scientific or technical report, spell out most terms and titles, except in the cases discussed in this chapter. You may also want to consult your discipline's style manual for guidelines.

www.mhhe.com/
awr3
For information
and exercises on
abbreviations, go to

Editing >
Abbreviations

Abbreviations and Grammar Checkers

Computer grammar or spelling checkers may flag an abbreviation, but they generally will not tell you if your use of it is acceptable or consistent within a piece of writing.

Abbreviations and Symbols

Some abbreviations and symbols may be acceptable in certain contexts, as long as readers will know what they stand for. For example, a medical writer might use *PT* (*physical therapy*) in a medical report or professional newsletter.

64a Abbreviate familiar titles that always precede or follow a person's name.

Some abbreviations appear before a person's name (*Mr., Mrs., Dr.*) and some follow a proper name (*Jr., Sr., MD, Esq., PhD*). When an abbreviation follows a person's name, a comma is placed between the name and the abbreviation. Some writers consider the comma before *Jr.* and *Sr.* to be optional. Spell out religious, government, and professional titles such as Rev. (Reverend) in academic writing and when they appear with only the last name.

- **Before names:** Mrs. Jean Bascom; Dr. Epstein

- **After names:** Robert Robinson, Jr.; Elaine Less, CPA, LL.D.

Do not use two abbreviations that represent the same thing: *Dr. Peter Joyce, MD.* Use either *Dr. Peter Joyce* or *Peter Joyce, MD.* Spell out titles used without proper names.

▶ Mr. Carew asked if she had seen the ~~dr.~~ *doctor.*

64b Use abbreviations only when you know your readers will understand them.

If you use a technical term or the name of an organization in a report, you may abbreviate it as long as your readers are likely to be familiar with the abbreviation. Abbreviations of three or more capital letters generally do not use periods: *CBS, EPA, IRS, NAACP, USA.*

FAMILIAR
ABBREVIATION   The EPA has had a lasting impact on the air quality of this country.

Note: In the body of a paper, you can use *U.S.* as an adjective (*U.S. Constitution*) but not as a noun (*I grew up outside of the United States.*)

CHARTING the TERRITORY

Scientific and Latin Abbreviations

Most abbreviations used in scientific or technical writing, such as those related to measurement, should be given without periods: *mph, lb, dc, rpm*. If an abbreviation looks like an actual word, however, you can use a period to prevent confusion: *in., Fig*. In some types of scholarly writing, the use of Latin abbreviations is acceptable (in parenthetical statements and notes).

UNFAMILIAR ABBREVIATION

After you have completed them, take these

the Human Resources and Education Center.
forms to ~~HREC~~.
      ^

Write out an unfamiliar term or name the first time you use it, and give the abbreviation in parentheses.

▶ **The Student Nonviolent Coordinating Committee (SNCC) was far to the left of other civil rights organizations, and its leaders often mocked the "conservatism" of Dr. Martin Luther King, Jr. However, the SNCC quickly burned itself out and disappeared.**

64c Abbreviate words typically used with times, dates, and numerals, as well as units of measurement in charts and graphs.

Abbreviations or symbols associated with numbers should be used only when accompanying a number: *3 p.m.*, not *in the p.m.; $500,* not *How many $ do you have?* The abbreviation *B.C.* ("Before Christ") follows a date; *A.D.* ("in the year of our Lord") precedes the date. The alternative abbreviations *B.C.E.* ("Before the Common Era") and *C.E.* ("Common Era") can be used instead of *B.C.* and *A.D.*, respectively.

6:00 p.m. or 6:00 P.M. or 6 PM	9:45 a.m. or 9:45 A.M. or 9:45 AM
498 B.C. or 498 B.C.E. or 498 BCE	A.D. 275 or 275 C.E. or 275 CE
6,000 rpm	271 cm

In charts and graphs, abbreviations and symbols such as = for *equals, in.* for *inches,* % for *percent,* and *$* with numbers are acceptable because they save space.

Note: Be consistent. If you use *a.m.* in one sentence, do not switch to *A.M.* in the next sentence.

64d Avoid Latin abbreviations in formal writing.

In formal writing, it is usually a good idea to avoid even common Latin abbreviations (*e.g., et al., etc.,* and *i.e.*). Instead of *e.g. (exempli gratia),* use *such as* or *for example.*

cf.	compare (*confer*)
et al.	and others (*et alia*)
etc.	and so forth, and so on (*et cetera*)
i.e.	that is (*id est*)
N.B.	note well (*nota bene*)
viz.	namely (*videlicet*)

64e Avoid inappropriate abbreviations and symbols.

Days of the week (*Sat.*), places (*TX* or *Tex.*), the word *company* (*Co.*), people's names (*Wm.*), disciplines and professions (*econ.*), parts of speech (*v.*), parts of written works (*ch., p.*), symbols (@), and units of measurement (*lb.*) are all spelled out in formal writing.

▶ The *environmental* (not *env.*) engineers from the Paramus Water *Company* (not *Co.*) are arriving in *New York City* (not *NYC*) this *Thursday* (not *Thurs.*) to correct the problems in the *physical education* (not *phys. ed.*) building in time for *Christmas* (not *Xmas*).

> **Exceptions:** If an ampersand (&) or an abbreviation such as *Inc., Co.,* or *Corp.* is part of a company's official name, then it can be included in formal writing: *Time Inc. announced these changes in late December.*

Use -*s,* not -'*s* to make abbreviations plural (two *DVDs*).

TEXTCONNEX

Digital Age Abbreviations and Acronyms

CD	compact disc
CD-ROM	compact disc read-only memory
DVD	digital videodisc
FTP	file transfer protocol
GB	gigabyte
HTML	hypertext markup language

TEXTCONNEX *(continued)*

HTTP	hypertext transfer protocol
IM	instant message
KB	kilobyte
MB	megabyte
URL	uniform resource locator
WWW	World Wide Web

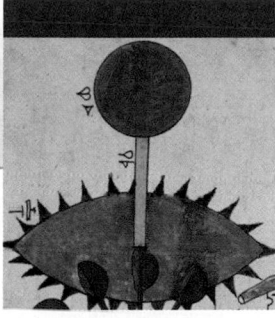

65 Numbers

65a In nontechnical writing, spell out numbers up to one hundred and round numbers greater than one hundred.

www.mhhe.com/ awr3

For information and exercises on numbers, go to

Editing > Numbers

▶ Approximately *twenty-five* students failed the exam, but more than *two hundred and fifty* passed.

When you are using a great many numbers or when a spelled-out number would require more than three or four words, use numerals.

▶ This regulation affects nearly *10,500* taxpayers, substantially more than the *200* originally projected. Of those affected, *2,325* filled out the papers incorrectly and another *743* called the office for help.

Round numbers larger than one million are expressed in numerals and words: 8 million, 2.4 trillion.

Use all numerals rather than mixing numerals and spelled-out words for the same type of item in a passage.

▶ We wrote to 132 people but only ~~sixteen~~ responded.
                                             16

> ***Exceptions:*** When two numbers appear together, spell out one and use numerals for the other: *two 20-pound bags.*

65b Spell out a number that begins a sentence.

If a numeral begins a sentence, reword the sentence or spell out the numeral.

► *Twenty-five* children are in each elementary class.

65c In technical and business writing, use numerals for exact measurements and all numbers greater than ten.

► The endosperm halves were placed in each of 14 small glass test tubes.

► A solution with a GA_3 concentration ranging from 0 g/mL to 10^5 g/mL was added to each test tube.

► With its $1.9 trillion economy, Germany has an important trade role to play.

65d Use numerals for dates, times of day, addresses, and similar kinds of conventional quantitative information.

- **Dates:** October 9, 2009; 1558–1603; A.D. 1066 (*or* AD 1066); *but* October ninth, May first
- **Time of day:** 6 A.M. (*or* AM *or* a.m.), a quarter past eight in the evening, three o'clock in the morning
- **Addresses:** 21 Meadow Road, Apt. 6J; Grand Island, NY 14072
- **Percentages:** 73 percent, 73%
- **Fractions and decimals:** 21.84, 6½, two-thirds (*not* 2-thirds), a fourth
- **Measurements:** 100 miles per hour (*or* 100 mph), 9 kilograms (*or* 9 kg), 38°F, 15°Celsius, 3 tablespoons, 4 liters (*or* 4 L), 18 inches (*or* 18 in.)
- **Volume, chapter, page:** volume 4, chapter 8, page 44
- **Scenes in a play:** *Hamlet,* act 2, scene 1, lines 77–84
- **Scores and statistics:** 0 to 3, 98–92, an average age of 35
- **Amounts of money:** 10¢, (*or* 10 cents), $125, $2.25, $2.8 million (*or* $2,800,000)
- **Serial or identification numbers:** batch number 4875, 15.20 on the AM dial
- **Telephone numbers:** (716) 555-2174
- **Surveys:** 9 out of 10

To make a number plural, add -*s*.

> *Note:* In nontechnical writing, spell out the names of units of measurement (*inches, liters*) in text. You can use abbreviations (*in., L*) and symbols (%) in charts and graphs to save space.

For MULTILINGUAL STUDENTS

Dates and Decimals

In American English, the day usually follows the month in dates: *May 9, 2009; 5/9/09.* Decimals are preceded by a period (one-tenth = 0.1), and commas are used within whole numbers longer than four numerals (twenty-two thousand three = 22,003). In four-digit numbers, the comma is optional: *4,010* or *4010. Hundred* is always singular following a number and plural when alone (*hundreds of years*).

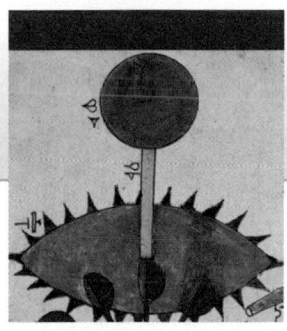

66 Italics (Underlining)

Italics, a typeface in which the characters slant to the right, is used to set off certain words and phrases. If italics is not available or if your instructor prefers, however, you can underline words that would be typeset in italics. MLA style requires italics.

www.mhhe.com/ awr3
For information and exercises on italics, go to
Editing > Italics

▶ Daniel Day-Lewis gives one of his best performances in *There Will Be Blood.*

▶ Daniel Day-Lewis gives one of his best performances in There Will Be Blood.

66a Italicize (underline) titles of lengthy works or separate publications.

Italicize (or underline) titles of long works or works that are not part of a larger publication.

TextConnex

Italics and Underlining

Italics may not be available in online environments. To indicate underlining, put an underscore mark or an asterisk before and after what you would italicize in a manuscript: Daniel Day-Lewis gives one of his best performances in _There Will Be Blood_.

On the Web, underlining indicates a hypertext link. If your work is going to be posted online, use italics instead of underlining for titles to avoid confusion.

Works That Should Be Italicized (or Underlined)

- **Books (including textbooks):** *The Color of Water, The Art of Public Speaking*
- **Magazines and journals:** *Texas Monthly, College English*
- **Newspapers:** *Chicago Tribune*
- **Comic strips:** *Dilbert*
- **Plays, films, television series, radio programs:** *Death of a Salesman, On the Waterfront, 24, Car Talk*
- **Long musical compositions:** Beethoven's *Pastoral Symphony* (*But* Beethoven's Symphony No. 6—the title consists of the musical form, a number, and/or a key.)
- **Choreographic works:** Balanchine's *Jewels*
- **Artworks:** Edward Hopper's *Nighthawks*
- **Web sites:** *Slate*
- **Software:** *Microsoft PowerPoint*
- **Long poems:** *Odyssey*
- **Pamphlets:** *Gorges: A Guide to the Geology of the Ithaca Area*
- **Electronic databases:** *Academic Search Premier*

In titles of lengthy works, *a, an,* or *the* is capitalized and italicized (underlined) if it is the first word, but *the* is not generally treated as part of the title in names of newspapers and periodicals in MLA or

---

Exceptions: Do not use italics or underlining when referring to the Bible and other sacred books.

Chicago style: the *New York Times*. If you are following APA or CSE style, however, you should treat *the* as part of the title.

Court cases may also be italicized or underlined, but legal documents and laws (*the Constitution*) are not.

▶ **In *Brown v. Board of Education of Topeka* (1954), the U.S. Supreme Court ruled that segregation in public schools is unconstitutional.**

▶ **He obtained a writ of habeas corpus.**

Do not italicize or underline punctuation marks that follow a title unless they are part of the title: I finally finished reading *Moby Dick*!

Quotation marks are used for the titles of short works—essays, newspaper and magazine articles and columns, short stories, short poems, and individual Web pages. Quotation marks are also used for titles of unpublished works when they are referred to within text, including student papers, theses, and dissertations. (*See Chapter 61, pp. 526–27, for more on quotation marks with titles.*)

66b Italicize (underline) the names of ships, trains, aircraft, and spaceships.

Queen Mary 2   *Montrealer*   *Spirit of St. Louis*   *Apollo 11*

Do not italicize any abbreviations used with the name, such as HMS or SS. Model names and numbers (such as Boeing 747) are not italicized.

66c Italicize (underline) foreign terms.

▶ **In the Paris airport, we recognized the familiar no smoking sign: *Défense de fumer*.**

Many foreign words have become so common in English that everyone accepts them as part of the language and they require no italics or underlining: rigor mortis, pasta, and sombrero, for example. (These words appear in English dictionaries.)

66d Italicize (underline) scientific names.

The scientific (Latin) names of organisms, consisting of the genus and species, are always italicized. The genus is capitalized.

▶ **Most chicks are infected with *Cryptosporidium baileyi*, a parasite typical of young animals.**

66e Italicize (underline) words, letters, and numbers referred to as themselves.

For clarity, italicize words or phrases used as words rather than for the meaning they convey. (You may also use quotation marks for this purpose.)

► **The term *romantic* does not mean the same thing to the Shelley scholar that it does to the fan of Danielle Steel's novels.**

Letters and numbers used alone should also be italicized.

► **The word *bookkeeper* has three sets of double letters: double *o*, double *k*, and double *e*.**

► **Add a *3* to that column.**

66f Use italics (underlining) sparingly for emphasis.

An occasional word in italics helps you make a point. Too much emphasis, however, may mean no emphasis at all.

WEAK	You don't *mean* that your *teacher* told the whole *class* that *he* did not know the answer *himself*?
REVISED	Your teacher admitted that he did not know the answer? That is amazing.

If you add italics or underlining to a quotation, indicate the change in parentheses following the quotation.

► **Instead of promising that no harm will come to us, Blake only assures us that we "need not *fear* harm" (emphasis added).**

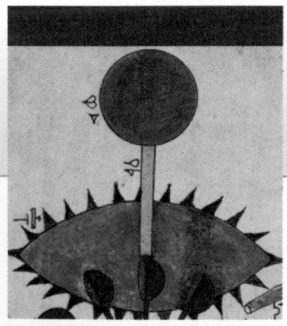

67 Hyphens

67a Use hyphens for compound words and for clarity.

www.mhhe.com/
awr3

For information and exercises on hyphens, go to

Editing > Hyphens

A hyphen joins two nouns to make one compound word. Scientists speak of a *kilogram-meter* as a measure of force, and professors of literature talk about the *scholar-poet*. The hyphen lets us know that the two nouns work together as one. As compound nouns come into general use, the hyphens between them tend to disappear: *firefighter, thundershower.*

A dictionary is the best resource when you are unsure about whether to use a hyphen. If you cannot find a compound word in the dictionary, spell it as two separate words. Whatever spelling you choose, be consistent throughout your document.

67b Use hyphens to join two or more words to create compound adjective or noun forms.

A noun can also be linked with an adjective, an adverb, or another part of speech to form a compound adjective.

accident-prone   quick-witted

Hyphens are also used in nouns designating family relationships and compounds of more than two words:

brother-in-law   stay-at-home

Compound nouns with hyphens generally form plurals by adding -s or -es to the most important word.

attorney general/attorney<u>s</u> general
mother-in-law/mother<u>s</u>-in-law

Some proper nouns that are joined to make an adjective are hyphenated.

the Franco Prussian war   of Mexican-American heritage

Hyphens often help clarify adjectives that come before the word they modify. Modifiers that are hyphenated when they are placed *before* the word they modify are usually not hyphenated when they are placed *after* the word they modify

▶ It was a *bad-mannered* reply.

▶ The reply was *bad mannered.*

Do not use a hyphen to connect -*ly* adverbs to the words they modify. Similarly, do not use a hyphen with -*er* or -*est* adjectives and adverbs.

▶ They explored the newly⁄discovered territories.

▶ This dress is better⁄looking in red.

In a pair or series of compound nouns or adjectives, add suspended hyphens after the first word of each item.

▶ The child care center accepted three-, four-, and five-year-olds.

67c Use hyphens to spell out fractions and compound numbers.

Use a hyphen when writing out fractions or compound numbers from twenty-one to ninety-nine.

three-fourths of a gallon   thirty-two

> *Note:* In MLA style, use a hyphen to show inclusive numbers: *pages 100-40.*

67d Use a hyphen to attach some prefixes and suffixes.

Use a hyphen to join a prefix and a capitalized word or a number.

un-American	pre-Columbian	pre-1970
mid-August	neo-Nazi	

A hyphen is sometimes used to join a capital letter and a word.

T-shirt	V-six engine

The prefixes *all-, ex-, quasi-* and *self-,* and the suffixes *-elect, -odd,* and *-something)* generally take hyphens.

all-purpose	president-elect
ex-convict	fifty-odd
quasi-scientific	thirty-something
self-sufficient	

Most prefixes, however, are not attached by hyphens, unless a hyphen is needed to show pronunciation, avoid double letters (*anti-immigration*), or distinguish the word from the same word without a hyphen: *recreate* (play) versus *re-create* (make again). Check a dictionary to be sure you are using the standard spelling.

67e Use hyphens to divide words at the ends of lines.

When you must divide words, do so between syllables. Pronunciation alone cannot always tell you where to divide a word, however. If you are unsure about how to break a word into syllables, consult your dictionary.

► **My writing group had a very fruitful *collab-oration.* [not *colla-boration*]**

Never leave just one or two letters on a line.

► **He seemed so sad and vulnerable and so *discon-nected* from his family. [not *disconnect-ed*]**

Compound words such as *hardworking, rattlesnake,* and *bookcase* should be broken only between the words that form them: *hard-working, rattle-snake, book-case.* Compound words that already have hyphens, like *brother-in-law,* are broken only after the hyphens.

> *Note:* Never hyphenate an abbreviation, a contraction, a numeral, or a one-syllable word.

TextConnex

Dividing Internet Addresses

If you need to divide an Internet address between lines, divide it after a slash. Do not divide a word within the address with a hyphen; readers may assume the hyphen is part of the address. Break an e-mail address after @. Check your style manual for specific guidelines.

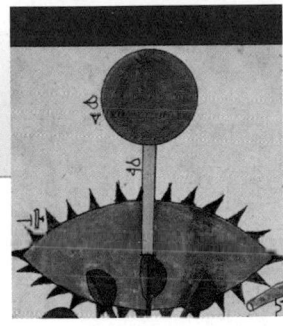

68 Spelling

Proofread your writing carefully. Misspellings creep into the prose of even the best writers. Use the following strategies to help you improve your spelling.

www.mhhe.com/
awr3
For information and
exercises on spelling,
go to
Editing > Spelling

- Become familiar with major spelling rules (*68a*).
- Learn to distinguish **homonyms**—words that are pronounced alike but that have different meanings and spellings (*68b*).
- Keep a list of words that give you trouble. Include tricks to help you remember how to spell particular words—for example, there is "a rat" in *separate*.
- If you are not sure how a word is spelled, look it up in the dictionary.

Spelling Checkers

Computer spell checkers are helpful tools. Remember, however, that a spell checker cannot tell *how* you are using a particular word. If you write *their* but mean *there,* a spell checker cannot point out your mistake. Spell checkers also cannot point out many misspelled proper nouns.

68a Learn the rules that generally hold for spelling, as well as their exceptions.

1. *i* before *e*

Use *i* before *e* except after *c* or when sounded like *a,* as in *neighbor* and *weigh.*

- *i* **before** *e:* believe, relieve, chief, grief, wield, yield
- **Except after** *c:* receive, deceive, ceiling, conceit
- **Exceptions:** seize, caffeine, weird, height, science, species

2. Adding prefixes and suffixes

- **Prefixes** do not change a word's spelling when attached.

- **Final silent** *e:* When adding a suffix that begins with a vowel, drop the final silent *e* from the root word. Keep the final *e* if the suffix begins with a consonant.

  force/forcing   remove/removable
  surprise/surprising   care/careful

  Exceptions: argue/argument, true/truly, change/changeable, judge/judgment, acknowledge/acknowledgment

---

Exception: Keep the silent *e* if it is needed to clarify the pronunciation or if the word would be confused with another word without the *e.*

dye/dyeing (to avoid confusion with *dying*)
hoe/hoeing (to avoid mispronunciation)

- **Final** *y:* When adding the suffix -*ing* to a word ending in *y,* retain the *y.*

  enjoy/enjoying   cry/crying

  To add other suffixes, change the *y* to *i* or *ie* when the final *y* follows a consonant, but not when it follows a vowel.

  happy/happier   defray/defrayed

- **Final consonants:** When adding a suffix to a word that ends in a consonant preceded by a single vowel, double the final consonant if the root word has only one syllable or an accent on the last syllable.

  grip/gripping   refer/referred

  Exceptions: bus/busing, focus/focused

- **-ly with words that end in -ic:** Add -ally.

  logic/logically   terrific/terrifically

  Exception: public/publicly

- **Frequently confused suffixes:** Be especially careful with words ending in -able/-ible, -ant/-ent, and -ify/-efy. Always check with a dictionary.

3. Forming plurals

Most plurals are formed by adding -s. Some are formed by adding -es.

When to Form the Plural with -es

SINGULAR ENDING	PLURAL ENDING
-s, -sh, -x, -z, "soft" -ch bus, bush, fox, buzz, peach	**-es** buses, bushes, foxes, buzzes, peaches
consonant + o hero, tomato	**-es** heroes, tomatoes
Exception: solo/solos	
consonant + y beauty, city	**change y to i and add -es** beauties, cities
Exception: a person's name—Kirby, the Kirbys	
-f, -fe leaf, knife, wife, life	**change f to v and add -s or -es** leaves, knives, wives, lives
Exception: Words that end in -ff and some other words that end in -f (staff, roof) form the plural by adding only an -s (staffs, roofs).	

Most plurals follow standard rules, but some have irregular forms (*child/children, tooth/teeth*), and some words with foreign roots create plurals in the pattern of the language they come from, as do these words.

    alumna/alumnae   datum/data
    alumnus/alumni   medium/media
    analysis/analyses   stimulus/stimuli
    criterion/criteria   thesis/theses

> ***Note:*** Some writers now treat *data* as though it were singular, but the preferred practice is still to recognize that *data* is plural and takes a plural verb: *The data are clear on this point: the pass/fail course has become outdated.*

Some nouns with foreign roots have regular and irregular plural forms (*appendix/appendices/appendixes*). Be consistent in using the spelling you choose.

Compound nouns with hyphens generally form plurals by adding *-s* or *-es* to the most important word.

mother-in-law/mothers-in-law

For some compound words that appear as one word, the same rule applies (*passersby*); for others, it does not (*cupfuls*). Consult a dictionary if you are not sure.

If both words in the compound are equally important, add *-s* to the second word: *singer-songwriters*.

A few words such as *fish* and *sheep* have the same forms for singular and plural. To indicate that the word is plural, you need to add a word or words that indicate quantity: *five fish, a few sheep*.

For MULTILINGUAL STUDENTS

American and British Spelling

Standard American spelling differs from British spelling for some words—among them *color/colour, canceled/cancelled, theater/theatre, realize/realise, check/cheque,* and *judgment/judgement*.

✓ **68b** Learn to distinguish words pronounced alike but spelled differently.

Homonyms sound alike but have different meanings and different spellings. The following is a list of common homonyms as well as words that are almost homonyms. For more complete definitions, consult the Glossary of Usage (*Chapter 50, pp. 432–40*) and a dictionary.

COMMON HOMONYMS and FREQUENTLY CONFUSED WORDS

accept: "to take willingly"
except: "to leave out" (verb); "but for" (preposition)

affect: "to influence" (verb); "a feeling or an emotion" (noun)
effect: "to make or accomplish" (verb); "result" (noun)

all ready: "prepared"
already: "by this time"

discreet: "tactful" or "prudent"
discrete: "separate" or "distinct"

cite: "to quote or refer to"
sight: "spectacle, sense"
site: "place"

desert: "dry, sandy place" (noun); "to leave" (verb)
dessert: "after-dinner course"

hear: "perceive by listening"
here: "at this place"

it's: contraction for *it is* or *it has*
its: possessive pronoun

loose: "not tight"
lose: "to misplace"

passed: past tense of *pass*
past: "former time"

peace: "quiet, harmony"
piece: "part of "

plain: "simple"
plane: "aircraft" or "tool for leveling wood"

precede: "to come before"
proceed: "to go forward"

principal: "most important" (adjective); "the head of an organization" or "a sum of money" (noun)
principle: "a basic standard or law" (noun)

their: possessive pronoun
there: adverb of place
they're: contraction for *they are*

to: indicating movement
too: "also"
two: number

weather: "atmospheric condition"
whether: "if it is or was true"

who's: contraction for *who is*
whose: possessive of *who*

your: possessive pronoun
you're: contraction for *you are*

CHECKLIST

Editing for Sentence Punctuation

As you revise, check your writing for proper punctuation by asking yourself these questions:

☐ Are commas used appropriately to separate or set off coordinated independent clauses; items in a series and coordinate adjectives; introductory sentence elements; nonessential sentence elements; direct quotations; and the parts of dates, addresses, titles, and numbers? (*See Chapter 57: Commas, pp. 501–11.*) Are any commas mistakenly used with sentence elements that should not be separated or set off? (*See Chapter 57: Commas, pp. 511–14.*)

☐ Are semicolons used appropriately to join independent clauses and to separate items in a series when the items contain commas? (*See Chapter 58: Semicolons, pp. 514–17.*)

☐ Are colons used appropriately after a complete sentence to introduce a list, an appositive, or a quotation; after one independent clause to introduce a second that elaborates on the first; and in business letters, ratios, and bibliographic citations? (*See Chapter 59: Colons, pp. 518–20.*)

☐ Are quotation marks used appropriately with other punctuation to identify brief direct quotations, dialogue, and the titles of short works? Are single quotation marks used appropriately to identify quotations within quotations? (*See Chapter 61: Quotation Marks, pp. 525–31.*)

☐ Are periods used appropriately at the end of sentences and in abbreviations? Are question marks and exclamation points used appropriately at the end of sentences and within quotations? Are brackets and ellipses used correctly to identify elisions and interpolations within quotations? Are dashes and parentheses used appropriately to insert or highlight nonessential information within a sentence? (*See Chapter 62: Other Punctuation Marks, pp. 531–37.*)

X CHECKLIST

Editing for Mechanics and Spelling

As you revise, check your writing for mechanics and spelling by asking yourself these questions:

☐ Are words and letters capitalized according to convention and context? (*See Chapter 63: Capitalization, pp. 538–43.*)

☐ Are abbreviations capitalized and punctuated in a consistent way? Are Latin abbreviations and non-alphabetic symbols used appropriately? (*See Chapter 64: Abbreviations and Symbols, pp. 543–47.*)

☐ Are numbers either spelled out or represented with numerals according to the conventions of the type of writing (non-technical or technical) you are engaged in? (*See Chapter 65: Numbers, pp. 547–49.*)

☐ Are italics (or is underlining) used appropriately for emphasis and to identify the titles of works, foreign words, and words used as words? (*See Chapter 66: Italics (Underlining), pp. 549–52.*)

☐ Are apostrophes used appropriately to indicate possession and to form contractions? Are any apostrophes misused to make a noun plural? (*See Chapter 60: Apostrophes, pp. 520–21.*)

☐ Are hyphens used appropriately to form compound words, in spelled-out numbers, and with certain prefixes and suffixes? (*See Chapter 67: Hyphens, pp. 552–55.*)

☐ Have you learned the rules for spelling (and their exceptions) and checked a dictionary for any words whose spelling you are unsure of? (*See Chapter 68: Spelling, pp. 555–59.*)

Shinjuku's Skyscraper District in Tokyo— featured in Lost in Translation— caters to an international, multilingual populace with signs in Japanese and English.

Grammar and rhetoric are complementary. . . . Grammar maps out the possible; rhetoric narrows the possible down to the desirable or effective.

—FRANCIS CHRISTENSEN

Basic
Grammar
Review

WITH TIPS FOR MULTILINGUAL WRITERS

12 Basic Grammar Review

Tips for Multilingual Writers

Tab 12: Basic Grammar Review
This section will help you answer questions such as:

Rhetorical Knowledge
How does sentence structure in some other languages differ from that of English? **(70)**
How does a sentence's purpose affect its type? **(72b)**

Critical Thinking, Reading, and Writing
How do I find the subject and predicate of a sentence? **(70a, b)**

Processes
During editing, should I add a comma after an *-ing* verb phrase? **(71b)**

Knowledge of Conventions
How do nouns function in a sentence? What are count and noncount nouns? **(69b)**
What are the five common sentence patterns in English? **(70b)**
How do verb tenses work with *if* (conditional) clauses? **(71e)**

Self-Assessment: *Take an online quiz at www.mhhe.com/awr3 to test your familiarity with the topics covered in Chapters 69–72. As you read the following chapters, pay special attention to the sections that correspond to any questions you answer incorrectly.*

 LEARNING in COLLEGE

What Was the Language of Your Ancestors?

Your native language or even the language of your ancestors may influence the way you use English. Even if English is your first language, you may be part of a group that immigrated generations ago but has retained traces of other grammatical structures. For example, the slang contraction *ain't,* brought here by Scottish settlers, may have meant *am not* at one time. Take note of the Tips for Multilingual Writers in this section. Some might help native speakers as well.

Written language, although based on the grammar of spoken language, has its own logic and rules. The chapters that follow explain the basic rules of standard written English.

565

www.mhhe.com/
awr3

For information and
exercises on problem
areas for multilingual
writers, go to

Editing >
Multilingual/ESL
Writers

Tip for Multilingual Writers:
Recognizing language differences

The standard structures of sentences in languages other than English can be very different from those in English. In other languages, the form of a verb can indicate its grammatical function more powerfully than can its placement in the sentence. Also, in languages other than English, adjectives may take on the function that articles (*a, an, the*) perform, or articles may be absent.

If your first language is not English, try to pinpoint the areas of difficulty you have in English. See whether you are attempting to *translate* the structures of your native language into English. If so, you will need to learn more about English sentence structure.

69 Parts of Speech

English has eight primary **parts of speech:** verbs, nouns, pronouns, adjectives, adverbs, prepositions, conjunctions, and interjections. All English words belong to one or more of these categories. Particular words can belong to different categories, depending on the role they play in a sentence. For example, the word *button* can be a noun (*the button on a coat*) or a verb (*Button your jacket now*).

www.mhhe.com/
awr3

For information and
exercises on parts of
speech, go to

Editing > Parts
of Speech

69a Verbs

Verbs carry a lot of information. They report action (*run, write*), condition (*bloom, sit*), or state of being (*be, seem*). Verbs also change form to indicate person, number, tense, voice, and mood. To do all this, a **main verb** is often preceded by one or more **helping verbs,** thereby becoming a **verb phrase.**

>   mv
> ► The play *begins* at eight.

>   hv   mv   hv mv
> ► I *may change* seats after the play *has begun.*

1. Main verbs

Main verbs change form (**tense**) to indicate when something has happened. If a word does not indicate tense, it is not a main verb. All main verbs have five forms, except for *be,* which has eight.

BASE FORM	(*talk, sing*)
PAST TENSE	Yesterday I (*talked, sang*).
PAST PARTICIPLE	In the past, I have (*talked, sung*).
PRESENT PARTICIPLE	Right now I am (*talking, singing*).
PRESENT TENSE THIRD-PERSON SINGULAR (OR -*S* FORM)	Usually he/she/it (*talks, sings*).

(For more on subject-verb agreement and verb tense, see Tab 10: Editing for Grammar Conventions, pp. 459–60 and 467–68, and the list of common irregular verbs on p. 468.)

 **Tip for Multilingual Writers: *Using verbs followed by gerunds or infinitives***

Verbs in English differ as to whether they can be followed by a gerund, an infinitive, or either. Some verbs, like *avoid,* can be followed by a gerund but not an infinitive. These constructions often express facts.

► We avoided ~~to climb~~ *climbing* the mountain during the storm.

Other verbs, like *attempt,* can be followed by an infinitive but not a gerund. Often these constructions convey intentions.

► We attempted ~~reaching~~ *to reach* the summit when the weather cleared.

Others can be followed by either a gerund or an infinitive with no change in meaning.

► We began climbing.

► We began to climb.

Still others have a different meaning when followed by a gerund than they do when followed by an infinitive. Compare these examples:

► She stopped eating. [She was eating but she stopped.]

► She stopped to eat. [She stopped what she was doing before in order to eat.]

The following lists provide common examples of each type of verb.

Some Verbs That Take Only an Infinitive

appear	fail	need	seem
ask	intend	plan	threaten
choose	learn	prepare	want
claim	manage	promise	wish
decide	mean	refuse	would like
expect			

Some Verbs That Take Only a Gerund

admit	forgive	regret
avoid	imagine	resist
consider	mention	risk
defend	mind	suggest
deny	practice	support
discuss	quit	tolerate
enjoy	recommend	understand
finish		

Some Verbs That Can Take Either a Gerund or an Infinitive

An asterisk (*) indicates those verbs for which the choice of gerund or infinitive affects meaning.

begin	like	start
continue	love	*stop
*forget	prefer	*try
hate	*remember	

> **Note:** For some verbs, such as *allow, cause, encourage, have, persuade, remind,* and *tell,* a noun or pronoun must precede the infinitive: *I reminded my sister to return my sweater.* For a few verbs, such as *ask, expect, need,* and *want,* the noun may either precede or follow the infinitive, depending on the meaning you want to express: *I want to return my sweater to my sister. I want my sister to return my sweater.*
>
> *Make, let,* and *have* are followed by a noun or pronoun plus the base form without *to: Make that boy come home on time.*

To make a verb followed by an infinitive negative, add *not* or *never* before the verb or before the infinitive. The location of *not* sometimes affects meaning:

▶ **He did not promise to write the report.**

▶ **He promised not to write the report.** [He said he would not write the

report.)

Verbs followed by a gerund always take the negative word before the gerund: *She regrets not finishing the assignment.*

---

2. Helping verbs that show time

Some helping verbs—mostly forms of *be, have,* and *do*—function to signify time (*will have been playing, has played*) or emphasis (*does play*).

(*See Tab 10: Editing for Grammar Conventions, pp. 471–74.*) Forms of *do* are also used to ask questions (*Do you play?*). Here are other such helping (**auxiliary**) verbs.

be, am, is	being, been	do, does, did
are, was, were	have, has, had	

 **Tip for Multilingual Writers:** *Matching helping verbs (do, have, be) with the appropriate form of the main verb*

Do, Does, Did

The helping verb *do* and its forms *does* and *did* combine with the base form of a verb to ask a question or to emphasize something. Any helping verb can also combine with the word *not* to create an emphatic negative statement.

QUESTION	*Do* you hear those dogs barking?
EMPHATIC STATEMENT	I *do* hear them barking.
EMPHATIC NEGATIVE	I *do not* want to have to call the police about those dogs.

Have, Has, Had

The helping verb *have* and its forms *has* and *had* combine with a past participle (usually ending in -*d, -t,* or -*n*) to form the *perfect tenses.* Do not confuse the simple past tense with the present perfect tense (formed with *have* or *has*), which is distinct from the simple past because the action can continue in the present. (*For a review of perfect tense forms, see Tab 10: Editing for Grammar Conventions, p. 472.*) To form a negative statement, add *not* after the helping verb.

SIMPLE PAST	Those dogs *barked* all day.
PRESENT PERFECT	Those dogs *have barked* all day. Those dogs *have not barked* all day.
PAST PERFECT	Those dogs *had barked* all day.

Be

Forms of *be* combine with a present participle (ending in -*ing*) to form the *progressive tenses,* which express continuing action. Do not confuse the simple present tense or the present perfect with these progressive forms. Unlike the simple present, which indicates an action that occurs frequently and might include the present moment, the present progressive form indicates an action that is going on right now. In its past form, the progressive tense indicates actions that are going on simultaneously. (*For a review of progressive tense forms, see Tab 10: Editing for Grammar Conventions, pp. 472–74.*)

SIMPLE PRESENT	Those dogs *bark* all the time.
PRESENT PROGRESSIVE	Those dogs *are barking* all the time.
PAST PROGRESSIVE	Those dogs *were barking* all day while I *was trying* to study.

When *be* is used as a helping verb, it is preceded by a modal verb such as *can* or *may: I may be leaving tomorrow.* When *been* is the helping verb, it is preceded by a form of *have: I have been painting my room all day.*

Forms of *be* combine with the past participle (which usually ends in *-d, -t,* or *-n*) to form the passive voice, which is often used to express a state of being instead of an action.

BE + PAST PARTICIPLE

PASSIVE	The dogs *were scolded* by their owner.
PASSIVE	I *was satisfied* by her answer.

When *be, being,* or *been* is the helping verb, it needs another helping verb to be complete.

MODAL VERB	The dogs *will be scolded* by their owner.
ANOTHER FORM OF *BE*	The dogs *were being scolded* by their owner.
FORM OF *HAVE*	The dogs *have been scolded* by their owner.

3. Modals

Other helping verbs, called **modals,** express an attitude toward the action or circumstance of a sentence:

can	ought to	will
could	shall	would
may	should	must
might		

Modal verbs share several characteristics:

- They do not change form to indicate person or number.
- They do not change form to indicate tense.
- They are followed directly by the base form of the verb without *to.*
- Sometimes they are used with *have* plus the past participle of the verb to indicate the past tense.

▶ We must ~~to~~ study now.

▶ He *must* have studied hard to do so well.

Some verbal expressions ending in *to* also function as modals, including *have to, be able to,* and *be supposed to.* These **phrasal modals** behave more like ordinary verbs than true modals, changing form to indicate tense and agree with the subject.

 **Tip for Multilingual Writers:** *Understanding the form and meaning of modal verbs*

Modals are used to express the following:

FUNCTION	PRESENT/FUTURE	PAST
Permission	*may, might, can, could* *May* I come at five o'clock?	*might, could* My instructor said I *could* hand in my paper late.
Polite request	*would, could* *Would* you please open the door?	
Ability	*can, am/is/are able to* I *can* (*am able to*) take one piece of luggage.	*could, was/were able to* I *could* (*was able to*) take only one piece of luggage on the plane yesterday.
Possibility	*may, might* She *may* (*might*) try to return this afternoon.	*might* + *have* + past participle His train *may* (*might*) *have* arrived already.
Expectation	*should* I have only one more chart to create, so I *should* finish my project today.	*should* + *have* + past participle The students *should have* finished the project by now.
Necessity	*must* (*have to*) I *must* (*have to*) pass this test.	*had to* + base form She *had to* study hard to pass.
Prohibition	*must* + *not* You *must not* go there.	
Logical deduction	*must* (*has to*) He *must* (*has to*) be there by now.	*must* + *have* + past participle You *must have* left early to make the noon bus.
Intention	*will, shall* I *will* (*shall*) go today.	*would* I told you I *would* go.
Speculation (past form implies that something did *not* happen)	*would, could, might* If she learned her lines, she *could* play the part.	*would* (*could/might*) + *have* + past participle If she had learned her lines, she *might have* gotten the part.
Advisability (past form implies that something did *not* happen)	*should* (*ought to*) You *should* (*ought to*) water the plant every day.	*should* + *have* + past participle You *should have* listened to the directions more carefully.
Habitual past action		*would* (*used to*) + base form When I was younger, I *would* ride my bike to school every day.

69b Nouns

Nouns name people (*Shakespeare, actors, Englishman*), places (*Manhattan, city, island*), things (*Kleenex, handkerchief, sneeze, cats*), and ideas (*Marxism, justice, democracy, clarity*).

► *Shakespeare* lived in *England* and wrote *plays* about the human *condition.*

1. Proper and common nouns

Proper nouns name specific people, places, and things and are always capitalized: *Aretha Franklin, Hinduism, Albany, Microsoft.* All other nouns are **common nouns:** *singer, religion, capital, corporation.*

2. Count and noncount nouns

A common noun that refers to something specific that can be counted is a **count noun.** Count nouns can be singular or plural, like *orange* or *suggestion* (*four oranges, several suggestions*). **Noncount nouns** are nonspecific; these common nouns refer to categories of people, places, or things and cannot be counted. They do not have a plural form. (*The orange juice is delicious. His advice was useful.*)

Count Nouns		Noncount Nouns	
cars	tools	transportation	equipment
computers	machines	Internet	machinery
facts	suggestions	information	advice
clouds	earrings	rain	jewelry
stars		sunshine	

 **Tip for Multilingual Writers:** *Using quantifiers with count and noncount nouns*

Consult an ESL dictionary if you have trouble determining whether a word is a count or noncount noun. If a word is a noncount noun, it will not have a plural form.

> *Note:* Many nouns can be either count or noncount depending on the context in which they appear.
>
> ► **Baseball** [the game: noncount] **is never played with two baseballs** [the object: count] **at the same time.**

Count and noncount nouns are often preceded by **quantifiers,** words that tell how much or how many. Quantifiers are a type of determiner. (*See p. 574 for a discussion of determiners.*) Following is a list of some quantifiers for count nouns and for noncount nouns, as well as a few quantifiers that can be used with both.

- **With count nouns only:** *several, many, a couple of, a number of, a few, few, each, every*

- **With noncount nouns only:** *a great deal of, much, not much, little, a little, less,* a word that indicates a unit (*a bag of sugar*)

- **With either count or noncount nouns:** *all, any, some, a lot of, no, enough, more*

Note: The quantifiers *a few* and *few* for count nouns and *a little* and *little* for noncount nouns all indicate a small quantity. In contrast to *a few* and *a little*, however, *few* and *little* have the negative connotation of *hardly any.*

▶ **The problems are difficult, and we have few options for solving them.** [The outlook for solving the problems is gloomy.]

▶ **The problems are difficult, but we have a few options for solving them.** [The outlook for solving the problems is hopeful.]

▶ **We have little time to find a campsite before sunset.**

[The campers might spend the night in the open by the side of the trail.]

▶ **We have a little time to find a campsite before sunset.**

[The campers will probably find a place to pitch a tent before dark.]

(*For help using articles with count and noncount nouns, see the section on pp. 574–76.*)

---

3. Concrete and abstract nouns

Nouns that name things that can be perceived by the senses are called **concrete nouns:** *boy, wind, book, song.* **Abstract nouns** name qualities and concepts that do not have physical properties: *charity, patience, beauty, hope.* (*For more on using concrete and abstract nouns, see Tab 9: Editing for Clarity, pp. 424–25.*)

4. Singular and plural nouns

Most nouns name things that can be counted and are singular or plural. Singular nouns typically become plural by adding *-s* or *-es: boy/boys, ocean/oceans, church/churches, agency/agencies.* Some have irregular plurals, such as *man/men, child/children,* and *tooth/teeth.* Noncount nouns like *intelligence* and *electricity* do not form plurals.

5. Collective nouns

Collective nouns such as *team, family, herd,* and *orchestra* are treated as singular. They are not noncount nouns, however, because collective nouns can be counted and can be made plural: *teams, families. (Also see Tab 10: Editing for Grammar Conventions, pp. 463 and 480–82.)*

6. Possessive nouns

When nouns are used in the **possessive case** to indicate ownership, they change their form. To form the possessive case, singular nouns add an apostrophe plus *s* (*'s*), whereas plural nouns ending in -*s* just add an apostrophe ('). *(Also see Tab 11: Editing for Correctness, pp. 520–24.)*

SINGULAR	insect	insect's sting
PLURAL	neighbors	neighbors' car

7. Determiners used with nouns

Determiners precede and specify nouns: *a* desk, *five* books. They include articles (*a, an, the*), possessives (*my, neighbors'*), demonstrative pronouns used as adjectives (*this, that, these, those*), and numbers as well as quantifiers (*see p. 572*). A singular count noun must have a determiner.

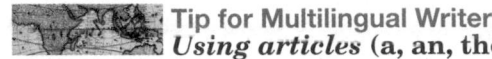 **Tip for Multilingual Writers:**
Using articles (**a, an, the**) *appropriately*

Articles in English express three basic meanings: indefinite (indicating nonspecific reference), definite (indicating specific reference), and generic (indicating reference to a general category).

Indefinite and definite meaning

A noun has an indefinite meaning, or a nonspecific reference, when it is first mentioned. To express an indefinite meaning with count nouns, use the **indefinite article** (*a* before consonant sound, *an* before vowel sound) for singular forms and no article for plural forms.

► I bought *a* new computer.

► I sold *an* old computer.

► I bought new computers.

Note: Noncount nouns *never* take the indefinite article.

    Knowledge
► ~~A knowledge~~ is a valuable commodity.
     ^

To express a definite meaning or a specific reference, use the **definite article** (*the*) with both noncount nouns and singular and plural count nouns. A noun has a definite meaning or a specific reference in a variety of situations.

- **When the noun identifies something previously mentioned:**

  I was driving along Main Street when *a* car [nonspecific reference] pulled up behind me. *The* car [specific reference to the previously mentioned car] swerved into the left lane and sped out of sight.

- **When the noun identifies something familiar or known from the context:**

  We could not play today because *the* soccer field was wet.

- **When the noun identifies a unique subject:**

  The moon will be full tonight.

- **When the noun is modified by a superlative adjective:**

  We adopted *the* most economical strategy.

- **When information in modifying phrases and clauses makes the noun definite:**

  The goal *of this discussion* is to explain article use.

Generic meaning

A noun is used generically when it is meant to represent all the individuals in the category it names. Singular count nouns used generically can take either an indefinite article or a definite article depending on the context.

► *A student* can use the Internet to research *a topic* efficiently.

► *The university* is an institution with roots in ancient times.

Noncount nouns and plural count nouns used generically take no article.

► *Television* may be harmful to young children.

► *Psychologists* believe that *children* should reduce the amount of time they spend watching television.

Articles and proper nouns

Most proper nouns are not used with articles.

► ~~The~~ Arizona is a dry state.

Some proper nouns, however, do take the definite article.

▶ *The* Civil War was a watershed event in American history.

Some other exceptions are the names of structures (*the White House*), names that include the word *of* (*the Fourth of July*), plural proper nouns (*the United States*), and many countries with names that are two or more words long (*the Dominican Republic*).

Whenever you encounter an unfamiliar proper noun, determine whether it is used with a definite article. (A dictionary may help you.)

69c Pronouns

A **pronoun** takes the place of a noun. The noun that the pronoun replaces is called its **antecedent.** Some pronouns function as adjectives. (*For more on pronoun-antecedent agreement, see Tab 10: Editing for Grammar Conventions, pp. 478– 82.*)

▶ The *snow* fell all day long, and by nightfall *it* was three feet deep.

The box on page 578 summarizes the different kinds of pronouns.

1. Personal pronouns
The **personal pronouns** *I, me, you, he, his, she, her, it, we, us, they,* and *them* refer to specific people or things and vary in form to indicate person, number, gender, and case. (*For more on pronoun reference and case, see Tab 10: Editing for Grammar Conventions, pp. 482–89.*)

▶ *You* told *us* that *he* gave Jane a lock of *his* hair.

2. Possessive pronouns
Like possessive nouns, **possessive pronouns** indicate ownership. However, unlike possessive nouns, possessive pronouns do not add apostrophes: *my/mine, your/yours, her/hers, his, its, our/ours, their/theirs.*

▶ Brunch is at *her* place this Saturday.

3. Reflexive and intensive pronouns
Pronouns ending in *-self* or *-selves* are either reflexive or intensive. **Reflexive pronouns** refer back to the subject and are necessary for sentence sense.

▶ Many of the women blamed *themselves* for the problem.

Intensive pronouns add emphasis to the nouns or pronouns they follow and are grammatically optional.

► President Harding *himself* drank whiskey during Prohibition.

4. Relative pronouns

The **relative pronouns** *who, whom, whose, that,* and *which* relate a dependent clause—a word group containing a subject and verb and a subordinating word—to an antecedent noun or pronoun in the sentence.

dependent clause

► In Kipling's story, Dravot is the man *who* would be king.

The form of a relative pronoun varies according to its **case**—the grammatical role it plays in the sentence. (*For more on pronoun case, see Tab 10: Editing for Grammar Conventions, pp. 485–89.*)

5. Demonstrative pronouns

The **demonstrative pronouns** *this, that, these,* and *those* point out nouns and pronouns that come later.

► *This* is the book literary critics have been waiting for.

Sometimes these pronouns function as adjectives: *This book won the Pulitzer.* Sometimes they are noun equivalents: *This is my book.*

6. Interrogative pronouns

Interrogative pronouns such as *who, whatever,* and *whom* are used to ask questions.

► *Whatever* happened to you?

The form of the interrogative pronouns *who, whom, whoever,* and *whomever* indicates the grammatical role they play in a sentence. (*See Tab 10: Editing for Grammar Conventions, pp. 488–89.*)

7. Indefinite pronouns

Indefinite pronouns such as *someone, anybody, nothing,* and *few* refer to a nonspecific person or thing and do not change form to indicate person, number, or gender.

► *Anybody* who cares enough to come and help may take *some* home.

Most indefinite pronouns are always singular (*anybody, everyone*). Some are always plural (*many, few*), and a handful can be singular or plural (*any, most*). (*See Tab 10, pp. 464 and 479–80.*)

PRONOUNS

PERSONAL (INCLUDING POSSESSIVE)

SINGULAR	PLURAL
I, me, my, mine	we, us, our, ours
you, your, yours	you, your, yours
he, him, his	they, them, their, theirs
she, her, hers	
it, its	

REFLEXIVE AND INTENSIVE

SINGULAR	PLURAL
myself	ourselves
yourself	yourselves
himself, herself, itself	themselves
oneself	

RELATIVE

who	whoever	what	whatever	that
whom	whomever	whose	whichever	which

DEMONSTRATIVE

this, that, these, those

INTERROGATIVE

who	what	which
whoever	whatever	whichever
whom	whomever	whose

INDEFINITE

SINGULAR		PLURAL	SINGULAR/PLURAL
anybody	nobody	both	all
anyone	no one	few	any
anything	none	many	either
each	nothing	several	more
everybody	one		most
everyone	somebody		some
everything	someone		
much	something		
neither			

RECIPROCAL

each other, any other, one another

8. Reciprocal pronouns

Reciprocal pronouns such as *each other* and *one another* refer to the separate parts of their plural antecedent.

▶ My sister and I are close because we live near *each other.*

69d Adjectives

Adjectives modify nouns and pronouns by answering questions like *Which one? What kind? How many? What size? What color? What condition?* and *Whose?* They can describe, enumerate, identify, define, and limit (*one person, that person*). When articles (*a, an, the*) identify nouns, they function as adjectives.

Sometimes proper nouns are treated as adjectives; the proper adjectives that result are capitalized: *Britain/British.* Pronouns can also function as adjectives (*his green car*), and adjectives often have forms that allow you to make comparisons (*great, greater, greatest*).

▶ The *decisive* and *diligent* king regularly attended meetings of the council. [What kind of king?]

▶ *These four artistic* qualities affect how an advertisement is received. [Which, how many, what kind of qualities?]

▶ *My little blue* Volkswagen died *one icy winter* morning. [Whose, what size, what color car? Which, what kind of morning?]

Like all modifiers, adjectives should be as close as possible to the words they modify. (*See Tab 9: Editing for Clarity, pp. 406–10.*) Most often, adjectives appear before the noun they modify, but **descriptive adjectives**—adjectives that designate qualities or attributes—may come before or after the noun or pronoun they modify for stylistic reasons. Adjectives that describe the subject and follow linking verbs (*be, am, is, are, was, being, been, appear, become, feel, grow, look, make, prove, taste*) are called **subject complements.**

BEFORE SUBJECT

The *sick* and *destitute* poet no longer believed that love would save him.

AFTER SUBJECT

The poet, *sick* and *destitute,* no longer believed that love would save him.

AFTER LINKING VERB

No longer believing that love would save him, the poet was *sick* and *destitute.*

 **Tip for Multilingual Writers:**
Using adjectives correctly

English adjectives do not change form to agree with the number and gender of the nouns they modify.

► Juan is an *attentive* father. Alyssa is an *attentive* mother. They are *attentive* parents.

Adjectives usually come before a noun, but they can also occur after a linking verb.

► We had a *delicious* meal.

► The food at the restaurant was *delicious.*

The position of an adjective can affect its meaning, however. The phrase *my old friend,* for example, can refer to a long friendship (*a friend I have known for a long time*) or an elderly friend (*my friend who is eighty years old*). In the sentence, *My friend is old,* in contrast, *old* has only one meaning—elderly.

Adjective order

When two or more adjectives modify a noun cumulatively, they follow a sequence—determined by their meaning—that is particular to English logic:

1. Determiner/article: *the, his, my, that, some*
2. Adjectives that express subjective evaluation: *cozy, intelligent, outrageous, elegant, original*
3. Adjectives of size and shape: *big, small, huge, tiny, tall, short, narrow, thick, round, square*
4. Adjectives expressing age: *old, young, new*
5. Adjectives of color: *yellow, green, pale*
6. Adjectives of origin and type: *African, Czech, Gothic*
7. Adjectives of material: *brick, plastic, glass, stone*
8. Nouns used as adjectives: *dinner [menu], computer [keyboard]*
9. Noun modified

Here are some examples:

► the small red brick cottage

► the tall African statues

► its striking arched Gothic stained-glass window

Present and past participles used as adjectives

Both the present and past participle forms of verbs can function as adjectives. To use them properly, keep the following in mind:

- Present participle adjectives usually modify nouns that are the agent of an action.

- Past participle adjectives usually modify nouns that are the recipient of an action.

► **This problem is *confusing*.**

The present participle *confusing* modifies *problem,* which is the agent, or cause of the confusion.

► **The students are *confused* by the problem.**

The past participle *confused* modifies *students,* who are the recipients of the confusion the problem is causing.

The following are some other present and past participle pairs that often cause problems.

amazing/amazed	frightening/frightened
annoying/annoyed	interesting/interested
boring/bored	satisfying/satisfied
depressing/depressed	shocking/shocked
embarrassing/embarrassed	surprising/surprised
exciting/excited	tiring/tired
fascinating/fascinated	

69e Adverbs

Adverbs often end in *-ly* (*beautifully, gracefully, quietly*) and usually answer such questions as *When? Where? How? How often? How much? To what degree?* and *Why?*

► **The authenticity of the document is *hotly* contested.** [How is it contested?]

Adverbs modify verbs, other adverbs, and adjectives. Like adjectives, adverbs can be used to compare (*less, lesser, least*). In addition to modifying individual words, they can be used to modify whole clauses. Adverbs can be placed at the beginning or end of a sentence or before the verb they modify, but they should not be placed between the verb and its direct object. Generally, they should appear as close as possible to the words they modify.

► **The water was *brilliant* blue and *icy* cold.** [The adverbs intensify the adjectives *blue* and *cold.*]

► **Dickens mixed humor and pathos *better* than any other English writer after Shakespeare.** [The adverb compares Dickens with other writers.]

► ***Consequently,* he is still read by millions.**

Consequently is a conjunctive adverb that modifies the independent clause that follows it and shows how the sentence is related to the preceding sentence. (*For more on conjunctive adverbs, see the material on conjunctions, pp. 588–89.*)

No, not, and *never* are among the most common adverbs. *Never* should not appear at the end of a sentence.

SAY *NO* ONLY ONCE

It only takes one negator (*no/not/never*) to change the meaning of a sentence from positive to negative. In fact, when two negatives are used together, they cancel each other.

►   They don't have ~~no~~ *any* reason to go there.

Tip for Multilingual Writers: *Putting adverbs in the correct place*

Although adverbs can appear in almost any position within a sentence, they should not separate a verb from its direct object.

►   Juan found ~~quickly~~ *quickly* his cat.

The negative word *not* usually precedes the main verb and follows the first helping verb in a verb phrase.

►   I have been ~~not~~ *not* sick lately.

69f   Prepositions and prepositional phrases

Prepositions (*on, in, at, by*) usually appear as part of a **prepositional phrase.** Their main function is to allow the noun or pronoun in the phrase to modify another word in the sentence. Prepositional phrases always begin with a preposition and end with a noun, pronoun, or other word group that functions as the **object of the preposition** (in *time,* on the *table*).

A preposition can be one word (*about, despite, on*) or a word group (*according to, as well as, in spite of*). Place prepositional phrases as close as possible to the words they modify. Adjectival prepositional phrases usually appear right after the noun or pronoun they modify and answer questions like *Which one?* and *What kind of?* Adverbial phrases can appear anywhere in a sentence and answer questions like *When? Where? How?* and *Why?*

AS ADJECTIVE   Many species *of birds* nest there.

AS ADVERB   The younger children stared *out the window.*

PREPOSITIONS and COMPOUND PREPOSITIONS

about	behind	in addition to	through
above	below	in case of	to
according to	beside	including	toward
across	between	in front of	under
after	beyond	in place of	underneath
against	by	in regard to	until
along	by means of	inside	up
along with	by way of	instead of	upon
among	down	into	up to
apart from	during	like	via
as	except	near	with
as to	except for	of	within
as well as	excluding	on	without
at	following	on account of	with reference to
because of	from	over	with respect to
before	in	since	

 **Tip for Multilingual Writers:**
Using prepositions

Every language uses prepositions idiomatically in ways that do not match their literal meaning. In English, prepositions combine with other words in such a variety of ways that the combinations can be learned only with repetition and over time (*see pp. 585–86*).

Idiomatic uses of prepositions indicating time and location

The prepositions that indicate time and location are often the most idiosyncratic in a language. Here are some common ways in which the prepositions *at, by, in,* and *on* are used:

TIME

AT   The wedding ceremony starts *at two o'clock.* [a specific clock time]

BY   Our honeymoon plans should be ready *by next week.* [a particular time]

IN   The reception will start *in the evening.* [a portion of the day]

ON The wedding will take place *on May 1.* The rehearsal is *on Tuesday.* [a particular date or day of the week]

LOCATION

AT I will meet you *at the zoo.* [a particular place]

You need to turn right *at the light.* [a corner or an intersection]

We took a seat *at the table.* [near a piece of furniture]

BY Meet me *by the fountain.* [a familiar place]

IN Park your car *in the parking lot* and give the money to the attendant *in the booth.* [on a space of some kind or inside a structure]

I enjoyed the bratwurst *in Chicago.* [a city, state, or other geographic location]

I found that article *in this book.* [a print medium]

ON An excellent restaurant is located *on Mulberry Street.* [a street, avenue, or other thoroughfare (not an exact address)]

I spilled milk *on the floor.* [a surface]

I watched the report *on television.* [an electronic medium]

Prepositions plus gerunds (-*ing*)

A gerund is the *-ing* form of a verb acting as a noun. A gerund can occur after a preposition (*thanks for coming*), but when the preposition is *to,* be careful not to confuse it with the infinitive form of a verb. If you can replace the verbal with a noun, use the gerund.

► I look forward to ~~win~~ *winning* at Jeopardy.

69g Conjunctions

Conjunctions join words, phrases, or clauses and indicate their relation to each other.

1. Coordinating conjunctions

The common **coordinating conjunctions** (or **coordinators**) are *and, but, or, for, nor, yet,* and *so.* Coordinating conjunctions join elements of equal weight or function.

► She was strong *and* healthy.

► The war was short *but* devastating.

► They must have been tired, *for* they had been climbing all day long.

(The section on conjunctions continues on page 587.)

COMMON IDIOMATIC EXPRESSIONS

COMMON ADJECTIVE + PREPOSITION COMBINATIONS

afraid of: fearing someone or something

anxious about: worried

ashamed of: embarrassed by someone or something

aware of: know about

content with: having no complaints about; happy about

fond of: having positive feelings for

full of: filled with

grateful to (someone) (for something): thankful; appreciative

interested in: curious; wanting to know more about

jealous of: feeling envy toward

proud/suspicious of: pleased about/distrustful of

responsible to (someone) (for something): accountable; in charge

satisfied with: having no complaints about

tired of: had enough of; bored with

COMMON VERB + PREPOSITION COMBINATIONS

apologize to: express regret for actions

arrive in (a place): come to a city/country (*I arrived in Paris.*)

arrive at (an event at a specific location): come to a building or a house (*I arrived at the Louvre at ten.*)

blame for: hold responsible; accuse

complain about: find fault; criticize

concentrate on: focus; pay attention

congratulate on: offer good wishes for success

consist of: contain; be made of

depend on: trust

explain to: make something clear to someone

insist on: be firm

(continued)

COMMON IDIOMATIC EXPRESSIONS *(continued)*

COMMON VERB + PREPOSITION COMBINATIONS (CONT.)

laugh at: express amusement

rely on: trust

smile at: act friendly toward

take care of: look after; tend

thank for: express appreciation

throw at: toss an object toward someone or something

throw to: toss something to someone to catch

throw (something) away: discard

throw (something) out: discard; present an idea for consideration

worry about: feel concern; fear for someone's safety or well-being

COMMON PARTICLES

Verb + preposition combinations that create *verb phrasals,* expressions with meanings that are different from the meaning of the verb itself. An asterisk (*) indicates a separable particle.

break down: stop functioning

*call off: cancel

*fill out: complete

*find out: discover

get over: recover

*give up: surrender; stop work on

*leave out: omit

look forward to: anticipate

look into: research

*look up: check a fact

look up to: admire

put up with: endure

run across: meet unexpectedly

run out: use up

stand up for: defend

turn down: reject

 **Tip for Multilingual Writers:**
Using direct objects with two-word verbs

If a two-word verb has a direct object, the preposition (particle) may be either separable (*I filled the form out*) or inseparable (*I got over the shock*). If the verb is separable, the direct object can also follow the preposition if it is a noun (*I filled out the form*). If the direct object is a pronoun, however, it must appear between the verb and preposition.

► I filled out ~~it~~. *it*

2. Correlative conjunctions

Correlative conjunctions also link sentence elements of equal value, but they always come in pairs: *both . . . and, either . . . or, neither . . . nor, not only . . . but also,* and *whether . . . or.*

► *Neither* the doctor *nor* the police believe his story.

3. Subordinating conjunctions

Common **subordinating conjunctions** (or **subordinators**) link sentence elements that are not of equal importance. They include the following words and phrases:

Subordinating Words

after	once	until
although	since	when
as	that	whenever
because	though	where
before	till	wherever
if	unless	while

Subordinating Phrases

as if	even though	in that
as soon as	even when	rather than
as though	for as much as	sooner than
even after	in order that	so that
even if	in order to	

Because subordinating conjunctions join unequal sentence parts, they are used to introduce dependent, or subordinate, clauses in a sentence.

► The software will not run properly *if* the computer lacks sufficient memory.

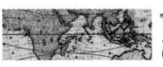 Tip for Multilingual Writers:
Using coordination and subordination appropriately

Do not use both subordination and coordination to combine the same two clauses, even if the subordinating and coordinating words are similar in meaning. Some examples include *although* or *even though* with *but* and *because* with *therefore.*

► Although I came early, ~~but~~ the tickets were already sold out.

or

► ~~Although~~ I came early, but the tickets were already sold out.

► Because Socrates is human, and humans are mortal, ~~therefore~~ Socrates is mortal.

or

► ~~Because~~ Socrates is human, and humans are mortal/; therefore, Socrates is mortal.

When you use a coordinating conjunction (*and, but, or, for, nor, yet, so*), make sure you use the conjunction that expresses the relationship between the two clauses that you want to show.

                                                            but
► My daughter's school is close to my house, ~~and~~ my office is far away.

In the revised version, *but* shows the contrast the writer is describing.

When you use a subordinating conjunction, make sure you attach it to the clause that you want to subordinate, not to the main idea. For example, if the main point is that commuting to work takes too much time, then the following sentence is unclear.

MAIN POINT OBSCURED	Although commuting to work takes two hours out of every day, I use the time to catch up on my reading.
MAIN POINT CLEAR	Commuting to work takes two hours out of every day, although I use the time to catch up on my reading.

(For help in punctuating sentences with conjunctions, see Tab 11: Editing for Correctness, pp. 503 and 514.)

4. Conjunctive adverbs

Conjunctive adverbs indicate the relation between two clauses, but unlike conjunctions (*and, but*), they are not grammatically strong enough on their own to hold the clauses together. A period or semicolon is also needed.

► Swimming is an excellent exercise for the heart and muscles; *however,* swimming does not help a person control weight as well as jogging does.

Common Conjunctive Adverbs

accordingly	as a result	certainly
also	besides	consequently

finally	likewise	similarly
furthermore	meanwhile	specifically
hence	moreover	still
however	nevertheless	subsequently
indeed	now	then
instead	otherwise	therefore

69h Interjections

Interjections are forceful expressions that often occur alone (as in the first example below). They are rarely used in academic writing except in quotations of dialogue.

▶ *"Wow!"* Davis said. "Are you telling me that there's a former presidential adviser who hasn't written a book?"

▶ Tell-all books are, *alas,* the biggest sellers.

 # **70** Parts of Sentences

Every complete sentence contains at least one **subject** (a noun and its modifiers) and one **predicate** (a verb and its objects, complements, and modifiers) that fit together to make a statement, ask a question, or give a command.

subject predicate
▶ The *children solved* the puzzle.

 ### Tip for Multilingual Writers: *Putting sentence parts in the correct order for English*

In some languages (such as Spanish), it is acceptable to omit subjects. In others (such as Arabic), it is acceptable to omit certain kinds of verbs. Other languages (such as Japanese) place verbs last, and still others (such as Hebrew) allow verbs to precede the subject. English has a distinct order for sentence parts that most sentences follow.

MODIFIERS + SUBJECT → VERB + OBJECTS, COMPLEMENTS, MODIFIERS
mod subj verb mod obj obj comp
▶ The playful kitten batted the crystal glasses on the shelf.

Changing a **direct quotation** (someone else's exact words) to an **indirect quotation** (a report on what the person said or wrote) often requires changing many sentence elements. When the quotation is a declarative sentence, however, the subject-before-verb word order does not change.

DIRECT QUOTATION	The instructor said, "You have only one more week to finish your papers."
INDIRECT QUOTATION	The instructor told the students that they had only one more week to finish their papers.

> *Note:* In the direct quotation, the verb *have* is in the present tense, but in the indirect quotation it changes to the past tense (*had*).

Changing a direct question to an indirect question, however, does require a word-order change—from the verb-subject pattern of a question to the subject-verb pattern of a declarative sentence.

DIRECT QUESTION	The instructor always asks, "Are you ready to begin?"
INDIRECT QUESTION	The instructor always asks [us] if we are ready to begin.

In an indirect quotation of a command, a pronoun or noun takes the place of the command's omitted subject, *you,* and is followed by the infinitive (*to*) form of the verb.

DIRECT QUOTATION: COMMAND	The instructor always says "[*you*] Write down the assignment before you leave."
INDIRECT QUOTATION: COMMAND	The instructor always tells *us* to write down the assignment before we leave.

In indirectly quoted negative imperatives, the word *not* comes before the infinitive.

DIRECT	The instructor said, "Do not forget your homework."
INDIRECT	The instructor reminded us *not* to forget our homework.

70a Subjects

The **simple subject** is the word or words that name the topic of the sentence; it is always a noun or pronoun. To find the subject, ask who or what the sentence is about. The **complete subject** is the simple subject plus its modifiers.

> simple subject
> ► Did *Sir Walter Raleigh* give Queen Elizabeth I the requisite obedience?
> [Who gave the queen obedience?]

> complete subject
> simple subject
> ► *Three six-year-old children* solved the puzzle in less than five minutes.
> [Who solved the puzzle?]

A **compound subject** contains two or more simple subjects connected with a conjunction such as *and, but, or,* or *neither . . . nor.*

> compound
> simple   simple
> ► *Original thinking* and *bold design* characterize her work.

In **imperative sentences,** which give directions or commands, the subject *you* is usually implied, not stated. A helping verb is needed to transform an imperative sentence into a question.

> ► [*You*] Keep this advice in mind.

> ► *Would* you keep this advice in mind?

In sentences beginning with *there* or *here* followed by some form of *be,* the subject comes after the verb.

> simple subject
> ► Here are the *remnants* of an infamous empire.

In questions, the subject may precede the verb (*Who* $\overline{\text{will go}}$?), follow

the verb (*Are you* very busy?), or appear between the helping verb and

main verb (Will *you* go?).

 ## Tip for Multilingual Writers:
Including only one subject or there
or it *in the subject position*

All English sentences and clauses except commands require an explicitly stated subject.

> *She said*
> ► The teacher told us to review sentence structure. ~~Said~~ we would have a
>
> quiz on it next class.

> ***Note:*** In commands, or imperative sentences, the subject, which is always *you,* is omitted.
>
> ► [*You*] Read the instructions before using this machine.

Unlike in some other languages, however, a pronoun cannot duplicate the subject.

► The teacher ~~she~~ told us to review sentence structure.

If the subject follows the verb, then the expletive *there* or *it* is needed in the subject position.

> *There is*
> ► ~~Is~~ a new independent radio station in our city.
> ^
>
> > *There* indicates existence or locality. The verb *is* agrees with the subject (*radio station*), which follows the verb.

> *It is*
> ► ~~Is~~ hard to find doctors who are willing to move to rural areas.
> ^

> ***Note:*** The pronoun *it* can also be the subject of a sentence about weather or environmental conditions (*It is cold in this house*), time (*It is three o'clock*), or distance (*It is five miles to the next filling station*). *There* is an expletive or adverb and cannot be used as a subject.

70b Verbs and their objects or complements

In a sentence, the **predicate** says something about the subject. The verb constitutes the **simple predicate.** The verb plus its object or complement make up the **complete predicate.**

Tip for Multilingual Writers: *Including a complete verb*

Verb structure, as well as where the verb is placed within a sentence, varies dramatically across languages, but in English each sentence needs to include at least one complete verb. (*See Chapter 69, pp. 566–71.*) The verb cannot be an infinitive—the *to* form of the verb—or an *-ing* form without a helping verb.

> *is bringing*
> ► The caterer ~~to bring~~ dinner.
> ^

> *are*
> ► Children running in the park.
>   ^

In some languages, linking verbs (verbs like *be, seem, look, sound, feel, appear,* and *remain*) may sometimes be omitted, but not in English.

> *look*
> ► They happy.
>   ^

Verb functions in sentences

Based on how they function in sentences, verbs are linking, transitive, or intransitive. The kind of verb determines what elements the complete predicate must include and therefore determines the correct order of sentence parts. Most meaningful English sentences use one of five basic sentence patterns:

- **SUBJECT + LINKING VERB + SUBJECT COMPLEMENT**
  New Yorkers are busy people.

- **SUBJECT + TRANSITIVE VERB + DIRECT OBJECT**
  The police officer caught the jaywalker.

- **SUBJECT + TRANSITIVE VERB + INDIRECT OBJECT + DIRECT OBJECT**
  The officer gave the jaywalker a ticket.

- **SUBJECT + TRANSITIVE VERB + DIRECT OBJECT + OBJECT COMPLEMENT**
  The ticket made the jaywalker unhappy.

- **SUBJECT + INTRANSITIVE VERB**
  She sighed.

Linking verbs and subject complements A **linking verb** joins a subject to information about the subject that follows the verb. That information is called the **subject complement.** The subject complement may be a noun, a pronoun, or an adjective.

> subj   lv   comp
> ► Ann Yearsley was *a milkmaid.*

The most frequently used linking verb is the *be* verb (*is, are, was, were*), but verbs such as *seem, look, appear, feel, become, smell, sound,* and *taste* can also function as links between a sentence's subject and its complement.

> subj   lv   comp
> ► That new hairstyle *looks* beautiful.

Transitive verbs and direct objects A **transitive verb** identifies an action that the subject performs or does to somebody or something else—the receiver of the action, or **direct object.** To complete its meaning, a transitive verb needs a direct object, usually a noun, pronoun, or word group that acts like a noun or pronoun.

NOUN	I threw *the ball.*
PRONOUN	I threw *it* over a fence.
WORD GROUP	I put *what I needed* into my backpack.

Most often, the subject is doing the action, the direct object is being acted on, and the transitive verb is in the **active voice.**

ACTIVE   *Parents* sometimes *consider* their *children* unreasonable.

If the verb in a sentence is transitive, it can be in the **passive voice.** In the following revised sentence, the direct object (*children*) has become the subject; the original subject (*parents*) is introduced with the preposition *by* and is now part of a prepositional phrase.

PASSIVE   Children are considered unreasonable by their parents.

Tip for Multilingual Writers: *Including only one direct object*

In English, a transitive verb must take an explicit direct object. For example, *Take it!* is a complete sentence but *Take!* is not, even if *it* is clearly implied. Be careful not to repeat the object, especially if the object includes a relative adverb (*where, when, how*) or a relative pronoun (*which, who, what*), even if the relative pronoun does not appear in the sentence but is only implied.

▶   Our dog guards the house *where* we live ~~there~~.

Transitive verbs, indirect objects, and direct objects   **Indirect objects** name to whom an action was done or for whom it was completed and are most commonly used with verbs such as *give, ask, tell, sing,* and *write.*

      subj   v   ind obj   dir obj
▶   **Coleridge wrote *Sara* a heartrending letter.**

Note that indirect objects appear after the verb but before the direct object.

Transitive verbs, direct objects, and object complements   In addition to a direct object and an indirect object, a transitive verb can take another element in its predicate: an **object complement.** An object complement describes or renames the direct object it follows.

>   dir obj   obj comp
> **His investment in a plantation made Johnson *a rich man.***

Intransitive verbs   An **intransitive verb** describes an action by a subject that is not done directly to anything or anyone else. Therefore, an intransitive verb cannot take an object or a complement. However, adverbs and adverb phrases often appear in predicates built around intransitive verbs. In the sentence that follows, the complete predicate is in italics and the intransitive verb is underlined.

> **As a recruit, I *<u>complied</u> with the order mandating short hair.***

Some verbs, such as *cooperate, assent, disappear,* and *insist,* are always intransitive. Others, such as *increase, grow, roll,* and *work,* can be either transitive or intransitive.

TRANSITIVE   I *grow* carrots and celery in my victory garden.

INTRANSITIVE   My son *grows* taller every week.

Tips   LEARNING in COLLEGE

Using the Dictionary to Determine Prepositions and Transitive and Intransitive Verbs

Your dictionary will note if a verb is *v.i.* (intransitive), *v.t.* (transitive), or both. It will also tell you—or show by example—the appropriate preposition to use when you are modifying an intransitive verb with an adverbial phrase. For example, we may *accede to* a rule, but if and when we *comply,* it has to be *with* something or someone.

71 Phrases and Dependent Clauses

A **phrase** is a group of related words that lacks either a subject or a predicate or both. Phrases function within sentences but not on their own. A **dependent clause**

**www.mhhe.com/
awr3**
For information and
exercises on phrases
and clauses, go to

Editing > Phrases
and Clauses

has a subject and a predicate but cannot function as a complete sentence because it begins with a subordinating word.

71a Noun phrases

A **noun phrase** consists of a noun or noun substitute plus all of its modifiers. Noun phrases can function as a sentence's subject, object, or subject complement.

SUBJECT	*The old, dark, ramshackle house* collapsed.
OBJECT	Greg cooked *an authentic, delicious haggis* for the Robert Burns dinner.
SUBJECT COMPLEMENT	Tom became *an accomplished and well-known cook.*

71b Verb phrases and verbals

A **verb phrase** is a verb plus its helping verbs. It functions as the predicate in a sentence: *Mary should have photographed me.* **Verbals** are words derived from verbs. They function as nouns, adjectives, or adverbs, not as verbs.

VERBAL AS NOUN	*Crawling* comes before walking.
VERBAL AS ADJECTIVE	Chris tripped over the *crawling* child.
VERBAL AS ADVERB	The child began *to crawl.*

Verbals may take modifiers, objects, and complements to form **verbal phrases.** There are three kinds of verbal phrases: participial, gerund, and infinitive.

1. Participial phrases

A **participial phrase** begins with either a present participle (the -*ing* form of a verb) or a past participle (the -*ed* or -*en* form of a verb). Participial phrases always function as adjectives. They can appear before or after the word they modify.

▶ *Working in groups,* the children solved the problem.

▶ *Insulted by his remark,* Elizabeth refused to dance.

▶ His pitching arm, *broken in two places by the fall,* would never be the same again.

2. Gerund phrases

A **gerund phrase** uses the -*ing* form of the verb, just as some participial phrases do. But gerund phrases always function as nouns, not adjectives.

► *Walking one hour a day* will keep you fit.
   subj

► The instructor praised *my acting in both scenes.*
   dir obj

3. Infinitive phrases

An **infinitive phrase** is formed using the infinitive, or *to* form, of a verb: *to be, to do, to live.* It can function as an adverb, an adjective, or a noun and can be the subject, subject or object complement, or direct object in a sentence. In constructions with *make, let,* or *have,* the *to* is omitted.

► *To finish his novel* was his greatest ambition.
   noun/subj

► He made many efforts *to finish his novel* for his publisher.
   adj/obj comp

► He needed *to finish his novel.*
   adv/dir obj

► Please let me *finish my novel.*
   adv/dir obj

71c Appositive phrases

Appositives rename nouns or pronouns and appear right after the word they rename.

► One researcher, *the widely respected R. S. Smith,* has shown that a child's
   noun   appositive

performance on such tests can be very inconsistent.

71d Absolute phrases

Absolute phrases modify an entire sentence. They include a noun or pronoun, a participle, and their related modifiers, objects, or complements. They may appear almost anywhere in a sentence.

► The sheriff strode into the bar, *his hands hovering over his pistols.*

71e Dependent clauses

Although **dependent clauses** (also known as **subordinate clauses**) have a subject and predicate, they cannot stand alone as complete sentences. They are introduced by subordinators—either by a subordinating conjunction such as *after, in order to,* or *since* (*for a more complete listing, see p. 587*) or by a relative pronoun such as *who, which,* or *that* (*for more, see the box on p. 578*). They function in sentences as adjectives, adverbs, or nouns.

1. Adjective clauses

An **adjective clause** modifies a noun or pronoun. Relative pronouns (*who, whom, whose, which,* or *that*) or relative adverbs (*where, when*) are used to connect adjective clauses to the nouns or pronouns they modify. The relative pronoun usually follows the word that is being modified and also points back to the noun or pronoun. (*For help with punctuating restrictive and nonrestrictive clauses, see Tab 11, pp. 503–07 and 512–13.*)

▶ Odysseus's journey, *which can be traced on modern maps,* has inspired many works of literature.

In adjective clauses, the direct object sometimes comes before rather than after the verb.

dir obj subj   v

▶ The contestant *whom he most wanted to beat* was his father.

2. Adverb clauses

An **adverb clause** modifies a verb, an adjective, or an adverb and answers the same questions adverbs answer: *When? Where? What? Why?* and *How?* Adverb clauses are often introduced by subordinators (*after, when, before, because, although, if, though, whenever, where, wherever*).

▶ *After we had talked for an hour,* he began to get nervous.

▶ He reacted *as if he already knew.*

3. Noun clauses

A **noun clause** is a dependent clause that functions as a noun. In a sentence, a noun clause may serve as the subject, object of a verb or preposition, or complement and is usually introduced by a relative pronoun (*who, which, that*) or a relative adverb (*how, what, where, when, why*).

SUBJECT	*What he saw* shocked him.
OBJECT	The instructor found out *who had skipped class.*
COMPLEMENT	The book was *where I had left it.*

As in an adjective clause, in a noun clause the direct object or subject complement can come first, violating the typical sentence order.

dir obj subj

▶ The doctor wondered *to whom he* should send the bill.

 Tip for Multilingual Writers: *Understanding the purposes and constructions of* if *clauses*

If clauses (also called **conditional clauses**) state facts, make predictions, and speculate about unlikely or impossible events. These conditional constructions most often employ *if,* but *when, unless,* or other words can introduce conditional constructions as well.

- Use the present tense for facts. When the relationship you are describing is usually true, the verbs in both clauses should be in the same tense.

STATES FACTS

If people *practice* doing good consistently, they *have* a sense of satisfaction.

When Meg *found* a new cause, she always *talked* about it incessantly.

- In a sentence that predicts, use the present tense in the *if* clause. The verb in the independent clause is a modal plus the base form of the verb.

PREDICTS POSSIBILITIES

If you *practice* doing good through politics, you *will have* a greater effect on your community.

- If you are speculating about something that is unlikely to happen, use the past tense in the *if* clause and *could, should,* or *would* plus the base verb in the independent clause.

SPECULATES ON THE UNLIKELY

If you *were* a better person, you *would practice* doing good every day.

- Use the past perfect tense in the *if* clause if you are speculating about an event that did not happen. In the independent clause, use *could have, might have,* or *would have* plus the past participle.

SPECULATES ON SOMETHING THAT DID NOT HAPPEN

If you *had practiced* doing good when you were young, you *would have been* a different person today.

- Use *were* in the *if* clause and *could, might,* or *would* plus the base form in the main clause if you are speculating about something that could never happen.

SPECULATES ABOUT THE IMPOSSIBLE

If Lincoln *were* alive today, he *would fight* for equal protection under the law.

Do not use *will* in *if* clauses.

► If you ~~will~~ study, you will do well.

72 Types of Sentences

Classifying by how many clauses they contain and how those clauses are joined, we can categorize sentences into four types: simple, compound, complex, and compound-complex. We can also classify them by purpose: declarative, interrogative, imperative, and exclamatory.

www.mhhe.com/awr3

For information and exercises on types of sentences, go to

Editing >
Sentence Types

72a Sentence structures

A clause is a group of related words that includes a subject and a predicate. **Independent clauses** can stand on their own as complete sentences. **Dependent,** or **subordinate, clauses** cannot stand alone. They function in sentences as adjectives, adverbs, or nouns. The presence of one or both of these two types of clauses, and their relation to each other, determines whether the sentence is simple, compound, complex, or compound-complex.

1. Simple sentences

A simple sentence has only one independent clause. Simple does not necessarily mean short, however. Although a simple sentence does not include any dependent clauses, it may have several embedded phrases, a compound subject, and a compound predicate.

INDEPENDENT CLAUSE

The bloodhound is the oldest known breed of dog.

INDEPENDENT CLAUSE: COMPOUND SUBJ + COMPOUND PRED

Historians, novelists, short-story writers, and playwrights write about characters, design plots, and usually seek the dramatic resolution of a problem.

2. Compound sentences

A compound sentence contains two or more independent clauses but no dependent clause. The independent clauses may be joined by a comma and a coordinating conjunction or by a semicolon with or without a conjunctive adverb.

► The police arrested him for drunk driving, *so* he lost his car.

► The sun blasted the earth; *therefore,* the plants withered and died.

3. Complex sentences

A complex sentence contains one independent clause and one or more dependent clauses.

independent clause   dependent clause

► He consulted the dictionary *because he did not know how to pronounce*

the word.

4. Compound-complex sentences

A compound-complex sentence contains two or more coordinated independent clauses and at least one dependent clause (italicized in the example).

► She discovered a new world of international finance, but she worked so hard investing other people's money *that she had no time to invest any of her own.*

72b Sentence purposes

When you write a sentence, your purpose helps you decide which sentence type to use. If you want to provide information, you usually use a declarative sentence. If you want to ask a question, you usually use an interrogative sentence. To make a request or give an order (a command), you use the imperative. An exclamatory sentence emphasizes a point or expresses strong emotion.

DECLARATIVE	He watches *Seinfeld* reruns.
INTERROGATIVE	Does he watch *Seinfeld* reruns?
IMPERATIVE	Do not watch reruns of *Seinfeld.*
EXCLAMATORY	I'm really looking forward to watching *Seinfeld* reruns with you!

CHECKLIST

Self-Editing for Multilingual Students

This checklist will help you identify the types of errors that can confuse your readers. Check the rules for those items that you have trouble with, and study them in context.

As you edit a sentence, ask yourself these questions:

☐ Do the subject and verb agree? (*See Chapters 53: Subject-Verb Agreement and 54: Problems with Verbs.*)

☐ Is the form of the verb or verbs correct? (*See Chapters 53: Subject-Verb Agreement and 54: Problems with Verbs, as well as the coverage of verbs in Chapters 69 and 70 and verb phrases in Chapter 71.*)

☐ Is the tense of the verb or verbs appropriate and correctly formed? (*See Chapters 53: Subject-Verb Agreement and 54: Problems with Verbs, as well as the coverage of verbs in Chapter 69.*)

☐ Do all pronouns agree with their referents, and are the referents unambiguous? (*See Chapter 55: Problems with Pronouns, as well as the coverage of pronouns in Chapter 69.*)

☐ Is the word order correct for the sentence type (for example, declarative or interrogative)? Is the word order of any reported speech correct? (*See Chapter 72 for sentence types and Chapter 70 for word order.*)

☐ Is the sentence complete (not a fragment)? Is the sentence a run-on or a comma splice? (*See Chapters 51: Sentence Fragments and 52: Comma Splices and Run-on Sentences.*)

☐ Are articles and quantifiers used correctly? (*See Chapter 69.*)

☐ Is the sentence active or passive? (*See Chapter 46: Active Verbs.*)

☐ Are the words in the sentence well chosen? (*See Chapters 47: Appropriate Language and 48: Exact Language.*)

☐ Is the sentence punctuated correctly? (*See the chapters in Tab 11: Editing for Correctness.*)

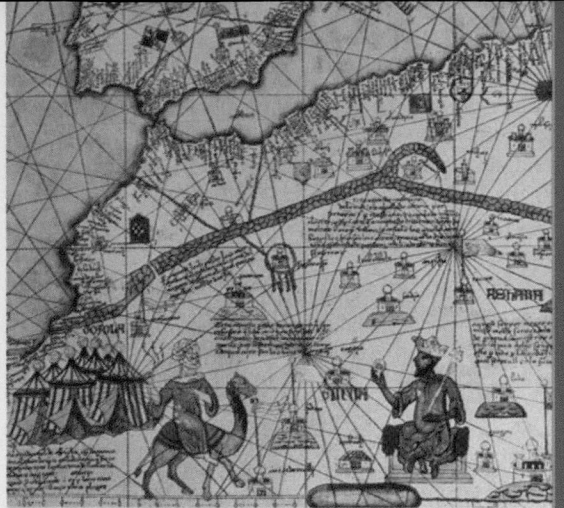

This fourteenth-century map features Mansa Musa, the greatest ruler of the Empire of Mali in West Africa. During his reign, Mali prospered as a hub of trade and learning.

13

To be able to be caught up into the world of thought—that is educated.

—EDITH HAMILTON

Further Resources for Learning

13 Further Resources for Learning

13 | Further Resources
for Learning

Timeline of World History

ca. 3000 BCE City of Babylon is founded; cuneiform script, the earliest known fully developed system of writing, emerges in ancient Mesopotamia.

3000

2500–2001 BCE Bow and arrow is first used in warfare; cotton is cultivated in Peru.

ca. 2660–1640 BCE Old and Middle Kingdoms of Egypt. Pyramids and grand monuments such as the Great Sphinx of Giza are built as royal tributes and burial structures.

2000 BCE *Gilgamesh,* ancient Mesopotamian epic, is composed (fullest extant *written* text of this epic dates from **seventh century BCE**): theme is futile human quest for immortality.

2000

ca. 1950 BCE Irrigation systems are in use in Chinese agriculture.

ca. 1850 BCE Oldest surviving Egyptian mathematics text shows that decimal system was in use.

1792–1750 BCE Rule of Babylonian king Hammurabi produces an orderly arrangement of written laws—the Hammurabi Code—among the first in the ancient world.

1200 BCE Olmec culture flourishes in Mexico (until **ca. 400 BCE**).

ca. 1000–80 BCE Varna system—precursor of caste system—evolves in India.

1000

776 BCE First recorded Olympic games are held at Olympia in Greece.

ca. 750 BCE *Iliad*—the earliest surviving example of Greek literature—and *Odyssey* are composed (ascribed to Homer).

700

Literary and cultural developments and events

Historical events

Advances in science and technology

Changes in everyday life

Break in timeline

600

551–479 BCE Life of Confucius, China's greatest philosopher.

ca. 500 BCE Many Old Testament books are transcribed.

Greeks adopt Ptolemaic model of cosmos, in which the sun revolves around the earth.

399 BCE Greek philosopher Socrates is tried and executed for corruption of youth.

387 BCE Greek philosopher Plato founds the Academy.

350 BCE Aristotle, student of Plato, writes *Poetics*, founds rival school, Lyceum; earliest portion of *Mahabharata* (Sanskrit heroic epic) is composed mid-century.

ca. 250 BCE Archimedes, founder of mathematical physics, writes *Measurement of the Circle* (includes concept of π).

215 BCE Construction of Great Wall of China begins.

23–13 BCE Roman poet Horace composes *Odes*.

30 Jesus is crucified by the Romans in Jerusalem.

ca. 560–480 BCE Life of Buddha (Siddhartha), founder of Buddhism.

508 BCE Athens becomes the world's first democracy.

500

461–429 BCE Reign of Pericles ushers in flowering of Athenian culture: Aeschylus, *Oresteia* (**458 BCE**); Sophocles, *Antigone* (**ca. 442–441 BCE**) and *Oedipus the King* (**ca. 429 BCE**); Euripides, *Medea* (**431 BCE**); Aristophanes, *Lysistrata* (**411 BCE**); Plato, *Republic* (**ca. 406 BCE**).

400

404 BCE Golden age of Periclean Athens ends with fall of Athens to Sparta.

356–323 BCE Life of Alexander the Great, king of Macedonia, who conquers the Persian Empire

300

ca. 300 BCE Euclid writes *Elements*, seminal work of elementary geometry.

ca. 250 BCE *Ramayana* (Sanskrit heroic epic) is composed mid-century.

200

ca. 200 BCE–500 CE Roman Empire encompasses the entire Mediterranean region.

100

27–19 BCE Roman poet Virgil composes the epic poem *Aeneid*.

0

8 Ovid composes *Metamorphoses*, a 15-volume poem based on Greek and Roman myths.

ca. 65–85 New Testament Gospels are composed.

ca. 300 Large towns exist in inland Niger Delta, later to develop into the Empire of Ghana in west Africa.

300

400

413–26 St. Augustine writes *City of God,* interpreting history in light of Christianity.

410 Visigoths sack Rome.

478 First Shinto shrine is built in Japan.

500

550–900 Mayan civilization reaches Late Classical phase: art, architecture, and writing flourish at Tikal and dozens of other city-states.

600

ca. 650–750 *Beowulf,* Old English epic, is composed.

622 Mohammed, founder of Islam, flees from Mecca to Medina, transforms Islam into religious and secular empire.

651–5 Koran or Qu'ran, the holy book of Islam, is codified.

700

718 Muslims are in control of most of Iberian peninsula; some Muslim influence remains until Christian forces gain control in **1492** with taking of Granada.

900

960–1279 Song Dynasty in China: flowering of arts and scholarship.

1000

ca. 978–1026 Life of Lady Shikibu Murasaki, Japanese author of *Tale of Genjii,* considered by many to be the world's first novel.

ca. 1100 *Song of Roland*, French epic poem, is composed.

1100

1096–1291 The Crusades, nine military expeditions in which European Christians attempted to reconquer the Holy Land (Palestine) from the Muslims, take place.

1200

ca. 1200 Zen Buddhism travels from China to Japan, becomes influential in Japanese politics, painting, landscape, and culture, especially in the tea ceremony.

ca. 1290–1918 Ottoman Empire, Muslim Turkish state comprising Anatolia, modern southeastern Europe, and the Arab Middle East and North Africa, is established.

1300

ca. 1300–1650 Renaissance in Europe: "rebirth" of arts and culture.

1307–21 Dante Alighieri composes *La Divina Commedia,* an epic poem describing his imaginary journey through heaven and hell.

1312–27 Empire of Mali in West Africa reaches its height under Mansa Musa, builder of the Great Mosque at Timbuktu.

1350

1347–51 "Black Death," an epidemic of the bubonic plague, rages in Europe, eventually claiming 25–50% of the population.

ca. 1370–1400 English poet Chaucer composes *The Canterbury Tales*, a collection of 24 tales with dramatic links.

ca. 1350–1400 Great Zimbabwe, a fabled stone city that controlled a large part of southeast Africa in medieval times, reaches its height.

1400

1431 Joan of Arc, leader of French army against the British in the Hundred Years' War, is burned at the stake for heresy by the British.

ca. 1438–1532 Inca Empire, largest native empire of the Americas, reaches its height in Central and South America; expansion ends with the Spanish invasion led by Pizarro.

1450

1453 Constantinople falls to Ottoman Turks, marking the end of the Byzantine Empire.

ca. 1455 Gutenberg Bible set and printed; Gutenberg's invention of movable type leads to book printing boom in Europe.

1484 Botticelli paints *Birth of Venus* for the Medici family of Florence.

ca. 1492 Christopher Columbus lands in the Bahamas.

1500

1499 Amerigo Vespucci lands in South America.

1503 Leonardo da Vinci, painter, inventor, and scientist, paints *Mona Lisa*.

1508–12 Michelangelo paints the ceiling of the Sistine Chapel in Rome.

1513 Niccolo Machiavelli writes *The Prince*, arguing for pragmatism over virtue in a ruler.

1517 Martin Luther's *95 Theses* introduces the Protestant Reformation in Europe.

1520 Gold, silver, and chocolate are brought from the Americas to Spain.

1532 Sugarcane is cultivated in Brazil.

1593–99 Shakespeare's sonnets are published, followed by *Hamlet* (**1600–1**) and *Othello* (**1604**).

1599 Globe Theater is built in London.

1600

1603 Kabuki is first performed in Japan by female entertainer Okuni.

1605 Miguel de Cervantes Saavedra writes his masterpiece *Don Quixote.*

1609 Tea is first shipped to Europe from China.

1611 King James Bible is published, becomes most popular version for more than three centuries.

1619 African captives are brought to Jamestown, Virginia, to be servants; slave system develops over the next 80 years.

1631–48 Taj Mahal, premier example of Mogul architecture, is built in Agra, India.

1637 René Descartes, called by some the founder of modern philosophy, writes *Discourse on Method* (from which comes *"Cogito, ergo sum"*: "I think; therefore, I am").

1651 Thomas Hobbes writes *Leviathan,* portraying human life in a state of nature as "nasty, brutish, and short" and offering as a remedy a social contract in which the ruler's power—for the sake of expediency—is absolute.

1625

1650

1675

1608 Galileo Galilei invents astronomical telescope, provides evidence to support Nicolaus Copernicus's theory that the earth and planets revolve around the sun.

1614 Pocahontas, Native American princess, marries tobacco planter John Rolfe.

1620 Pilgrims sail for America and found Plymouth Colony.

1632 Rembrandt van Rijn, prolific Dutch painter, paints his first major portrait, *The Anatomy Lesson of Dr. Tulp.*

1642–1648 English Civil War pits Parliamentary forces under Oliver Cromwell against Charles I: Charles I is defeated and beheaded in **1649.**

1667 John Milton writes *Paradise Lost,* an epic poem describing man's "first disobedience" and the promise of his redemption.

1687 Isaac Newton publishes *Principia,* in which he codifies laws of motion and gravity not modified until the twentieth century.

1690 John Locke publishes *Essay Concerning Human Understanding,* in which he espouses an empiricist view of philosophy (limiting true knowledge to what can be perceived through the senses or through introspection).

ca. 1688–1790 The Enlightenment, an intellectual movement committed to secular views based on reason, takes hold in Europe.

1700

ca. 1701 Peter the Great begins westernization of Russia.

ca. 1740s Culmination of the Baroque era in music: Vivaldi, *The Four Seasons;* Bach, *Brandenberg Concertos;* Handel, *Messiah.*

1740

1750

1755–73 Samuel Johnson publishes *Dictionary of the English Language.*

Johann Sebastian Bach

1760

1767–87 Sturm und Drang ("Storm and Stress"), a literary and intellectual movement in Germany that prefigures Romanticism (**ca. 1789–1825** in England).

1761 Jean-Jacques Rousseau publishes *The Social Contract,* in which he praises the natural goodness of human beings but insists on the need for society to attain true happiness.

1769 James Watt patents a steam engine.

1770

ca. 1770 Industrial Revolution begins, fueled by steam power: first steam-driven cotton factory (**1789**) and first steam-powered rolling mill open in England (**1790**).

1775–81 American Revolution: hostilities begin at Lexington and Concord, Massachusetts, in 1775, although the Continental Congress will not officially vote for independence until 1776.

1780

1776 "Declaration of Independence" is approved by the Continental Congress on July 4.

Adam Smith publishes *Causes of the Wealth of Nations,* advocates regulation of markets through supply and demand and competition.

1781 Immanuel Kant publishes *Critique of Pure Reason,* an attempt at reconciling empiricism and rationalism, and for many the single most important work of modern philosophy.

1780s–90s Height of the Classical era in music: Mozart writes the opera *Don Giovanni* (**1787**); Haydn establishes the form of the symphony with *The Clock Symphony* (**1794**).

1788 Bread riots occur in France.

1789 William Blake's *Songs of Innocence,* followed by *Marriage of Heaven and Hell* (**1790**) and *Songs of Experience* (**1794**), ushers in early Romanticism in England; Olaudah Equiano's *The Interesting Narrative of the Life of Olaudah Equiano, or Gustavus Vassa, the African,* one of the first slave narratives, is published.

1790

1789–99 French Revolution transforms France from a monarchy to a modern state.

1792 Mary Wollstonecraft publishes *A Vindication of the Rights of Woman,* an early work of feminism.

1793 Queen Marie Antoinette and King Louis XVI of France are guillotined.

ca. 1795–1825 English Romantic poetry flourishes with the work of William Wordsworth (**1770–1850**), Lord Byron (**1788–1824**), Percy Bysshe Shelley (**1792–1822**), and John Keats (**1795–1821**).

1798 Thomas Malthus's *An Essay on the Principle of Population* stirs interest in birth control and concerns about overpopulation.

1799 Rosetta Stone is found in Egypt, making it possible to decipher hieroglyphics; perfectly preserved mammoth is found in Siberia.

1800

1800 Alessandro Volta produces first battery of zinc and copper plates.

1803 Beethoven composes *Third Symphony (Eroica)*, marking the start of his dramatic middle period.

1804–6 Lewis and Clark expedition from St. Louis to the Pacific fuels westward expansion in the USA.

1804 Napoleon becomes emperor of France.

1807 Hegel publishes *Phenomenology of Spirit,* which introduces the concept of "master-slave" dialectic.

1808 Goethe publishes *Part 1* of *Faust,* a drama about a man who sells his soul for knowledge and power.

1810

1812 Noah Webster's *American Dictionary of the English Language* helps standardize spelling of American English.

1813 Mexico declares independence from Spain, becomes a republic in **1824.**

1813 Jane Austen publishes her novel *Pride and Prejudice.*

1815 Napoleon is defeated by British and Prussian forces at Waterloo.

1818 Mary Shelley publishes horror classic *Frankenstein.*

1820

ca. 1821 Cherokee leader Sequoya codifies the Cherokee alphabet.

1823 Monroe Doctrine closes Western Hemisphere to colonial settlements by Europe.

ca. 1825 Katsushika Hokusai, great Japanese printmaker, creates *Mt. Fuji on a Clear Day.*

1830

1830–42 Auguste Comte, founder of philosophical positivism, writes *The Course of Positive Philosophy,* advocates application of scientific method to social problems.

1830 Church of Jesus Christ of Latter-day Saints (Mormons) is founded by Joseph Smith.

1831 Nat Turner leads a group of fellow slaves in the largest slave revolt in North America.

1833 Charles Babbage designs an "analytical engine," prototype of the modern computer.

1836 Samuel Colt puts his revolver into mass production, revolutionizes manufacture of small arms.

1837 Ralph Waldo Emerson, American transcendentalist, delivers "The American Scholar," an address expressing American literary independence.

1837–1901 Queen Victoria reigns in England, Ireland, and India.

1838 Charles Dickens publishes *Oliver Twist,* the first of many novels that sharply criticize abuses brought on by the Industrial Revolution in England.

1839 Daguerreotypes, forerunners of modern photographs, are developed by L. M. Daguerre and J. N. Niepce in France.

1840

1841 First university degrees granted to women in USA.

1840s Rise of Romantic movement in France, Germany, and Italy.

1843 Søren Kierkegaard, Christian existentialist philosopher, publishes *Either / Or.*

1843 Richard Wagner composes *The Flying Dutchman,* an opera expressing his ideal of the *Gesamtkunstwerk* ("total work of art").

1844 Samuel Morse invents the telegraph.

1847 Charlotte Brontë publishes *Jane Eyre;* Emily Brontë publishes *Wuthering Heights;* Anne Brontë publishes *Agnes Grey.*

1850

1848 Seneca Falls Convention for Women's Suffrage is held in USA; Karl Marx and Friedrich Engels write *Communist Manifesto,* a pamphlet exhorting workers to unite against capitalist oppressors.

1855 Walt Whitman publishes first edition of *Leaves of Grass,* creates a new American style for poetry.

1857 French poet Charles Baudelaire publishes *Flowers of Evil,* one of the seminal works of modern poetry.

1859 Charles Darwin publishes *On the Origin of Species,* establishes theories of evolution and natural selection ("survival of the fittest").

ca. 1860 Louis Pasteur invents pasteurization process, advances germ theory of infection, discovers rabies and anthrax vaccines (**1880s**).

1860

1860–65 Emily Dickinson writes most of her poetry; creates a new rhythm and vernacular for American verse.

1861–65 U.S. Civil War pits northern against southern states.

1863 "Emancipation Proclamation" frees all slaves in states rebelling against the federal government.

1865 U.S. President Abraham Lincoln is assassinated.

1865–69 Leo Tolstoy publishes *War and Peace,* an epic of the Napoleonic invasion of Russia.

1867 Universal Exposition in Paris introduces Japanese art to the West.

1867–94 Publication of Karl Marx's *Capital*, a political and economic treatise providing the theoretical basis of socialism.

1868 Overthrow of Tokugawa Shogunate, followed by the Meiji Restoration and establishment of a new government, signals emergence of Japan as a major world power.

1869 U.S. transcontinental railroad is completed.

1870

1874 First exhibition of French Impressionism in Paris is held; notable exponents include Monet, Renoir, Pissarro, Degas, and Cassatt.

1875 Alexander Graham Bell invents the telephone.

1877 Thomas Edison invents the phonograph.

1879 Thomas Edison invents the lightbulb.

1880

1878 In Boston, Mary Baker Eddy founds Church of Christ, Scientist, a religion emphasizing divine healing.

1883–85 Friedrich Nietzsche writes *Thus Spake Zarathustra*, which expounds on the concept of *Übermensch* (superman).

1890

1889 Eiffel Tower is built for Paris Exposition.

1893 Fabian Society, a socialist group that includes Irish playwright George Bernard Shaw, is established.

1893 X rays are discovered.

1895 Louis and Auguste Lumière project brief motion pictures on a screen to a paying audience in Paris; based on Thomas Edison's technology, their Cinématographe became the prototype of the movie camera.

ca. 1895 Charles "Buddy" Bolden, New Orleans cornet player and band leader, begins playing improvised music later known as jazz.

1898 Marie and Pierre Curie isolate radium and polonium.

1900

1903 Orville and Wilbur Wright make their debut power-driven flight near Kitty Hawk, North Carolina.

1907 Albert Einstein first publishes equation $E = mc^2$, deduced from his theory of special relativity, ushering in revolution in physics and astronomy.

1907 Pablo Picasso's *Les Demoiselles d'Avignon,* first Cubist painting, ushers in new artistic aesthetic.

1908 Henry Ford introduces the Model T; demand for cars induces the company to introduce assembly-line technique.

1910

1910 International Psychoanalytic Association is founded by Sigmund Freud and others; Freud's theories of the unconscious begin to gain popular recognition.

1913 *The Rite of Spring,* ballet with groundbreaking music by Igor Stravinsky and choreography by Vaslav Nijinsky, is first performed.

1914 Serbian nationalist assassinates heir to the Austro-Hungarian Empire in Sarajevo, sparking World War I.

1915 Margaret Sanger opens the first birth control clinic in USA.

1914–21 James Joyce writes *Ulysses,* a masterpiece of modernist literature; publication in USA is delayed until **1933** because of obscenity charges.

1915 British passenger ship *Lusitania* sunk by German submarine, fueling American sympathy for war efforts of Britain, France, and Russia.

1917 USA enters World War I; Russian Revolution: Bolsheviks led by Vladimir Lenin seize power.

1918 Romanian poet Tristan Tzara writes manifesto for Dada, avant-garde artistic movement established in part in reaction to the senseless slaughter of World War I.

1918–19 Influenza epidemic kills 22 million worldwide.

1918 Treaty of Versailles ends World War I; death toll approaches 15 million worldwide; race riots rock major U.S. cities.

1920

1920 Nineteenth Amendment to the U.S. Constitution grants women suffrage.

ca. 1920 Arnold Schoenberg invents 12-tone system of musical composition.

1922 First fascist government formed by Benito Mussolini in Italy.

1920s Harlem Renaissance: flowering of African American literature and the arts, particularly jazz, centered in New York City.

1924 Joseph Stalin succeeds Lenin as head of Soviet Union.

1927 Martin Heidegger publishes *Being and Time,* a founding work of existentialist philosophy; Martha Graham, pioneer of modern dance, opens a dance studio in New York.

1929 Virginia Woolf, central to the Bloomsbury literary group, publishes feminist work *A Room of One's Own.*

1930

1927 Charles Lindbergh makes first solo, nonstop transatlantic flight; Werner Heisenberg develops Uncertainty Principle, which, together with Theory of Relativity, becomes basis of quantum physics; first successful transmission of an image via "television" occurs.

1930s The Great Depression, precipitated by a stock market crash in **1929,** begins in USA and spreads abroad; in response, President Roosevelt introduces "New Deal" measures based on Keynesian economics.

1933 Adolf Hitler becomes chancellor of Germany, gradually assumes dictatorial power.

1931 Incompleteness Theorem is developed by the mathematician and philosopher Kurt Gödel.

1936–39 Spanish Civil War.

1935 African American Jesse Owens wins four gold medals in track at the Berlin Olympics.

1939 World War II begins shortly after Germany's invasion of Poland; Hitler's Nazis begin program of extermination of "undesirable" elements, including dissidents, homosexuals, Gypsies, and especially Jews; 6 million Jews die in the ensuing Holocaust.

1940

1941 Japan bombs Pearl Harbor, and USA enters World War II.

1943 Jean-Paul Sartre, existentialist philosopher, publishes *Being and Nothingness.*

1945 USA drops atomic bombs on Hiroshima and Nagasaki, Japan— World War II ends; United Nations is formed; Soviet Union occupies Eastern Europe.

1947 India and Pakistan gain independence from Britain.

1948 Mahatma Gandhi, Indian nationalist and spiritual leader, is assassinated; Pakistan-India wars ensue.

1949 Communists seize mainland China; Mao Zedong becomes first chairman of the People's Republic of China.

1950

1949 Simone de Beauvoir publishes *The Second Sex,* a groundbreaking study of women's place in society.

1950–55 Jonas Salk develops polio vaccine.

1950s–70s Height of the "Cold War," in which USA and Soviet Union face off—mutual military buildup and threat of nuclear annihilation create a "balance of power."

1953 J. D. Watson and F. H. C. Crick determine the structure of DNA, launching the modern study of genetics.

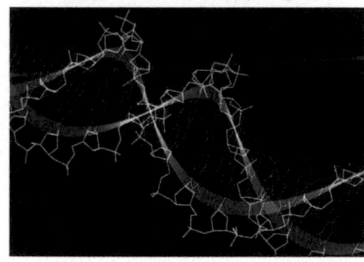

1956 Soviet Union crushes revolt in Hungary.

1959 Cuban Revolution: Fidel Castro overthrows Batista regime.

1962 Cuban missile crisis—Soviet missile-building in Cuba precipitates tense standoff with USA, ultimately resolved through diplomacy; César Chávez organizes the National Farm Workers Association (NFWA).

1960

1961 Berlin Wall erected; USA stages failed "Bay of Pigs" invasion of Cuba.

1963 Martin Luther King, Jr., delivers "I Have a Dream" speech to crowd of 250,000 at the Lincoln Memorial; President John F. Kennedy is assassinated in Dallas.

1964 U.S. involvement in Vietnam War escalates with Tonkin Gulf Resolution; Malcolm X is assassinated in New York; Watts riots roil Los Angeles.

1966 Mao Zedong's Cultural Revolution begins, aiming to revitalize communist zeal; Black Panther Party is founded in Oakland, California.

1968 Martin Luther King, Jr., is assassinated in Memphis, Tennessee.

1969 American astronaut Neil Armstrong becomes first man to walk on the moon.

1970

1971 East Pakistan (now Bangladesh) declares independence from West Pakistan.

1974 President Richard Nixon resigns as a result of the Watergate scandal.

1973 *Gulag Archipelego* by Alexander Solzhenitsyn is published in Paris; it is a massive study of the Soviet penal system based on author's firsthand experience.

1975 Bill Gates and Paul Allen build and sell their first computer product, creating Microsoft.

1975 Wave of former colonies—Mozambique, Surinam, Papua New Guinea—gain independence.

1975–79 Vaccination programs against smallpox eradicate the disease worldwide.

1979 Islamic revolution in Iran: Shah flees, Khomeini comes to power.

1980

1981 First cases of acquired immune deficiency syndrome (AIDS) in the USA are reported in New York and California.

1982 Benoit Mandelbrot publishes *The Fractal Geometry of Nature,* contributing to chaos theory.

1986 Chernobyl nuclear power plant disaster spreads fallout over Soviet Union and parts of Europe.

1990

1989 Pro-democracy protests in Tiananmen Square, China, are quashed by government crackdown; Berlin Wall is demolished; Eastern Europe is democratized.

1991 Soviet Union is dissolved, making way for looser confederation of republics.

1995 Internet boom hits—number of people online grows exponentially.

2000

2000 Initial sequencing of human genome completed.

2001 Hijacked planes fly into 110-story World Trade Center Towers in New York City and the Pentagon in Washington, D.C.—thousands die, USA invades Afghanistan in "war on terrorism."

2004 Massive Indian Ocean tsunami devastates coastal communities from Indonesia to Somalia.

2005 Voters in France and Holland reject the proposed constitution for the European Union.

Hurricane Katrina overwhelms U.S. Gulf coast and forces the evacuation of New Orleans.

2006 YouTube.com launches, enabling anyone with an Internet connection to post and view digital video files.

2007 Al Gore and the International Panel on Climate Change win the Nobel Peace Prize for their work on global warming.

2008 Barack Obama becomes the first African American to win a national party's presidential primary.

Selected Terms from across the Curriculum

*Here is a sampling of terms that commonly appear in academic **discourse**. Each of the words printed in bold has its own entry.*

alienation Being estranged from one's society or even from oneself. First used in psychology, the term was adapted by Karl **Marx** (1818–1883) in his writings on the relationship of workers to the products of their labor. In the twentieth century, **existentialist** philosophers used the word to mean an individual's loss of a sense of self, his or her *authenticity,* amid the pressures of modern society. *See also* **Marxism.**

archetype A model after which other things are patterned. The psychoanalyst Carl Jung (1875–1961) used the term to denote a number of universal symbols—such as the Mother or the universal Creator—that inhabit the collective unconscious, the elements of the unconscious that are common to all people.

Aristotelian Relating to the writings of Aristotle (384–322 BCE), Greek philosopher and author of works on logic, ethics, rhetoric, and the natural sciences. Aristotle established a tradition that values **empirical** observation, **deductive reasoning,** and science. This tradition can be contrasted with **Platonic idealism.**

bell curve In statistics and science, a graph in which the greatest number of results are grouped in the middle. If a math test is graded on a bell curve, for instance, most students will receive B's and C's, whereas only a few will receive A's or F's. Plotted on a graph, the curve will evoke the shape of a bell.

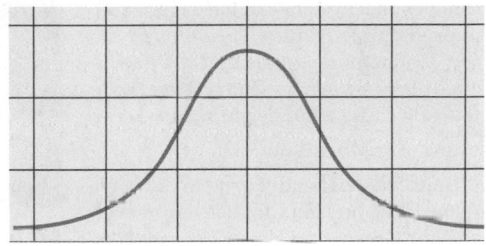

A bell curve.

binary oppositions Paired terms conventionally treated as stable and logical opposites, such as *light / dark* and *man / woman.* Certain **postmodern** trends in philosophy and literary theory, notably **deconstruction,** seek to expose the "artificiality" of these and other **constructs** that shape the way we see the world. *See also* **structuralism.**

black hole From astronomy, a region in space-time where matter is infinitely dense and dimensionless and where the gravitational field is so strong that nothing can escape from it. The term is often used metaphorically to indicate something that is limitless or unresolvable.

Boolean logic (after the English mathematician George Boole, 1815–1864) A specialized algebra developed for the analysis of logical statements, used extensively in the development of the modern computer. A computer performs everything from simple math to Internet searches by means of Boolean logic, which uses **variables** and operators such as AND, OR, NOT, IF, THEN, and EXCEPT.

bourgeois Of or relating to the middle **class.** The term is used in **Marxist** analysis to represent the capitalist class. *Bourgeois* commonly connotes an excessive concern with respectability and material goods.

canon Originally referring to a code of laws established by the church, the canon now typically refers to a collection of books deemed necessary for a complete education. Current debate tends to focus on the exclusion from the canon of works by and about women and people of color. *See also* **multiculturalism.**

capitalism An economic system that emerged during the Industrial Revolution of the nineteenth century and offered private individuals the ownership of industry as well as unregulated market freedom. Today capitalism includes Keynesian economic models that allow government to regulate industry, particularly regarding such concerns as the minimum wage, tariffs, and taxes.

case study An intensive investigation and analysis of a person or group; often the object of study is proposed as the model of a certain phenomenon. Originally used in medicine, the term is now also common in psychology and business.

chaos theory A branch of mathematics used to describe highly complex phenomena such as weather or the flow of blood through the body. Chaos theory starts with the recognition that minute changes in a system can have large and unpredictable results. The *butterfly effect,* for instance, states that the flap of a butterfly's wings in China could theoretically cause a hurricane in New York.

class *See* **Marxism.**

classical Originally used to describe the artistic and literary conventions of ancient Greece and Rome. *Classical (or classicism/neoclassicism)* is also used for periods and products in the sciences, social sciences, philosophy, and music marked by straightforwardly rational

An image generated from the Mandelbrot set, an aspect of chaos theory.

models that describe the workings of the universe and human society as logical and ultimately harmonious. *See also* **modernism, postmodernism.**

colonialism A policy by which a nation extends and maintains political and military control over a territory, often reducing it to a state of dependence. Begun as a way of acquiring resources such as spices, precious metals, and slaves, later instances of colonialism—such as the U.S. occupation of the Philippines from 1898 to 1946—have served mostly political or strategic purposes. *Postcolonial* refers to a state (or a cultural product or even a state of mind) that reflects former colonial occupation. *See also* **imperialism.**

constant In mathematics, science, and general usage, a factor that does not change. A mathematical or scientific constant is a quantity assumed to have a fixed value within a specific context. In physics, for example, the speed of light in a vacuum is 186,000 miles per second and is denoted by the constant c. Thus, in Einstein's famous equation $E = mc^2$, c is a constant and m, standing for any mass, is a **variable.**

construct (*noun*) Something that is shaped by culture ("constructed") but sometimes assumed to be "natural." For example, some might hold that the idea of gender ("maleness" and "femaleness") is a construct rather than the essential or inborn quality that past generations often assumed it to be.

contingent In logic, that which is true only under certain circumstances. In common usage, contingent often connotes that which has happened or can happen only as a result of a long, perhaps improbable sequence of events. Whenever you think, "It could easily have been different," you are feeling a sense of *contingency.*

correlation In statistics, a number that describes the relationship between two variables. In a *positive correlation,* the variables increase in tandem—for example, the higher a student's IQ, the better his or her scholastic performance. In a *negative correlation,* one variable increases while the other decreases—for example, the more green tea consumed, the lower the incidence of cancer.

counterculture *See* **culture.**

cross section A sample meant to be representative of a whole population. *See also* **longitudinal.**

culture Knowledge, beliefs, behavior, arts, institutions, and other products of work and thought that characterize a society. Within a dominant culture there may exist many *subcultures:* groups of particular ethnicity, age, education, employment, inclination, or other factors. A *counterculture* is a form of subculture whose values and lifestyle reject those of the dominant culture. *See also* **relativism.**

Darwinism British naturalist Charles Darwin's (1809–1882) theory of the historical evolution of species based on *natural selection,* or "the survival of the fittest." Where insects living within the bark of trees constitute a major food source, for instance, birds with longer, more pointed beaks tend to survive longer and produce more offspring, who then pass on longer, sharper beaks to ensuing generations.

deconstruction A method of literary criticism whose best-known theorist, Jacques Derrida (1930–2004), postulated that texts rest on **binary oppositions** such as *nature/culture, subject/object,* and *spirit/matter* that have been incorrectly assumed to be true; in exposing this fallacy, Derrida revealed the illogic of texts thought to be logical and coherent. Although often associated with **postmodernism** and the debate about the **canon,** deconstruction is in a philosophical sense a radical form of skepticism. In more common usage, to *deconstruct* something is to analyze it intensively, exposing it as (perhaps) something unexpected.

deductive reasoning Reasoning to a conclusion based on a previously held principle. *Inductive reasoning,* on the other hand, is the process of deriving a conclusion based on data. **Empiricism** holds that all knowledge is derived from sense experience by induction, whereas *rationalism* claims that knowledge can be deduced from certain a priori (presumptive) claims.

demographics (from the Greek *demos,* "people," and *graphia,* "writing") The quantitative study of human populations. A demographic study of a city might include the rate at which its population is growing, the size and distribution of its middle **class,** or the number of its families who have access to the Internet.

determinism In philosophy and science, the doctrine that every event is *determined,* or entirely shaped by earlier events, and that given complete knowledge of prior events and the laws that govern them, all future events can be predicted. Something described as *overdetermined* is thought to be shaped by more than one equally significant cause. Usually contrasted with free will, determinism is a feature of eighteenth- and nineteenth-century **classical** thought. In science, determinism has come to be opposed by the *indeterminism* of **quantum physics.**

dialectic In philosophy, history, and the humanities, the use of logical oppositions as a means of arriving at conclusions about ideas or events. *Dialectical reasoning* is most often associated with the philosophies of Georg Hegel (1770–1831) and Karl **Marx** (1818–1883). According to Hegel, any human idea or *thesis* (for example, the sun circles the earth) naturally gives rise to an opposing idea or *antithesis* (the earth circles the sun), and these ideas resolve into a new idea or *synthesis* (the earth revolves around the sun but in an ellipse). Hegel's famous *master/slave dialectic* describes a seeming paradox: a slave holds power over his master because the master could not hold power without the slave. Marx extended dialectical reasoning in his theory of dialectical **materialism,** which analyzes not opposing ideas but contradictory class interests.

discipline A field of study with common research methods, approaches to creating knowledge, and written genres: for example, sociology, chemistry, art history. Sometimes, members of multiple disciplines come together to address a complex issue, such as global warming, from different perspectives.

discourse *Discourse* is most often used in English to denote writing and speech. *Discourse* can also refer to habits of expression characteristic of a particular community or to the content of that expression ("The *discourse* of experimental science does not often allow the use of the personal pronoun *I*").

discourse community *See the Charting the Territory box on p. 421.*

ecosystem A principal unit of study in ecology, the science of the relationships between organisms and their environments. All parts of an ecosystem are interdependent, and even small perturbations of one part (such as might be caused by pollution) can have profound effects on all of the other parts—a phenomenon often studied in **chaos theory.**

empiricism (from the Greek *empierikos,* "experienced") A philosophical trend, developed in large part by the philosophers John Locke (1632–1704) and David Hume (1711–1776), that data derived from experience or the senses are the ultimate source of knowledge, as opposed to reason, tradition, or authority. *Empirical* data are data gained through observation or experiment. Especially in medicine and psychology, *empirical* is often contrasted with *theoretical.* In its emphasis on observation and experience, empiricism is a conceptual cousin of **inductive reasoning** and **Aristotelianism.**

Enlightenment An intellectual movement committed to secular views based on reason that established itself in Europe in the eighteenth century (ca. 1688–1790).

epistemology The study of the nature of knowledge, its foundations and limits.

ethos (Greek for "character, a person's nature or disposition") The spirit or code of behavior peculiar to a specific person or group of people—for example, "part of the college student ethos is to stay up late drinking cola and eating Captain Crunch." Ethos is one of the parts of Aristotle's **rhetorical triangle** (**ethos-logos-pathos**): in order to argue effectively, a speaker or writer must communicate a credible **persona** and a coherent perspective.

existentialism A strain in philosophy that emphasizes the isolation of the individual in an indifferent universe and stresses the individual's freedom (and responsibility) to determine his or her own existence. Having roots in the philosophies of Friedrich Nietzsche (1844–1900) and Martin Heidegger (1889–1976), existentialism was extremely influential in France after World War II, where French intellectuals like Jean-Paul Sartre (1905–1980) and Albert Camus (1913–1960) argued that by making conscious choices and taking responsibility for one's acts, one could overcome the otherwise absurd nature of the universe.

Mussolini and Hitler.

fascism (from the Italian *fascio,* "group") A name for the form of government established by Benito Mussolini (1883–1945) in Italy and Adolf Hitler (1889–1945) in Germany. Arising in response to economic and political upheaval in Europe after World War I, both governments centralized authority under a dictator, exerted strong economic controls, suppressed opposition through censorship and terror, and implemented belligerent nationalist and racist policies.

feminism The principle that women should enjoy equal political, economic, social, and cultural rights and opportunities. Mary Wollstonecraft's *A Vindication of the Rights of Woman* (1792) was a pioneering feminist work. The *suffrage movement,* which demanded that women be granted the right to vote, emerged following the first women's rights convention in Seneca Falls, New York, in 1848, and had achieved its goal in the United States and Europe by the early twentieth century. The *women's movement* that began in the 1960s initiated a new wave of feminism that focused on rectifying political, economic, social, and cultural inequalities between women and men.

Freudian Relating to the theories of Sigmund Freud (1856–1939), the Viennese neurologist who invented psychoanalysis. A Freudian interpretation focuses on the unconscious emotional dynamics that are played out in a particular situation; in the study of literature, a Freudian interpretation focuses on such dynamics as they are represented in the **text.** Freud identified three areas of personality. The ego is the conscious self, the id embodies desire and instincts, and the superego represents internalized social rules and curbs the id and ego. *See also* **repression, unconscious.**

game theory (also sometimes called *decision theory*) A mathematical method for analyzing situations of conflict or competition so as to determine a winning strategy. Game theory is useful not only in *true games* such as poker but also in business management, economics, and military strategy. *See also* **zero sum game.**

geometric progression A sequence of numbers determined by multiplying or dividing each number in succession by a **constant.** For example, *1, 4, 16, 64, 256* is a geometric progression with a constant multiplier, or coefficient, of 4. *Arithmetic progressions* proceed more slowly by adding or subtracting a constant: for example, *1, 4, 7, 10, 13* is an arithmetic progression with a constant *addend* of 3.

globalization The process by which communication and transportation technologies have made the world seem smaller and more interconnected. In economics, *globalization* refers to the way these advances have made national borders far less relevant in determining markets. The *anti-globalization* movement aims to protect workers from exploitation by multinational corporations, to prevent job loss among domestic workers, and to counter cultural homogenization. The presence of a McDonald's in Beijing is a good example of the effects of globalization.

hegemony Generally, the dominance of one nation or state over its neighbors. The Italian Marxist Antonio Gramsci (1891–1937) and his followers often used the term to refer to the dominance of the capitalists over the working **class.** *Hegemony* is now also used to describe a theory that has dominance in a particular field of study: "Dualism has long exercised hegemony in Western thought."

humanism (also *secular humanism*) A movement traditionally associated with Renaissance philosophers who deemphasized the role of religion or God in society while celebrating the achievements of human beings. There are *humanistic* branches of psychology, theology, and other disciplines that move the role of the human individual to the forefront of their studies.

hypothesis A statement that can be shown to be true or false either experimentally (in science) or through the use of logic (in other disciplines). For example, a simple hypothesis that light is necessary for the survival of a certain plant could be proved or disproved by trying to grow the plant in a dark closet.

icon In **semiotics,** a sign that looks like what it refers to. A picture of the globe used to signify the earth or a line drawing of a suitcase indicating where to go to get your luggage at an airport are icons. Historically, an icon was a small picture of a religious figure, usually Jesus or the Virgin Mary.

idealism In philosophy and psychology, the notion that the mind determines ultimate reality, an idea that can be traced to **Plato** (428–347 BCE).

ideology A set of beliefs about the world (and often how it can be changed) espoused by an individual, group, or organization; a systematized worldview. **Capitalism,** for example, is an ideology. In the work of the Marxist critic Louis Althusser (1918–1990), an *ideology* is that which allows the individual to find his or her place and sense of self-worth within a given society.

imperialism One country's imposition of political and economic rule on other countries. The British annexation of several countries in Africa in the nineteenth century is an example of this brand of imperialism. Today the term has been broadened to include the exportation of dominant cultural products and values. For example, some people in Europe and other parts of the world see the influx of American films into their markets as a form of *cultural imperialism. See also* **colonialism.**

inductive reasoning *See* **deductive reasoning.**

laissez-faire (French for "allow to act") Generally, noninterference in the affairs or conduct of others. In economic and political theory, the idea that governments should not intervene in markets. The concept is based on the **classical** economic theory developed by Adam Smith (1723–1790) and others, which argues that an *invisible hand*—supply and demand, and competition—is sufficient to guide economic markets.

logos (Greek for "word") In Aristotle's **rhetorical triangle,** the topic of the argument or argument itself.

longitudinal A study in which the same group of subjects is examined over a long period of time. A *longitudinal study* could, for example, be conducted to test the rate of obesity over time among a certain group of schoolchildren.

Marxism The economic and political doctrine put forth by Karl Marx (1818–1883) and Friedrich Engels (1820–1895). It centers on the **class** struggle between the proletariat (the working class) and the **bourgeoisie** (capitalists, those who own the *means of production*). (*Class* refers to social and/or economic standing in society. Marx saw class as economically based, although many have argued that family, cultural background, and education affect it.) Marxism predicts that the working class will wrest the means of production from the bourgeoisie and cede them to the state, which will distribute goods equitably.

materialism In philosophy, the belief that physical matter is all that exists and that so-called higher phenomena—for example, thought, feeling, mind, will—are wholly dependent on and **determined** by physical processes. Since the **Enlightenment,** almost all scientists have been materialists. In history and economics, the dialectical materialism of Karl **Marx** (1818–1883) held that **cultural** phenomena are determined wholly by economic conditions.

mean (also *average*) The sum of a set of numbers divided by the number of terms in the set. For example, the mean of the set (1, 2, 3) is 2 because its sum (6) divided by the number of terms (3) equals 2.

median The middle term in an ordered set of numbers. For example, the median of the ordered set (2, 6, 10, 12, 15) is 10 because there are two numbers (2 and 6) below 10 and two (12 and 15) above 10.

meta- A prefix often used to suggest "moving beyond," "going up a level," or "transcending." Thus, *metaphysics* is the branch of philosophy that deals with questions that cannot be resolved by physical observation, such as whether God exists.

modernism Often used in opposition to classicism or neoclassicism when denoting periods in the sciences, social sciences, philosophy, and music, *modernism* as a trend in thought represents a break with the certainties of the past, among them a confidence that everything can be known. *Modern* science has been characterized by highly counterintuitive theories such as **relativity**—according to which there is no absolute way to measure time—and **quantum physics**—according to which you can know the speed or the position of a subatomic particle but never both. In literature, the **stream of consciousness** and/or *free association* style of *modernist* writers like Virginia Woolf (1882–1941) and James Joyce (1882–1941) broke decisively with the storytelling conventions of the late-nineteenth-century, or Victorian, novel. Thus, some critics believe that **postmodernism** is really only the development of a trend begun in the modernist era.

Virginia Woolf.

multiculturalism The view that many cultures, not just the dominant one, should be given attention in the classroom and in broader society. The debate on multiculturalism is related to the debate on the **canon.**

nature-nurture controversy A debate about whether genetic (*nature*) or environmental (*nurture*) factors have the upper hand in determining human behavior. Experimental studies involving fraternal and identical twins raised together and apart have been undertaken to investigate the issue, but fundamental questions about method and the small **samples** involved have left the question unresolved. This debate pervades countless topics studied in the social sciences, among them questions of gender difference, intelligence, poverty, crime, and childhood development.

object/subject In philosophy and psychology, the *subject* does the observing or experiencing, while the *object* is that which is observed or experienced. Throughout history, this philosophical dualism has been studied, refined, and debated extensively. In **Freudian** and post-Freudian psychology, an *object* is an external person or thing that gratifies an infant and is therefore loved.

objective Pertaining to that which is independent of perception or observation, as opposed to *subjective,* which pertains to that which is determined by perception or observation. The old philosophical puzzle—If a tree falls in the woods, and no one is there to hear it, does it make a sound?—plays on the notions of philosophical *objectivity* and *subjectivity.*

Oedipus complex The psychological notion expounded by Sigmund **Freud** (1856–1939) that describes the unconscious sexual longing of a son for his mother and his unconscious wish to kill his father, his rival for possession of the mother. The name is a reference to Sophocles' play *Oedipus Rex.* Freud also wrote of the *Electra* complex, which describes the similar sexual longing of a daughter for her father.

ontology Generally, the study of being and human consciousness.

paradigm A theoretical framework that serves as a foundation for a field of study or branch of knowledge. Darwinian evolution, Newtonian physics, and Aristotle's chemistry are all examples of scientific paradigms. *Paradigm shifts* designate the transition from one paradigm to another, usually with a profoundly transformative effect. For example, the shift from Newtonian physics to quantum physics might be termed a *paradigm shift.*

pathos (Greek for "suffering, experience, emotion") In Aristotle's **rhetorical triangle,** the feelings evoked in the audience by an argument.

persona (Latin for "mask") An assumed or public identity, as distinct from the *inner self;* a character adopted for a particular purpose; in literature, the voice or character of the speaker.

Platonic Following the teachings of the Greek philosopher Plato (428–347 BCE), Platonic **idealism** is a system that attempts to show a rational relationship between the individual, the state, and the universe, governed by what is good, true, and beautiful. Only a reflection of the truth can be perceived, and the gap between the ideal and its reflection motivates human consciousness. It can be contrasted with the **Aristotelian** tradition, which values empirical observation and scientific reasoning. In common usage, a *platonic relationship* is a close friendship that does not have a sexual component.

pluralism In everyday language, a condition of society in which multiple religions, ethnicities, and subcultures coexist peacefully. *Pluralism* can also refer to any philosophical system that proposes that reality is made up of a number of distinct entities. The pragmatist William James (1842–1910) and the analytic philosopher Bertrand Russell (1872–1970) were prominent *pluralist* thinkers.

postcolonial *See* **colonialism.**

postmodernism A cultural trend that seeks to expose the artificiality of the **constructs** that defined earlier periods of cultural production while confessing—indeed, in some cases even boasting of—an inability to replace them with an authentic substitute. One of the hallmarks of *postmodern* cultural products is *pastiche,* or *collage,* a form that borrows from other trends and emphasizes the disjuncture between disparate elements. *See also* **modernism.**

praxis Often used as a substitute for *practice* in ordinary usage, and opposed to **theory.** In the work of Antonio Gramsci (1891–1937), the "philosophy of praxis" outlined the refinements to Marxism that were necessary to make it relevant in the twentieth century.

qualitative research Research that focuses on observing what people say and do. Qualitative research methods include observation, interviews, surveys, and focus groups. In contrast, *quantitative research* depends on numerical data. Quantitative research methods include counting, measuring, analyzing statistics, and reporting the results in charts, graphs, and tables.

quantitative research *See* **qualitative research.**

quantum physics A theoretical branch of physics that deals with the behavior of atoms and subatomic particles. The work of such pioneers as Max Planck (1858–1947), Niels Bohr (1885–1962), and later Werner Heisenberg (1901–1976) has had a profound impact on the way we understand such things as the relationships between matter and energy. *See also* **relativity.**

relativism The belief that the meaning and value of all things are determined by their *context*—their relationship to other things in that time and place—rather than that things have inherent or absolute meaning or worth. *Moral relativism* is the idea that different people, groups, nations, or cultures have differing ideas about what constitutes good and evil and that those differences must be respected. *Cultural relativism* is the position that there is no absolute point of view from which one set of cultural values or beliefs can be deemed intrinsically superior to any other. *See also* **culture, humanism.**

relativity In physics, the theory expounded by Albert Einstein (1879–1955), which states that all motion is relative and that energy and matter are convertible. The famous formulation $E = mc^2$ equates energy (E) with matter (m) multiplied by the speed of light (c) squared. Einstein's work directly challenged two cornerstones of **classical** physics—that motion is an absolute and that energy and matter are two completely different entities.

repression In **Freudian** psychology, the process that keeps unacceptable desires, fears, and other troubling material (such as memories of traumatic experiences) from reaching (or returning to) consciousness. *See also* **unconscious.**

Albert Einstein.

rhetoric In classical times, the art of public speaking. Currently, the term more broadly encompasses *language* or *speech,* often in a derogatory context (as in "The mayor's speech was so much empty *rhetoric*"), as well as the study of writing and the effective use of language.

rhetorical triangle Aristotle's description of the context of argument, consisting of **ethos** (roughly, the character of the speaker), **logos** (the topic of the argument or the argument itself), and **pathos** (the feelings evoked in the audience).

sample A subset or selection of a group from a population. In a *random sample,* each subject is chosen in ways that replicate pure chance, and all members of the population have an equal chance of being selected for the sample.

scientific method A process involving observations of phenomena and the conducting of experiments to test ideas suggested by those observations. The development of the scientific method, a specialized form of trial and error, ushered in the scientific revolution of the seventeenth century. Francis Bacon (1561–1626), René Descartes (1596–1650), and especially Galileo Galilei (1564–1642) are most often credited with developing its constituent procedures: (1) choosing a question or problem (for example, what causes yellow fever); (2) developing a **hypothesis** (the disease is caused by a bacteria or virus transmitted by mosquitoes); (3) conducting observations and experiments (noting **correlations** between mosquito populations and incidence of yellow fever); (4) examining and interpreting the data (high correlations exist between incidence of yellow fever and that of the *A. aegypti* mosquito); (5) affirming, revising, or rejecting the hypothesis; and (6) deriving further experiments and hypotheses from it (microscopically examining the bodies of *A. aegypti* and yellow fever victims to try to find a virus or bacteria present in both).

secular Not having to do with religion or the church; deriving its authority from nonreligious sources. *See also* **humanism.**

semiotics The theory and study of signs and symbols. According to semiotics, meaning is never inherent but is always a product of social conventions, and **culture** can be analyzed as a series of sign systems. *See also* **structuralism.**

skepticism The belief that nothing can be held true until grounds are established for believing it to be true. René Descartes (1596–1650), one of the founders of modern philosophy, expressed this attitude in his famous statement *"Cogito, ergo sum"* ("I think, therefore I am").

Socratic method Repeated questioning to arrive at implicit truths, a teaching method used by the Greek philosopher Socrates (470?–399? BCE), who influenced **Plato.**

solipsism Philosophical theory that the self is the only thing that can be known and verified and therefore is the only reality.

standard deviation A measure of the degree to which data diverge from the **mean.** A high standard deviation means a greater range of results. Thus, in a **bell curve,** a tall, skinny curve represents a smaller standard deviation than does a wide, flat curve.

statistical significance A value assigned to a research result as a measure of how likely it is that the result reflects mere chance. The higher the statistical significance, the less likely it is that chance determined the outcome. The results of studies employing large numbers of subjects typically have a higher statistical significance than do those of studies of a small number of subjects.

stream of consciousness A **modernist** literary technique in which the writer renders the moment-by-moment progress of a character's or narrator's thoughts. Among those writers who have used the technique are James Joyce (1882–1941) in *Ulysses,* Virginia Woolf (1882–1941) in *Mrs. Dalloway,* and Marcel Proust (1871–1922) in *Remembrance of Things Past.*

structuralism An analytical method, today often subsumed under **semiotics,** that is used in the social sciences, the humanities, and the arts to examine underlying deep structures in a **text** by close investigation of its constituent parts (often termed signs). For example, in *narratology* (the study of narratives), myths, folktales, novels, paintings, and even comic books are reduced to their essential structures, from which are derived the rules that govern the different ways in which these narratives tell their stories. In *structural* approaches, the individual works under study are commonly considered less important than the universal structures that underlie them. This tendency has opened the approach to charges of anti-**humanism.** Michel Foucault (1926–1984) and other *poststructuralists* have challenged structuralists' belief in the possibility of revealing essential structures of knowledge and reality through this type of study. *See also* **semiotics, deconstruction.**

subculture *See* **culture.**

subjective *See* **objective.**

sublime Inspiring awe; impressive; moving; of high spiritual or intellectual worth. Michelangelo's painting on the ceiling of the Sistine Chapel is often cited as an example of the *sublime* in art; in nature, mountains such as Kilimanjaro have been described as *sublime.*

symbiosis In biology, a prolonged association and interdependence of two or more organisms, usually to their mutual benefit. *Parasitism*

The ceiling of the Sistine Chapel.

occurs when one organism benefits at the expense of another. In general usage, *symbiotic* is used metaphorically to denote a mutual dependency and benefit between people, organisms, or ideas.

taxonomy Any set of laws and principles of classification. Originating in biology, taxonomy includes the theory and principles governing the classification of organisms into categories such as species and phyla. Today a literary critic might compose a "taxonomy of literary styles."

teleology In philosophy, religion, history, and the social sciences, an explanation or theory that assumes movement or development toward a specific end. For instance, Christianity is profoundly *teleological* because it looks toward the second coming of Christ.

text In common academic usage, anything undergoing rigorous intellectual examination and analysis. Texts may be oral works such as speeches, visual works such as paintings, everyday objects like toys, and even human behavior. Analysis is often called "reading the text," even if the text is not a written work. *See also* **semiotics.**

theory A statement devised to explain a collection of facts or observations; also, the systematic organization of such statements. Theory is commonly contrasted with *practice* or **praxis.**

topography The physical features of a region. In cartography and surveying, maps and charts are the graphic representations of topography.

trope A figure of speech. In literary criticism, the term is often used to refer to any technique that recurs in a **text.** Comparing women's faces to flowers is a common trope in Renaissance poetry.

typology The systematic study and classification of individuals in a group according to selected characteristics. In psychology, Carl Jung (1875–1961) developed a personality typology that uses characteristics such as extraversion and introversion. The Myers-Briggs assessment tools, based on Jung's typologies, are used in psychotherapy and employment settings. *See also* **archetypes.**

uncertainty principle An important theory in **quantum physics** formulated by German physicist Werner Heisenberg (1901–1976) that places an absolute, theoretical limit on the accuracy of certain pairs of simultaneously recorded measurements. This principle prevents scientists from making absolute predictions of the future state of certain systems. Heisenberg's principle has been applied to philosophy, where it is called the *indeterminacy principle.*

unconscious In the **Freudian** theory of the mind, the repository for repressed desires, fears, and memories. Ordinarily inaccessible to the conscious mind, the repressed material in the unconscious nevertheless has a powerful impact on conscious behavior and thoughts. *See also* **repression.**

variable In mathematics, a variable is a term capable of assuming any set of values. In algebra, it is represented by a symbol such as x, y, p, or q. In experimental research, the *dependent variable* is measured for change precipitated by an *independent variable* determined by the experimenter. A *random variable* is a numerical value determined by chance driven experiment or phenomenon. The value can be predicted according to the laws of probability but is usually not known until after the experiment has been completed.

zero sum game Any competitive situation where a gain for one side results in a loss for the other side. This term originated in **game theory** but is now in common use. In a *zero sum economy,* any economic gain is offset by an economic loss.

Index

Index for Multilingual Writers

Credits

Text Credits

TAB 1: p. 6: Adapted from Robert S. Feldman, *P.O.W.E.R. Learning: Strategies for Success in College and Life,* Second Edition. Copyright © 2003 The McGraw-Hill Companies, Inc. Reprinted with permission. **p. 8: Fig. 2.1, bottom:** *Misused Statistics,* Second Edition by Herbert F. Spirer, Louise Spirer and Abram J. Jaffe. Copyright 1998 by Taylor & Francis Group LLC - Books. Reproduced with permission of Taylor & Francis Group LLC - Books in the format Textbook via Copyright Clearance Center. **p. 17:** Definition of "haze." Copyright © 2006 by Houghton Mifflin Company. Adapted and reproduced by permission from *The American Heritage Dictionary of the English Language,* Fourth Edition.
TAB 2: p. 22: Checklist from Maimon, Elaine P., Peritz, Janice H., Yancey, Kathleen, *The New McGraw-Hill Handbook.* Copyright © 2007 The McGraw-Hill Companies, Inc. Reprinted with permission. **p. 25:** Nat Hentoff's "Misguided Multiculturalism" in *The Village Voice,* July 19–25, 2000, pp. 29–30. Copyright © 2000, Village Voice Media. Reprinted with the permission of the Village Voice and Nat Hentoff, staff writer, Village Voice/author, *The War on the Bill of Rights and the Gathering Resistance* (7 Stories Press). **p. 42:** Maimon, Elaine P., Peritz, Janice H., Yancey, Kathleen, *The New McGraw-Hill Handbook.* Copyright © 2007 The McGraw-Hill Companies, Inc. Reprinted with permission. **p. 48: Fig. 5.3:** Microsoft® Internet Explorer screen shot reprinted with permission from Microsoft Corporation. **p. 55: bar graph:** Used with permission from Gary Klass. **p. 56: diagram:** From Clarke & Cornish, "Modeling Offenders' Decisions," in *Crime and Justice,* volume 6, Tonry & Morris, eds., 1985, p. 169. Copyright © 1985 University of Chicago Press. Used by permission of the publisher, University of Chicago Press. **p. 62:** Excerpt from Robert Reich, "The Future of Work," as found in *Harper's* Magazine, 1989. Reprinted with permission. **p. 64: Fig. 6.6:** Graph as found in the State of the News Media report by the Project for Excellence in Journalism, a project of the Pew Research Center, www.stateofthemedia.com. Based on Nielsen Media Research data. Reprinted with permission. **p. 66: Fig. 6.7:** From Lahey, Benjamin, *Psychology: An Introduction,* Ninth Edition, 2007, Fig. 12.2, p. 466. Copyright © 2007 The McGraw-Hill Companies, Inc. Reprinted with permission. **p. 67: Fig. 6.8:** Cintara Corporation, a full service branding agency. With permission. **pp. 69–70:** Text only from Damian Robinson's "Riding into the Afterlife" in *Archaeology,* Volume 57, Number 2, March/April 2004. Courtesy of Archaeology Magazine. **p. 69:** From Jonathan Fast's "After Columbine: How People Mourn Sudden Death" in *Social Work,* vol. 48, no. 4, October 2003. Copyright 2003, National Association of Social Workers, Inc., *Social Work.* Reprinted with permission. **p. 77: Fig. 7.1:** Microsoft® Word screen shot reprinted with permission from Microsoft Corporation. **p. 78: Fig. 7.2:** Microsoft® Word screen shot reprinted with permission from Microsoft Corporation. **p. 87: Fig. 7.3, top & bottom:** © 1998 Glencoe/McGraw-Hill. *Mathematics: Applications and Connections, Course 2.* Used with permission. **p. 91–93:** Maimon, Elaine P., Peritz, Janice H., Yancey, Kathleen, *The New McGraw-Hill Handbook.* Copyright © 2007 The McGraw-Hill Companies, Inc. Reprinted with permission. **p. 94: Fig. 8.1:** Microsoft® Word screen shot reprinted with permission from Microsoft Corporation. **pp. 102–104:** Maimon, Elaine P., Peritz, Janice H., Yancey, Kathleen, *The New McGraw-Hill Handbook.* Copyright © 2007 The McGraw-Hill Companies, Inc. Reprinted with permission. **p. 106: Fig. 8.2:** Screen shot from Process & Product: Reflections, © 2006 Ken Tinnes. http://www.students.niu.edu/~z120512/104.M70/eportfolio/Reflections/Process/process.html. Reprinted with permission.
TAB 3: p. 118: Canetto, Silvia Sara, et al. From "Love and Achievement Motives in Women's and Men's Suicide Notes." *Journal of Psychology,* Vol. 136, Issue 5, pp. 573–6, September 2002. Reprinted with permission of the Helen Dwight Reid Educational Foundation. Published by Heldref Publications, 1319 Eighteenth St., NW, Washington, DC 20036-1802. Copyright © 2002. **pp. 140–149:** Maimon, Elaine P., Peritz, Janice H., Yancey, Kathleen, *The Brief McGraw-Hill Handbook.* Copyright © 2008 The McGraw-Hill Companies, Inc. Reprinted with permission. **p. 141:** From Gloria Ladson Billings, *The Dreamkeepers: Successful Teachers of African American Children,* San Franscico: Jossey-Bass,

Explorer screen shot reprinted with permission from Microsoft Corporation. Screen shot from Reuters.com, "Companies seek alternatives to plastic chemical" by Will Dunham, Wed Sep 17, 2008 8:52pm EDT. Photos reproduced with permission from Reuters. Microsoft® Internet Explorer screen shot reprinted with permission from Microsoft Corporation. Adapted from Maimon, Elaine P., Peritz, Janice H., Yancey, Kathleen, *The New McGraw-Hill Handbook.* Copyright © 2007 The McGraw-Hill Companies, Inc. Reprinted with permission. **p. 281:** Excerpt from "Trumpet Player," from THE COLLECTED POEMS OF LANGSTON HUGHES by Langston Hughes, edited by Arnold Rampersad with David Roessel, Associate Editor, copyright © 1994 by The Estate of Langston Hughes. Reprinted by permission of Alfred A. Knopf, a division of Random House, Inc., and of Harold Ober Associates Incorporated. **p. 320** Courtesy of the Louis Armstrong House Museum, Queens College. Used with permission.
TAB 7: APA Foldout: From *Exploring Agrodiversity* by H. Brookfield. Copyright © 2001 Columbia University Press. Reprinted with permission of the publisher. Table of contents and article excerpt from Epstein, J. (2002). A voice in the wilderness. *Latin Trade,* 10(12), 26. Reprinted with permission of Latin Trade. Screen shot of Wiley Interscience web site and abstract for: Soares-Filho, B., Alencar, A., Nepstad, D., Cerqueira, G., del Carmen Vera Diaz, M., Rivero, S., et. Al. (2004). Simulating the response of land-cover changes to road paving and governance along a major Amazon highway: the Santarém-Cuiabá corridor. *Global Change Biology* 10 (5), 745–764. Reprinted with permission of the publisher, Wiley-Blackwell. Microsoft® Internet Explorer screen shot reprinted with permission from Microsoft Corporation. The U'was Reject Consulation Process and Ecopatrol's Oil Project on Their Reserve in Columbia by Atossa Soltani/Amazon Watch, 10/23/2006, http://www.amazonwatch.org/newsroom/view_news.php?id=1240. Reprinted with permission. Microsoft® Internet Explorer screen shot reprinted with permission from Microsoft Corporation.
p. 351, graph: From National Institute of Space Research (2002). In D. Kalmowitz, B. Mertens, S. Wunder, and P. Pacheco, Hamburger Connection Fuels Amazon Destruction: Cattle Ranching and Deforestation in Brazil's Rain Forest. Reprinted with permission from the Center for International Forestry Research (CIFOR).
TAB 8: pp. 380, 383–386: Adapted from Maimon, Elaine P., Peritz, Janice H., Yancey, Kathleen, *The New McGraw-Hill Handbook.* Copyright © 2007 The McGraw-Hill Companies, Inc. Reprinted with permission.
TAB 9: p. 420: From Maimon, Elaine P., Peritz, Janice H., Yancey, Kathleen, *The New McGraw-Hill Handbook.* Copyright © 2007 The McGraw-Hill Companies, Inc. Reprinted with permission. **p. 430: Fig. 49.1:** By permission. From the Merriam-Webster Online Dictionary © 2008 by Merriam-Webster, Incorporated (www.Merriam-Webster.com).
pp. 441–442: Maimon, Elaine P., Peritz, Janice H., Yancey, Kathleen, *The New McGraw-Hill Handbook.* Copyright © 2007 The McGraw-Hill Companies, Inc. Reprinted with permission. **p. 459:** Maimon, Elaine P., Peritz, Janice H., Yancey, Kathleen, *The Brief McGraw-Hill Handbook.* Copyright © 2008 The McGraw-Hill Companies, Inc. Reprinted with permission. **p. 480:** Maimon, Elaine P., Peritz, Janice H., Yancey, Kathleen, *The Brief McGraw-Hill Handbook.* Copyright © 2008 The McGraw-Hill Companies, Inc. Reprinted with permission. **p. 495:** Maimon, Elaine P., Peritz, Janice H., Yancey, Kathleen, *The New McGraw-Hill Handbook.* Copyright © 2007 The McGraw-Hill Companies, Inc. Reprinted with permission. **p. 537:** Reprinted with the permission of Scribner, a Division of Simon & Schuster, Inc., and of A P Watt Ltd on behalf of Gráinne Yeats, from *The Collected Works of W.B. Yeats, Volume I: The Poems, Revised* edited by Richard J. Finneran. Copyright © 1928 by The Macmillan Company. Copyright renewed © 1956 by Georgie Yeats. All rights reserved. **pp. 560–561:** Maimon, Elaine P., Peritz, Janice H., Yancey, Kathleen, *The New McGraw-Hill Handbook.* Copyright © 2007 The McGraw-Hill Companies, Inc. Reprinted with permission.
Resources for Writers Foldout: World Map: Maimon, Elaine P., Peritz, Janice H., Yancey, Kathleen, *The Brief McGraw-Hill Handbook.* Copyright © 2008 The McGraw-Hill Companies, Inc. Reprinted with permission.

Photo credits
Preface: p. v: Adam Crowley/Getty Images; **p. vi:** Getty Images.

Quick Guide to Key Resources

BOXES FOR MULTILINGUAL STUDENTS

Using Another Language to Explore Ideas *(p. 44)*
State Your Thesis Directly *(p. 51)*
Peer Review *(p. 76)*
Learning about Cultural Differences through Peer Review *(p. 133)*
Designing a Web Site Collaboratively *(p. 170)*
Applying for a Job *(p. 189)*
Researching a Full Range of Sources *(p. 209)*
Questioning Sources *(p. 227)*
Cultural Assumptions and Misunderstandings about Plagiarism *(p. 244)*
Adverbial Modifiers and Subject-Verb Order *(p. 415)*
Usage Problems *(p. 425)*

Sections of Special Interest to Multilingual Students *(p. 445)*
Avoiding Fragments *(p. 449)*
Adding a Subject Pronoun to a Dependent Clause *(p. 452)*
Nonstandard Irregular Verb Forms *(p. 469)*
When Not to Use the Progressive Tenses *(p. 473)*
Nouns and Gender *(p. 478)*
Using Adjectives *(p. 491)*
Dealing with Punctuation, Mechanics, and Spelling *(p. 501)*
Long Numbers *(p. 510)*
Capitalizing the Pronoun I *(p. 540)*
Dates and Decimals *(p. 549)*
American and British Spelling *(p. 558)*

THE MOST COMMON ERRORS

TAB 9 Editing for Clarity
Missing words *(Ch. 39a, p. 395)*
Mixed constructions *(Ch. 40a, p. 397)*
Confusing shifts (person and verb tense) *(Ch. 41a, 41b, and p. 405)*
Faulty parallelism *(Ch. 42a, p. 404)*
Dangling modifiers *(Ch. 43e, p. 410)*
Wrong word *(Ch.48f, p. 427)*

TAB 10 Editing for Grammar Conventions
Sentence fragments *(Ch. 51a and p. 448)*
Comma splices and run-ons *(Ch. 52a, p. 454)*
Subject-verb agreement *(Ch. 53a and p. 461)*

Pronoun-antecedent agreement *(Ch. 55a and p. 481)*
Pronoun reference *(Ch. 55b, p. 482)*
Pronoun case *(Ch. 55d and p. 485)*

TAB 11 Editing for Correctness
Comma needed with introductory word group *(Ch. 57a, p. 501)*
Comma needed in compound sentence *(Ch. 57c, p. 503)*
Commas needed for nonrestrictive clause *(57e, p. 506)*
Incorrect use of apostrophe with possessive pronoun *(Ch. 60c, p. 523)*
Incorrect capitalization *(Ch. 63a, p. 539)*
Spelling error (homonym) *(Ch. 68b, p. 558)*

SECTIONS ON VISUAL RHETORIC

2. Learning in a Multimedia World
   a. Persuasive power of images *(p. 7)*
   b. Multimedia elements *(p. 7)*
4. Reading, Thinking, Writing: The Critical Connection
   a. Reading critically *(p. 22)*
   b. Thinking critically *(p. 27)*
5. Planning and Shaping
   e. Considering visuals *(p. 54)*
6. Drafting Text and Visuals
   b. Developing ideas and using visuals *(p. 58)*
   d. Integrating visuals effectively *(p. 72)*
7. Revising and Editing
   h. Revising visuals *(p. 85)*
   k. Learning from one student's revisions *(p. 91)*
8. Designing Academic Papers and Portfolios
   c. Thinking intentionally about design *(p. 95)*
   d. Compiling an effective print or electronic portfolio *(p. 101)*
11. Arguments
   b. Writing an argument as a process *(p. 127)*
   c. Student paper: Argument *(p. 132)*

12. Other Kinds of Assignments
   b. Lab reports *(p. 142)*
   d. Essay exams *(p. 147)*
13. Oral Presentations
   b. Drafting your presentation *(p. 153)*
14. Multimedia Writing
   b. Analyzing images *(p. 158)*
   d. Creating multimedia presentations *(p. 161)*
   e. Creating a Web site *(p. 163)*
15. Service Learning and Community-Service Writing
   b. Brochures, posters, and newsletters *(p. 175)*
20. Finding and Creating Effective Visuals
   a. Finding and displaying quantitative data *(p. 220)*
   b. Searching for images *(p. 221)*
21. Evaluating Sources
   b. Questioning Internet sources *(p. 221)*
29. MLA Style: Paper Format *(p. 310)*
33. APA Style: Paper Format *(p. 348)*

abbr	Faulty abbreviation **64**
ad	Misused adjective or adverb **56**
agr	Problem with subject-verb or pronoun agreement **53, 55a**
appr	Inappropriate word or phrase **47**
art	Incorrect or missing article **69b**
awk	Awkward
cap	Faulty capitalization **63**
case	Error in pronoun case **55d, e**
cliché	Overused expression **48d**
coh	Problem with coherence **7g**
com	Incomplete comparison **39c**
coord	Problem with coordination **44**
cs	Comma splice **52**
d	Diction problem **47, 48**
dev	More development needed **6b, c**
dm	Dangling modifier **43e**
doc	Documentation problem APA **31, 32** Chicago **35. 36** CSE **37** MLA **26, 27**
emph	Problem with emphasis **44**
exact	Inexact word **48**
exam	Example needed **6b**
frag	Sentence fragment **51**
fs	Fused (or run-on) sentence **52**
hyph	Problem with hyphen **67**
inc	Incomplete construction **39**
intro	Stronger introduction needed **6c**
ital	Italics or underlining needed **66**
jarg	Jargon **47c**
lc	lowercase letter needed **63**
mix	Mixed construction **40**
mm	Misplaced modifier **43a–d**
mng	Meaning not clear
mood	Error in mood **54j**
ms	Error in manuscript form **8** APA **33** Chicago **36** MLA **29**
num	Error in number style **65**
¶	Paragraph **6c**

p	Punctuation error
,	Comma **57a–j**
no ,	Unnecessary comma **57k–o**
;	Semicolon **58**
:	Colon **59**
'	Apostrophe **60**
" "	Quotation marks **61**
. ? !	Period, question mark, exclamation point **62a–c**
— ( ) [ ] . . . /	Dash, parentheses, brackets, ellipses, slash **62d-h**
para	Problem with a paraphrase **24c, e**
pass	Ineffective use of passive voice **46b**
pn agr	Problem with pronoun agreement **55a**
quote	Problem with a quotation **24e, 61b, g**
ref	Problem with pronoun reference **55b**
rep	Repetitious words or phrases **38b**
run-on	Run-on (or fused) sentence **52**
sexist	Sexist language **47e, 55a**
shift	Shift in point of view, tense, mood, or voice **41**
sl	Slang **47a**
sp	Misspelled word **68**
sub	Problem with subordination **44**
sv agr	Problem with subject-verb agreement **53**
t	Verb tense error **54f**
trans	Transition needed **7g**
usage	See Glossary of Usage **50**
var	Vary your sentence structure **45**
vb	Verb problem **54**
w	Wordy **38**
ww	Wrong word **48f**
//	Parallelism needed **42**
#	Add a space
∧	Insert
◡	Close up space
×	Obvious error
??	Unclear

Contents